CHINA ART NOW

Acknowledgments

First of all, my warmest thanks to the artists, some of whom are close friends of long standing. All of the artists welcomed me with good grace and enthusiasm, and, obviously, this book would not have been possible without their generous help. I would also like to express my most sincere thanks to the Délégation aux Arts Plastiques. Without the unwavering support of Bernard Blistène from the very beginning of the project, with the help of Guy Ansellem and later Martin Bethenod, we would not have been able to travel to China to photograph the works and carry out in-depth interviews with the artists. Thanks also to Chantal Cusin-Berche and Marion Sauvaire. I must also express my gratitude to Florence and Daniel Guerlain, whose extremely generous financial aid enabled me to travel to China, Venice, the Netherlands, and the United States. Thanks also to Olivier Poivre d'Arvor and Alain Rainaudo of the Association Française d'Action Artistique, who have been unstinting with both time and friendship, in particular in opening doors in embassies that might otherwise have remained shut. I owe a great deal also to Raymond Rocher, the French cultural attaché in Guangzhou, and his superb assistant Françoise Chen, and likewise to Claude Hudelot, the French cultural attaché in Shanghai and his equally superb assistant Wang Amandine. Warmest thanks to Patrick Michel, the former French cultural attaché in Beijing, who gave generously of his time, and whose marvelous sense of humor is matched only by his professionalism. I must also express my deepest thanks to his fantastic team, Loraine Tambrun, Aurélie Arf, and Fan Xiuying. I am delighted that this book gave me the opportunity to make the acquaintance of Jean Poncet, now working in Australia. He knows Shanghai like the back of his hand, and his love of this marvelous city is truly infectious. Thanks also to Lorenz Helbling (Shanghart Gallery), Davide Quadrio (BizArt), Zhang Wei (Vitamin Gallery), and Béatrice Leanza (CHAW, Beijing), whose help and readiness to answer a constant stream of questions were utterly invaluable. This book would not have been possible without my fabulous team of translators and interpreters. My warmest thanks to Fan Xiuying, Loraine Tambrun, Li Hua, Wang Amandine, Cyrille Sayag, and Marion Bertagna. I must also express my gratitude to the gallery owners and specialists who taught me a great deal about contemporary Chinese art, and who gave me permission to include works from their collections: Jacqueline Frydman at the Passage de Retz Gallery, Alain Fleischer at Le Fresnoy, Alain Sayag at the Centre Pompidou, and Daniel and Florence Guerlain of the Fondation Guerlain. Last but certainly not least, my most grateful thanks to André Morin, who photographed some of the works in Venice, where he was accompanying Yan Pei Ming, as well as the works of Wang Jian Wei at the Musée d'Art Moderne in Paris.

Published with the support of the Fondation d'art contemporain Florence and Daniel Guerlai, and with the help of a grant from the Centre national des arts plastiques.

Editor's note: The pinyin spellings of names have been used throughout with the exception of historical figures such as Mao Tse-tung, where the Wade-Giles form has been adopted.

Translated from the French by
Susan Pickford

Copyediting
Chrisoula Petridis

Typesetting
Les Éditions de l'Après-Midi

Color Separation
Penez Édition, Lille

Simultaneously published in French as
L'Art Contemporain Chinois

26, rue Racine
75006 Paris

www.editions.flammarion.com

04 05 06 4 3 2 1

FC0440-04-IV
ISBN: 2-0803-0440-2
Dépôt légal: 04/2004

Printed in Italy

Michel Nuridsany

CHINA ART NOW

Photography by Marc Domage

Flammarion

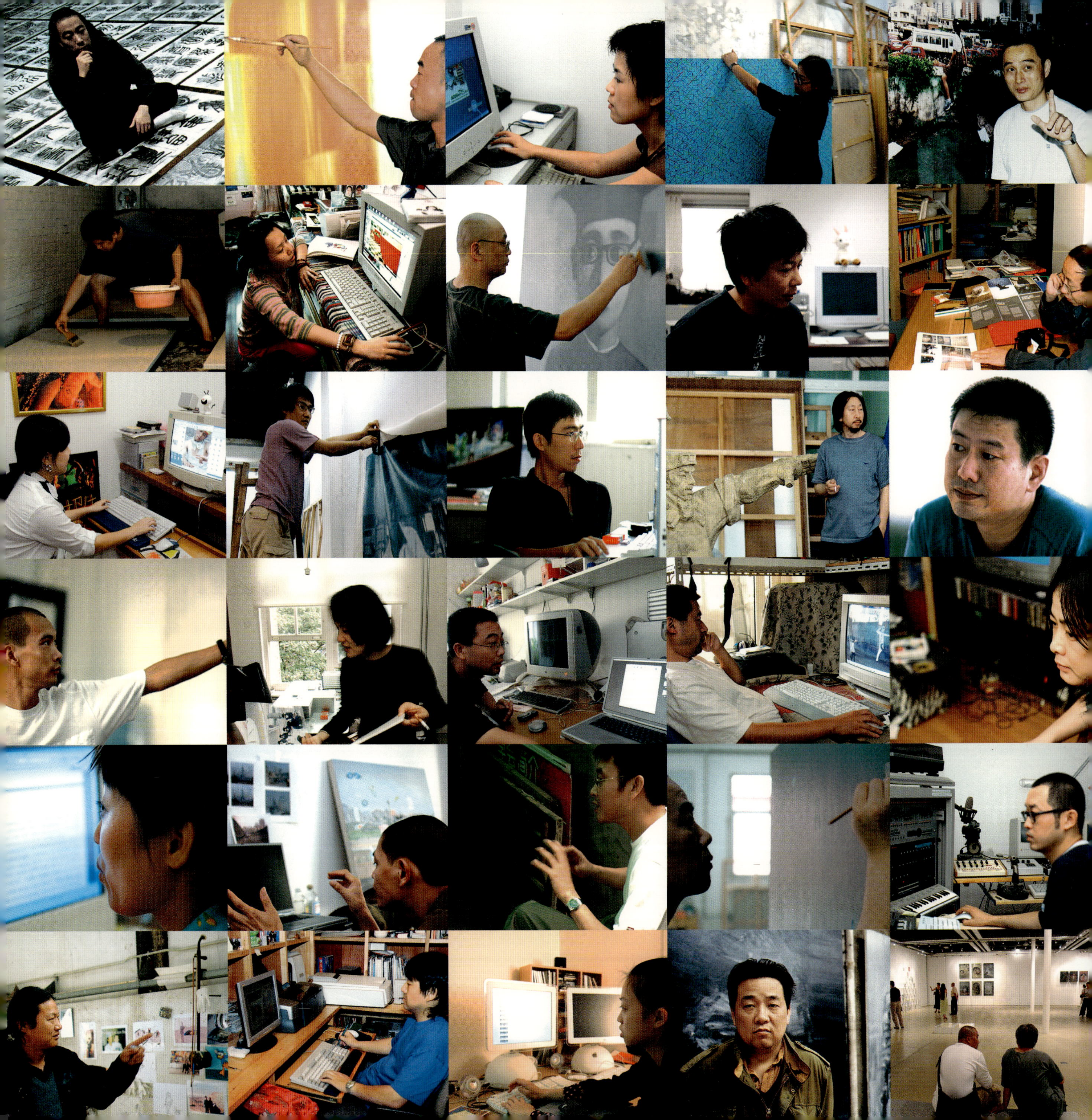

CONTENTS

FACING PAGE: GU WENDA, CHEN WENBO, CUI XIUWEN, DING YI, WENG PEIJUN, THE LUO BROTHERS, LING YUE, ZHANG XIAOGANG, ZHU JIA, HUANG YONG PING, CAO FEI, YAN LEI, XU ZHEN, WANG GUANGYI, ZHOU CHUNYA, ZHEN GUOGU, KAN XUAN, YANG ZHENZHONG, ZHANG PEILI, YANG FUDONG, CHEN LINGYANG, CHEN SHAOXIONG, WANG JIANWEI, ZHENG HAO, FENG MENGBO, WANG DU, SONG DONG, ZHOU YI, YAN PEI MING (MING).

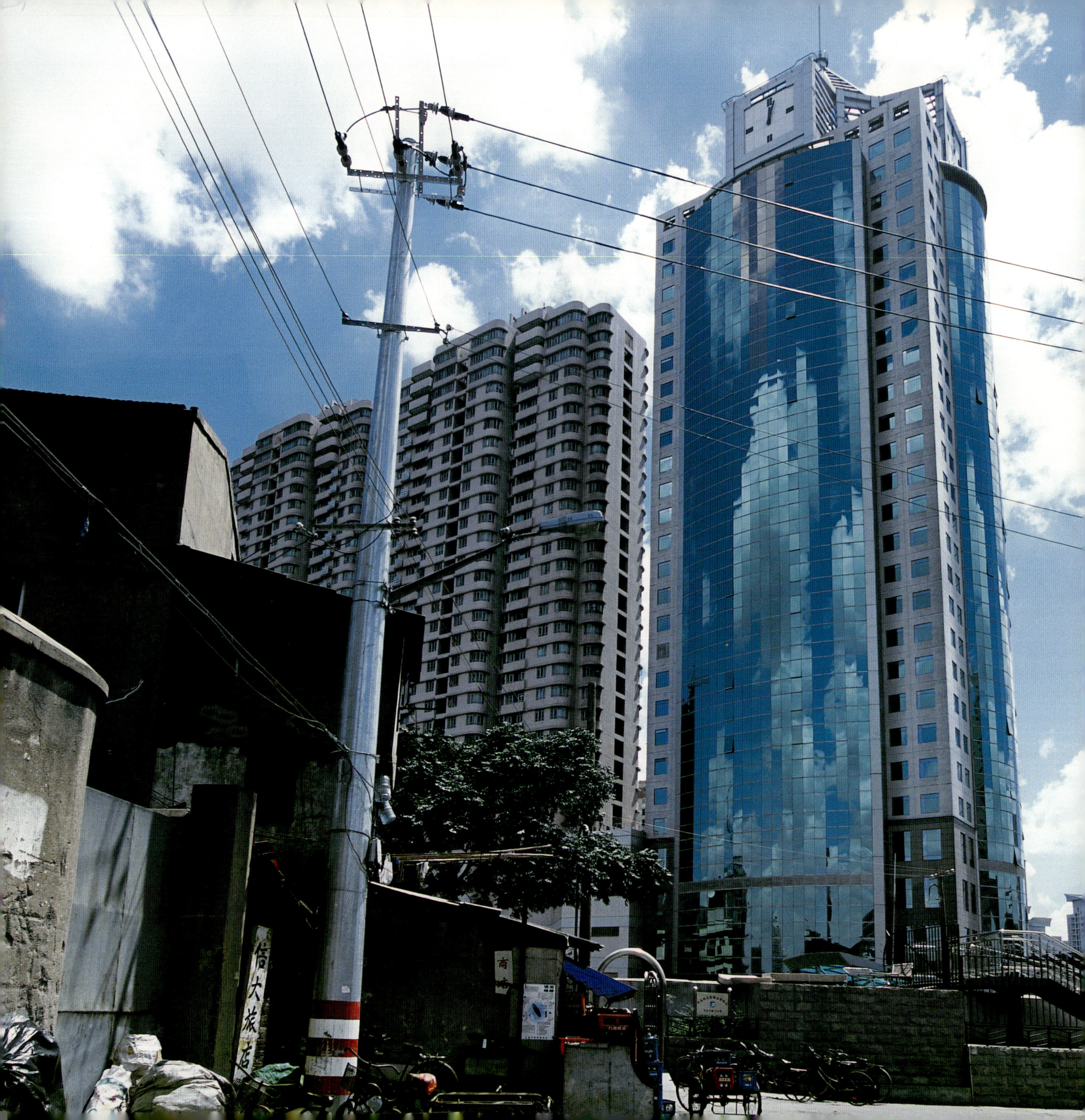
信大旅店

Wed., Jan. 31.—Dined with Goethe. "Within the last few days, since I saw you," said he, "I have read many and various things; especially a Chinese novel, which occupies me still, and seems to me very remarkable." "Chinese novel!" said I; "that must look strange enough." "Not so much as you might think," said Goethe; "the Chinamen think, act, and feel almost exactly like us; and we soon find that we are perfectly like them." . . . "But," said I, "is this Chinese romance one of their best?" "By no means," said Goethe; "the Chinese have thousands of them, and had already when our forefathers were still living in the woods."

Conversations of Goethe with Eckermann, translated by John Oxenford. London: G. Bell & Sons, 1874.

PREFACE

Here's an interesting statistic. When President Jiang Zemin gave the closing speech at the Communist Party congress in November 2002, he used the word "new" ninety-seven times, while the word "class" featured a mere five times. ¶ Welcome to modern China. ¶ Today, everything is new in China. Even the rainy season has somehow decided to begin a month earlier than it used to. Chinese society is in a constant state of flux, although certain aspects of life are—so far, at least—still considered beyond question, such as the place of the Communist Party. However, even official party vocabulary is beginning to thaw. Recently, a Cantonese weekly news magazine pointed out that where previously independent artists and self-employed professionals would have been labeled lazy and idle, now they are termed "social classes working towards the edification of socialism." Entrepreneurs are no longer "capitalists" and "exploiters." Mao's "mass line" has become "moral citizenship." ¶ The first Chinese astronaut, Yang Liwei, also broke with tradition when he said publicly that he had not been able to see the Great Wall of China from space. It had long been claimed that the Great Wall was the only man-made object visible from the moon. And so another carefully constructed "truth" crumbles into dust. ¶ The face of Chinese cities is changing thanks to the skyscrapers that are being built on every available plot of land. In cities all over China, atmospheric old neighborhoods are being torn down and replaced with soulless high-rises. The brand-new millionaires are discovering the joys of unbridled capitalism and the ease with which a kickback or two will open doors. It is as if China has decided to make up for decades of Communist rule overnight: no wonder some people are going over the top. ¶ I was having dinner with a friend one evening in Dondzhimen Street in the neighborhood of Dong Cheng in a restaurant where the spicy shrimp was particularly succulent. As I paid, I asked for a copy of the menu. My friend, Patrick Michel, the then cultural attaché in Beijing, asked me when I expected to be back in the city. Two months, I said. His response? "Then don't bother with the menu. In two months' time, this restaurant will have been replaced by a high-rise." ¶ It is true that new neighborhoods have sprung up practically overnight. The outbreak of SARS in early 2003, which sent the world media into a frenzy, killed 774 people in Beijing. The sense of paranoia proved just as infectious. A whole new quarter sprang up around the central lake, because people thought that the pure air would keep them safe from the virus. And since everything was closed everywhere else in Beijing, the new buildings were quickly followed by bistros, nightclubs, and restaurants—all within the space of three months. The health crisis seems to have come to an end, but the new neighborhood has remained, and grown. ¶ Two words sum up modern China: dynamism and vitality. Everything is larger than life. Everyone is eager for novelty, and everything has to be bigger, bolder, and brasher. ¶ Picture yourself in the heart of Beijing. There are skyscrapers all around. The vast avenues are almost as broad as they are long—six, eight, even twelve lanes of traffic. You see first one, then several, Mercedes. In fact, every other person seems to be driving one. The traffic snarls are endless. No one rides a bicycle any more. Your eye is drawn to an elderly couple shuffling along the sidewalk. They are so gray that they are almost transparent: gray skin, empty eyes, short, bristly haircuts, old Mao suits hanging off their skeletal frames. They are survivors. They pause to look in at the window of a shiny new restaurant, all glittering chrome and neon lights. The customers are teenagers: girls in miniskirts with dyed yellow hair and nose rings, and boys with slicked-back hair. They giggle, jostle each other, drink Coca-Cola, and French kiss. It is a Pizza Hut restaurant. ¶ Andy Warhol's declaration that, "The most beautiful thing in Tokyo is McDonald's. The most beautiful thing in Stockholm is McDonald's. The most beautiful thing in Florence is McDonald's. Peking and Moscow don't have anything beautiful yet" is light-years from modern Beijing, where there is a McDonald's on practically every street corner. Customers can also buy at Armani, Cartier, and all the top names. ¶ When I first visited Shanghai in 1996, there were already a few supermarkets and luxury goods boutiques, but they were generally poorly stocked and even faintly depressing. Today, the shelves are full, and the stores are crowded from morning to night. You have to book ahead for a table in any of the trendy restaurants that are just as expensive as any in Paris, London, or New York. The hottest restaurant in Beijing is currently South Silk Road. It is easy to find. Just look for the tall tower that carries an enormous neon sign boasting its name, SOHO. The American dream has arrived in China! Next door is an even more expensive and exclusive club, where the diners go to finish the evening. A quarter of an hour's drive away is a huge disco, the Banana Club, where all the bright young things come to flash their cash. Prostitution is obvious and shameless, as is drug-taking. The floor vibrates to the pounding beats of the latest remix to hit DJs' decks everywhere from Venice Beach to Roppongi. ¶ Beijing is like New York in the 1960s: the place to be. The key ingredients are the energy of youth and the optimism of the Kennedy era, the first man on the moon, and Warhol's Factory. ¶ Yes, energy is the word that best sums up modern China. Energy buzzes in Beijing, Shanghai, Guangzhou, and many of the lesser cities. Energy in the economy, in the conquest of space, and in contemporary art. A wind of eccentricity is blowing through China. There is also a slight sense of anxiety bubbling under the effervescent surface, because although freedom is gaining ground, life is still very much under surveillance. ¶ Shanghai recently lost the battle with Beijing for the 2008 Olympic Games, but was awarded the 2010 Universal Exhibition as a consolation prize. The city is working on two major projects as proof of its dynamism and modernity: a train network on magnetic rails and contemporary art. Beijing wants to avoid being outmaneuvered at all costs, and so held its first biennial in the fall of 2003. It was not a resounding success, but then again neither was the first Shanghai Biennial in 1996. Today, the most important aspect is the radical shift in the official attitude to contemporary art, which just a few years ago was decried as "spiritual pollution" but is now seen as a foremost way for China to signify its openness, dynamism, and innovation to the rest of the world. ¶ Change is indeed in the air in China. But that is no reason for ignorance. I was recently talking to a woman who thought herself an expert in Chinese contemporary art because she speaks Mandarin. She obviously thought I would agree when she told me, "Nowadays, there's nothing interesting going on in France. It's all happening in China." It was an idiotic thing to say. First of all, there is plenty going on in France—you just have to keep abreast of developments. Secondly, as concerns the Chinese situation, I think the best thing would be to repeat what Huang Yong Ping told me recently when he was explaining why he called the group he founded in 1985–86 Xiamen Dada. I asked why he called the group Dada, and why a radical young Chinese artist should choose to associate himself with a movement dating from the 1920s, some sixty-five years after the event. His answer: "Chinese contemporary art was fifty years behind the times compared to Western art. We believed that a reference to Western art was essential if Chinese contemporary art was to exist. So we had to take up a position in relation to Western art. For me, Dada was the most radical movement. When I wrote one of my earliest texts, in a magazine that never made it past the first issue, I called it Post-Modern Xiamen Dada, to indicate that although we were behind the times, we were still in touch with all the latest developments." That is where Huang Yong Ping saw himself. His answer was more precise, more subtle, and more intelligent than the woman I spoke to. ¶ It should be pointed out that in Europe and the United States, "Chinese contemporary art" generally means the few artists who have made fleeting appearances at two or three biennials—Istanbul or Venice, nothing too far afield—whose names are instantly forgotten as soon as the event is over. Xu Zhen's name was on everybody's lips at the 2001 Venice Biennale thanks to the video *Rainbow*—but who could remember it six weeks later? Strangely, people generally recalled the name of Yang Fudong, whose beautiful black-and-white film *An Estranged Paradise* won praise at the Documenta in Kassel. Why should he be singled out? There is an unknown quantity at work. ¶ A few years back, Westerners held Chinese art at arm's length, citing concerns over human rights in Tibet. Today, China and contemporary Chinese art are the height of fashion. Forget Tibet and those bothersome human rights protestors. But it is still *de rigueur* to adopt a supercilious tone and to refer to the problems of contemporary Chinese art to show that one is in the know. ¶ For example, how many times have I heard it said that it is a problem that Chinese art is bought only by foreign collectors? ¶ Well, there is a grain of truth here, but no more than that. It was true up until 2001 or 2002. The artists themselves say that one hundred percent of their sales were to foreign collectors. It was the only way they could live from their art. But over the last couple of years, Chinese museums have begun buying works as well—only a few so far, and without going through a gallery, preferring to negotiate a lower rate directly with the artist. The museums are building up their collections. The museum in Guangzhou under the direction of Wang Huangsheng is a remarkable example. Meanwhile, a few private individuals are taking their first timid steps as collectors. ¶ We should be wary of viewing contemporary art separately from the art market and the economy as a whole. Just like in New York, Chicago, Los Angeles, Tokyo, and London, nouveau riche entrepreneurs are investing some of their wealth in contemporary art as a way of acquiring a veneer of culture and sophistication. Wang Guangyi says that forty percent of his total sales are now to Chinese clients. Other artists say their figure is around the five percent mark. It's a start. And at the rate things are moving in China, just imagine what the figures will be in ten years. ¶ We should also remember that to begin with, Impressionist works sold far better in Russia and America than in France. Contemporary Chinese art is not the only case where homegrown collectors have failed to spot artistic potential. ¶ The second problem so-called experts like to bring up is that contemporary Chinese art is nothing but an imitation of international art. To which the only answer is: So what? It's a typically Western thing to say. When van Gogh copied Japanese prints by Hiroshige and Hokusai, was this not an imitation of international art? And when Picasso drew on African art in the *Demoiselles d'Avignon*? What else should we call it? Influence, borrowing, copying? Whether we like it or not, globalization is here to stay, in art as well as in the economy. Xu Zhen, Yang Zhenzhong, and Kan Xuan have their Western equivalents in Matthew Barney, Maurizio Cattelan, Claude Lévêque, and Pipilotti Rist. ¶ Japanese industrialists began by copying Leica cameras before inventing better models of their own and becoming world leaders in the camera market, when the Germans began copying their innovations in turn. ¶ In the 1940s, American artists drew heavily on French, Russian, and German art from the years after 1910, before finding their own feet in the 1950s, 1960s, and 1970s, when American art was as original and successful as any on the planet. ¶ The same goes for Chinese art today. ¶ When an artist like Wang Guangyi sees the huge size of the works on show at the Venice Biennale, he quickly grasps that large-format works have more of an impact than smaller ones. Does this make him any less original? ¶ Anyway, when critics carp at imitations, whom are they referring to? Artists working in the early 1990s? Wake up. It's now 2004. While there's no denying that the artists active in the Political Pop Art were heavily influenced by American Pop Art, Warhol in particular, I could give you the names of dozens of artists in Europe who followed the same path. But whom was Xu Zhen supposed to be imitating? And Kan Xuan? And Yang Zhenzhong, and Chen Shaoxiang, and Yan Lei, and Zhou Yi, and Feng Mengbo? And while we're at it, what about the rest of the younger generation—the ones included in the present book, at least? And among the older generation, what about Song Dong and Zhang Xiaogang, to name but two? Anyone who says Chinese art today is derivative is simply out of touch. ¶ I should note that when Chinese art historians go to great lengths to point out how original early twentieth-century Chinese oil painting is compared to European works of the same period, or when a critic as on the ball as Shao Dazhen unquestioningly accepts Huang Binhong's judgment that "the thought behind Fauvism is close to the power of the line in antique Chinese painting," it is hard to know whether to laugh or cry at such absurd displays of nationalist arrogance. ¶ The third problem that is often raised is whether Chinese art should be read from a critical, political standpoint. ¶ This is a more complex question. All too often, Chinese artists (at least in front of interpreters) will only say what they think we want to hear. They used to listen to critics interpreting their works from an almost exclusively political or antiestablishment point of view with patient smiles. Today, their patience with this approach has begun to wear thin and they are not afraid to show it. Zhang Xiaogang, who paints families in black and white linked with a thin red line, speaks for many others when he says, "People interpret my work from a political point of view, but I am looking for something more mysterious within my own family. If all I want to do is criticize, then I can no longer paint." ¶ Zhang Peili has criticized avant-garde Chinese artists who, in his opinion, laid too much importance on producing works that proclaimed their Chinese-ness in accordance with what they thought the Western art world wanted from them. "Chinese artists spend too much time wondering about their identity," he says. He would much prefer it if "artists were to remain natural." ¶ Easier said than done in a society that is constantly changing and a country that is in a permanent state of flux. ¶ Having said that, there is no denying that Political Pop Art (if not other movements) did lay itself open to such readings. The artists active in the Political Pop Art movement were seen as antiestablishment figures and were thus popular in the West. ¶ Problem number four: How can a French critic hope to understand artistic developments in a country where he is unfamiliar with the language and sometimes the culture? ¶ It's a matter of hard work, enthusiasm, and awareness, as always. Chinese culture is as hard to grasp as French culture (which, incidentally, many French critics, curators, and observers know less about than they think) or Brazilian, or American, or any other culture. Which is not to say that Chinese culture is hermetic, esoteric, and utterly inaccessible for foreign critics, as many Chinese observers and commentators would like us to believe. Chinese art—and contemporary art in particular—has a history. To know it well, you must study it from its origins, trace its development, and plunge into it today by meeting the artists. This goes for any culture—French, American, whatever. This is the only way to get inside a culture. ¶ So what is the best place to begin a study of Chinese contemporary art, if so many critics have got it wrong? ¶ The best place to begin is by being politically incorrect. As far as I am concerned, there is only one place to begin, and that is with Mao Tse-tung. Other critics have staked claims for 1989 or 2000. Some of the most eminent specialists have settled on 1985: we will see why shortly. But the first great event that set Chinese art on the road to the point of effervescence it reached in 1985 was launched by the Great Helmsman. He set the wheels in motion. ¶ Mao Tse-tung imposed the model of Soviet Socialist Realism. "Revolutionary!", as everyone said in the 1980s when the Citroën AX was the first car to drive along the Great Wall. The tradition of literati painting was beginning to die out as Xu Beihong accused it of being a relic of the nineteenth century and devoid of content and Lin Fengmian, in the 1930s, said it was an art that claimed to draw on form while in fact neglecting it. To begin with, Mao made artists give up traditional ink and paper in favor of canvas and oil paints. They were an extraordinary discovery in 1950s China, and opened up unimagined vistas. ¶ It is true that oil painting had been introduced to China in the early years of the century, particularly with the return of students sent to Europe in 1919 and the founding of art schools more or less in the Western tradition. However, the country was so unstable—with a revolution in 1911, the anti foreign May Fourth Movement in 1919, war against Japan from 1937 to 1945, then the war of liberation and the founding of the People's Republic—that attempts to introduce Western techniques such as oil painting were unsuccessful, at least in artistic terms. Some critics have been tempted to over estimate the importance of the Jesuit missionary and (mediocre) artist Catiglione (1688–1766) whose exotic paintings are on display at a museum in Taipei. He was followed by other Europeans who started a trend—it is too minor to be termed a school—for paintings combining Western and Chinese techniques at the Qing court in the eighteenth century. The Western contribution to these works was a remarkable use of light and shadow and perspective as well as the choice of contemporary events as their principal subjects. The paintings were naturally subject to the strict control of the emperor himself, who accepted or refused the works offered to him. The literati artists frowned on Western painting, which they perceived as little more than a handicraft because the use of oil paints allows the artist to go over and improve on his first brushstrokes, while the skill of brush-and-ink painting on paper lies in the sheer virtuosity of the brushstroke. ¶ The Cultural Revolution changed everything. The Chinese artists I interviewed had a more complex and finely shaded approach than I had expected to an event that swept away all the old traditions, paradoxically making it easier for China to open to the world when Mao's death in 1976 brought the whole disastrous experiment to an end. The old traditions, which would doubtless have hindered China's embrace of modernity, had been destroyed or survived only as hollow shells of their former selves. ¶ China's opening to the rest of the world began gradually but quickly gathered steam. As always, as in Europe in the early years of the twentieth century and America in the early 1960s, economic change was accompanied by artistic developments. Once Mao died, the floodwaters could no longer be held back and Deng Xiaoping decided to liberalize the economy—which had an impact on the art scene earlier than is generally acknowledged by historians, many of whom underestimate the role of the Star Group. ¶ 1979. The members of the Star Group were the first artists after the Cultural Revolution to take their art out of the official circuit and into the private sphere, such as the homes and offices of foreign diplomats, and the street. Other groups were doing the same in Czechoslovakia and the USSR for the same reasons. These were the beginnings of experimental art in China—closer to punk art than anything else. The defining characteristic of punk rockers was their burning desire to put their message across from the stage, even if they could not play more than three chords on the guitar. The Star Group had the same visceral need, and were a deeply interesting phenomenon, whatever the critics who wrinkle their noses in disgust at their name might think. ¶ The problem faced by these artists who had very little in the way of formal training was how and where to get their message across. They began by organizing discussions in each others' apartments and holding what they called "informal exhibitions." They made a name for themselves in September 1979 by hanging their works on the park railings outside the National Museum of Art in Beijing. A crowd soon gathered. The police stepped in. The exhibition was banned two days later because it had not been granted prior permission. The Star Group struck back one month later, on October 1, the anniversary of the Revolution, by bringing twenty artists along to Behai Park and holding a public demonstration. One year later, with the help of a far-sighted critic who belonged to the semi-official Association of Chinese Artists, they were granted permission to hold an exhibition on the top floor of the National Museum of Art. It attracted eighty thousand visitors in just sixteen days. ¶ In 1981 it was the turn of the city of Xi'an to hold its first exhibition of contemporary art. ¶ It is absolutely vital to read these events in the light of the political climate of the day. It was a crucial moment in Chinese history. Mao and the Cultural Revolution were both dead. In 1979, Deng Xiaoping, rehabilitated in 1977, announced a new economic policy for China and visited the United States, while entering into armed conflict against Vietnam. Deng Xiaoping was a clear-sighted and wily politician who had a long-term vision for China's future. ¶ 1980 saw the creation of the Special Economic Zones designed to bring in foreign technologies and capital. The zones were immediately criticized for being a modern version of the concessions granted by China to foreign interests in the late nineteenth and early twentieth century at the time of the Opium Wars. But from 1979 to 1984, the proponents of reform had the upper hand. They set about decollectivizing farmland and abolishing the people's communes while liberalizing trade and local crafts. ¶ Having said that, in 1978, the most daring, anti conformist artistic venture was an exhibition of landscapes from the Musée d'Orsay in Paris—hardly groundbreaking stuff. But China had never seen the like. "It was the first time we ever saw a major exhibition," Ding Yi recalls. "For the first time, we were seeing European paintings other than in reproductions." Chinese artists discovered a style of painting free of the pressure to produce a heroic version of the lives of workers and farm laborers. It was a slow beginning. One year later, an exhibition of European-style paintings was banned. In 1982, a dispute broke out over the inauguration of an abstract sculpture on the Gezhou dam, and an artists' association with several thousand members launched a campaign against what they called "spiritual pollution"—in other words, the Western influence in contemporary art. The campaign gathered momentum until, in 1984, a vast "national art exhibition" was organized in nine cities with the avowed aim of eliminating spiritual pollution from the art world. In Shanghai, an exhibition of experimental paintings was closed by the police four days after it opened. However, the tide was turning. In 1983, the National Museum of Art in Beijing had chosen to show works by Picasso and Munch. The 1984 national exhibition gave rise to the new wave of experimental art, which started in 1985 in reaction to the official event. ¶ The period prior to 1985 was a time of uncertainty but also of vibrant experimentation and great enthusiasm. Chinese artists discovered Surrealism, Picasso, and Duchamp, all at once. Unofficial exhibitions were being organized left, right, and center despite police repression. All this points to the importance of the years prior to 1985; yet despite all this vibrant artistic activity, a number of critics have stubbornly decided that contemporary Chinese art began in 1985, not before, while even more have settled on 1989 as the key date. ¶ I must say I find the point of view that contemporary art began in China only in 1989 quite simply absurd, even if it was the date of the key exhibition *China/Avant Garde*. A better case could be made for 1985, although not one I happen to find convincing. ¶ 1985 was marked by an event that had a major impact on the art world: the government relaxed the laws on cultural censorship. As a result, the number of exhibitions increased dramatically and groups of artists were founded all over China—eighty have been listed to date. A cheap magazine of four, sometimes eight, pages, entitled *Fine Art in China*, made its first appearance. It was the work of a young team of journalists passionate about art. It was sold all over the country and played a major part in creating the sense of an artistic community on a national scale. The government, while not exactly approving, turned a blind eye. Wang Du explains, "By then they had understood that China had to develop its economy, otherwise the whole country would go down the drain. So as long as you didn't directly attack Communism, they'd pretty well leave you alone." Fine Art in China talked art and creative tendencies, not politics. ¶ It was a time of idealism and euphoria. Experimenting and innovation were the watchwords. It was a fascinating time, when artists were racing to catch up on all those lost years. They were very politically and morally aware, having spent their formative years under the Cultural Revolution. The various avant-garde art movements and groups all felt that they had an important part to play. Maybe even vital. "We were innocent," Wang Du says. "We tried to talk about life in as natural a way as possible." They held performances that lasted three days. Reinvented art from scratch. Reinvented life itself. It was a time of great riches. ¶ The Rauschenberg exhibition, at which the artist himself was present, shown first in Beijing, then Lhasa, had an enormous impact. At the National Gallery in Beijing, the exhibition of progressive young artists at the forefront of the New Wave 85 gave avant-garde a form of official approval. Shanghai held the first exhibition of the *New Figurative Art*, featuring, among others, a certain Zhang Xiaogang. The exhibition was later shown in Nanjing. Hangzhou organized New Space 85 with works by Zhang Peili. Not all parts of China were equally progressive. In Taiyuan, in Shanxi province, an exhibition of works by the Three Steps Studio was shut down by the police just a few hours after it opened, despite the official relaxing of censorship laws. The Zero Group was founded in Changsha in Hunan province at around this time, as was Wang Guangyi's Northern Group, whose importance can hardly be overestimated. ¶ 1986 was marked by student protests, the foundation of a Surrealist group, exhibitions by the Zero Group in the streets of Shenzhen, the creation of the Xiamen Dada group by Huang Yong Ping, a display of installation art in Hangzhou—a hotbed of progressive art—and the inauguration of the Salon of Southern Chinese Artists founded by Wang Du. Nearly all of the artists at the forefront of the contemporary art scene today were beginning to make a name for themselves. ¶ 1987: a student demonstration in Tiananmen Square is heavily criticized by the People's Daily. The National Gallery of Fine Arts in Beijing organizes an exhibition entitled *Let's Turn to the Future*, including works by avant-garde young artists. In Changchun, in Jilin province, Wang Guangyi founds the first biennial for groups of artists in northern China. ¶ 1988 saw a worrying reversal of fortunes for art when the hard-liner Li Peng became prime minister. The party line was stated loud and clear: "The state controls the market, and the market guides companies." But the tide could not be turned back. Performances were held along the Great Wall of China. Xu Bing had an exhibition in the National Gallery in Beijing. In 1989, the flagship exhibition *China/Avant Garde* brought together 185 artists from all over China, whose works were shown over three floors in the National Gallery in Beijing. It covered everything from traditional painting and abstract oil painting to installations and performances. Xiao Lu decided to turn her installation into a performance by shooting at it, after which the exhibition was closed—but only temporarily. In Hong Kong and Taipei, the Star Group celebrated its tenth anniversary in the Hanart TZ Gallery. Thousands of miles away in Paris, the exhibition *The Magicians of the Earth* featured three Chinese artists, including Huang Yong Ping. This was the first time that contemporary Chinese artists had participated in a major exhibition outside China. ¶ From a political point of view, progress between 1984 and 1988 was checkered. The reforms begun in the countryside reached the cities where an economic sector beyond state control began to evolve. After Gorbachev's visit to Beijing, relations between China and the USSR returned to normal. Tensions rose between China and Tibet, on the other hand, when riots in Tibet led to the proclamation of martial law. ¶ 1989 was a turning point in Chinese history. It was marked by what has come to be called the Beijing Spring, with students declaring an unlimited strike to demand press freedom and the right to open dialogue with government. Deng Xiaoping ordered the demonstrations to be crushed with tanks and machine guns on June 4. ¶ The needless tragedy was condemned by the rest of the world. But very quickly—even as early as 1992—it was being whispered that the events of Tiananmen Square, rather than halting the transformation of the economy championed by Deng Xiaoping, actually set in motion a policy of developing a genuine market economy and all that that implied in terms of opening China's borders. But the positive buzz of 1985 had gone. The new freedom was still very much under surveillance. Still, Jiang Zemin thought it worthwhile to maintain close contacts with the intellectual and artistic milieus, letting it be known that the government would tolerate a certain degree of impertinence, as long as it remained "tolerable"—in other words, superficial. The message came across loud and clear. A (relatively large) proportion of the artists active in Political Pop Art decided to take advantage of the crumbs of freedom being offered, cynically exploiting the small window of opportunity given to them. ¶ Fifteen years after the tragedy of Tiananmen Square, Jean-Luc Domenach, an expert in Chinese politics, produced the following analysis of the situation: "Observers noted that the bloody repression of the democratic movement put an end to hopes that the opening up of economic perspectives would lead to a concomitant opening up of Chinese politics, thus allowing developments more in keeping with the social and political state of China: free of the demographic threat, the Communist Party thus felt free to embrace a type of development that was more and more inspired by the capitalist world, fed by its own integration into the global market." ¶ In fact, this can be compared to the situation of Japan in the Meiji era, when the country also wielded enormous control over the opening of its borders, choosing to let in Western science as a means of ridding itself of Western influence. In 1992, in Shenzhen, in a speech of the utmost significance, Deng Xiaoping made two major points: first, that China would continue to develop toward a market economy, and second, that China's future still lay in socialism adapted to the country's needs. There was no mistaking his meaning. ¶ Jean-Luc Domenach's analysis continues: "The Communist leaders discovered that in order to save their power and bring their national mission to fruition, they had to change both their internal strategy, by making their priority a more classical style of economic development, and their external strategy, by opening up their borders to adopt from the West the economic models and capital necessary for their development. Contrary to what had been hoped, it proved impossible to free China from the burden of underdevelopment without borrowing from the Western masters who had caused them so much suffering in the past." He goes on to drive his point home: "The troubles caused by the 'democratic movement' in 1989, however widespread they might have been, did not represent a real risk for the Communist government for one minute. The range and precision of the checks were the most obvious limits placed on the new policy of openness, in particular the political and intellectual limits, which Western human rights campaigners so rightly criticize. But the fact is often overlooked that these checks in fact guaranteed the duration and the vigor of this policy of openness and its expansion, both in territorial and social terms. If the Chinese Communist Party had not been in charge of the policy of openness, if it had not been benefiting from it, if it had not been convinced of its own capacity to slow it or even put a stop to it altogether, there is no way the Communists would have pushed it so far." ¶ Ten years after Deng Xiaoping's speech in Shenzhen, China is now officially one of the world's economic powerhouses, with an (official) annual growth rate of nine percent. It joined the World Trade Organization in 2001 after thirteen long years of negotiation. One consequence of this is that China relies on external stability, as the country is particularly dependent on Arab countries for its energy supplies, and internal stability for its export balance and to keep the necessary foreign capital flowing in. It is now out of the question for China, caught up in a web of international economic relationships that it cannot risk breaking, to start playing the sort of political games that might result in a shift in the balance of the economic scales. It is out of the question to play the troublemaker and start objecting to alliances on moral, idealistic, ideological, or any other grounds. ¶ Stability is the new watchword. Everything is geared towards maintaining the precious economic stability, at the cost of any number of concessions and compromises. Hail to the new consumer society! ¶ In the catalog for the magnificent China exhibition held at the Centre Pompidou in Paris in 2003, the brilliant young Chinese critic Pi Li drew on a series of concrete examples to demonstrate how the standard of living has risen in China since 1980. In the early 1980s, a "good life" was measured by the possession of three essential objects: a watch, a bicycle, and a sewing machine. A few years later, a cassette recorder also became a vital lifestyle accessory. By the end of the 1980s, the three essential possessions were a color television, a refrigerator, and a washing machine. But while there is clearly a world of difference between a watch and a washing machine in terms of purchasing power, Pi Li notes that lifestyles hardly changed. The 1990s were a different matter. He notes, "A new way of looking at material possessions became noticeable, reflecting a new way of thinking. The appearance of the first cellular phones, cable television, and the Internet have changed the way Chinese people communicate, and increasing urbanization has thrown their lives into turmoil. Traditional old homes with courtyards have given way to apartment buildings. Life in the old courtyards, where everyone knew everyone else's business—something which the Cultural Revolution pushed over the limit into absurdity—are vanishing. Even the power of the neighborhood committees is being eroded. Cable TV, the Internet, and pirated DVDs are letting Chinese people open up to new forms of entertainment, news, documentaries—in short, to the whole world." ¶ Except that in 2000, the National People's Congress promulgated laws against unfettered access to the Internet. ¶ Stability was still the watchword. The collapse of the USSR and the Communist regimes in central Europe and the fall of the Berlin Wall—all in the same year as the tragedy of Tiananmen Square—were uppermost in the Chinese leaders' minds. They meant instability and disorder. ¶ The period of greatest disorder in China (others might call it the biggest social experiment in history) was the Cultural Revolution. ¶ I would like to spend a few moments examining the role of the Cultural Revolution, even if chronologically it preceded the topic under discussion, since it serves today's leaders as a political, economic, and even ideological counterexample. They claim that no price is too high to pay to avoid descending into the chaos of post-Communist Russia and Central Europe, with all the disastrous consequences for the economy that this would have entailed. Yet they refuse to take the next logical step of disavowing Chairman Mao. The Chinese leaders dare not knock their homegrown version of Lenin and Stalin all rolled into one from his pedestal. ¶ Let's look at these ten years, one of the darkest periods in Chinese history. With the exception of a few of the youngest, the artists in the present work lived through the Cultural Revolution and were profoundly influenced by it in one way or another. Let us not forget that the collective madness of the Cultural Revolution was similar in scope (if not necessarily in terms of the proportion of the total population affected) to the madness of the Khmer Rouge, which led to one of the worst genocides of the twentieth century. But the Cultural Revolution went deeper still. ¶ I do not propose to devote much time to the majority of artists who said that it was fun, they were just kids, they didn't understand what was at stake, they were allowed to travel all over the place by train without paying, they could criticize their teachers, they could skip classes as often as they liked—when there were classes, that is—and no one would punish them. Their parents were always in political meetings and didn't have enough time to look after them. They grew up in total freedom. In fact, these reminiscences are a way of refusing to address the question. ¶ I also intend to skip over the rote, official answers I was given by some interpreters who talked of the "generation that did not labor in the fields," and the notable lack of reaction by a journalist interviewing Wang Jian Wei when the artist explained that "there was a movement that encouraged young people to move to the countryside to labor in the fields." ¶ On the other hand, I would like to take a closer look at Wang Guangyi's claim that the Cultural Revolution opened his, and many other people's, eyes. "It was a time when people thought a lot," he said, implying that the consumer society hardly encourages people to think about what they are doing. It may be the case, as I have been told, that Wang Guangyi—generally considered to be close to the Chinese authorities—tells all Westerners this as a way of throwing them off the track. But since anything can throw you off the track, in this case, I see no reason to not listen to him. The aim of the Cultural Revolution was to forge a new race of men. Some men—more than might now be ready to admit it—believed in the ideal. It overturned a whole raft of old ideologies and tried to bring about a permanent state of revolution. It was an epic dream. What makes ideologies dangerous is not their essence, but their excesses. Zhou Chunya even dared to affirm that without the Cultural Revolution, modern China would not exist, since prior to it Chinese society was very inward looking: it took a revolution to open China to the world. ¶ When I mentioned this to Feng Mengbo, he dismissed the idea impatiently, saying it was as stupid as saying the modern world would not be as it is without the World War II. But is it as stupid as all that? There is no denying that the World War II did change the world utterly, particularly Europe, whose national frontiers were radically altered and which attained its current modernity through a painful process that destroyed many of its old structures and had a profound and lasting impact on the outlook of the entire continent. ¶ Maybe this is what the historian Yves Chevrier meant when he wrote "Mao's revolution rediscovered the traces of the ancient empire, but also brought about modernity by killing off Chinese tradition." ¶ Destroying traditions. It is a phrase that rings horribly true to many people—including many of China's foremost thinkers—as modern consumer society tightens its grip on China, changing behavioral patterns and ways of thinking, at a time when many people are beginning to ask questions about Chinese identity and the place of their country in a world where globalization is spreading like a pandemic, and others are arguing for a return to specifically Chinese values to prevent China from losing its identity, forgetting her glorious past and neglecting chances for her future. ¶ As far as

I can tell, two major tendencies or artistic schools have arisen from the period from the start of the Cultural Revolution to the post-Tiananmen era: Political Pop Art, which springs, at least in part, from propaganda painting, and the post-Cultural Revolution utopia of the mid-1980s, which chose performance and occasionally video as a means of expression. ¶ Let us begin by looking at the Cultural Revolution. It gave rise to a school of propaganda art that was simple and effective, as all propaganda painting is, almost by definition. It drew people in, challenged their beliefs, overturned long-held aesthetic notions, and showed that the old emperor had no clothes on. First and foremost, art had to be accessible. It had to mean something, to instruct, guide, and move the masses. The grace and finesse of literati painting was outdated. A parallel can be drawn with Andy Warhol's Pop Art in the United States. ¶ Wang Du told me how there were portraits of Chairman Mao everywhere, and that all art was meant to serve as propaganda. Many of the artists I spoke to in the course of my research started out painting propaganda portraits of the Great Helmsman. Zhou Chunya, for example, earned a living painting Mao's portrait for an "art company" for three years. Yan Pei Ming explained that each neighborhood had its own committee and propaganda bureau, which the locals had to keep going. Each week, someone was put in charge of the painting activities, and often it was him. He would paint copies of propaganda pictures and posters to hand out—and that was all he ever painted. By 1974, Yan Pei Ming was a full-fledged propaganda painter, producing large-scale murals of Mao in schools and factories. The portraits were always red, said to be a positive color. The exultant, heroic, combative style has had a lasting impact on his work, which shares the dynamism of the works of his early career. ¶ The simplified realist technique common to the artists who began their careers as propaganda painters led many of them to take up Political Pop Art in the 1980s. The movement became more cynical after the tragedy of Tiananmen Square and the government's attempts to cover up what had happened. Fang Lijun's work is a typical example. Other artists, including the Luo Brothers, started a highly kitsch movement called Gaudy Art, which did not set out to be overtly political or cynical, but which deliberately adopted an often humorous posture of almost aggressively bad taste. ¶ This Chinese take on Pop Art burst onto the scene at the Guangzhou Biennial in 1992. The biennial was sponsored by wealthy industrialists from Guangzhou and Shenzhen, and was the first major event in the art world to be held without government support. The sponsors were given art works in return for their financial support and were thus able to begin building up a collection. Were they trying to jump-start interest in the art market, as has often been claimed? Did they really believe in the potential of the Chinese art market? ¶ Political Pop Art has always sold well, and it proved a wise choice for the investors to bet on. Over the years, it has come to be seen as emblematic of its era. The works, characterized above all by their veiled allusions to and criticisms of contemporary Chinese politics, were felt to be daringly antiestablishment, and as they were first shown just as Chinese artists were granted permission to participate in exhibitions abroad, they were a surefire hit. Their popularity proved such that for many Westerners, Political Pop Art and contemporary Chinese art are synonyms. ¶ Could it be said that Chinese performance art developed as an expression of dissatisfaction with the ambiguities of Political Pop Art? To begin with, it was one of the very few ways Chinese artists could give expression to their creativity when all official channels were closed to avant-garde art. When performance art developed into an original kind of body art, it became the medium for expressing the artist's thoughts on existence and idealism rather than identity. It thus represented a challenge to the blunt-edged criticism of Political Pop Art, which was increasingly being manufactured with one eye on the international art market. Thus Chinese art split into two streams, one commercial, with a few remarkable, but limited, successes, and the other much more avant-garde and experimental, using performance and video to create an extraordinarily dynamic and inventive movement. ¶ Performance art is not designed to appeal to potential buyers. One of the finest Chinese artists working in this field is Zhang Huan, now based in the United States. In 1994, he suspended himself from the ceiling by his feet after having made a small cut in his throat. The blood trickled down onto a wood-burning stove and filled the room with a peculiar smell. Another of his famous performances, entitled *12 m²*, involved him coating his naked body with honey and brine, then staying perfectly still for hours on end in an overheated toilet invaded by hordes of flies and mosquitoes before running to jump into a nearby lake where his body was swallowed up by the smooth surface of the water. What was the point of this work? To test his own powers of resistance and his moral attitude. ¶ In 1996, on the evening of December 31, Tiananmen Square was quite empty, except for the artist Song Dong. He lay face down on the ground in the freezing cold, and simply breathed for forty minutes. He just lay there, breathing. A thin layer of ice formed on the ground beneath him, showing the trace of where he had been lying, but vanishing by the next morning. This performance can be read as an allegory of artistic activity in general. It could also be a simple expression of the "temptation to exist," as the French philosopher Émile Cioran wrote. ¶ The history of performance art in China has yet to be written. It is not a recent or temporary phenomenon. Today, young artists are still producing works of great vitality and significance. As the genre is constantly renewing itself, it is progressing ever further into the territory of questions about human existence, being, the world, and reality that young artists see through unsullied eyes, going straight to the heart of the matter. They share the idealism of the mid-1980s, but with a more lighthearted approach. ¶ One of the most talented artists of the young generation, Xu Zhen, filmed himself sniffing the nooks and crannies of his girlfriend's body while she did the same to him. What is this, if not exploring reality in its most immediately material form—a reality that is far from self-evident in a country that was for decades dominated by ideological discourse and disconcerting lies. So the only place to begin is at the beginning and with what is closest at hand—your own body and that of your loved one. ¶ Would it be appropriate to call this new realism, a new way of looking at and describing reality? The performances by Xu Zhen, Liang Yue, Yang Zhenzhong, Kan Xuan, and Song Dong are all ways of grasping at truths. In Mao's China, reality was only seen through the trick mirrors of ideology and false statistics—just as in the West, our vision of the Gulf War and its aftermath was similarly distorted. Reality must be invented. It is not an easy undertaking. ¶ Questions about national identity and mind-numbing speeches about the distinctiveness of the Chinese character have fallen out of favor. The young generation couldn't care less. They have no problem with drinking Coca-Cola while eating with chopsticks, wearing jeans and cheap traditional padded jackets, reading books in English and then switching to Chinese ideograms. Yan Lei, for example, dismisses the question with a shrug: What is worth keeping in our traditions? ¶ For a Chinese artist working today, there are other questions that are more immediate, in particular issues of independence, or rather the lack of it, vis-à-vis the foreign market. All too often, this gives rise to either over zealous attempts to second-guess Western taste, or out-and-out anti-Western racism. ¶ Yan Lei addresses this question in two controversial works that lambaste both the Westerners who hop over to China on a flying visit to check out the latest developments in the art world, and his Chinese colleagues whose greatest ambition in life is to be invited to Documenta. ¶ *May I See Your Work?* was always the first thing specialists in the international art scene utterly convinced of their own importance would say to any Chinese artist the first time they met. At least, that was the impression they gave Chinese artists in the mid-1990s—predatory judges. The lack of independence of the Chinese artists meant they could not afford to respond as they honestly wished to the question "May I see your work?"—one short phrase that meant glory or oblivion. The result was a work in which the feeling of exasperation shines through, which gives it a strength of impact that was recognized immediately in both China and Europe. Tension crackled through the work. ¶ The 1997 performance *Invitation* bristles with the same exasperation. This time, the object of the artist's ire was the Documenta exhibition in Kassel, the ultimate aim of all Chinese artists. Yan Lei send a hundred or so artists a letter on notepaper with the Documenta logo announcing that the director of the festival would soon be coming to China, and giving a contact number, which was in fact the number of a payphone. Of course, there was no reply when the artists called the number, a metaphor for the way the organizers of the Kassel exhibition failed to meet the expectations of Chinese artists, who, Yan Lei says, were more interested in getting accepted for Documenta than in producing decent work. The letter was so convincing that when the truth came to light, most of the artists who fell for it were extremely angry, and the ones who had not been sent the letter in the first place even more so. It was an enormous scandal that strained diplomatic relations between China and Germany for a while. Yan Lei was forced to publish a letter apologizing for the work. Could anything be more revealing about the dependence of contemporary art on foreign support? ¶ Today, things have changed. Chinese artists are regularly invited to Documenta as well as other international art events such as the biennials in Venice, São Paulo, and Gwangju. The relationship between Chinese artists, critics, and curators, and those of other countries is no longer defined by subservience, but equality—most of the time. ¶ The most visible proof of this change in attitudes is the number of international exhibitions where Chinese curators such as Hou Hanrou, Fei Dawei, and Pi Li are invited to take part, and on a smaller scale the Shanghai exhibitions *Art for Sale* and *Twins*, where the German artist Alexander Brandt was invited to co-curate alongside Yang Zhenzhong and Xu Zhen. ¶ Another sign of the times is the number of Chinese artists who now manage galleries, such as the Long March Foundation and Space in Space 798. Until recently, all of the major Chinese galleries were run by Swiss, Dutch, Italian, or Australian managers with the sole exception of Li Liang at Eastlink. ¶ *Art for Sale* and *Post-Sense Sensibility* in 1999, *Fuck Off* in 2000, and *Twins* in 2002—these four major exhibitions, along with the new-look Shanghai Biennial in 2000 and Guangzhou Triennial in 2002, are proof of the marked improvement in the outlook of Chinese contemporary art. Further proof, if it were needed, was to be found at the 48th Venice Biennale in 1999, organized by Harald Szeeman, which featured twenty Chinese artists. ¶ In Shanghai, a city that has earned a reputation for rampant consumerism, the exhibition *Art for Sale* was held in a vast department store, with a catalog designed to look like a supermarket promotional brochure. It brought together thirty-three artists and featured an art supermarket where the works came in cans. It was a great success, bringing in over one thousand visitors in just two days. On the third day, the police intervened to evict the organizers who had, of course, been less than entirely truthful in their application for permission to the Cultural Bureau. Song Dong dressed up in yellow as the character Mr. Banana—nearly all department stores in Shanghai have their own mascot. He spent two days parading through the store with a megaphone and little flag, inviting shoppers to come and look at the works of art tucked away on the shelves among the other products, explaining their significance and their price. ¶

The exhibition *Post-Sense Sensibility: Alien Bodies and Delusion* went much further. It was organized by a group of artists from the Central Academy of Fine Arts in Beijing and was held in the basement of an apartment block in the same city. As is often the case with such exhibitions, the address was only divulged at the very last minute. Featuring works by some twenty artists, it was heavily influenced by the recent London exhibition *Sensation* whose catalog Qiu Zhijie had brought back from Holland. It was not for those with a nervous disposition or weak stomach. In the cellars, Zhu Yu hung a human arm from the ceiling, clutching a long rope, which trailed on the floor. Xiao Yu put together a hybrid monster of various animal body parts and the head of a human fetus. A little further on, in a separate cellar space, visitors were shocked to discover a work by the Beijing artist Sun Yuan, featuring a bed on which was placed a block of ice containing a man's head, while the body of a still-born child lay on the ice as if snuggling up to the head. How much further could the boundaries of taste be pushed back? ¶ Much, much further, it soon turned out. At the *Fuck Off* exhibition, Zhu Yu recorded a performance of himself cleaning, cooking, carving, arranging on a plate, and finally eating the body of a still-born fetus. There was no trick photography. The work was so shocking that it gave rise to a rumor that the International Olympic Committee had decided against awarding the games to Beijing because of this act of cannibalism. In fact, as it turned out, the rumor was unfounded. The artist defended himself by saying that it was a deeply artistic act designed to challenge moral, social, and religious taboos, while others claimed that the work was a reaction against the commercialization of Chinese art by the Western art market. ¶ Whether or not you believe that this work went beyond the bounds of acceptability, the exhibition *Fuck Off*, featuring ten of the twenty-nine artists selected for the present book—Xu Zhen, Yang Zhenzhong, Chen Lingyang, Ding Yi, Chen Shaoxiang, Zhen Guogu, Yang Fudong, Song Dong, Cao Fei, and Liang Yue—certainly had the greatest impact of any recent exhibition in China. Curated by Ai Weiwei and Feng Boyi at the Eastlink Gallery, it was held during the first international biennial in Shanghai. The controversial poster (or rather web banner) giving the biennial's URL claimed that "the biennial awaits your visit," while the accompanying picture was of three call girls putting on their make-up ready to do business. The Chinese title for the *Fuck Off* exhibition translated as "No taking part." ¶ The least controversial and probably the best of the recent major exhibitions was *Twins*, curated by the trio behind *Art for Sale*, Xu Zhen, Yang Zhenzhong, and Alexander Brandt. It was held during the official opening of the Fourth Shanghai Biennial. Each work was placed to echo another, forming an astonishing circuit where, for example, a color painting by Zhen Guogu faced the same subject executed in black and white. On the day the exhibition opened, visitors were given the address and an exact time to arrive by cell phone. In a corridor running parallel to the one used by the visitors to the show, again forming a mirror effect, old men, teenagers, students, and workers, all dressed in striped uniforms like prisoners or madmen, followed the visitors noiselessly like a shadow. Meanwhile, assistants were hired to push around fake pillars mounted on castors so that the exhibition space was in a permanent and utterly fascinating state of flux. A little over a year later, still very much impressed by what I had seen, I decided that *Twins* was one of the best contemporary art exhibitions of the last ten years. ¶ This fantastic spurt of energy led to the opening of many galleries, often vast, modern, innovative spaces. They were generally well-thought-out designs making the best use of abandoned lots and old warehouses and factories, in both Beijing and Shanghai. ¶ In Shanghai, Moganshan Street is where it is all happening, just a stone's throw from where the Shanghart Gallery's twenty-thousand-square-foot (two-thousand-square-meter) warehouses stood until they were recently demolished and replaced by a skyscraper. Now, Ding Yi's huge studio is on the left. Next door are the storage facilities and a large wing of the Shanghart Gallery, managed by Lorenz Helbling, who started off in a hotel lobby in 1996 and now runs what has become the biggest gallery in Shanghai and probably all of China. Shanghart is the only Chinese gallery apart from Courtyard to take part in international art fairs. Almost immediately opposite are Eastlink, where *Fuck Off* was held, and the extremely dynamic gallery BizArt, in premises of around six thousand square feet (six hundred square meters). Actually, BizArt is not strictly speaking a gallery, but rather a center specializing in multimedia, which works in art, consulting, production and coproduction, and a program of artists in residence in cooperation with the British Council, among a whole range of other activities. Xu Zhen, BizArt's brilliant young art director, and Davide Quadrio, the equally dynamic and brilliant director, are the brightest, sharpest, and most innovative duo in the Chinese art world today. Shanghart, BizArt, and Eastlink are the three heavyweights in contemporary Chinese art. ¶ At the entrance to Space 798, the place to see and be seen in Beijing, where tourists cluster after a visit to the Forbidden City and the Great Wall, the streets are lined with pleasant apartment blocks with rows of large satellite dishes along the ground. Then there is a long road straight ahead, with an unbelievable clutter of abandoned factories, fashionable galleries, consultants, and design studios on either side. But what draw the crowds are the fabulous galleries. One of the first to arrive in the neighborhood was a rather small Japanese undertaking, the Tokyo Beijing Art Project. Many artists live here in lofts, such as Chen Wenbo and Chen Lingyang. There is the trendy At Café, where you can order an Italian espresso, Brazilian roast, or French café, for thirty yuans. (I wonder briefly what they mean by French café.) The tables are cutting-edge modern designs, the snacks keep the artists happy, and the walls are decorated with old quotes by Chairman Mao to encourage the workers to greater efforts for the good of the Revolution. ¶ Similar old communist slogans are to be found in the aptly named Space Gallery, which has a 13,000-square-foot (1,200-square-meter) hall near a modest photograph gallery. Nearby are another building, twice as large as Space, and a soon-to-open icily chic French restaurant named Sit. Just up the street is the Long March Foundation Gallery. On my most recent visit in August 2003, Yan Lei and Chen Wenbo were the featured artists. By the front door was a stand selling Chinese and English art reviews and Long March T-shirts. ¶ In Canton, Wang Wei's Vitamin Gallery opens onto a marketplace. It is an interesting and dynamic art space, if a little difficult to get to. Wang Wei prefers not to use the term gallery, since the center works in a range of different areas. ¶ Among the more traditional galleries is Courtyard, near the Forbidden City in Beijing, which is as well known for its restaurant and fine French wines as it is for its artworks, shown in the basement. Among the artists to have shown there are Cao Fei, the Luo Brothers, and Chen Wenbo. CAAW, also in Beijing, is one of the oldest, best, and best-organized galleries, although it is terribly unprepossessing from the outside, with grim walls as uninviting as a prison. Ding Yi, Yan Lei, and Zhen Guogu, along others, have all shown here. ¶ Who buys Chinese art today? Ding Yi explains that there are two types of buyers: firstly, those that intend to found a museum, and who want to buy a number of works representing the different periods of all the major artists, and secondly, a larger category of buyers who want a work of art that will go with the color scheme in their new office. The numbers of buyers in this second category are constantly increasing, and must thus be provided for. However, ninety-five percent of collectors of contemporary Chinese art are foreign. The foremost collector in the world today is the former Swiss ambassador to Beijing, Uli Sigg. Buyers on his scale are few and far between, but have played an important part in bringing contemporary Chinese art to international prominence. ¶ Collectors in general do not buy much in the way of video art, and collectors of Chinese art are no exception. While Zhang Peili, who shot the first Chinese video art work in 1988, says he makes a comfortable living from his sales, and while the Guangzhou Museum has built up a decent collection of video art, these are unusual examples. Yet Chinese video art is some of the most stimulating in the world, in my opinion. Maybe this is because it is mostly the work of extremely young artists who are disenchanted with politics—Xu Zhen even says, "we don't give a fuck about politics"—because they did not live through the Cultural Revolution as the older artists did, and so they are free of many of the influences that weigh down so much of the art from a few years back. Young artists are now producing videos that are fun, unburdened by existential anguish, and much better able to hold their own on the international art scene than painting or sculpture, which have practically died out anyway. The impressive works by some incredibly young artists discussed in the present work are ample evidence of their inventiveness. In particular, video seems to me the best medium to portray a certain way of life and a certain type of behavior, which may seem odd but that's the way things are today. They display great subtlety, imagination, humor, and grace, with digressions, sidesteps, zooms, and fast-forwards that are full of charm and audacity, surprises, and marvelous ingenuity. ¶ And what can I say about the superb, untamed calligraphy of Zhen Guogu and his gang, which is closer to graffiti than to the refined, restrained art of lettering that it supposedly derives from? For the new generation of Chinese artists, life is something to be sucked dry, to the very last drop. ¶ I was surprised, then, to hear a number of people I admire greatly, both in China and elsewhere, saying that there are no longer any artists in China of the stature of those who made their mark a few years back—in the past. Maybe the shoulders of the new generation aren't quite as broad, but I firmly believe that with the honorable exception of three or four artists, the artists who achieved prominence in the 1980s, in China or elsewhere, were never as original or in tune with their times as today's generation. Never was a generation so crazily, dynamically inspired. ¶ Look at Yang Zhenzhong, look at Kan Xuan, look at Xu Zhen, look at Zhen Guogu, Cui Xiuwen, Zhou Yi, Liang Yue, and Yang Fudong. But it would be pointless to list them all. Read the book, and you will see what I mean.

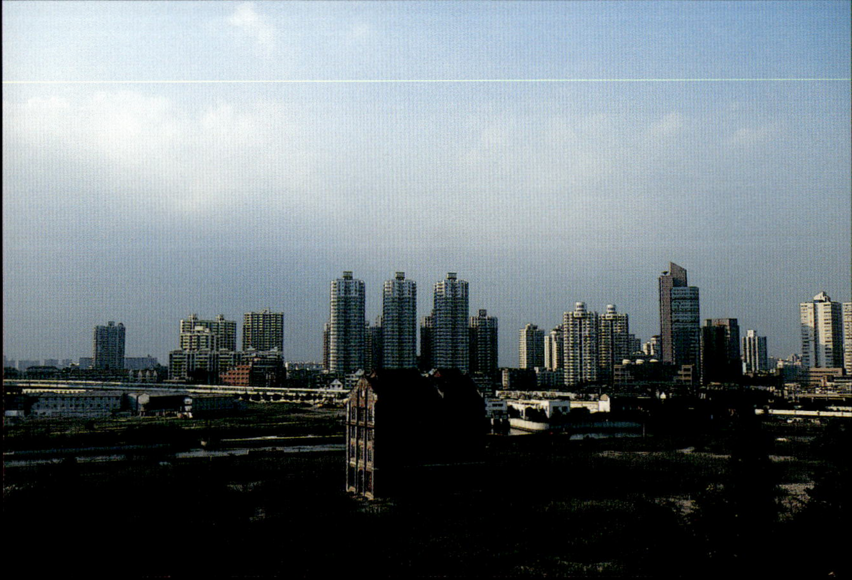

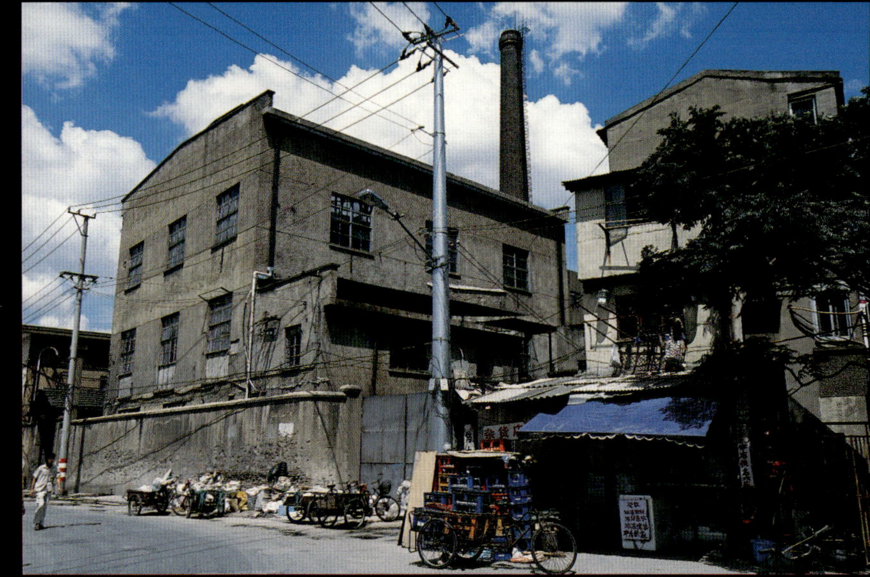

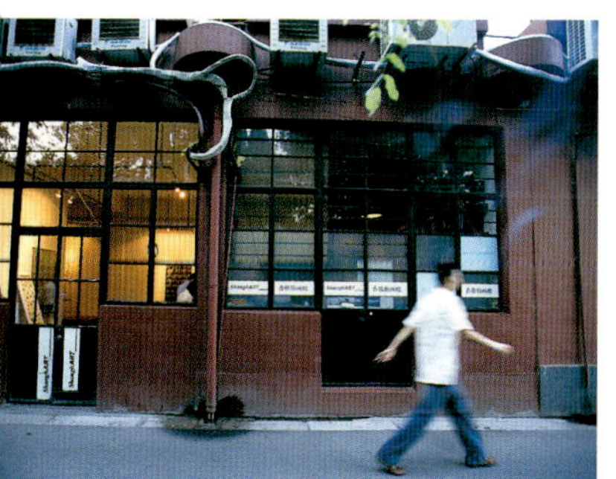

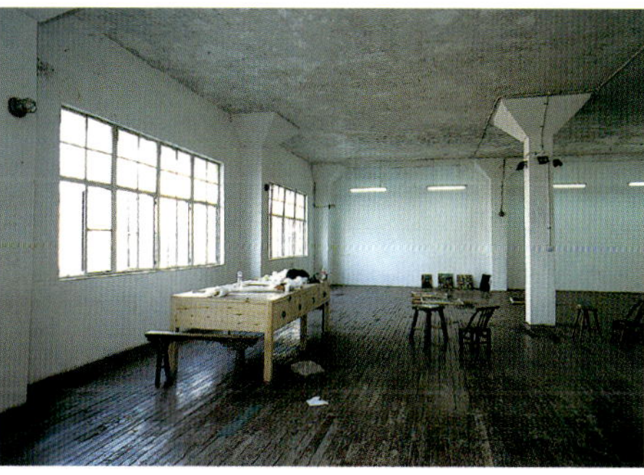

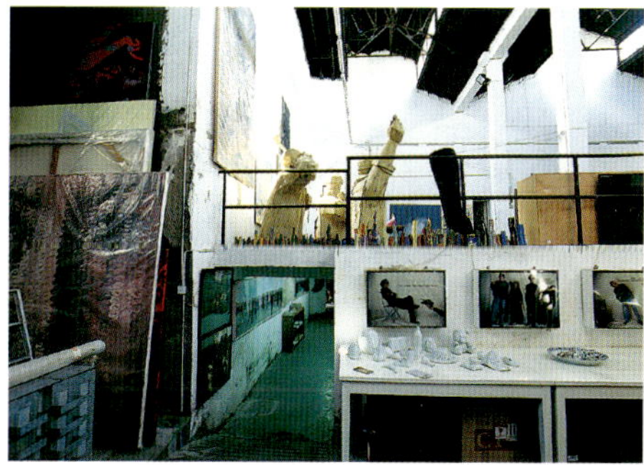

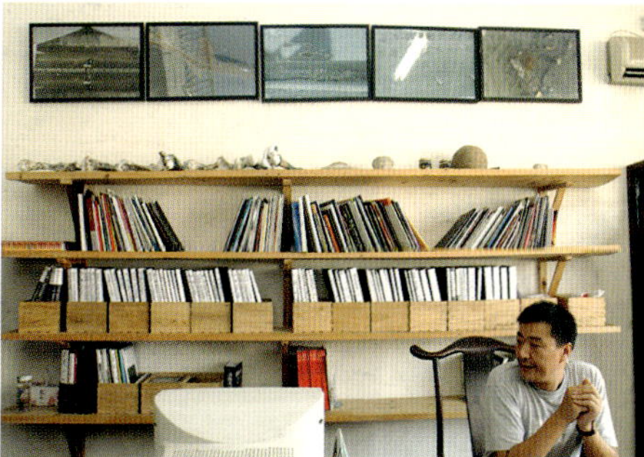

50 MOGANSHAN ROAD, BUILDING 6, SIXTH FLOOR: THE EASTLINK GALLERY AND ITS MANAGER LI LIANG, RIGHT, ONE OF THE FEW CHINESE GALLERY DIRECTORS. LI LIANG ORGANIZED THE CONTROVERSIAL EXHIBITION *FUCK OFF*.

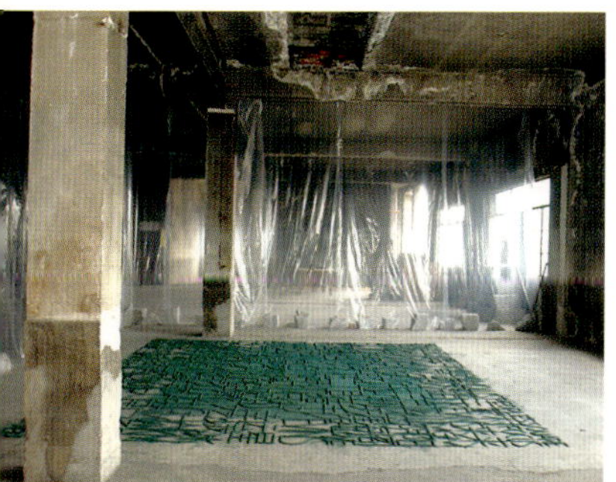

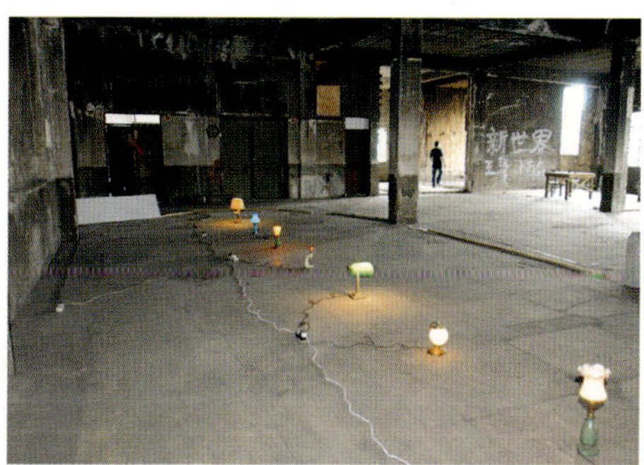

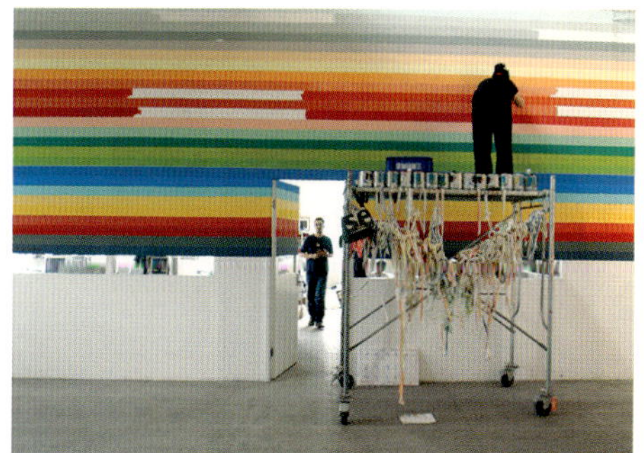

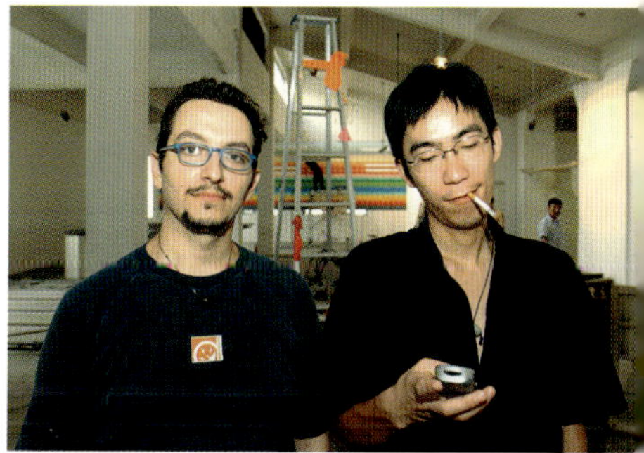

DAVIDE QUADRIO AND XU ZHEN, RESPECTIVELY DIRECTOR AND ARTISTIC DIRECTOR OF THE DYNAMIC BIZART CENTER, IN THEIR NEW PREMISES AT 50 MOGANSHAN ROAD, BUILDING 7, FIFTH FLOOR.

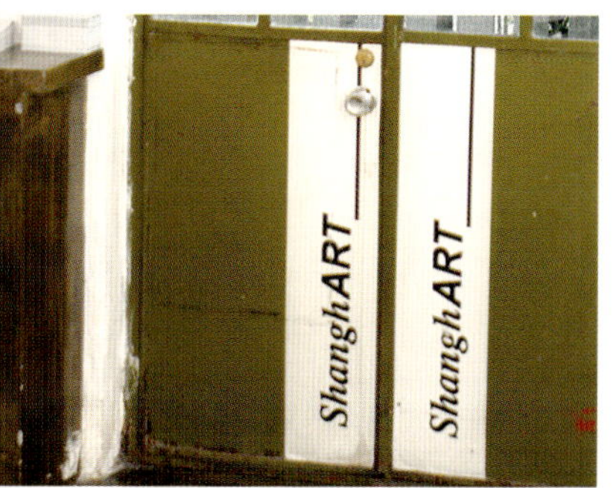

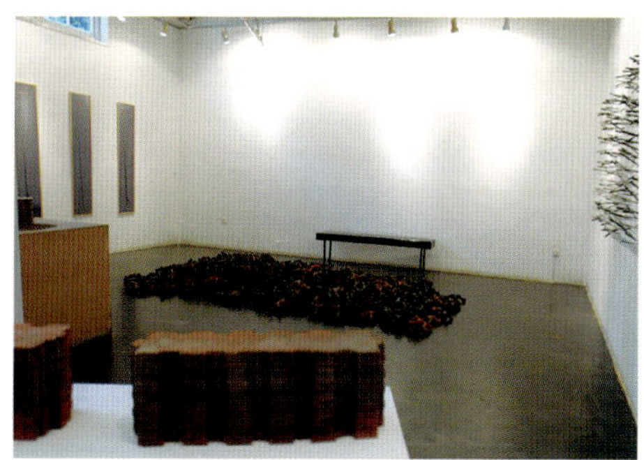

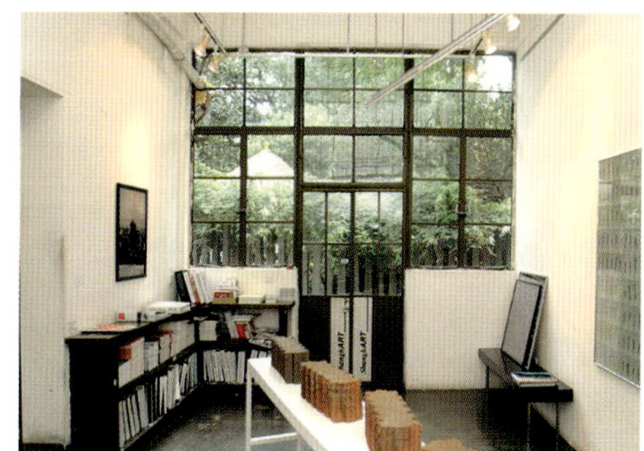

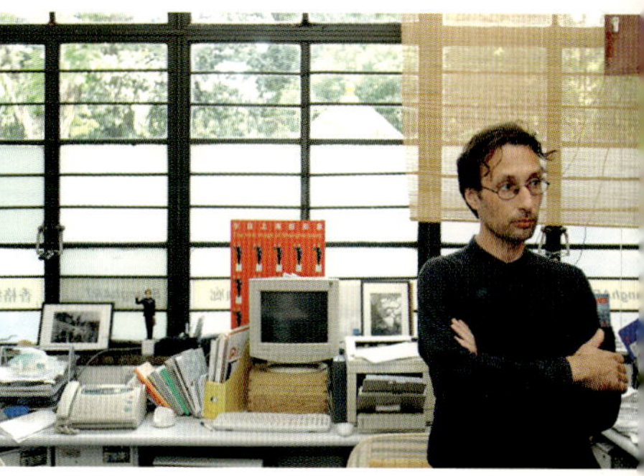

LORENZ HELBLING, DIRECTOR OF THE SHANGART GALLERY, IN THE PREMISES ON GAOLAN ROAD IN FUXING PARK. THE EXHIBITION SPACE AND ARCHIVES ARE AT 50 MOGANSHAN ROAD.

FACING PAGE: SHANGHAI

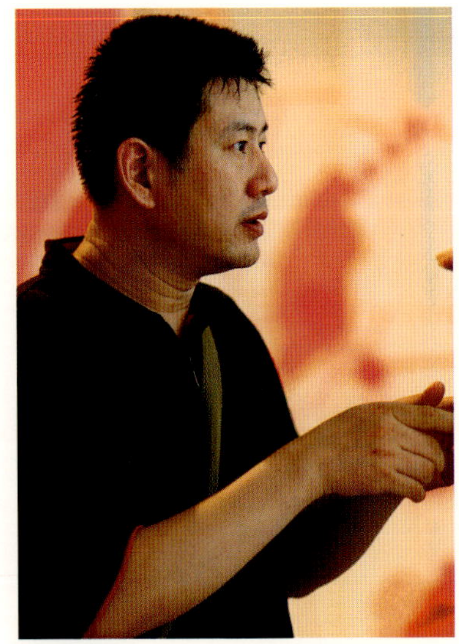

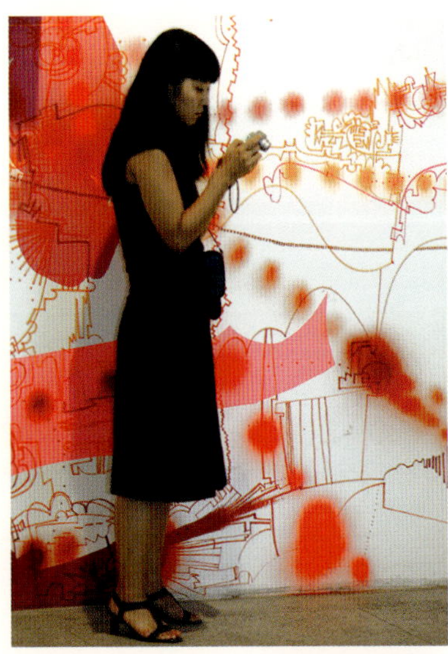

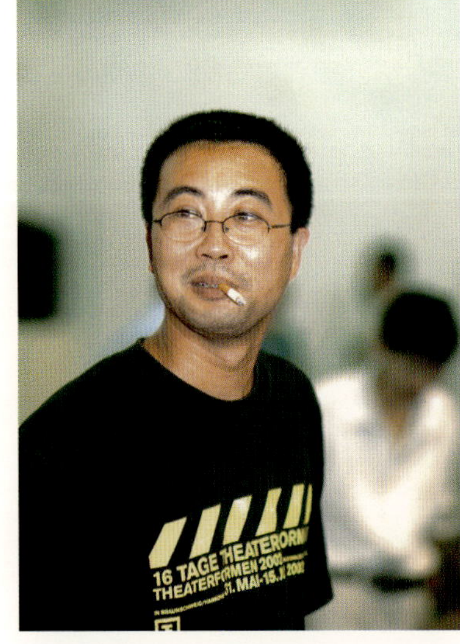

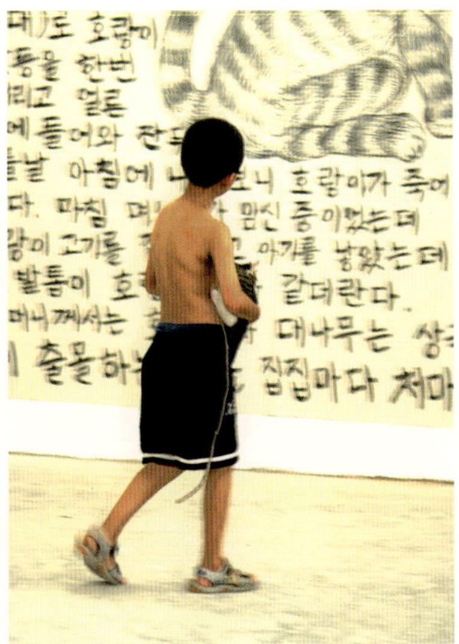

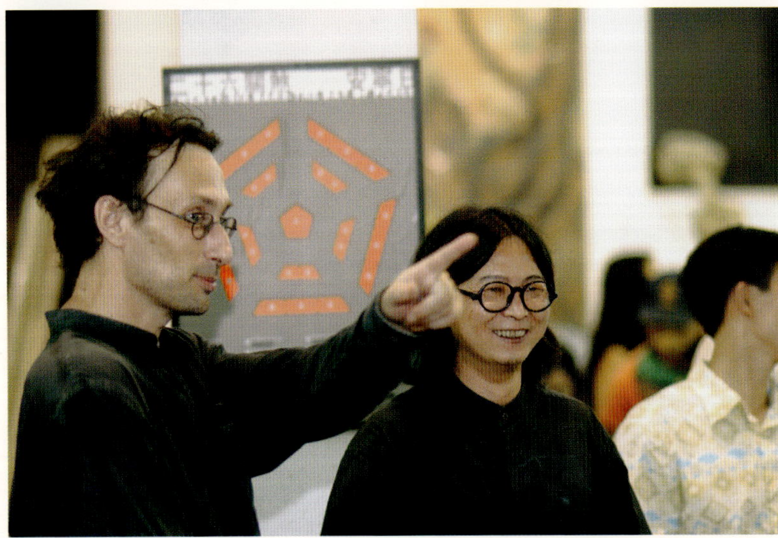

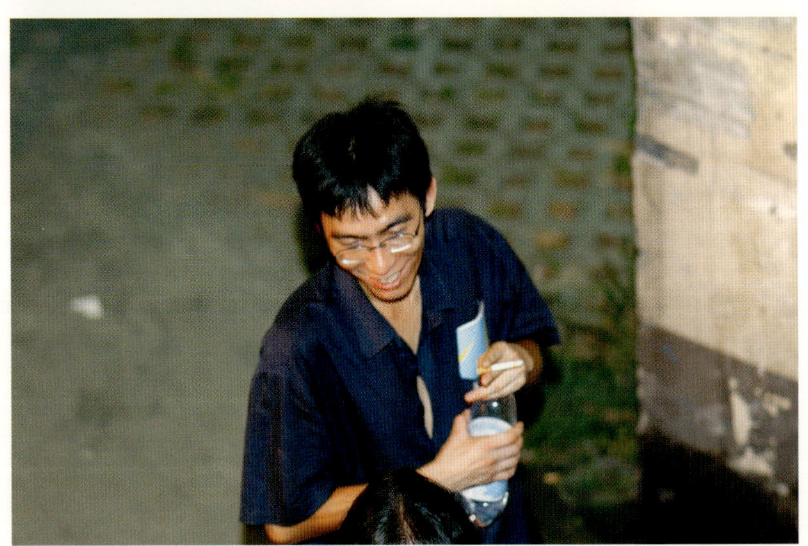

A VERNISSAGE AT 50 MOGANSHAN ROAD AT THE EASTLINK GALLERY. TOP: ZHOU CHUNYA, YANG ZHENZHONG, AND TWO GUESTS. LATER THE SAME EVENING, A VERNISSAGE AT THE SHANGART GALLERY. BOTTOM: LEFT: LORENZ HELBLING AND DING YI WITH XU ZHEN ON THE RIGHT.

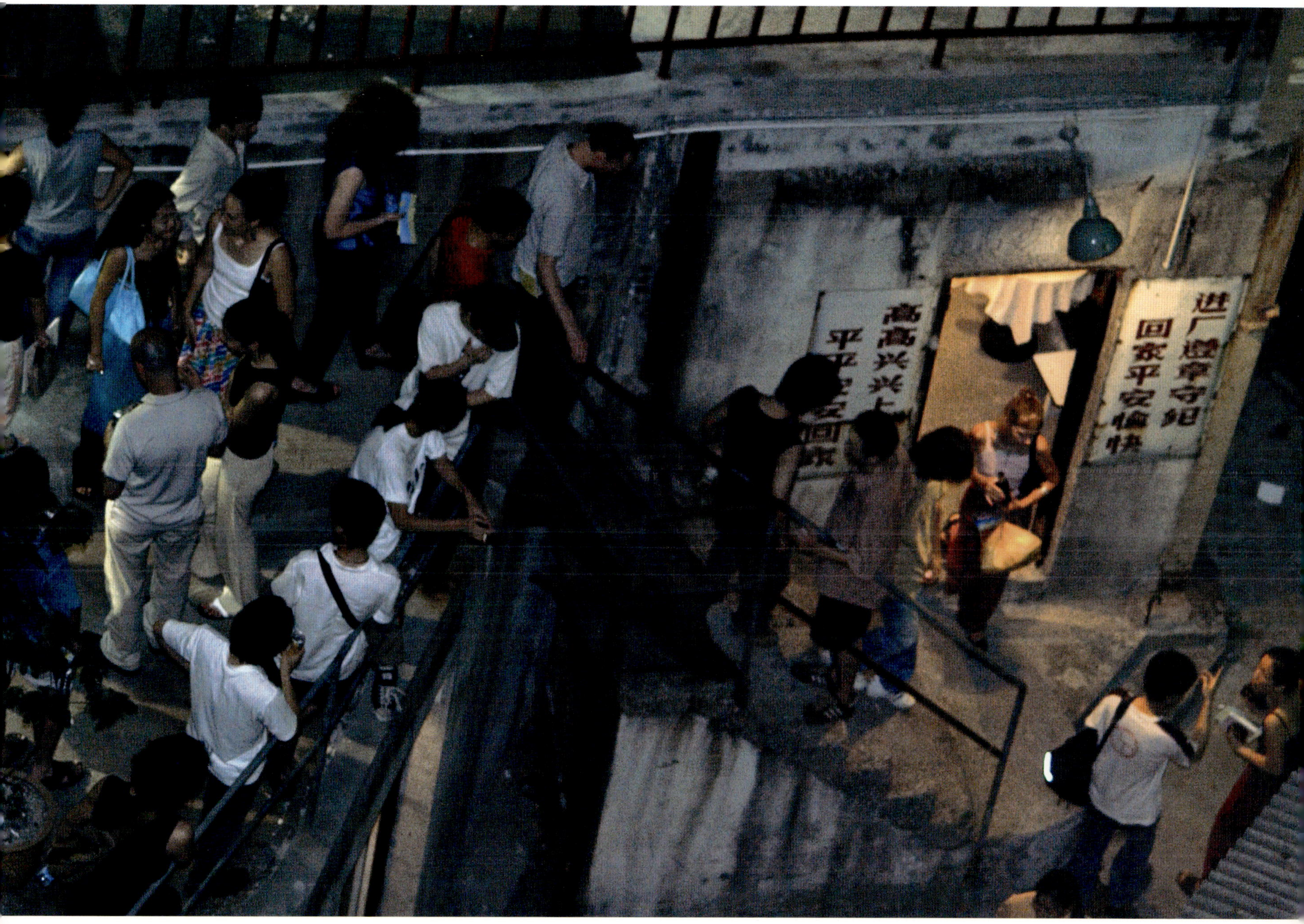

OUTSIDE THE GALLERY. BY 2006, THE WASTELAND AROUND THE GALLERIES WILL HAVE BEEN REPLACED BY HIGH-RISES.

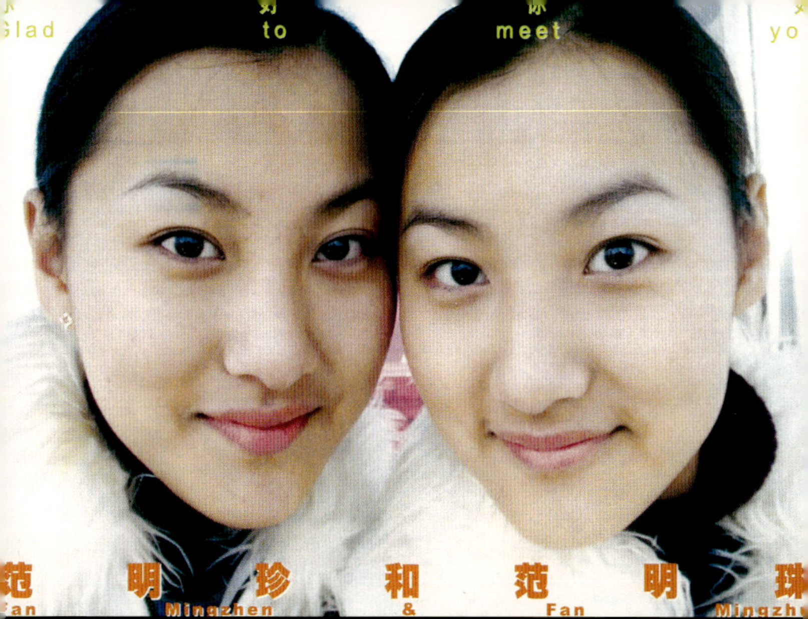

Glad to meet yo

范 明 珍 和 范 明 珠

Fan Mingzhen & Fan Mingzh

Kan Xuan, Liang Yue, Liu Wei, Shi Qing, Tang Maohong, Wang Wei, Xu Tan, Xu Zhen, Yang Fudong, Yang Zhenzhong, Zheng Guogu, Zhu Yu

阚萱 梁玥 刘韡 石青 唐茂宏 王卫 徐坦 徐震 杨福东 杨振忠 郑国谷 朱昱

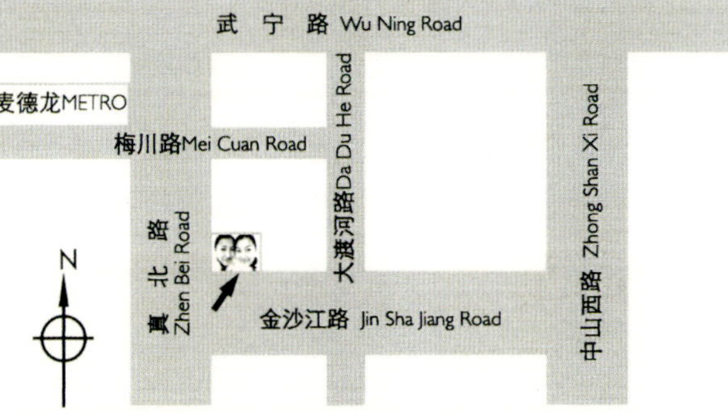

地址：上海 金沙江路1508号2楼
时间：2002年11月23日16:00-20:00, 11月24日10:00-17:30
Address: 2th floor, 1508 Jin Sha Jiang Road, Shanghai
Opening: 23 Nov. 2002 16:00-20:00, 24 Nov. 10:00-17:00

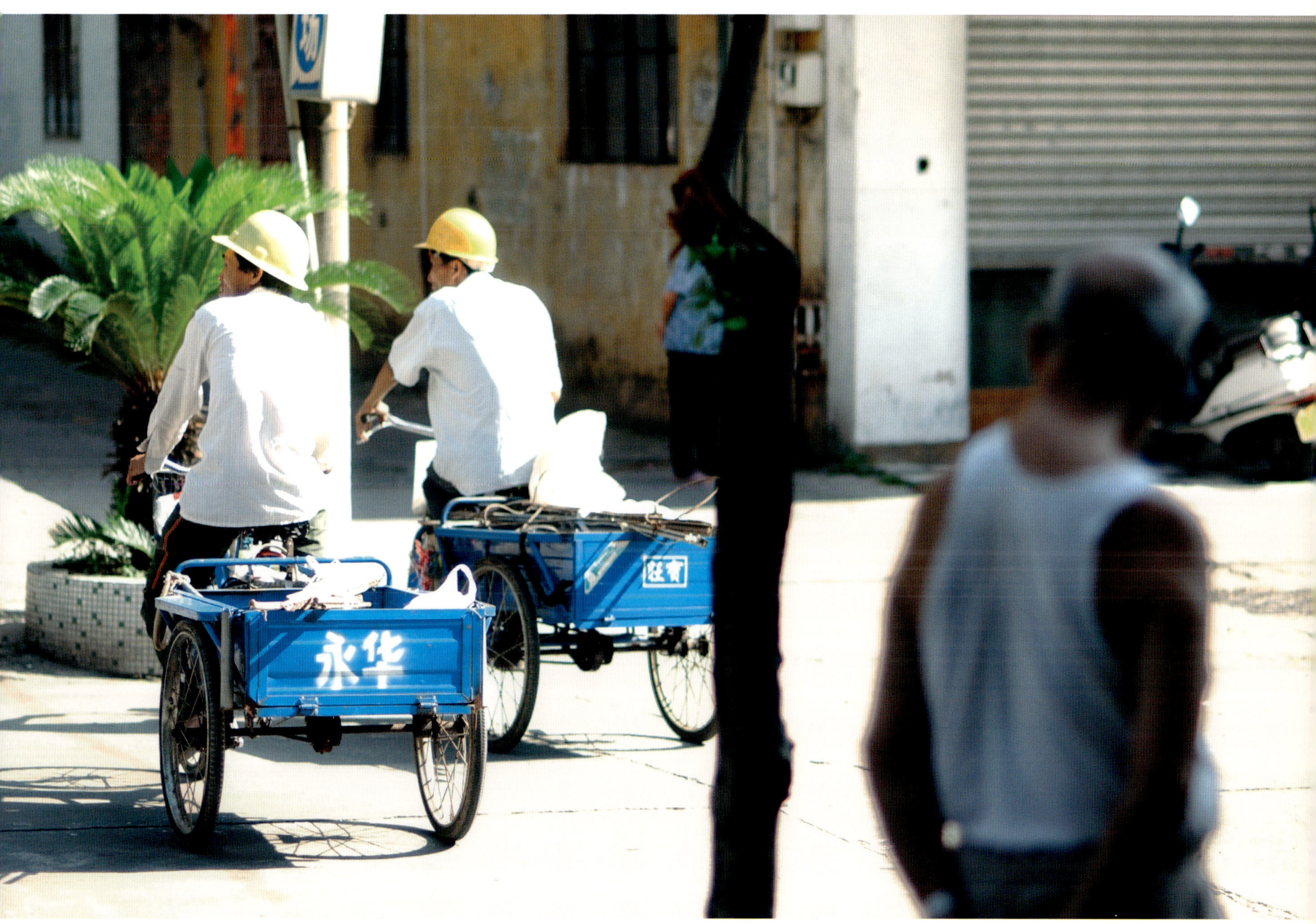

FACING PAGE: LEFT: AN INVITATION TO THE EXTRAORDINARY EXHIBITION *TWINS* ORGANIZED BY YANG ZHENZHONG, XU ZHEN, AND ALEXANDER BRANDT DURING THE FOURTH SHANGHAI BIENNIAL IN 2002.
ABOVE: A GUANGZHOU STREET SCENE, NOT FAR FROM THE VITAMIN GALLERY.

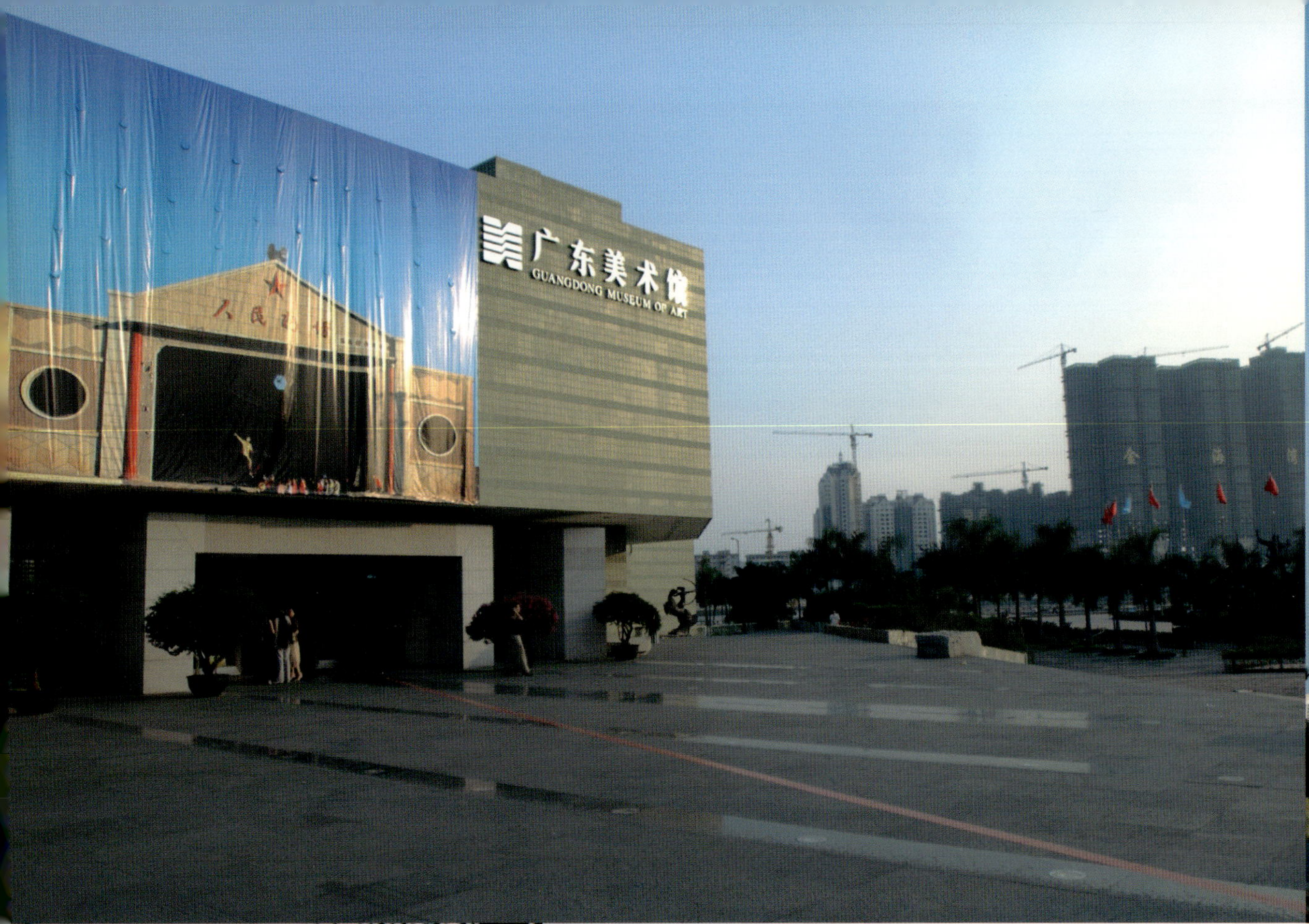

广东美术馆
GUANGDONG MUSEUM OF ART
金 海 湾 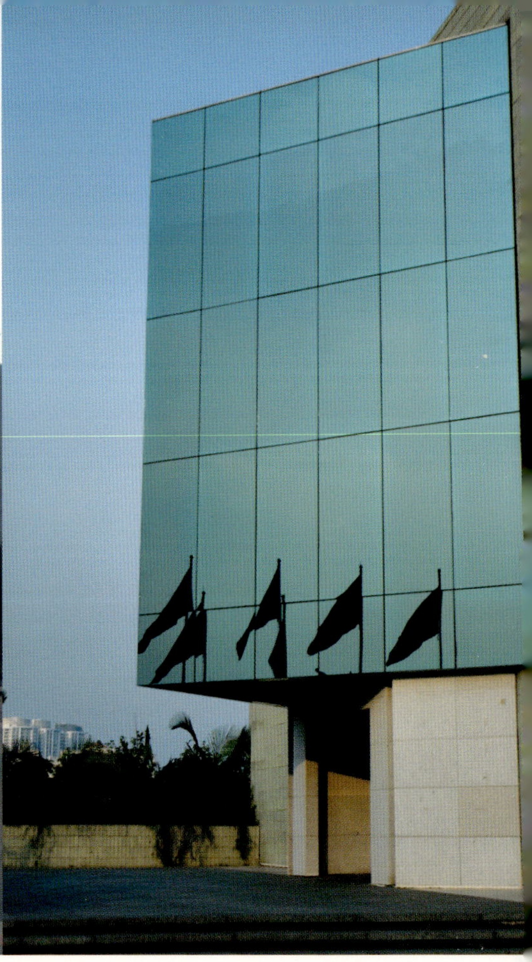 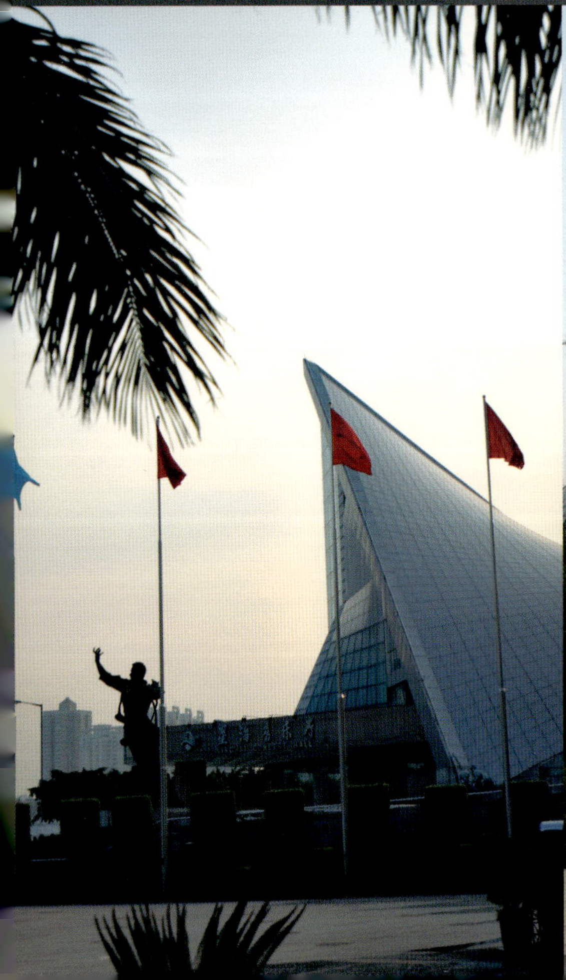 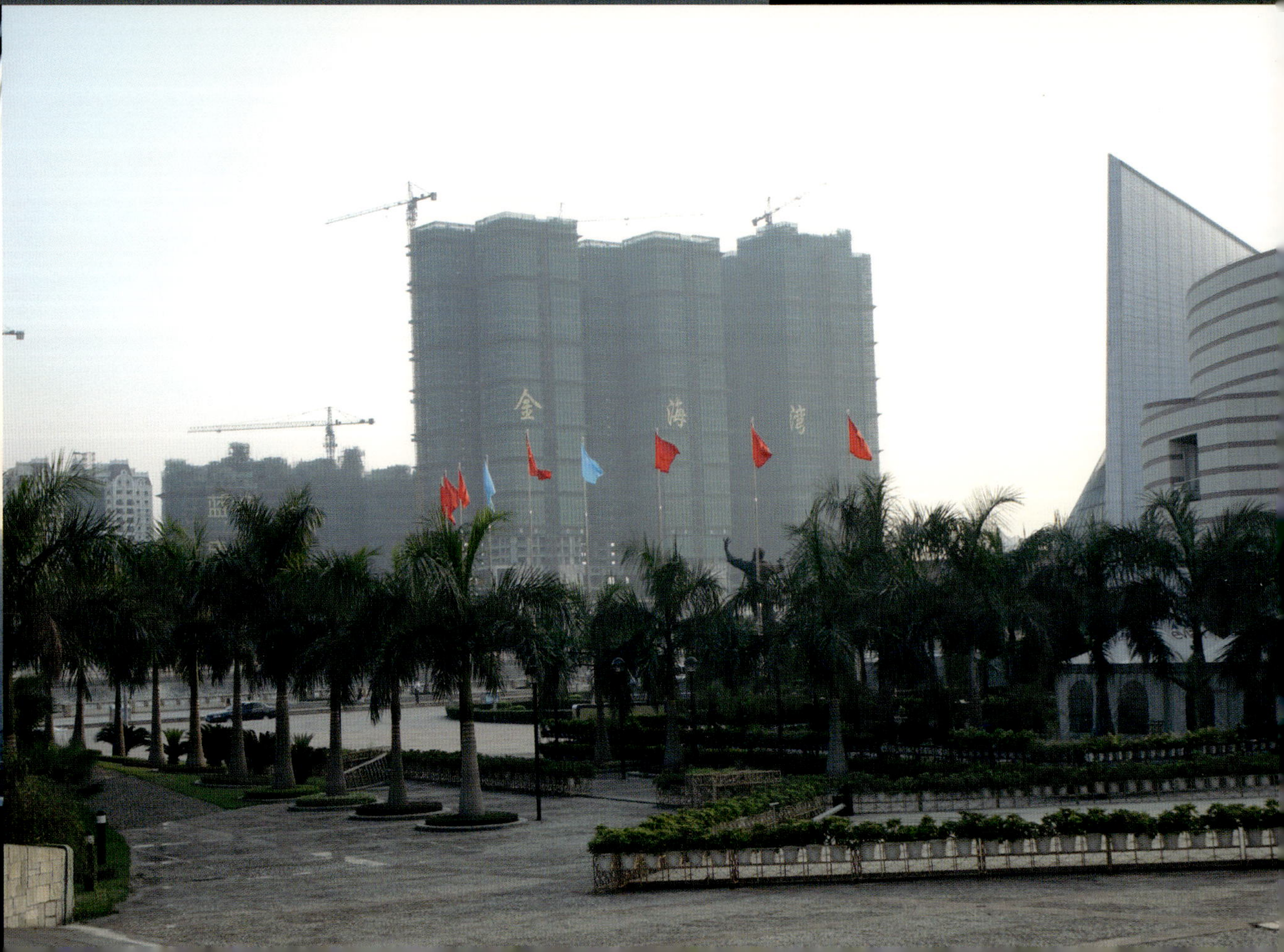
金 海 湾

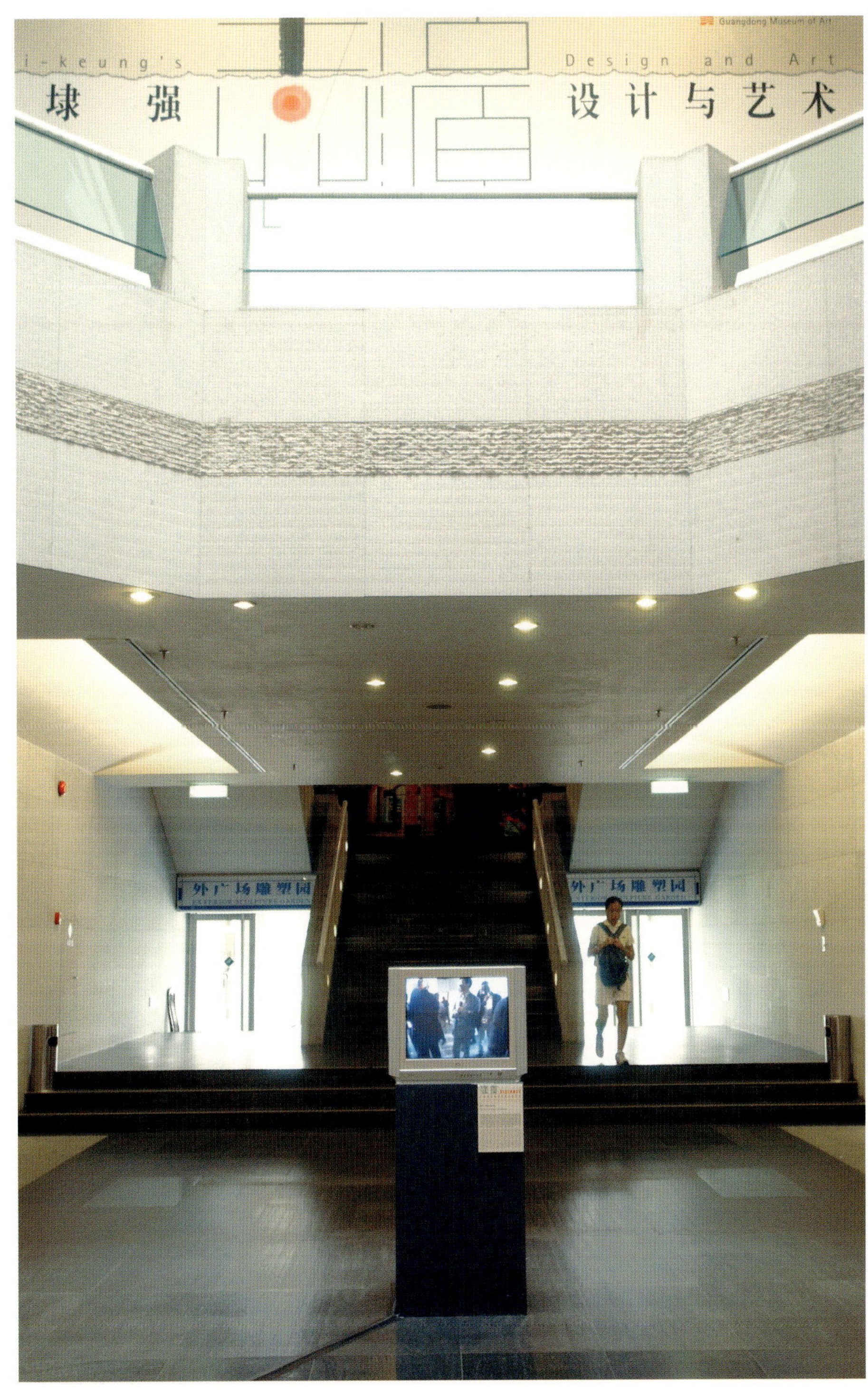

THE EXTERIOR, FACING PAGE, AND INTERIOR, ABOVE, OF THE GUANGDONG MUSEUM OF MODERN AND CONTEMPORARY ART IN GUANGZHOU, CURATED BY WANG HUANGSHENG. IN THE FOREGROUND, A VIDEO BY SONG DONG.

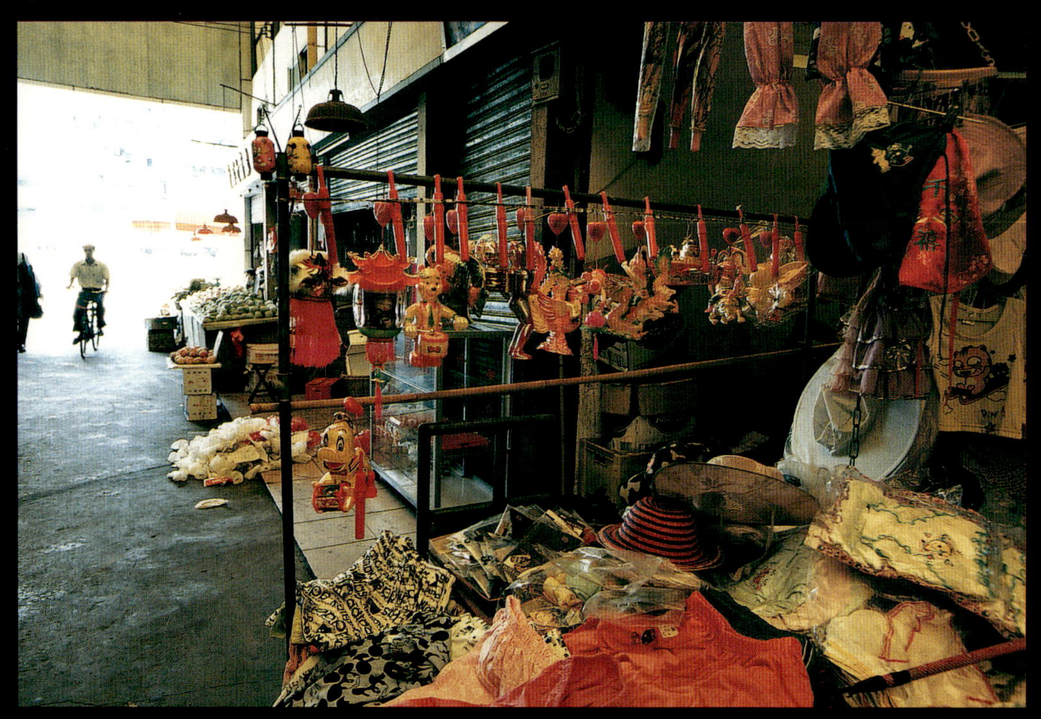

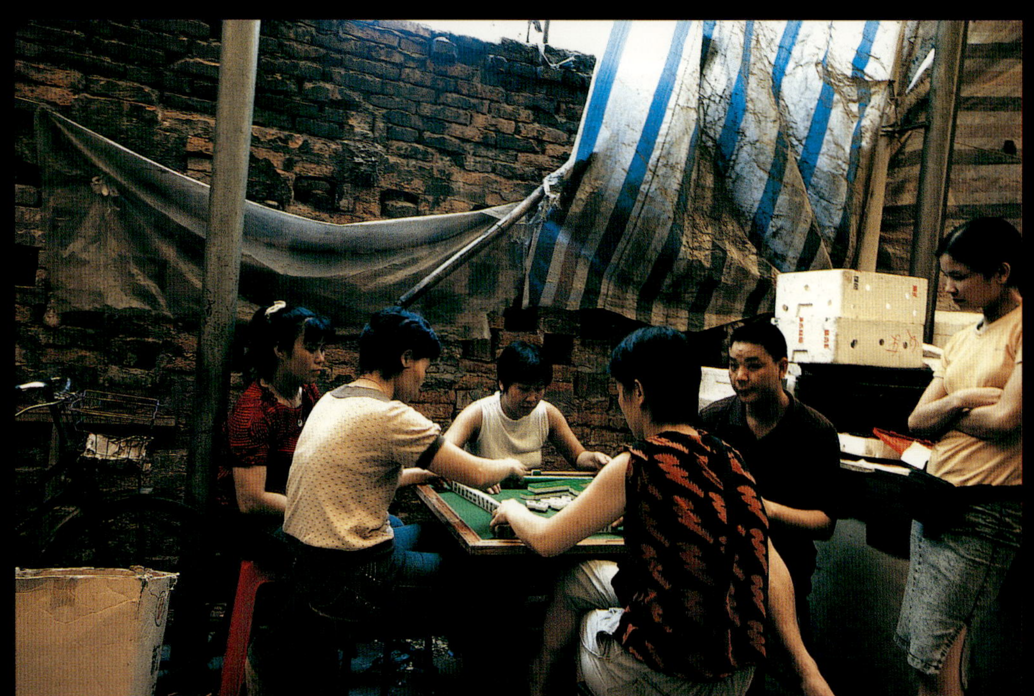

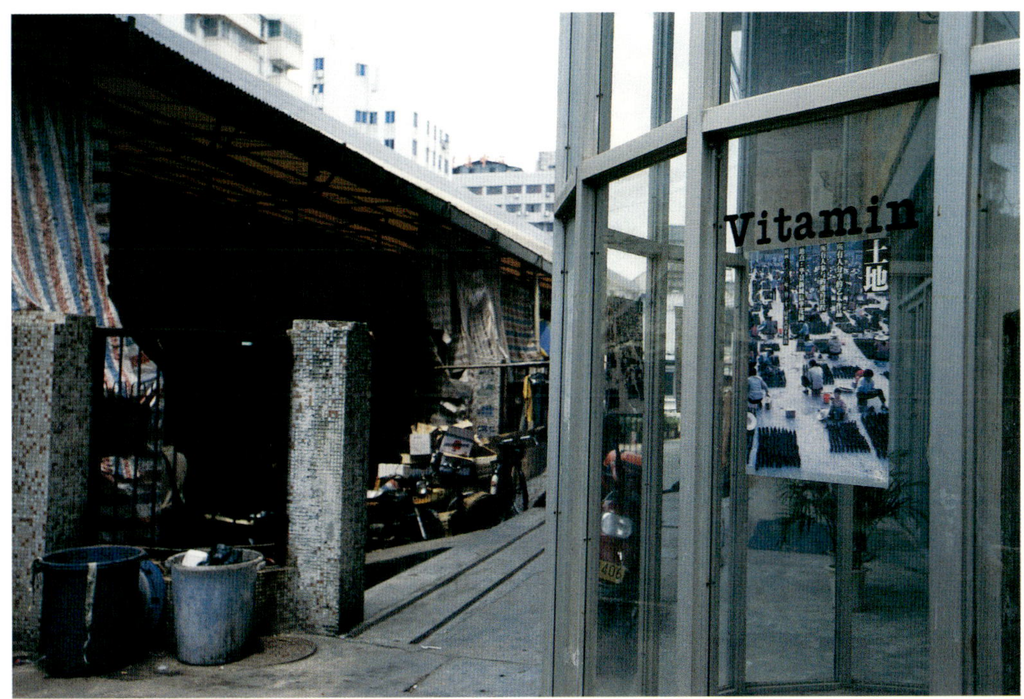

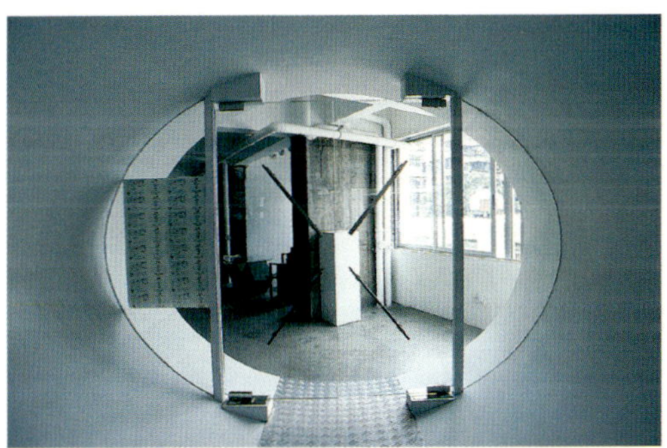

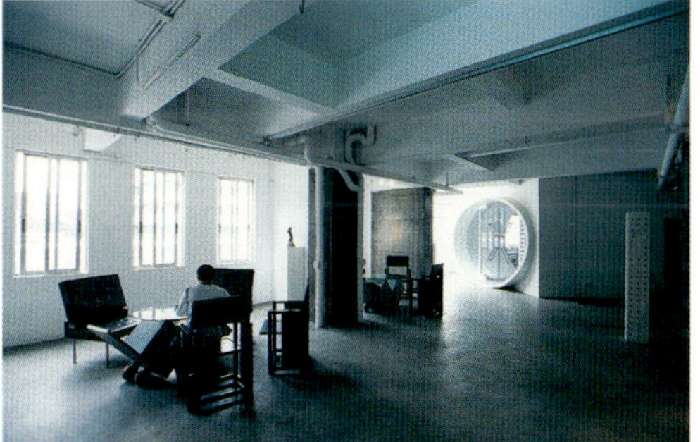

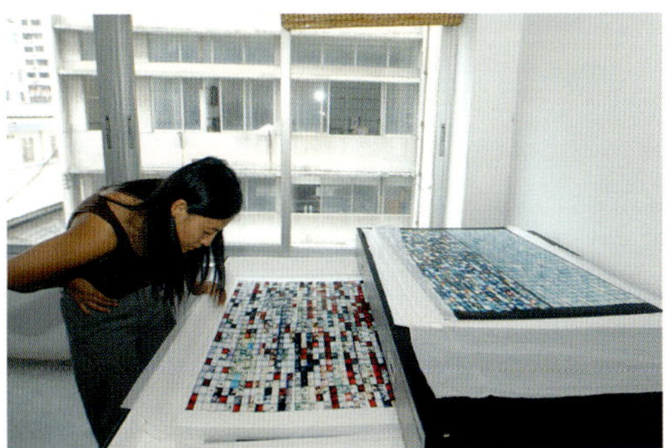

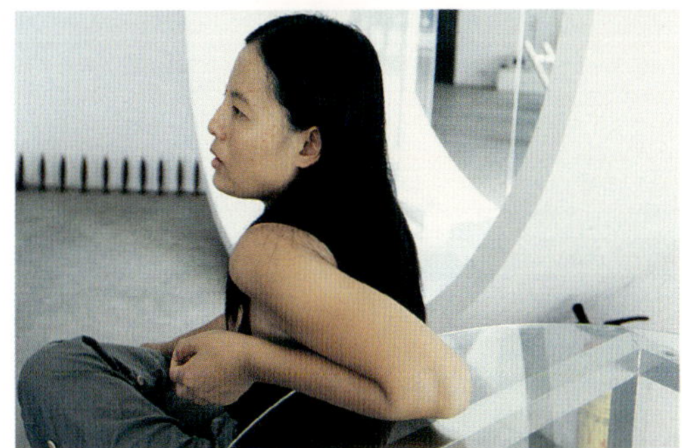

FACING PAGE: THE GUANGZHOU MARKET THAT IS HOME TO THE VITAMIN GALLERY. TOP: THE ENTRANCE TO THE GALLERY. CENTER: THE CUTTING-EDGE GALLERY INTERIOR. BOTTOM: THE DIRECTOR ZHANG WEI, LOOKING AT PHOTOGRAPHS BY ZHEN GUOGU IN FRONT OF SCULPTURES BY THE SAME ARTIST.

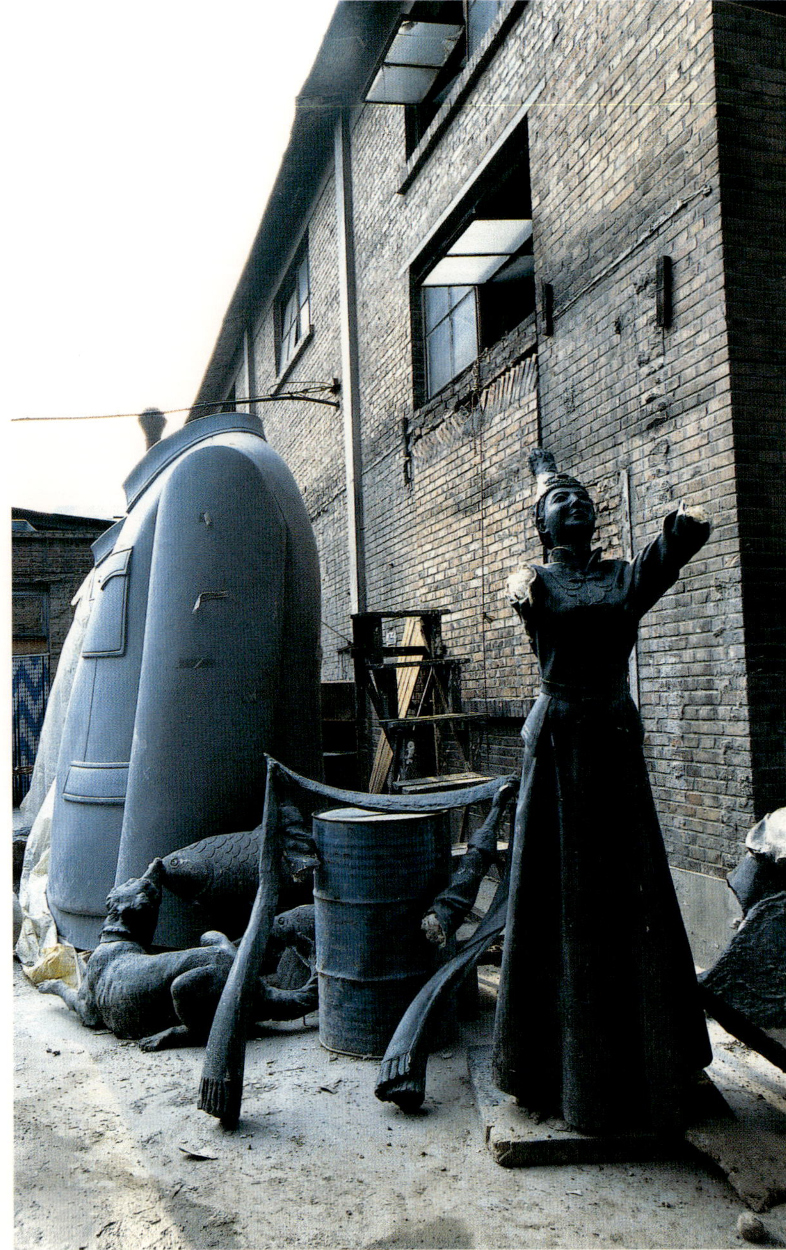

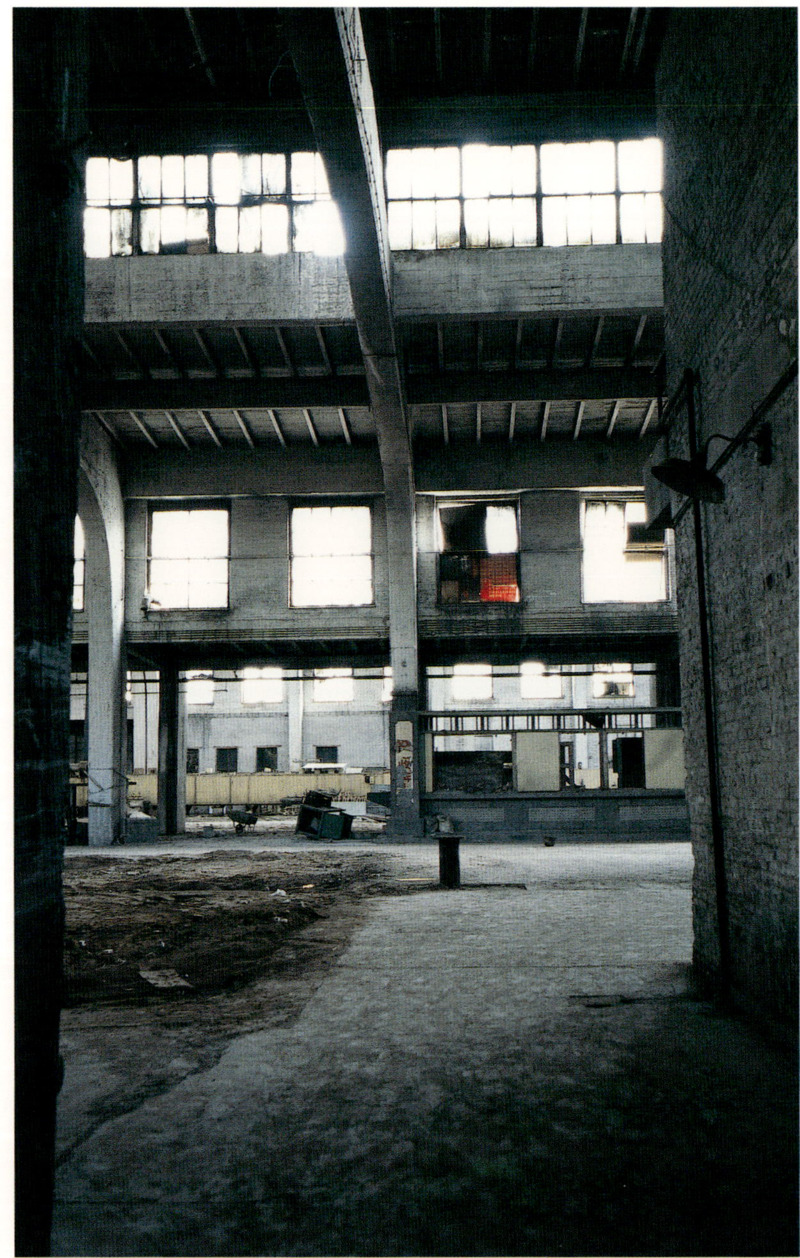

SPACE 798, ONE OF THE MOST FASHIONABLE PLACES IN BEIJING. OUTSIDE, ONE OF SUI JIANGUO'S "HERITAGE COATS" SEEMS TO LIE ABANDONED. RIGHT: A NEW GALLERY UNDERGOING BUILDING WORK. HOW LARGE WILL IT BE? IT IS BOUND TO BE HUGE, IN ANY CASE.

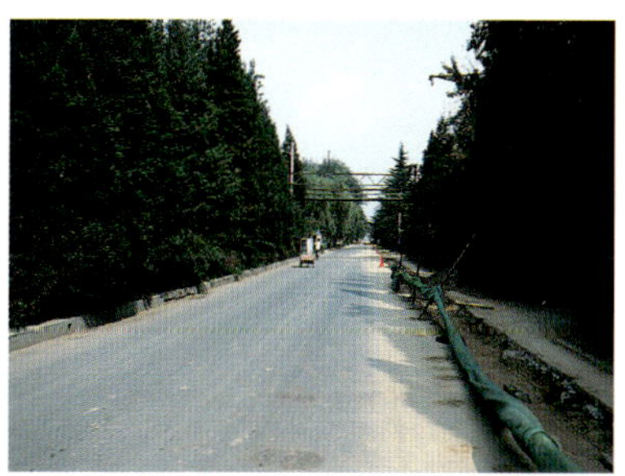
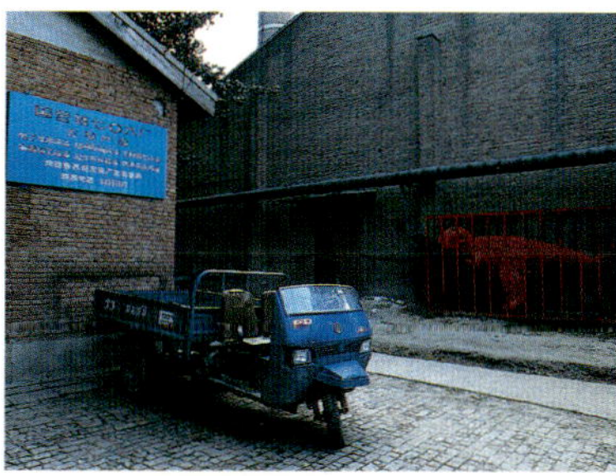
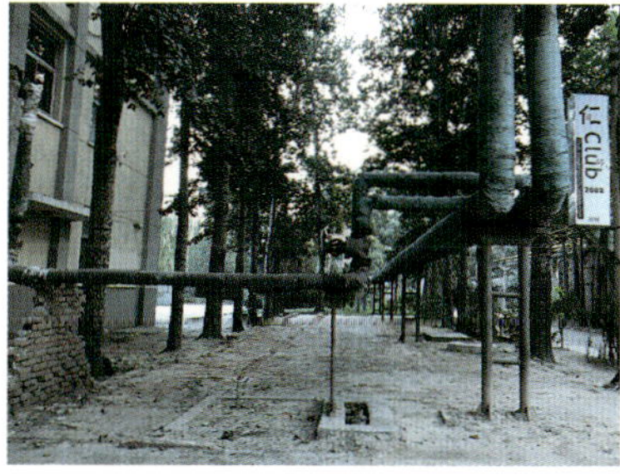

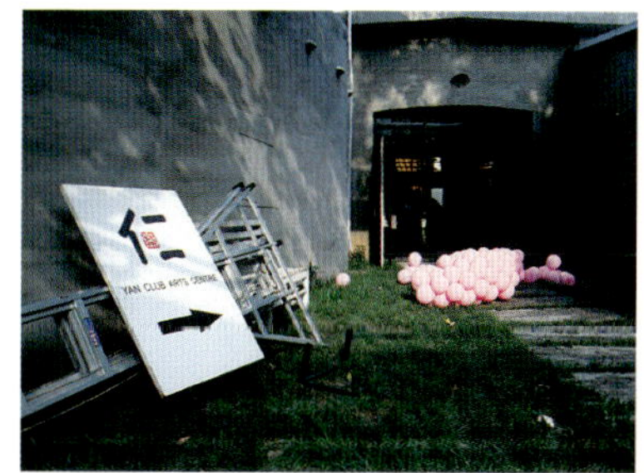

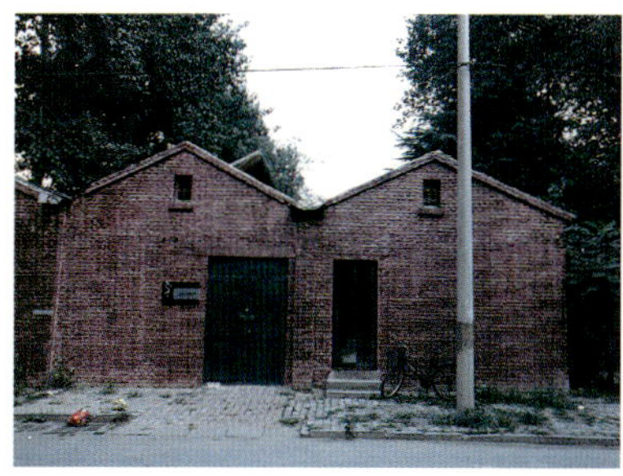
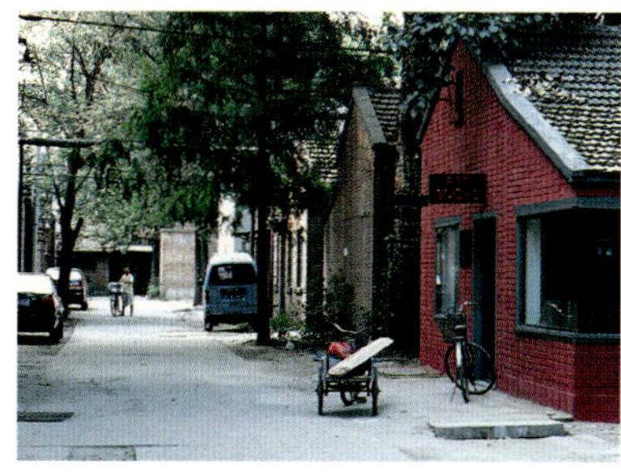
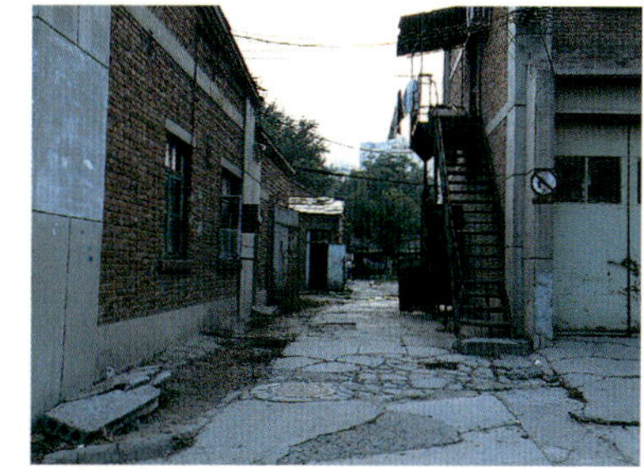
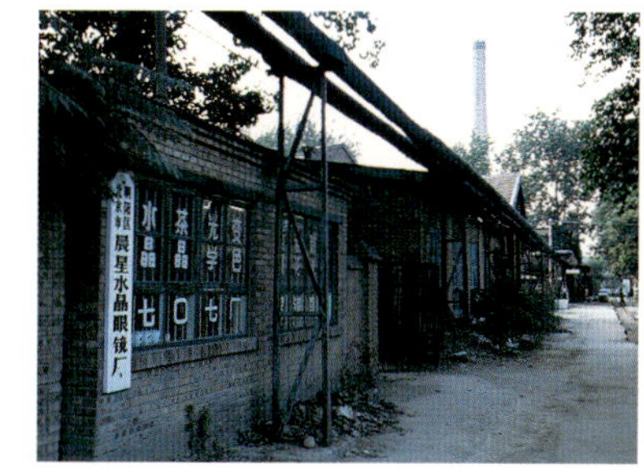

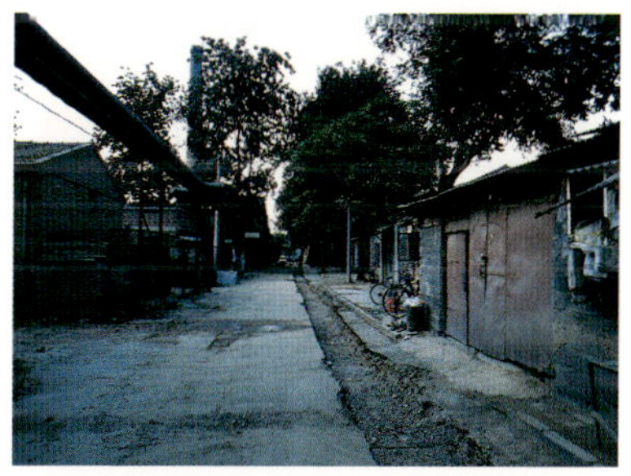
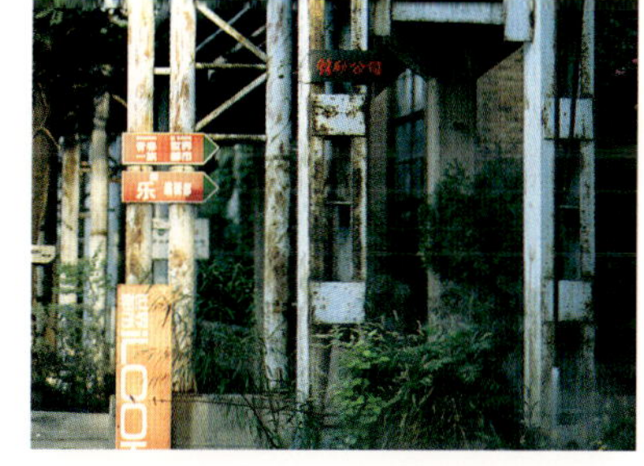
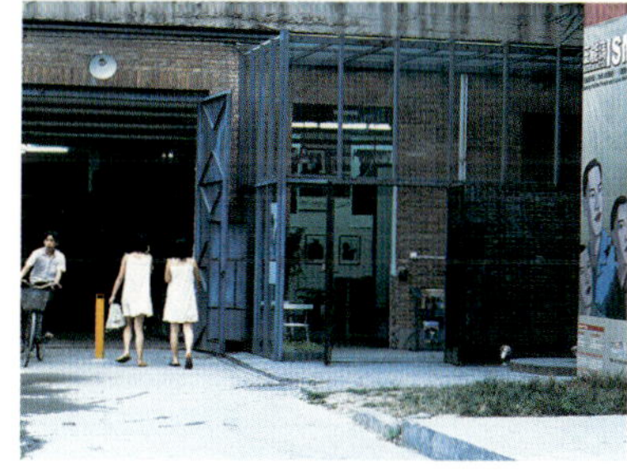
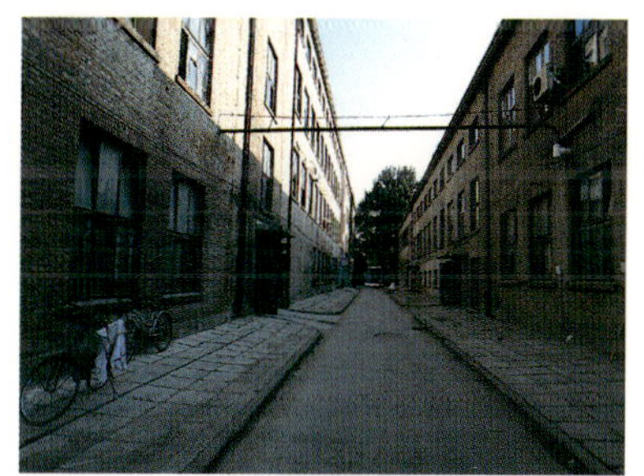
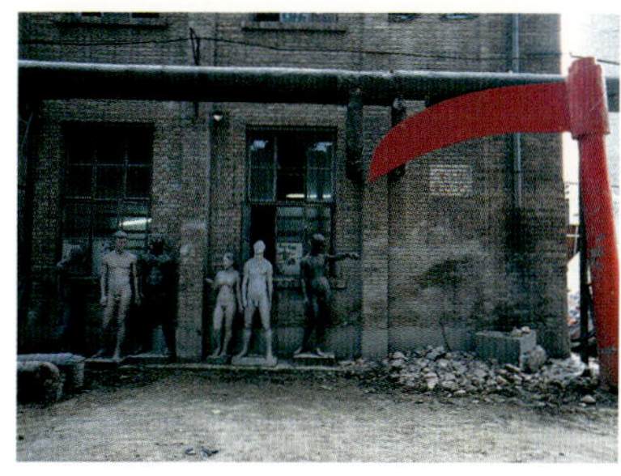
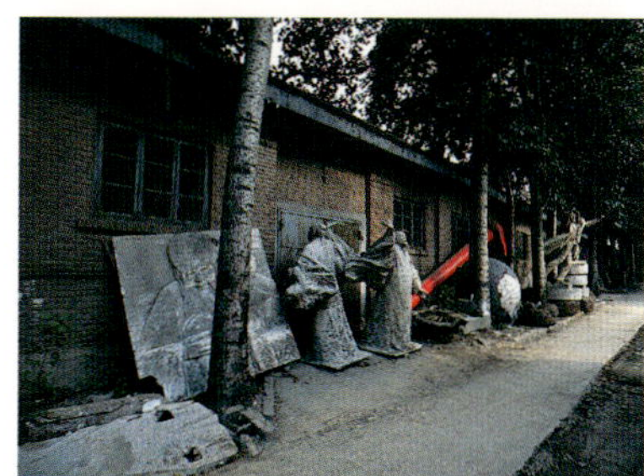
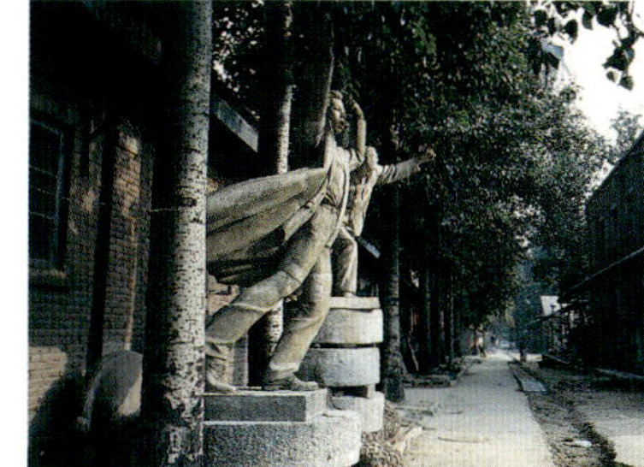
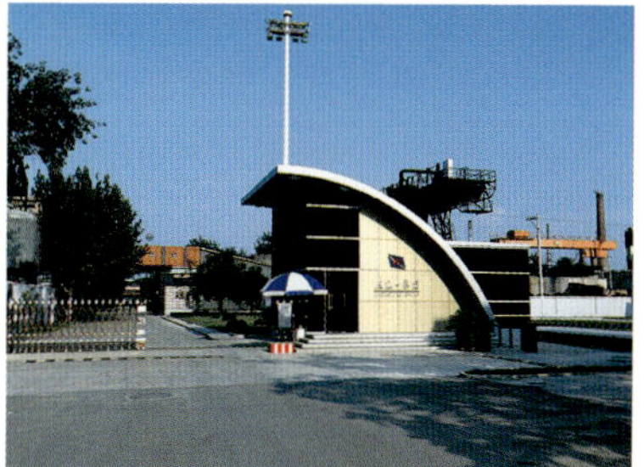

STROLLING THROUGH SPACE 798, WHERE GALLERIES ARE SPRINGING UP AMONG THE HALF-BUILT LOTS AND ABANDONED FACTORY SITES. A FEW OF THE FACTORIES ARE STILL IN BUSINESS.

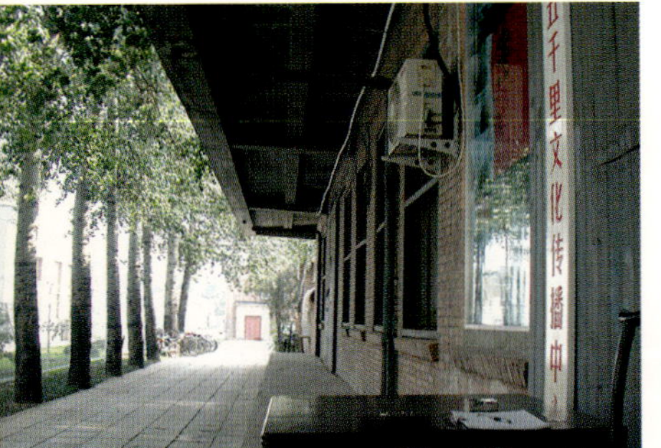
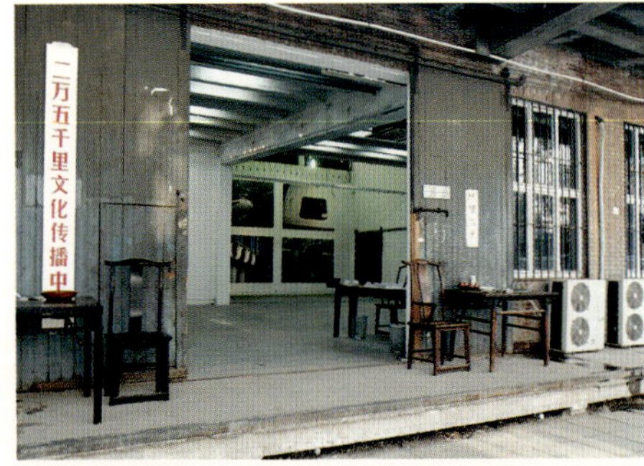

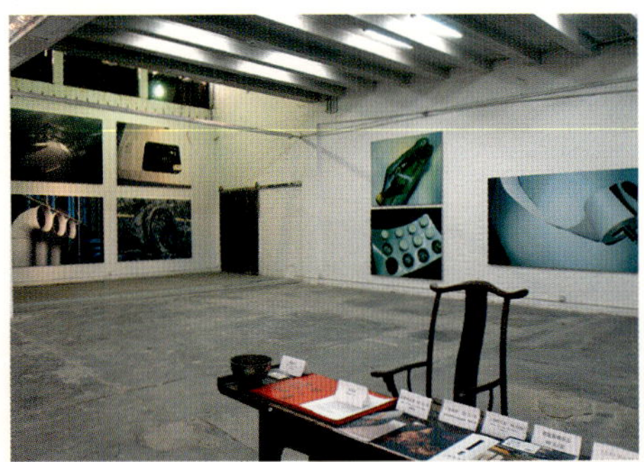
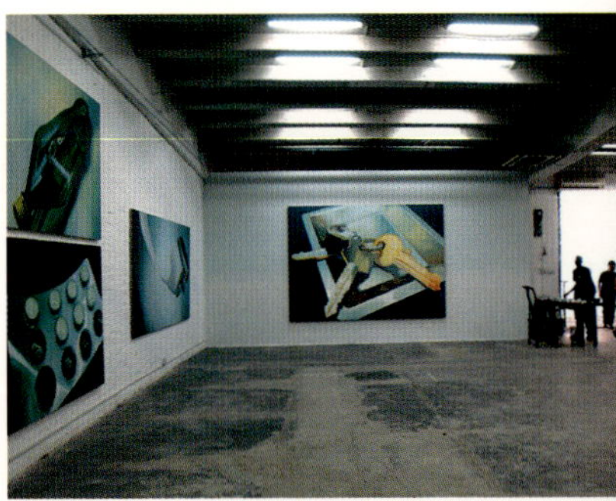

THE NEW LONG MARCH FOUNDATION GALLERY IN SPACE 798, FEATURING PAINTINGS BY YAN LEI AND CHEN WENBO.

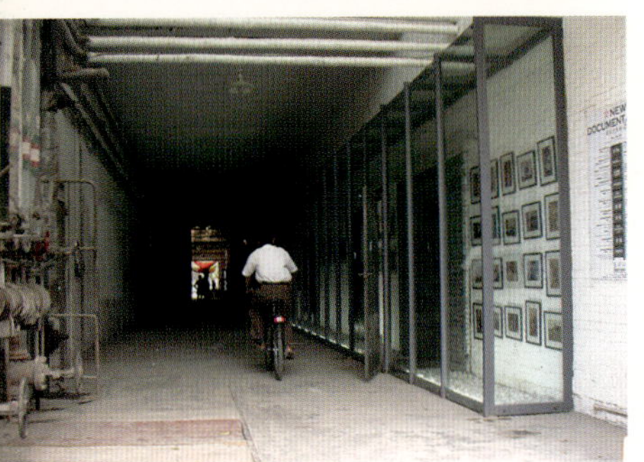
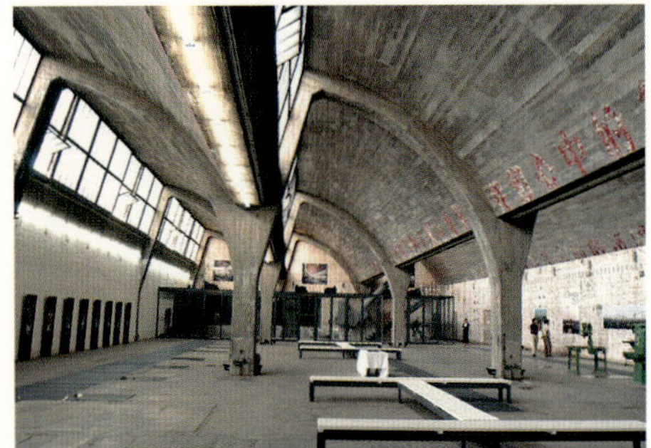
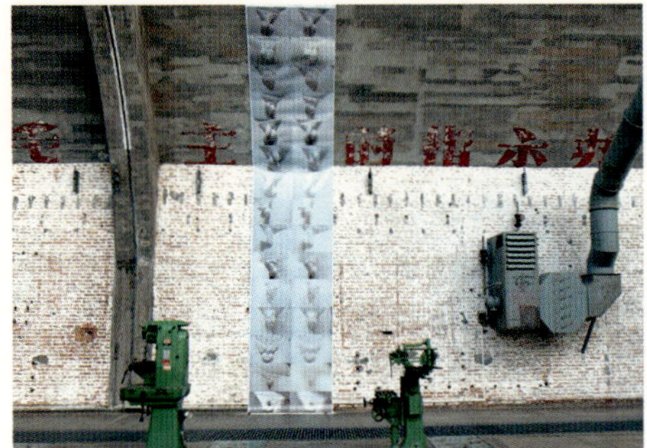
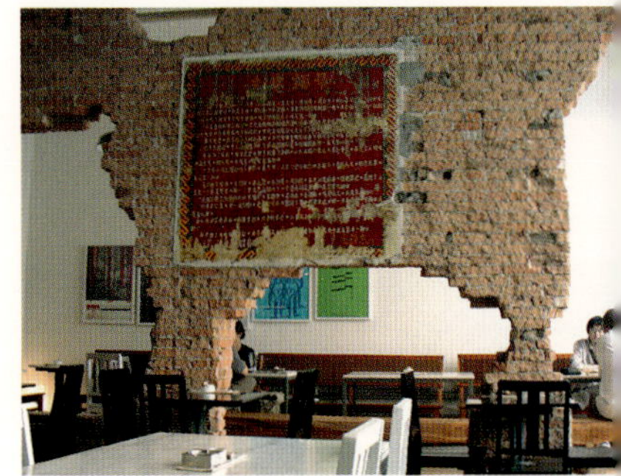

SPACE 798: THE ENTRANCE TO THE BRAND-NEW SPACE GALLERY, AND THE GALLERY INTERIOR. FAR RIGHT: THE AT CAFÉ.

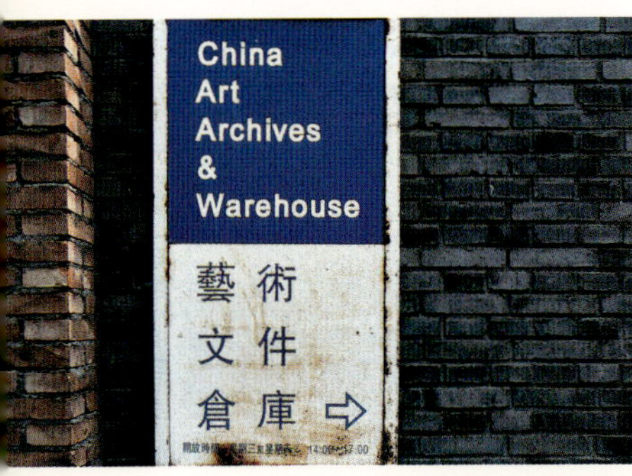

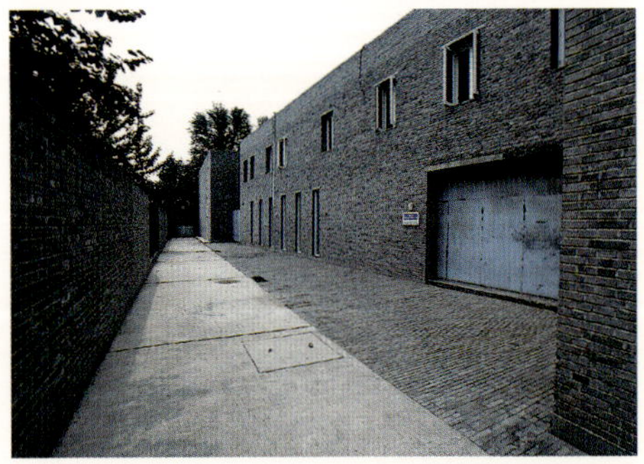
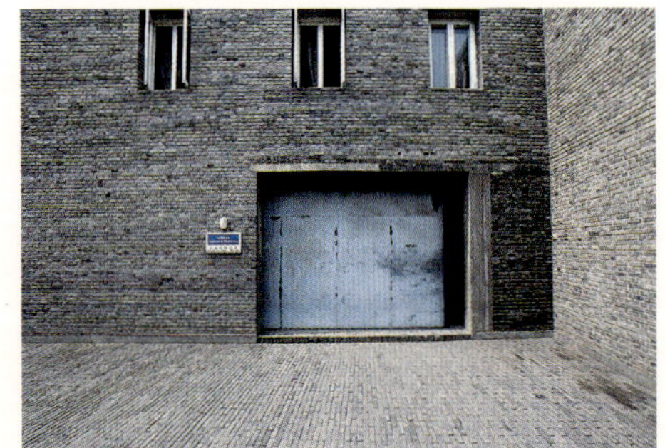
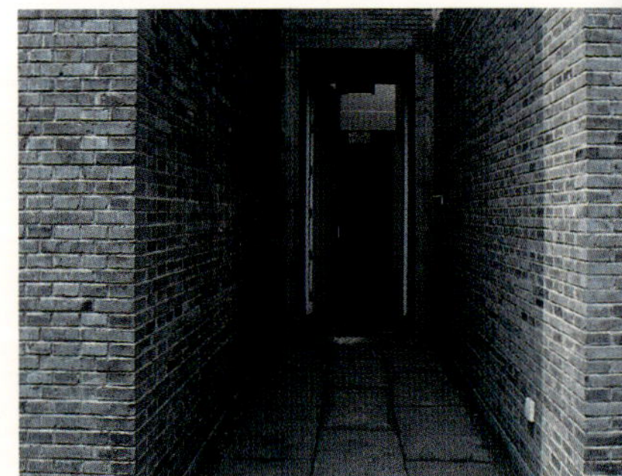

THE ODDLY UNINVITING EXTERIOR OF THE CAAW GALLERY, ONE OF THE OLDEST AND MOST INTERESTING GALLERIES IN BEIJING, NOT FAR FROM THE ROAD TO THE AIRPORT.

FACING PAGE: A STONE'S THROW FROM THE FORBIDDEN CITY, THE COURTYARD GALLERY. THE COURTYARD IS ONE OF THE FEW CHINESE GALLERIES, ALONG WITH SHANGART, TO TAKE PART IN INTERNATIONAL ART FAIRS. THE GALLERY IS IN THE BASEMENT OF A RESTAURANT FAMOUS FOR ITS FRENCH WINES. THE RESTAURANT AND GALLERY BOTH BELONG TO THE SAME OWNER. A WORK BY THE LUO BROTHERS HANGS ON THE WALL.

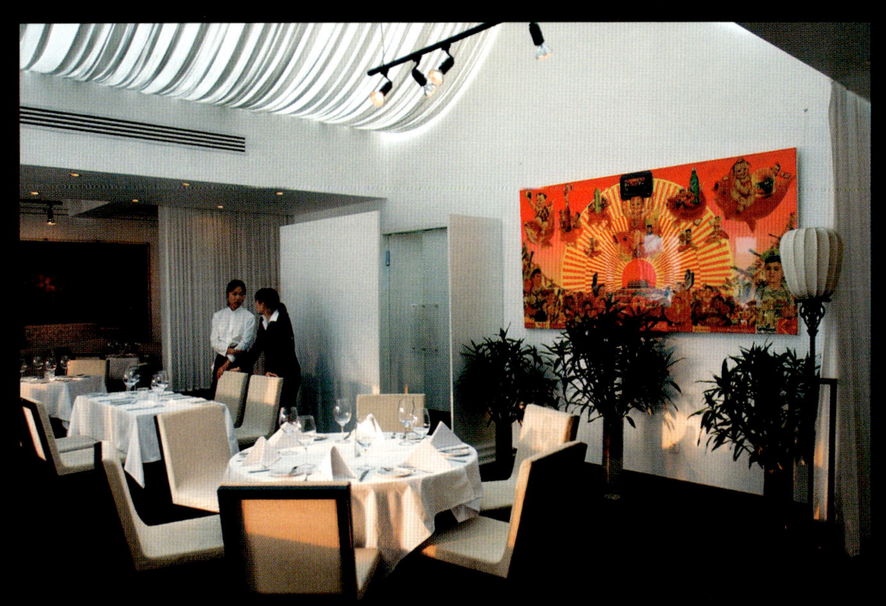

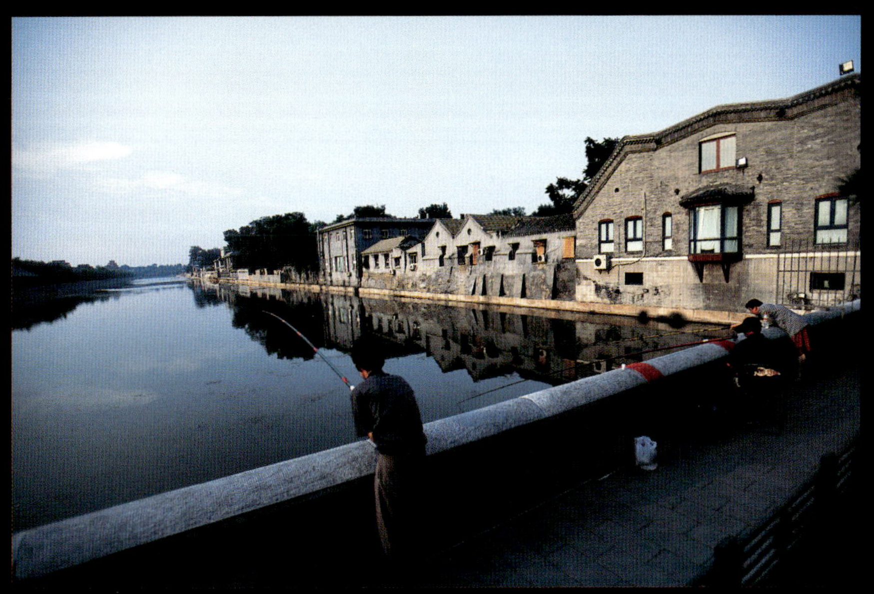

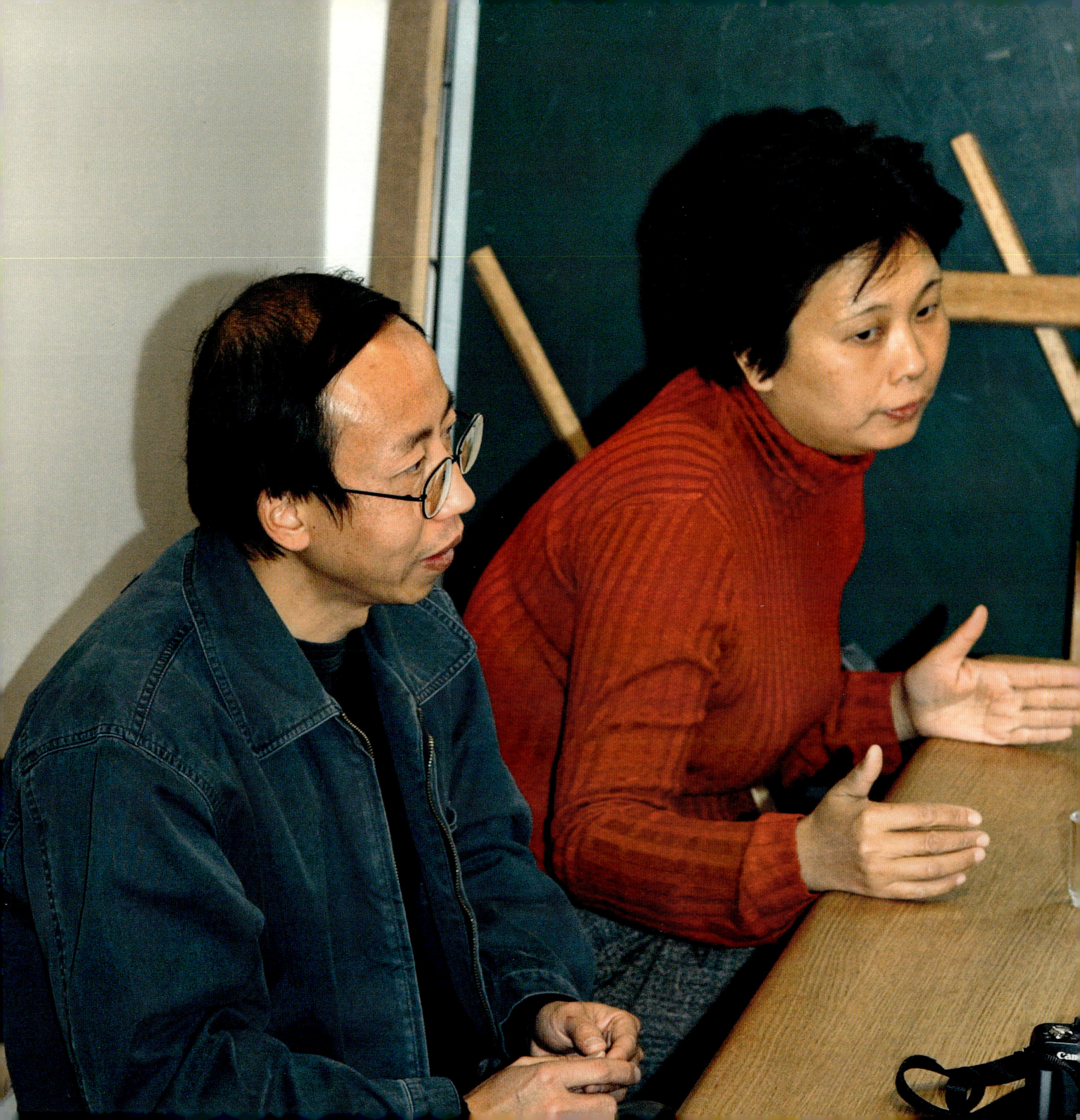

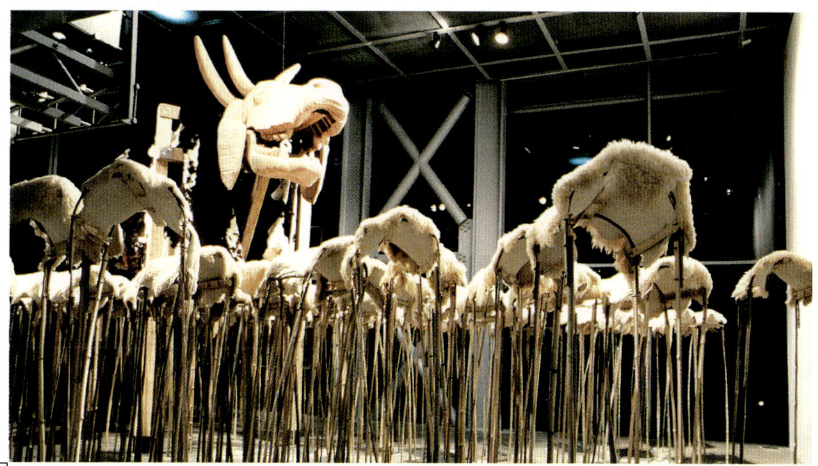

HUANG YONG PING

This is the best place to start. He is the best. "In my opinion, the greatest Chinese artist is Huang Yong Ping," says Yan Pei Ming, not generally known for his lavish praise of other artists. "He has enormous power. He is incredibly influential in China. He has a great aura, but he's discreet. He knows all the right people, but he's humble and never proud." I should add that he is an artist through and through and that he is extremely, extraordinarily intelligent. ¶ He is small and stooped. He wears glasses, and has a long lock of hair brushed carefully over his bald spot. This meek, mild appearance hides a will of steel and the unyielding artistic vision that marks out the very greatest artists. ¶ He has been living in France for fifteen years, became a French citizen in 1999, but still has difficulties in expressing himself in French. I interview him through the intermediary of an interpreter, who is a native of Beijing. Because Huang Yong Ping comes from Xiamen, much further south, she sometimes finds it hard to understand him and has to ask him to repeat himself several times. It is not an easy task, communicating with Huang Yong Ping. ¶ Having said that, when you overcome the various hurdles, it is a genuine pleasure to discover his extraordinary clarity of thought, the swift certainty of his taste, and the acuity and depth of his critical eye. ¶ His rise to the top was remarkably quick, helped by his unerring choice of exhibitions at which to showcase his work. *Magicians of the Earth* in 1989, *Base* at the Fondation Cartier in the suburbs of Paris in 1990, *Avant-Garde China* in Berlin in 1993, *Our Century* at the Ludwig Museum in Cologne in 1995, *Manifesta 1* in Amsterdam in 1996, the Gwangju biennial in South Korea and the Johannesburg biennial in 1997, *Cities on the Move* in Bordeaux, *Inside Out: New Chinese Art* in New York in 1998, the Venice Biennale in 1999, and the first Guangzhou triennial in 2002. He works with only a very few galleries, but there again only the very best: Barbara Gladstone in New York in the United States and Art et Public in Switzerland for Europe. He has no gallery in France or in China. He does not need them. ¶ This list of successes does not mean that Huang Yong Ping's life in the art world has been a bed of roses. He has been at the center of a number of scandals, and his works have been banned. He is now living in exile. He has overcome extraordinary difficulties. He seems to be violently opposed to any form of compromise when artistic freedom is under threat in any way. ¶ Huang Yong Ping says, "The artist's work is a knife without a handle and a double-edged blade." This one sentence sums up his vision of art, his approach to life, what we might even call his strategy, perfectly. Having said that, none of his other works highlight his statement that "artists don't have a safety net" to the same extent as *Bat Project* and the scandal it caused. It was a powerful, subtle project that drew heavily on current affairs. ¶ To grasp the full implications of the work, we need to remember that on March 3, 2001, an American EP-3 spy plane, a marvel of technology that could listen in on any radiotelephone conversation, caused a Chinese fighter plane to crash and had to make an emergency landing at Hainan airport. It should also be remembered that the Chinese Embassy in Belgrade had been bombed by the Americans in 1999 and that according to Russian radar stations, sixty "reconnaissance flights" by American (or NATO) planes had been recorded over Russian and Chinese territorial waters. ¶ It was in this highly sensitive political context that the United States negotiated the return of the American pilots held in China, and then of the plane itself. On May 24, China agreed to a proposal by the US government to dismantle the "reconnaissance plane," as the spy plane was euphemistically referred to, before returning it to the United States. Huang Yong Ping says, "The idea of this plane being dismantled and put inside another to be sent back to the United States was like a work of art. I thought it should stay in China. That's how the seeds of *Bat Project* were sown. But how to do it? You need a lot of space, equipment, and money to build a plane. Then, around that time, I was invited to an exhibition in Shenzhen organized with the aid of the French government. We got the money together and started work on the project, showing half of the dismantled plane." ¶ The idea for this "ready-made" work came to Huang Yong Ping from life. He says, "Life often presents us with similar works of art, but it's up to us to grab hold of them, and you have to be patient enough to wait for them to come to you. It's important to be able to deconstruct. In fact, it can be described as power deconstructing itself." ¶

FACING PAGE: THE ARTIST AND HIS WIFE IN HIS STUDIO IN PARIS. ABOVE: *SHEEP PERIL*, AN INSTALLATION CREATED IN 1997 AT THE FONDATION CARTIER POUR L'ART CONTEMPORAINE.

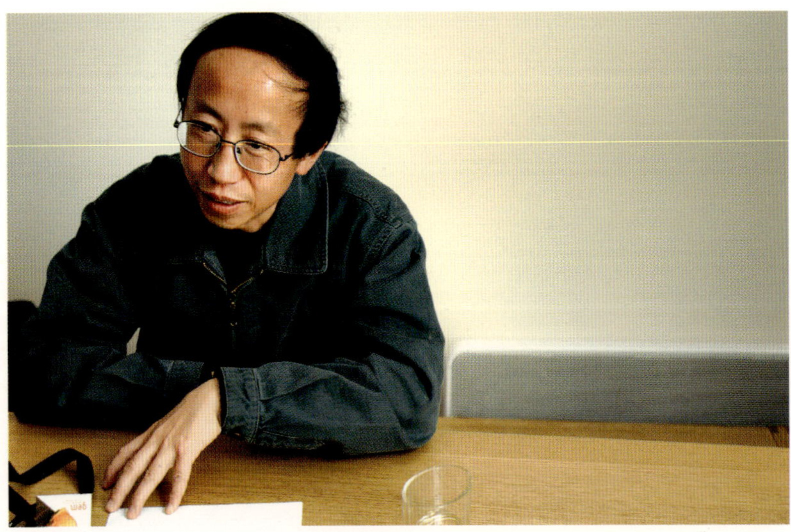

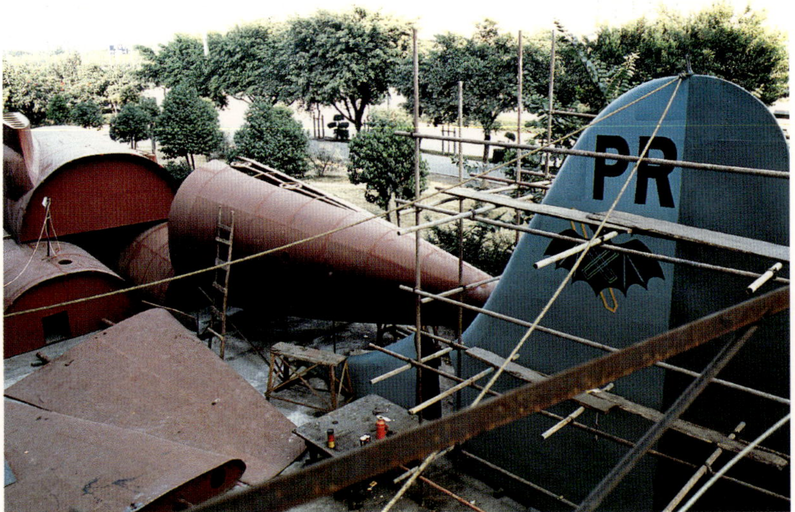

Designed before 9/11, but presented after the attacks on the World Trade Center, the work showed the plane chopped in half as it was returned to the United States. It caused a great deal of embarrassment for the Chinese and French governments, who were anxious not to be seen as provoking the Americans in what was, after all, a semi-official exhibition. There were negotiations, traps, and lies. The Americans put on the pressure. Then the work was simply censored. Pure and simple. Huang Yong Ping's contribution was removed from the exhibition. ¶ In an interview that was destined to be printed in the exhibition catalog, but which was censored at the same time as the work of art, Huang Yong Ping presented the piece as "a kaleidoscopic symbol expressing a rejection both of globalization and the rampant Americanism that now dominate the world. The work says what it says. It's up to the audience to decide what their own personal opinion is." ¶ The (unfinished) airplane was handed over to the Chinese authorities "for safekeeping" and has been inaccessible, even for Huang Yong Ping, ever since. He is furious. A number of artists, including Daniel Buren, Anne and Patrick Poirier, Radi Designers, and the ten Chinese artists participating in the exhibition immediately put together a petition to express their support for Huang Yong Ping, against his "unjust and ridiculous" exclusion, and "against an unacceptable restriction of the freedom of expression." There was a stormy press conference, which was cut short almost before it had a chance to get underway. ¶ "I have already been censored in China, in Fujian province in 1987," Huang Yong Ping reminds me, with a sardonic laugh. "The exhibition only lasted two hours. I asked the visitors to bring into the museum all sorts of objects that they found outside. The museum director said my method was 'aesthetically unacceptable,' and he had the exhibition closed down after two hours." He adds, bitterly, "But at least that time, I was able to show my work!" ¶ The 1987 exhibition was one of two that the group founded by Huang Yong Ping managed to organize, more or less, in Fujian province. It was not dissimilar to one that the group had held a year earlier, in a less tense atmosphere and a more favorable political context, in a sort of art center in Xiamen. They had brought together an exhibition of paintings, photographs, and installations, and at the end of the show they set fire to all the exhibits and then photographed them like any other performance. ¶ One time, Huang Yong Ping explained to me, "In any case, we couldn't sell them. Back then, in China, there was no structure in place for the works to go anywhere. So we thought, why not just burn them instead?" And why not make a radical gesture of the auto-da-fe? ¶ Another time, he told me, "For the artist, the work of art is both extremely important and completely devoid of significance. The artist can destroy it whenever he likes." ¶ The extreme attitude of an artist who cuts straight to the quick and never falters. ¶ The extreme attitude of a group, Xiamen Dada, which put down roots in a provincial corner of China with the aim of being as provocative as possible. ¶ Xiamen, 1985–86. Let us pause for a moment in the city where, as it happens—or perhaps the choice was deliberate—Huang Yong Ping was born. ¶ He points out that "The Chinese ideogram for Xiamen depicts a door with a sort of worm in the middle. The region of Fujian is quite remote because of the hills, which make keeping in contact with the cities and artists of the north rather difficult." OK. Actually, Xiamen is open to the sea, and owes its wealth to the emigrants from all over Fujian province who pass through the port on their way to the Philippines, Singapore, Malaysia, and Indonesia. Xiamen and the whole region maintain close links with these expatriates who have played an important role in the modernization of the province, since the Chinese government encourages them to invest in their homeland. Taiwanese investment

LEFT: THE ARTIST IN HIS STUDIO. ON THE RIGHT IS THE WORK IN PROGRESS *BAT PROJECT*, A MODEL OF PARTS OF THE U.S. EP-3 SPY PLANE THAT COLLIDED WITH A CHINESE FIGHTER PLANE ABOVE THE CHINA SEA ON APRIL 1, 2001.

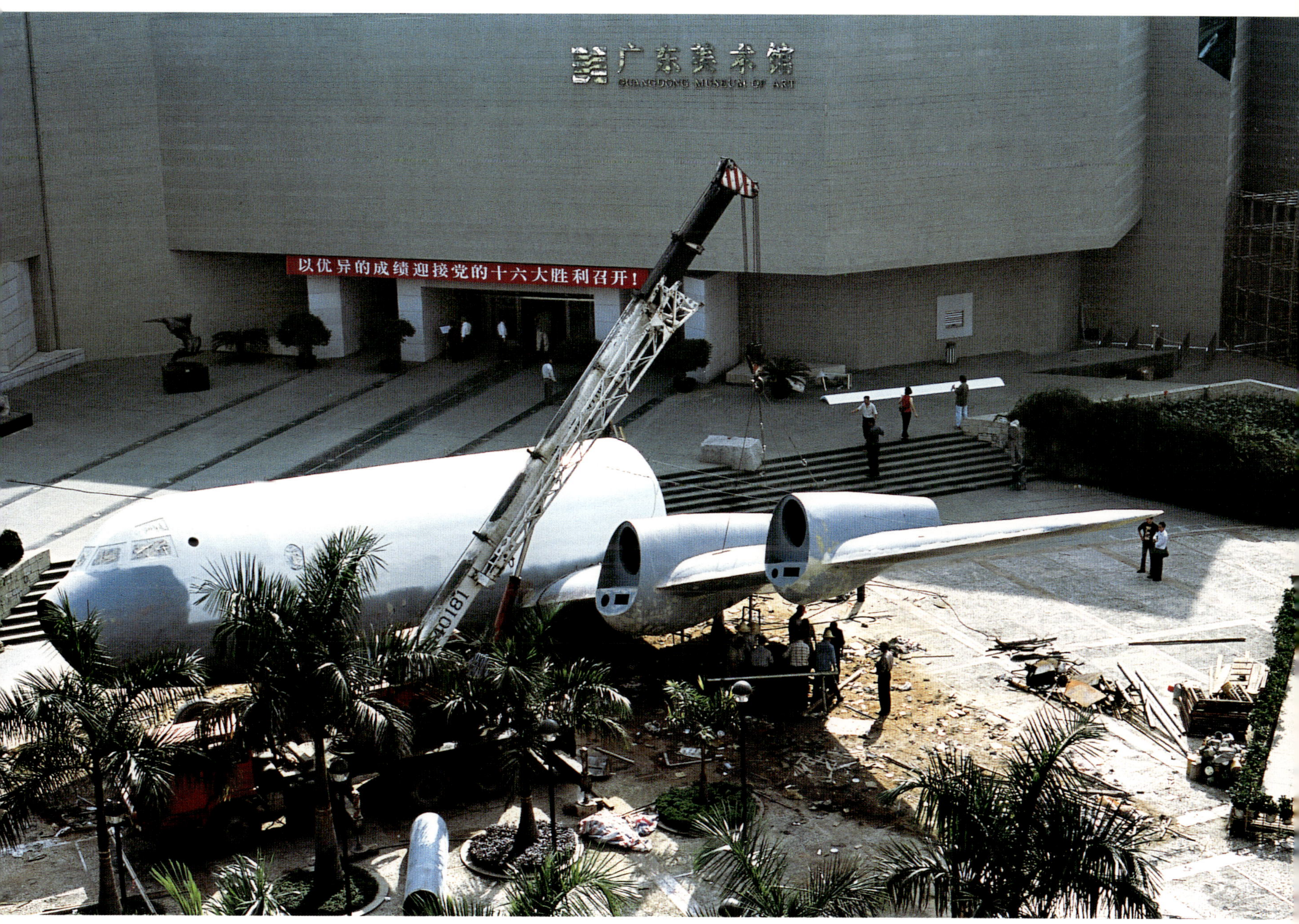

WORK IN PROGRESS ON *BAT PROJECT* OUTSIDE THE GUANGDONG MUSEUM IN GUANGZHOU FOR THE FIRST TRIENNIAL, HELD IN 2002, BEFORE THE PROJECT WAS HALTED IN WHAT CAN ONLY BE DESCRIBED AS AN ACT OF CENSORSHIP AFTER SEPTEMBER 11. THE ONLY QUESTION IS WHO MADE THE DECISION TO STOP THE WORK BEING SHOWN.

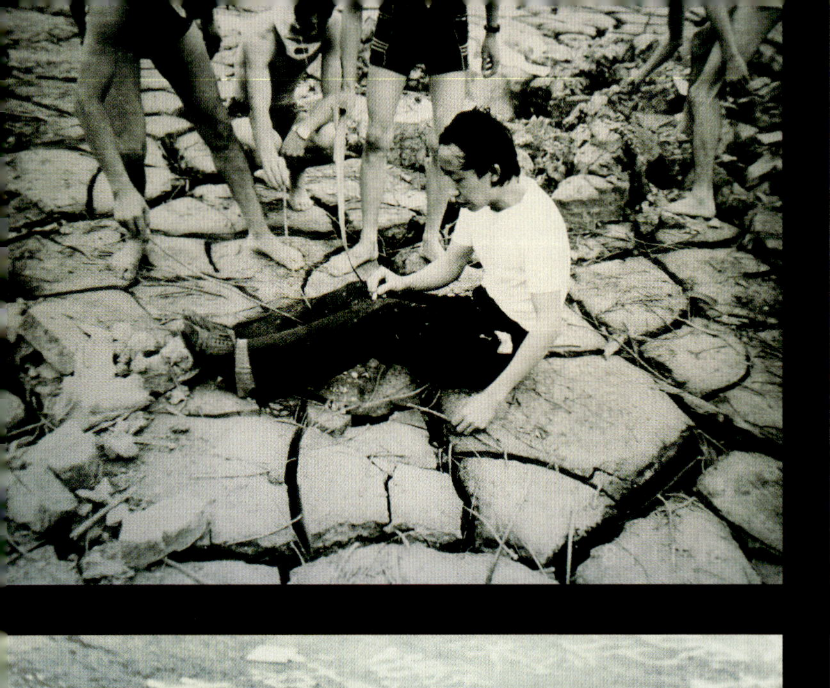

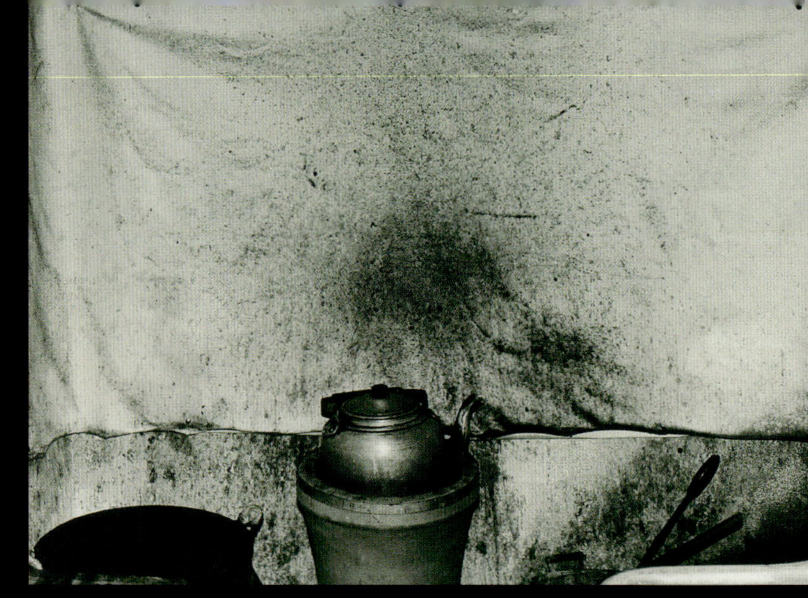

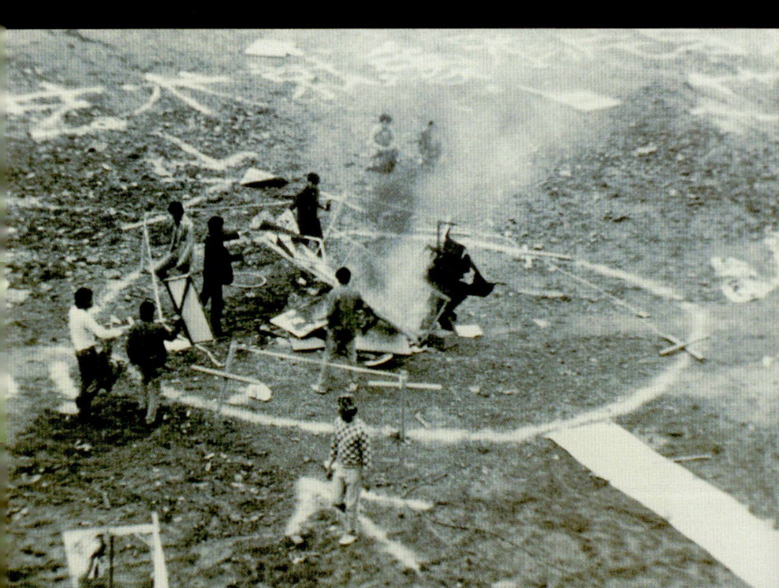

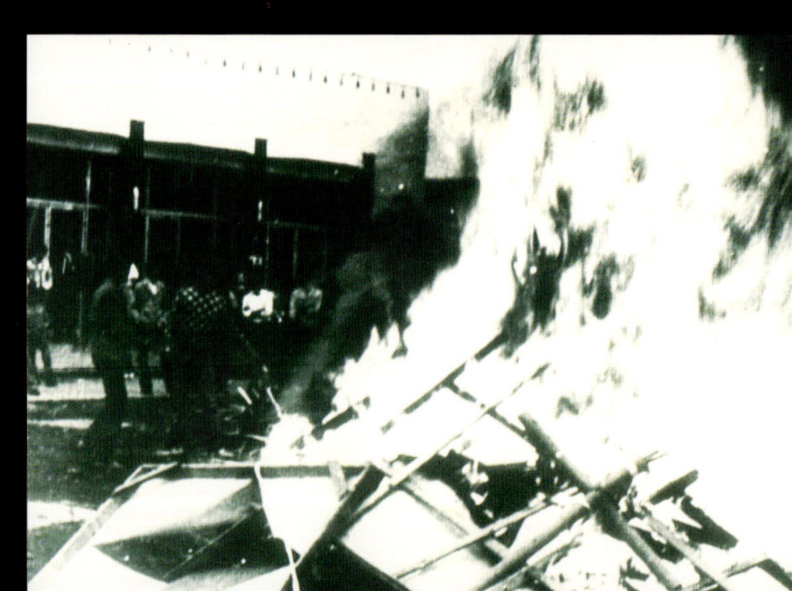

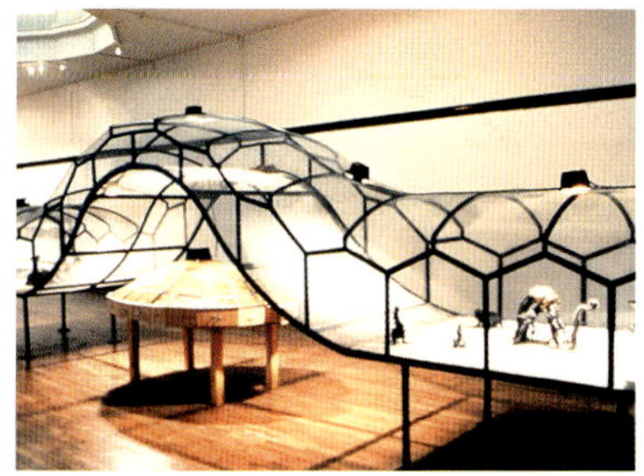
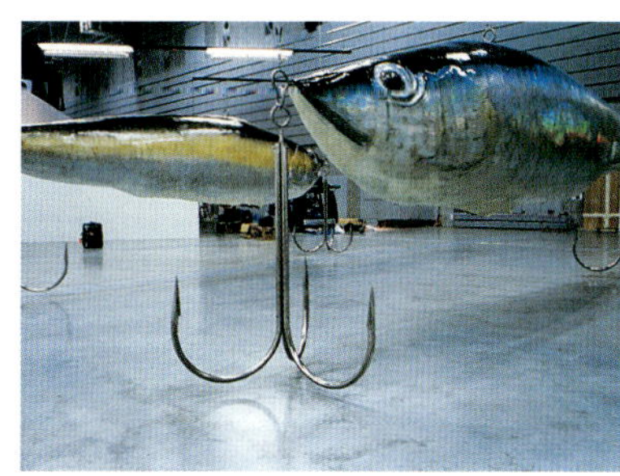
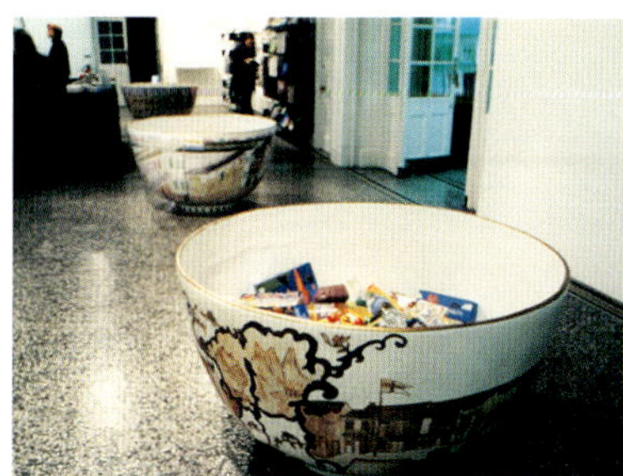
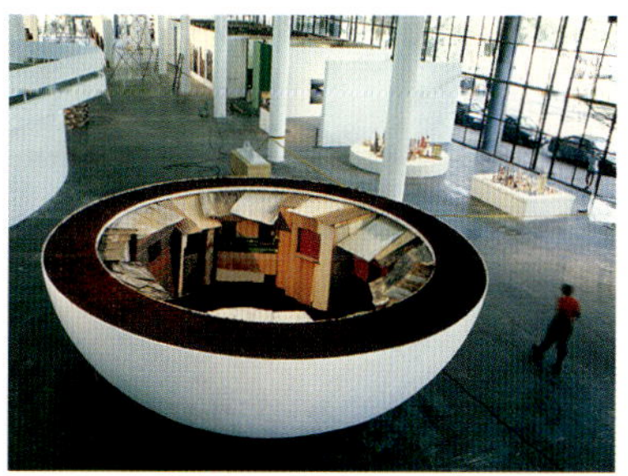

FROM LEFT TO RIGHT: *THE BRIDGE AND THE THEATER OF THE WORLD*, MUSÉE NATIONAL DES ARTS D'AFRIQUE ET D'OCÉANIE, PARIS, 1993–95. *TWO KINDS OF FOOD*, YO KOHAMA, 2001. DA XIAN—*THE DOOMSDAY*, CAMDEN ARTS CENTRE, LONDON, 1997. THE EXHIBITION AT THE SÃO PAULO BIENNIAL, 2002.

and tourism—Taiwan is about sixty miles (one hundred kilometers) away—represent another major source of wealth for the region. ¶ Xiamen is a relatively large port with a population of 1.4 million. The streets are winding and narrow. The Portuguese arrived here in the sixteenth century, followed by the British, the French, and the Dutch. The port was closed to foreign vessels from 1750 to the start of the Opium Wars. In August 1841, thirty-eight British ships forced entry into the port, leading the way for Japan and the Western powers to set up consulates on the nearby island of Gulang, which thus became a foreign enclave in Chinese territory. It was a Japanese possession from 1938 to 1945. In 1949, the islands of Jinmen and Xiao Jinmen, off the coast of Xiamen, were occupied in turn by Kuomingtang troops. In 1958, when the People's Army carpet bombed these islands, the security pact between Taiwan and the United States threatened to lead to an all-out war between China and the United States. Even as recently as 1996, when missiles were fired off the coast of Taiwan, the United States sent warships to the region. ¶ It would be naïve to think that Huang Yong Ping's attitude is entirely the result of this turbulent history, which has stoked nationalist or indeed anti nationalist feeling in the region, but it cannot be wholly ignored as a contributing factor. ¶ Huang Yong Ping's father was a storekeeper in a city that thrived on commerce. He sold tea. It was a large family, with seven children. Huang Yong Ping was a late addition: his father was sixty when he was born. His father, who wrote with a calligraphy brush all his life, loved painting. ¶ Huang Yong Ping was twelve when the Cultural Revolution began. "I saw it from the outside," he says. "Children had no part to play in that revolution. Whatever people say, the Cultural Revolution was truly a part of the wider revolution. It wasn't important." Not important! I exclaim. He explains, "It was important, but in its form. It was utopian." ¶ He and his group Xiamen Dada preferred to focus on important questions about the nature of culture and how it should be part of life. ¶ Huang Yong Ping's real debut was in 1985 or 1986, when he founded the Xiamen Dada group with five friends and ten or so other artists who were occasional participants. Why did he call it Dada, fifty years after the original movement? ¶ "Chinese contemporary art was fifty years behind the times compared to Western art. We believed that a reference to Western art was essential if Chinese contemporary art was to exist. So we had to take up a position in relation to Western art. For me, Dada was the most radical movement. When I wrote one of my earliest texts, I called it *Postmodern Xiamen Dada*, to indicate that although we were behind the times, we were still in touch with all the latest developments." The group lasted two years. As I have already said, in that time it organized two exhibitions and brought out a review, which never got past the first issue. ¶ Huang Yong Ping was immediately drawn to the idea of expressing himself through installations. Why? He looks at me. A glint of mischief lights up his eyes: "They say that when you don't have a talent for painting, you do sculpture, when you don't have a talent for sculpture, you do installations, when you don't have a talent for installations, you do videos, and when you don't have a talent for video art, you become an exhibition curator." On a more serious note, he tells me that at the School of Fine Arts, whenever he had to paint an object, he asked himself why he couldn't just cut out the middleman and place the object directly on the canvas. ¶ 1989 was a key year. He was invited to participate in one of the most controversial exhibitions of the day, but which has since become something of a legend: *Magicians of the Earth*. Huang Yong Ping put two books, a *History of Chinese Art* and a *History of Modern Western Art*, in a washing machine for two minutes, then displayed the resulting papier-mâché. The work dated from 1987. "Washing

FACING PAGE: TOP LEFT: *TROUSER WITH FIRE CRACKERS*, A 1986 PERFORMANCE BY HUANG YONG PING. TOP RIGHT: *DUST COLLECTION*, 1987. BOTTOM LEFT: A PERFORMANCE BY THE XIAMEN DADA GROUP AT THE PEOPLE'S PALACE IN 1986. BOTTOM RIGHT: THE GROUP BURNING THE WORKS ON SHOW.

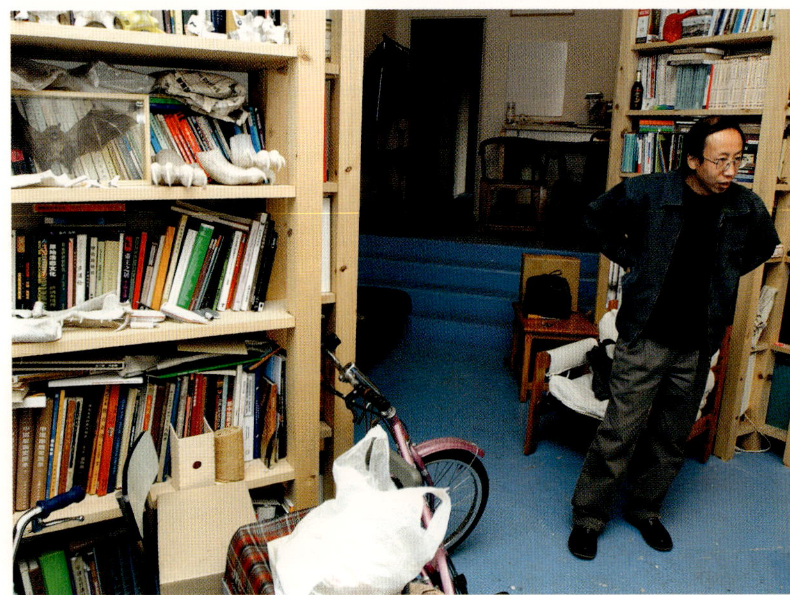

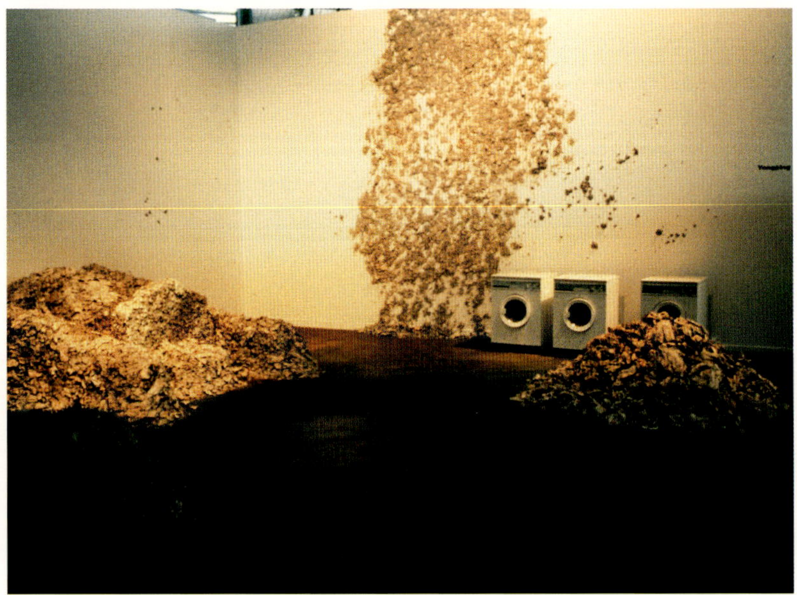

books does not mean washing culture, but on the contrary, making it dirtier," he said at the time. Today, when I ask him to expand on this idea, he says simply, "Normally, washing machines are there to make things clean, but I used it for the opposite effect. Once the books had been washed in the machine, they were still able to be read by anyone willing to make the effort, but they were totally different. In that sense, dirtiness is important. The content of the book changes once it has been washed." ¶ Bringing the two books together in a sort of mulch may also have been a way of resolving the problem of dialogue between East and West by reducing it to burlesque absurdity. The most striking thing about the work is the way Huang Yong Ping managed to reverse a given process, dirtying an object with the help of a washing machine. He often works on this theme of reversing processes. ¶ What does the catalog have to say? It devotes two pages to the work, entitled *Reptiles* (1989), including a sketch of the project and a descriptive commentary: "Papier-mâché, washing machine, books, newspapers, and photographs. The shape of the tomb is reminiscent of an animal creeping along on its belly (like a tortoise, the Chinese symbol of longevity). Culture is like a tomb, but it still lives, creeping along the floor, ugly as a tortoise. Washing newspapers: washing culture. The 'concept of culture' must always be washed and dried again and again." ¶ Another commentary on the same page presents a paradox. "A Chinese proverb says, 'In the olden days, nothing important was ever written on paper.' Fortunately, I believe art to be something quite unimportant. For me, this proverb is very important. I would like everything to remain ambiguous." ¶ His attitude to his earlier works is a prime example of this ambiguity. When he left Xiamen to take part in the exhibition *The Magicians of the Earth*, he did not know that he would be obliged to stay in France because of political turmoil and the tragedy of Tiananmen Square. Of course, he left all his early works behind. His family took them for trash, old rags, and useless junk, and threw them all out. Chinese people are accustomed to throwing out whatever they consider to be old junk. Some of Huang Yong Ping's major early works were thus destroyed. When he set fire to his own works in 1986, how did he feel? Did he feel that they had outlived their usefulness? "No," he says, "You have to look at it from both sides. If you set your sights very high, no single work is of any importance whatsoever. They are all ephemeral. If you look at things from a practical point of view, it's important to keep a record." ¶ Back then, alongside the paintings in his studio, he kept a canvas behind the stove, which was a record of all the cooking he did, assemblages and juxtapositions of various objects and pictures which, as transparencies or superimposed, showed both sides of pages of illustrations taken from books on Chinese art. The illustrations he chose all followed the rules set out in the *I Ching*, the Book of Changes. ¶ Huang Yong Ping arrived in Paris in April 1989. The exhibition was held in May. On June 4, student demonstrations in Tiananmen Square were brutally crushed. ¶ I asked him why he chose not to return to China when the political situation calmed down. "I received a lot of invitations, including a one-year scholarship to work in Aix-en-Provence. I was invited to the United States. As time passed, I received still more invitations. So I stayed. If I hadn't stayed in France, maybe I would not have known as much as I do today." ¶ He has even been granted French citizenship. Changing nationality is a big step. But Huang Yong Ping says it was no big deal. "Nationality is nothing more than a piece of paper. Even if it's important when you want to travel, it's still just a piece of paper." ¶ He was granted citizenship after he was chosen to represent France at the forty-eighth Venice Biennale. Yan Pei Ming told me when we discussed the strange choice

LEFT: HUANG YONG PING IN HIS STUDIO APARTMENT. RIGHT: *REPTILE*, 1989.

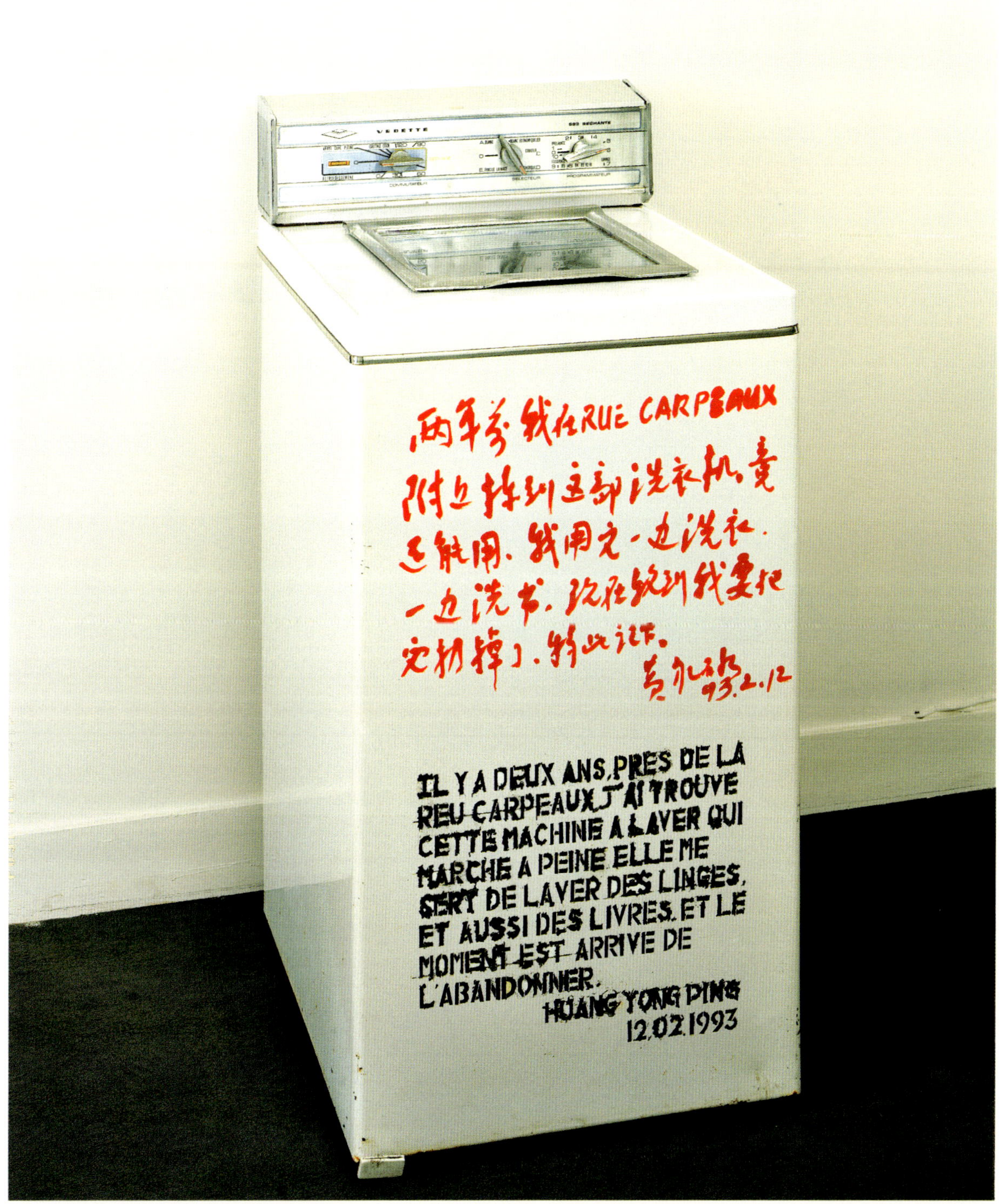

A VARIATION DATING FROM 1993 ON THE WASHING MACHINE SHOWN AT THE EXHIBITION *THE MAGICIANS OF THE EARTH* IN 1989 IN THE GRAND HALL OF LA VILETTE. THE TEXT READS: TWO YEARS AGO I FOUND THIS WASHING MACHINE, NEAR TO THE RUE CHAPEAUX, TO WASH MY CLOTHES AND BOOKS—IT HARDLY WORKS—THE TIME HAS COME TO GET RID OF IT. HUANG YONG PING 12.02.1993.

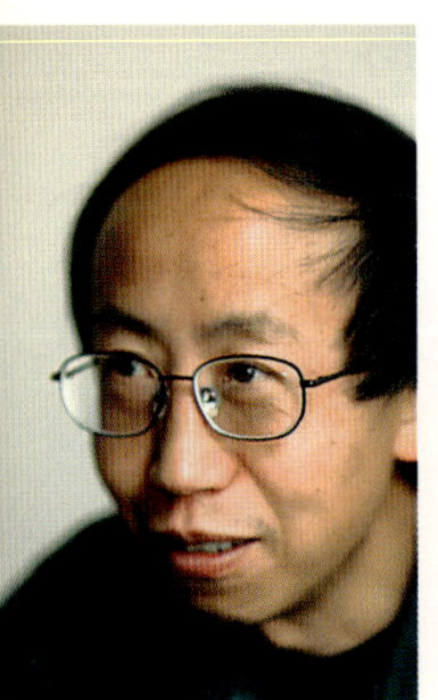
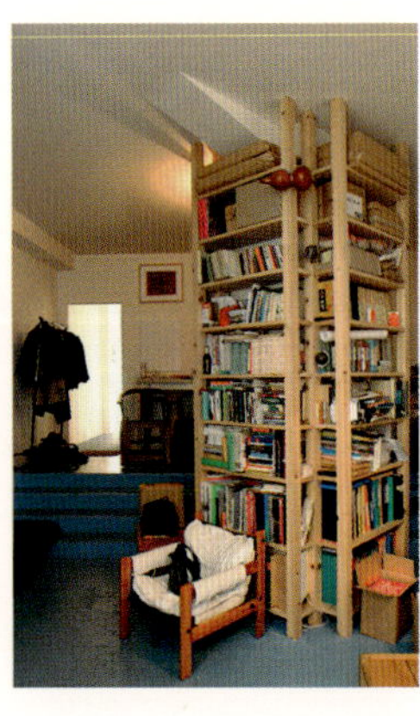
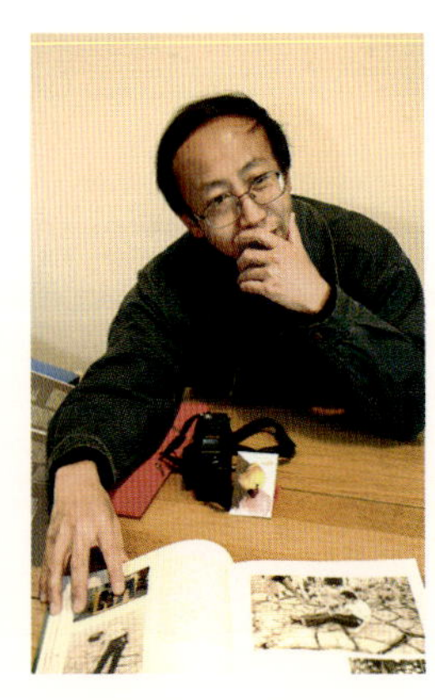
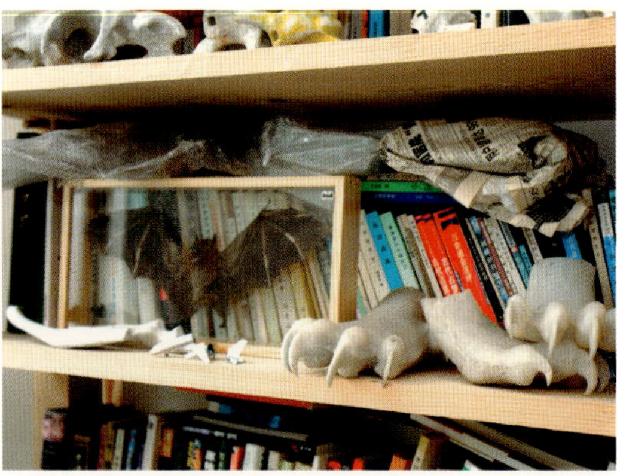
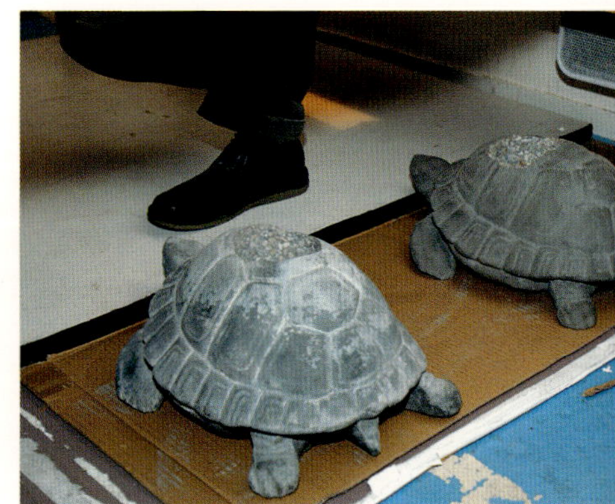

of Huang Yong Ping, a Chinese artist, to represent France: "Everything Huang Yong Ping does is a question of strategy. His monsters displayed high up were Chinese symbols that the French couldn't understand. He thought to himself, I'm representing France, so I'll be inscrutably Chinese. That's just Huang Yong Ping's nature. No other artist is as sly as he is. He is really crafty. He was in the French pavilion. At the time, he didn't even have a French passport. He only got it after the Biennale." ¶ What were the sculptures he exhibited? What did they show? Were they made by Huang Yong Ping himself? Were they traditional subjects? What was his purpose in showing them? ¶ To begin with, there were nine of them in all, perched on pillars, some of which were forty-five feet (fifteen meters) tall, breaking through the roof and sunk into the floor in ruins. On each pillar he placed one of the traditional animal figures that symbolize natural disasters in the classic Chinese text the *Shanhaijing,* as well as protection against these scourges. "I had no other choice," says Huang Yong Ping. But, he insists, having said that, the most important thing to note is that his monsters were displayed outside the pavilion, beyond the disputed space that was a symbol of the conflict between Jean-Pierre Bertrand and himself. At the entrance, on a chariot, used by the Chinese for measuring time and indicating directions, he displayed a man placed on an empty compass, the chariot indicating the end of a millennium stripped of all discernible ideologies. ¶ At the same time, nearby Kosovo was torn by war. It was even debated whether the Biennale should be held under such circumstances. Did Huang Yong Ping take this into account in his work? "No," he says, leaving no room for doubt. "My work always questions culture, and in this case in particular, the role of the Venice Biennale, which is organized by the state. There is also a clash of cultures there." ¶ His own culture is that of the *I Ching,* the Book of Changes, and of the Tao, which he contrasts with the omnipotence of Western culture. He used the *I Ching* in 1992, for example, by using a small turntable to fix the price of a series of works, from five to five hundred thousand French francs. In 1993, he used the *I Ching* again for the exhibition *Silent Energy,* at the Museum of Modern Art in Oxford. The outcome, *Quian* and *Gu,* meant that he had to use insects in his work. From then on, insects have been a recurring feature of his work. In June 1995, at *Asiana* in Venice, he once again turned to the *I Ching.* The answer he got was "Come back in three years." 1995 + 3 = 1998. Wrong: Huang Yong Ping took part in the Venice Biennale in 1999. "No," he retorts. "I returned in 1998 to see the site of the pavilion and to think about my project." ¶ The Tao, which Huang Yong Ping is reluctant to talk about, is different in that it is "less concrete," he says, but more complete and therefore less easy to discuss. It is a way of thinking and living. "It's hidden. It has no meaning. It brings about associations of ideas, which enabled me to be creative, for instance." He evidently finds it hard to explain precisely what he means. "Tao means you often approach things from the opposite angle. It's very important for artists." ¶ Both in his life and in his art, Huang Yong Ping creates nodes of tension and elaborates alternative solutions to the dominant ideologies (in current geopolitical terms, that means American and European ideology), which establish the truth and try to pin it down forever. He presents another point of view, a different way of seeing, a way of living that allows him to question stereotypical channels of thought. Maybe that is why for him, none of his works is of particular importance on its own—rather, what counts is his oeuvre as a whole. His oeuvre is a living state of flux, a constantly evolving living being.

ABOVE: HUANG YONG PING IN HIS STUDIO WITH SOME OF THE ELEMENTS HE USES IN HIS WORKS. FACING PAGE: ONE MAN, NINE ANIMALS, 1999. ALTHOUGH NOT YET OFFICIALLY A FRENCH CITIZEN, HUANG YONG PING WAS SELECTED TO REPRESENT FRANCE AT THE VENICE BIENNALE IN 1999.

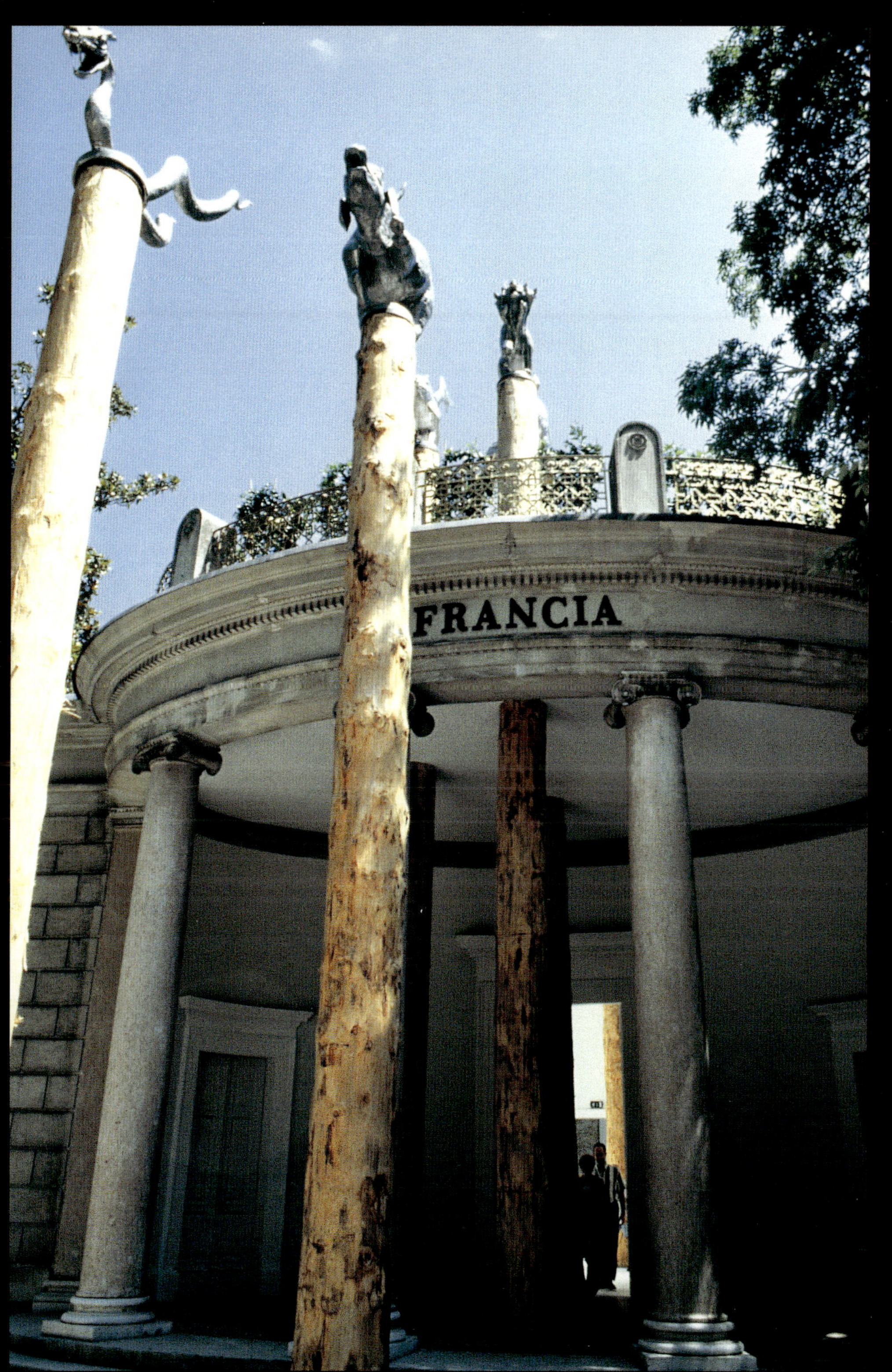
FRANCIA

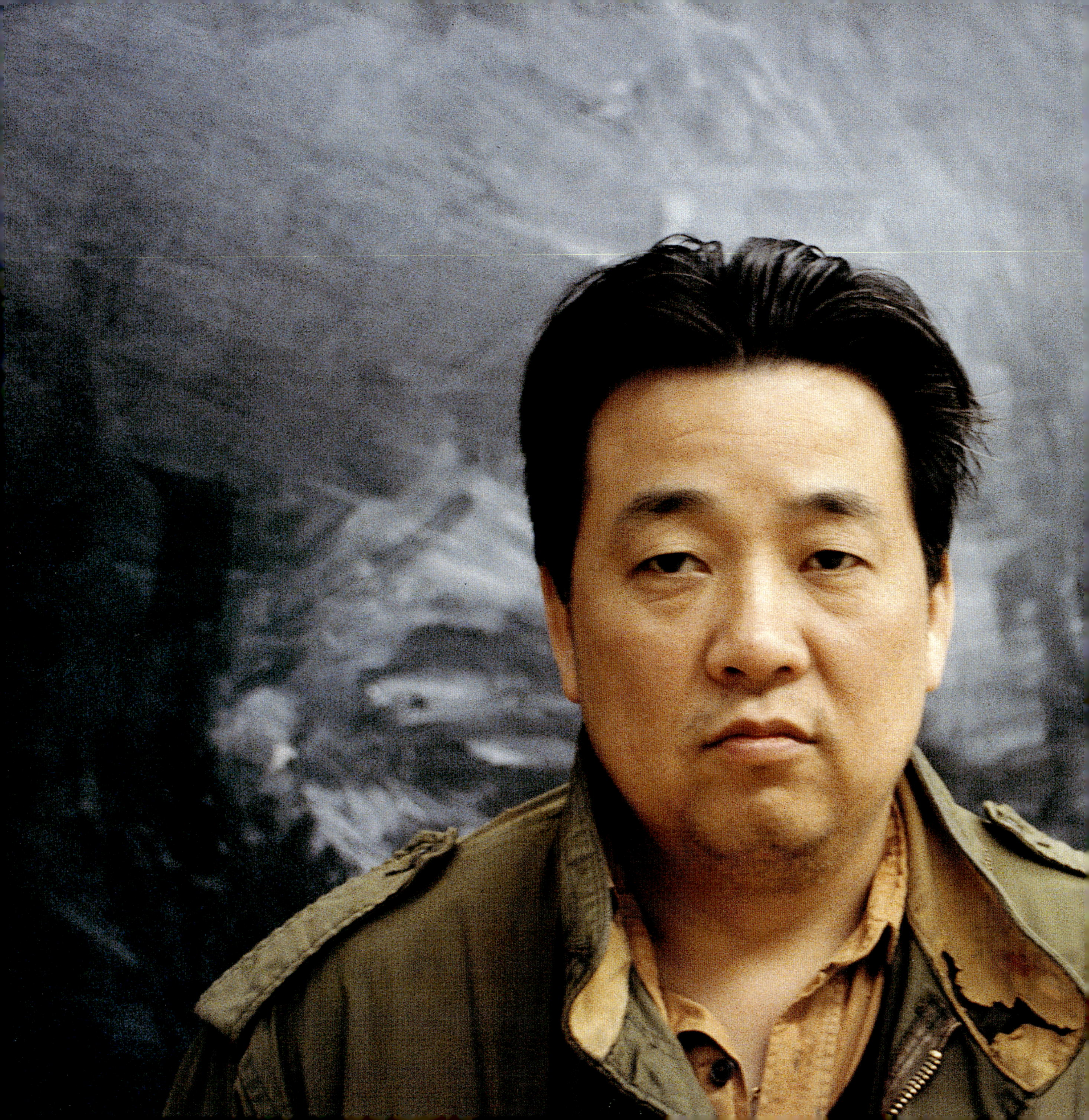

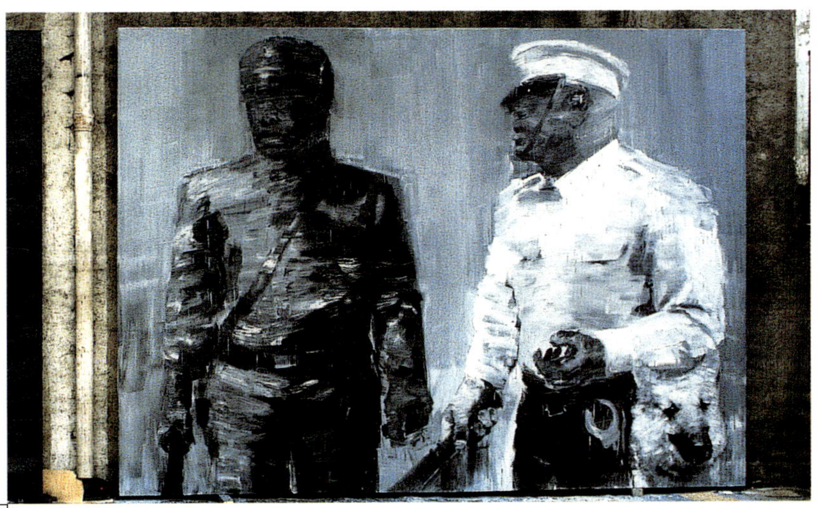

YAN PEI MING

"Painting takes time. That is the limit of my work. But," he adds, in a much more cheerful tone, "if there is a good chance, I jump at it!" Yan Pei Ming is a prudent man, taking small steps forward, as he often says, and yet at the same time, he is impressively dynamic. ¶ We are outside one of his studios in Dijon, opposite the Elton bar, very close to the station. He sticks his key into a hidden keyhole high up to the right of the door, then another keyhole in the center of the door, then a third in the normal position, then a fourth at the bottom of the door. He opens it. "It smells of paint. You can see why I don't want that at home." ¶ He lives a short distance away, in rue Buffon, right in the city center, in an odd-looking house with a tall, thin façade. He bought it in 1998 and has completely remodeled the interior, where there are surprises around every corner. We walked through the living room to the dining room with its Chinese-style Lazy Susan table, then on to the tiny courtyard with three trees, then the office and the little studio where he works on his ink and charcoal drawings. This is where he keeps his archives—the nerve center of his little world. The whole family shares in his work: his mother cooks for him, his wife is his secretary, and his brother is in charge of storing the works and wrapping and transporting them. ¶ Back to the second studio that Yan Pei Ming has just unlocked. The smell of paint is not the only thing that hits you: the canvases immediately grab your attention. They are huge, impressive. They are being sent to Venice this week for the Biennale. There are brushes, armchairs, stepladders, a table on castors, and pots of paint lying about everywhere. The floor is covered in splashes of paint. Canvases are propped up against the walls. It is May 20, 2003. Yan Pei Ming's whole contribution to the exhibition is in this room—all oil paintings in black and white. Anti-riot police, self-portraits in dark glasses or dressed as a hooligan, an airport, a view of Shanghai. ¶ All new works. ¶ The policemen resemble the "invisible man" painted a while before, with uncertain brushstrokes, the peaks of their caps hiding their gaze, the helmets seeming to meld with the eyes, the cheeks, the nose, blended by the rapid brushstrokes as the artist blurs the lines. They are wholly impersonal in their anti-riot gear. ¶ Facing up to them are a group of equally blurry hooligans, including a self-portrait. Yan Pei Ming also included a self-portrait in his work *108 Brigands*, painted at the Villa Médicis, the French cultural center in Rome that awards grants to its artists in residence, in 1993. ¶ Yan Pei Ming is a figurative painter. He plays with the boundaries of resemblance, painting figures that are at a certain distance from the original but which are still close enough to be recognizable. This halfway house makes the issue of identification a thorny one. ¶ This is the first time he has painted his home city of Shanghai. It is immense, in the form of a nineteenth-century building in the Bund district in the foreground at the bottom of the painting. The modern city floats dreamlike at the top of the canvas. ¶ He tells me, "When I left Shanghai, it was like that," pointing to the nineteenth-century building. "When I returned, it was like that," indicating the modern cityscape. "When I left, there was a field where all these skyscrapers now stand; when I returned, there were no more fields, no more peasants, nothing. It was a totally different city. Why have I waited until now to paint it? Because I wanted to wait until I was excited by it. The city and the world have changed. It's both a memory and the present." ¶ The title of the painting of Shanghai is *International Landscape*. While the painting itself is a close likeness of the city—anyone who has been to Shanghai will recognize it thanks to two or three landmarks—the title takes a step back from the city. We will come back to this point later. ¶ In a corner of the studio is a radio. Does he like to listen to music as he works? No: he listens to *France Info*, the twenty-four-hour news station. ¶ "I got into the habit when I moved to France. I couldn't speak very good French, so I listened to *France Info* to learn. Now I have it on as background noise. Without it, I find it impossible to work. And when I'm working, I like to know what's going on in the world. I find it helps me to keep a precise track of time." ¶ Yan Pei Ming also has a third studio in Dijon, tucked away and more discreet than the other two. It is just a little house with closed shutters. Nothing special.

FACING PAGE: THE ARTIST IN ONE OF HIS STUDIOS IN DIJON. ABOVE: *ANTI-RIOT COPS*, 2003, SHOWN AT THE VENICE BIENNIAL. PHOTOGRAPHS BY ANDRÉ MORIN.

He opens four or five locks, we go in—and still nothing special. The room is a bit poky, decorated 1950s-style, and horribly petit bourgeois. But outside is a vast, empty warehouse with a glass roof. Wait a minute—not quite empty: on the left I can see a few small paintings up against the wall, and there is a sort of round podium where he worked on preparatory pieces for *International Airport*, a painting currently on show on the Place de la Libération, opposite Dijon's art museum. To my right there is a sort of alcove where wrapped canvases are piled high. They are works by Yan Pei Ming's former students, acclaimed at the Sparta Gallery in Chagny, France, in 2002. ¶ He has just bought his fourth studio, in the suburbs of Paris. ¶ Why does he need so many studios? ¶ "They are indispensable. Over the last few weeks, I've been working on five exhibitions at the same time: two in Dijon—one at the art museum of recent portraits and a few nudes and the other, *International Airport,* at the Consortium—one at the art museum in Besançon of portraits of Mao. In a week I'll be showing some drawings in Geneva, and then in three weeks, the Venice Biennale. For weeks, I've been running from one studio to another. How else could I manage? At home, I work on the drawings for Geneva. I did the paintings for Venice in the first studio we visited. The project for the Consortium on Place de la Libération I worked on in the little house, along with some other ongoing projects. As your work develops, all that becomes necessary. You also need more help. You can't do everything yourself. It is a lot of work organizing five exhibitions at the same time, wrapping up the works, sorting out transport, looking after the books, keeping track of what is going where and when it is supposed to be returned. At the moment, I need to wrap the six paintings for the Venice Biennale that are going next week. They're so big that it takes six people to handle them. It's impossible to do it all alone. You know, American artists all hire two or three assistants as soon as they start working. It's very rare in France. I suppose it's a difference of mentalities. Americans know how to make the most of their potential." ¶ Yan Pei Ming is acknowledged all over the world as a consummate professional. The exhibition at the Dijon art museum will soon be shown together with works from the Geneva and Besançon exhibitions at the FRAC (Regional Fund for Contemporary Art) in the Champagne-Ardennes region, then on from there to Shanghai, Guangzhou, and Canberra. The Consortium show, co-organized with the Grande Halle de la Villette art center in Paris, is showcasing his work in a tent on the loveliest square in Dijon. It is later to be shown in Paris. ¶ The museum exhibition features portraits of Chairman Mao, his father, and self-portraits. There are also plenty of nudes. These are not often shown, I believe. I happen to know that the sitters were prostitutes. Yan Pei Ming met them through a friend who works in a Chinese restaurant and who used to take the dishes the girls ordered over to the all-night bar where they worked. Sometimes Ming would go along. They would clap him on the shoulder and say, "So, Ming, how's the painting?" When he asked them to pose for him, they put aside their distrust for anything out of the ordinary and accepted with good grace. ¶ But why nudes? Ming says, "Because I wanted to paint portraits of women. Since my style of painting is rather brutal, it was difficult to identify the sitters of the ones I had done until then. You could never tell if it was a man or a woman. I said to myself that to be sure it was a woman, I'd better paint nudes. And nudes are the most classical subjects. Portraits, nudes, and landscapes—all my subjects are classics." ¶ Yes, but the classicism is completely neutralized. ¶ Like when he paints a landscape and calls it *International Landscape*. A strange sort of classicism. ¶ *International Airport* seems to make more sense. But Yan Pei Ming painted this series after his landscapes, which he depicted as cliché-ridden models. ¶ This very obviousness is a source of ambiguity, especially since the tent where

FACING PAGE: *MAO*, 1991.

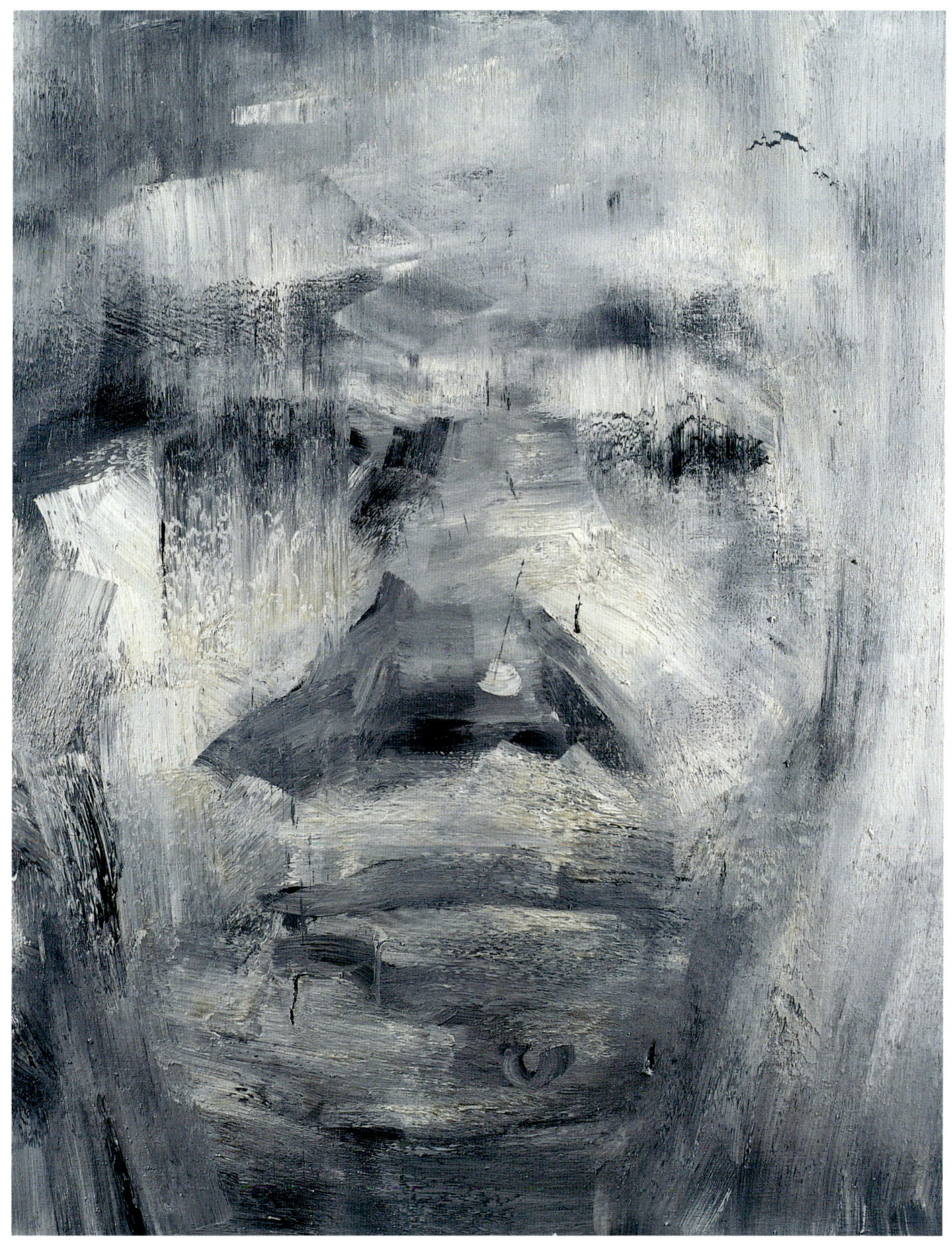

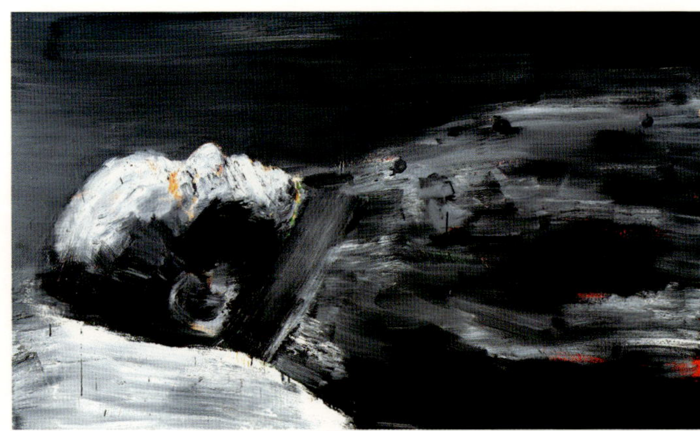
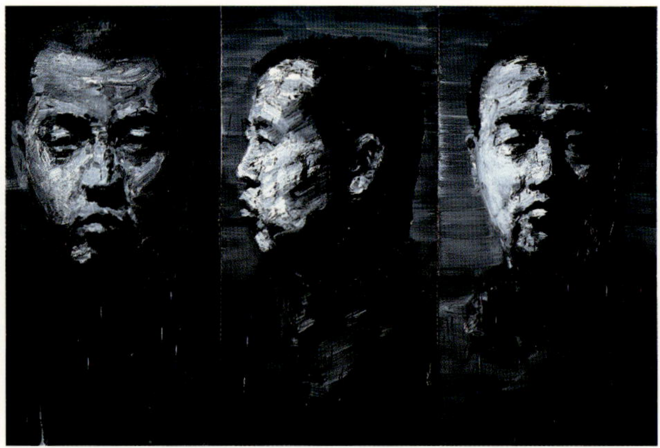
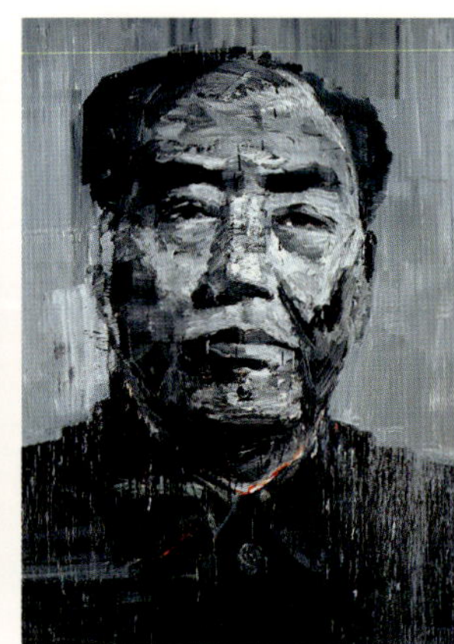

International Airport is being shown certainly has something of the fairground about it. Yan Pei Ming chose to set up his tent in the center of the square, with a booth at the entrance selling tickets priced at one euro. You are shown into the exhibition through two sets of doors by an usherette who lights the way to the center of the space with a flashlight. You climb onto a sort of podium and lean on the railings. Gradually, the lights come on and reveal a 360° painting of an airport with dozens of planes waiting to take off and one in the air. This is *International Airport*. I have heard that the name is a reference to *International Landscape*, which Yan Pei Ming worked on from 1996, and which (coincidentally?) had its first airing at the Consortium, which is now co-organizer of this show. ¶ What is *International Landscape*? An ideal place. A commonplace. An indeterminate place without borders, which could be anywhere and nowhere. ¶ Hence the title. ¶ Yan Pei Ming explains, "It's always very simple: a tree, a little house, sometimes a lake. Like a perfect chromolithograph. When you ask people to describe a landscape, they describe a lake, a house, some trees. It's as simple as that." ¶ Simple? No. Because when Yan Pei Ming was living in Shanghai, even in the darkest days of the Cultural Revolution, he must have had some knowledge of landscape painting. He had to free himself of this experience and take a step back. ¶ He sweeps the suggestion away when I question him about it. "History is history. It's the past. Chinese painting hasn't evolved at all for the last three hundred years. It's difficult to make it evolve. We should forget it and move on." ¶ But how? By sheer willpower. By fighting against the easy temptations of talent. By becoming international. By closing off the past and the lure of nostalgia. ¶ Anyway, as they say, nostalgia ain't what it used to be. ¶ What is Yan Pei Ming's past? ¶ His parents were workers. His father worked in a suburban slaughterhouse. ¶ 1960s Shanghai, at the start of the Cultural Revolution. Shanghai is as vibrant as ever. Open to the sea, to foreigners, to the surrounding countryside. A fabulous melting pot, like New York. "There wasn't a single Shanghai man born and bred in my whole neighborhood. Everyone spoke a different dialect," Ming recalls. ¶ People spent their lives outside in the streets. Doors were always left open. Ming probably saw his first paintings at about eight, through the open door or window of his neighbor's home. His neighbor was a docker, and copied portraits of Mao. ¶ Ming was hooked. ¶ He remembers, "It was magic! Copying a portrait of Mao, all properly squared up. I was fascinated. I could get to grips with the idea of painting a table or a chair. But this guy with his copies of Mao just enthralled me. And gradually, we saw more and more of each other." ¶ Then came the Cultural Revolution. It's strange how different artists have differing views of this shattering event. Ming begins by excusing himself, then explains, "I was very young, but it was really a fabulous time for me. I remember that near us there lived a fairly bourgeois family with a lovely house with a red roof, a tiny courtyard, and a garden. It was tiny, maybe fifteen feet (five meters) by eighteen feet (six meters), but back then it seemed big to us, and we dreamed of having a garden like that. It was protected by barbed wire to keep us out. We kept asking why they had such a nice house and garden, and not us? One day, the Red Guards requisitioned it. Finally we were allowed in. We didn't think about the hurt to the family—we were just thrilled." ¶ He would go to school either in the morning or the afternoon. There were too many children in Shanghai, not enough classrooms, and not enough teachers. The authorities put in place a system where half the children would go in the morning and half in the afternoon; when they were not in school, they did their homework in halls where teachers would keep an eye on them. The children would let each other know whose turn it was to go to school. ¶ Ming began painting when he was ten. His talent was quickly recognized. He tells me,

FROM LEFT TO RIGHT: *MAO ZEDONG'S REMAINS*, 2002. *SELF-PORTRAIT*, 2000, FROM FAGGIONATO FINE ARTS, LONDON. *OFFICIAL PORTRAIT*, 2000. PHOTOGRAHS BY ANDRÉ MORIN.

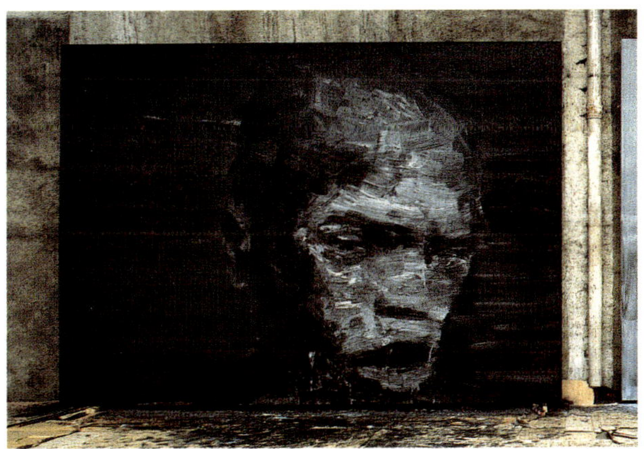

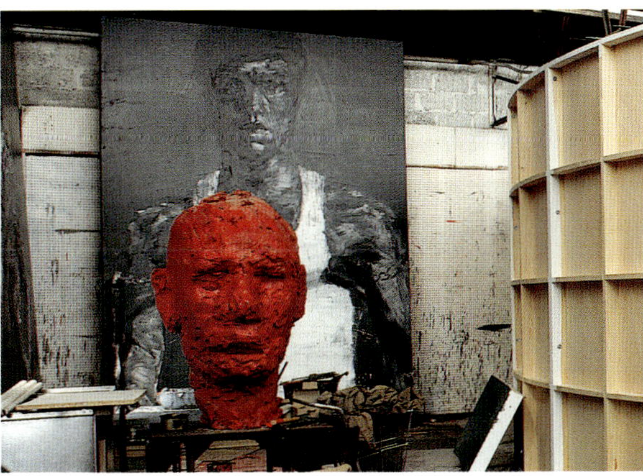

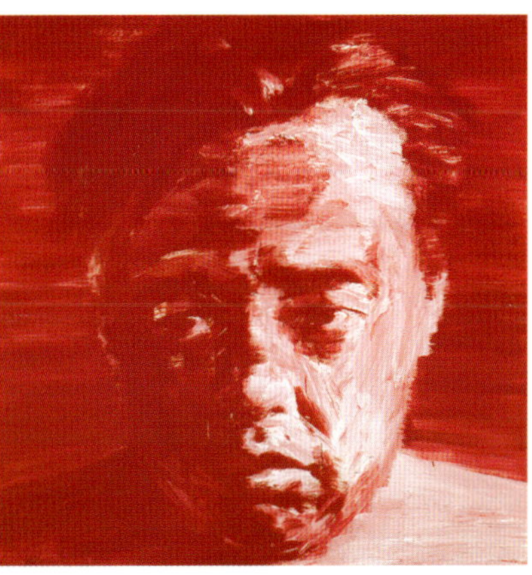

"In every neighborhood, there was a committee and propaganda bureau, which organized activities. Every week someone was put in charge of painting. Often, it was me. At home, they noticed my talent very quickly. Then the neighbors knew, then the whole neighborhood, then the school. I have always been able to attract an audience." ¶ What did he paint? Copies of pictures handed out to children, propaganda posters. If the SARS virus had been around in those days, everyone would have had to paint health education posters. That was the sort of thing Ming was painting. ¶ Where did he learn to paint? In school? No, there was no art room. Not put off by this, Ming organized lessons at the age of twelve. He found himself a teacher and explained what he wanted to learn. Together, they cleared out a tiny shed measuring seven feet (two and a half meters) by nine feet (three meters), and called it their studio. They got together a group of a dozen pupils. They had no money for even the most basic materials, so Yan Pei Ming went out collecting paper and other waste to sell. At that time, everything had a price in China. He then bought brushes and paints. So the adventure began. ¶ When he moved on to high school, he found that again there was no art room—and again, he set one up with the help of an art teacher. "By the time it had been going three years, it was the best-known studio in all of Shanghai. Little by little, it acquired a superb reputation," he laughs. ¶ 1974. Ming became a propaganda artist, painting vast murals of Chairman Mao in schools and factories. Always in red, a good, positive color. He found it oddly exalting, dynamic, heroic, and energetic. Mao died in 1976. ¶ How does Yan Pei Ming remember the event? "That day, for the first time, I painted a portrait of Mao in black and white," he says in the same tone he told me how the Cultural Revolution had been good to him. "Before, it was forbidden to paint Mao in black and white. For the Chinese, black and white are the colors of death and mourning." ¶ In Beijing, just a few days after Mao's death, the art scene—still in its very early days—began to break free of the yoke, staging a number of artistic events. But not in Shanghai. The most avant-garde art about in Shanghai in those days was abstract art of the Paris school, imported via Hong Kong and Taiwan. Artists showed their work in parks or buildings transformed into galleries for the occasion. ¶ In 1980, Yan Pei Ming left for Paris. He was twenty. He had failed the entrance examination for the Shanghai School of Fine Art, probably at the interview stage. He recalls, "I couldn't say a word. I was struck dumb. I think I stuttered. I was so emotional." He continues, "I find it difficult to express myself, so I have always had to work much harder than everyone else just to be able to speak. This problem is a real handicap. When I was little, I really found it hard. So I tried to find something to replace oral expression. I focused on pictorial expression instead. I devoted all my energy to building a career in the visual arts. I thought it was the only line of work where you didn't need to speak. But when I arrived in France, it was the complete opposite: I had to explain everything. I found it deeply unsettling." ¶ He came to France because he had an uncle already living in Paris. He took the entrance exam to the School of Fine Arts in Paris, and failed again. ¶ How did he end up in Dijon? Simply because he needed a job, and found one there as general helper in a Chinese restaurant. ¶ He was quickly accepted at the Dijon School of Fine Arts. There he discovered teaching methods radically different from everything he had known in China. Like he said, everything needed explaining. He didn't understand what the teachers wanted from him. He didn't speak much French. All he learned was one piece of advice drummed into the students by the teachers: be different from the others. In China, teachers said the exact opposite. So all in all, it was a good thing to take on board. ¶ Meanwhile, he was making progress. He had his first exhibition in 1982 in a framing shop. "It was crap," he says. Maybe, but it was a start. He was

FROM LEFT TO RIGHT: STUDIO IN DIJON IN 2003. *SELF-PORTRAIT*, 2003. PHOTOGRAPHS BY ANDRÉ MORIN.

to have other exhibitions, just as much "crap," and all the while he was learning. ¶ He was on his way. ¶ Yan Pei Ming does not only have a superb grasp of strategy, but he also has an instinctive feel for what is important, good, of decent quality—in short, what counts. ¶ At the time, the vogue at his college in Dijon, as elsewhere in France, was for free figuration: Robert Combas and so on. All his fellow students were crazy about it. But not Yan Pei Ming. "It wasn't a means of expression, just a grimace. What I found thrilling was work by people like Lavier or Toroni." ¶ As I said before, Yan Pei Ming has a gift for not taking his eye off the ball. He keeps on moving forward at his own pace, and in so doing has garnered an impressive résumé. ¶ When he first got off the train in Dijon in 1981, he didn't know a single person there, and he had a bad stammer. Yet straight away he found the only stage for contemporary art in the whole region, the Consortium, founded in 1978. He made himself indispensable by helping out as often as possible. That is how he met Bertrand Lavier, who at that time was far from being the star he is today, and who proved a very helpful contact. ¶ In 1988, Yan Pei Ming was selected to take part in an event hosted by the ARC studios in Paris, and also studied for a year at the prestigious Institute for the Plastic Arts under Pontus Hulten. In 1990, he was given an exhibition at the Villa Arson in Nice, and in 1991 his works were on show at the *Mouvement 2* exhibition at the Centre Pompidou Center in Paris. That same year, he also had his first solo exhibition at the Galerie Anne de Villepoix in Paris, then at the Anciens Établissements Sacrés gallery, in Liège, Belgium. He was also invited to take part in the seventh edition of the prestigious International Art Workshops organized by the Loire region. In 1994, he was awarded a grant as artist in residence at the Villa Médicis, the French cultural center in Rome, and then he became a familiar face on the Biennial circuit: he has been to Venice and Lyon twice, Gwangju and Shanghai once, and at the Pantheon in Paris in 1999. ¶ The work shown there was *Eulogy to Metissage*. It featured twenty-one orphans from Soweto, twenty-one children from Réunion, and twenty-one children from the poor Paris suburb of Aubervilliers. ¶ His work has been shown at numerous galleries: Arndt and Partner in Berlin, Art et Public in Geneva, Bernier in Athens, Rodolphe Janssen in Brussels. Only the very best. ¶ Yan Pei Ming has not put a foot wrong. ¶ He knows exactly what he wants and how to get it—which he always does. ¶ It is a gift that should never be underestimated. ¶ His real debut was at the Galerie Anne de Villepoix in 1991, with the first public exhibition of his portraits of Mao since he had left China. "Because back then, I wanted to make a splash. I was a complete unknown in Paris. The portraits of Mao gave people an idea of who they were dealing with." ¶ Actually, Yan Pei Ming never stopped painting portraits of the Great Helmsman. First in China, and more recently in France, where visitors, friends, and collectors can see them in his studio. But "I didn't dare to show them," he says. And he certainly didn't dare make a whole exhibition out of them. What's more, they were all in black and white. ¶ He certainly made a splash. Visitors to the Paris exhibition were split exactly down the middle: half loathed the paintings, or the portraits, or both. The others tuned in immediately to what was at stake in the paintings. Jean Brolly, an admirer of Buren, Toroni, and Rutault, began to collect Ming's work. ¶ His Mao is very different from Andy Warhol's—Mao as an icon or star like any other, a machine among the machines. His Mao is me, you, our father, a dictator, a hero, everything, nothing—he is what we make of him. Like his curious painting "without qualities" (to paraphrase the title of Robert Musil's famous novel), which is either fabulously expressive or absolutely neutral, like his strokes

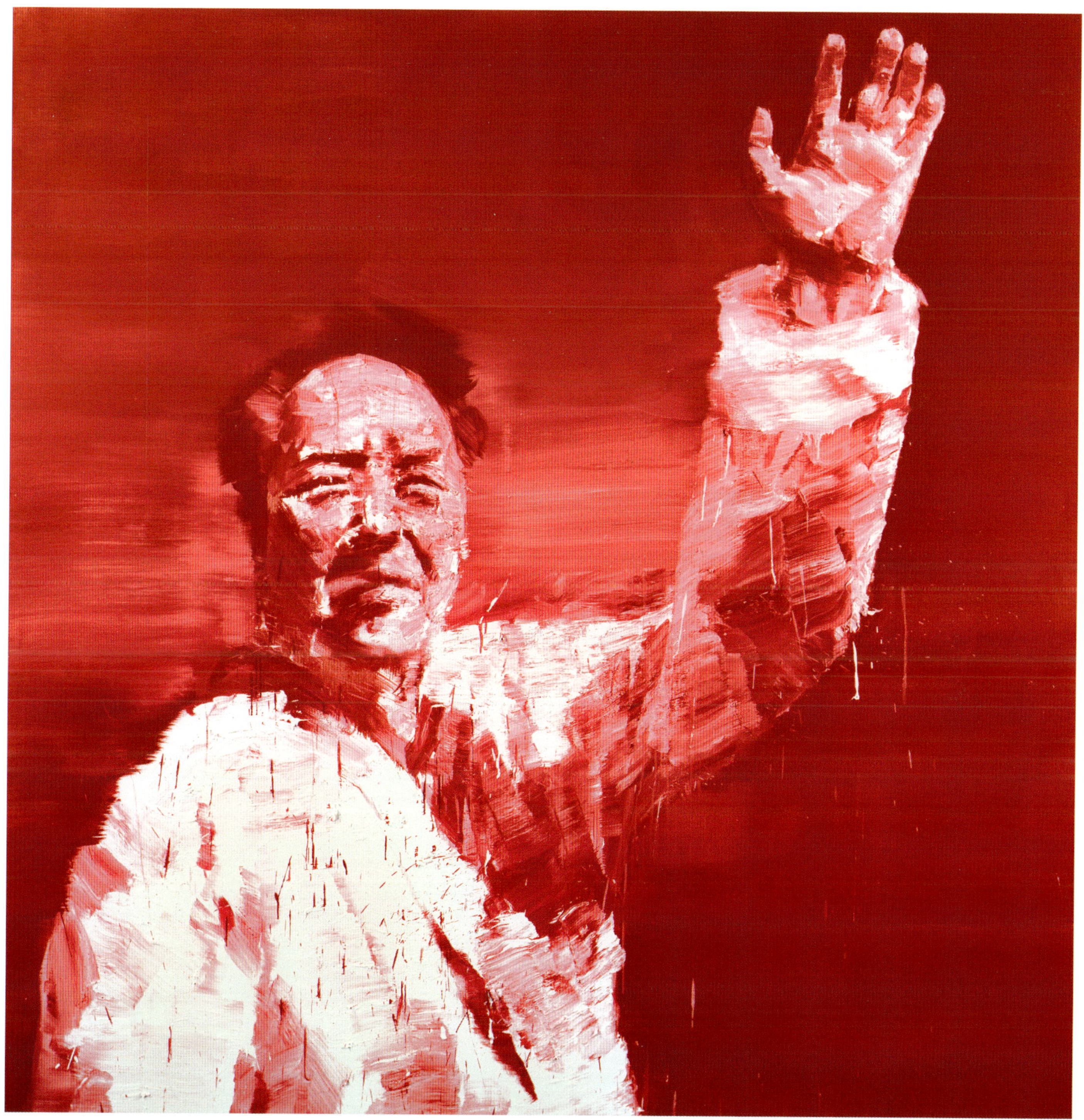

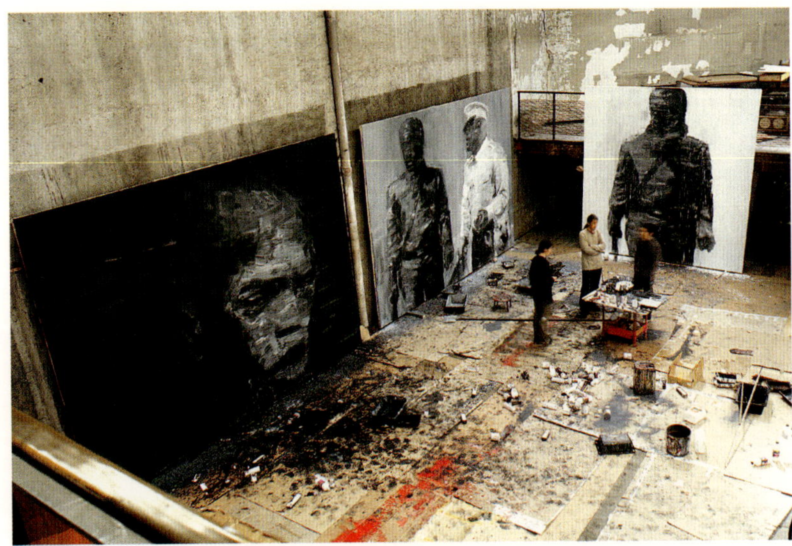

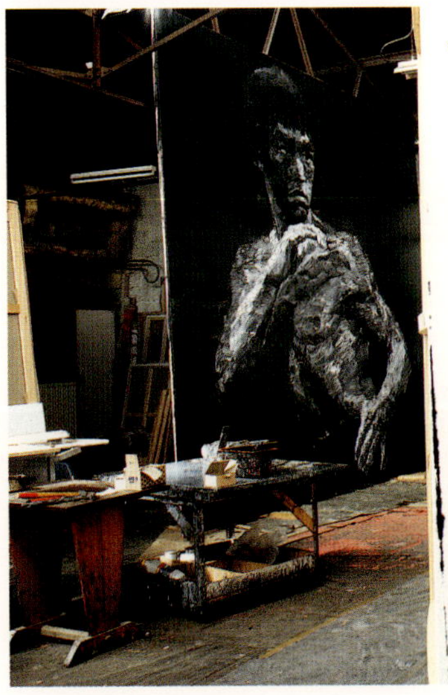

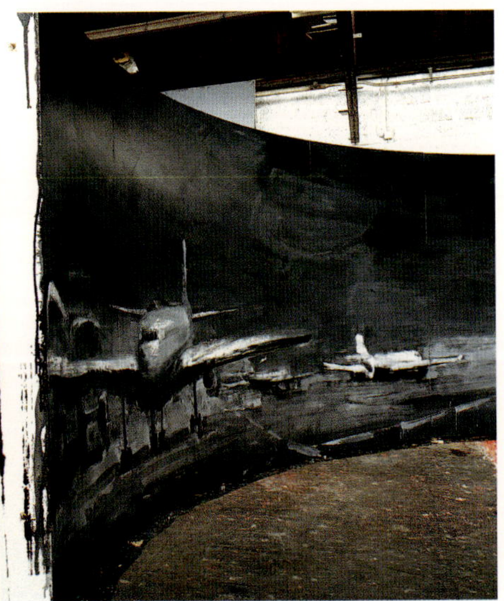

that could be the van Gogh strokes Lavier used to paint over his pianos and pieces of furniture, like the black and white that is the color of death, but is above all the absence of color. ¶ Sometimes he added a touch of red, a magnificent Chinese vermilion, but reminded people that in China, "red is the color of propaganda paintings." ¶ Having seen an exhibition at the Besançon art museum in May 2003 that featured a retrospective of Yan Pei Ming's Mao portraits, it is astonishing to note the variety of ways he has interpreted this most famous of faces. He has kneaded it, boxed it, magnified, dismantled, caressed, slapped it, and put it back together again, rebuilding it after taking it apart, just barely keeping a few recognizable features to make it identifiable. ¶ "For me, Mao is a sort of laboratory. I try all sorts of new things out using his portrait." ¶ He has his subject so much at his fingertips, has painted and repainted it so often, wearing it almost to the bone, that in the end it melts away and becomes pure painting, like the poet Paul Valéry's fruit that melts into pure *jouissance*. ¶ Mao is a painting, and thus becomes the act of painting. ¶ A "head," as Giacometti would have said. ¶ Yan Pei Ming eventually (naturally?) moved on to portraits of his own father. He showed forty or so of these portraits at the Durand-Dessert gallery in Paris, each with a little notice describing it as "the craziest," "the most loving," "the most powerful," "the most stubborn," "the most perspicacious," "the deafest," "the gentlest," and so on. He alternated positive and negative statements, and most significantly, called the exhibition *Portrait of an Unknown*. ¶ "I don't see too much of a difference between Mao and my father," he says, gliding from the better-known to the lesser-known personality in an ambiguous way. He confides, "In China, we were always being told that Mao was more important than our own fathers. But I didn't agree with that." Then he said, "Of course, Mao is the father." ¶ What is the truth? ¶ Both statements are true. ¶ Mao and the father figure meld into one, the masses, where the Great Helmsman is stripped of his particularities and becomes pure image, as does the father: he is both a father and a "man without qualities," at the same time "gentle" yet "selfish," "loving" and "stubborn." The two father figures meld together in anonymity. "I am a man without a name," says Don Juan at the start of the earliest known literary version of the legend, by Tirso de Molina. The artist's father and Mao are both men without names. ¶ Ming often paints himself as his own father. Is this a question of a transfer of identity, or of the fluidity of personality? ¶ Yan Pei Ming says, "When I paint a portrait, it is a perfectly autonomous entity. It does not represent a given person in particular." ¶ I remember reading somewhere that he once said, "I work with the notion of the anti-portrait." I remind him of this, and he bursts out laughing. "When I first started to work in France fifteen years ago, portraits were taboo. Because I painted a lot of them, I invented this word, anti-portrait, to describe all my paintings. But really, they were just normal portraits. Inventing this new term meant the possibilities opened up again. I could paint portraits and just call them anti-portraits. I was free." ¶ In the 1950s, Eugène Ionesco and Samuel Beckett coined the term anti-theater. Was he perhaps influenced by them? Yan Pei Ming claims to be a disciple of Willem de Kooning. He admires the sense of urgency that radiates from his powerful paintings, which almost punch and scream. Ming paints extremely fast himself, taking just two afternoons to complete a portrait and a week for a landscape. Sometimes he completes a work in just half a day. He does not begin with the background and then add in the figures over it, but rather paints everything at the same time—a bit of background, then part of a figure, then the whole outline, then he returns to the background. "I always paint

FROM LEFT TO RIGHT: A VIEW OF MING'S HUGE STUDIO IN DIJON WHERE YOU CAN SEE, *ANTI-RIOT COPS*, 2003. *BRUCE LEE: THE WAY OF THE DRAGON*, 2000. *INTERNATIONAL AIRPORT*, 2003. PHOTOGRAPHS BY ANDRÉ MORIN.

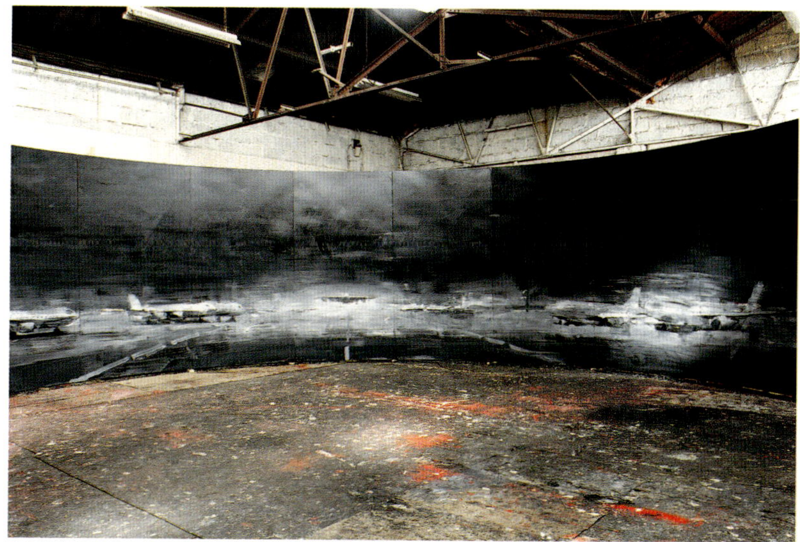

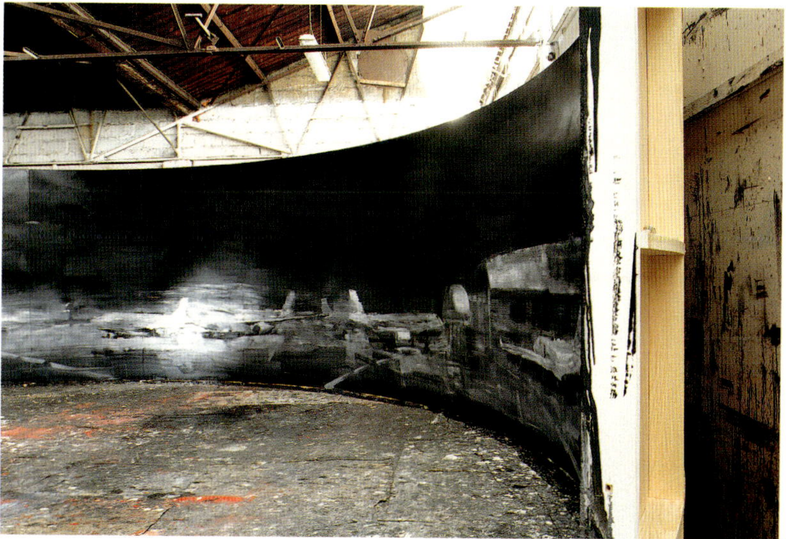

everything at once," he says. He likes to maintain a sense of physical proximity to the canvas. ¶ What are the traces of de Kooning's influence? ¶ I am always a little mistrustful of the influences artists claim for themselves, as they often use them to mask their true sources of inspiration. Yan Pei Ming's work reveals the general influence of Lavier and more specific traces of Warhol, notably in his work *Têtes mises à prix (Prices on their Heads)*, featuring a number of skulls. He is also deeply influenced by Christian Boltanski. ¶ This influence remains in the background for much of the time, but is evident in a work completed in 1991, produced in collaboration with students at the Montpellier School of Fine Art. The work is highly reminiscent of a piece produced by Boltanski at a school in Lentillères, near Dijon, in 1973. Yan Pei Ming sketched each student in less than five minutes, and called the resulting work *Anonymous Portraits: 108 Brigands*. ¶ "When I started work on *108 Brigands* in Montpellier, I was like a painting machine. All the students just filed past. It took me three days to do 108 portraits. My work is far more efficient than Andy Warhol's. Back then, I was still marking out my territory through painting." ¶ The title *108 Brigands* is a reference to an enormously long tale called *By the Water*, which is the first book children in China read. It is similar in theme to *Robin Hood*, with a band of noble-hearted brigands who steal from the rich to give to the poor. It is an eternal theme of justice and retribution found in cultures all over the world. ¶ Yan Pei Ming says his work in Montpellier was a rehearsal, a preparatory stage. "Then one day, I got to work on the real version, on canvas. In Montpellier, I painted directly on the wall. When the paintings finally faded two or three years later, I did a similar work at the Villa Médicis, where I was artist in residence, with portraits of everyone who came to see me in my studio—my fellow artists in residence, other artists just passing through, my friends, everyone." ¶ I foolishly mention that Andy Warhol used to film, or had his friends film, everyone who came to the Factory. Yan Pei Ming immediately raises a number of objections—"But I paint," "Well, there aren't that many ways to go about it," "It's close, but actually quite different." ¶ And how is it "different"? In almost every way, actually. The influences that we critics often make a game of spotting have been chewed over and spat out again by Yan Pei Ming. He has forgotten, or at least tried to forget, all the burdensome details: where he comes from. What he once was. ¶ For example, some critics have noted a similarity to calligraphy in his paintings. He used to be an expert calligrapher, but now he rejects the reference entirely: "It's a language we use to talk to each other, and that's all." A language that is marvelously intimate, but "out of date," he informs me peremptorily. "Magnificent, but non-transmissible. It is a local language that is used but that no one can understand. Nowadays, English is an international language, or oil painting, or installations, or video, or the image. Calligraphy is a regional language." ¶ He even goes so far as to refuse to consider himself Chinese. ¶ "You've known me for fifteen years, but when people who don't know me see my paintings, they'd never guess that they were done by a Chinese man. But when people know I'm Chinese, they say 'Oh, it's obvious, only someone Chinese could have painted that.' Typical." ¶ He tells me again that what left the deepest impression on him in China was his time as a propaganda artist, painting as quickly as possible with fat brushes. Perfect images. Images that talk to people. That is where he is coming from. ¶ Apart from that, he says, "I am on the side of today's language. I use oil paints like other artists use video. As far as I am concerned, there's no difference."

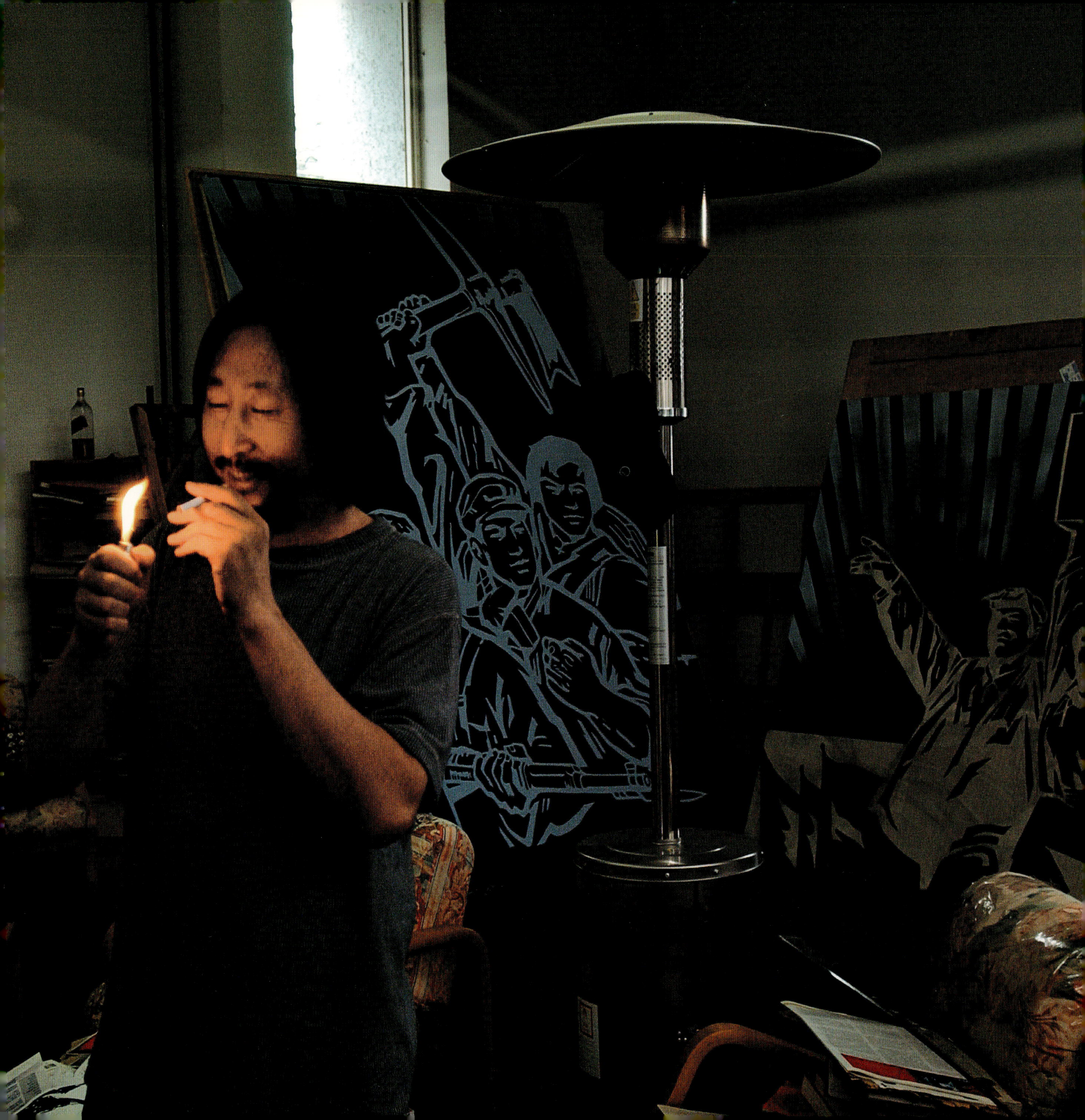

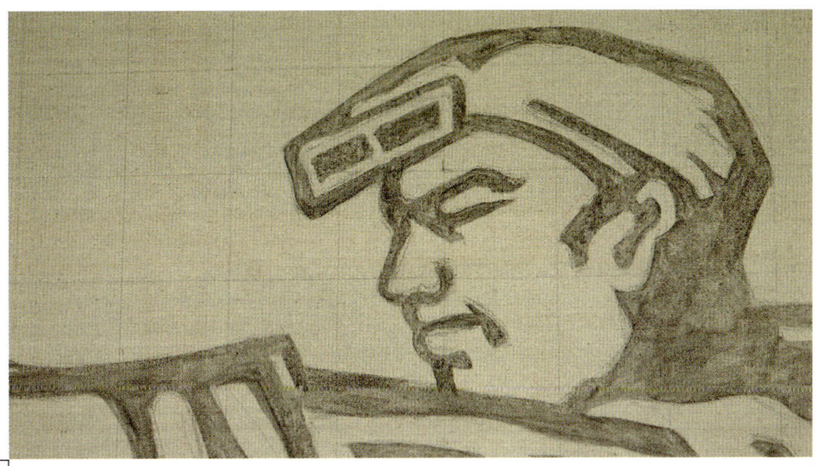

WANG GUANGYI

Wang Guangyi is a poker player, sparing with his words, only speaking in brief, clipped phrases. He is one of the most influential artists on the modern Chinese art scene. He and his work have become emblematic of an art that opposes, links, and confronts two visions of society, Communist and liberal, the political propaganda of the Chinese Cultural Revolution and advertisements for a Western-style consumer society—one dominated by socialist realism, the other by the aesthetic of efficiency of commercial art. ¶ Wang Guangyi is the undisputed star of so-called Chinese Political Pop Art. ¶ It is strange, then, to see him being saluted by a guard or young soldier at the entrance to the upscale housing complex as we drive in on our way to his studio. Why the salute? I ask. "Don't make anything of it," he smiles, "the guard salutes every time one of the residents enters or leaves." Oh. ¶ We had settled on an appointment in a hotel, not far from where he lives, halfway between his home and his studio, about twenty miles (thirty kilometers) southwest of Beijing city center, at the end of a very boring stretch of freeway lined with greenhouses. He chose this neighborhood because it is so quiet. ¶ His hair is a little on the long side. He has a straggly beard. He is wearing a good leather jacket and drives a Mercedes—not the cheapest model, either. ¶ He flatters me with a few words of French—"*Mademoiselle, vous êtes très jolie*" ("Young lady, you are very pretty")—to show that he is polite, that he has been to France, and that he enjoyed his time there. ¶ The studio is a one-story building with high ceilings. The flagged courtyard is open to the sky. It is filled with his own sculptures of workers and peasants from the waist up, their muscles bulging, holding hammers or brushes. They are overgrown with climbing plants. ¶ His studio is bright and airy. He comes here almost every day to spend the afternoon. There are chests for transporting sculptures lying around on the floor. At the far end is a forest of sculptures begun in 2001. Facing them, a number of frames. On a chair, I can see a canvas—a yellow background with a group of enthusiastic young people figured on it in black outline. Beside it stands an empty easel. Apparently the painting is unfinished. Why isn't it on the easel? "Because I only use the easel for small formats. I'm used to working like that. I prop the canvas on the chair and I begin laying out the figures." ¶ Only after that does he include a brand logo. "Cardin?" he wonders aloud, maybe seeking my approval, adding that since the young people in the painting are smiling and because France is a "romantic" country, he thought of Cardin as an image of romantic happiness. ¶ Another unfinished painting shows a group of obviously more aggressively enthusiastic youths. He plans to add a typically American logo—something like McDonald's. ¶ Isn't this a peculiar way of working, especially as he has just said that he is painting the clash of civilizations? Wouldn't it be more logical to work on the two clashing images simultaneously? ¶ No, he explains to me in his deep, pleasant voice. He begins by sketching out the characters, and then, depending on the result—their facial expressions and the general atmosphere of the work—he decides what will work well with them. ¶ On the wall are paintings that were well received at the 1993 Venice Biennale, in São Paulo in 1994, in Bonn in 1996, and in Berlin in 1998. They depict young men with powerful arms and women with clear gazes. They are smiling at the radiant future that awaits them all. Stuck over them are the international brand logos—Mobil, Pepsi, Fedex, Gucci—that claim to make our lives radiant today. "*Gucci, c'est français?*" ("Is Gucci French?") he asks me. ¶ He lights an extremely modern-looking gas stove. It is January, and it is very cold. ¶ I spot a ceramic cup full of cigarette butts. Wang Guangyi smokes cigarettes with blue filters. An armchair sags under a teetering pile of magazines. On the table are scattered paper cups, bottles of water, and a book on Andy Warhol. Well, well. ¶ What does he like most about his fellow Pop Artist? Like everyone else, the notion of accumulation in series. But when he compares Warhol's Maos with his own, painted three or four years later, all he is willing to say is that Warhol didn't live in China under the Great Helmsman. ¶ Wang Guangyi did experience life under Chairman Mao. He was born in 1958 in Heilongjiang province, in the far northwest of China. Next stop Russia. The climate is subarctic. Every January, the region hosts a strange festival of ice lanterns. The temperature can fall as low as -63°F (-53°C). Life is difficult,

FACING PAGE: THE ARTIST AMONG HIS LATEST WORKS IN HIS STUDIO, STANDING IN FRONT OF A WOOD-FIRED STOVE, VITAL DURING THE DIFFICULT WINTER MONTHS. ABOVE: A SKETCH THAT CLEARLY SHOWS HOW THE ARTIST ROUGHS OUT THE OUTLINES OF HIS DRAWINGS.

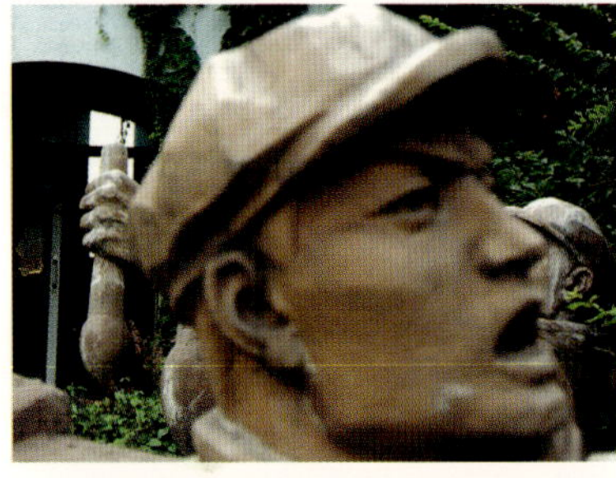
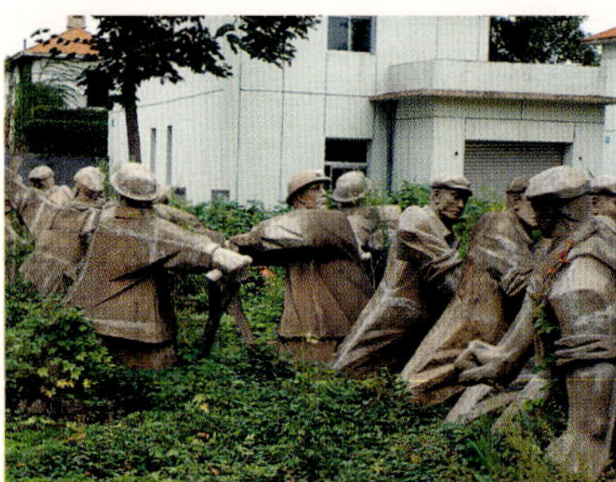
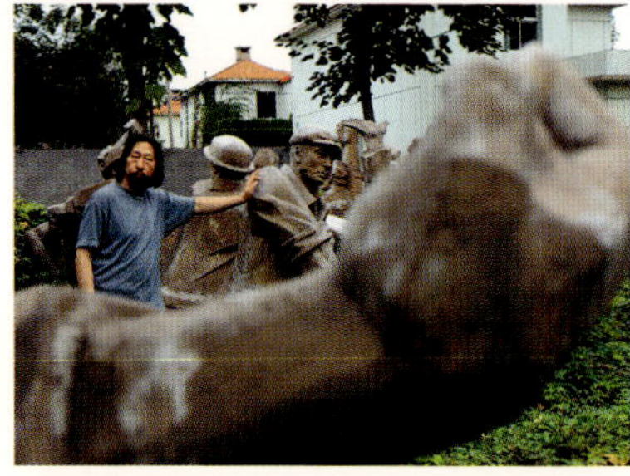
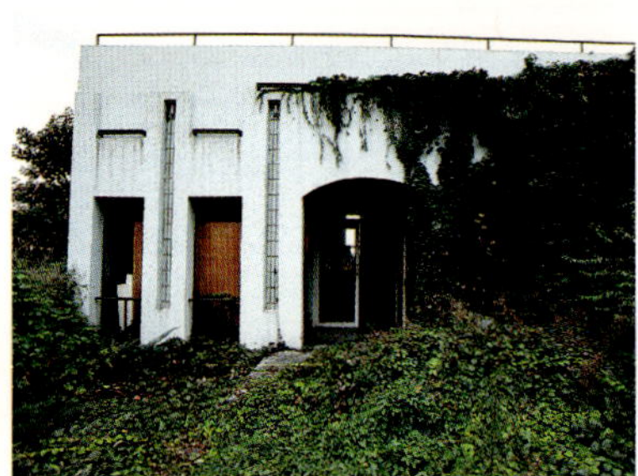
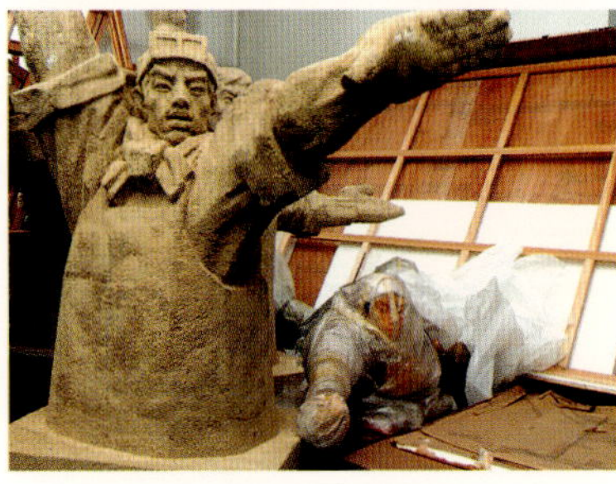
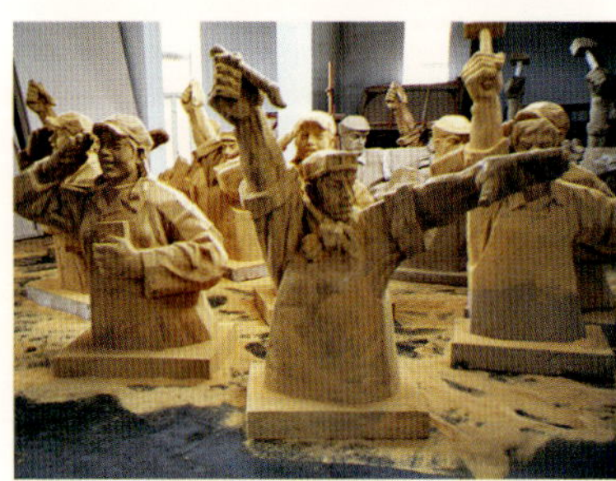
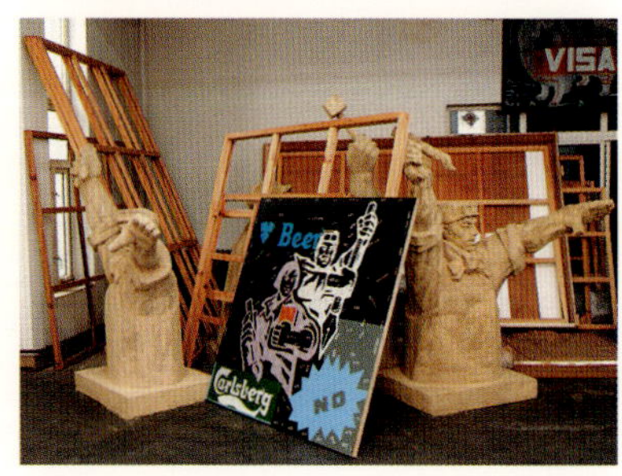

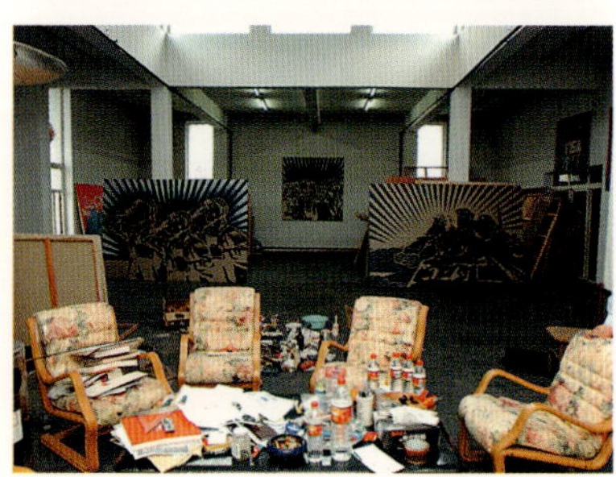

and the people have garnered a reputation for robustness, even ruggedness. ¶ Wang Guangyi is certainly robust and rugged. Sometimes he plays it up a little, like when he poses for my camera. ¶ His family was entirely made up of workers. He discovered his artistic vocation thanks to an early love of drawing. Is that all, I inquire? Oh yes, he remembers, when the Cultural Revolution began when he was nine, one event left a deep impression on him. Every child in every class had to come up with propaganda drawings. The best pupil from each school was selected to take part in a collective series of posters. He was chosen, but he messed up his drawing. From that day on, his one overriding wish was to improve. ¶ That day—and that whole incident—left him with a strangely positive take on the Cultural Revolution. "It opened my eyes," he says. When I express my astonishment, thinking I must have misunderstood, he explains: "It was good in that it opened people's eyes to new things. It was a period when people thought a lot. For the country in general, of course, it left deep traumas, but it also developed certain aspects of art." He repeats, "The Cultural Revolution opened my eyes." ¶ Maybe this should open our eyes to what Wang Guangyi's vision of art is based on, beyond what we can see. ¶ Another time, he gave a more measured interpretation. "I think that the Cultural Revolution was neither good nor bad, but full of significance. This word gives a more precise idea of what it meant for me." ¶ I mentioned this conversation to a friend of mine, a specialist in Chinese contemporary art, now resident in France. He smiled and nodded, saying, "You were being manipulated. It's an old habit of Guangyi's, especially when he's dealing with a Westerner." ¶ Maybe. Probably. Almost certainly. But does his art probe the Communist values of enthusiasm and the liberal values of consumerism with the same degree of criticism? In Russia and the former Soviet bloc, it's not necessarily the old stalwarts of the Communist regimes who are disappointed by the way freedom has turned out, with the rise of the mafia, a shameless plutocracy, pornography, drugs, and unemployment taking the place of the old ills, and who have come to look back on the old days with a certain degree of rose-tinted nostalgia. ¶ It must also be said that many artists consider Wang Guangyi to be uncomfortably close to the powers that be—or at least, that was the impression he gave. ¶ So are we right to interpret his work as placing political propaganda and the marketing strategies of our consumer society on the same footing, reading them both as "mind control strategies"? It is far from certain that this is the case. ¶ Although from where I am standing, it certainly seems an unavoidable conclusion. ¶ After all, some of his paintings feature, alongside the Gillette, Coca-Cola, Pepsi, Parker, Nokia, Davidoff, Time, and Swatch logos, a prominent "no," black on white or white on black. ¶ And another thing: in the painting in which two workers affront a Parker logo, a white "no" on a black background is painted next to the half-open mouth of the top worker, while the second, lower down, is brandishing his clenched fist—but thrusts forward in his other hand a foregrounded calligraphy brush. ¶ One day, in the company of an excellent interpreter, I probed Wang Guangyi to see if it really was a question of the clash of two ideologies. He corrected me: "No, two cultures." I asked the same question two or three times, rephrasing it each time to be sure of his answer and that subtleties were not being lost in translation, but each time he gave me the same answer. Then I asked him again if he considered himself to be a critic. "No," he replied. "It's not my goal to say this is good, or that is bad. My place is that of an observer. What I am showing is the confrontation, the meeting, of two civilizations, two worlds, clashing." ¶ An answer

ABOVE AND FACING PAGE: SCULPTURES OUTSIDE WANG GUANGYI'S STUDIO, COVERED IN VEGETATION. THEY ARE MADE OF REINFORCED FIBERGLASS STUDDED WITH MILLET SEED, GIVING THEM AN EARTHY, OCHER APPEARANCE.

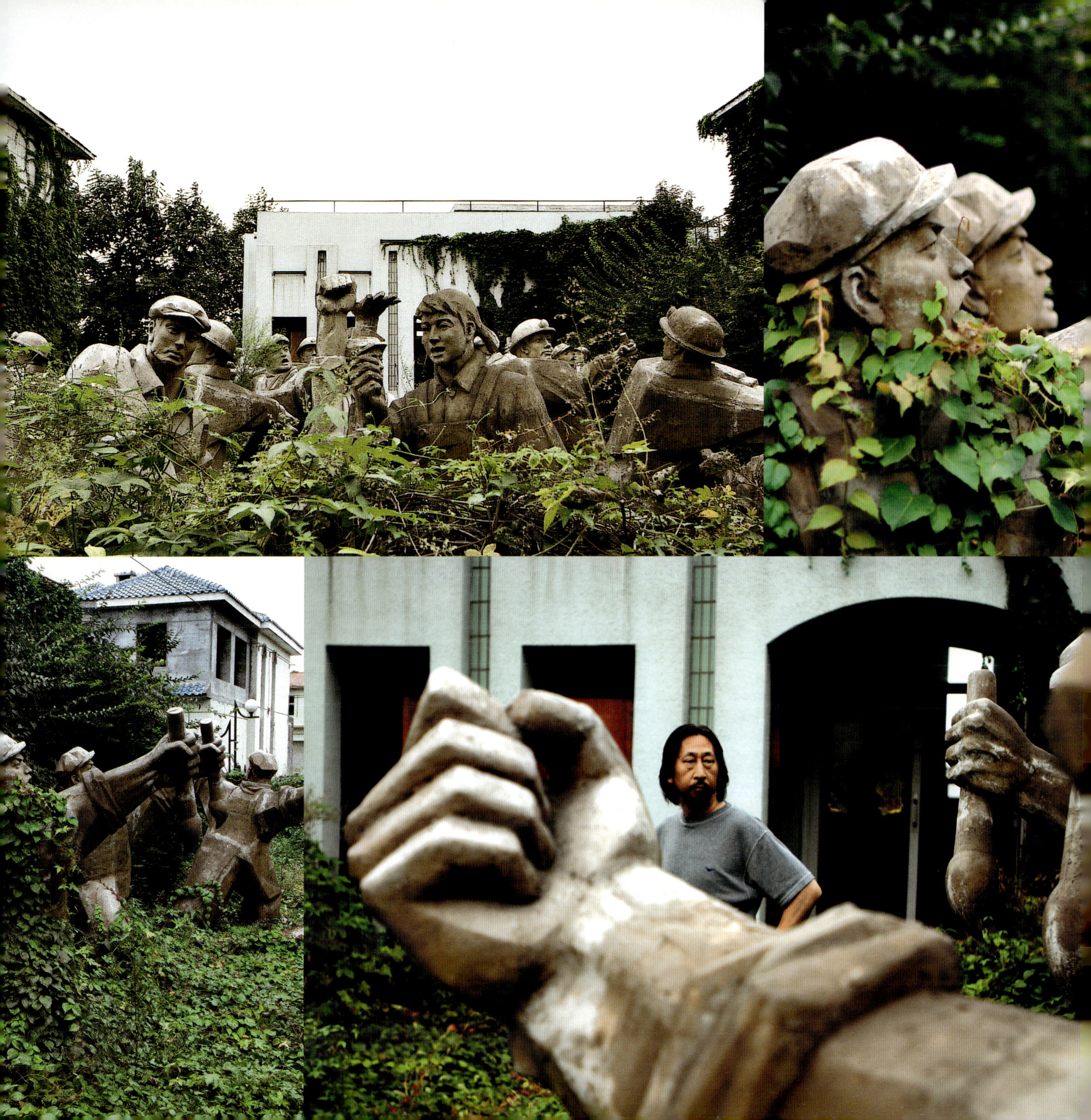

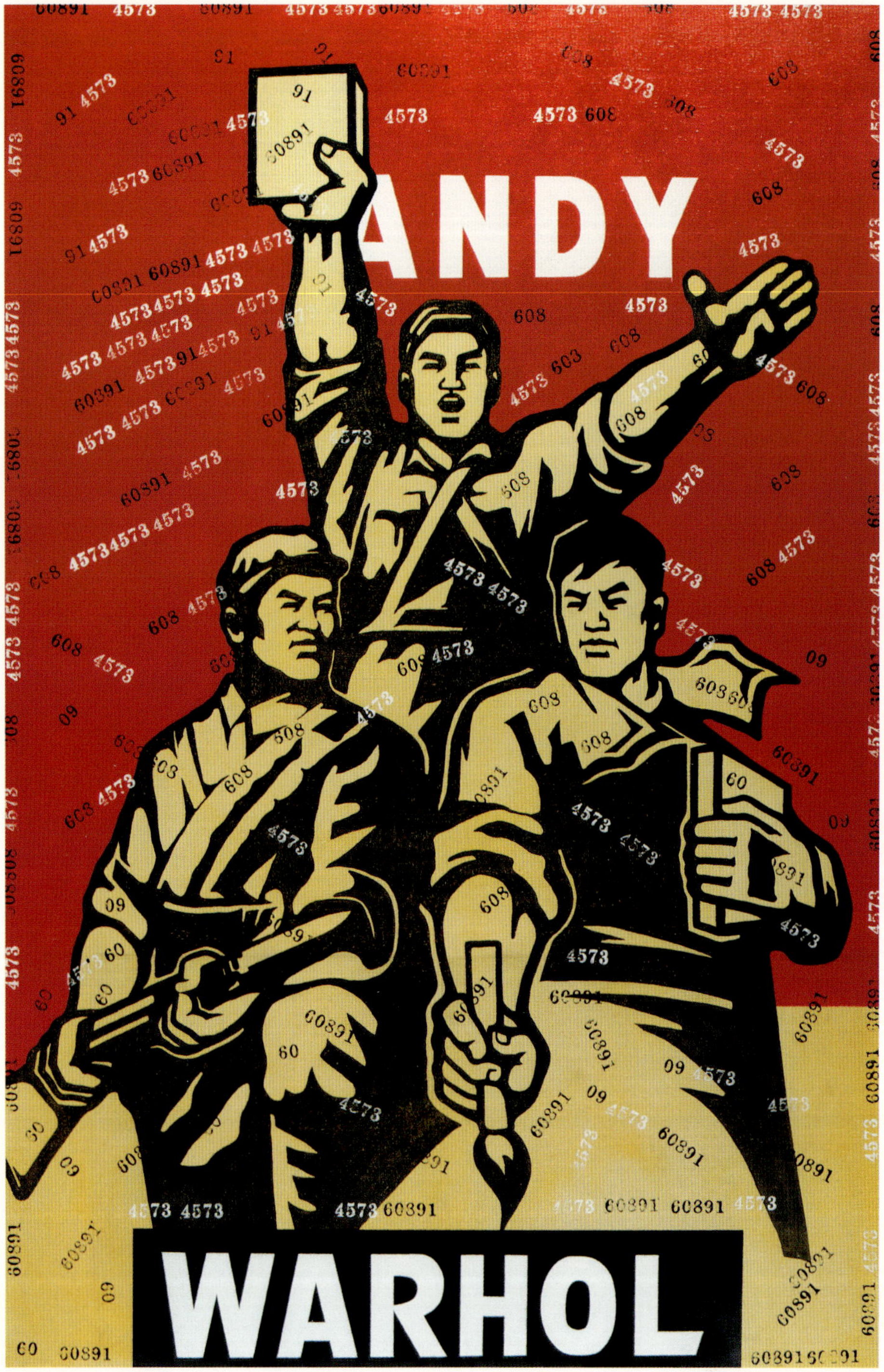

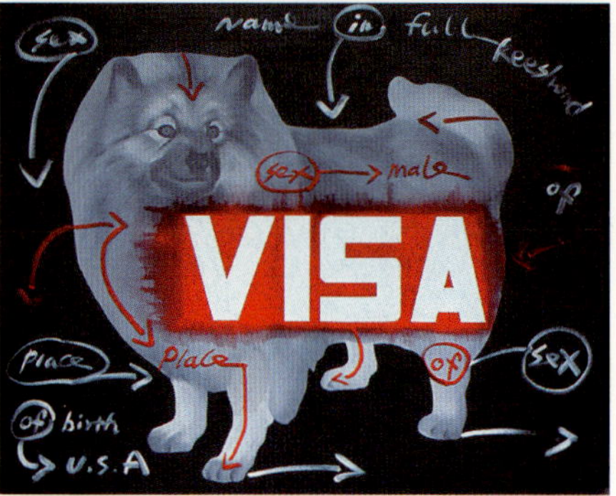

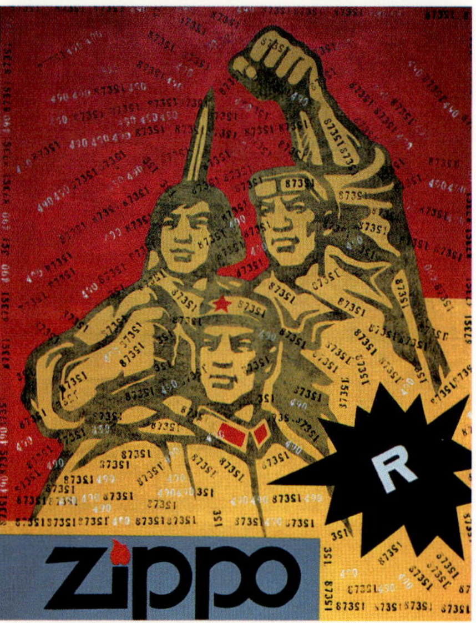

FACING PAGE: WANG GUANGYI'S BEST-KNOWN WORK, *GREAT CRITICISM: COCA-COLA*, 1990–92. THE WORK MADE IT ONTO THE COVER OF *FLASH ART* IN 1992. ABOVE LEFT: *GREAT CRITICISM: WARHOL*, 2002, AND *CARLSBERG*, 1996, WITH THE CHARACTERISTIC "NO" OF THE EARLIER YEARS, AND *ZIPPO* WITH THE *R* TYPICAL OF HIS EARLIER WORK.

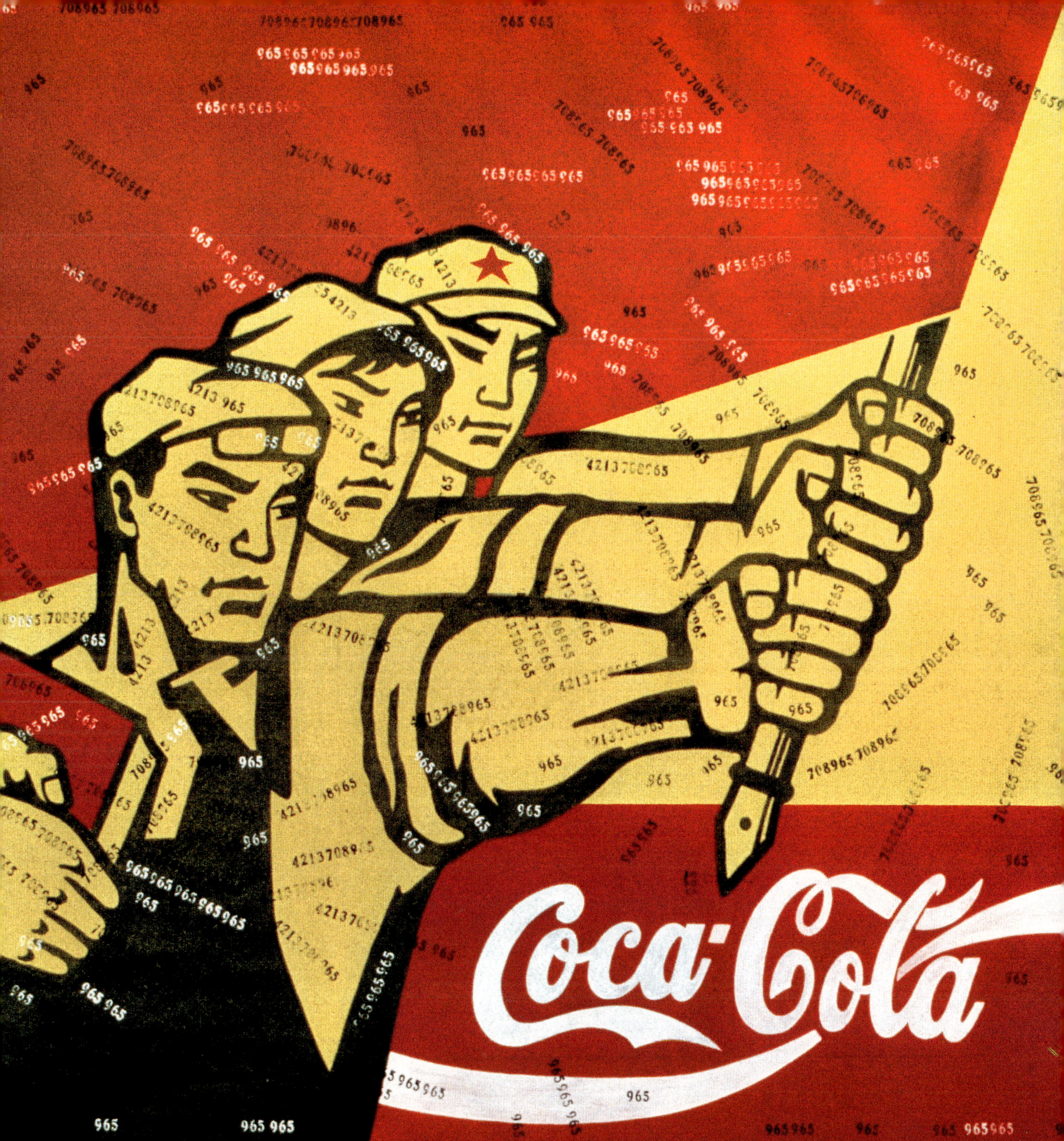
Coca-Cola

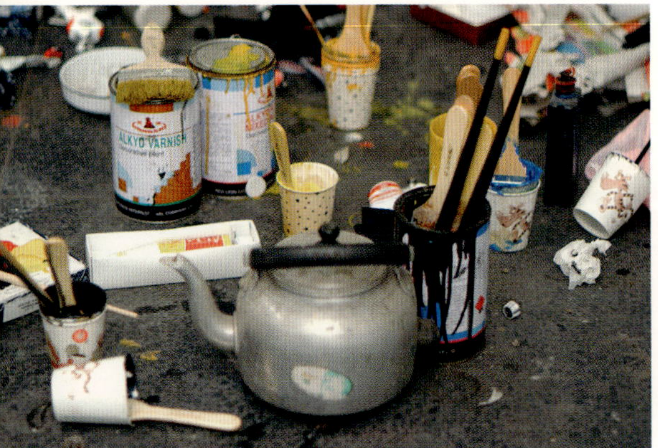

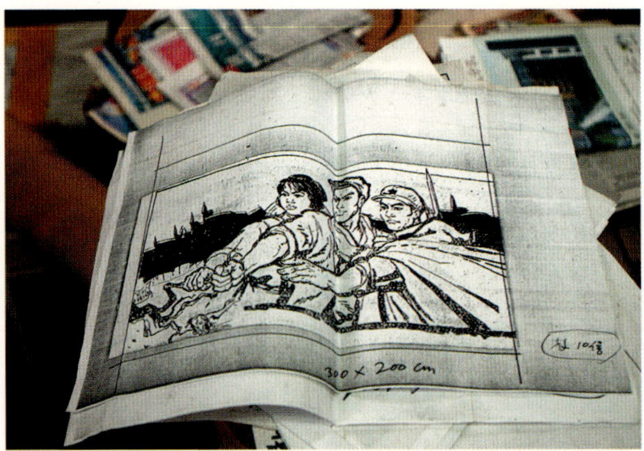

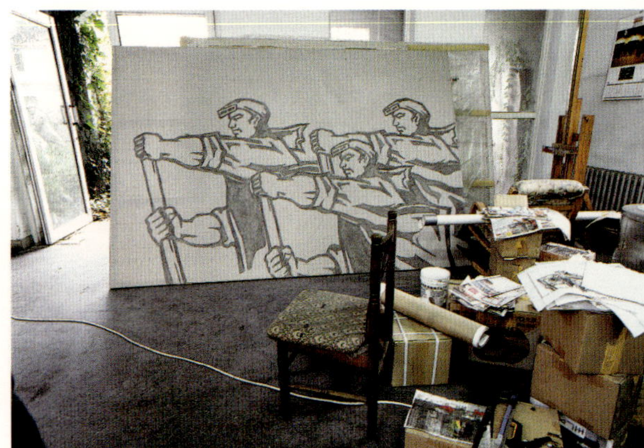

that just throws the debate open even further and muddies the waters. ¶ He started at a communal school in Harbin, a city of nine million people, capital of Heilongjiang province, which has several Orthodox churches and a large Russian minority. The Great Cultural Revolution started when Wang Guangyi was nine. He "naturally" took part in the movement as a Little Red Guard, then a Red Guard. He then began to study art more regularly and took lessons at the Municipal Children's Palace. ¶ Like all other high school children with qualifications, Wang Guangyi was a "young intellectual" and was thus sent to be reeducated on the land, laboring in the fields. When he was not working, he spent his time sketching landscapes. In the late 1970s, he joined a team building a railway. At the same time, college entrance examinations were reinstated. Before, entrance was restricted to good Communists. He gained entrance to the Zhejiang Academy of Fine Arts in Hangzhou, a city of six million people southwest of Shanghai. The Chinese have a saying: "In the sky there is Paradise; on earth are Souzhou and Hangzhou." ¶ The teaching was extremely traditionalist, but he learned what he needed to know—how to understand the history of art, and how to express himself. "I began to realize that the way I saw the problems and issues of the world were not the same as in the West," he says. "I also learned at university a very sophisticated way of expressing what I had to say." He refuses to say whether socialist realism is "good" or "bad," but concedes that the exaltation it shows corresponds to something inside him. ¶ He studied oil painting at university for four years. His research focused on classical art, but gradually evolved. After his marriage in 1984, he returned to Harbin, where he founded the Northern Art group. At the time, avant-garde art movements were springing up all over China. He was appointed to a position at the Harbin School of Architecture, and in 1985 he began work on his *Ice Deserts*, a more or less Surrealist series reminiscent of Giorgio De Chirico, probably influenced by the Ice Lanterns Festival. ¶ These paintings—generally a palette of blues—depict vaguely humanoid forms frozen in swathes of space as empty as Salvador Dali's earliest canvases. They form hypnotic, rectangular clouds. It was a far from indifferent beginning: it was an affirmation. A star was born. He was to shine ever brighter until he achieved the international recognition he enjoys today. ¶ The following year, he moved to Zhuhai, where he was offered a teaching position at the art institute, and where he organized slide shows and symposiums on what has been called the new wave of Chinese art. The same year, he began to explore the possibility of revising the canons of classical Western art, reworking Jacques-Louis David's *Death of Marat* and several other masterpieces of Renaissance and seventeenth-century French and Italian art. His art already expressed his determination not to kowtow to Western art, adopting a position that was neither subordinate nor dominant, but equal, untainted by fear or arrogance. How did he do this? He used a layer of black paint that he left to drip over a reproduction of the painting. This was his way of expressing how he, as a modern man, perceived history. "It was a way of turning the page," he says, "of affirming, the man that I am today is dealing with his own life, and not the past." ¶ Turning over a new leaf, one might say. ¶ In 1988, he revised the iconic effigy of Mao Tse-tung. The Great Helmsman died in 1976. Warhol transformed him into a Hollywood icon in 1984. What did Wang Guangyi do four years later? He reduced him to a mere outline, like a puppet—but still immediately recognizable by every Chinese man and woman, and in fact by the whole world. The idea was not to put Mao in a cage, as some critics have jokingly suggested. Nor was he trying to outdo Warhol. Wang Guangyi

CENTER: THE BOOK WANG GUANGYI TAKES MANY OF HIS FIGURES FROM. RIGHT: THE FIRST STAGE IN WANG GUANGYI'S PAINTINGS: THE LOGO IS ADDED LATER. FAR LEFT: THE ARTIST'S MATERIALS LIE SCATTERED AROUND A TEAPOT.

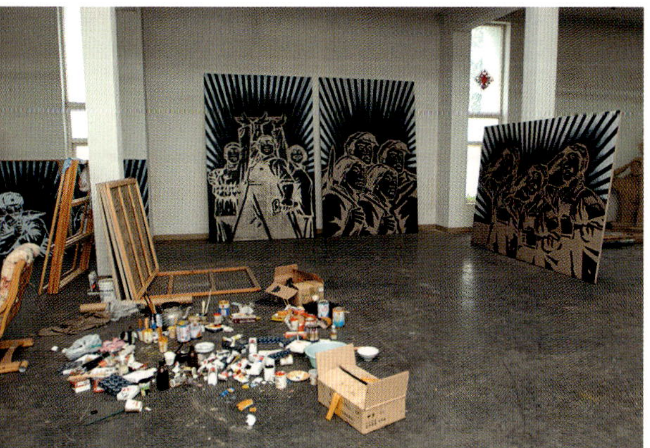

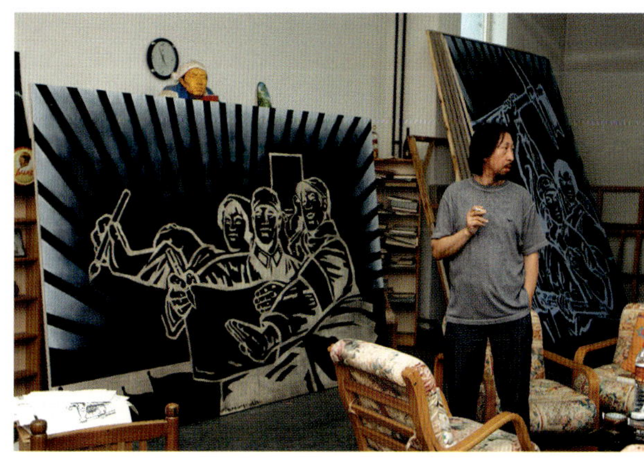

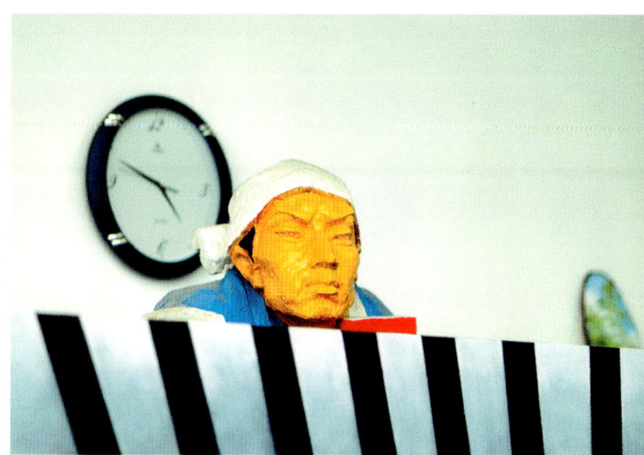

wanted to lay bare the machinery. He was going through a deconstructionist phase. ¶ This is how the work should be read: "Warhol did not know Mao." For Warhol, Mao was the most iconic figure of the day, and that was enough. For Wang Guangyi, like for millions of Chinese, Mao was more than just a picture in a magazine. He imprinted many emotions on every Chinese soul, not all of them negative. "Even ten years after his death, the imprint was still there," I heard on several occasions. ¶ The grieving process (if it can be termed such) took the form of a series of works that Wang calls conceptual, and that I would call analytical. Wang Guangyi lays the familiar silhouette out flat and exposes the brain and the thought processes, like the wiring and circuitry in a computer. He deconstructs and flays the figure. He shows that the king is hollow and the puppet just that—a puppet. This beautiful series, painted in the late 1980s, bears further witness to his talent, which it would be shortsighted to restrict to the *Great Criticism* series of the 1990s and beyond. ¶ In fact, it would be a good idea to take stock of the progression of his best-known series. Wang Guangyi did not settle straight away on the highly efficient style, which consists of a background of rows of numbers against which are juxtaposed figures borrowed from the visual vocabulary of the propaganda posters of the Cultural Revolution, and brand logos. ¶ To begin with, Wang Guangyi carried on using his grid system, for example, in one of the first in the *Great Criticism* series, dating from 1990, which shows three red revolutionaries against the orange background, behind a black grid with a large white *R* on a black backdrop right in the center. *R* for revolution? Another painting shows three representative Chinese characters—a young Red Guard, a worker, and a female peasant—together brandishing a large red book against a background of a red flag inscribed with three Chinese ideograms, white on a black background, at the bottom of the painting. We are still a long way from the clash of civilizations that he was later to explore. ¶ The first Western logos made their appearance a few months later, mixing with Chinese ideograms. A timid Kodak, then some bolder Maxwell House Coffees and Nestlé Coffees put in an appearance, but always alongside Chinese characters. There are often numbers as well, but in no apparent order. Together, they give the impression that the times are changing rapidly, and cannot be pinned down. ¶ The human figures that appear in the paintings at this stage are not as confident as they were to become a few months or years later—far from it. ¶ In order to reach the stage of perfect simplicity that appeared particularly from the mid-1990s onwards, Wang Guangyi not only had to strip out a lot of unnecessary detail, but also to decide once and for all what the true meaning of the series was—although it had had the same name, *Great Criticism*, from the outset. ¶ He did not just hesitate over stylistic matters. ¶ It might be the case that his increasing popularity with overseas collectors led him to include more and more English vocabulary and European and American logos in his paintings from the mid-1990s. ¶ What is even more likely to be the case is that he was led to do this by developments in Chinese politics and the economy, which saw a wave of Western consumer products wash over China, causing people to take up clear positions either for or against the omnipresence of these foreign brands. ¶ We must not forget that Wang Guangyi has also worked on installations. ¶ In 2002, a book about his work was published in Hong Kong. The book, every stage of which appears to have been approved by the artist, gives a prominent place to his installations, which are given equal coverage with his paintings, whether for the 1990s or the early 2000s. Wang Guangyi obviously considers them a major part of his work. ¶

CENTER, WANG GUANGYI IN FRONT OF HIS NEW SERIES *ETERNAL GLORY*. RIGHT: AN ENLARGED DETAIL. FAR LEFT: A VIEW OF HIS STUDIO.

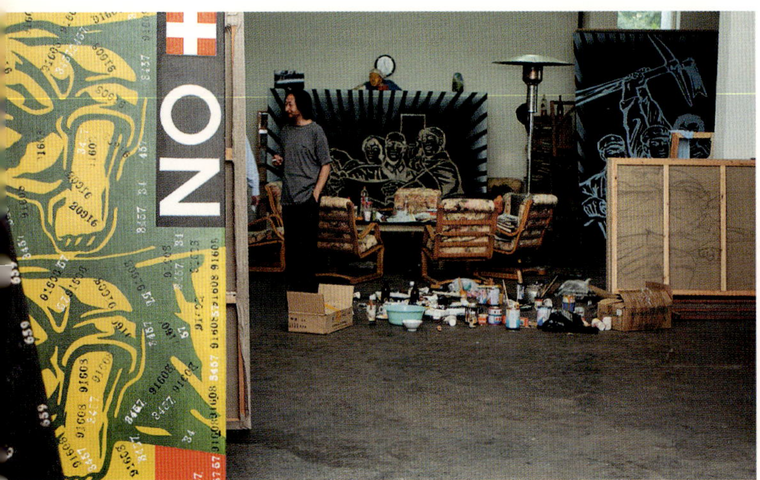

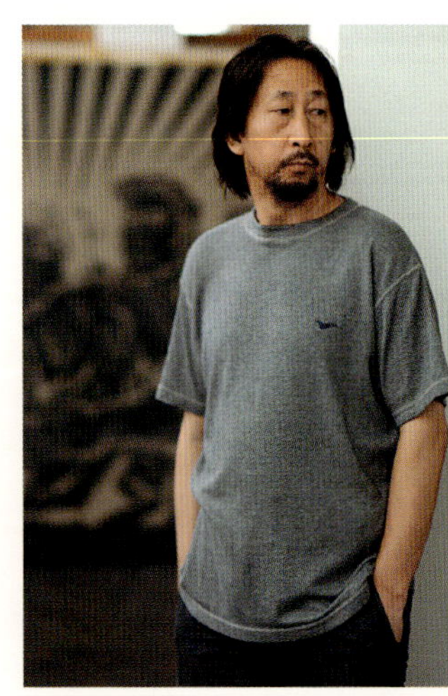

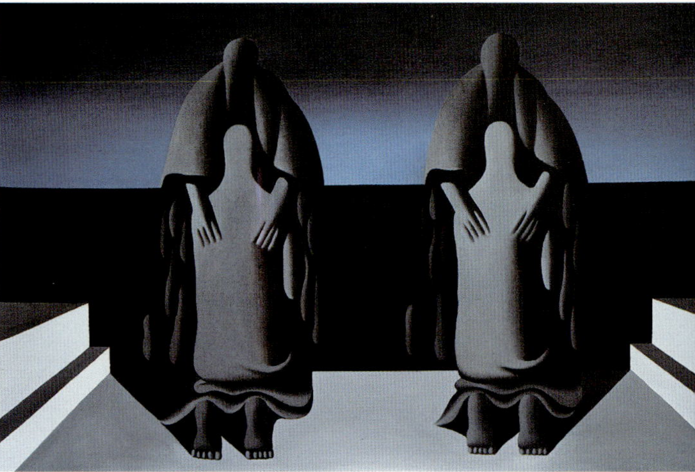

Funnily enough, he told me that he generally preferred to show his installations abroad, where they are more easily accepted, rather than in China, where people were more accepting of his painting. ¶ One of his installations, shown in Hamburg, juxtaposes official anti war posters from 1960s China, building materials and spades made in Germany, a jacket hung on some scaffolding, and shoes lying in the midst of all the materials. The work, dated 2001, was entitled *Elementary Education*. Wang says, "Sometimes it is easier for me to express some of my ideas in an installation, at other times through a painting. Here, the installation represents a building site. I included spades and information notices like the ones you used to find in schools all over China and on building sites wherever there were a lot of people. Always harping on the same points. Even when they were resting, the workers had to look at them. All the time." ¶ So his installations are like a staging of reality, then? ¶ Yes, sort of. For Wang Guangyi, installations are loaded with simple, direct meaning. Even if we should note that in a nice ironic twist, the spades were not made in China, as we might have expected, but in Germany. ¶ Wang says, "What I like in installations is their directness. You build something, people come to see it, and in the end, you dismantle it. You get rid of it. Finished." ¶ Is it worth reiterating at this point that spades were a major feature of the artistic vocabulary of Joseph Beuys, one of the greatest installation artists of the second half of the twentieth century? And that Mao was one of Warhol's idols at the end of his life? And that Wang Guangyi's debt to both Beuys and Warhol is immense? ¶ He seems to recognize this fact himself with two paintings dated 2002, where their names feature instead of the usual logos. Let's take a closer look: having taken the place of the usual Coca-Cola or Parker logos, they have not just been relegated to product status (which would have delighted Warhol), but more importantly, they are equated with products *imported into China*. ¶ In Wang Guangyi's world, this is precisely what China is opposed to, with its workers, soldiers, and intellectuals, armed with their socialist convictions and the Little Red Book. ¶ They could almost be called enemies. ¶ Which is anything but a homage. ¶ Wang Guangyi told me on several occasions that what is happening today in China is like what happened in the United States after World War II, when American artists began copying the Russians and the Europeans, or at least drawing inspiration from them, without ever admitting that that was what they were doing. ¶ It is up to China to find her place. It is up to Wang Guangyi to conquer his place, with his own powerful talent. ¶ Wang Guangyi is a determined man. ¶ Recently, he moved almost all of his impressive sculptures out of the studio and into the garden. He needed the studio for a new, large-format series of canvases, which dominate the space with their raw power. The title of the series? ¶ *Eternal Glory*. ¶ On ecru canvas, he has painted the same determined workers, the same victorious peasants, but this time in black and white, like a negative of a photograph. ¶ The logos have vanished. ¶ These heroic black figures fill me with a strange feeling of gloom, as if I was in mourning for a certain type of image, a certain ideology, which no longer had the strength to stand up to the ideology that now reigns supreme: the ideology of consumption. ¶ Funereal black and white. ¶ It is impossible not to be reminded of Warhol's inversions. ¶ Wang Guangyi inaugurated this magnificent series with an exhibition in Basel. ¶ He tells me that he will be working on the series for another two years. Wang Guangyi is an organized, forward-looking artist.

FACING PAGE: LEFT: *MAO TSE-TUNG BEHIND A BLACK GRILLE*, 1989. RIGHT: ONE OF WANG GUANGYI'S MOST RECENT WORKS, *ETERNAL GLORY*, 2003. ABOVE, FAR RIGHT: ONE OF THE OLDEST WORKS, *POST CLASSICAL: THE RETURN OF TRAGIC LOVE*, 1986, AND, ON THE LEFT, A VIEW OF THE STUDIO.

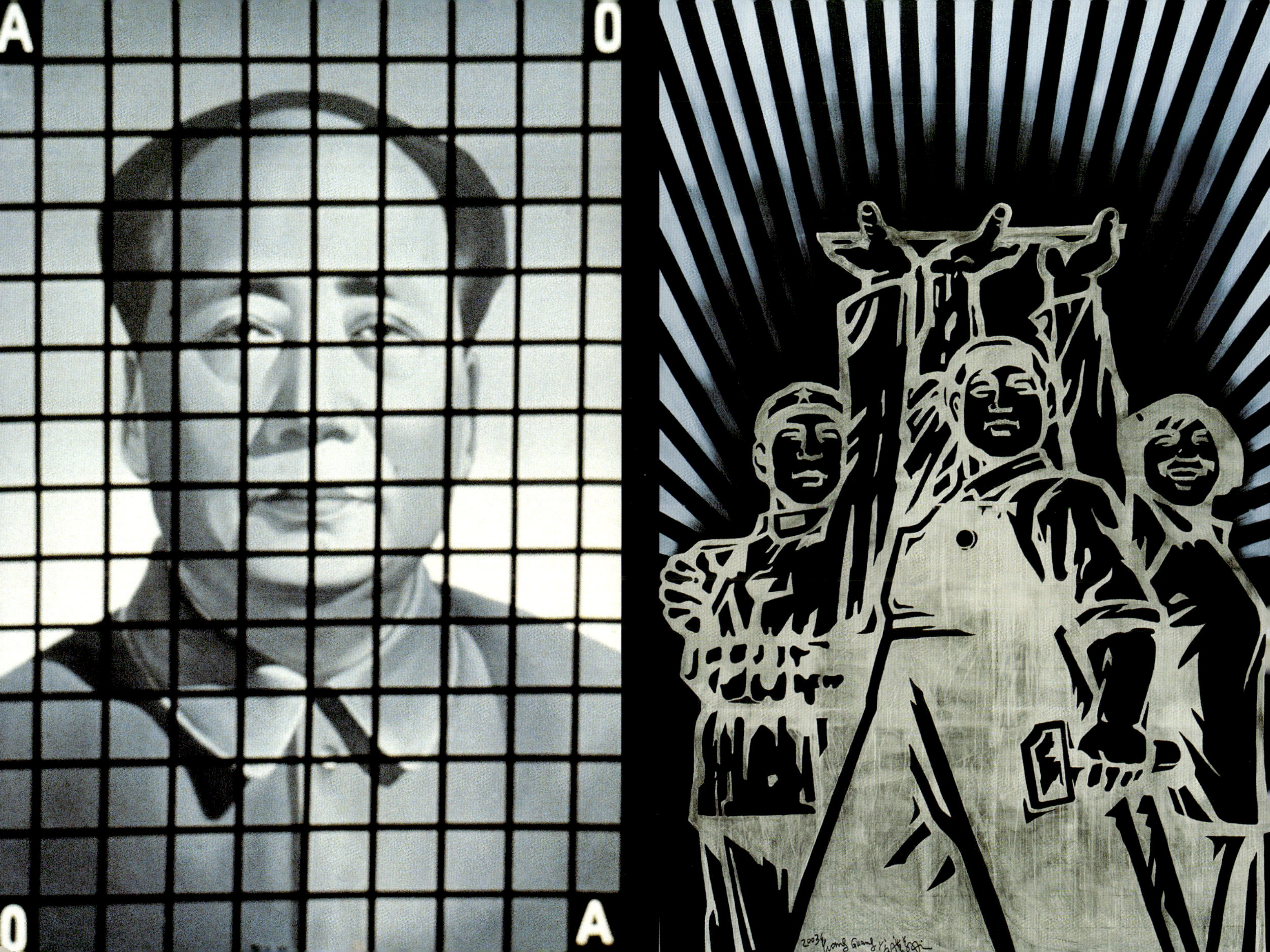
A
O
O
A

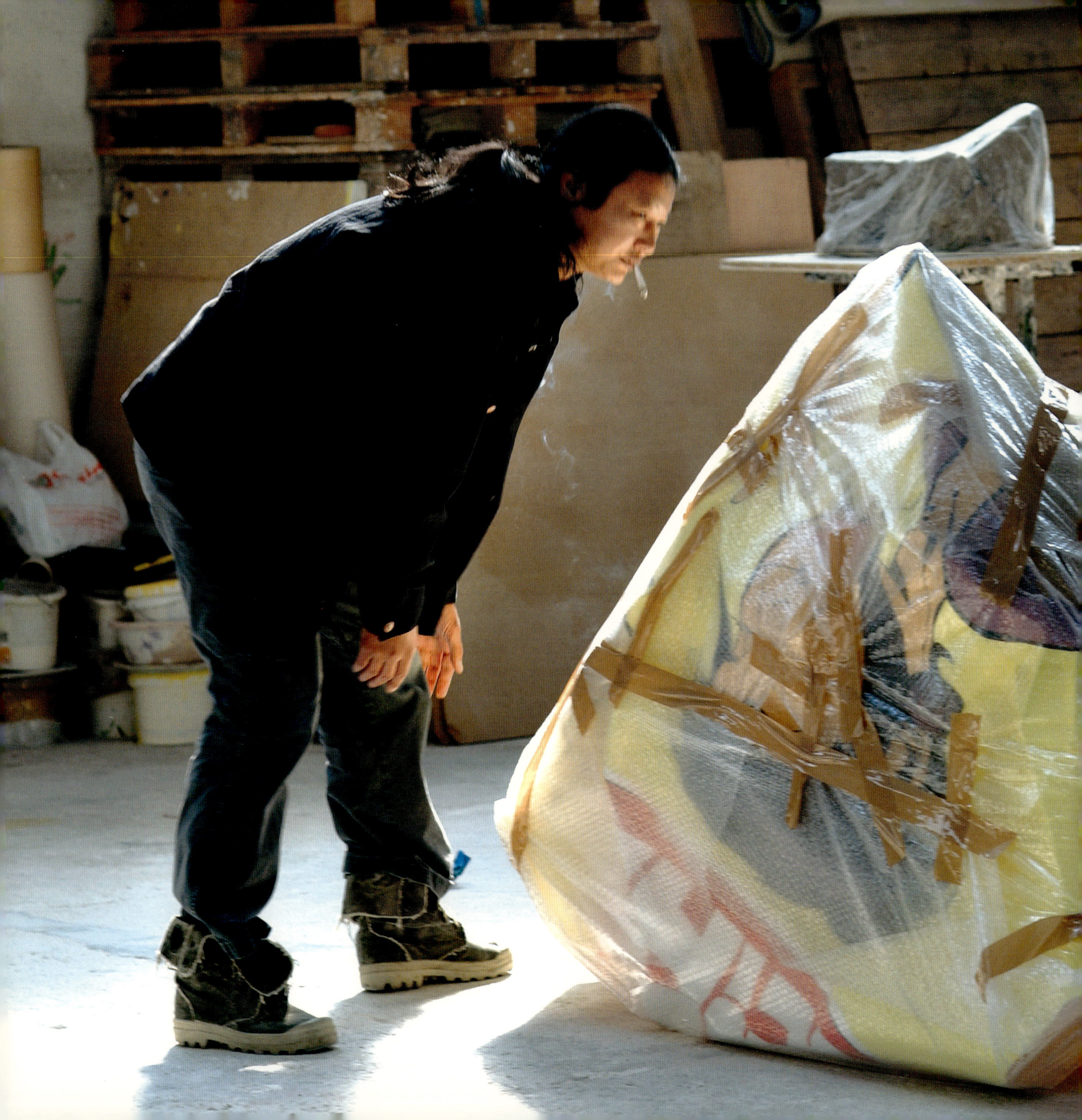

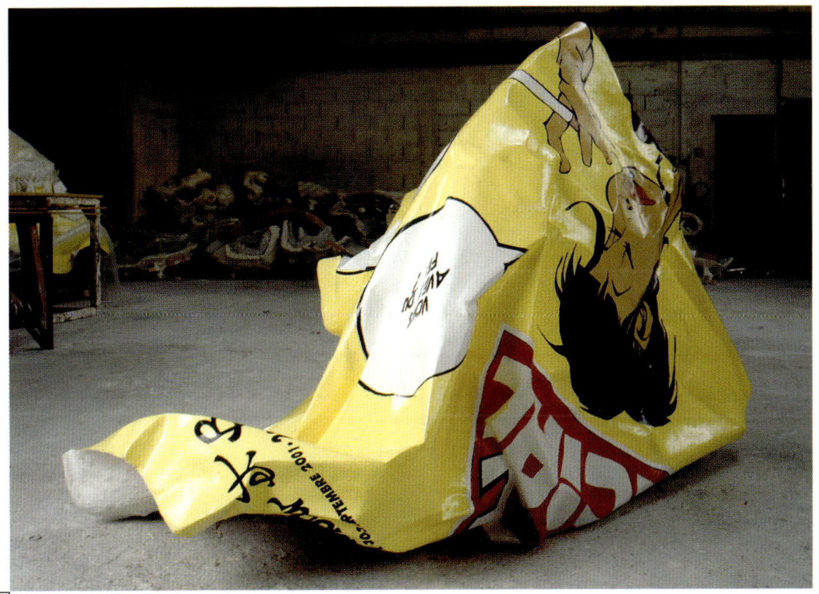

WANG DU

"Shut up, you don't know what you're talking about!" Wang Du shouted across the table. A friend had invited him to a dinner party, and one particular guest, who prided himself on his knowledge of China and Chinese contemporary art, was showing off—until Wang Du's little outburst. That's what I like about him. He doesn't bother with niceties. He has a brutal frankness that I find extremely refreshing. ¶ He is forty-eight, but looks much younger with his jet-black ponytail. He is a tall man, and reminds me of a wolf on the steppes, drinking hard late into the night. ¶ He has had a studio in Alfortville, a suburb of Paris, for three years now. He bought the space in a 6,500 square-feet (600 square-meter) former factory with a fifteen-year loan, and swears he has not touched a thing since. The studio is a vast loft-like space. On the left is a sort of dining room taken up with a tremendously long table for raucous parties with his friends and an office space where he tries to keep his papers and so on in order. On the right is the studio itself, with a concrete floor, a glass ceiling—and that is practically all. There are a few tools hanging from the wall and one or two works in progress in the center of the room. ¶ Wang Du strides across the space with his long legs. He feels at ease here. ¶ What brought him to Alfortville, I inquire? ¶ "Love," he murmurs, with a timid smile. ¶ Flashback. Let's begin at the beginning. Wang Du was born in 1956 in Wuhan, in Hubei province, central China. "It used to be the third biggest city in China. Bigger than Guangzhou. Wuhan has a long, long history. Very cultural," he tells me with evident pride, when I confess to being unfamiliar with this city, which he tells me is undergoing something of a renaissance. Wuhan straddles the Yangtze River, 625 miles (1,000 kilometers) east of Shanghai. ¶ I ask about his parents. "Workers," he answers, a little too quickly. Later he told me how his father encouraged him to draw, that his parents were cultivated people, and that his father was actually a foreman rather than a worker—well, the factory boss, to be strictly accurate. ¶ "When I was six, I drew a lot," he says. "I wanted to be a great painter. My parents encouraged me. Whenever I showed them a good drawing, my father would shout, 'Bravo!' He loved painting." ¶ The Cultural Revolution began when he was nine. "There were portraits of Chairman Mao everywhere. The only art we saw was propaganda. People followed Mao, because he knew how to exploit their resentment. When children reached the age of thirteen, they had to reenact the Long March of the 1930s. It was claimed that it would teach them about China. It was madness. Children took the train without paying. There were a million of them in Tiananmen Square. Fortunately, it only lasted three years. It was really getting out of hand." ¶ For Wang Du, as for many other adults, his memories of that period of his childhood are not unpleasant. They did not have to go to school, they played, and pretended to be soldiers. But should we believe these neatly arranged memories, more carefully filtered than they might care to admit? ¶ 1966—76: the Cultural Revolution was in full swing. Given such a context, how could anyone want to be an artist, since in those days, the status and prospects of an artist were hardly encouraging. They were in the service of the people and its leaders in particular; they had to quash their own artistic impulses to churn out cliché-ridden propaganda

FACING PAGE: WANG DU WATCHES CAREFULLY AS ONE OF HIS WORKS IS WRAPPED TO BE TRANSPORTED TO AN EXHIBITION.

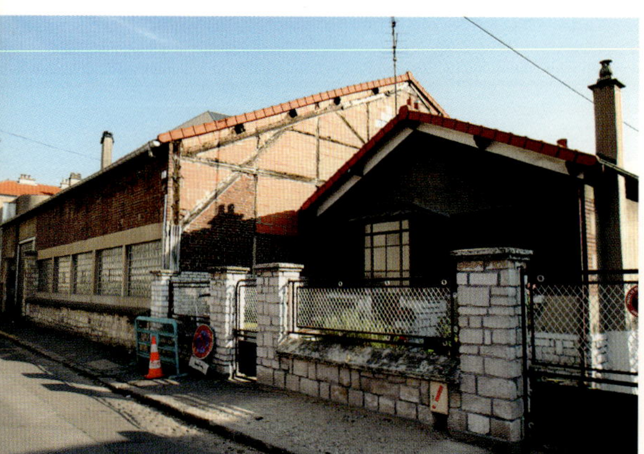

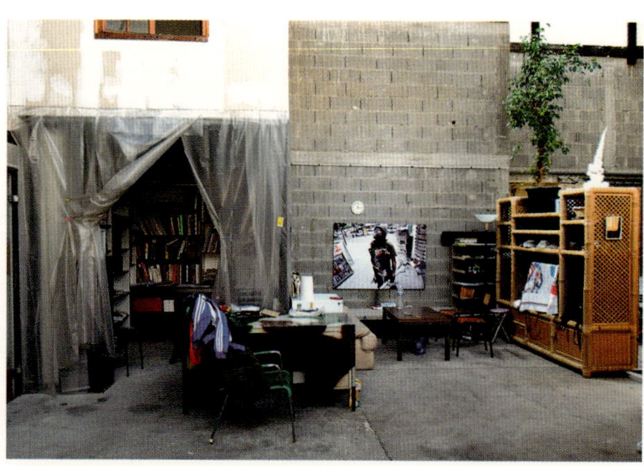

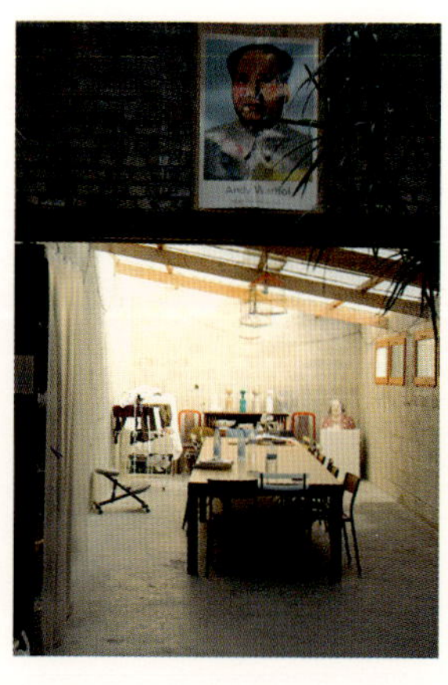

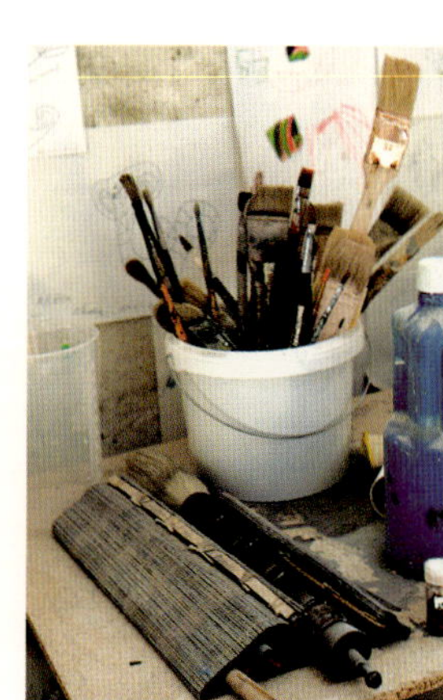

to educate the masses. Copy, not invent. ¶ So between the ages of sixteen and twenty-four, Wang Du first labored in the mines, then worked for China's second largest steel company. He spent his days producing posters and decors. He painted for himself at night. In 1976, the year Mao died, he had his first exhibition as an "official young amateur." ¶ After the Cultural Revolution, things got easier as students were once again allowed to write entrance examinations for university and hope to win a place on merit, rather than their political connections. Wang Du headed for Guangzhou. He failed the examination in 1977, but succeeded on his second try in 1981. The universities were vastly oversubscribed in the years after the collapse of the Cultural Revolution. There was huge competition to get in, especially since each university admitted a majority of students born in the city, with a few places reserved for the wider region and a tiny number for students from elsewhere in China. ¶ None of this made Wang Du's path easier. He finally enrolled at the Guangzhou School for the Fine Arts, which had departments for Western painting and sculpture as well as traditional Chinese painting. Like many other schools, it had a fairly traditional approach, and very soon Wang Du grew disillusioned: he had come to university to have his horizons broadened, but he quickly discovered he was in the wrong place. "I had to begin over with things I had already done and that led to a clash with the school. I don't take orders well," he says, with a wolfish smile. ¶ It was a crazy, unsettled time, with a strange feeling of freedom and rediscovered intelligence, after the madness of the Cultural Revolution. Deng Xiaoping launched his new economic policy. The future appeared a little brighter. ¶ In 1977 and 1978, the first unlicensed performances began to take place in makeshift venues, and against the odds, artists began to organize unofficial exhibitions. The first art collectives got off the ground. Of course, all of this was still very much an underground movement. ¶ It was a confusing time, but rich in terms of artistic experiments, enthusiasm, and opportunities. In one fell swoop, Chinese artists discovered Surrealism (which influenced contemporary painting), Picasso, and Duchamp. People were finally able to talk freely, debate, and argue about art. ¶ Wang Du clashed with his teachers about pretty much everything, and left university in 1985 without his diploma. He created his first performance at the end of that same year, while teaching drawing in a school of architecture. ¶ It was a time of great effervescence. The powers that be turned a blind eye. "They understood that China had to develop its economy, otherwise it would go down the drain. So, as long as you weren't directly attacking Communism, they let you get on with it." ¶ A cheap magazine—sometimes four pages, sometimes eight—called *Fine Art in China* began to appear. It was written by young journalists and critics, and was designed to forge a bond between artists of the same age. ¶ Then there was Southern, the group founded by Wang Du together with a dozen other artists, intellectuals, and philosophers. They were united by one ideal: to think together, work together, and share. "We did a performance that lasted three days," remembers Wang Du. "We were constantly transforming the space. We were having fun. We were innocent. We tried to talk about life as naturally as possible. I believed that the human heart was the best material for art. We were—I was—very idealistic." ¶ But why performances? Did they have any idea what had been done—indeed, what was going on right then—in that domain? ¶ Yes, Wang Du assures me: "But nobody had an idea what art might become. And nobody was interested. We didn't have anything to

WANG DU'S STUDIO IN THE PARIS SUBURBS. FROM LEFT TO RIGHT: AN EXTERIOR VIEW OF THE FORMER FACTORY. WANG DU'S ARCHIVES. THE LONG TABLE THAT SEATS TWENTY. THE ARTIST'S MATERIALS.

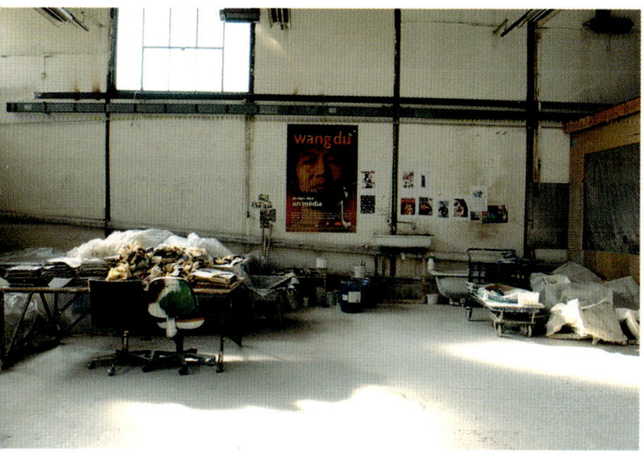

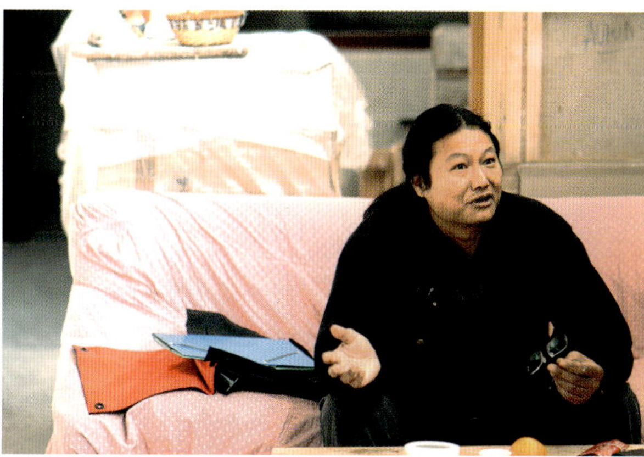

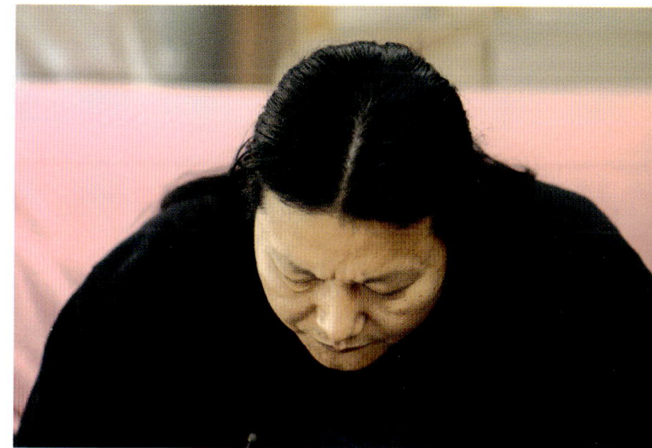

show that was radical enough to interest anybody. We wanted to create something powerful. I had had enough of the academic tradition. I wanted to show off to people." ¶ At the same time, elsewhere in China, other artists—Huang Yong Ping, Wang Guangyi—were exploring the same ground. It is pointless trying to date one earlier than the other. Anyway, we all know how common backdating works and movements is in the art world. Suffice it to say that, suddenly, a number of groups seemed to spring from nowhere, all at the same time. ¶ After this spectacular performance, Wang Du did not show his works for a year. Every month, he organized a conference at Guangzhou library on a range of subjects, calling on researchers, intellectuals, and artists to participate. ¶ One day in late 1987, Wang Du tells me, "A young man who often sat in the front row, and who seemed specially interested, came up to me after one of the conferences and said, 'Dear Mr. Wang, I have been sent by the Ministry of the Interior. I think you should put a stop to your conferences.' I asked why. He replied, 'There is no reason why. As you have seen, I have been present at every conference, and personally, I am with you, but my job is to warn you to stop, otherwise you could suffer serious consequences. I will not be able to help you.' We held a little party, sticking the candles together, and we stopped the conferences. Otherwise we would have gone to prison." ¶ Wang Du was to spend some time in prison nonetheless, in 1989, but for other reasons. He was a young drawing teacher. He spoke out at a demonstration, not against the regime or the government, as has been claimed, but against corruption. For Wang Du, it is an important distinction to make. He was arrested and sentenced to nine months' hard labor. ¶ That was in September. The following August, he left for Paris, where he has been ever since—for love. ¶ In Guangzhou, he met and married a French journalist who was writing a book. When Wang Du left prison, they decided to leave China; because of his time in prison, Wang Du knew he would be under constant surveillance. He preferred to leave, and the marriage certificate gave him the wherewithal to move to France. ¶ He had no problem finding somewhere to live: the newlyweds simply moved into the bride's apartment. She was also well-connected in the art world: one of her friends owned a gallery in rue Jacob in Paris. She bought one of Wang Du's paintings. The price has stuck in Wang Du's memory: "Ten thousand francs." Shortly after, she showed the painting as part of a group exhibition. Wang Du was taking his first steps in the French art world. ¶ In 1992, soon after his arrival in France, Wang Du made an important new friendship. He went to Lausanne, Switzerland, to see the magnificent exhibition *Post Human* organized by Jeffrey Deitch. He had been to the Documenta in Kassel shortly before, but had not been impressed. It was just another exhibition—a bit bigger, better known, more influential than others, but also more unwieldy and backward-looking. *Post Human* was a different kettle of fish—it was lively and refreshing, and in phase with the world of today. He reports in his *Wang Du Magazine Number 1* that "The idea at the base of Jeffrey Deitch's thinking is that in contemporary society, hi-tech research, such as bio-genetic engineering, has a far greater impact on human lives than history and culture." For Wang Du, both the premise and the conclusions were intriguing. "The idea presupposes that today, human evolution is not a gradual, natural process, but rather artificial and rapid. And the changes are not just physical. Our intellect is changing just as radically." ¶ His discreet exhibition at the Galerie Anne de Villepoix over the course of a weekend showed little

LEFT: THE POSTER ON THE WALL CLAIMS "I AM AN ART MEDIUM." WANG DU'S ARTISTIC VISION IS BUILT ON THIS AFFIRMATION. THE TABLE IS COVERED WITH CRUMPLED NEWSPAPER, WHICH HE USES FOR THE LARGE-FORMAT WORKS SHOWN ON THE PRECEDING PAGES.

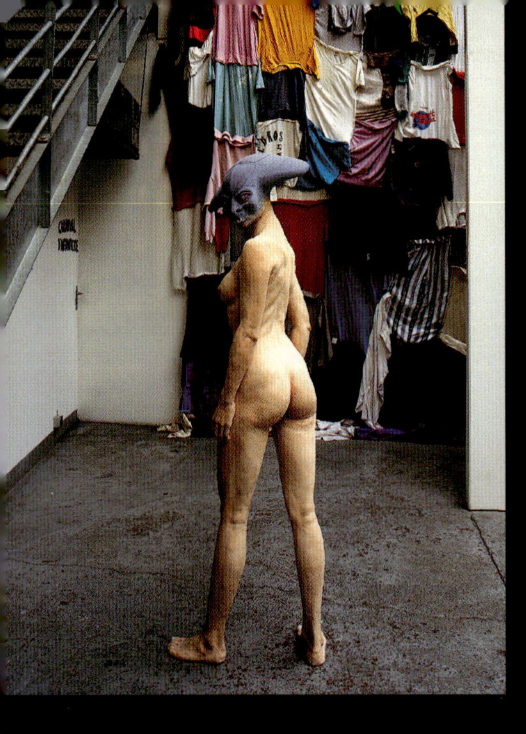
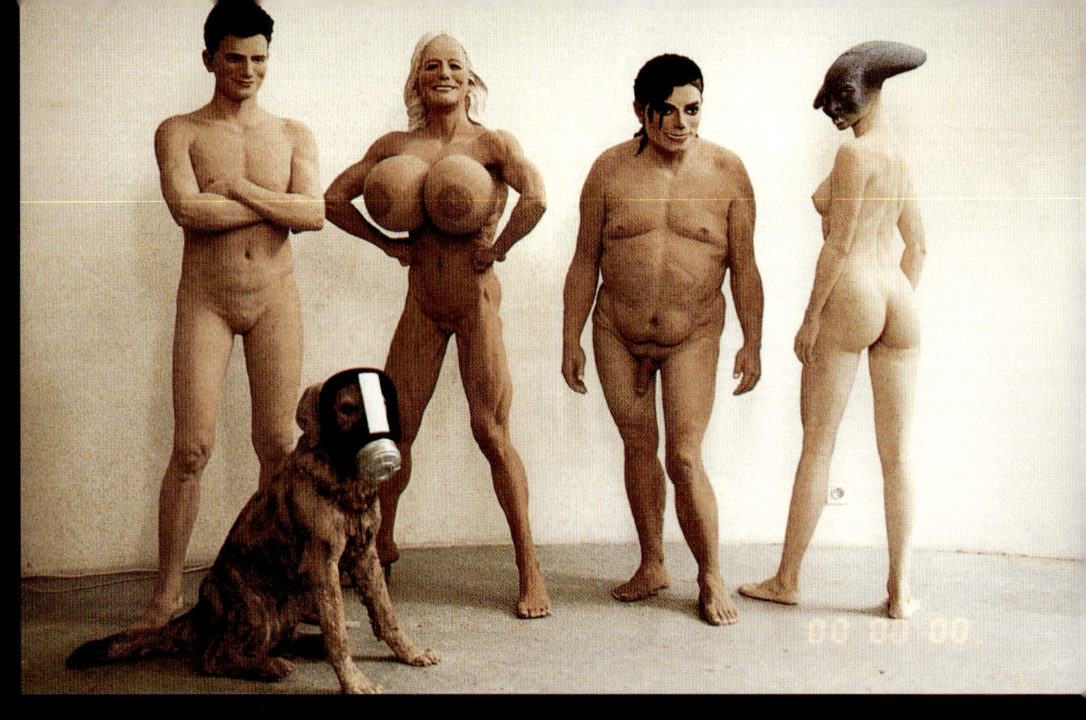
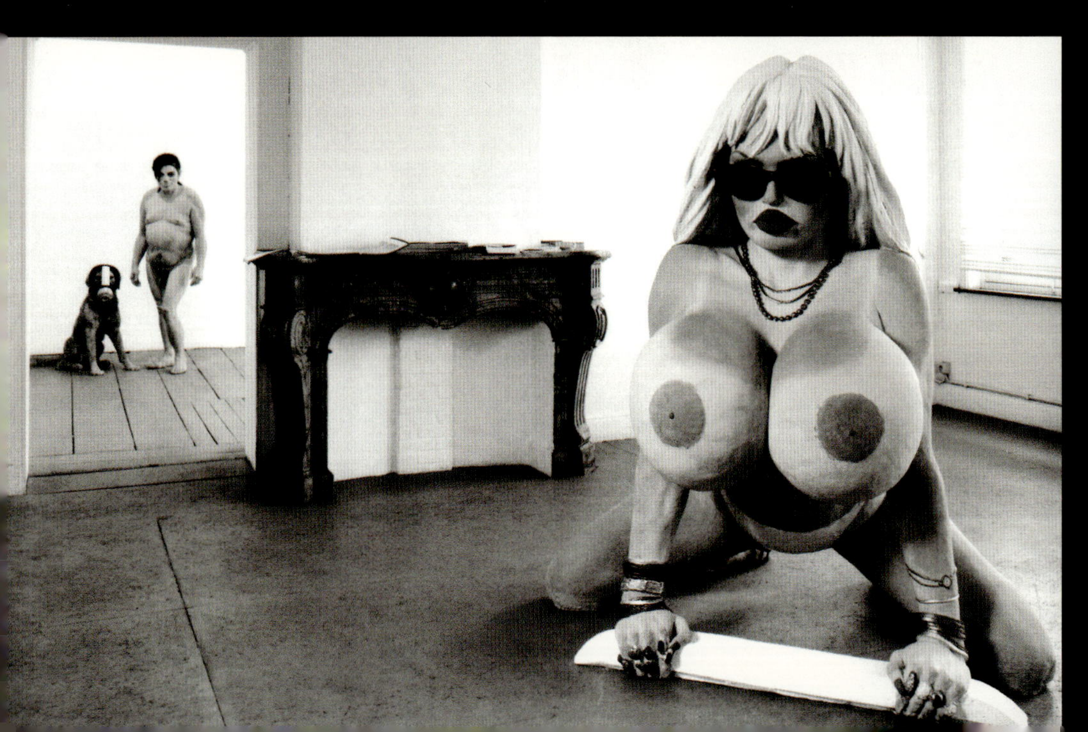
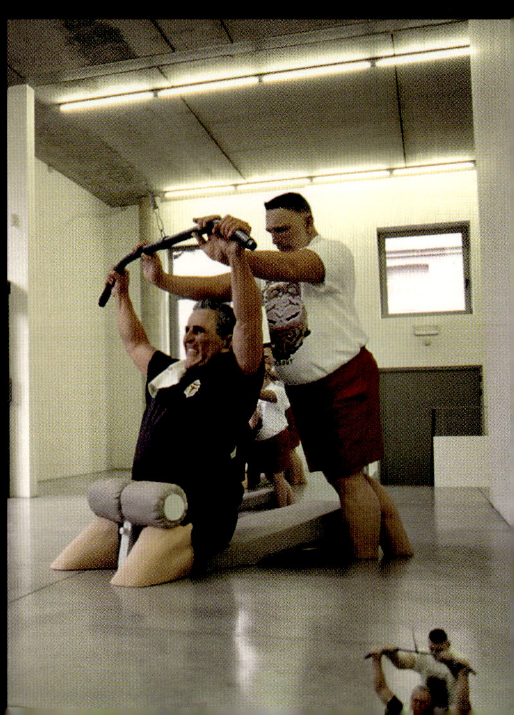

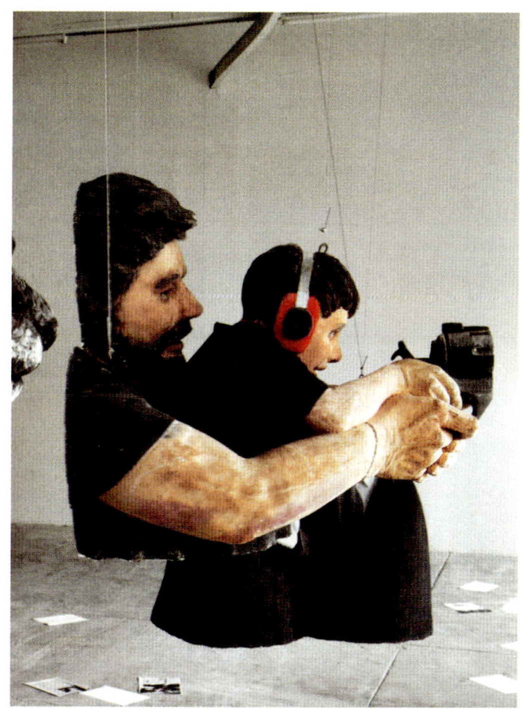

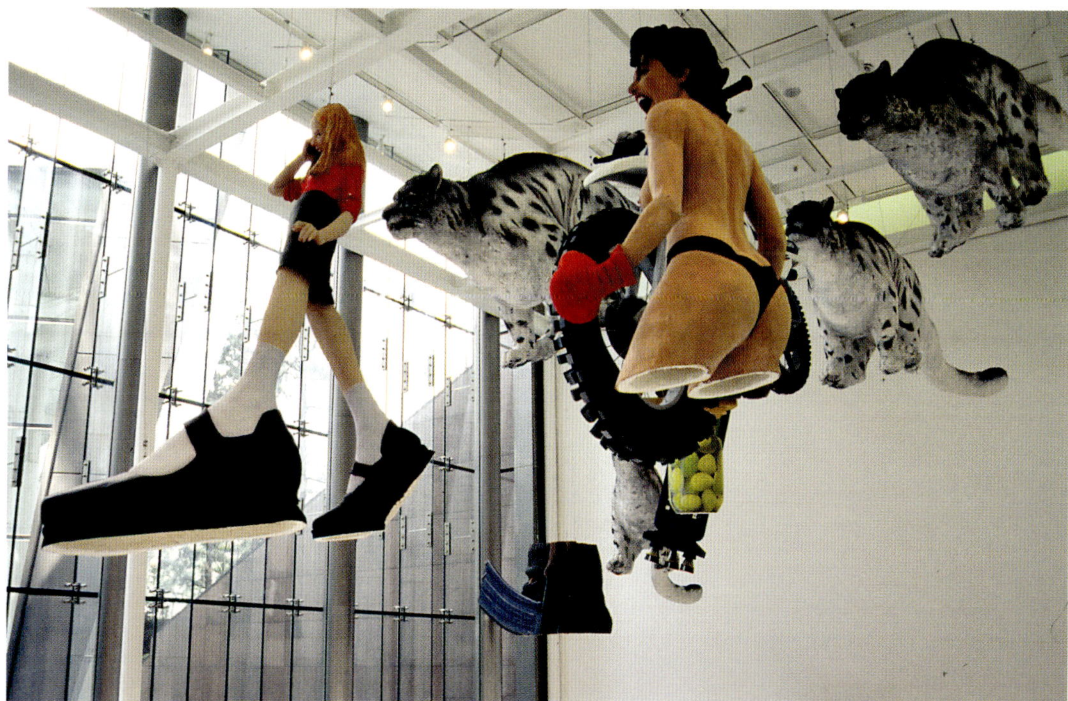

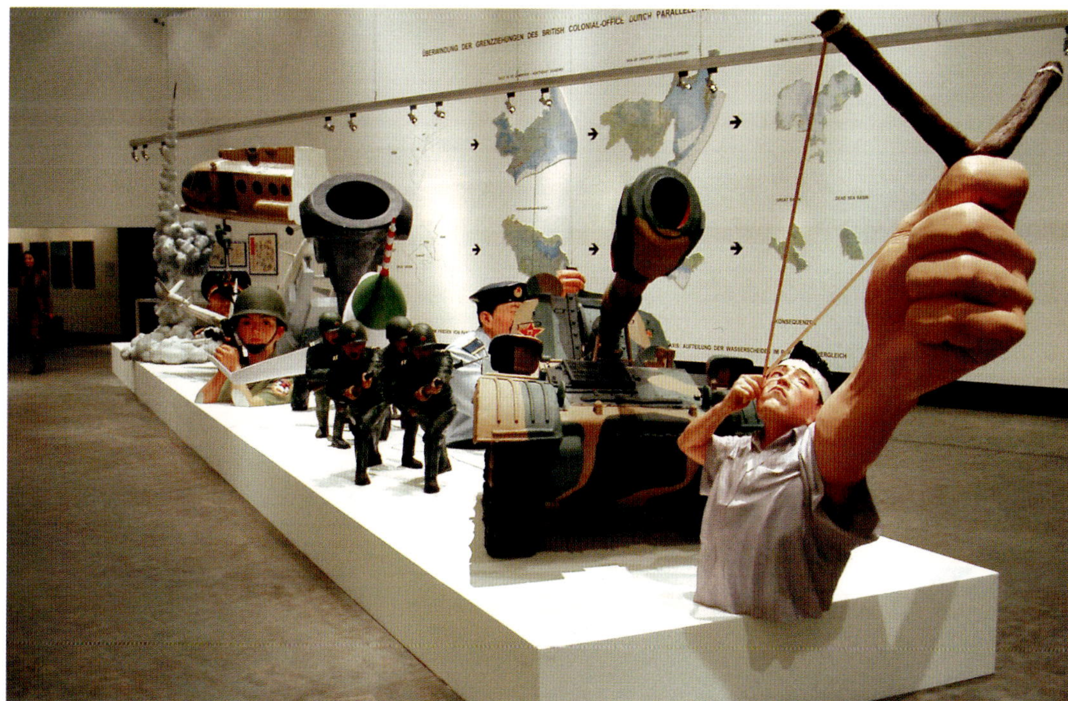

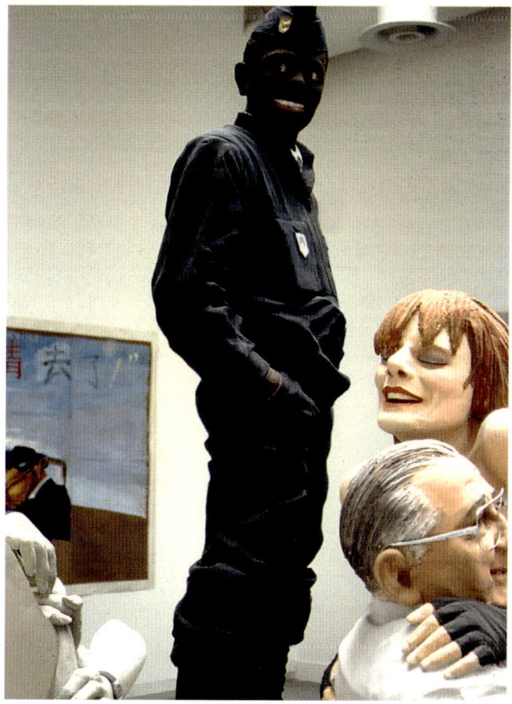

FACING PAGE: *FAMILY*, 1997. ABOVE TOP: *DISPOSABLE REALITY*, 2000. BOTTOM RIGHT: *FLEA MARKET* AT THE VENICE BIENNIAL, 1999. BOTTOM LEFT: *DÉFILÉ*, 2000.

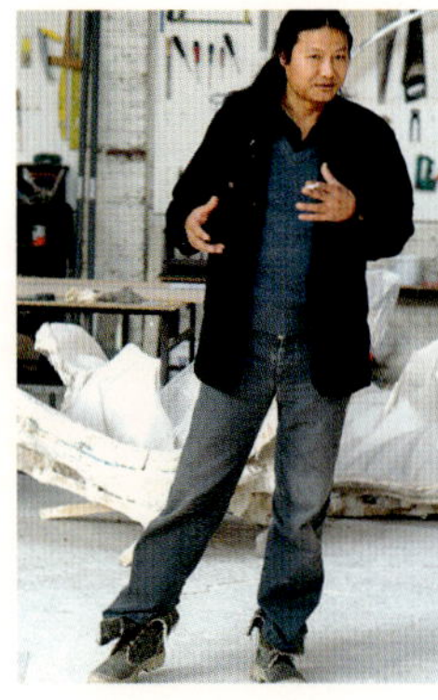
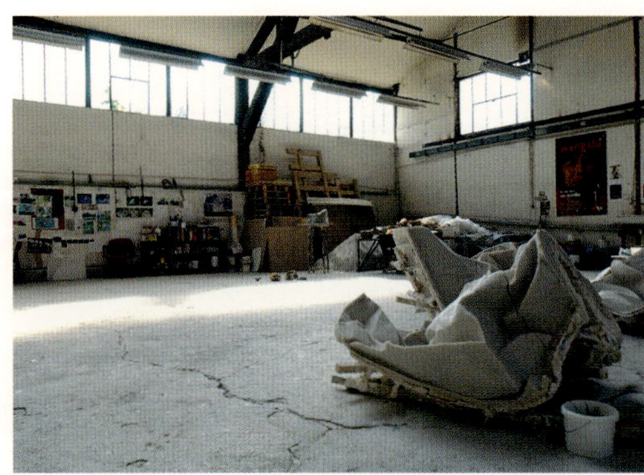
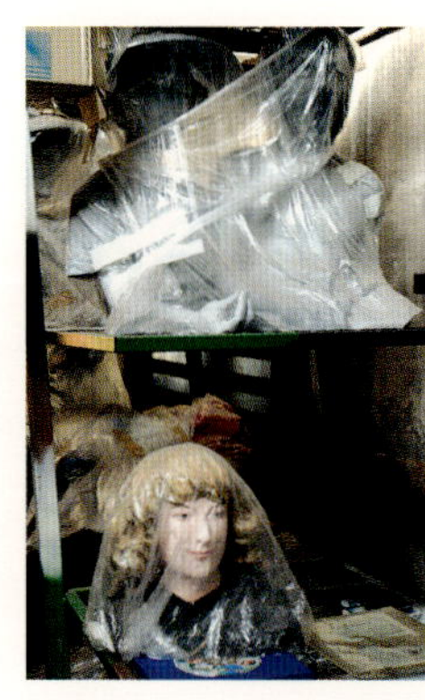
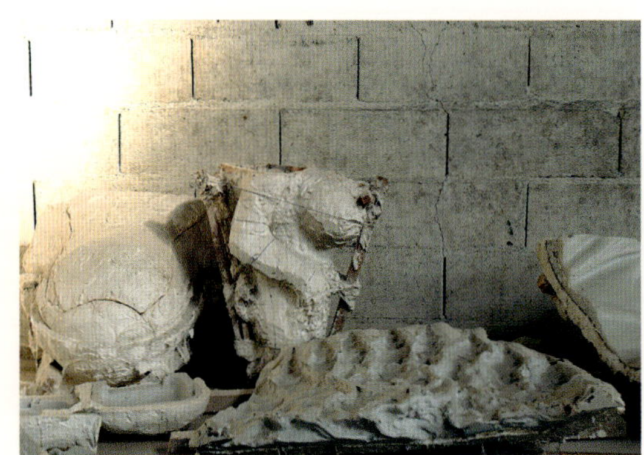

sign, however, of the huge impact *Post Human* had had on him. Entitled *Relics*, it was a collection of eighteen three-dimensional painted images (not sculptures, he insists) drawn from scenes of his daily life as a recent immigrant—problems with the language of his new home country, difficulties in reading the newspaper, getting simple things mixed up. ¶ He took the bull by the horns and made this confusion the basis of his reflection. *Relics* shows perfectly mediocre images taken from newspapers and "mummified," as he says. This was the first step towards his current artistic practice. ¶ In 1997, at the Albert Baronian Gallery in Brussels, he showed works that betray the influence of *Post Human*, with a family of nude figures placed in the four corners of the gallery space, which has odd fireplaces built into the walls. A family of monsters? No: a normal family of today or tomorrow, where scientific progress means we are all free to choose our own face and gender, to improve or alter our bodies as we wish—or in accordance with the canons of desirability foisted upon us by consumer society. ¶ Wang Du says, "Transforming your body has become a way of adapting to modern society where technical and scientific developments and information have taken the place of thoughts and life, in order to take on a new personality." ¶ The father, with a large beer belly, seems to listlessly wallow in mediocrity. He has chosen Michael Jackson's face—ironic, given the pop star's predilection for extreme plastic surgery. The mother has enormous breasts swollen with silicone injections and implants; her body bulges with muscles thanks to her keep-fit program designed to keep her flesh young and tender. The son dislikes the notion of gender differences and, deciding that all human ills come from the sexual impulse, has simply got rid of his genitals. The daughter believes that differences between people and thought systems stem from the shape of their brains, and so has chosen the face of an alien she saw at the cinema. Finally, the dog is wearing a gas mask, since (Wang Du tells me) it believes that people in high society use gas masks for their bizarre rituals. ¶ The next major step in Wang Du's artistic career was the itinerant exhibition *Cities on the Move*, shown in Vienna, Bordeaux, New York, Louisiana, London, and Bangkok in 1997 and 1998. This exhibition shows the first timid signs of Wang Du's desire to explore the media, through advertising or, more accurately, subvertising. He was inspired by a picture he found in a magazine of a Dutch prostitute, the Queen of Amsterdam. He reproduced the image in three dimensions, and placed ten of the resulting sculptures in unexpected corners around the exhibition. Like the Asian prostitutes waiting on street corners for sex tourists that we have all become accustomed to seeing on our TV screens, Wang Du put a Western prostitute in a similar situation for the wealthy men of Shanghai to lust over. *Cities on the Move* showed the dangers of the high-speed, high-density urban development that is taking over much of Asia. ¶ Wang Du also dotted around the exhibition space—and even outside—constructions like the watchtowers along the Great Wall of China. They contained loudspeakers that broadcast soundtracks recorded over a week by the artist on a tour of various Chinese cities, in busy places such as restaurants, karaoke bars, the subway, and train stations, and conversations with prostitutes. ¶ The critics made various references to the aggressiveness of this soundtrack. But Wang Du sees it as an attempt to open a dialogue. How, I ask? ¶ Since Marshall McLuhan, who influenced Warhol, who in turn influenced everybody else, we have been told that the medium is the message and that information makes all things equal. Warhol figured this by his unique

THE ARTIST IN HIS HUGE, UNTIDY STUDIO.

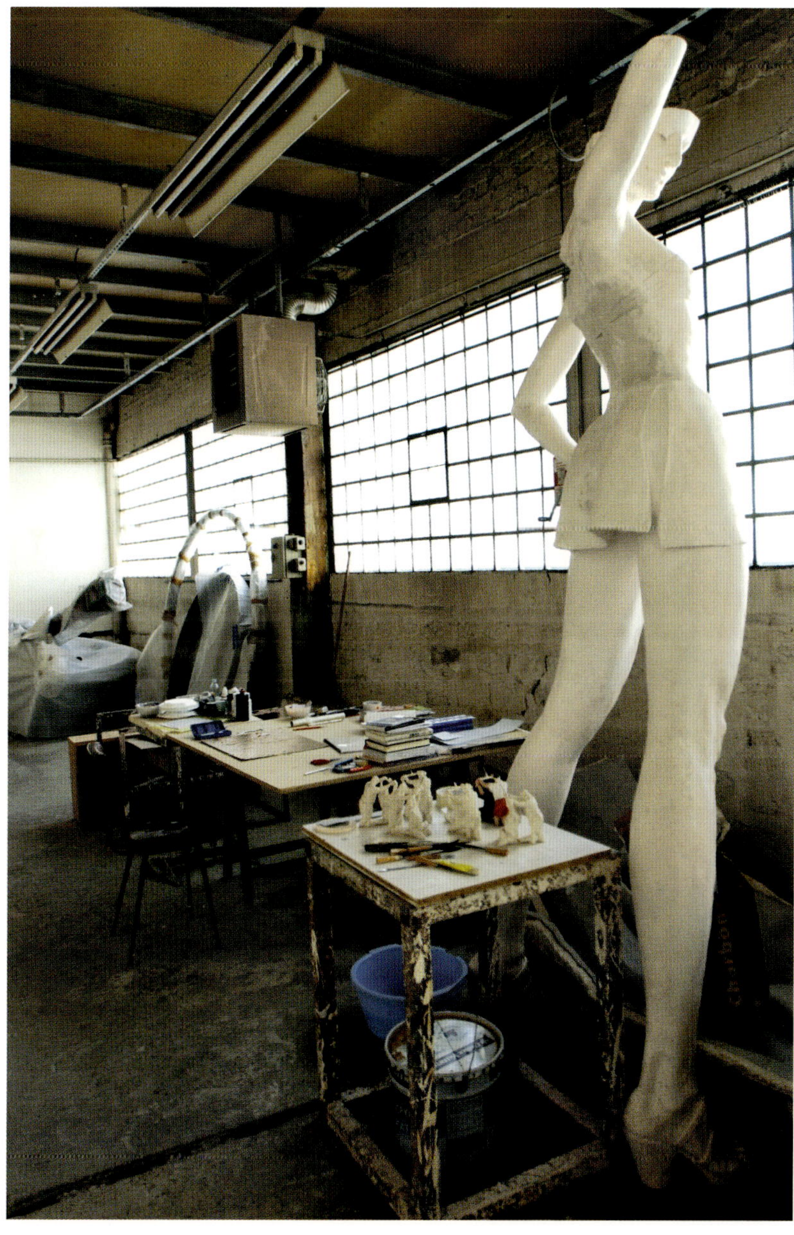

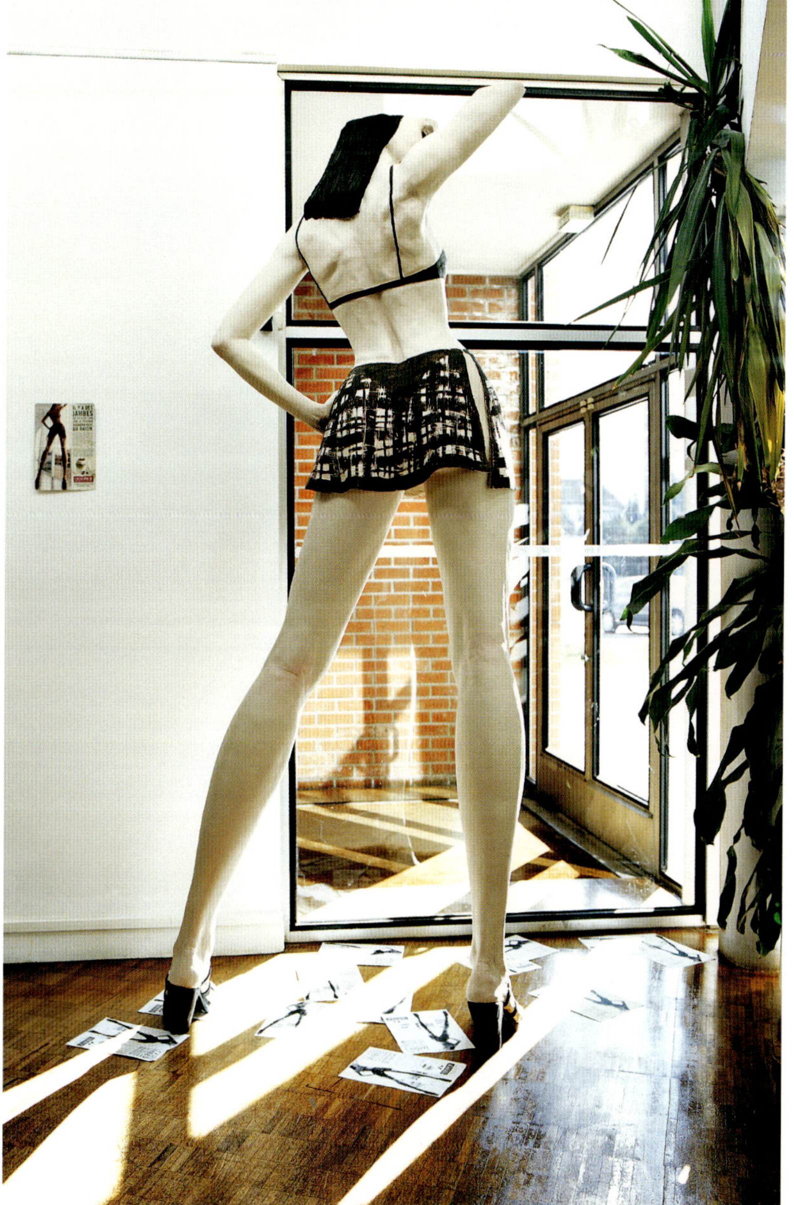

LADY'S LONGLEGS, 1999. LEFT: THE WORK IN PROGRESS. RIGHT: THE COMPLETED WORK IN GOUACHE ON SHOW IN THE GALLERY.

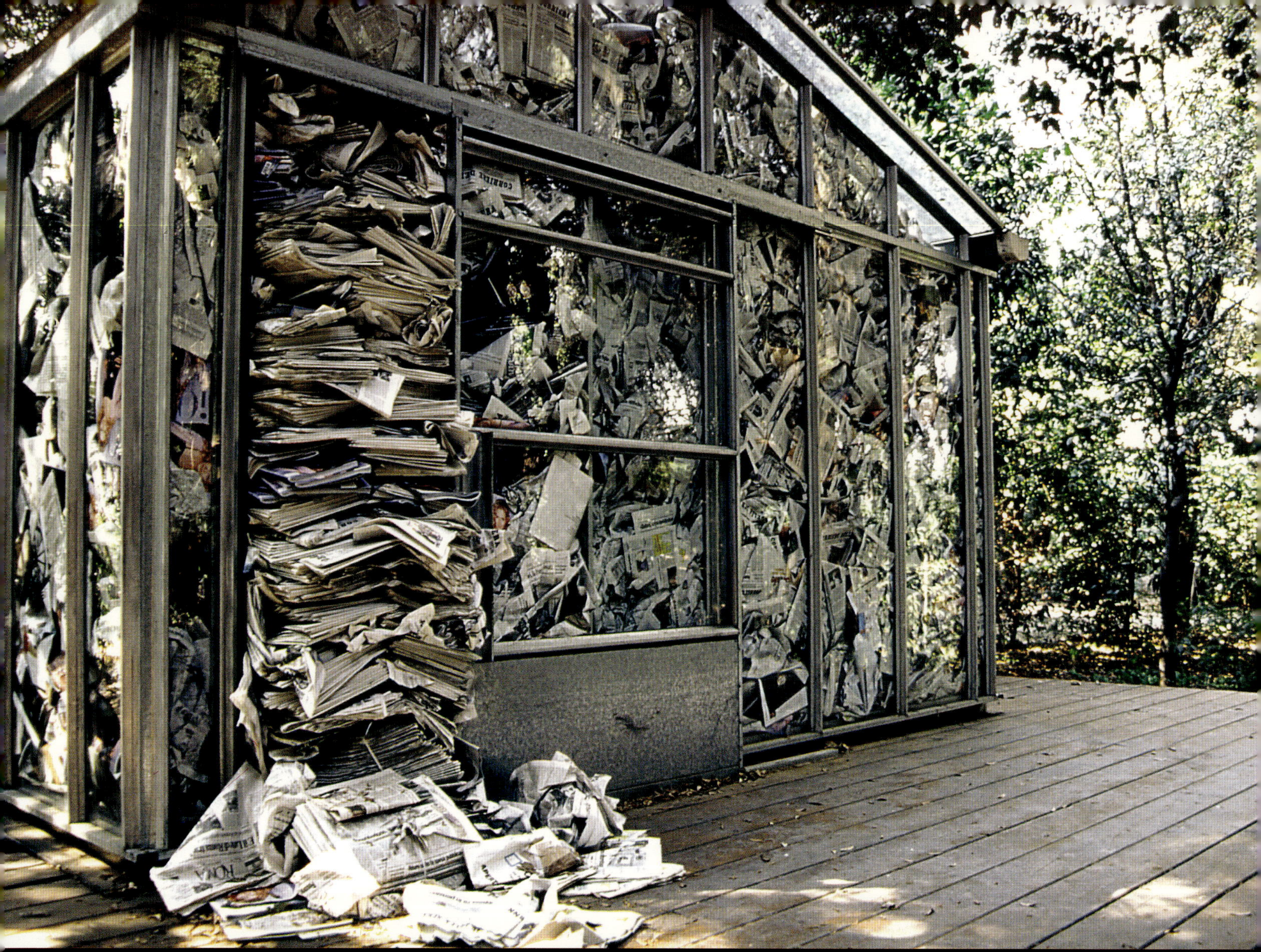

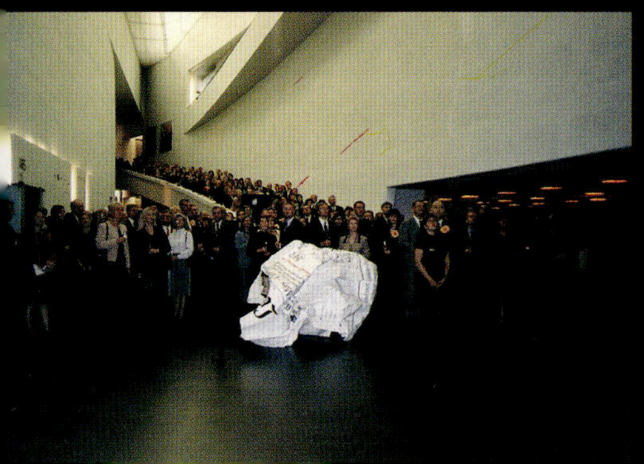

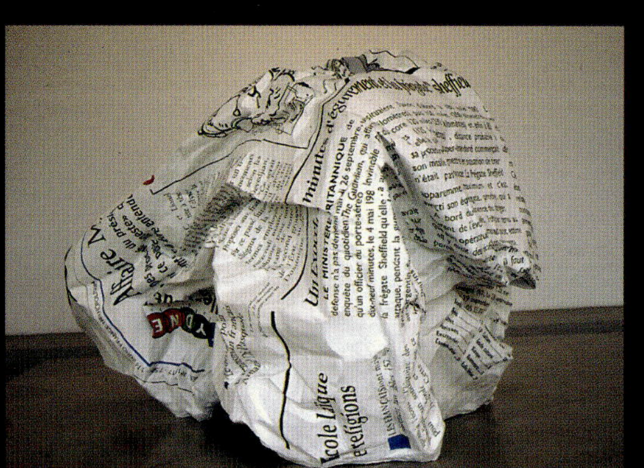

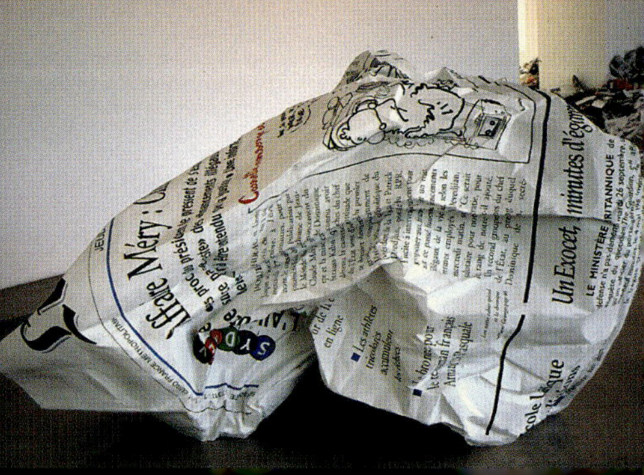

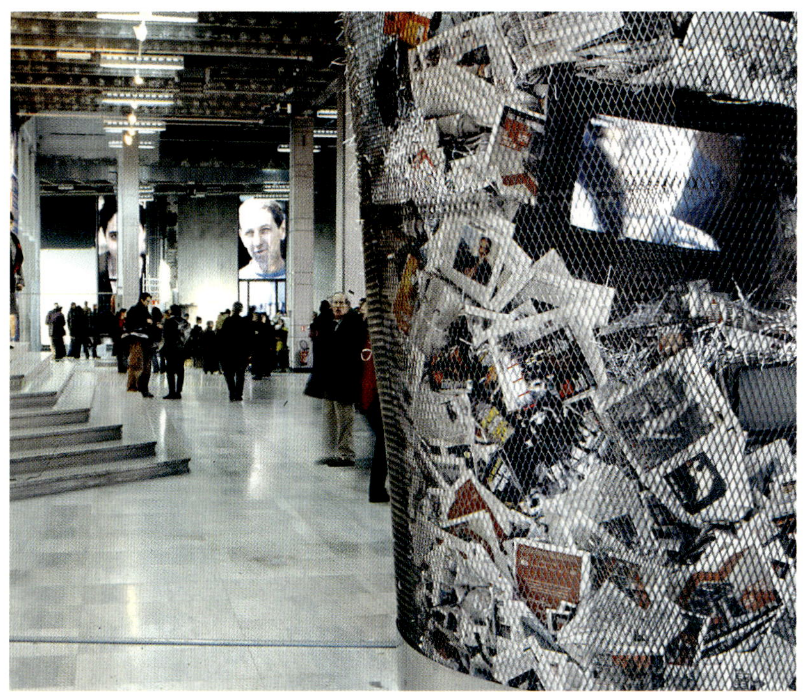

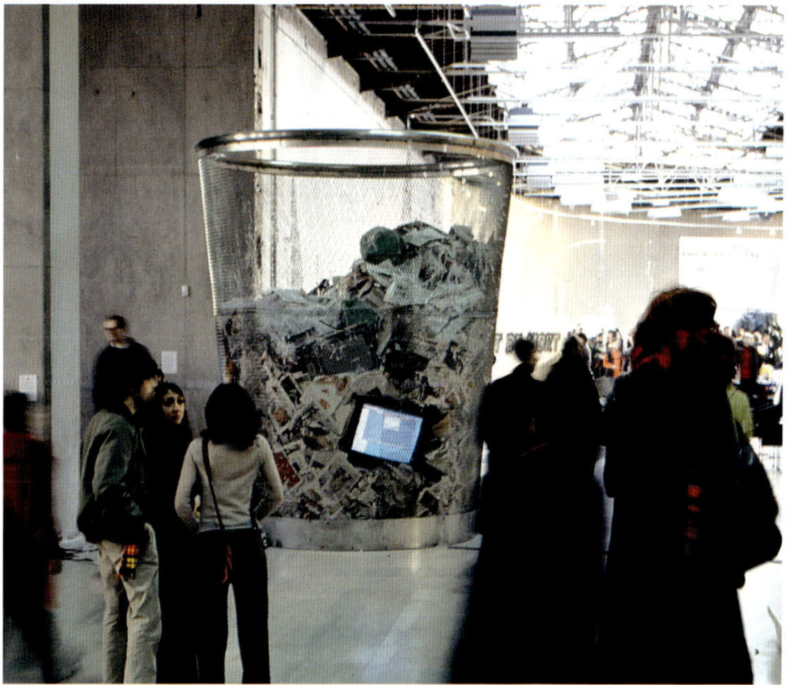

accumulation of images that puts Marilyn Monroe on the same footing as the electric chair. Wang Du chooses to focus on the frame, demonstrating how he picks out a slice of reality and rejects the extraneous elements in the name of choice. He is authoritarian and decisive. ¶ Of course, some ten years ago, Wang Du saw the astonishing cutouts by Bertrand Lavier, such as an enormous piece of farm machinery cut out exactly like in the advertising image. It is a way of demonstrating what reality looks like today, seen through a camera lens, through photography itself, through advertising, through the media. ¶ Wang Du latched onto this idea. One of his friends told me, "Wang Du is highly intelligent, extremely sharp, very bold, free, and uncompromising. He feels things and expresses them right away." He shook up the process of transferring reality as filtered through the media back into actual reality, and made it unmistakably his own, organizing reality differently—on a table like a flat plan to decide page layout, for example, or hanging in the air. ¶ Wang Du says, "We are living in an unreal world created by the media. Since 1994 I have developed each of my projects in the same way, like an editor in chief deciding the layout of a newspaper. I choose the subject, the size of the pictures, and the text. In fact, I organize my projects just like the media do with reality." ¶ In 1999, he presented *Flea Market—Secondhand News for Sale* at the Venice Biennale. On a table twenty-seven feet (nine meters) long and three feet (one meter) wide, he presented a series of snippets from international news stories, cutting from Yasser Arafat to Monica Lewinsky to demonstrate the effects of this information overload: chaos. ¶ *Disposable Reality* at the Dijon Consortium (France) in 2000, organized in conjunction with his Genevan gallery *Art et Public*, explored similar themes. The exhibition was transferred after a few months to the Rodin Gallery in Seoul, an odd museum built to house two Rodins bought in Paris in the 1990s. ¶ The Consortium proudly presented *Disposable Reality* as Wang Du's most monumental work to date. It consists of eighteen plaster pieces painted with gouache, some up to six feet (two meters) tall, hanging from the ceiling. Wang Du hired an army of assistants, some flown over from China, and worked in the Usine (Factory) art studios in Dijon for two months solid. ¶ What is immediately striking, apart from the usual mixture of elements chosen completely at random to underline the impossibility of producing meaning from chaos, is the way information and advertising are placed on the same footing. ¶ A woman who has undergone a mastectomy, wearing boxing gloves. A jar of olives. A nude blonde bombshell squatting in front of a computer logged on to a porn site. A motorbike. President Chirac with his Chinese counterpart Jiang Zemin. A cell phone. An American father taking his son to the local shooting gallery. A Lebanese soldier, his face masked, carrying a Kalashnikov. Half a dozen snow leopards bounding across the room. ¶ These elements have all been taken from the magazines that accompany Wang Du's exhibitions. The cell phone, sleek as a rocket and with the energetic slogan "Launch off," comes from a Panasonic ad. The nude blonde was originally a photograph in a magazine article on cyber-sex. The woman with the mastectomy was in the gossip magazine *Paris Match*. The snow leopards were taken from an article entitled "They reign in secret over the Himalayas" in a current affairs magazine. The Lebanese soldier was in the weekly newspaper *The European* for April 18–24, 1996. ¶ Wang Du and his assistants work from photographs. "Easy," he says, almost boastfully. They begin with a metal framework that they then cover in plaster

FACING PAGE: *INSANITY*, 2002. ABOVE: *NO COMMENT*, PALAIS DE TOKYO. WANG DU SEES HIMSELF AS A JOURNALIST INVESTIGATING THE ROLE OF JOURNALISTS IN TODAY'S MEDIA.

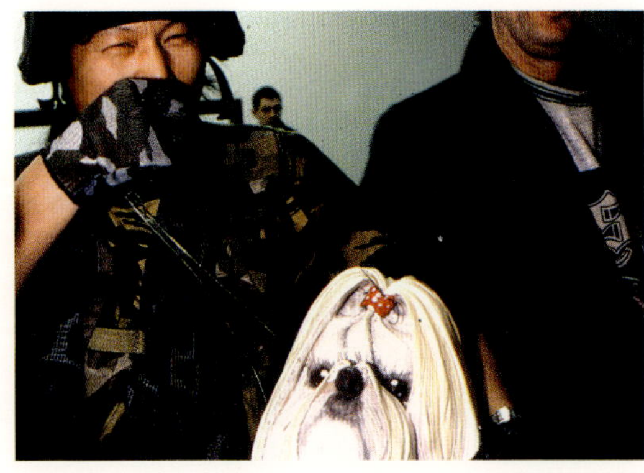

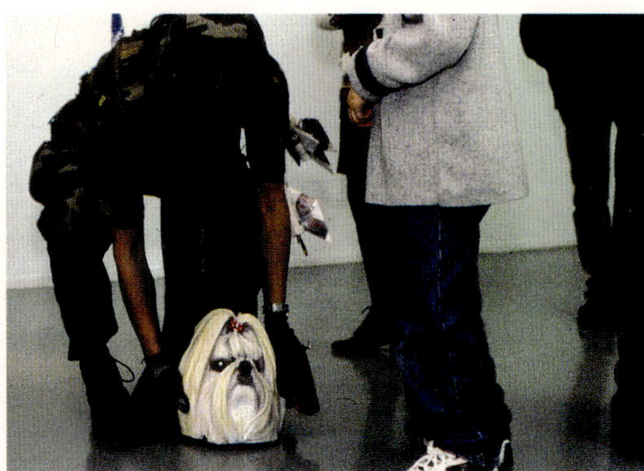

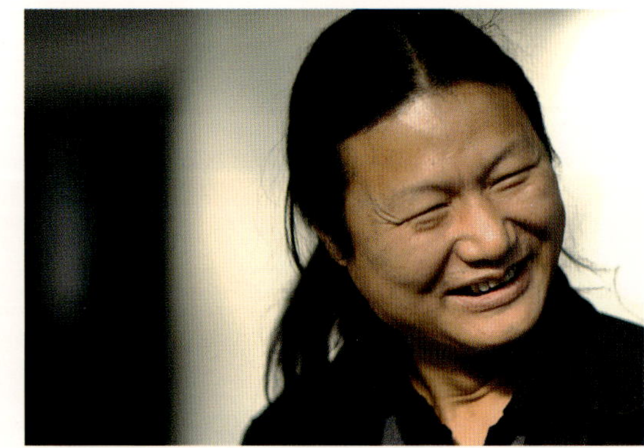

and resin. It doesn't need to be exact—in fact, it's not a bad thing to maintain a certain distance between the original and the copy. There just has to be a certain degree of resemblance. The final stage is a coat of gouache. "The cheapest available, to match the worthlessness of the information," he says. ¶ Some people find this blunt, couldn't-care-less attitude rather off-putting. But just think of Warhol, who told anybody who would listen how once his input was over, he just left his works, even if the ink on the silk screens was dribbling. He would talk absently about how horror and its opposite were both marvelous. There were just one or two essential points that he would not brook compromise on—including the concept of the work as a whole. As for the rest—well, that was just the rest. This is a fair summary of Wang Du's attitude. But the comparison breaks down after a certain point. It's a matter of personalities. Wang Du is a dynamic, powerful hitter. He looks curiously uninvolved, but his wish is to be provocative. ¶ Today, faced with a filtered, stunted, deformed version of reality that is edging ever closer to fiction, faced with ever more sophisticated media manipulation, where can he go next? Wang Du has made a decision. He wants to be the barbarian within the gates, a guerilla fighter. He wants to produce his own media to smoke out the truth and learn to deconstruct their logic, the better to make them cough up their secrets. Turn the situation around to make people think. ¶ In *Strategies en chambre*, he turns newspapers into ultra-sophisticated weapons in what looks like a children's sandpit. He says, "In *Flea Market*, I am putting information back on sale." ¶ The last time I visited him at home, in July 2003, there were oversized sheets of newspaper lying around, crumpled on the floor. He has been making a lot of these recently—crumpled images, crushed by reader-consumers. A way of consuming. ¶ His most recent works are flying carpets made from magazine headlines about the Columbia shuttle. Columbia, Columbus, Christopher Columbus, the man who discovered America. He is probing the question of the colonization of space, in his own humorous way. ¶ Dare I say it? Deep down, Wang Du—married Heaven only know how may times, and with children scattered all over the globe—is a deeply faithful person. To his art, at least. Today, he still involves elements of performance as he did as a young artist just starting out. From time to time, he prowls through exhibitions—his own or other people's—dressed in leopard-skin, like a derisory guerilla soldier. I remember seeing him at the opening of *Paris pour Escale* at the Musée d'Art Moderne in Paris in 2000, dressed in combat fatigues ("Camouflaged like reality," he told me), complete with gun and helmet, walking his dog—a 3-D copy of a Shih Tzu, or "lion dog," a charming (or intensely annoying, depending on your point of view) cross between a Lhasa Apso and a Pekinese. It had a little bow in its "hair" and made the front page of *Animal Junior* magazine. The irony is irresistible.

WALKING MY DOG, 2000, A PERFORMANCE WITH A REMOTE-CONTROL SCULPTURE IN POLYESTER RESIN, IN THE MUSÉE D'ART MODERNE IN PARIS. THE WHITE DOG IS MODELED ON A SHIH TZU. WANG DU IS WEARING CAMOUFLAGE TO REFLECT HOW REALITY IS DISGUISED. FACING PAGE: WANG DU BELIEVES IN A THEORY OF FAST INFORMATION ON THE SAME LINES AS FAST FOOD. TODAY'S MEDIA CUT OUT THE MIDDLEMAN. HE COMPARES THIS TO THE DEVELOPMENT OF SUPERMARKETS, WHICH DID AWAY WITH SALESPEOPLE TO GIVE CUSTOMERS DIRECT ACCESS TO THE PRODUCTS THEY WANTED.

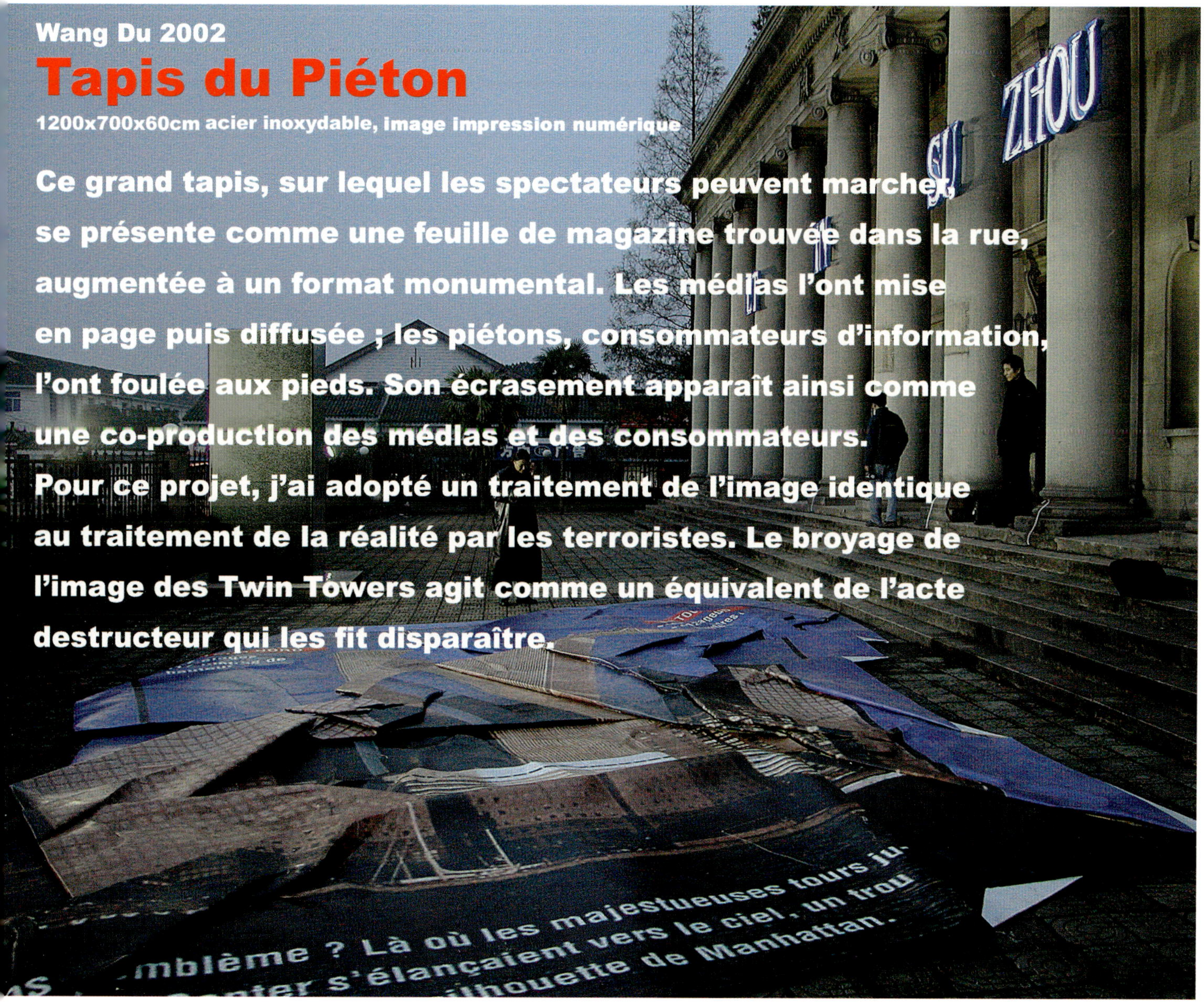

Wang Du 2002

Tapis du Piéton

1200x700x60cm acier inoxydable, image impression numérique

Ce grand tapis, sur lequel les spectateurs peuvent marcher, se présente comme une feuille de magazine trouvée dans la rue, augmentée à un format monumental. Les médias l'ont mise en page puis diffusée ; les piétons, consommateurs d'information, l'ont foulée aux pieds. Son écrasement apparaît ainsi comme une co-production des médias et des consommateurs. Pour ce projet, j'ai adopté un traitement de l'image identique au traitement de la réalité par les terroristes. Le broyage de l'image des Twin Towers agit comme un équivalent de l'acte destructeur qui les fit disparaître.

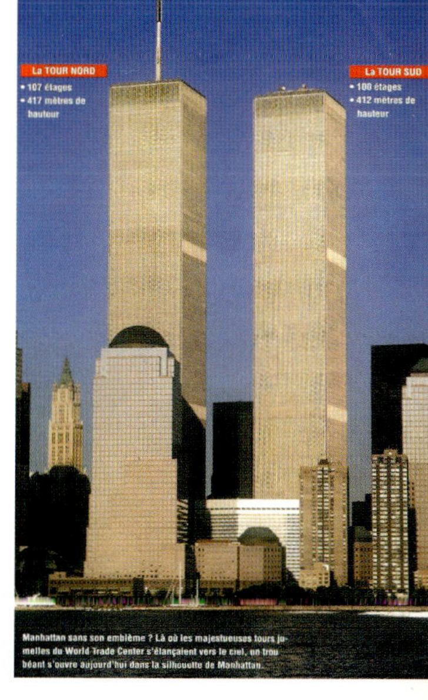

Tapis du piéton
Wang Du 2002

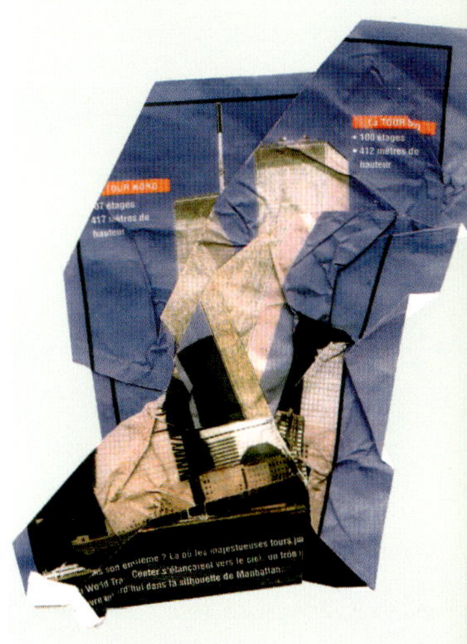

THE TEXT READS: THIS ENORMOUS FLOOR COVERING, WHICH VISITORS CAN WALK ON, IS BASED ON A PAGE FROM A MAGAZINE FOUND IN THE STREET, ENLARGED TO AN ENORMOUS SIZE. THE MEDIA HAVE CREATED AND DISTRIBUTED IT AND PEDESTRIANS AND CONSUMERS HAVE TRAMPLED IT UNDER THEIR FEET. ITS DESTRUCTION REPRESENTS A CO-PRODUCTION BY THE MEDIA AND CONSUMERS. FOR THIS PROJECT I ADOPTED A TREATMENT OF AN IMAGE THAT IS IDENTICAL TO TERRORISTS' TREATMENT OF REALITY. THE CRUSHING OF THE IMAGE OF THE TWIN TOWERS ACTS AS AN EQUIVALENT TO THE ACT OF DESTROYING THEM.

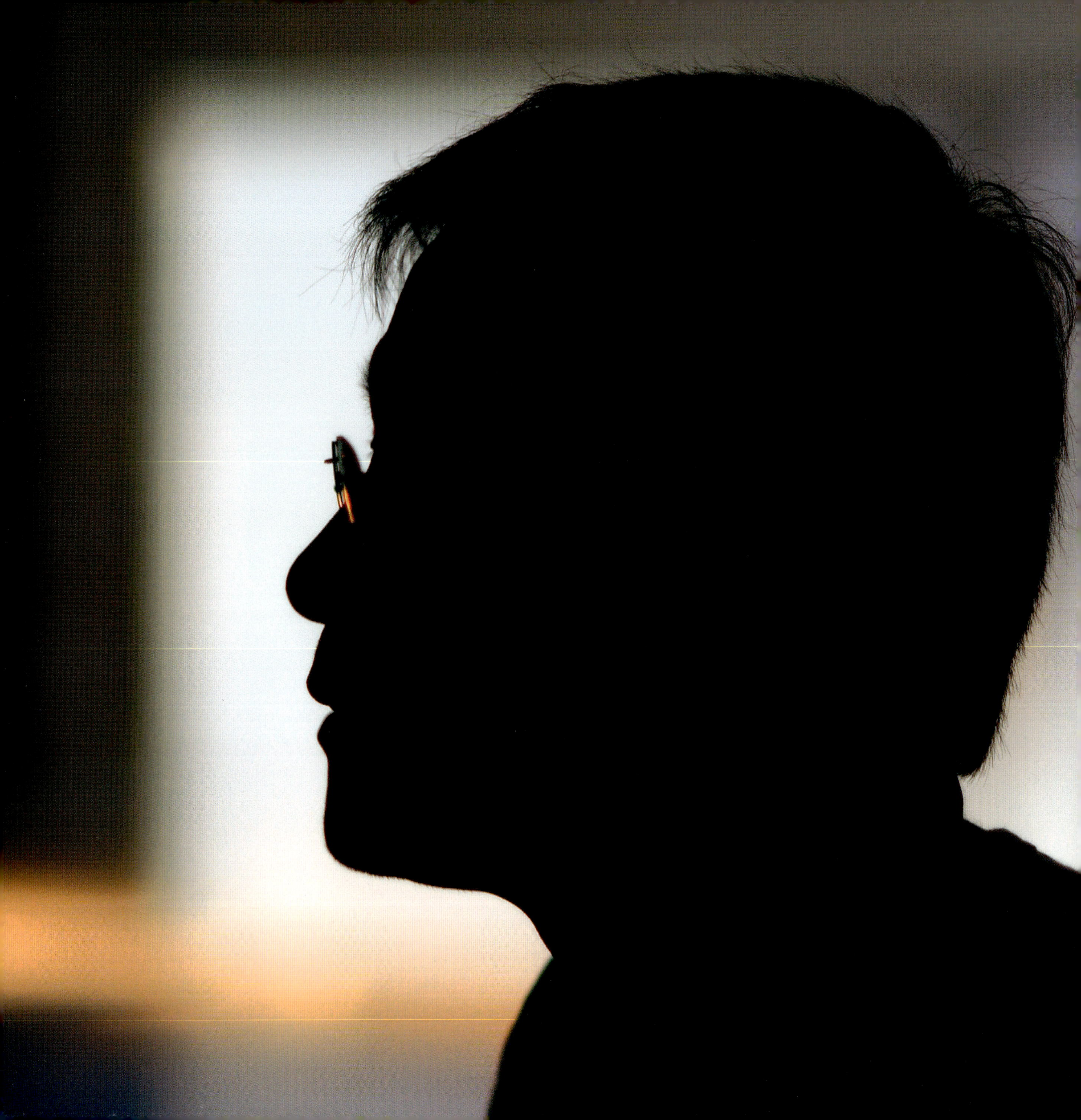

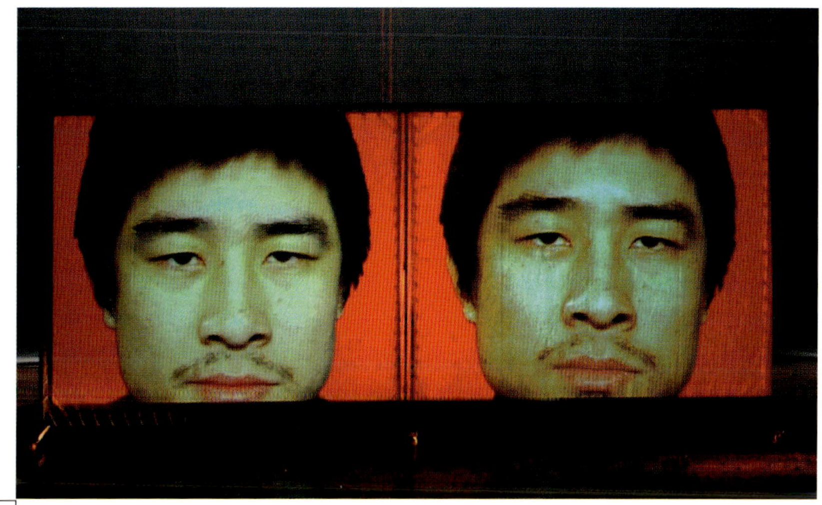

WANG JIAN WEI

"I've never done any performances, but that doesn't mean to say that I have never given any." That is what Wang Jian Wei told me—or at least what one of the best interpreters said at one of my meetings with him. A brief pause. A smile. Then the explanation. "In all I do, I take care not to be affirmative, fixed, fastened to one particular state. I prefer to position myself between things." ¶ Is that why he has filmed so many city squares where people gather or simply pass through? If he is interested in apartments, gatherings, and people, is it to shed light on similar processes and other forms of passage? He is a rather solitary artist, drawn to examine the relationship between public and private space. Gaps. Divisions. Interstices. ¶ Wang Jian Wei has been filming squares for four or five years, observing what goes on and finding food for thought. Squares where everyone goes to spend time, just hang out, forget themselves. ¶ In the 1960s, he remembers how they were built, here and almost everywhere else, for political reasons, to host marches, speeches, and meetings. In the years that followed, these reasons gradually disappeared, as did many of the squares themselves. In the early 1990s, new squares were built, but this time with lawns that the people were forbidden to walk on. Apparently the lawns had no real function—or at best a very vague one, symbolizing the city that surrounded them. The problem was that all the squares looked identical. ¶ So, Wang Jian Wei asked himself, what might their symbolic power be? ¶ He watches the people in the squares with sensitivity, his lens following a young woman holding a bunch of flowers waiting for a bus or a flute seller playing as he cuts his way through the crowds. He captures the fleeting moments that normally vanish into oblivion as soon as they are past—men and women locked in their dreams, following their vision through crowds of people they do not even notice. ¶ That is what I like most about Wang Jian Wei's art—careful attention followed by reflection, and not vice versa. ¶ But where does this fascination come from?

FACING PAGE: SHADOW PLAY FOR A DISCREET ARTIST WHO GENERALLY AVOIDS THE CHINESE ART SCENE. ABOVE: TWO TV SCREENS SHOWING TWO FACES AS PART OF THE MULTIMEDIA WORK *CEREMONY*, 2003.

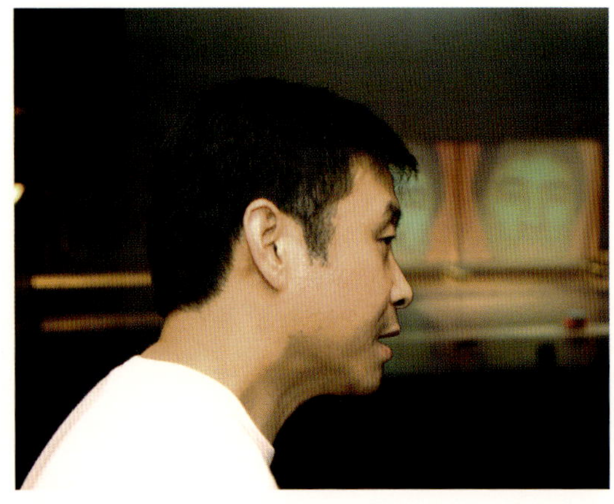

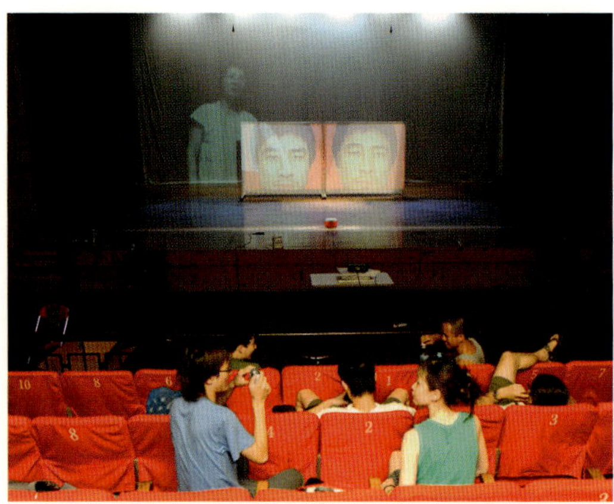

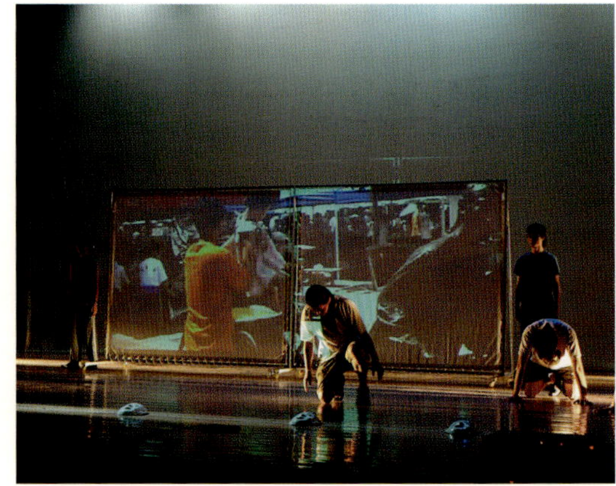

Why so many questions, and so much intense concentration? ¶ If an explanation is really required, it resides in Wang Jian Wei's history, in his personal itinerary, in his unique, incommunicable life experience, which feed his work and determine the conditions of its existence. ¶ As he says himself, "Video is just a technique. It all depends on the artist who uses it to express what he has to say. And what he has to say is closely bound up with his body, his ideas, and especially his culture." Banal? Yes. But the reality behind the words is less so. ¶ Wang Jian Wei's family is as far removed from the world of art as it is possible to be—his parents were both in the army. As a child, Jian Wei enjoyed drawing and painting. So far, so good. And if he preferred staying quietly at home to draw, so much the better. At least he wasn't about to pick up bad habits from the local ruffians. That is what his parents thought. ¶ Later, after high school, he was sent to work on the land as a "young intellectual," as one of my interpreters euphemistically put it (she, too, had undergone "reeducation"). It was the tail end of the Cultural Revolution. ¶ A typically Communist youth. A typically Communist education. Completely cut off from tradition. No knowledge whatsoever of life in the West. ¶ So where does the extreme finesse of his vision comes from? What about the superb subtlety, the delicate intelligence, and the gentle modesty that make his work so seductive and at the same time highly impressive? How did all this come about? His constant gravity, even in moments of hilarity, has its roots in a deep, secret, yet torn and divided place shared by all those who lived the Cultural Revolution as a terrifying experience. How best to describe it? Death in the eyes and under the skin that even the brightest smile cannot quench. ¶ Can he empathize with Wang Guangyi when he says that in spite of all the collateral damage it caused, the Cultural Revolution at least "opened people's eyes"? No, he says, "The Cultural Revolution completely destroyed their loyalty. Mao's famous rallying cry, 'The revolution is always right,' broke all the rules and pushed people to do anything and everything." My interpreter, very knowledgeable about the Chinese art scene, adds that I should take Wang Guangyi's words with a pinch of salt, as he is known for being provocative, particularly when talking to Westerners. ¶ Wang Jian Wei's break with the Revolution came when he was being "reeducated" in the fields. He made what Thomas Bernhard, in his memoir *Breath*, called "a decision." Alongside the hard physical labor of his reeducation program, he decided to carry on drawing and painting. It was not always easy, after the days of backbreaking labor and the accompanying mental and spiritual exhaustion. He told me, "In those days, I was not aware of what I was doing, but now, looking back, I believe it was already an individual choice. I was demonstrating that I could make my own choices even in such a situation." From our vantage point, it does not seem like much, but back then, it was an act of resistance. ¶ Those were dreadful times in China. Everything was in short supply, whether material goods, intellectual stimulation, or spiritual nourishment. Wang Jian Wei was terribly isolated and extremely fearful for his future, over which he had no control. Instead, his future lay in the hands of the ignorant peasants who held almost all the posts of responsibility. ¶ So, carrying on with his painting was a way of imposing his own choice on a future that lay out of his hands. In spite of everything. He told me, "Painting was a way of wanting to create a different life." ¶ He spent two years divided between these two parallel worlds—a public life working alongside the peasants and a private life painting. It was his secret haven, an almost absurd oasis in a world that

REHEARSALS FOR *CEREMONY*, 2003, BEIJING. WANG JIAN WEI TOOK GREAT CARE WITH THE LIGHTING IN PARTICULAR. THE ACTORS GAVE HIM LESS TROUBLE SINCE THEY FOLLOWED HIS EVERY ORDER TO THE LETTER.

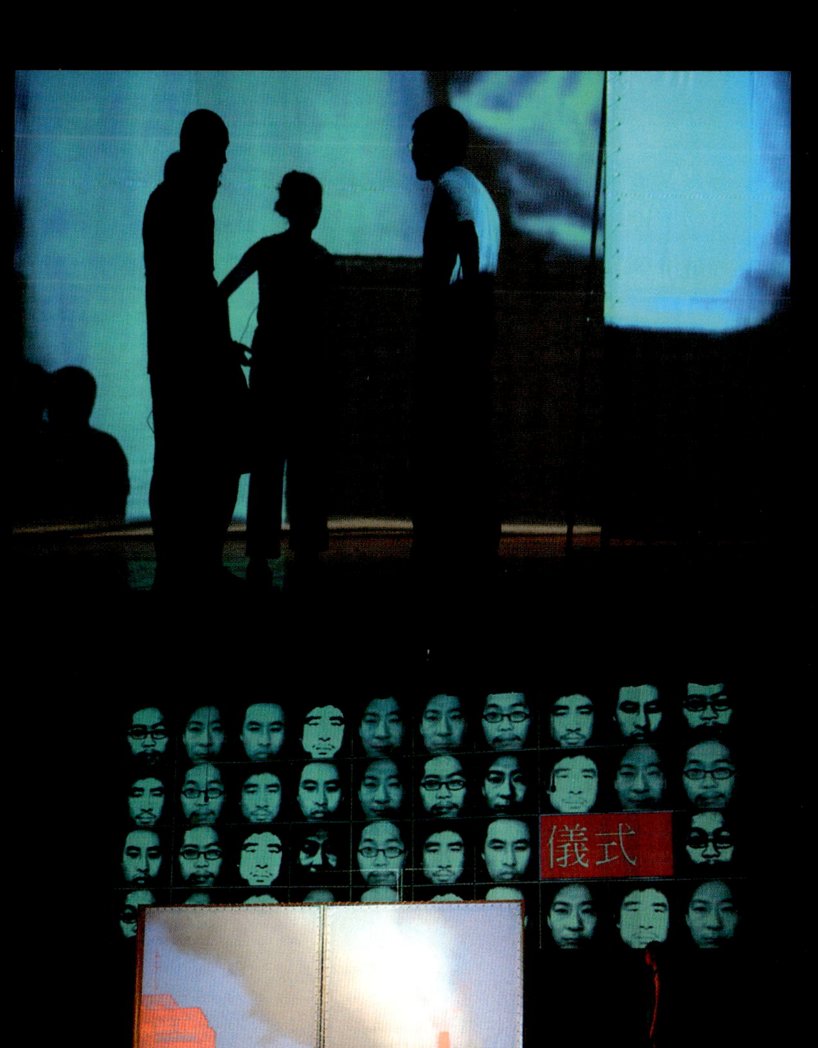
儀式

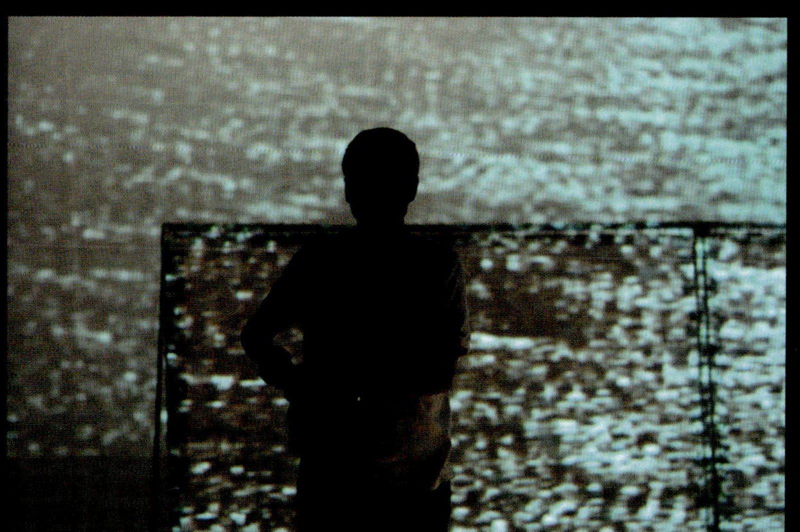

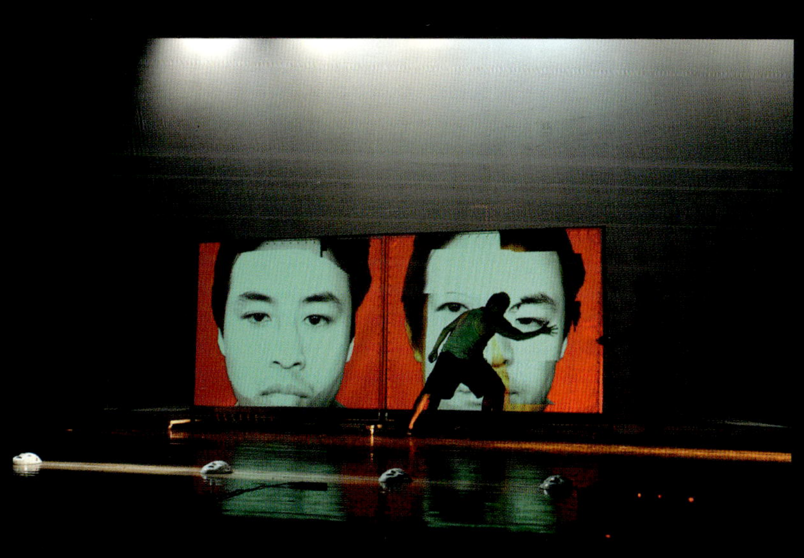

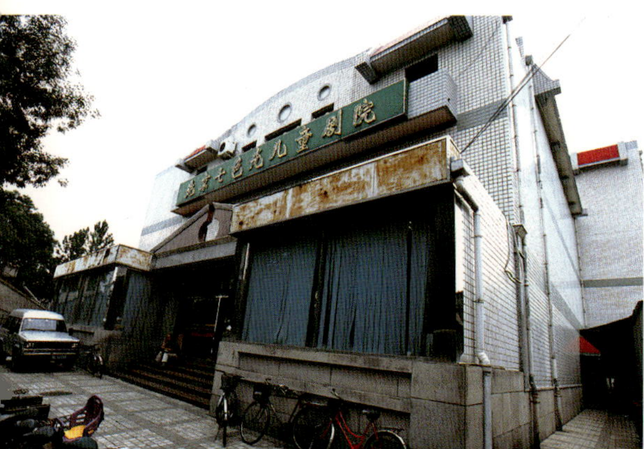

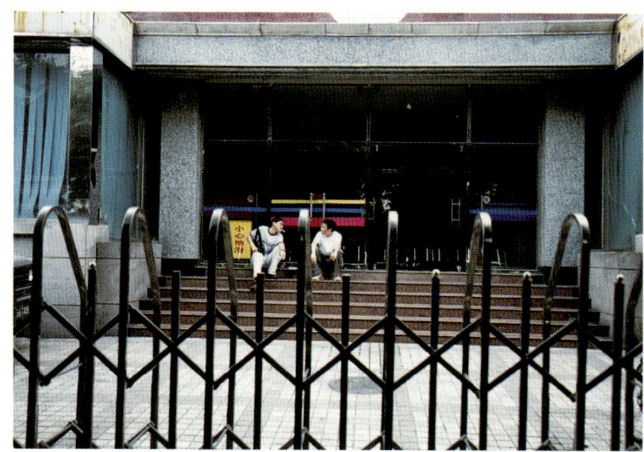

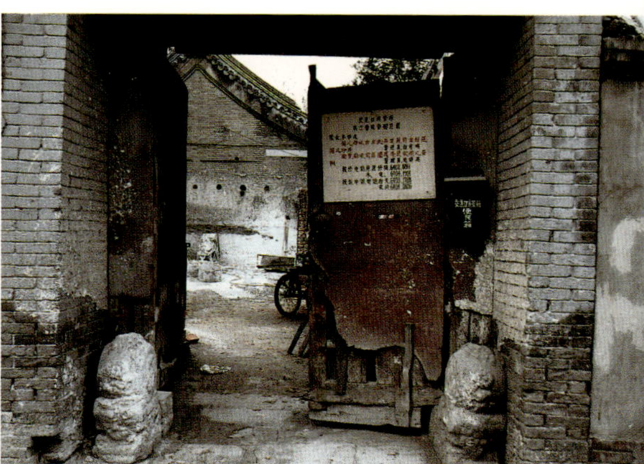

denied him the right to be who he was. ¶ There is probably something of this in his films of squares and the people in them, people who, one way or another, choose to be alone in the midst of a crowd. ¶ "I hated farm laboring, which I found exhausting in every way. So, I decided to join the army, thinking it would be exciting, but it was worse. Not only did we have to work even harder, but on top of that, there was no freedom whatsoever." ¶ His parents were in the army, which meant he escaped the worst treatment. He was told, "Being able to paint is no use on the land, so we'll find you a place in the army where you can use your skills." ¶ So he spent six years drawing up topographical maps. ¶ That was twenty-two years ago, he says with a hollow laugh. He is now forty-four. ¶ Eventually the political situation eased and he was able to leave the army to become an "independent painter." He spent his time studying, painting, and reading: Jean-Paul Sartre, Albert Camus, Roland Barthes, Michel Foucault—"I've read practically all his books. The notion of the archeology of the text is fundamental for me. I have been very influenced by French philosophy. I learned a new way of looking at things—the relationships between things. Bonds." In fact, he read everything he could lay his hands on, from Niels Bohr and books on science to sociology texts. Between 1985 and 1987, China began to open up to the West. Wang Jian Wei describes himself as a sponge, absorbing new thoughts. He spent practically all his time reading. ¶ This led him to ask questions about the history of his own country. He rediscovered traditional Chinese art, such as frescoes painted in caves. He painted in oils, in the Soviet realist style. ¶ Having read so much, and thought about what he read, he felt an overwhelming need to express his thoughts and ideas. He tried to do so through painting for two or three years, feeling his way round the medium, but finally had to admit defeat. He gave up painting. ¶ Wang Jian Wei made his first video in 1995. It was as if someone had turned the lights on. Success. Perfect harmony between the idea, the way of life, and the form. ¶ The question of form is fraught. As Goethe said, "Everyone can see the subject; the background appears only to those concerned; but the form is a mystery for almost everyone." ¶ Wang Jian Wei accepts this, saying that above and beyond what he has already done in this medium, he is looking for a new language for and through video. His multimedia creations, projected on cloth screens and featuring live actors, represent an opening onto another facet of his art that is also rooted deep inside him. ¶ His installation *Connection* is already a remarkable piece. The two screens placed facing each other were awarded a prize in the video category at the Foire Internationale d'Art Contemporain (FIAC), France's international contemporary art fair, in 2003. One of the screens shows families sitting on very similar sofas in more or less the same position, with almost identical objects on the coffee table beside the sofa. They appear fascinated by the other screen, which shows a montage of scenes from DVDs, put together by Wang Jian Wei. ¶ He visited three families and asked them which DVDs they watched. Most of the films were well-known, big-budget American productions on the twin themes of violence and love. He took scenes from about thirty of these films to make his own movie, awash with violence and love. ¶ Previously, he filmed a recently finished building and the three families just moving in. These were the same families he filmed in front of the television. The first said they were going to decorate their apartment to make it stand out from the others. Wang Jian Wei filmed the apartment, its furniture, household appliances, and knickknacks. Then he went

THE OLD NEIGHBORHOOD OF BEIJING—OR WHAT IS LEFT OF IT—WITH CHRYSANTHEMUM ROAD AND THE RAINBOW CHILDREN'S THEATER IN THE CENTER. *CEREMONY* WAS REHEARSED AND PERFORMED IN THIS THEATER.

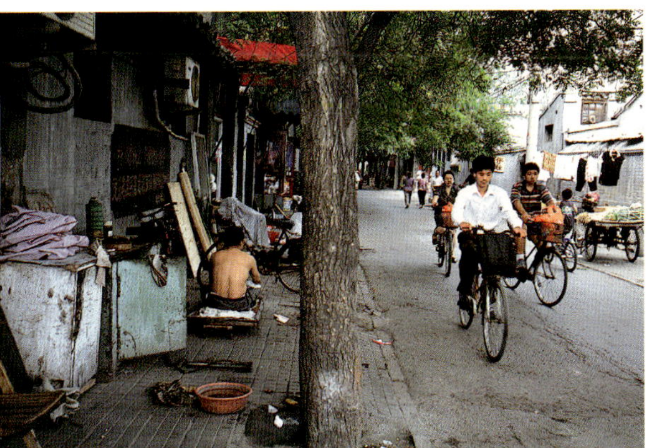

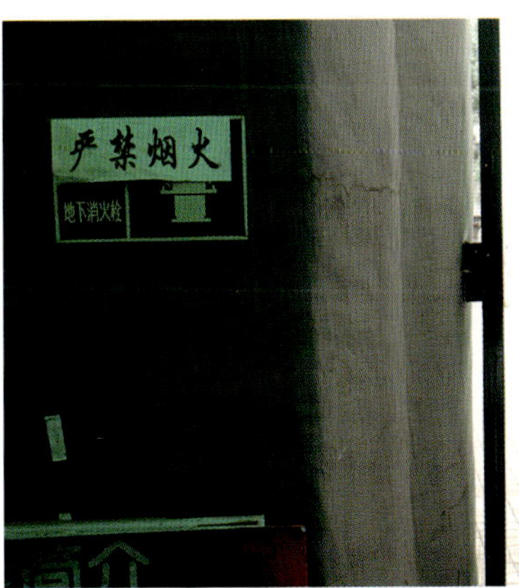

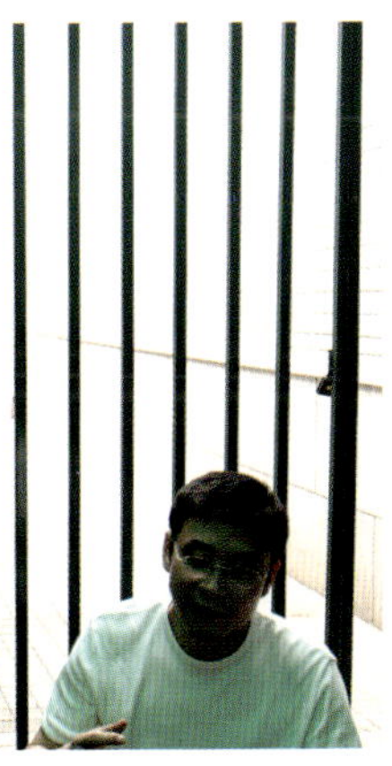

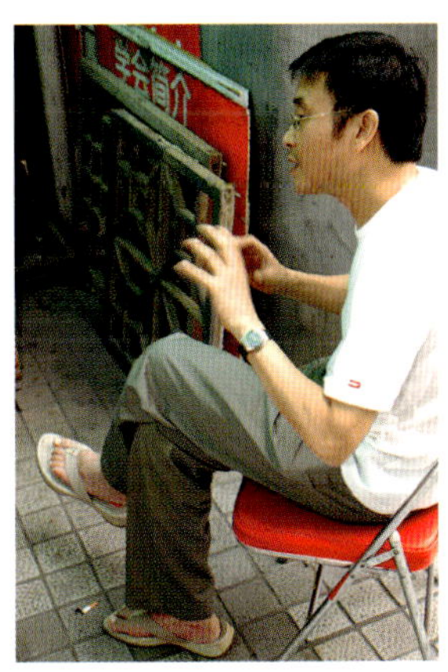

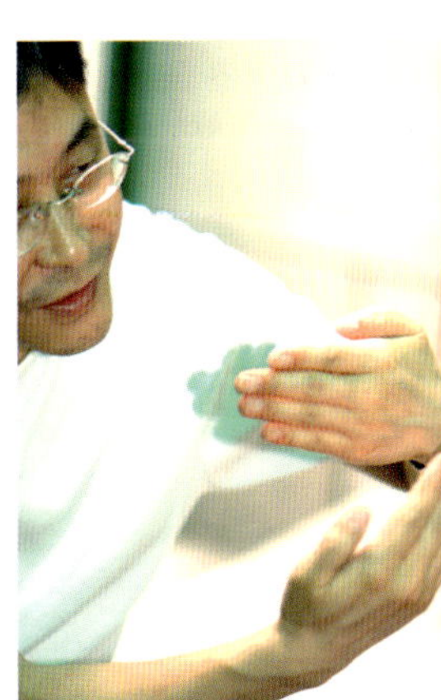

to the second apartment, where the family told him exactly the same thing—they wanted to decorate in an unusual and original way. He noted the sheer conformity and similarities between the families, and beyond them, their adherence to an overarching model. This is not far removed from Christian Boltanski. This is the very heart of Wang Jian Wei's art, which is founded not on an ideological or sociological belief, but on his own sensitivity to this way of life. ¶ He then turned to the third family, which confirmed his impression. "In the end," he says, "no one wants to be like everyone else, but everyone is. The private sphere has maybe become public. There are no profound differences." ¶ He explored the same territory with his film of the crowds on Tiananmen Square, where everyone adopts the same pose in front of the Tiananmen Gate, two fingers raised in a victory V for the camera. Wang Jian Wei asks them why. Nobody knows. "Everybody does it, so I just do it too," they answer. ¶ Wang Jian Wei notes, "The Chinese are scared of not being like other people. If they do not conform, they feel threatened." ¶ Is there a way back up this slippery slope? ¶ Of course. Nothing is unavoidable. Luckily, Wang Jian Wai believes, reality is illogical. ¶ "In my work, I ignore logic in order to learn to distrust anything that is too convincing or obvious." ¶ It is about deconstruction, he says. ¶ At the ARC exhibition in Paris in February 2003, where the lucid, analytical Wang Jian Wei was working in collaboration with the romantic Yang Fudong, he found it almost impossible to "deconstruct" the tightly knit, unwieldy stagings designed by the architect Chang Yung Ho. Instead, he looked beyond them to create his own bond between the two works he was showing, *Square* and *Theater*. The Chinese word for square literally translates as "stage for the masses," and theater as "stage for the theater." ¶ In 1999, Wang Jian Wei spent eleven hours filming on Tiananmen Square during the celebrations to mark the fiftieth anniversary of the foundation of the People's Republic of China. Most of the film is of people taking photographs of each other. Poses. Attitudes. A human comedy. In counterpoint to these images of people putting themselves on show and striking poses, he cut the film with archive images of marches on the same square. A different sort of spectacle. ¶ *Theater* is in two parts. It recounts a folktale that is instantly familiar to anyone of Wang Jian Wei's generation, who know all the ins and outs by heart: *The Girl with White Hair*. The story recounts the adventures of a poor young girl (the equivalent of the woodcutter's daughter in our Western fairy tales) and a wealthy landowner (the prince). It was held up during the Revolution as a perfect example of class struggle, and was frequently put on in theaters. During the Cultural Revolution, the Communist Party first adapted it as an opera, then a film and a ballet. It caught Wang Jian Wei's attention because of the gradual textual transfer from one political context and one medium to the next. ¶ He put together a compilation of various versions of the tale: sung, danced, and acted. He then filmed his own version, "as it was originally told," he says, juxtaposing the contradictory realities of past and present. ¶ He told me, "In the West, you have been distinguishing between reality and representation since Plato. In China, we still believe that what we see must be real." ¶ Images are astonishingly powerful. When the image changes, so does the truth. ¶ I watched Wang Jian Wei's most recent work, *Ceremony*, in late summer 2003, in the Dong Cheng district in the heart of the old Beijing city center, which is full of little Muslim restaurants serving food I have never seen anywhere else on earth and with pictures of the Ka'aba on the walls. The film was on show in the Children's

INSIDE THE THEATER, WANG JIAN WEI EXPLAINING THE INSPIRATION FOR THE WORK AND ACTING OUT TWO OF THE KEY LINES: "FORGETFULNESS KILLS," AND "NO, IT'S REMEMBRANCE THAT KILLS."

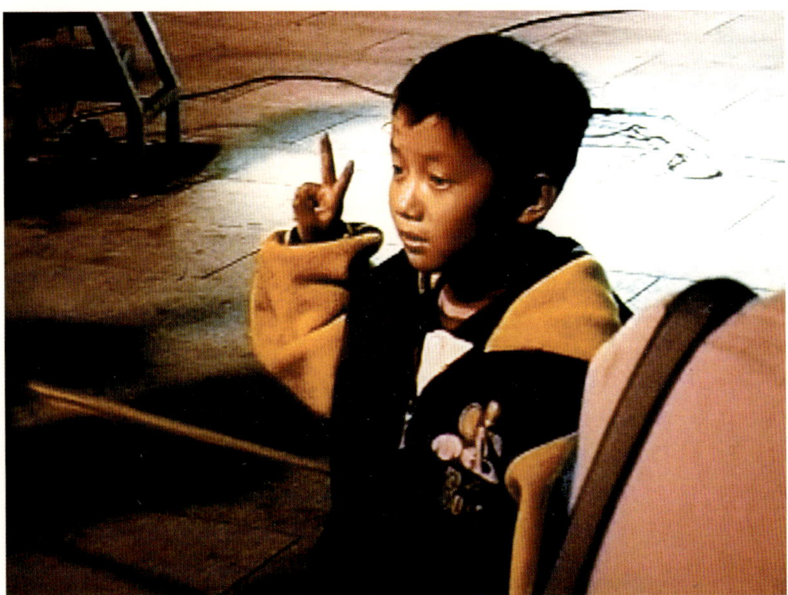

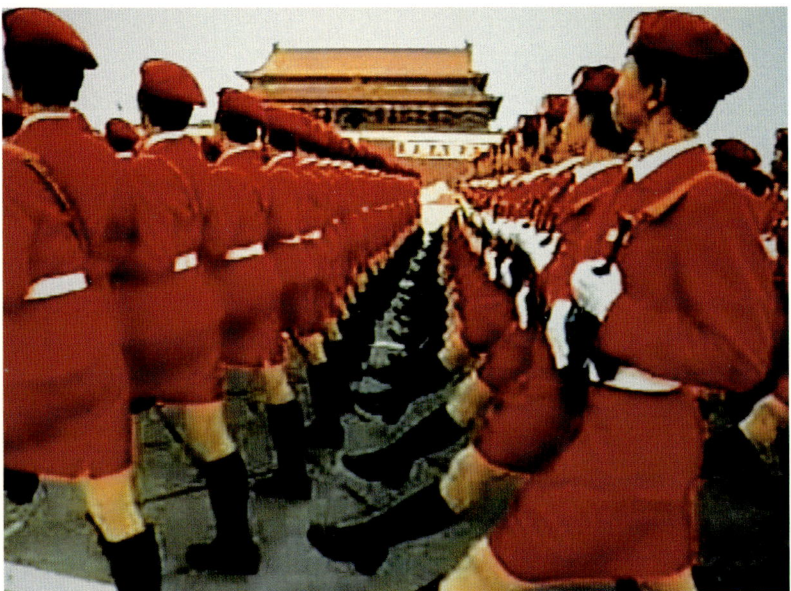

Rainbow Theater at 50 Juerhutong (Chrysanthemum) Street. ¶ Why this theater? Wang Jian Wei had had some trouble with the censors, who criticized him for producing a work that was designed neither as a play nor as dance, but rather as a blend of the two and the questionable medium of "multimedia." He had thus been forced to opt to call the piece a play, to avoid serious difficulties. After that, the remaining problems were small beer. ¶ That is where I watched the rehearsals, including the dress rehearsal, for Wang Jian Wei's most all-around work, with actors, sound, and photo and video projections. The work is based on a famous episode in Chinese history, recounting how Cao Cao, a tyrannical Han dynasty emperor who reigned in the second and third centuries, was seriously insulted in front of the whole court by a storyteller and tambourine player. Cao Cao immediately decided to kill the insolent man, but with typically Chinese cunning he sent him to visit one of his most irascible vassals, who did not hesitate to have the storyteller assassinated for the tiniest criticism. ¶ Cao Cao had been prime minister during an extremely troubled period of Chinese history, when several factions of noblemen were fighting for power and laying the country to waste. Cao Cao shamelessly claimed undying loyalty to the emperor, who was no more than a puppet in his hands. This helped him unite the northern provinces of the empire behind him so that he could usurp the throne. In Chinese tradition, he is held up as an example of a bloody tyrant. In fact, the story has given rise to a proverb: "A usurper will never keep his word." ¶ This tale was the basis for Wang Jian Wei's work. On rereading the life of Cao Cao, he realized that the story was taken up in the court chronicles of the Han dynasty, the *History of the Three Kingdoms*, a collection of oral tales handed down from father to son, and *Kuang Gu Shi Yang San Nong*, a traditional play. ¶ Wang Jian Wei stresses that the different accounts of the episode each tell a different version of the tale. As he wrote in his play, "History is memorized according to need." One character cries, "Forgetting is death." Another replies, "No, memory is death." A third says, "It is very fashionable to pass off falsehoods as truth." All ways of denouncing the manipulation of history. ¶ On stage, there are two screens placed next to each other. Sometimes they move apart, sometimes they screen the characters. They are constantly on the move. There are masks and masked characters, a drum, and projections of photos and videos showing portraits that have been tampered with like the old pictures of Stalin in which those who fell out of favor were airbrushed out of history. ¶ It is a brutal, violent, and yet wholly allusive work. ¶ Wang Jian Wei's previous stage work, *Screens*, examined the society of shams and pretences that was China under Chairman Mao—but also the China of the socialist market economy, and beyond that, the world as it is today. ¶ As Wang Jian Wei often says, "I have had enough of China, the Eternal Nation, the political China that foreigners love so much. I wish that in Europe and America, people would think of China as a modern country with modern people. As complex as everywhere else in the world today."

SQUARE, PRESENTED AT THE ARC IN PARIS. FACING PAGE: TOP: THE VIDEO *CONNECTION* BROUGHT WANG JIAN WEI FAME IN FRANCE. BOTTOM: *OBSERVE*, 2002 WAS BOTH AN INSTALLATION AND A PERFORMANCE.

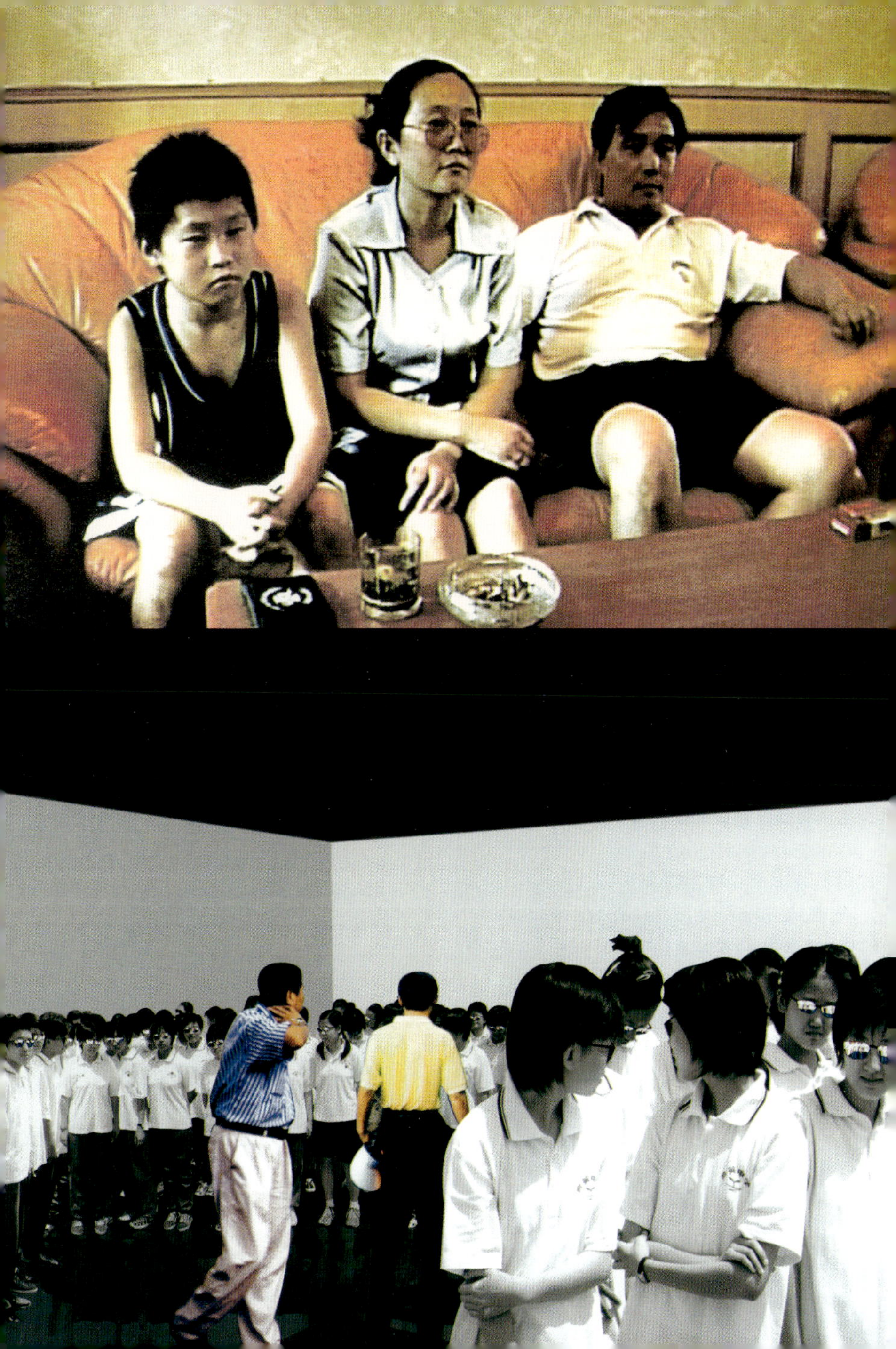

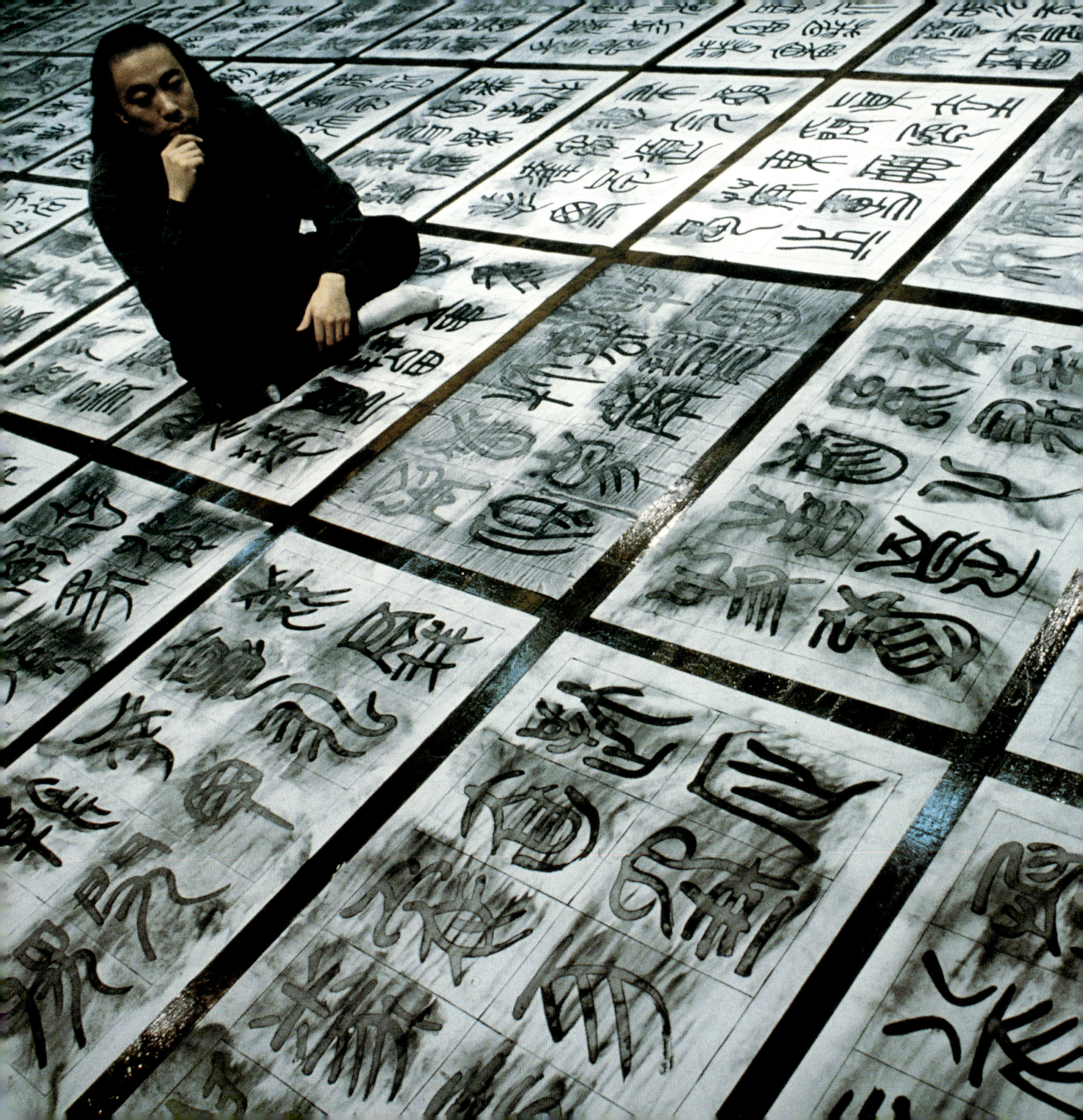

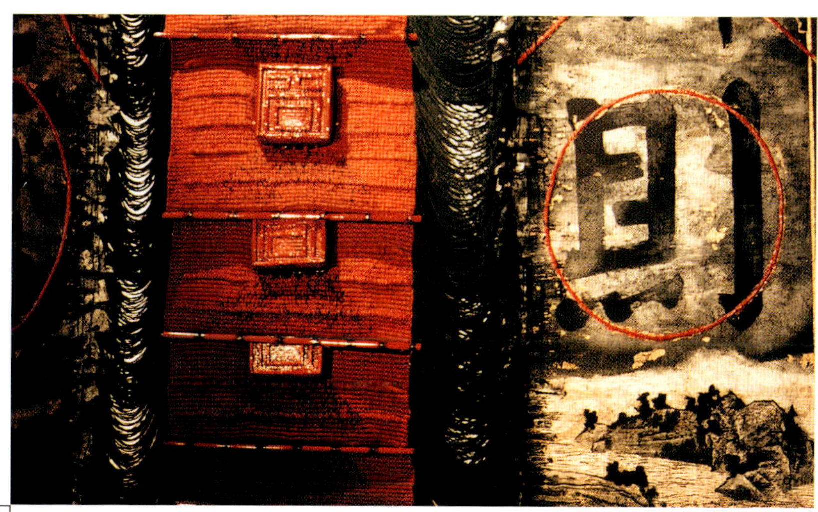

GU WENDA

Say the name Gu Wenda, and one thing immediately springs to mind—hair, just as Joseph Beuys has become synonymous with felt, César with crushed and compacted cars, and Dan Flavin with neon. These artists have integrated their material into their work to such an extent that it has become their own, and no one else can ever use it. They are more than owners of the material: they have acquired the sole rights to it. ¶ Gu Wenda throws individual hairs into the air, weaving an infinitely delicate tapestry. The word "spidery" comes irresistibly to mind. Having woven the piece, he unfurls it, hangs it from the ceiling, arranges its folds into various monumental, astonishing shapes. In the finely woven network of hairs, combed more or less smooth, ideograms appear and disappear, forming a Jamesian "figure in the carpet." ¶ At the moment, Gu Wenda is wandering through the streets of Brooklyn, where he moved in 1999 to live with his new wife, Kathryn Scott. Not the rough, tough Brooklyn where taxi drivers fear to tread, not the Brooklyn where penniless artists shiver in modern-day garrets, toward Williamsburg, where he has his enormous studio. No: we're right beside the famous bridge, strolling along the riverside promenade, in Brooklyn Heights, one of the finest historical neighborhoods in New York, as proclaimed by the February 2001 issue of *Homestyle* magazine, which did a feature on Kathryn and Gu's elegant home (Kathryn is a fashionable interior designer). The article breathlessly describes Kathryn's family history: she grew up in Houston, Texas, and can trace her family tree back to the Revolutionary War. ¶ Actually, Kathryn Scott and Gu Wenda are used to having their home appear in special-interest magazines. Generally, the articles explain in great detail how she bought the place in 1987 and spent more than two years fixing it up, how she met Gu Wenda at a post-vernissage party where she was reluctantly accompanying friends who were keen collectors of Chinese objets d'art, how two years later, she spent her Saturdays studying Chinese and began work all over again on her split-level apartment to make it a home for both of them. ¶ Gu Wenda is the very picture of the successful artist. Apart from his Williamsburg studio, he has two others in China, one in Xi'an, the other in Shanghai, where women weave the hair he collects. He has eight part-time assistants, having discovered the advantages of working for both the American and Chinese art markets. He poses for the camera with easy grace, a broad smile showing off his charming dimples, although the magazine he is posing for has nothing to do with the art world. There is not much trace left of the lean, angry young man who left China with just twenty-five dollars—the maximum amount the authorities would permit—in his pocket. ¶ That was in 1987. He immigrated to the United States on a student visa that he had been waiting for for five years. It was his first time on an airplane. He was 32. Today, he is 49. ¶ His parents were bank employees, and his maternal grandparents worked in wool. Art was a large part of his upbringing: his paternal grandfather was an actor and his sister a musician. Both proved a major influence on the young Gu Wenda. His mother was a keen amateur singer and painter, and made sure that her young son grew up with an appreciation of culture. ¶ His paternal grandfather had enormous influence over Gu Wenda. He was a well-known actor who was the first to introduce dialogue and speech into Chinese theater, which was traditionally sung. Imposing the new style was a challenge; it was even harder to gain acceptance as one of the few Chinese theater actors to appear in films. ¶ Gu Wenda's sister was an even bigger influence. She studied the cello in a special music school. He still remembers fondly how his family would hold a party to celebrate the New Year. His sister and a friend of hers would perform a cello and piano duet, while his mother would sing in a delightful soprano voice. His sister also gave Gu Wenda plenty of books. When their father saw the first book she brought back for her brother, he murmured, "That's a dangerous book." ¶ It was the height of the Cultural Revolution. ¶ His grandfather was sent to be "reeducated" in the countryside, where he died alone, far from his family. As a member of the Communist Party, Gu Wenda's father was not authorized to attend the funeral. His maternal grandparents were also sent to undergo a "reeducation" program. ¶ Gu Wenda has two or three crystal-clear memories of the Cultural

FACING PAGE: GU WENDA SITTING ON HIS *MYTHOS OF LOST DYNASTIES-FORM #C:*, AN EXAMPLE OF PSEUDO-CALLIGRAPHY, HANGZHOU ACADEMY OF ART, 1983–87. ABOVE: *WISDOM COMES FROM TRANQUILITY*, AN INSTALLATION CREATED IN HANGZHOU IN 1995.

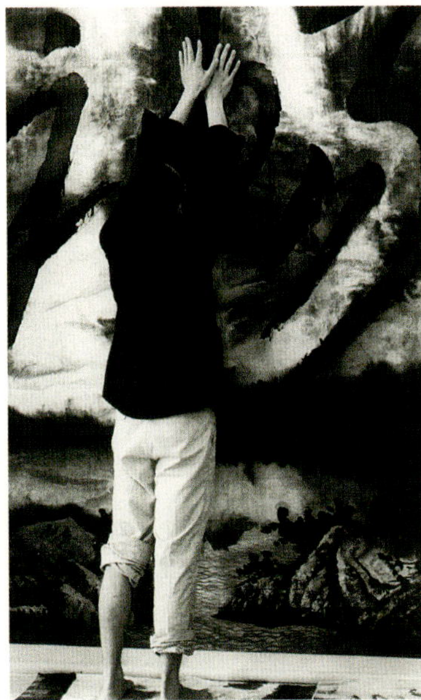

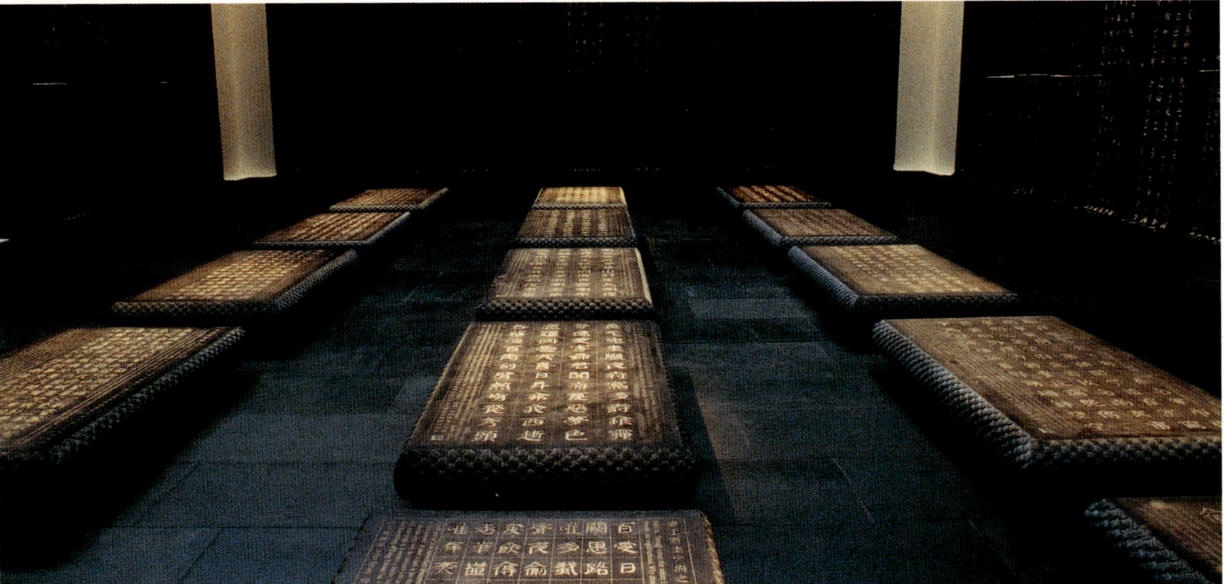

Revolution. Red Guards bursting into his parents' house to search for hidden gold or family treasure. Other guards rifling through his grandfather's papers, coming across an unpublished manuscript on cinema and the theater, and taking it away with them. It was lost forever. Every single member of the family had to denounce the grandfather's "bourgeois" activities and write their criticisms on the outside of the house. His mother, who loved painting in watercolor, finishing a black-and-white portrait of Mao that she hung on the wall. Himself as a boy, hanging small flags on either side of the portrait. Yang Pei Ming told me that he could only paint Mao in black and white once the Great Helmsman's death had been announced. "Before, we couldn't. For the Chinese, black and white are the colors of death." Gu Wenda's mother must have known this. In any case, the Red Guards decided that the little flags made the painting look out of proportion, and forced the little boy to tear the whole thing down from the wall. ¶ Despite all this, as a boy, Gu Wenda was simply fascinated by the Red Guards and dreamed of becoming one himself when he grew up. Eventually, he did. ¶ Looking back, what does he remember of his time as a Red Guard? Funnily enough, his memories are pretty positive. He remembers the way they wanted to change people's attitude to their mother tongue; young men without any specific training set out to simplify Chinese calligraphy in order to create a new, living language. Gu Wenda tells me that it was this, above all, that marked him most deeply. ¶ More than once, talking about the following few years, he told me about how "people lost what they believed in." ¶ He was sent to study wood carving. He hated it—or at least he hated the way it was taught in that particular school. "It wasn't art," he says, "just applied art. All you can do carving wood is make tables, chairs, and lamps." He dreamed of art, fame, and glory, and spent hours painting brush-and-ink landscapes for himself. Once the course in wood carving was over, he was destined to follow the twenty-five other students to a wood-carving factory. Fortunately for him, he was the only student in his class to be sent to design school—maybe because he had been such a reluctant student of wood carving. By another stroke of good fortune, his studies there left him enough time to carry on with his landscape painting, keeping the spark alive. His efforts were encouraged by a teacher who gave him lessons privately and who became his master in all things artistic, encouraging him to adopt a more modern style. This marked the beginning of his subsequent career. Later, he was to study landscape painting with Lu Yanshao at the Hangzhou National Academy, where he studied traditional Chinese techniques in the most traditional setting imaginable. Under the influence of his private tutor, Gu Wenda could not help but have a highly critical attitude to these hidebound methods and the dead weight of tradition that they implied. Today, his attitude is more accommodating. "How can you rebel against tradition if you don't know what the traditions are?" he asks. ¶ In the early 1980s, Gu Wenda invented ideograms that resembled Chinese ideograms, that were painted like Chinese ideograms, but were no more true ideograms than a glass of root beer is a glass of bourbon. His ideograms meant nothing at all. They were pure, empty signs, unburdened by any form of signification. ¶ He says that the idea came to him as he was trying to decipher some ancient manuscripts usually only understood by highly specialized academics, totally cryptic for the average Chinese reader. The ideograms may have been invented by the first emperor. Gu Wenda found that rather than being a source of difficulty, the fact of not being able to read the ancient symbols was a strangely liberating experience. He decided to invent his own language. And why not? After all, artists invent new shapes and objects every day, so why not a new language, particularly when, as in the case of Chinese,

FROM LEFT TO RIGHT: *SPEECHLESS #1*, 1985, PERFORMED AT THE HANGZHOU ACADEMY OF ARTS. *FOREST OF STONE STELES-RETRANSLATION AND REWRITING OF TANG POETRY*, 1993–2001, XI'AN. FACING PAGE: *UNITED NATIONS-CHINA MONUMENT: TEMPLE OF HEAVEN*, 1997–98.

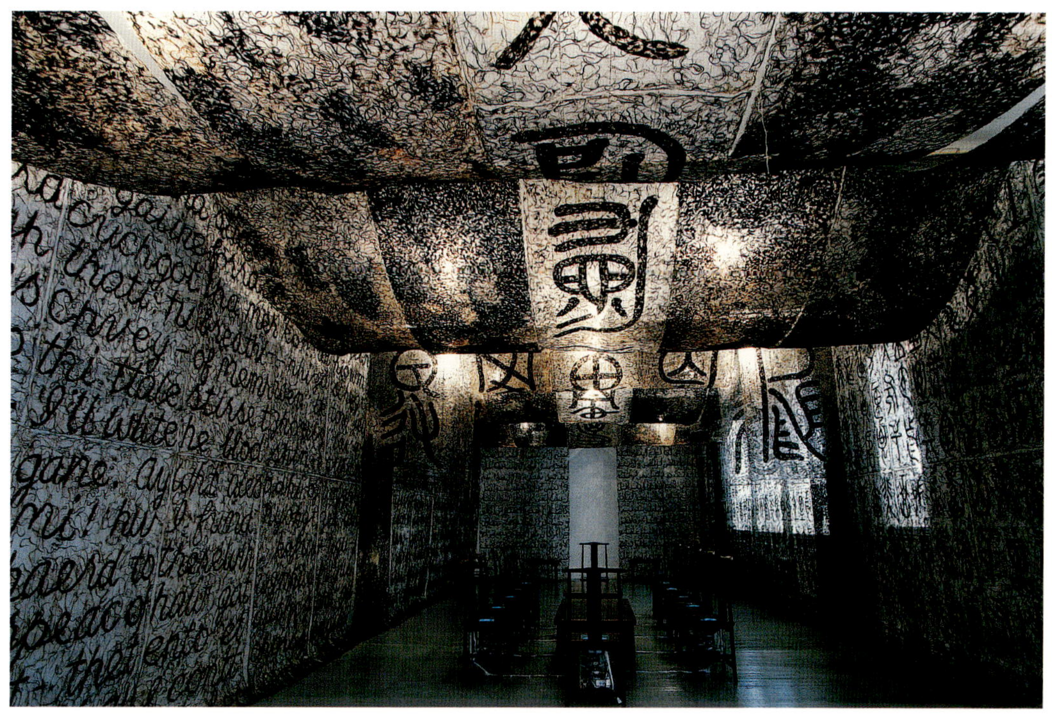

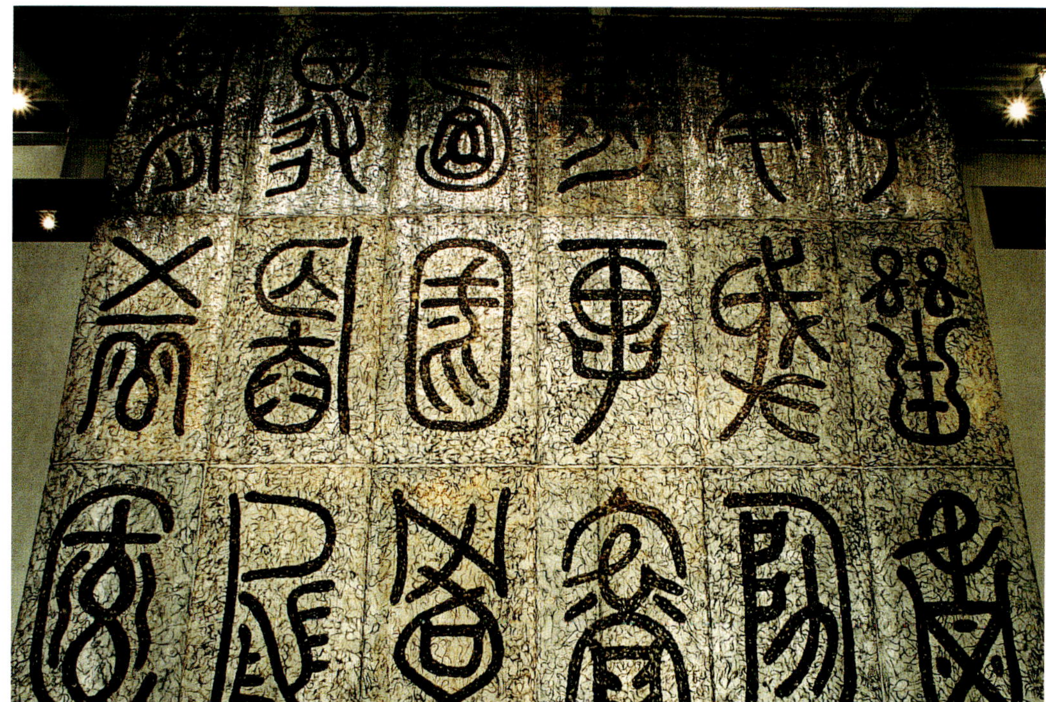

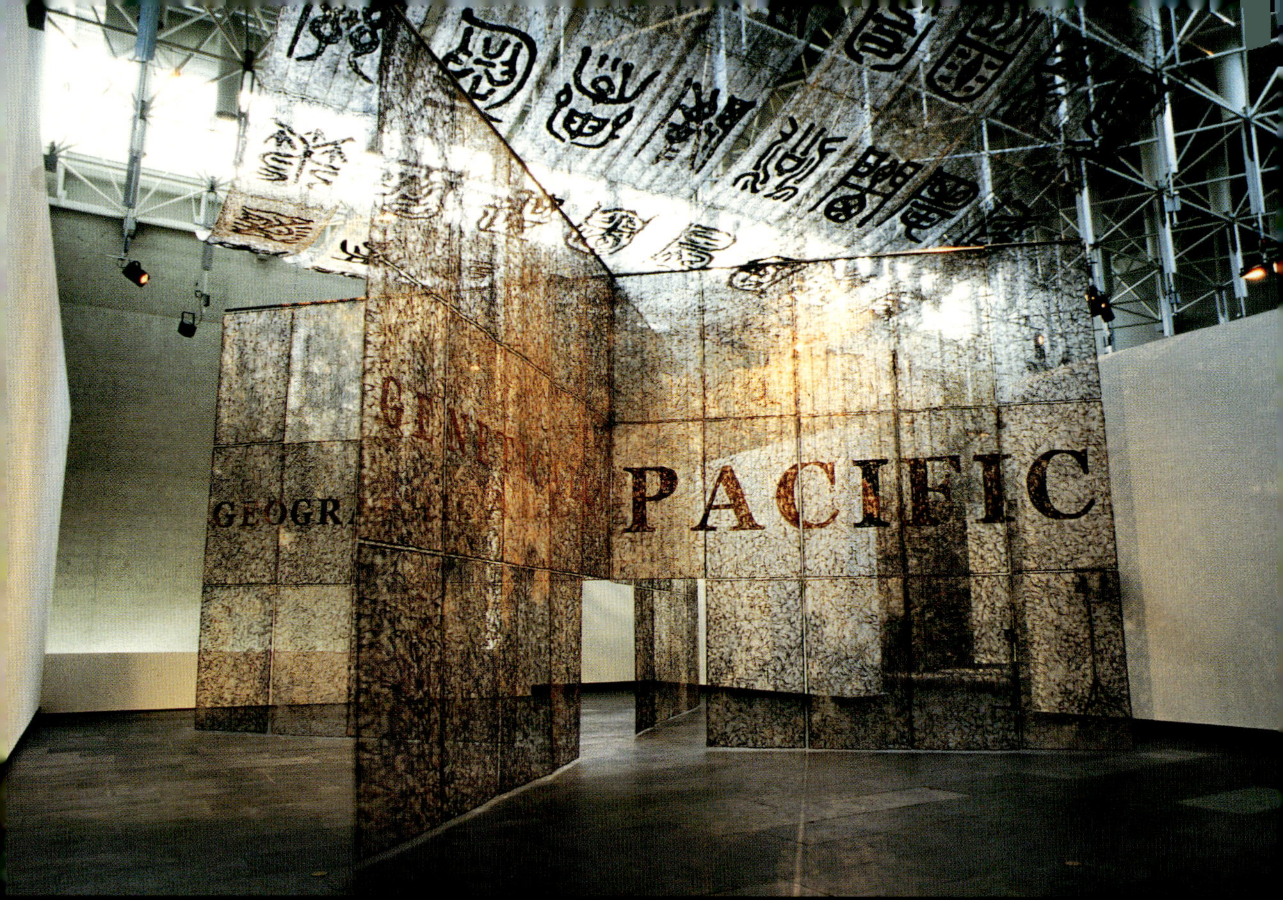

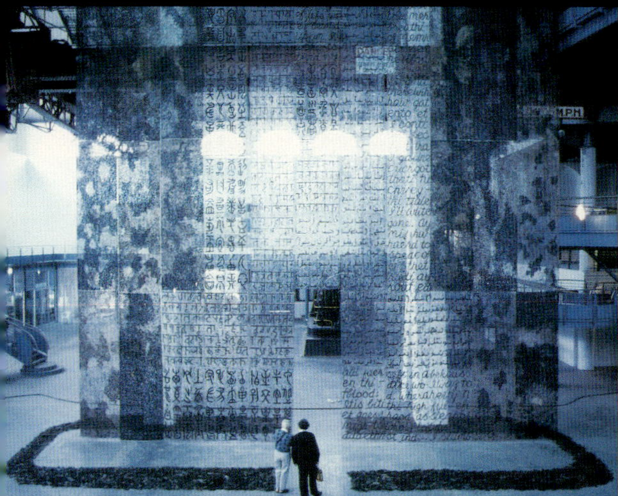

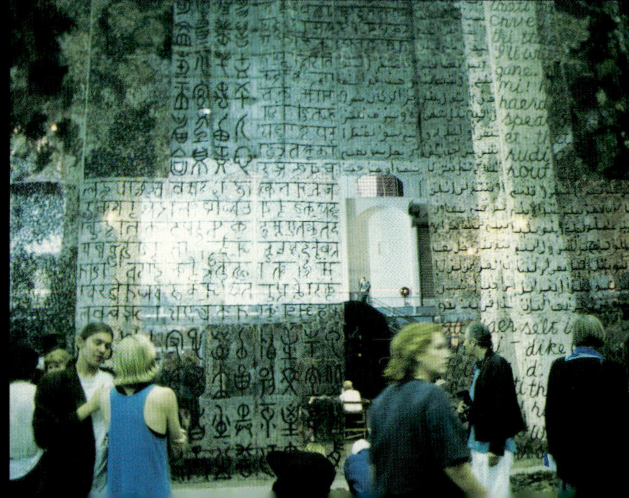

the written form is so adaptable? And, as we have already seen, the Red Guards had already simplified the language. So why shouldn't Gu Wenda try? ¶ One year before Gu Wenda left for the United States, in 1986, he announced that he was going to put on an exhibition of extremely large paintings of ideograms of his own invention in the city of Xi'an. The day before the exhibition opened, the People's Propaganda Department came to inspect the works on display. Because they were unable to read the ideograms, they at once suspected that the show was critical of the authorities and shut it down before it even had a chance to open. Gu Wenda firmly denied any "direct" political intention in his works. At the time, he was studying Wittgenstein's philosophy of language with great pleasure and was more interested in the conceptual possibilities of language than in any sort of political debate. What he was trying to do was to reconnect with an ancient Chinese tradition. After a few days of toing and froing, the exhibition was granted permission to go ahead, but only professional artists were authorized to attend. The Chinese propaganda department moves in mysterious ways. ¶ 1987. Gu Wenda sets off for the United States. He insists that he did not leave China for political reasons, but because New York was the center of the universe as far as contemporary art was concerned and he wanted his work to be known internationally. ¶ Fortunately, Gu Wenda had a good friend and mentor to guide him when he arrived: the dean of the University of Utah School of Medicine, who was also a keen art collector. The two met when the dean was on vacation in China and discovered a passion for contemporary Chinese art. He set about collecting with the help of the art critic Peter Selz, who put him in touch with Gu Wenda. In 1986, Gu Wenda asked his new friend to help him. The dean bought several of his works. Sadly, he died three weeks before Gu Wenda set out for the United States, but made sure that there would be some money waiting for his Chinese friend when he arrived. ¶ He stayed first in San Francisco for a week, where he obtained a document that allowed him to visit the artists at Toronto's York University for three months. He then returned to San Francisco for a further three months before heading to New York. There, he stopped working on his art almost entirely for a year while he learned English, giving a few lessons here and there to earn a meager living. He also spent some time as artist in residence at the University of Minnesota. ¶ Gu Wenda first began to work with hair in the spectacular creation *United Nations* in 1993. The inspiration for using this unusual material lay in his work on the body, begun in China shortly before his departure. He saw this theme as an important part of his campaigning for human, in particular homosexual, rights. Having called language into question and reached the outer limits of dematerialization in his earlier work, he decided to turn to works that explored their own materiality in a frank, unabashed manner. As he explored this notion, he became aware that the human body lay at the center of all his artistic concerns. Not necessarily his own body, as is the case with the proponents of Body Art. Gu Wenda has not mutilated his own penis, slit his skin with a knife, or tortured his body. He worked with all sorts of bodily fluids: semen, placenta, menstrual blood. The resulting work was *Oedipus Refound #5: The Enigma of Blood,* which incorporated used sanitary napkins sent to him by sixty women in sixty different countries, placed on white cushions under glass in a quasi-medical or anthropological presentation, with explanatory letters, reports, and diagrams. The work did not go down well with feminists. Gu Wenda came up against the limits of free speech in the home of the First Amendment. No institution in the country would agree to show his work. He was to all intents and purposes barred for being too "wild," he says—too politically incorrect. American feminists were not about to accept a man making light of their periods. ¶ He also discovered at this time how something can be perceived in radically different ways from one culture to another; for while in China, placenta is frequently used as an ingredient in traditional remedies, Americans found his use of it in art extremely shocking. He is generally reluctant to tell people that the

FACING PAGE: TOP: *UNITED NATION-AUSTRALIA MONUMENT*, 2001, NEW YORK. BOTTOM: *UNITED NATIONS-AFRICA MONUMENT: THE PRAYING WALL OF THE WORLD*, 1997, JOHANNESBURG BIENNIAL.

placenta came from a woman who had aborted a handicapped fetus. Gu Wenda: courting controversy considered as one of the fine arts. ¶ His work on hair evolved out of these experiences. For while hair can have religious connotations, and piles of hair immediately call to mind scenes from concentration camps, Gu Wenda places his work in such a humanist, multiracial perspective, calling it the *United Nations Project*, that there can be no room for ambiguity. However, once bitten, twice shy—he made sure to make a public announcement that all the hair had been duly collected from hairdressers. And since some people might like to know whether their own hair had made it into the finished tapestry, he displayed at the entrance the names of all the participating hairdressers so that visitors could check. ¶ The work was designed to evolve over time. To begin with, Gu Wenda worked at a national level. In each country that he visited, he made "monuments" of hair from local people, referring to local history. The first stage of the *United Nations Project* was in Lodz, Poland, where the local Jewish community was soon up in arms about what it saw as an untimely reminder of the concentration camps and the Holocaust. The exhibition was closed after just twenty-four hours. Gu Wenda then made the work more international in scope, incorporating objects, scripts, and cultural references from all over the world. In Lyon, France, for the 2000 biennial, he presented an installation of hair curtains, which included texts imitating Latin, Chinese, Arabic, and Hindi script, with furniture that was a cross between the Ming dynasty and Louis XV. The American project was the most complex of all. He collected hair from Chinatown, Park Avenue, Washington, San Francisco, and the Native American reservations. The itinerary around the States ended with a final ceremony in New York, the melting pot. But, Gu Wenda says, "I'm not in a hurry to finish." ¶ Surprisingly, Gu Wenda's use of hair has caused almost as much scandal as his use of menstrual blood and placenta, in Lodz, in Sweden and Russia, and particularly in Israel where protests were held outside the exhibition. But nowadays he is better armed to argue with his critics, and he often convinces them, reminding them that when Europe's Jews were being turned away from countries all over the world, only the gates of Shanghai remained open, and declaring that his project is absolutely not designed to refer to the tragedy of the Shoah, but rather as a reference to a Utopia where humankind, united at last, can live in harmony. He adds, for good measure, that without Jewish hair, his Utopia would be incomplete. ¶ He tells me that he was not entirely satisfied with his creation until he hit upon the idea of the United Nations. He explains that there are three attitudes that an immigrant can adopt: turn his back on his own traditions, struggle to preserve them come what may, or try and adapt. *United Nations* is a way of bringing all cultures into his work. That is why the project appealed to him so much: it was universal, not typically Chinese. ¶ In the last ten years, *United Nations* has incorporated some twenty countries on five continents, forming a sort of chain throughout the world. ¶ When he came up with the idea of painting with a brush made from human hair, he said he was painting "with human genes." He claimed to be convinced that it was totally different from traditional painting. He painted with his enormous brush of human hair in public, dressed in a long red gown. Gu Wenda is nothing if not spectacular. When it is not banned or booed, his work demands applause. ¶ Finally, it is worth noting that he almost never refers to other Chinese artists. When I mention Xu Bin or Chen Zhen, he skirts the issue, avoiding even saying their names if he can help it. ¶ Maybe he feels that he is the only Chinese artist worthy of interest, the only one of any note. ¶ Or maybe rather he feels different—hardly Chinese anymore, but not yet American, either.

FACING PAGE: *INK ALCHEMY*, 1999–2001, USING INK MADE FROM GROUND HAIR FROM CHINESE DONORS, SHERMAN GALLERY, AUSTRALIA.

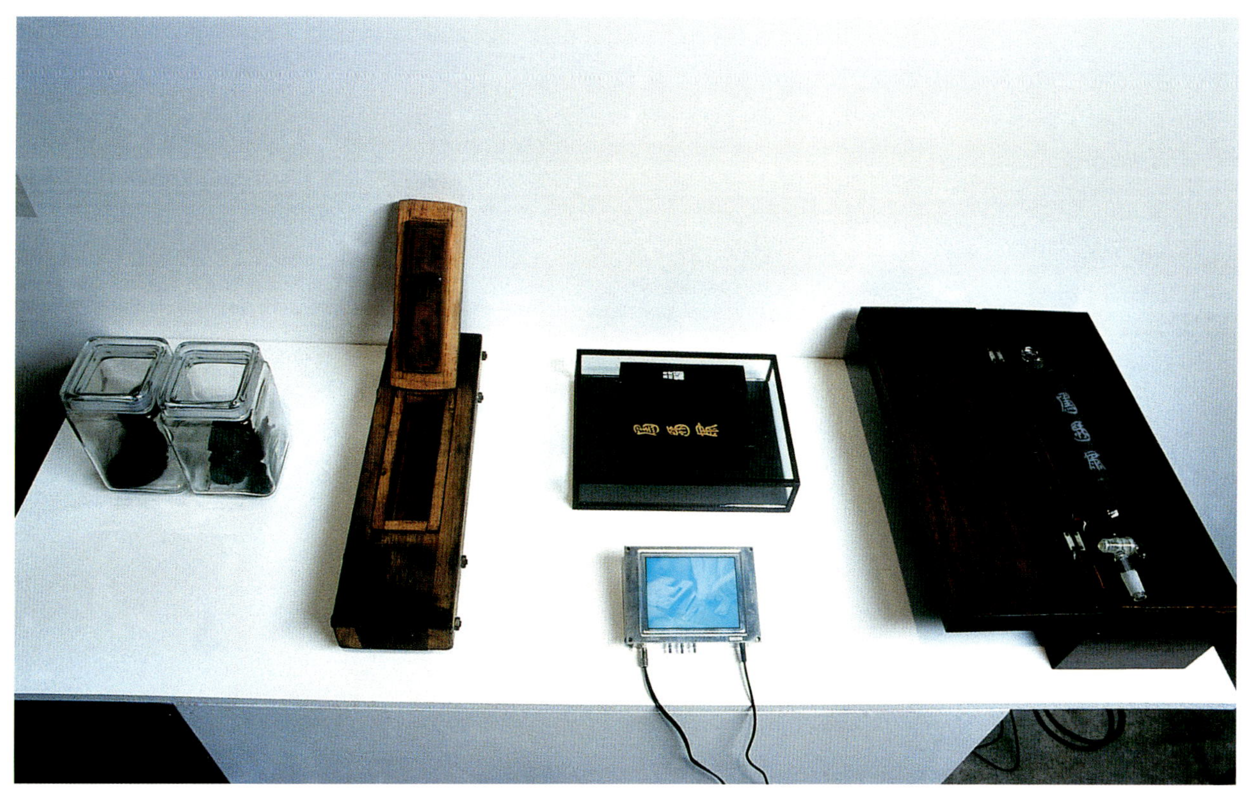

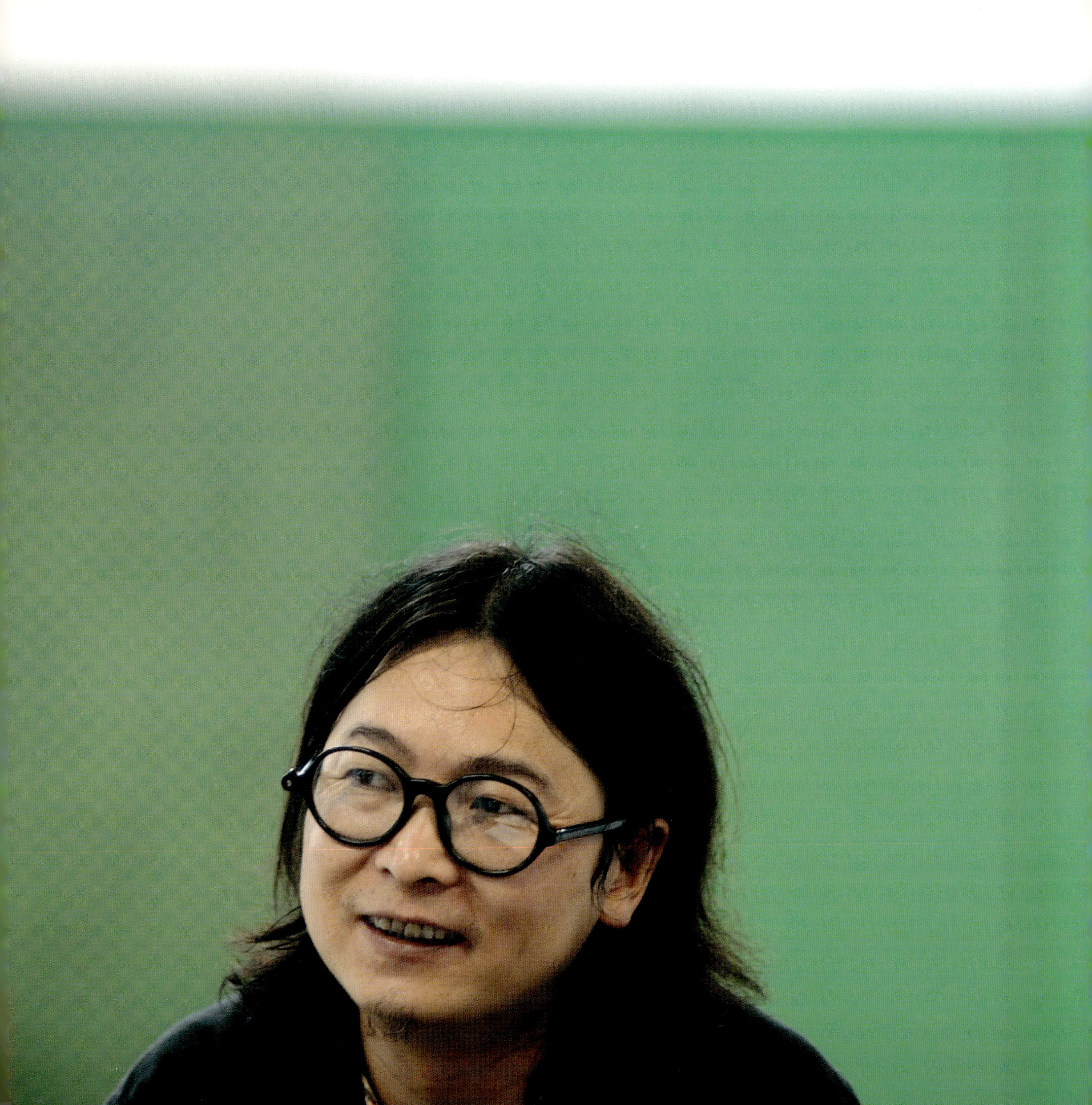

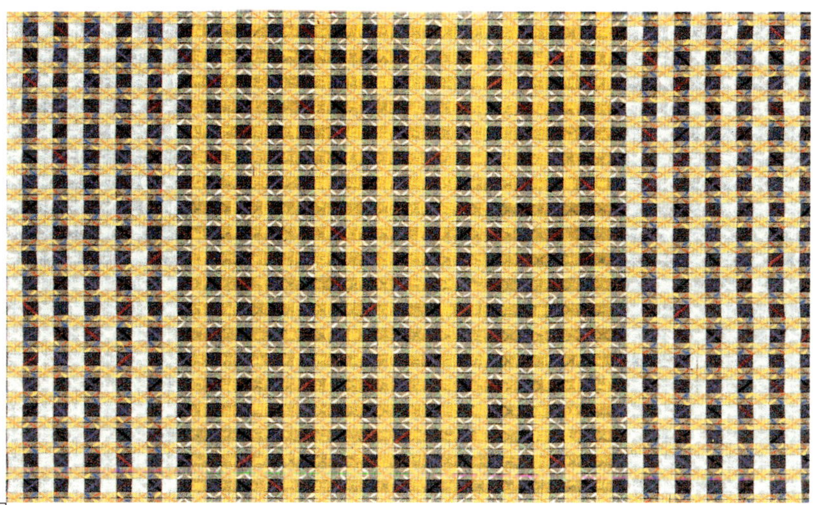

DING YI

Marcel Duchamp and Andy Warhol are big news in China, like everywhere else. But Ding Yi wanted to talk about Maurice Utrillo, famous for his legendary alcoholism as much as for his paintings of Montmartre street scenes. ¶ Utrillo was the biggest influence on Ding Yi's formative years as an artist. ¶ I am wide-eyed with amazement. Did I hear right? He says it again. Utrillo? But why? "Because," Ding Yi says, "what he showed us of Paris looked very much like the Shanghai of my formative years, or at least Hangkou in Xuhui district. By imitating him and painting Shanghai so that it resembled his Paris, my technique improved." He glances up as if to check the impact his words have had on me. The look on my face must be priceless: I can't believe my ears. I ask if he has kept any of these paintings or any reproductions. Yes, he has some copies. *View of Dalian Street* (1983) and *Street with Red Houses* (1983) are, as he said, Utrillo with a Chinese twist. They have the same naivete, meticulously analyzed, drawn, and colored. ¶ We are in a studio at 50 Moganshan Road, in the same street as the three major galleries: Eastlink, Shanghart, and BizArt. Ding Yi has been working here for two years, but from the look of the studio, he could have been here forever: the shelves are stacked with neat rows of little paint pots; there is an old table down the middle of what was formerly a tailor's workshop. Ding Yi is sitting on an old Qing chair. He is rather short and is dressed in black, as always. He has five o'clock shadow. His hair, black as his glasses, is long. ¶ He was born in 1962, and was thus four when the Cultural Revolution began, in an atmosphere that he says was "very heavy." There were paintings of Mao and propaganda posters everywhere—including just outside his house. Every year, artists were sent to renew the paintings on the bulletin boards. "That's how I began to want to paint pictures," he says. "I was at primary school, where there were no art lessons at all. I copied comics and did quite a good job. In my class, my school friends told me that I was talented. I was good at art. But back then, no one knew anything about art or Chinese painting, and even less about foreign art. What did it mean to say someone was talented?" ¶ Several people have told me that, in those days, often the only available means of artistic expression was drawing on blackboards in chalk. That is how the young Ding Yi began. He told me how in each classroom, there were two blackboards—one for the teacher, and the other for the children to write and draw on. Actually, the children's blackboard was reserved for the most

FACING PAGE: DING YI IN HIS STUDIO, AS ALWAYS, DRESSED IN BLACK WITH ROUND GLASSES AND LONG HAIR. UNLIKE MANY CHINESE ARTISTS, HE KEEPS MANY OF HIS OLDER WORKS IN HIS STUDIO. ALL OF HIS CREATIONS ARE ENTITLED *APPEARANCE OF CROSSES*.

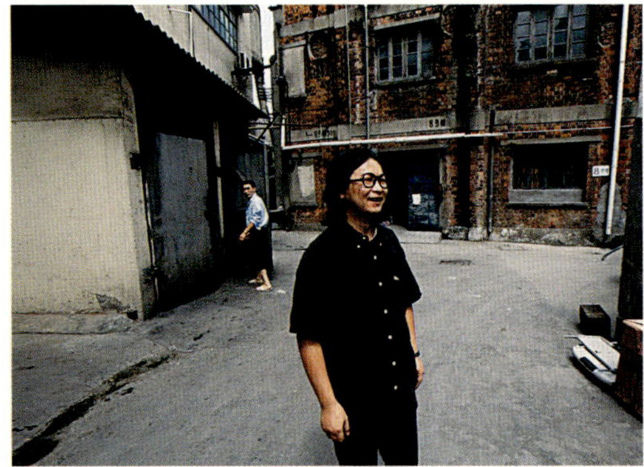

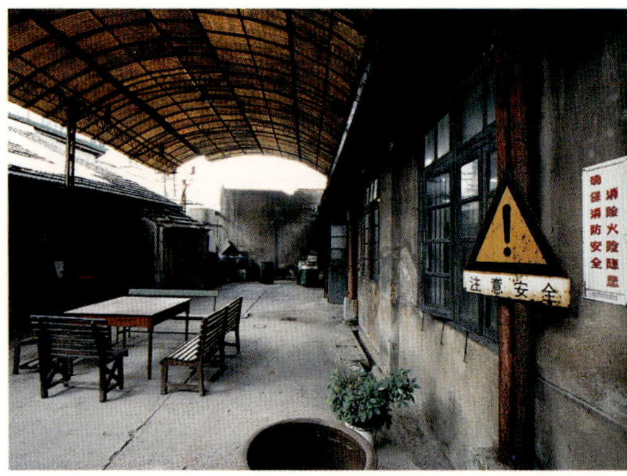

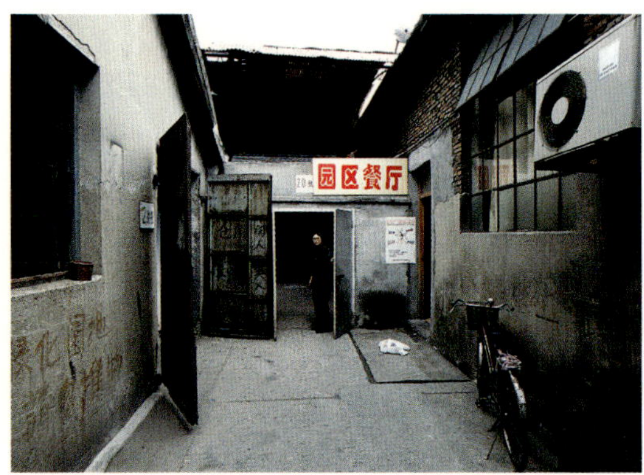

talented children who supplied the drawings for the whole class. It was the same in high school. Only a very few students used the children's blackboard. They felt it to be a real privilege, as it meant they were dispensed from politics class. Ding Yi smiles at the memory. "It was a real pleasure," he laughs. ¶ In his third year of high school, the students decided to start an arts club. That is when Ding Yi set his heart on becoming an artist. He studied at the Shanghai School of Fine Art, specializing in design, like many other young artists. He painted in his free time. ¶ He had a family relative who worked in Japan, whom he asked to send him art magazines, catalogs, and books, on Maurice Utrillo in particular. ¶ In those days, there were close political ties between China and the USSR. China was heavily influenced by its vast neighbor—even in terms of art. Those were the days of Socialist Realism. At the same time, China was slowly opening up to the West. The process was tortuously slow. In 1978, the most daring exhibition was a collection of Impressionist landscapes from the Musée d'Orsay in Paris. It's hard to believe today, but this exhibition had an enormous impact on an entire generation of artists. "It was the first time we had seen a large exhibition. And finally, there in front of us, we discovered European art," Ding Yi remembers fondly. ¶ It was a breakthrough, but a very isolated one. In 1979, a European-style exhibition was banned. But too late: the dam had been breached. The younger generation began to experiment with new ways of creating art. Information was flooding in from all sides and new directions were being explored. Five or six years later, new artistic groups were flourishing all over China. ¶ By now, it was 1983—84. Ding Yi recalls, "In those days, every exhibition had a political dimension and they all took place on one of the many national festivals: May 1, Labor Day, or August 1, the holiday celebrating the founding of the Red Army, or October 1, the national holiday. When I went to these exhibitions, I saw that my own level was much better." ¶ 1984, 1985, and 1986 were vital years for art and artists in China. Prior to that, information was scarce, or nonexistent. But in the mid-1980s, artists became impatient and began kicking against the constraints, trying out a whole range of new styles. ¶ Ding Yi tells me, "There was a peculiar atmosphere in Shanghai. Although there were art schools everywhere, there was simply nothing new happening. Back then, Shanghai was very quiet, very calm—the opposite of today. ¶ Like so many other artists, Ding Yi began with performances. He shows me a few photographs of these. Doesn't he have any slides? He gives me a sad smile. "Back then, we were very poor." ¶ In 1986, one of his first performances was to wrap a long stretch of bright yellow cotton around two people sitting on a bench. Of course, in China, yellow is traditionally associated with religion; it was the color worn by the king. The performance took place outside the newly built Shanghai art museum. "Yes, it was new, but it represented tradition, while I represented modernity," he says. "The performance was planned not so much as a dialogue as a confrontation." I point out that, actually, he was wrapping things just like Christo. Yes, that's true, he laughs. ¶ He also talked to me about the influence of Fernand Léger, which, I must say, was not apparent to me in his works. He says, "This influence certainly exists. In the 1930s, Léger painted workers and machines. Maybe that was what marked me to begin with. In those days, I was influenced by a lot of people, but none of them proved to be decisive." ¶ The first series of *Appearance of Croce* dates back to 1989. To begin with, his paintings were cold, impersonal, industrial, based on his design experience. His inspirations were Mondrian

DING YI'S STUDIO IS AT 50 MOGANSHAN ROAD, NEAR THE THREE MOST IMPORTANT GALLERIES IN SHANGHAI. HIS OWN GALLERY IS SHANGART, NEXT DOOR TO THE STUDIO.

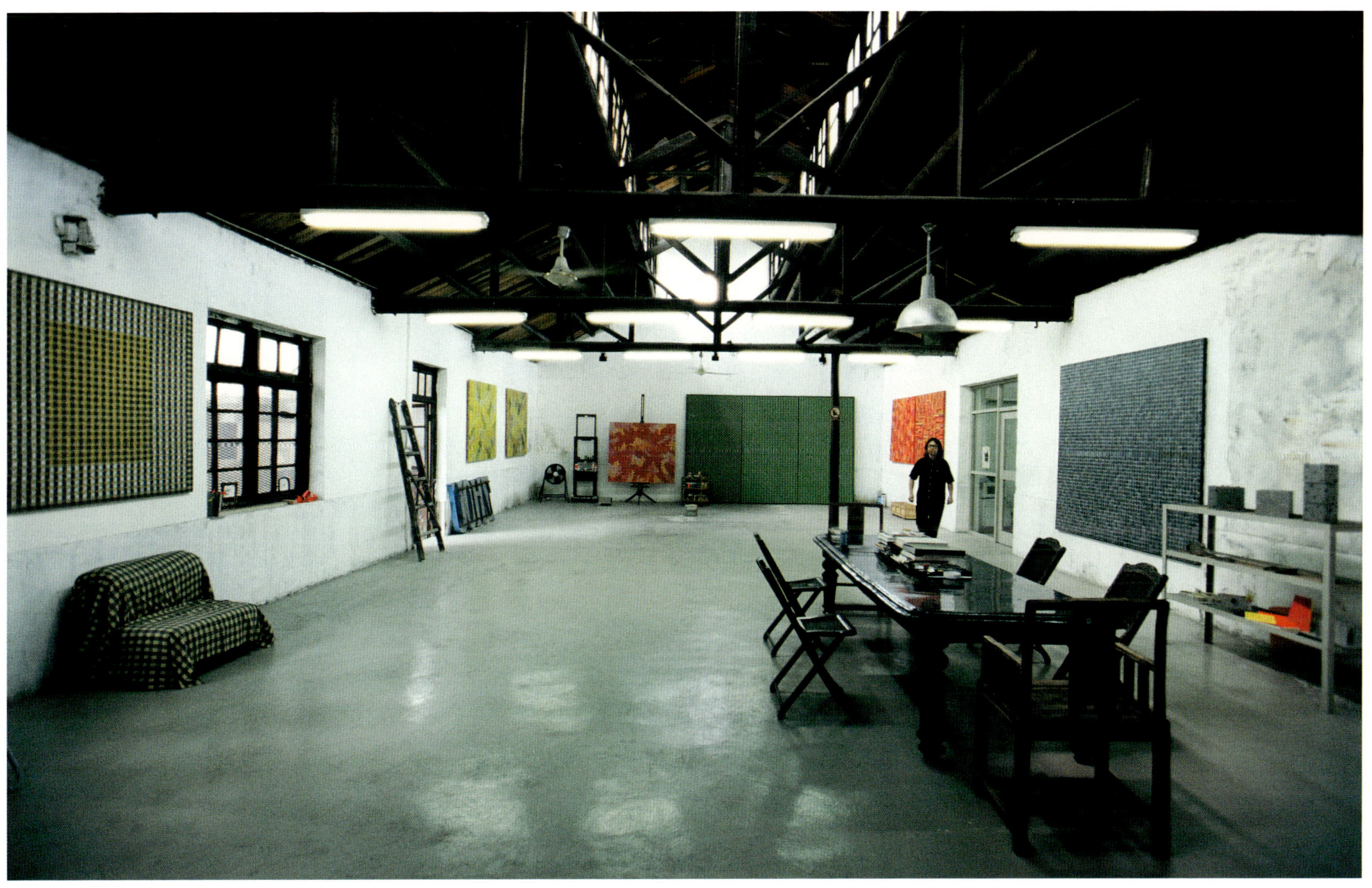

DING YI HAS BEEN RENTING HIS STUDIO FROM A CLOTHING FACTORY FOR TWO YEARS. AT THE END OF THE LONG WORKTABLE IS A QING CHAIR. SEVERAL OF HIS PAINTINGS CAN BE SEEN ON THE WALL.

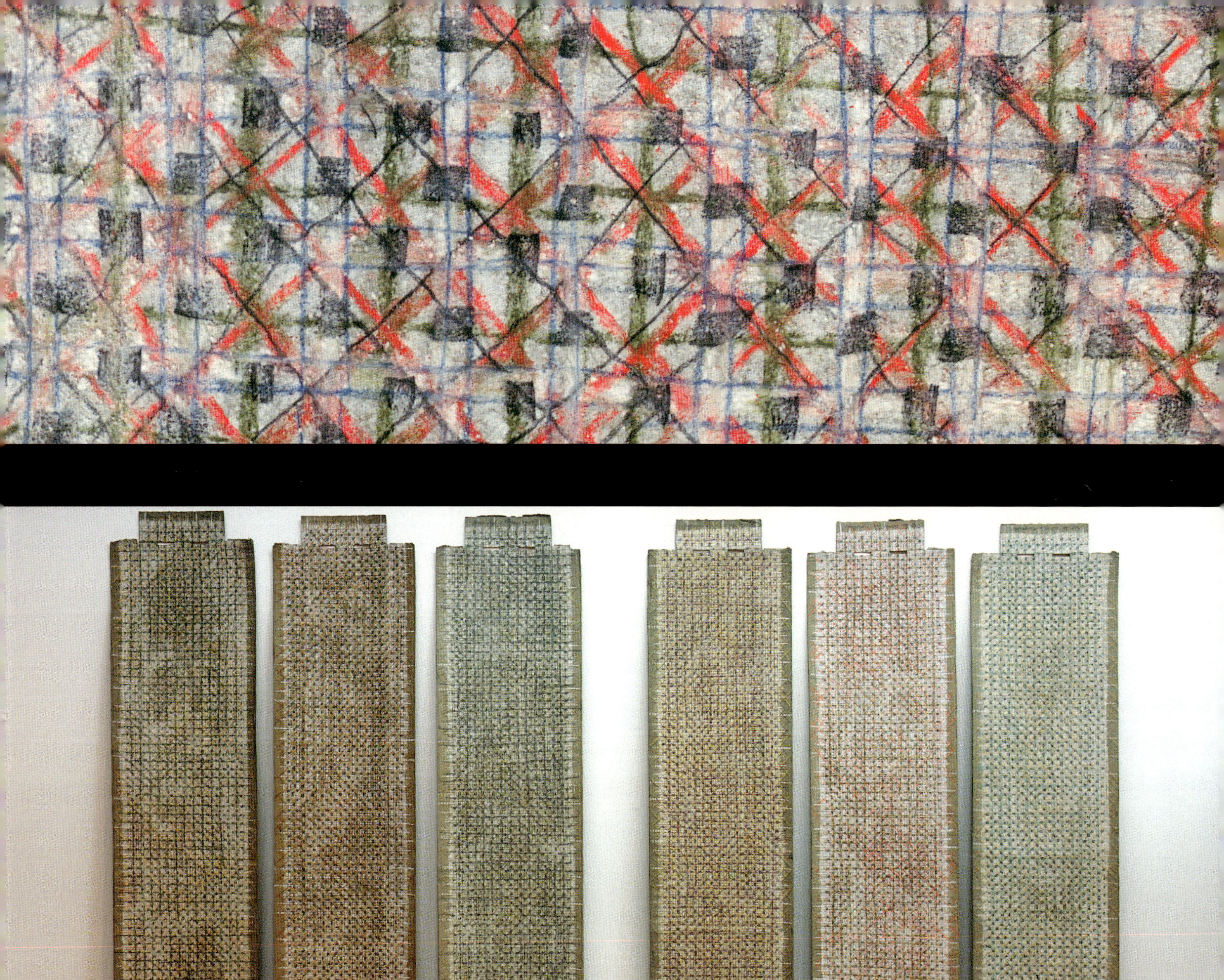

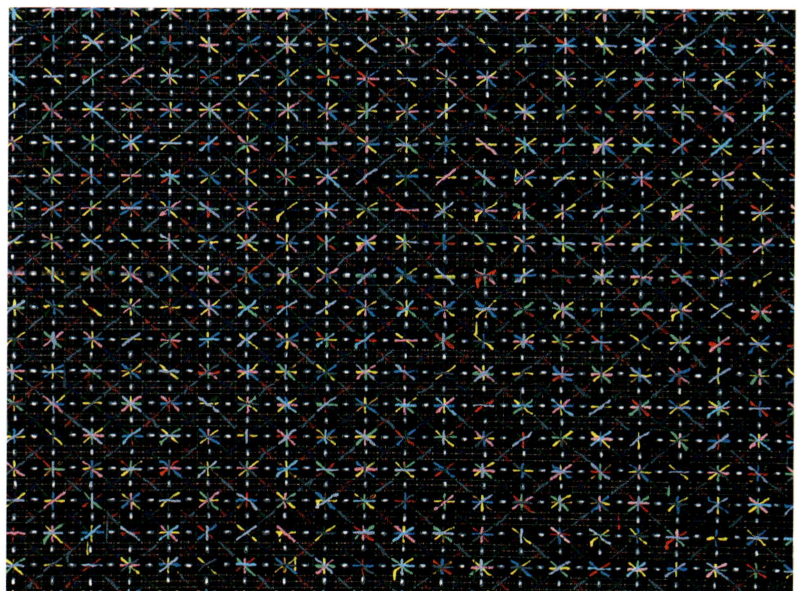

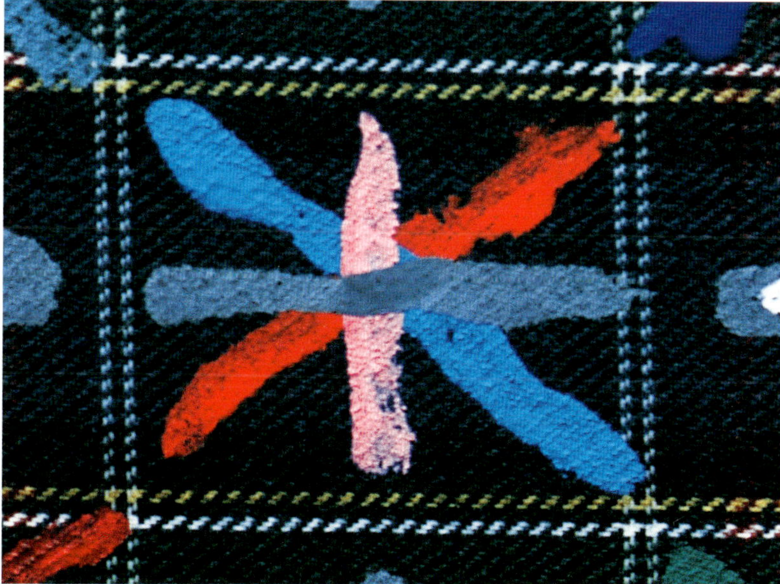

and Stella. His use of abstraction is based on his character, his artistic judgment, and his own personal history. Abstract art is rather uncommon in China. He tells me how after his studies, he began working for a toy company. "Three years later, in 1986, I decided to leave the company and go back to studying painting. I chose to specialize in Chinese painting." Why? "Because I had seen how, in the 1930s, the contact between Chinese and European art had given rise to some very interesting developments. I knew quite a lot about European art, but very little about Chinese art. It was the opportunity I had been waiting for to learn more about this domain, and to counterbalance the influence of European art." ¶ So Ding Yi began studying Chinese art in 1987. He made a fundamental discovery: "I realized that this artistic style did not correspond to the modernity of contemporary Chinese society. I was unsettled by this. I didn't know what to do or how to find my way out of the maze. I decided to forget everything I had ever learned on both the European and Chinese sides and to explore a completely different route." ¶ A return to first principles. In 1988 and 1989, he worked on a combination of art and design, with shapes drawn with a ruler that were to become the crosses of the series *Appearance of Croce*. Ding Yi says, "In these works, I simply reject all sentiment, all feeling, all trembling in the fingers." In the work he shows me, thin strips of white and gray cross at right angles on a blue background. The strips change color at the point where they meet and form a neutral pattern of quadrilaterals on the canvas. ¶ The cross is a very simple shape: two lines crossing at right angles. It is really an allover covering of a colored background. "The cross is simply the basic element of composition of my works," he says. "The cross is what gives the image of abstraction." ¶ Crosses immediately call Malevich and Beuys to mind. Does he feel he owes them anything? No. No more than he does the repetitive activities of the 1970s. "It might look repetitive, but in my mind, it's actually an augmentation. It's not the same thing. Buddhists do the same thing when they pray with beads." ¶ Would it be accurate to talk of an American influence through their design on the one hand, and the impersonal aspect on the other? "No. Back then, in China, the fashionable styles were Expressionism and Surrealism, two schools where emotions play an important role. What I did was in opposition to that." ¶ From 1991 onward, there are signs of a slight development in his work, a first move away from the very minimalist style, but without quite turning his back on his rejection of the excessive emotionalism of Expressionism. "I was trying to recreate a kind of industrial precision," he says. "But at that time, I started to question the value of this precision. Technical precision does not imply precision of thought. So then, while you might note that the lines are, say, a little clumsy, you can still tell that the spirit is perfectly precise. That's the important thing." ¶ His artistic vision moved onto a higher plane in 1997, when he discovered a new material: tartan. Tartan is characterized by its lines, pattern, and colors. "I took advantage of what this industrial product had to offer," he says. He began painting crosses over tartan, sometimes following the patterns, sometimes going against them, sometimes echoing them. In 1997 and 1998, he always left a margin to showcase the cloth used as a background. ¶ In the first works, we can see that he used chalk to trace out his crosses. Is this the influence of the blackboards he drew on as a child? "I can see why you might think so, but it's not the case," he says. And very quickly, he changed style. "For three years, it was a real challenge. I created about a hundred works of art, each in a different style." His current

FACING PAGE: SEVERAL FABULOUS WORKS IN CHALK ON CARDBOARD BY DING YI DATING FROM 1996 AND 1997, NOW IN THE CAAW GALLERY. THEY DATE FROM BEFORE THE ARTIST'S DISCOVERY OF TARTAN, WHICH HE NOW USES, DRAWING HIS OWN CROSSES OVER THE PATTERN OF THE FABRIC, AS ABOVE.

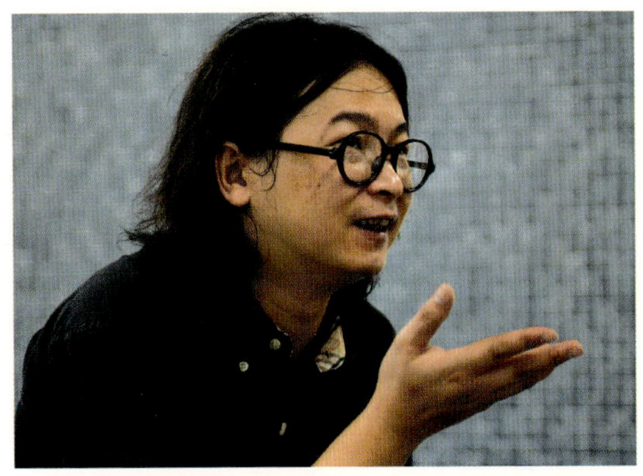

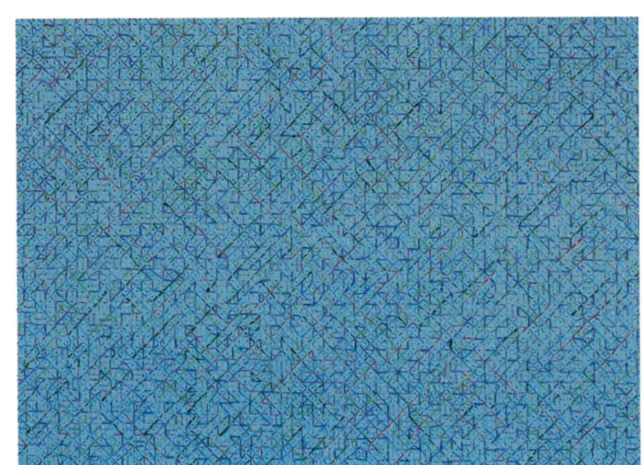

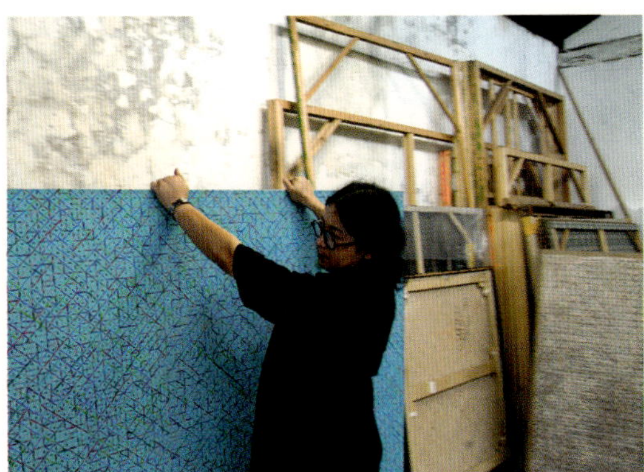

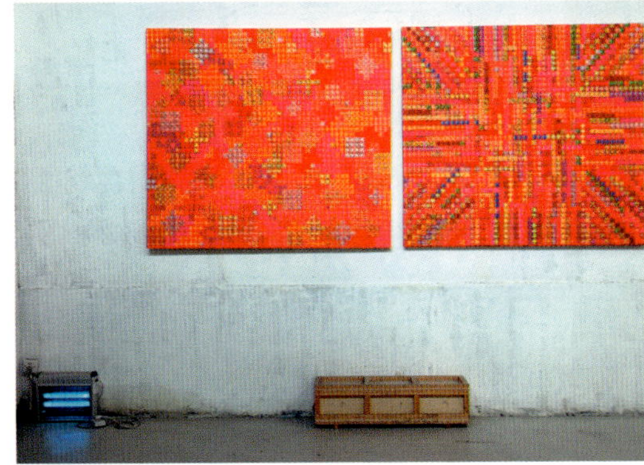

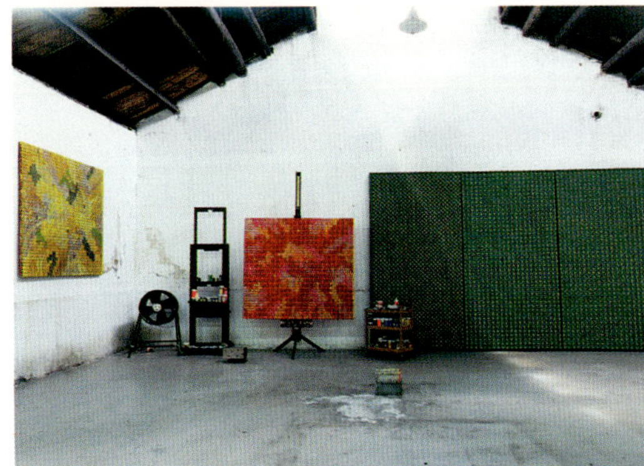

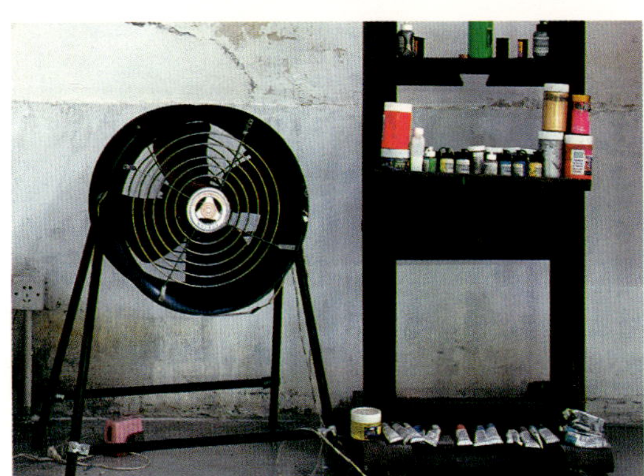

FACING PAGE: VARIATIONS ON THE SIMPLEST OF THEMES: A SERIES OF CROSSES IN EVER MORE FLUORESCENT COLORS THAT REPRESENT SHANGHAI BY NIGHT, ACCORDING TO DING YI. ABOVE: SOME RECENT WORKS. TOP RIGHT: THE ARTIST WITH A WORK DATING FROM 1997.

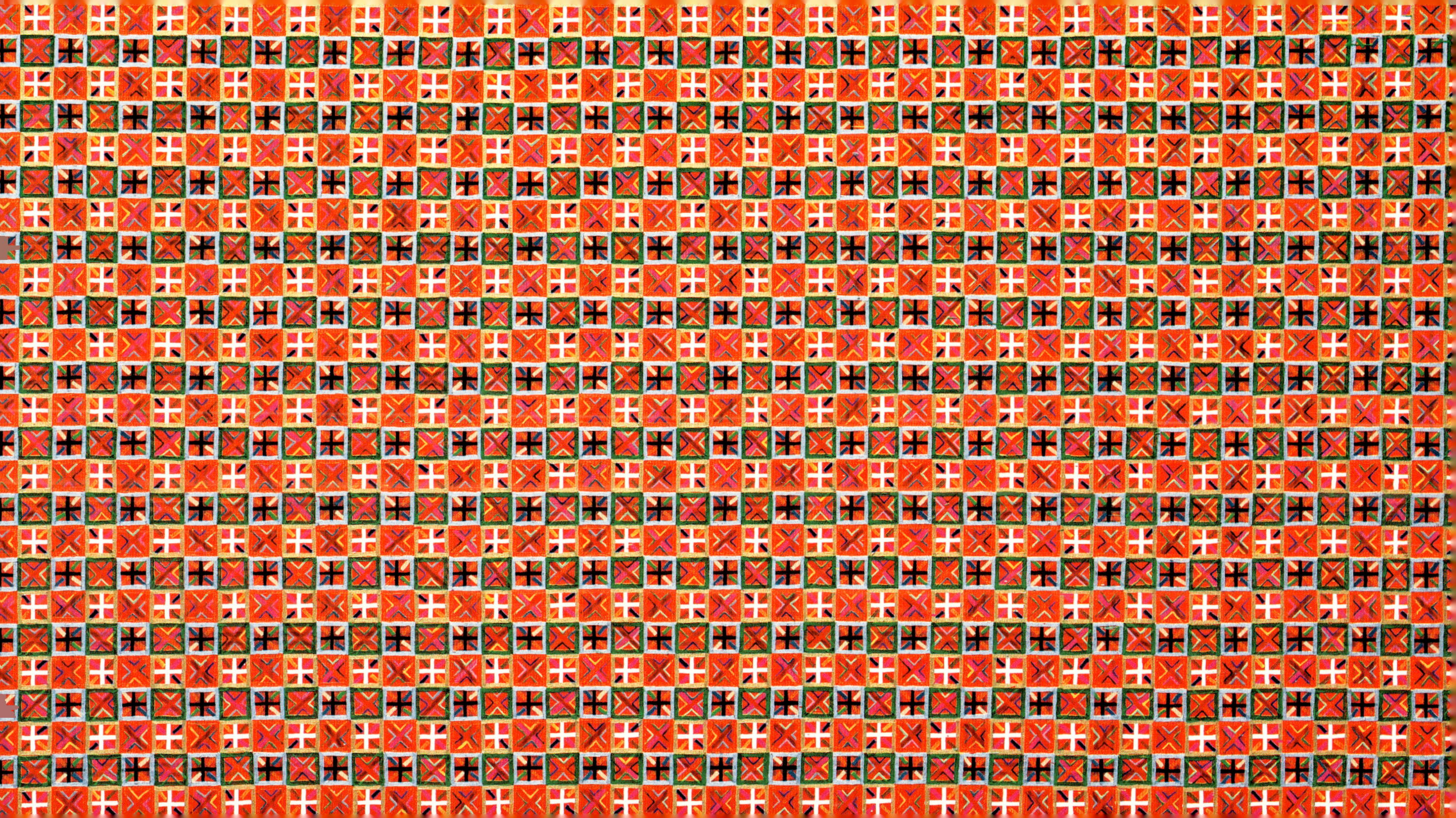

choice of color is bright fluorescent shades. ¶ In 1998, at the second Shanghai Biennial, he met an art teacher from Vancouver. The two started chatting. The Canadian told him that Shanghai today is a lot like Paris in the 1920s or 1930s, but that modern artists do not seem to go with the modern Shanghai. In 1920s and 1930s Paris, artists painted the city they saw around them. In Shanghai, artists seem very keen to keep their distance from the city. "This notion had a very strong impact on me," Ding Yi says in an intense voice. ¶ He told himself that he had to connect his art to the period he was living in. His first decision was to move from his studio in the suburbs to one right in the heart of Shanghai: "The better to feel the city, with its brash advertising." He paints in fluorescent colors borrowed from the streets and the television. In neon-bright hues. ¶ And today? He is still doing the same thing, painting the same motifs with acid-bright colors that seem to fill the air with crackling electricity. ¶ How does an artist like him make a living? Apparently he is not suffering particular hardship. He rents his studio from a textiles company. He sells his canvases through two of the most reputed galleries in Shanghai and Beijing, Shanghart and CAAW. On average, he sells a dozen or so works—his entire annual output—for about ten thousand dollars. Ninety-five percent of his works are sold abroad, only five percent remaining in China. These figures are similar for most Chinese artists—and even then, only recently have Chinese collectors been able to buy even five percent of the works. ¶ Ding Yi says, "There are two types of art collectors in China, among the wealthiest sector of the population. The first is the people who buy with the intention of founding a museum one day. They want to buy works by all the most important artists, and preferably several dating from different periods. The second group is bigger: it consists of people who buy art to go with the interior design of their office." Since Ding Yi's work is considered decorative, his future is assured from that point of view. ¶ What about the museums? In China, they are just beginning to buy art and build up their collections. But since their budgets are tiny, they drive a hard bargain with the artists directly, without consulting the galleries. What does Ding Yi think about this? "I accept because I am not very prolific," he says. "But it's not the museums that are doing me a favor, but the opposite." Ding Yi also has a further source of income: he teaches at the School of Fine Arts, where he studied. ¶ Ding Yi, a fervent admirer of Mondrian, is one of just a handful of abstract painters in China. With an almost obsessive consistency, and just as constant—and highly subtle—variations, he has been painting crosses for over ten years. He gives each work the same title: *Appearance of Croce*. ¶ I have heard it said that his work is akin to calligraphy. It is not an obvious comparison. But when you have become fully imbued with the meditative and spiritual dimension of the undertaking, you begin to see where the comparison comes from. His alternation of crosses and Xs is, after all, reminiscent of computer languages. His work is calligraphy for the computer age, where words are transformed into binary code, then electronic or optical pulses, traveling ever faster.

FACING PAGE: TOP LEFT: *OUTSIDE-INSIDE*. TOP RIGHT: TUBES OF PAINT TO SHOW THAT DING YI IS A GENUINE ARTIST. BOTTOM LEFT: THE WORK SEEMS TO PICK UP THE PATTERN OF THE FABRIC COVERING THE ARMCHAIR. BOTTOM RIGHT: DING YI SITTING IN THE QING ARMCHAIR.

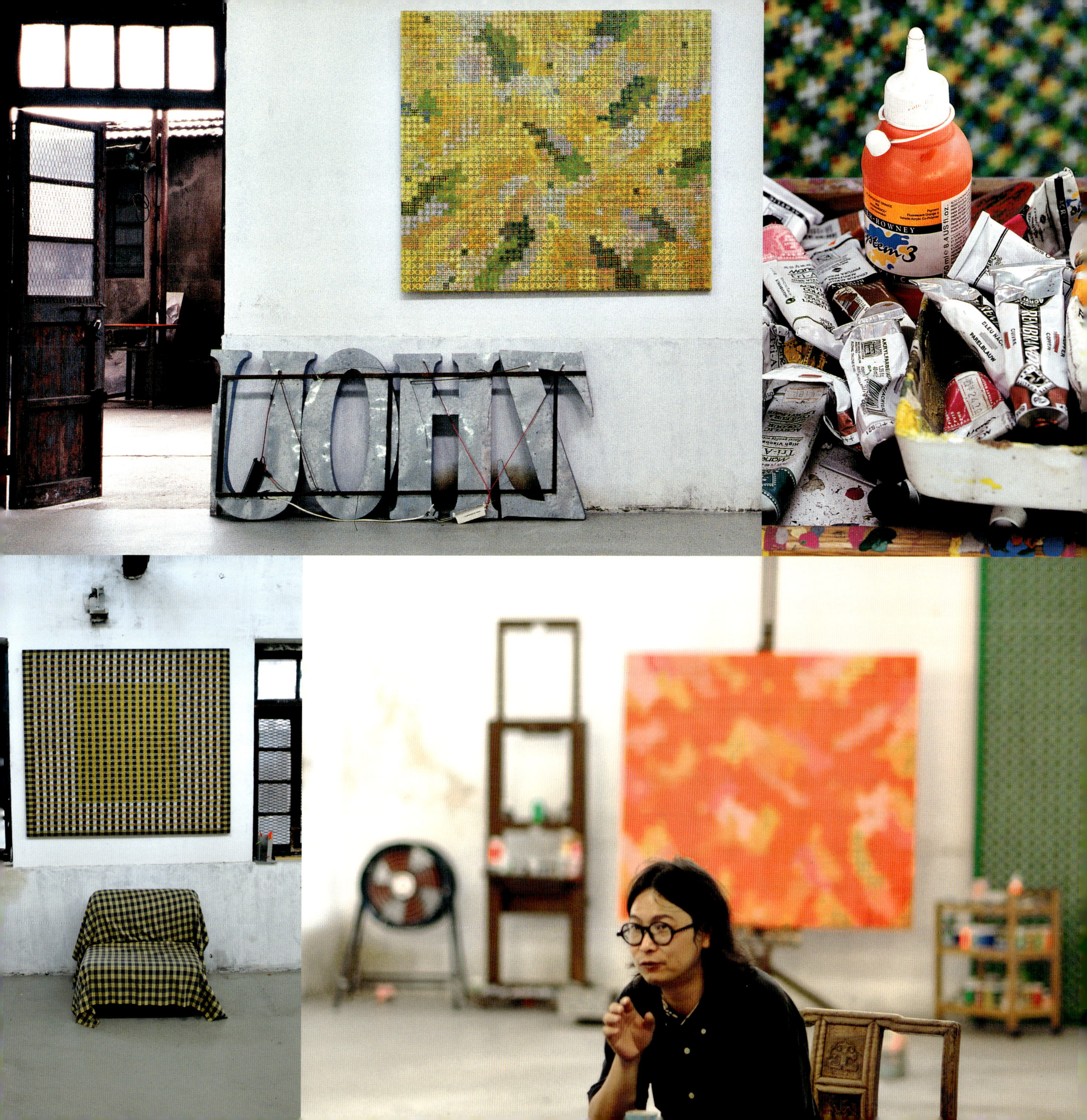

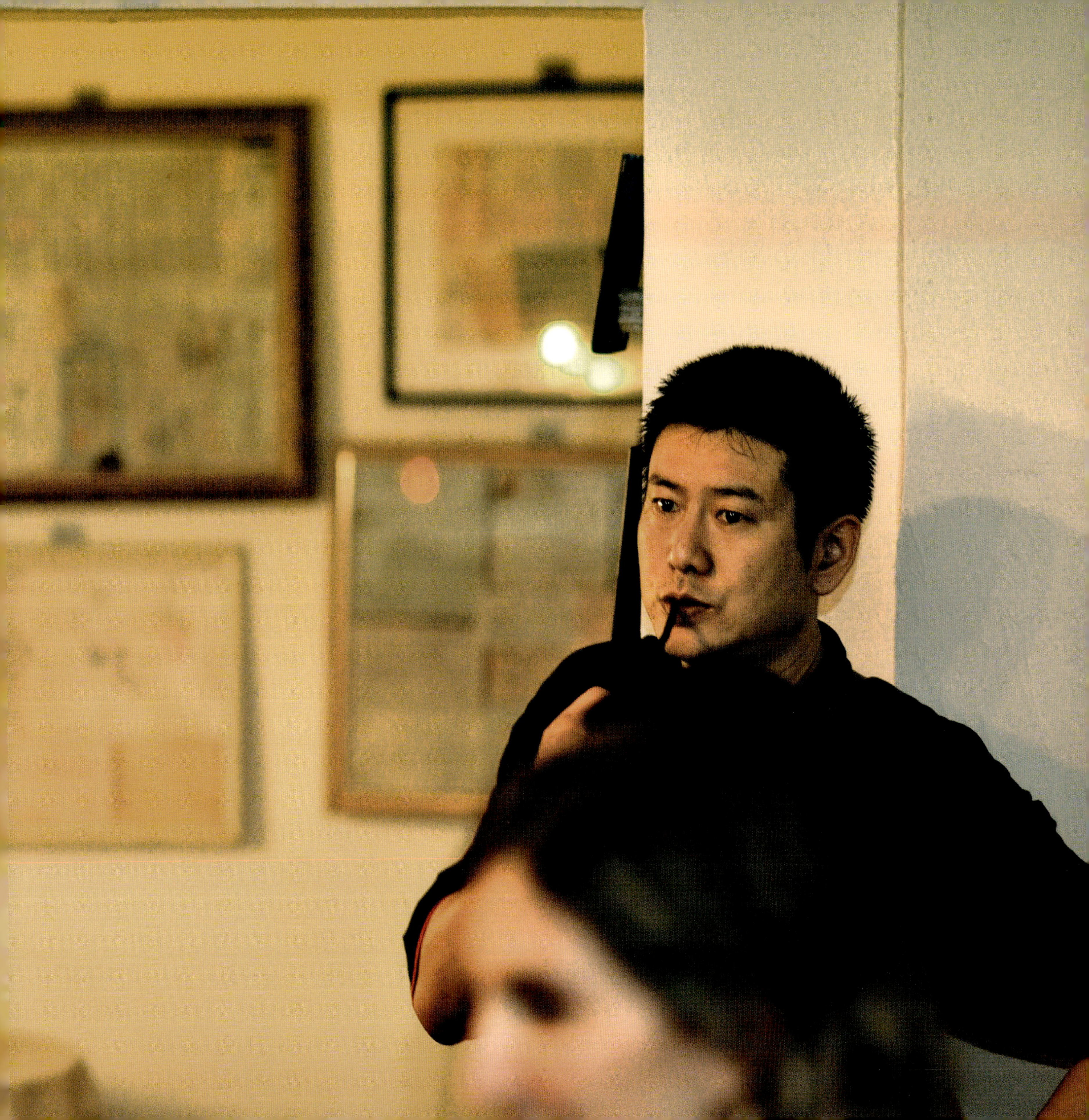

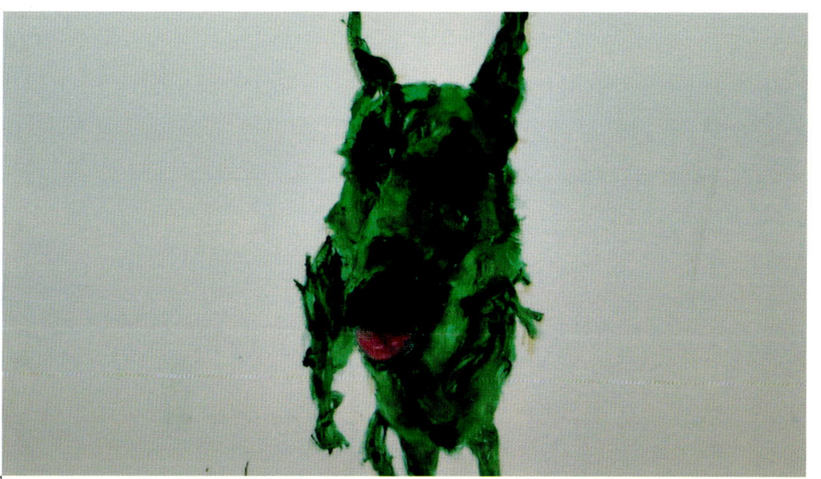

ZHOU CHUNYA

October 11, 2003. A news agency has just announced that from now on, forty breeds of dog are banned in China, including German shepherds and Dalmatians. Poor Zhou Chunya. He is still suffering because of his love of dogs in general, and German shepherds in particular. He thought that now that he was famous, and with the market economy in full swing, he would finally be able to buy a house with a garden, and the German shepherd of his dreams. And then came the press announcement. ¶ When I saw him in Beijing in August 2003, he was radiant with happiness at the thought of soon having his own dog, and the house and land to go with it. True happiness was within his grasp. The other dog, the one in his paintings, Hei Gen (Black Root), wasted away and finally died in 1999, without ever leaving the fifth-floor apartment in Chengdu where Zhou Chunya has always lived and worked. ¶ It should be noted that my intention is not to paint a picture of a shy, solitary man at ease only when he is alone with his dog. He is a frequent visitor to Beijing, which is a fair distance from Chengdu. He is a familiar face at vernissages and is on friendly terms with a number of artists, painters in particular. Zeng Hao is a good friend. ¶ In fact, I first met Zhou Chunya when he was visiting Zeng Hao. While I was interviewing Zeng Hao, the cell phone in his pocket rang. He held it close to his ear. Zeng Hao smiled, began chatting, listened, replied, listened again, explained something at great length. Apparently someone was calling him from a taxi and was in need of directions to his studio, the interpreter explained. "It's Zhou Chunya," Zeng Hao announced. ¶ The first impression you get of Zhou Chunya is of a tall, somewhat bulky man. His hair is cut short and sticks out at comical angles. He has a more than passing resemblance to a bear—solid yet cuddly. His face is open and expressive. He is not a great one for talking, but when you ask him questions, he talks easily. No hesitations, no regrets. He is very clear. ¶ I began this text by writing about his dog. It is a major feature of his life. Almost all of Zhou Chunya's work is based on this aspect of his life. He has been called a Chinese Wegman. It is a tempting comparison at first sight, but in fact his art has little in common with Wegman's apart from the dog—which he paints green. ¶ So why green? "It happened in 1997, quite by chance," Zhou Chunya explains. "I was putting on a green undercoat to paint over, and I just thought it looked good like that. And when I painted the genitals and mouth in red, I thought the contrast was particularly striking. Over the years, I've accentuated this aspect, using more acid greens and brighter, more raw-looking reds." ¶ When he was given the dog as a gift, it was a cute little puppy. Very rapidly, it became a less cute, fully grown German shepherd. It is hard to find out whether German shepherds were already banned in China at that time. I have had differing reports. But in any case, owning such a dog was not looked on favorably by the authorities. ¶ Are German shepherds aggressive by nature? Zhou Chunya says not, but as a precautionary measure, either because he was obliged to or because he was given to understand that it would be better all around, he kept the dog shut up in his little apartment. Gradually, the animal wasted away and eventually died in 1999. Zhou Chunya was deeply pained by his loss. For two years, he found it impossible to paint his dog, either from memory or from a photograph. Eventually, he was able to begin painting dogs again, but I can still sense the underlying pain that has never quite left him. During those two years, he painted rocks, more of which later. "I painted other things, but I like talking about my dog. In any case, I share most people's opinion when they say that the dog series is their favorite," he says. In 2001, he began painting dogs again, based on his hundreds of photographs and from other dogs. The green dog (a bitch, in fact) shown at the Centre Pompidou's 2003 China exhibition was painted from a live "model." Zhou Chunya says, "My dog was a male. My biggest regret is not having been able to mate him with a bitch. He wasn't really happy." ¶ This was in Chengdu. Chengdu, where he lives, and where I never managed to go and see him. Chengdu, a large city in the mountains, not far from Tibet, where the weather is mild and the cuisine spicy, as in most of Sichuan. Chengdu, where people leave to make their fortune and return to the city when they retire, as life here is pleasant and the people friendly. ¶ Zhou Chunya was born in 1955 in the city of Chongqing, the main industrial center in southern China, 190 miles (three hundred kilometers) southeast of Chengdu. Chongqing's streets are steep and

FACING PAGE: ZHOU CHUNYA VISITING BEIJING. HE NORMALLY LIVES IN CHENGDU, NEAR THE BORDER WITH TIBET. ABOVE: THE GREEN DOG THAT BROUGHT HIM FAME AND EARNED HIM COMPARISONS WITH THE US ARTIST WILLIAM WEGMAN.

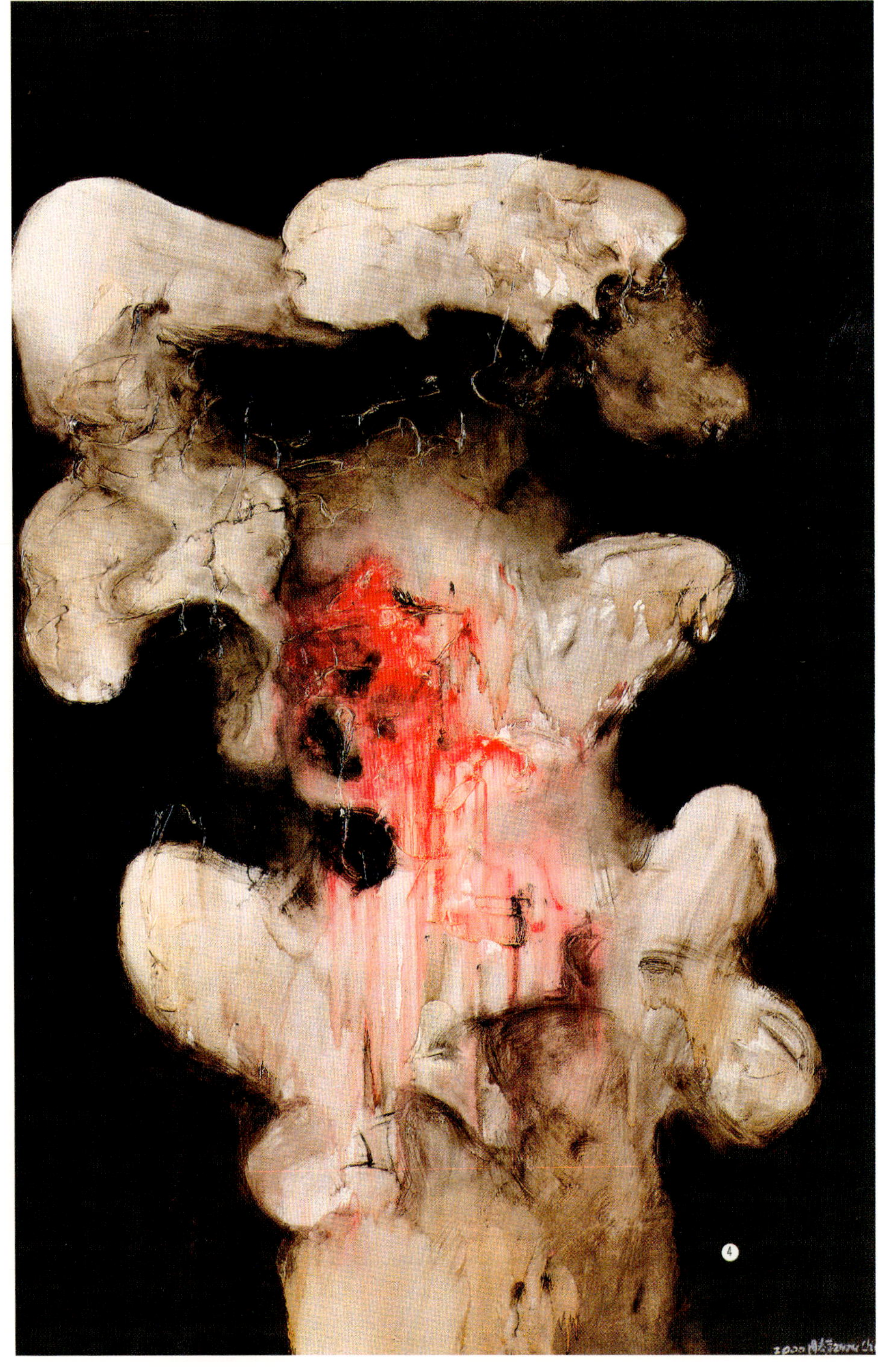

TAI LAKE STONE, 2000, A PAINTING FROM THE SERIES OF WORKS ON THE TAIHU ROCKS THAT ZHOU CHUNYA BEGAN AFTER THE DEATH OF HIS DOG. HE SAYS THAT, FOR HIM, STONES ARE LIKE LIVING BEINGS.

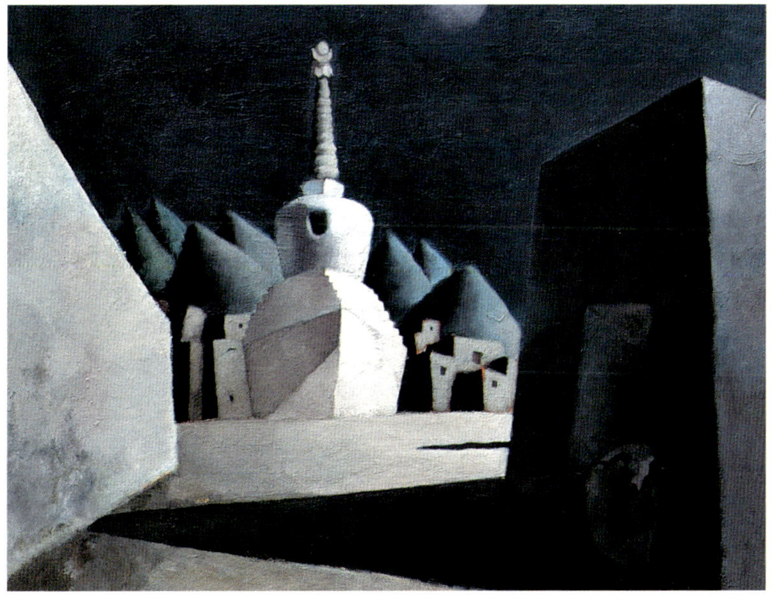

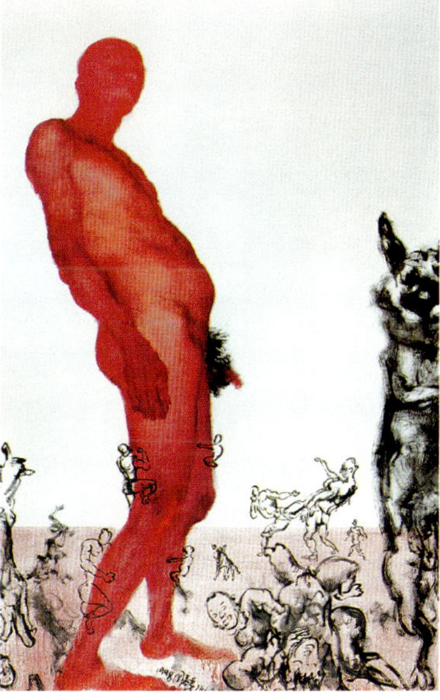

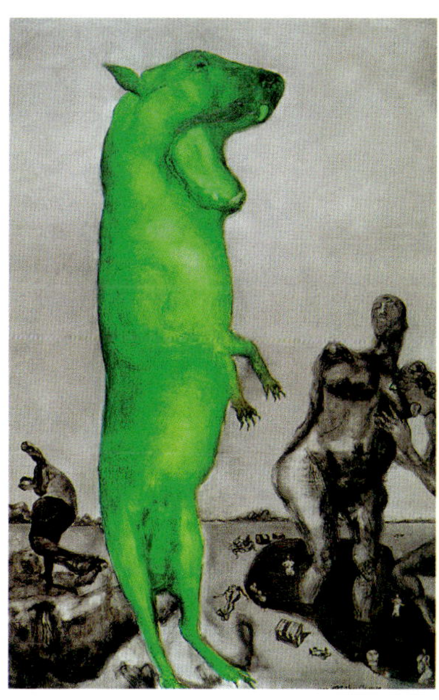

narrow: there are two cable lifts but no bicycles. The city is renowned for its sweltering summers. ¶ Actually, Zhou Chenya's parents left Chongqing shortly after his birth. He spent his entire childhood in Chengdu. His parents were civil servants. His father was a literary critic who worked at the Writers' Foundation. He was a Communist intellectual. His mother followed the Communists from Shanghai to Sichuan where she worked in a music school as the party representative. "I grew up surrounded by culture," Zhou Chunya says, forgetting the highly charged political atmosphere that was also an integral part of his childhood. ¶ His father collected works of art and encouraged his son's love of painting as soon as it became apparent. Sadly, he died when Zhou Chunya was fourteen. He says, "The two biggest tragedies in life are losing your father and losing your dog." He lost both. He adds quietly, "The Cultural Revolution hurt my father very badly." ¶ I venture to ask his opinion on the subject of the Cultural Revolution. "The Cultural Revolution?" He pauses for a few moments. "I was eleven when it began. I didn't really understand what was happening, but I felt instinctively that it was changing the lives of Chinese people a great deal." Another pause. "Without the Cultural Revolution, China would not be where it is today. Before, Chinese society was very isolated. Afterwards, things began to open up. But the Cultural Revolution also had a lot of very negative sides. It destroyed many traditions and many of the old ways wholesale. Today, most young people have neither their traditional culture nor Western culture. It's a complex question. Like the personality of Mao, who was a great man. Yet he did a lot of very bad things, too." ¶ Zhou Chunya began painting when he was sixteen. From 1971 to 1974, he studied at one of the few remaining schools of fine art, named July 5th, after the date of one of Chairman Mao's key speeches. "I had a small grant and I had enough to eat meat two or three times a week in a period of the utmost poverty," he says. At the art school, the only authorized source of inspiration was the life of the peasants, workers, and soldiers, painted in the Soviet Social Realist style. Zhou Chunya was lucky: his father had instilled in him a love of oil painting and an appreciation of the Soviet Social Realism school, which in the 1970s was tending to replace traditional Chinese painting. ¶ For three years after the end of his studies, he worked for an "artistic company," churning out countless portraits of Mao. It was propaganda painting, pure and simple, and Zhou Chunya worked at it diligently. He had no qualms about making a living from propaganda. ¶ In 1977, he began studying again, this time alongside Zhang Xiaogang, at the Academy of Fine Arts in Chongqing, which reopened at the end of the Cultural Revolution. He discovered Western Realist art and Impressionist painters such as Courbet and Monet. ¶ In 1980, he moved to Tibet to work on a series of paintings of various tribes in their traditional costumes. His works from this period are a rather charming blend of Impressionism and Realism. These paintings were very much appreciated in the 1980s, at a time when Zhou Chunya was moving toward a more metaphysical approach, Fauvism, and Expressionism. ¶ He also painted flowers as a way of exploring the notion of pure color. "It was a time of ideology. It was not absolutely negative. It gave my generation a lot of idealism and determination." ¶ In 1986, he was invited to Germany by a friend who was living there at the time. He visited museums and galleries, learned German very quickly, talked to many people, observed them, and tried to understand. "I loved German art, but I didn't like life in Germany at all," he now says. It hardly mattered. He was immediately bowled over by his discovery of the Neo-Expressionist art of Baselitz and Kiefer. In 1987, after a year's break, he started painting again—not green dogs, but red horses and blue cows. ¶ At this point, his life was turned around

FROM LEFT TO RIGHT: *WHITE STUPA*, 1986, WHICH ZHOU CHUNYA PAINTED ON A JOURNEY IN WESTERN CHINA AT A TIME WHEN RESEARCHING CHINA'S TRIBAL MINORITIES WAS A WAY TO GET AWAY FROM SOCIALIST REALISM. *HUMAN FIGURE 3*, 1998. *LOVER UNDER THE MOON*, 1997.

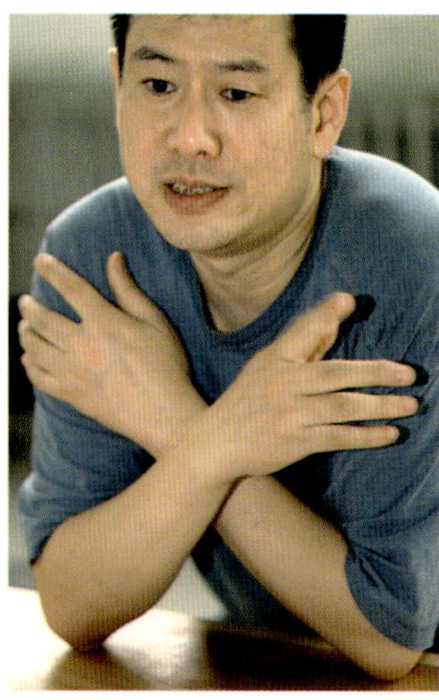

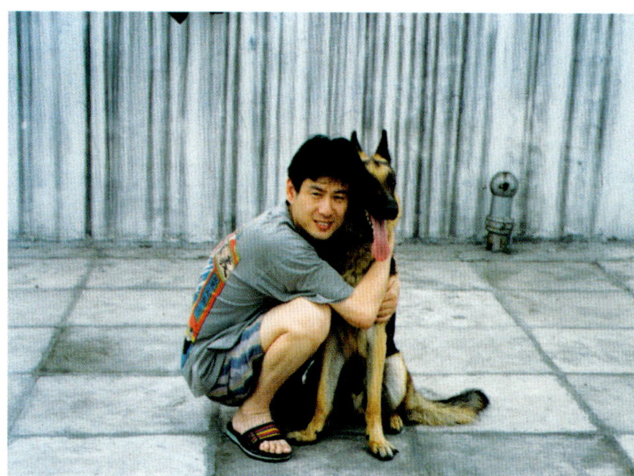

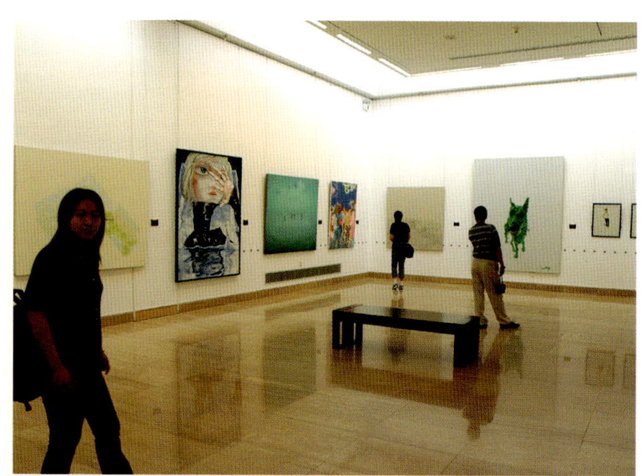

again by a mysterious cassette that he was sent from China, of two friends playing traditional Chinese airs on old musical instruments. He was deeply touched, and decided to work at reviving the old Chinese artistic values that he had suppressed since childhood. He settled down to study Chinese art as he never had before, deeply troubled by his ignorance of his own country's traditions. ¶ He graduated from Kassel and returned home shortly before history was made in Tiananmen Square by the euphoria and tragedy of those few days. He returned to Germany a year later, before finally coming back to Chengdu. ¶ In 1992, he produced a number of fantastical, extravagantly colored paintings of the rocks that he decided to make his principal subject from then on. He gradually stopped going to Tibet, devoting himself instead to the fabulous gardens of Suzhou or Lake Tai Hu, taking photographs of interesting rock formations and producing paintings based on the photographs. What is most striking about his paintings is that they give the rocks volume rather than shape, thanks to the play of light and shadows. They are heavily anthropomorphized, with red splashes where the genitalia would be. He says, "I see the rocks as living beings." All of these paintings were shown in 1993 at the *Chinese Experience* exhibition in Chengdu. ¶ Some critics have over-hastily pronounced that Zhou Chunya's subjects are Chinese, but that he paints them in a Western manner. In an era dominated by Political Pop Art, Zhou Chunya feels the need above all to express himself, as shown in the highly erotic series dating from 1994. Working on the edge of the tradition that sees rocks as a metaphorical, miniaturized representation of mountains—a metaphor traditionally expressed in ink—Zhou Chunya preferred to stick with oils, which allowed him to demonstrate all his force and vigor. ¶ In 1995, so the story goes, a friend gave Zhou Chunya a puppy, which he christened Hei Gen. It was love at first sight. He loved the dog so much that he let it share his bed and even claimed he could read its mind. But the German shepherd grew quickly and was soon far too large for his small apartment. To the end of its life, it was Zhou Chunya's principal—indeed, almost his only—model. ¶ He painted the dog sitting, standing, lying with its paws in the air, enormous tongue lolling from its jaws, baring its teeth, blended with its shadow, tucked away in a corner of the canvas, its legs folded underneath it, with bright red gums and equally red genitals. ¶ In 1997, he produced one of his most famous paintings, showing Hei Gen standing on its hind legs, like a terrible avenging angel against a background of corruption. The title of the work was *Lover under the Moon*. The dog is green and the human figures black. Then realism takes over and the shapes become more deformed; limbs are distorted, the paint runs, flows, spatters. Zhou Chunya tried out large format paintings, up to eight feet by six feet (250 centimeters by 200 centimeters). Another success. He rode on the crest of the wave until 1999 when Hei Gen—by then an icon almost as famous as William Wegman's Man Ray—died. ¶ Zhou Chunya was as desolate as if he had lost a brother or a child. He returned to his rocks and painted "red men" with highly sexual connotations. In 2001, his period of mourning over, he began to live again. He was seized with a hurricane of energy, painting frenetically, throwing drawings based on photographs or other sources down on the paper dogs, monsters, and golems. Magic evocations of a lost supernatural love. ¶ It is easy to see that they are just simulacra. But somehow, they blend into a lyrical, sacrificial offering. Pure incandescence.

THE GREEN DOG, IN THE NATIONAL MUSEUM OF MODERN AND CONTEMPORARY ART IN BEIJING (PICTURED ABOVE), WAS A GERMAN SHEPHERD CALLED HEI GEN. THE ANIMAL HAS TAKEN ON MYTHICAL STATUS SINCE ITS DEATH. FACING PAGE: *YOUNG BITCH*, 2002.

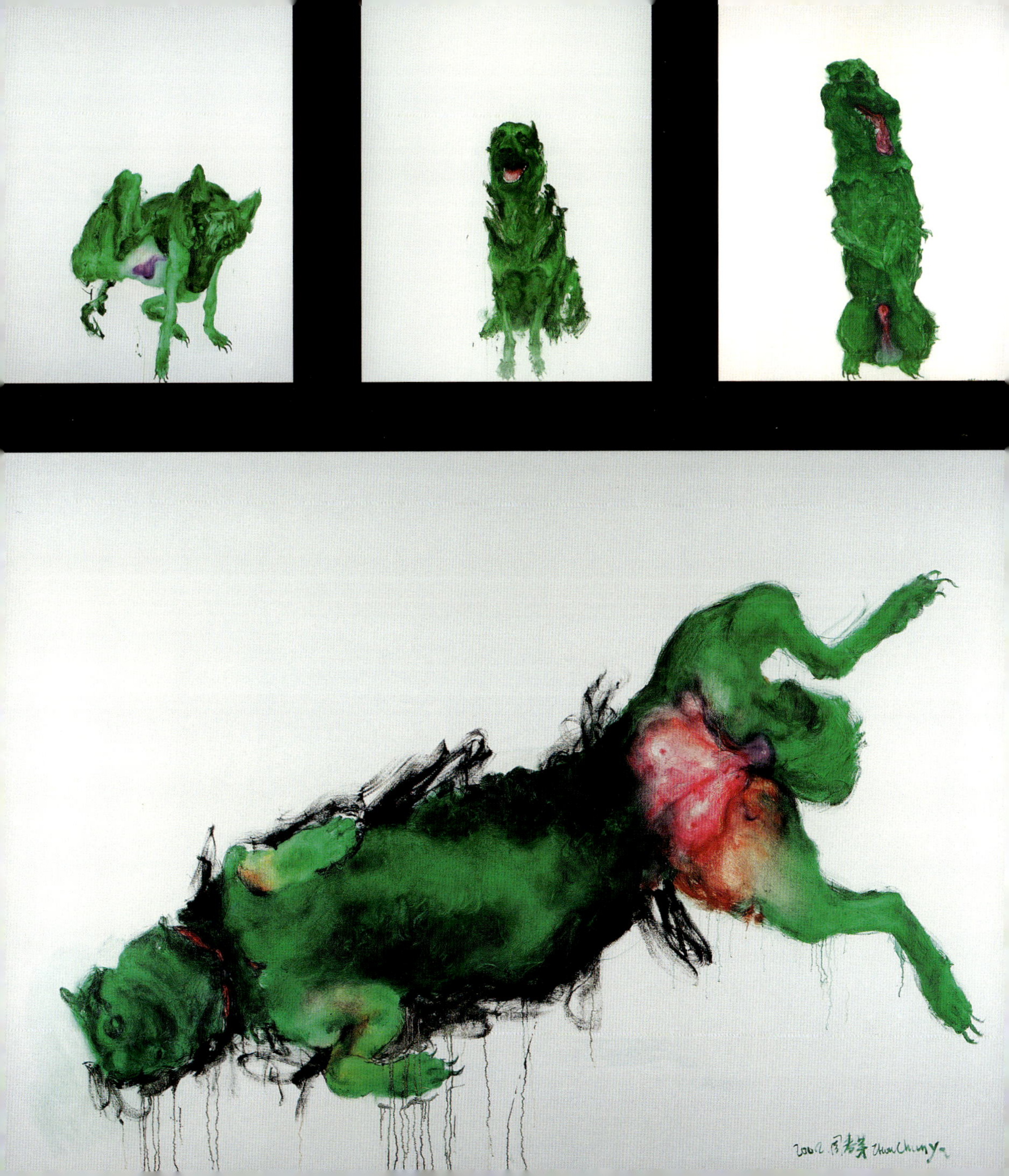

2002 周春芽 Zhou Chunya

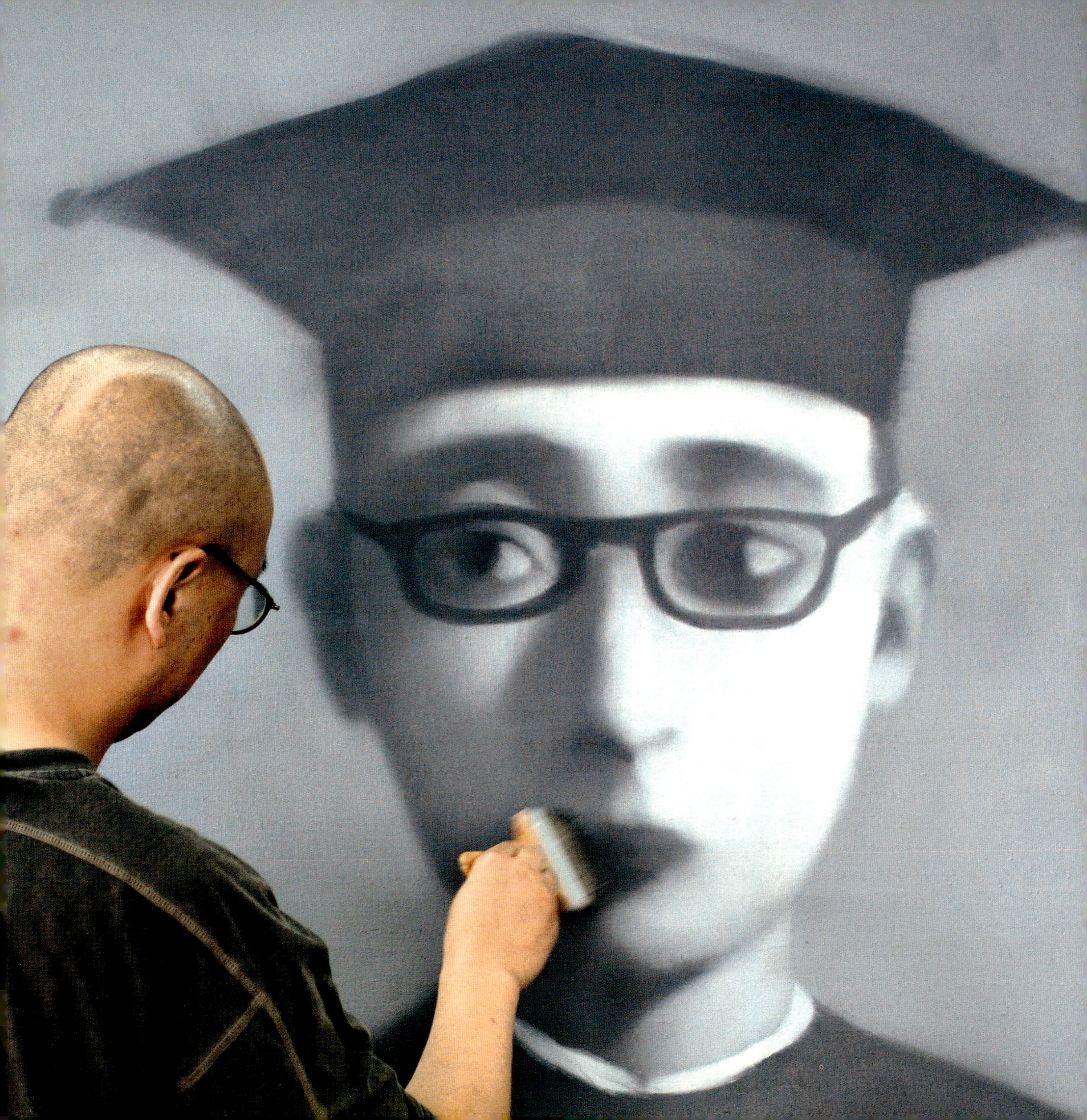

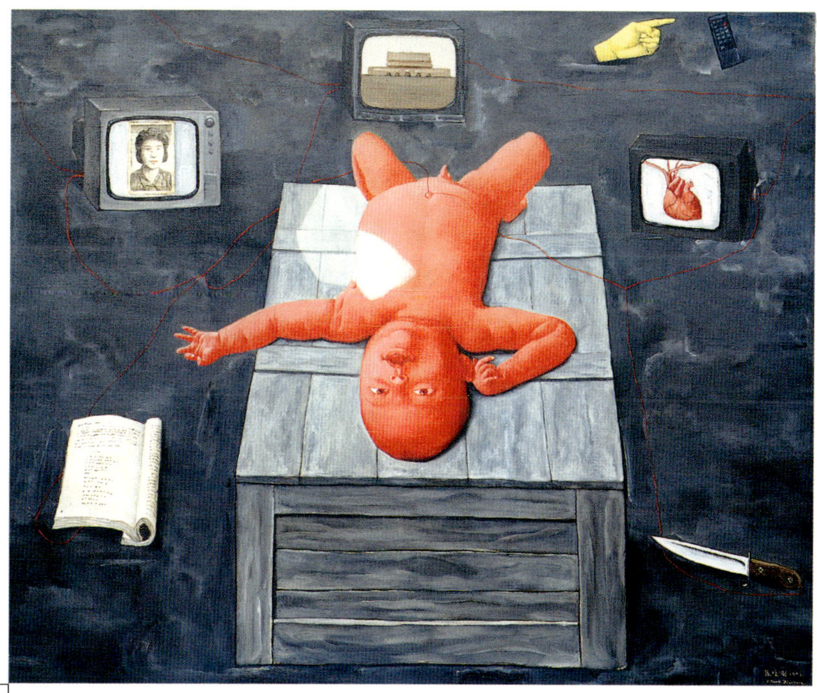

ZHANG XIAOGANG

The driver has brought me to the northeast corner of Beijing, to a part of the suburbs where the houses are almost outnumbered by fields. He has never been to this part of the city before, and we get hopelessly lost. We stop several times to telephone or to ask for directions. Finally we end up on a road with a field to the right, and low, one- or two-story buildings on the left. We pull up by a large gate surrounded with name plaques for the Imagine Gallery, Red Gate Arts and Studio, and Shangrillart. Have we arrived? We push the gate open. I recognize the former Mustard project, an ambitious building program set up just two years ago by a local yuppie who hoped to make this outlying suburb a magnet for Beijing art lovers. I first visited the site back when the work was beginning. Today, the covered "street" is full of hippie-chic studios and unlikely looking galleries. A girl dressed in what look like rags but are probably the work of some top designer points the way to Zhang Xiaogang's studio, on a street parallel to the one outside the gate. ¶ I noted down the name of the neighborhood, Biegao, in the village of Cuigezhuang. Did I write it down right? Here we are. The entrance is hardly inviting. Behind the gateway we find the doorman who looks after a "street" very similar to the first. The buildings are all in pink brick. On the left is a row of identical studios that bear a striking resemblance to enormous prison cells. There are twelve in total, with seven artists working in them. Further on, more studios are being built. I ask whether the artists have bought the studios, or whether they just rent them. Apparently the answer is rather complicated. Someone explains that the studios belong to the local farmers. It is not quite clear whom the land belongs to, the government or the local authorities. In any case, there is no way the artists can buy their studios. ¶ "I haven't been here for two months, so it's a bit dusty," Zhang Xiaogang warns us before we go in. The floor is concrete; the walls are painted white. A number of fluorescent strip lights bathe the studio in a harsh glow. It is a vast space, practically empty but for two canvases on easels and one propped against the far wall, with the painted side hidden. Zhang Xiaogang is working on the two paintings on the easels. He always has several paintings in the works—sometimes four or five, sometimes just two, like today. They are nearly finished. Along the right-hand wall are a cupboard, a small structure built of bricks, two very modern chairs, and a sofa. In the center of the studio are a table and chairs, also the work of a modern designer. ¶ He started renting the studio in February 2002. He has two others, one in Yunnan province, where his parents live, and one in Chengdu, where his daughter lives. Wherever he is, he works according to the same rhythm, getting up late, painting all the afternoon, and then staying up very late. He produces about thirty paintings a year. ¶ He was born in 1958 in Yunnan province, like his friend Zeng Hao, but his family moved away when he was four. He grew up in Sichuan, a little further north. The Cultural Revolution began when he was eight and living in Chengdu with his parents, who were both civil servants. It lasted throughout his formative years until he was eighteen. He says

FACING PAGE: ZHANG XIAOGANG AT WORK IN HIS STUDIO. HE USES A VERY SOFT BRUSH AND RUNNY PAINT. ABOVE: *RED BABY*, 1993, WHICH HE SEES AS ONE OF HIS MOST IMPORTANT EARLY PAINTINGS.

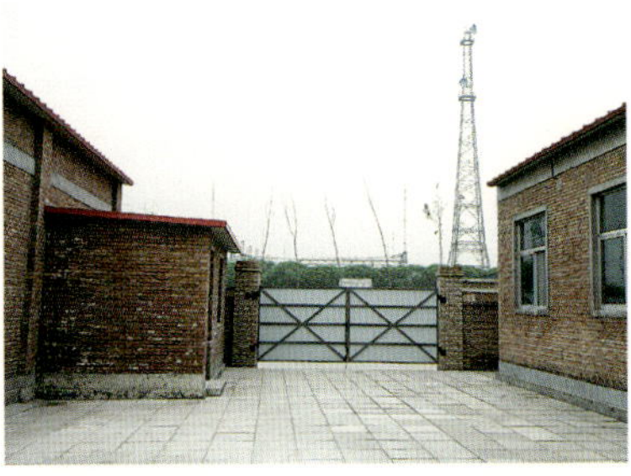

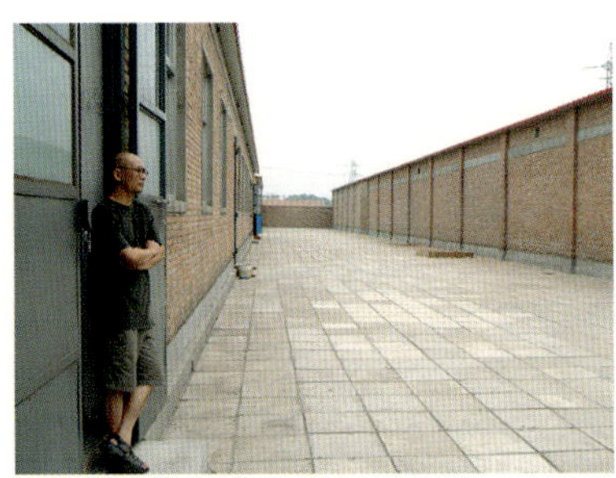

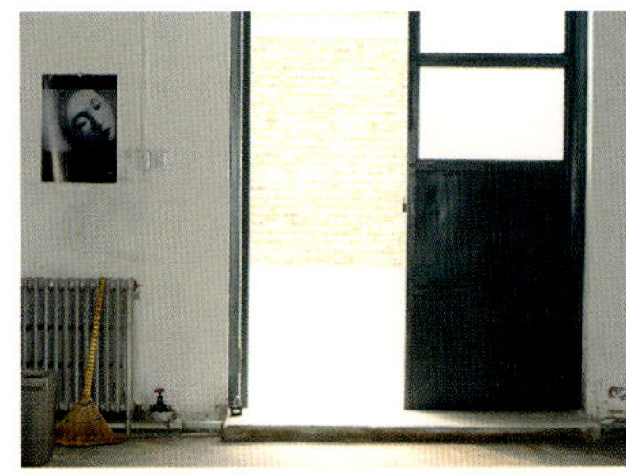

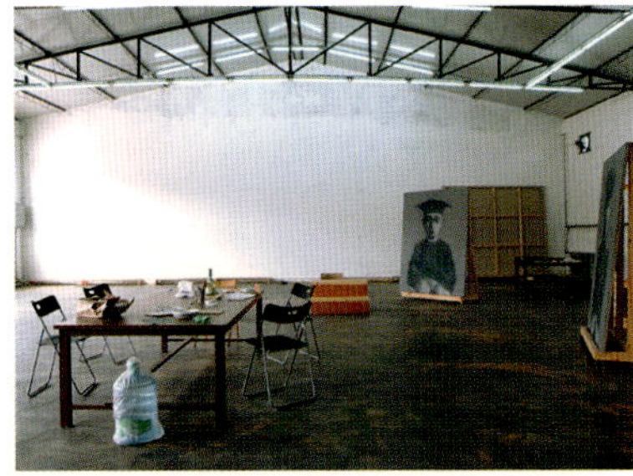

pretty much the same thing as most of the other artists about the Cultural Revolution. (I'm almost tempted to believe that they passed the word around, or that the Western perception of events is completely skewed, or that the experience was simply beyond description). "To begin with, it was fun. When you're eight, it's great not having to go to school. It was pretty good." Then the internal struggles between revolutionary factions began. There were demonstrations. People were beaten up in the streets. By 1972, the situation was desperate. Zhang Xiaogang's parents were arrested and imprisoned for three years. Zhang Xiaogang had three siblings, and the four children looked after each other and got through the darkest times. He is reluctant to talk about his past, but someone else told me that in the final years of the Cultural Revolution, he was sent to be reeducated with peasants in a remote village in Yunnan province. This period of his life affected him deeply. ¶ Eventually, Zhang Xiaogang was accepted at the Sichuan School of Fine Art. He says, "I couldn't choose where to study, but as it happens, it was the third-best school in China. I learned a lot of important things there, and it certainly changed my life." ¶ It was far from easy to be accepted into art school back then. In 1977, the first year after the Cultural Revolution, the art schools were authorized to reopen, and there were vast numbers of applicants. Most of the places were reserved for applicants from the region. Only two places were available for students from Yunnan, one for oil painting, and one for engraving. Zhang Xiaogang was accepted to study oil painting. ¶ His principal subject back then was the Tibetan people and their traditional lifestyle, which he painted in a folk realist style, vaguely influenced by Expressionism. It was rather a brave choice in a time when art was dominated by Socialist Realism. "But the lives and traditions of the people I was painting didn't actually interest me all that much," he says. "What I did find thrilling was their—and my—emotion at the grandiose spectacle of nature." ¶ He graduated in 1982. "Getting into the school was incredibly difficult, but getting my diploma was actually very easy," he says. But once he had his diploma, what next? "I looked for work all over the place, but I couldn't find anything. I wanted to teach, but all the jobs went to people who had a more classical style than me." ¶ He began working for a dance troupe, designing costumes and scenery. "I was seen as something of an oddity in the troupe," he laughs. "The dancers clearly didn't understand where I was coming from or what I was up to. But it was a very important time for me. That was when I learned about Western painting." ¶ Four years later, he was offered a teaching post. Together with a few friends, he founded a group of figurative artists. In those days, artists were setting up groups and schools all over China as a reaction against the dryly academic style that still dominated the art world and condemned these upstarts as nothing more than spiritual pollution. ¶ For example, Cheng Cong Lin, the School of the Wound, was founded in reaction to the Cultural Revolution, while Gao Xiao Hua, the School of the Countryside, brought together artists who painted the lives of peasants. Artists in northern China founded the school of reasonable painting, while Zhang Xiaogang and his friends specialized in what they called sensitive painting. Together with two friends from Kunming, Mao Xuehui and Ye Yongqing, he set up the New Images group. ¶ The group was influenced by Surrealist painting. Zhang Xiaogang particularly admired Magritte. Although it is not generally acknowledged, Surrealism was a major influence on many Chinese artists of Zhang Xiaogang and Wang Guangyi's generation. They found in Surrealism an echo of the fantasy, imagination, and sense of wonder that are so prevalent in Chinese literature. Zhang Xiaogang says, "Chinese philosophy and religion are both highly poetic and sensitive." ¶

FROM LEFT TO RIGHT: THE ENTRANCE TO THE STUDIOS WHERE ZHANG XIAOGANG WORKS ALONGSIDE ZHENG HAO IN THE NORTHEAST OF BEIJING. ZHANG XIAOGANG AT THE ENTRANCE TO HIS STUDIO. THE DOOR TO THE STUDIO AND A VIEW OF THE INTERIOR.

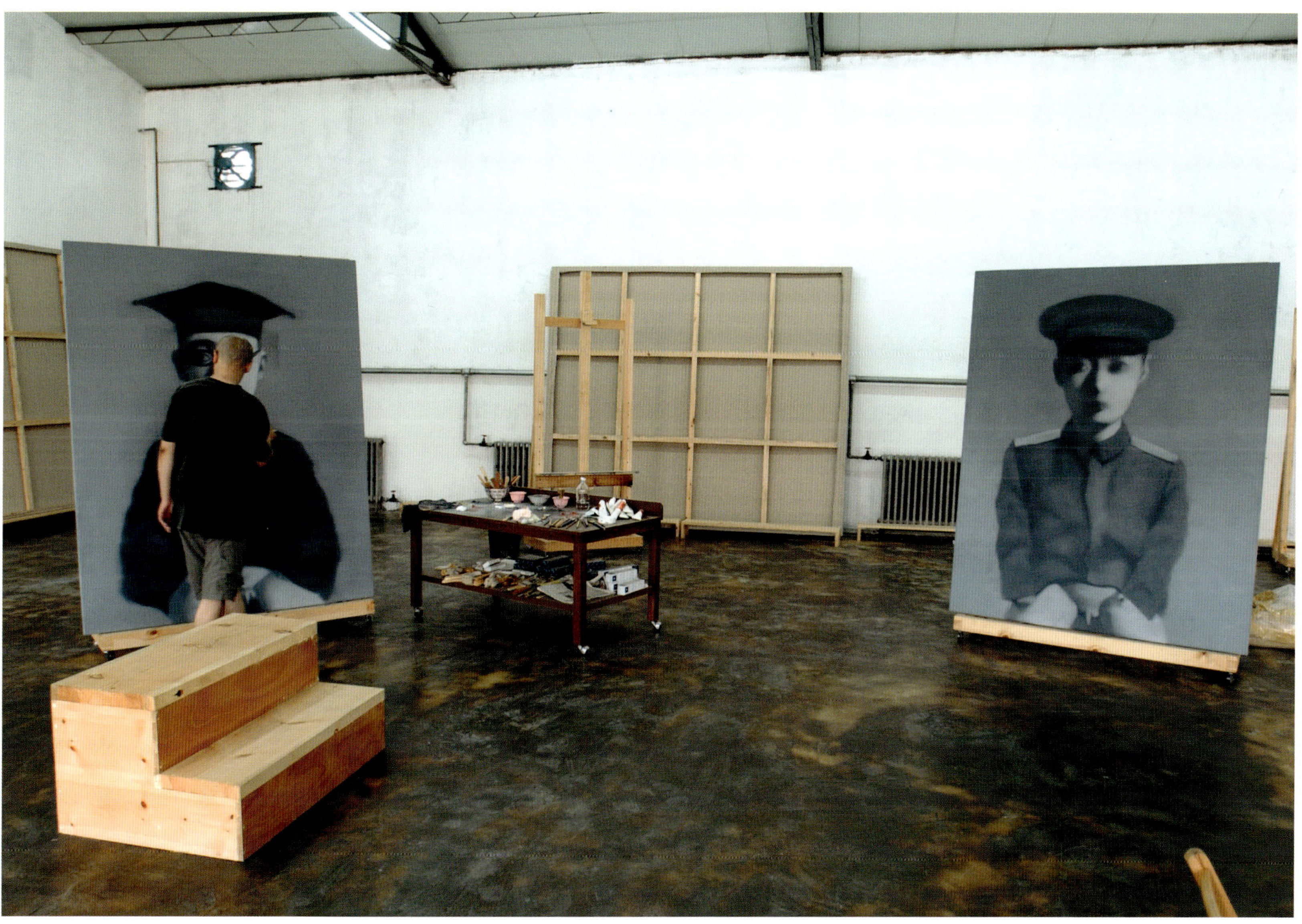

ZHANG XIAOGANG HAS PRACTICALLY FINISHED THESE TWO WORKS. THE SET OF WOODEN STEPS ARE FOR REACHING THE TOP OF THE BIGGER CANVASES. TUBES OF PAINT AND BRUSHES LIE ON THE TABLE ON CASTORS.

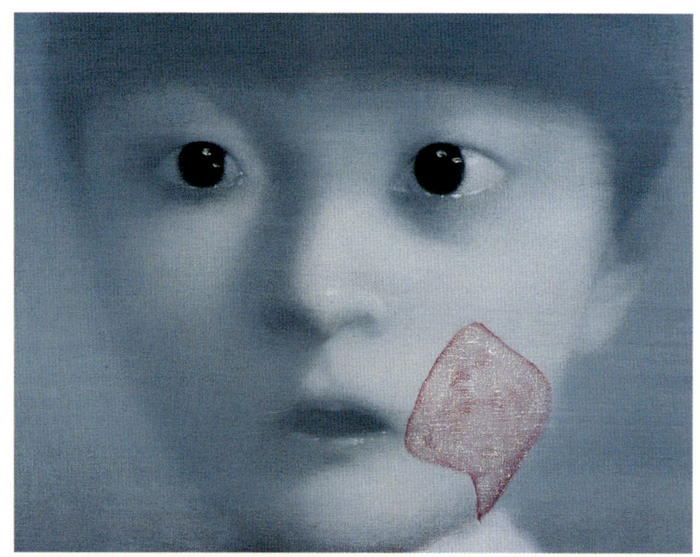

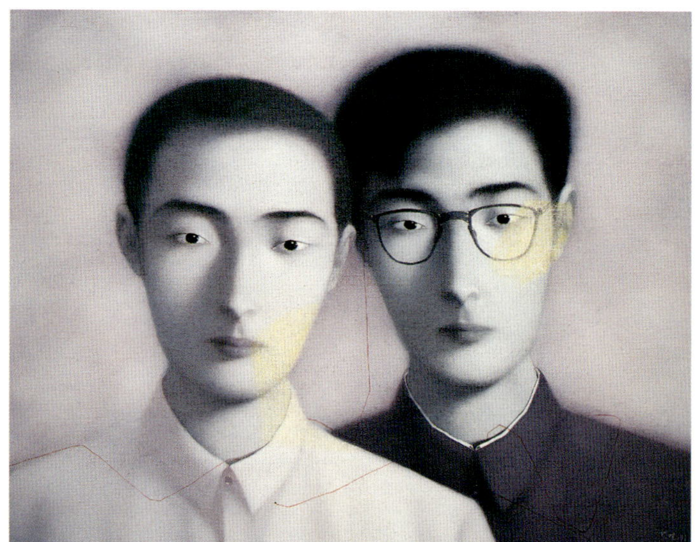

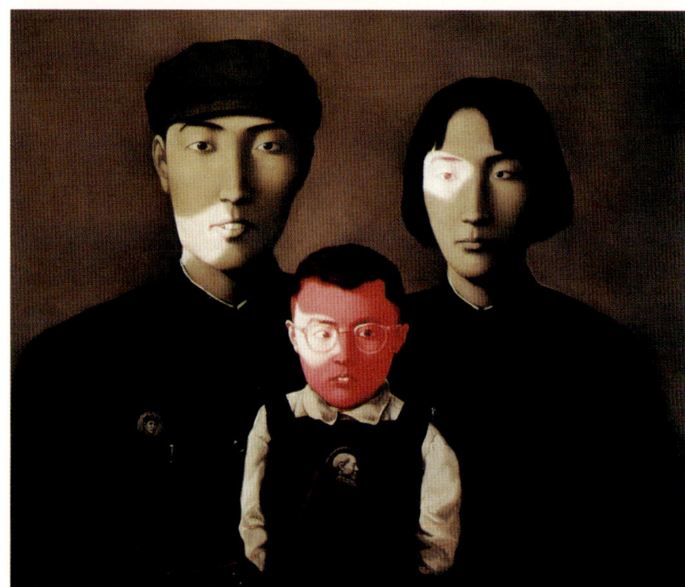

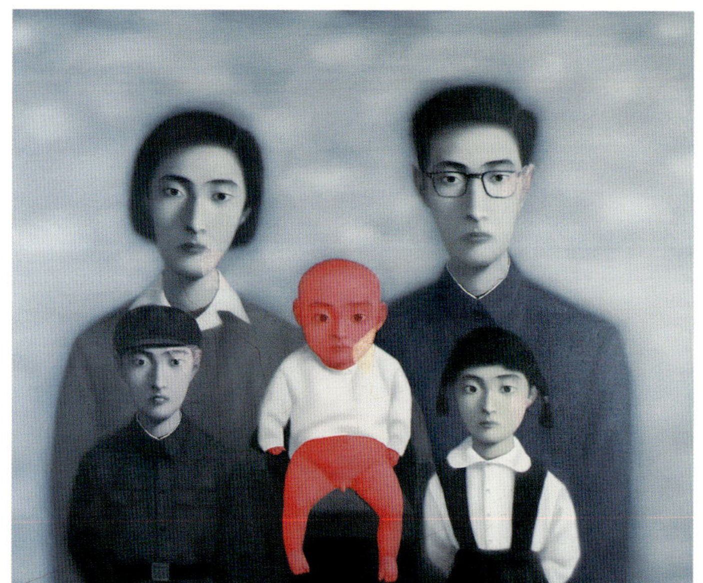

TOP LEFT: *MY DAUGHTER*, 2000. TOP RIGHT: *COMRADES*, 1996. BOTTOM LEFT: *BIG FAMILY*, 1994. BOTTOM RIGHT: *BIG FAMILY*, 1999. FACING PAGE: *BIG FAMILY*, 2001.

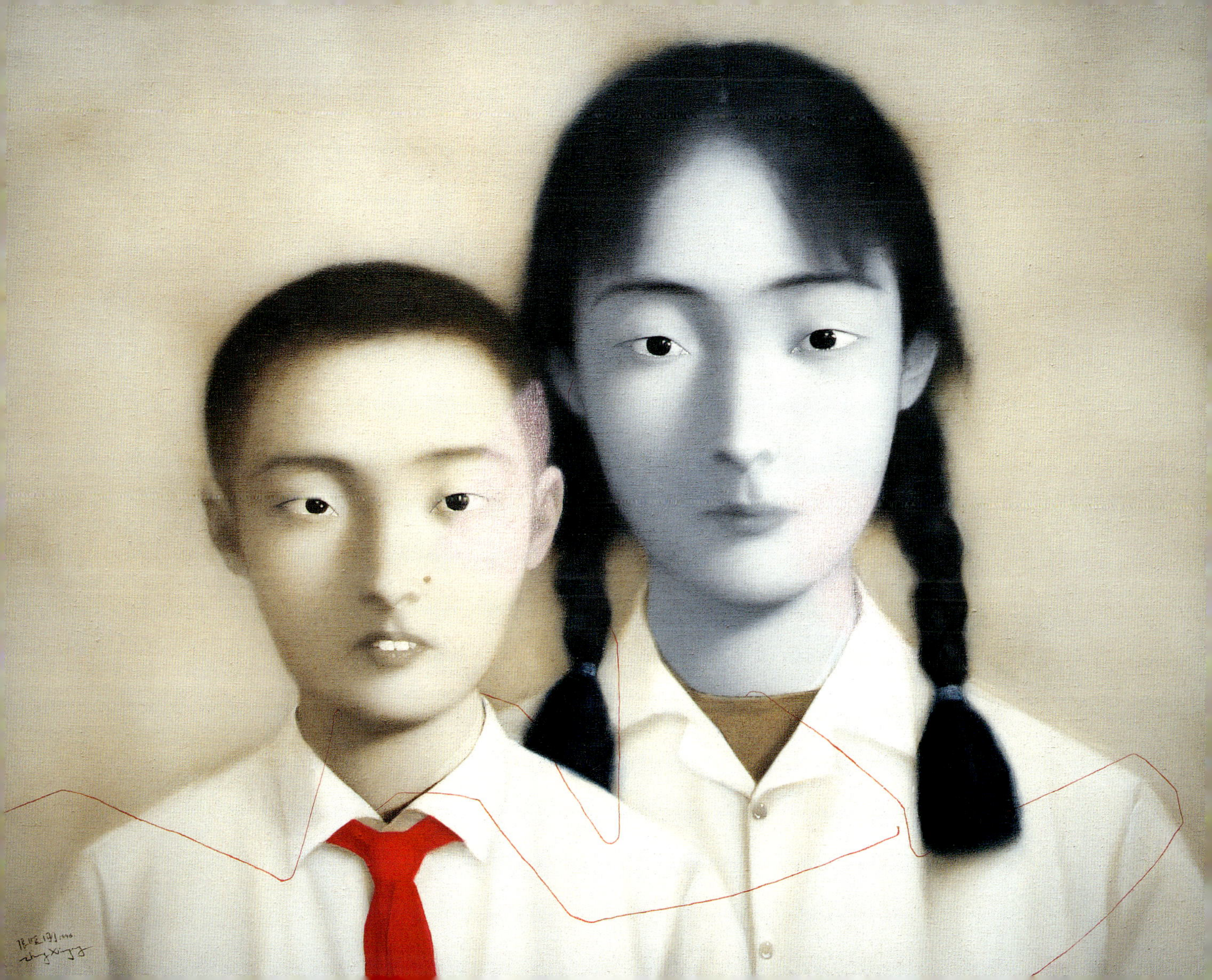

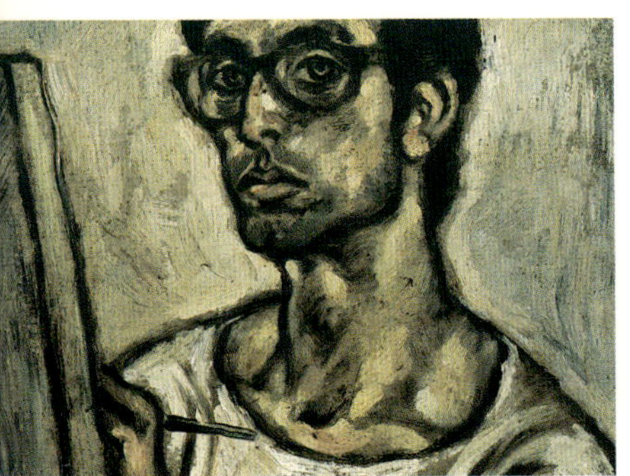

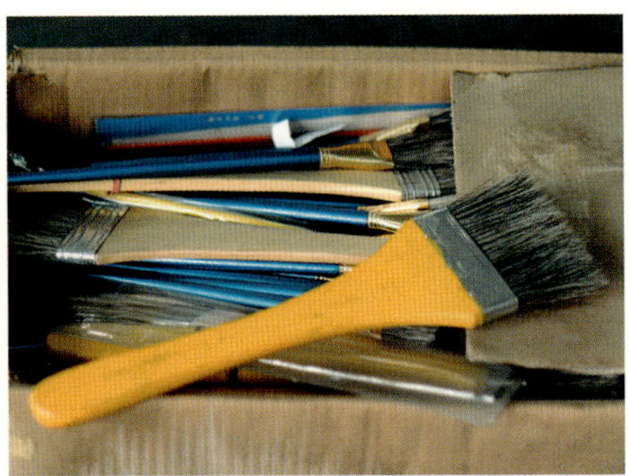

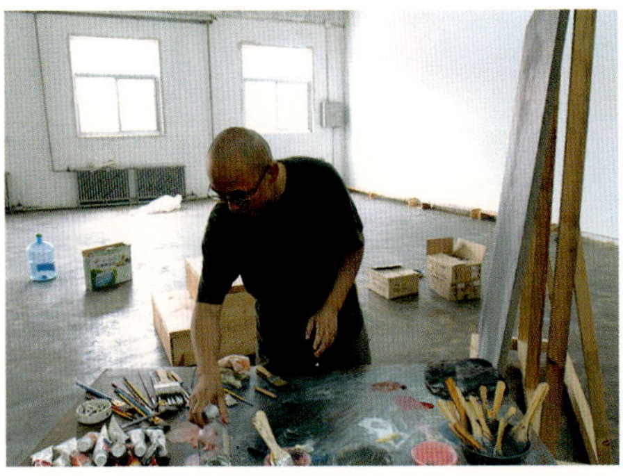

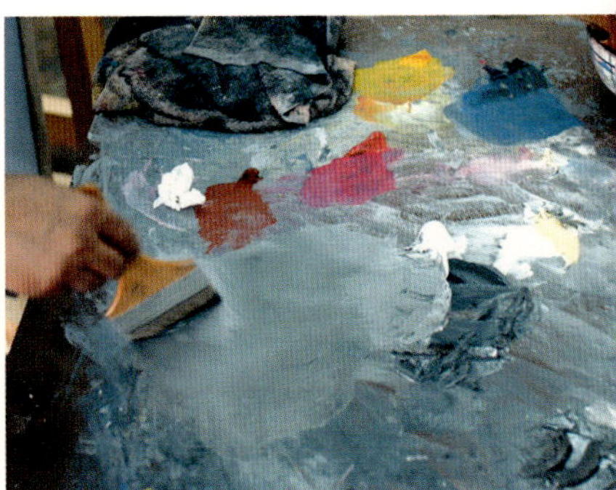

I found out from one of his friends—he never talks about it himself—that in about 1983, Zhang Xiaogang split up with a girlfriend and suffered a bout of depression that took the form of an overdose of philosophy, music, and alcohol. It is hard to say which had the most profound effect on him, although his drinking landed him in the hospital for two months. His time there gave rise to a series of drawings, *Ghosts between Black and White, a Hospital Diary*. This experience gave him a more personal vision of Surrealism shaded with Expressionism. ¶ Both Zhang Xiaogang and China then entered a calmer phase, punctuated with occasional political crises, before the tragedy of Tiananmen Square changed the face of China. ¶ Zhang Xiaogang spent 1991 traveling. He gave up working and spent all his time thinking. He was dissatisfied with the increasingly emotional nature of the path he had traced for himself. The appearance of Political Pop Art at that time gave him a fresh impetus. He painted his famous *Red Baby* in 1993. He has said of this painting that he put all of his secrets into it. All the memories of his childhood, buried for nearly two decades, came flooding back. ¶ I should mention at this point that even as a small boy, Zhang Xiaogang had found his mother a mystery. One day, his father sat him and his siblings down and explained that she was suffering from something called schizophrenia. From that day on, the whole family gathered round and protected her as if she were a child. Clearly not wishing to expand on the subject, Zhang Xiaogang simply says, "Her illness got worse during the Cultural Revolution. When I moved away from home, my mother wrote me strange letters that some people would no doubt call incoherent, but that I thought were full of poetry. I had the urge to find out who she really was. I wanted to find out about my parents when they were young." ¶ He found the photographs of his parents as a young couple in 1993. He discovered that his mother had been a very pretty girl, that she had a romantic streak, and that she loved music, but that due to circumstances she had become a civil servant. "Society changed her into a different person. Personal needs and the demands of society are two very different things. The relationship between individuals and society worries me and yet I find it enormously interesting," he insists. His mother sat for him. "I was not very close to my father, but my mother was very important." It was at this time that he produced the acclaimed series *Big Family*. ¶ "People interpret my work from a political point of view, but I am looking for something more mysterious within my own family," he explains. I wish I had a dollar for every time someone had complained about the tendency of Western critics to interpret all Chinese contemporary art through the lens of politics. Yet when I try to avoid the trap of seeming overly critical of Chinese society by saying that Western consumer society also threatens individual expression, he replies, "If all I want to do is criticize, then I can no longer paint." ¶ If you look at his older works side by side with more recent paintings from the series *Big Family* or *Blood Lines*, it is clear that his older paintings had an internal tension. They are brightly colored and the paint is laid on thick. In the later works, the colors are muted and the layer of paint is thinner. Today, his works are almost exclusively in black and white, like old photographs. "Closer to dreams," he says, adding, "Black and white are the shades of memory, when the colors have faded." ¶ The family he paints is to all appearances a typical revolutionary family—asexual, dressed in Mao suits, their gaze glassy and dismal. They are depicted in gray against a gray background. They could be clones—father, mother, and their only child in the middle. Of course, in China, couples are only allowed to have one child. The atmosphere of the painting is depressingly calm and unruffled. All emotion is crushed beneath a dull acceptance of reality.

FROM LEFT TO RIGHT: A SELF-PORTRAIT DATING FROM 1983. A SELECTION OF THE ARTIST'S MATERIALS. ZHANG XIAOGANG MIXES HIS COLORS DIRECTLY ON THE TABLE IN HIS STUDIO.

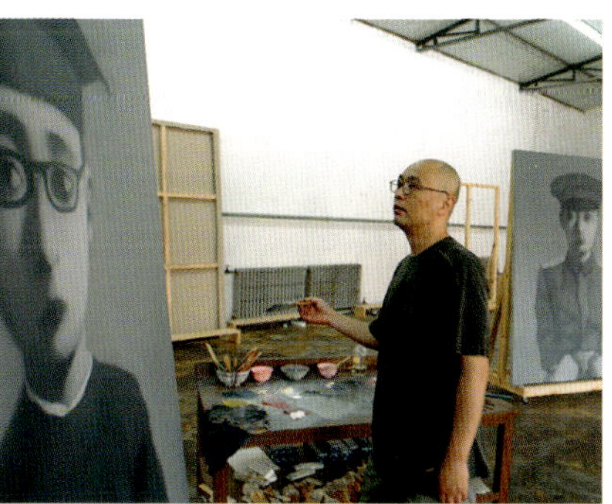

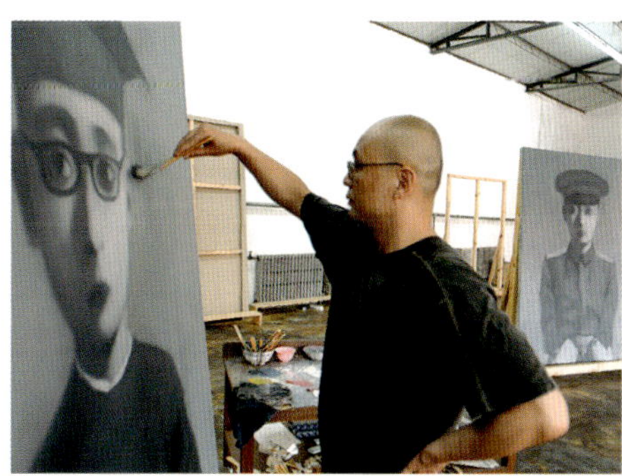

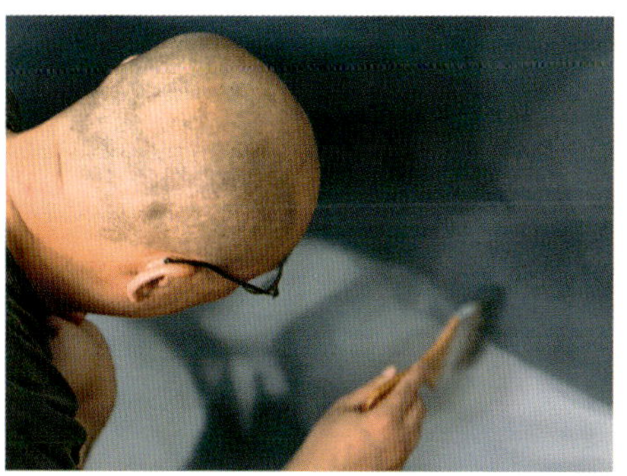

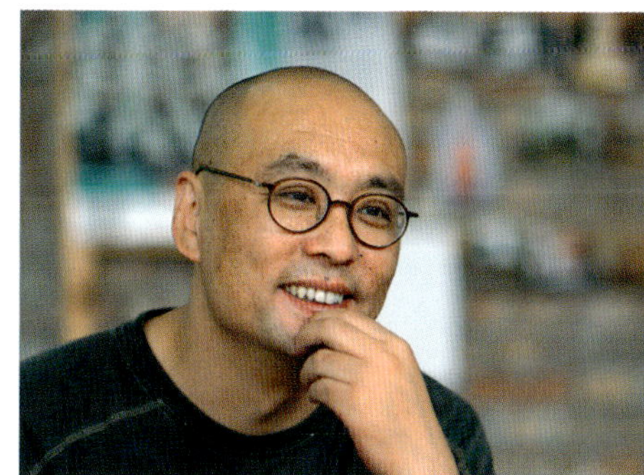

Nothing unexpected, no rough edges. Even the surface of the paint is smooth and soft. ¶ Zhang Xiaogang says, "We are all dependent on each other. The bonds between us are complex, subtle, and long-lasting. They are made of constraints and numbness." I point out at this moment that Confucianism dictates that the state should be run as one big family. "Yes," he nods, "but the first thing we learn is to protect ourselves, how to shut ourselves in a secret place, all the while pretending to be in perfect agreement with the other members of the family." ¶ The characters in his painting are linked by a barely visible red line—the bloodline, critics say. "That's true, but that's not all," Zhang Xiaogang says. "The line also represents historical and cultural bonds." ¶ At this point I ask him why so many of his models have a mark on their cheek, temple, or lips or are slightly disabled in some way. Many of them are cross-eyed. "There are physical faults, and then there are moral faults," he says laconically. What about these points of light? "Sometimes I put them in for dramatic effect. But primarily, they represent the passing of time. The things that remain with us over time." ¶ The cross-eyes and other minor infirmities symbolize a way for individuals to hold onto their own unique self in a system that imposes uniformity. It is a universal desire. It is depicted as a negative presence in the glassy, inexpressive gazes of the people in the paintings who have turned all their hopes and desires inwards, along with their memories, their suffering and their secrets. ¶ These paintings leave the viewer with a curious feeling of unease, although their formal beauty is undeniable. Their chilly smoothness is reminiscent of photography, and matches the impersonal nature of the subjects. ¶ Zhang Xiaogang seems to have a rather careless approach to questions of technique. "I use thin oil paint," he says. "I use Chinese paint, or foreign brands when I've been traveling. Nowadays I can afford the more expensive brands. I use wolf-hair brushes," he explains, although he doesn't look terribly sure. "The most important thing is that they must be soft to give as smooth a surface as possible. Before, I worked very quickly. Less so now. I used to paint one picture after another. Now I work on up to five at once. Sometimes I have to wait for two weeks for the painting to dry before adding another layer. I put on three or four layers in all." ¶ It is this deftness of touch and the use of several layers that make the paintings so light and yet so deep, like wells of memory. They are at the same time so realist and yet so sadly dreamy, as Zhang Xiaogang's mother must have been. Her presence haunts the whole of his subtle, powerful oeuvre. ¶ Today, Zhang Xiaogang is one of the best-known Chinese artists in the West. His paintings are very much in demand. He sold his first work in 1988 to a Japanese student for three hundred yuans—about three thousand yuans or three hundred dollars in today's money. The average monthly salary back then was 150 yuans. "It was an absolute windfall, just before I got married," he says, smiling at the memory. Today, he tells me, his paintings sell for an average of forty thousand dollars. ¶ He earns a comfortable living. But he is still troubled with a sense of unease and a tendency to introspection, as well as the curious blend of remarkable singularity and common sense shared by many great artists today. ¶ If a work by Andy Warhol is shown in a group exhibition, all the other works fade into insignificance beside it. His Marilyns and Coca-Colas are always the focal point. The same goes for Zhang Xiaogang. Maybe this is because the oeuvres of both artists reflect the tension between violent expressiveness (death for Warhol, and the death of the individual for Zhang Xiaogang) and an equally powerful sense of impersonality or neutrality. ¶ And beyond that, the realm of secrets.

THE CANVAS AND THE GRAY SMOOTHNESS OF THE PAINT. THE QUICK, LIGHT STROKES OF THE BRUSH. THE ARTIST'S SMILE.

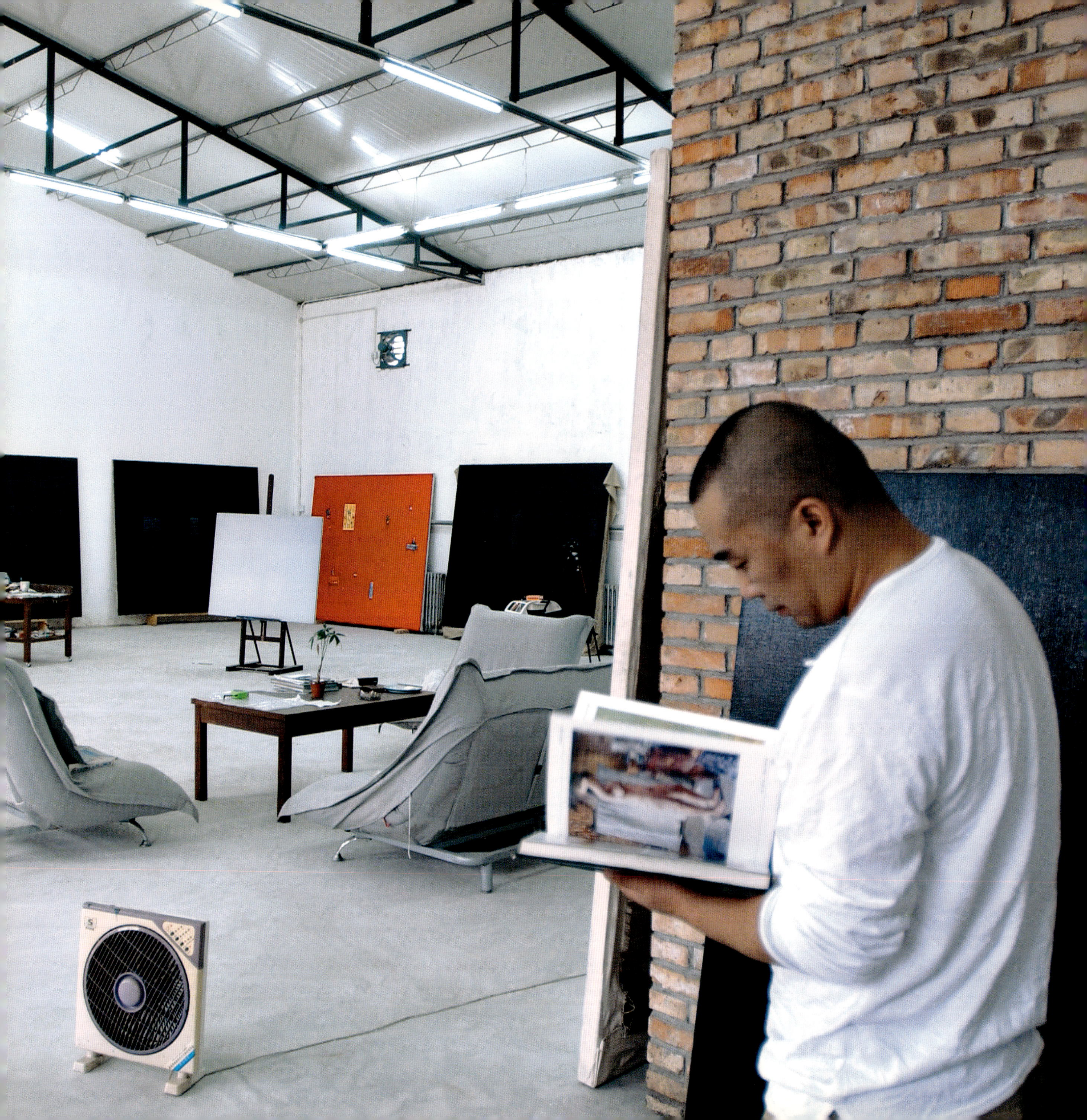

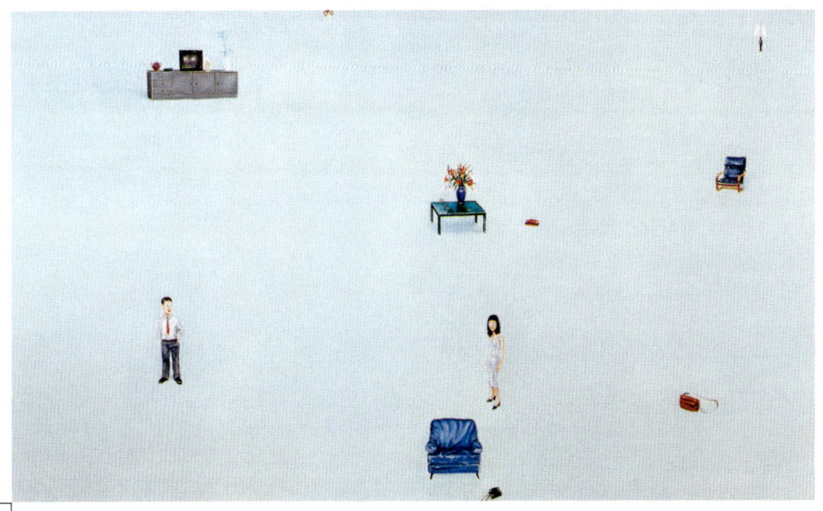

ZENG HAO

"Painting? My parents pushed me into it. I was almost forced to start painting. I didn't even enjoy it that much—you could say I wasn't very keen. When all the other children went out to play, my father sent me off to paint." Zeng Hao's opening gambit is unexpected, to say the least. He is in his early forties, and has a gentle, sad smile. His whole body is an expression of his timidity. He was born in 1963 in Kunming, a city of four million people, at an altitude of nearly one and a quarter miles (two thousand meters) in the remote Yunnan province on the border with Laos and Vietnam. Zeng Hao's father pushed his son to paint by taking him to an outlying village where he was cut off from the world. ¶ "I began to enjoy painting when I was about eighteen, after high school, when I began studying at the Institute of Fine Art in Sichuan," he explains. ¶ He claims that his childhood was fairly happy. Note the use of the adverb "fairly." His parents were strict—probably extremely strict. They were both university lecturers. None of his childhood memories seems to stand out. "My father loved me very much," he says, maybe a little defensively. ¶ Given his age, he could get away with saying that he has no memory of the Cultural Revolution, that he was too young. He was three when it began. But like many of the other artists I have interviewed, he said that, for the children, it was fun—adding, again like many of the others, that he and his friends no longer went to school. He hinted that his parents—both from very wealthy families—stopped going to the university, which saved them from being sent to prison. They seized on his father's illness—he still does not know if it was real or feigned—as an excuse to seek refuge in his mother's home village. ¶ His parents were protective—maybe overly so. I get the feeling that looking back, Zeng Hao cannot help blaming them. "It was just too much for me," he says about their constant worrying. In high school, he rebelled, becoming disruptive and neglecting his potential, until eventually he was moved away from his parents. "I was so happy to be free! I was so happy that there was no one to look after me!" he says. ¶ It's hard to imagine this placid, calm man rebelling. But then he tells me how in the time after the Cultural Revolution, pupils had to stay in school studying, sometimes as late as 9:30 P.M. He would sneak out with his friends and cut off the electricity. "My rebellion wasn't aimed against anyone in particular, other than my parents," he says. ¶ In 1989, he was awarded a diploma in painting from the Central Academy of Fine Art in Beijing. "Those years of study were particularly important. They taught me to tame art and to love painting after all those years of being forced to do it. They taught me to step out of the shadow of my over-protective education and to be more open and free. Those years were the basis for everything.

FACING PAGE: ZHENG HAO IN HIS BEIJING STUDIO, NEXT DOOR TO ZHANG XIAOGANG. ABOVE: DETAIL OF THE PAINTING *12:30 P.M., JANUARY DATE 2001*, 2001.

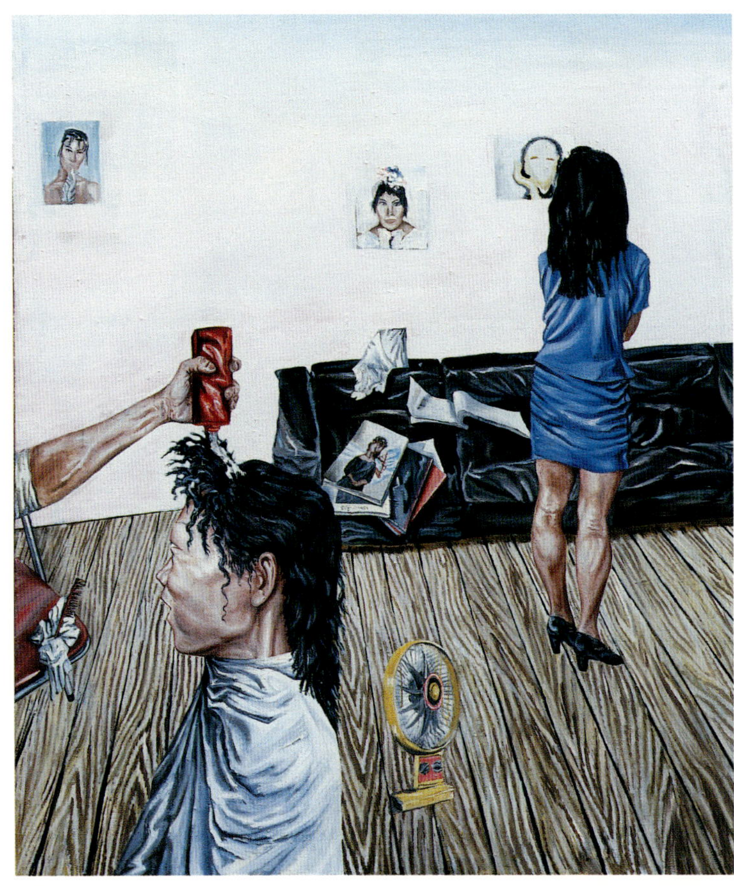

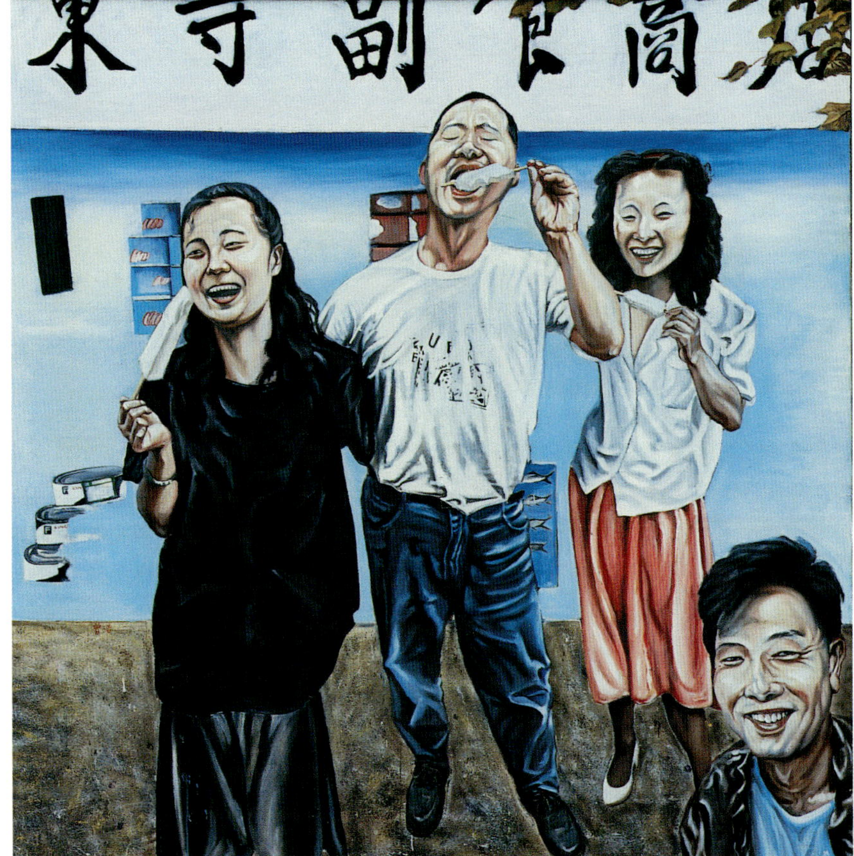

LEFT: *HAIR WASH*, 1994. A CRITICAL LOOK AT A NEW LIFESTYLE CHARACTERIZED BY NEW POSSESSIONS. THE QUICK, CASUAL FRAMING OF THE SCENE IS TYPICAL OF ZHENG HAO. RIGHT: *ICE CREAM*, 1994.

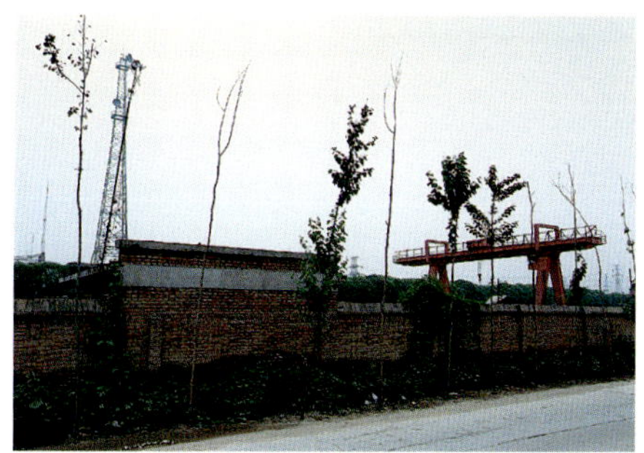
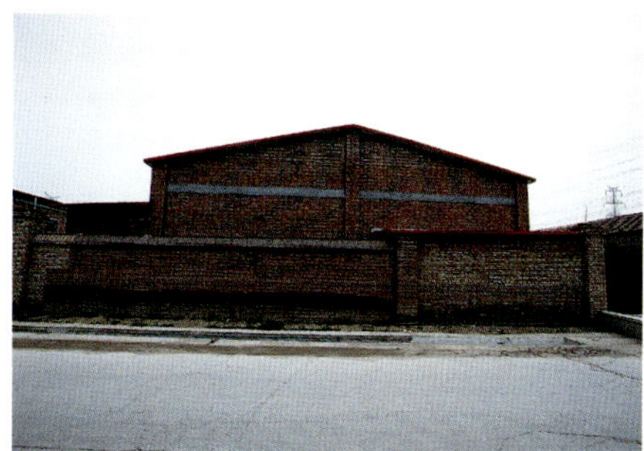
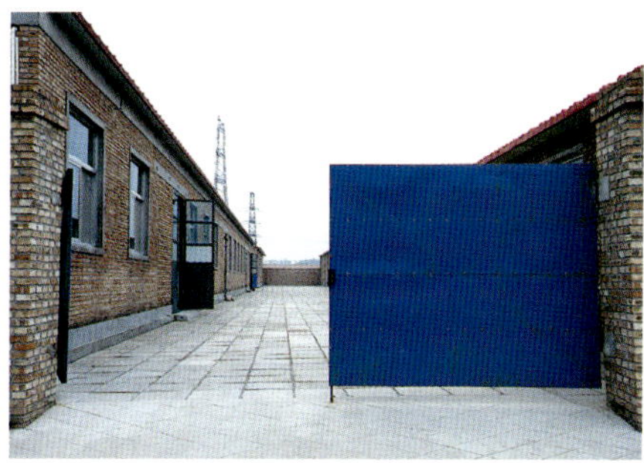
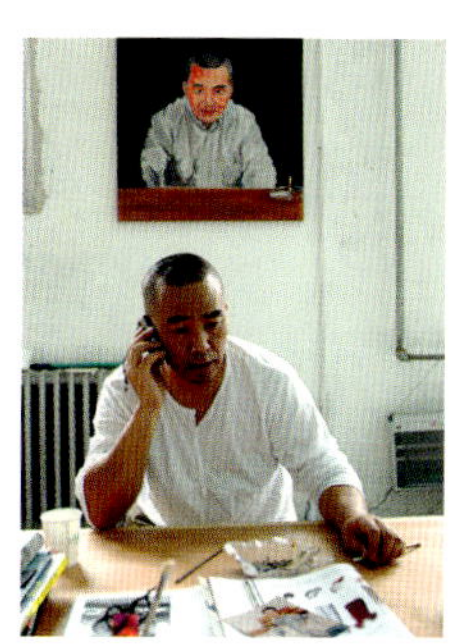

They showed me what was going on in the art world in China and gave me the opportunity to meet other artists. Zhang Xiaogang, for instance. I met him when I was sixteen." ¶ We are having this conversation in a corner of northeastern Beijing, in an outlying suburb that bears some resemblance to the suburbs of Paris in the 1950s. We are in his studio, which as it happens is practically right next to Zhang Xiaogang's. They both moved into this neighborhood in February 2002, because it is spacious and airy, if not particularly attractive. The studios are lined up along a long, straight road, and look out onto an enormous brick wall. A little further on, more studios are being built. The ambience changes as soon as we step inside. The lighting, the glass roof, the whitewashed walls, the canvases propped in corners, the photos pinned on the wall in one corner alongside his plants, a sofa, chairs, and a table, all go to make a pleasant impression of warmth. ¶ This new studio is infinitely more cheery than the tiny studio where I first met Zeng Hao, which from the outside could have been a prison, with its huge gate and circular corridor. I sit down at his table. On the table are piled magazines. Zeng Hao has been cutting out people and objects to use as models for his paintings. He serves me tea. He sits down and carries on telling me about his past. "When I got my diploma, I spent a year doing nothing. I went traveling in northern Sichuan, then I became a teacher in Kunming, then in the department of oil painting in the Guangzhou Academy of Fine Art. It's good being a teacher, as it leaves you with plenty of free time. Over a period of two years, I taught about two months' worth of lessons in all. Because I was young, the older teachers presumed I had no experience and so they didn't give me much to do. I put all my energy, all my efforts, into my own painting. I think the head of the school admired me for that." ¶ It was at this time, in around 1992, that Zeng Hao began producing works characterized by a light, deft humor and subtle formal innovations, freely demonstrating a new way of living alone, in a couple, or as part of a communal group. "Prior to that, education was too serious. It's become more relaxed since then, which is definitely a good thing," he says. His 1994 painting *Hair Wash* shows, first and most strikingly, a hardwood floor—still a rarity in China—and the improbably off-center figure of a young woman depicted from the chest up, wrapped in a towel, her hair wet. A second figure is depicted only in the form of a mysterious forearm and hand, holding a bottle of what appears to be some kind of shampoo, which is being poured onto the girl's head. On the floor is a kind of electric fan. On the wall in the background are some portraits. A girl is shown from behind looking at one of them. She is wearing a miniskirt and high heels, and her hair is permed. ¶ *Summer* (1992) is just as remarkable in terms of the way it plays with framing. The foreground is a mysterious thin strip covered in more or less legible writing, which seems to be pushing back the couple that the viewer expects to find in the foreground. The entire left side of the painting is filled with a vast pile of panties, which are the real focal point of the work (which, like *Hair Wash*, also features a portrait on the wall). Zeng Hao's *Balloon* series is also noted for its humor. One canvas, for example, features three people in the foreground, side by side. The first is shown from the neck up, the second from the chest, and the third from the waist. Behind them is a row of balloons—pale green, vermilion, baby blue—and then a fuzzy background, possibly showing a floor and some crazily angled walls. ¶ *Make Up* (1995) could well be one of the paintings linking Zeng Hao's earlier works with the ones that made him famous, which he likewise produced in 1995. The canvas is cut sharply in two. The top half shows a tiny woman in a dress with a low-cut neckline against a pale orange background. She

FROM LEFT TO RIGHT: A NUMBER OF VIEWS FROM THE BUILDING WHERE ZENG HAO HAS A STUDIO. THE STUDIO IS IN AN ALMOST RURAL SUBURB. EXTERIOR VIEWS OF THE STUDIOS. ZHENG HAO EXPLAINING THE ROUTE TO ZHU CHUNYA BY TELEPHONE.

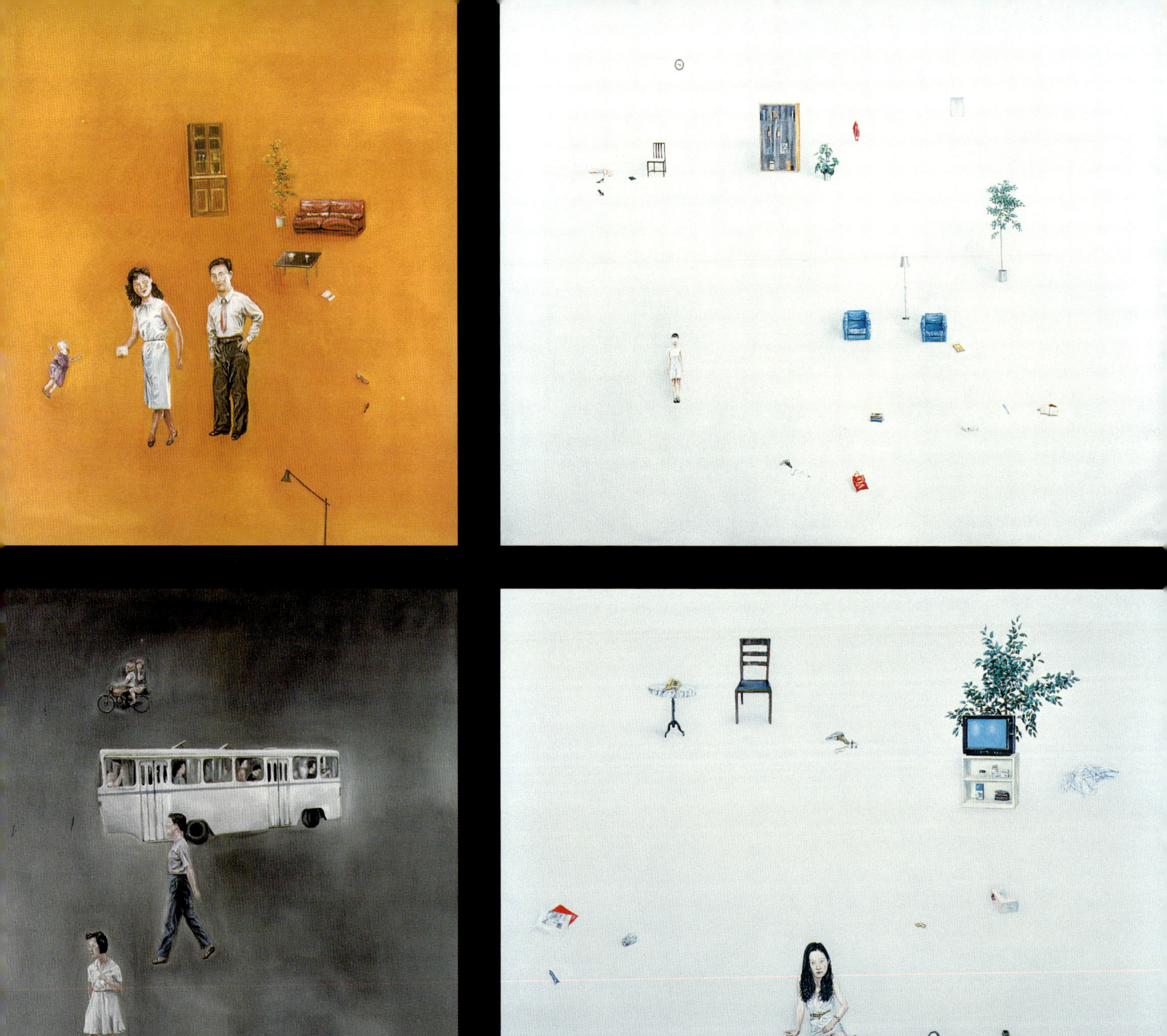

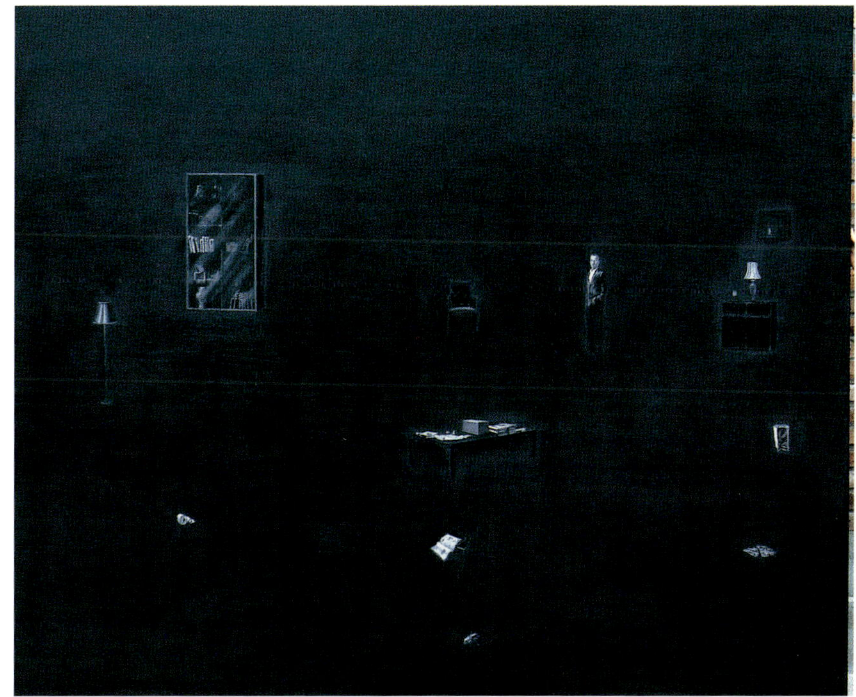

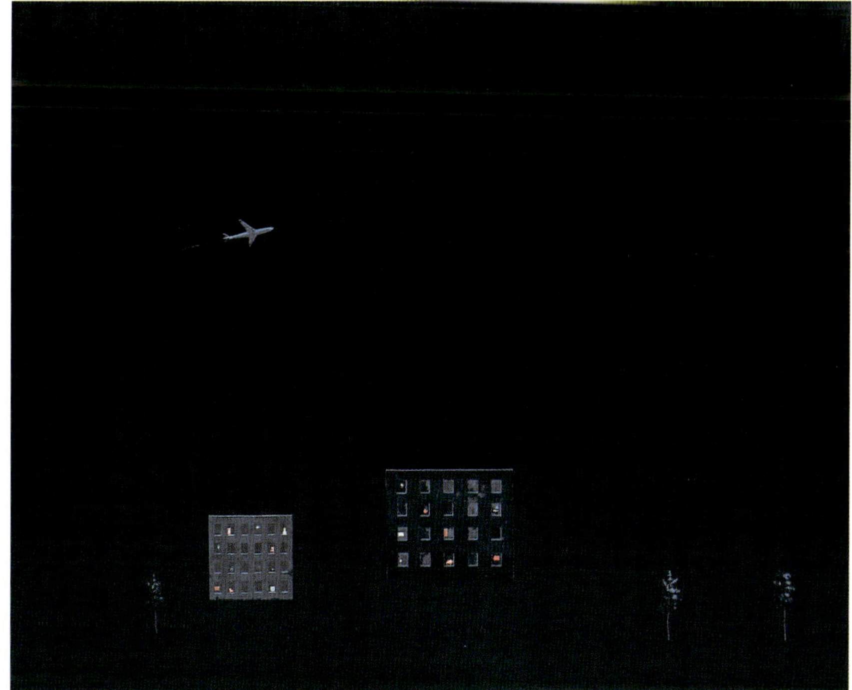

ABOVE: TWO CANVASES COMPLETED IN 2003, PLAYING WITH THE BOUNDARIES BETWEEN VISIBILITY AND INVISIBILITY, DEPICTING A STREET SCENE IN BEIJING IN VERY DARK TONES. FACING PAGE: NOTE THE CHANGE IN STYLE BETWEEN THE WORK ON THE TOP LEFT, *THE AFTERNOON OF SUNDAY*, 1995, THE BOTTOM LEFT, *SEPTEMBER THE TWENTIETH*, 1996, AND THOSE MORE RECENT WORKS ON THE RIGHT.

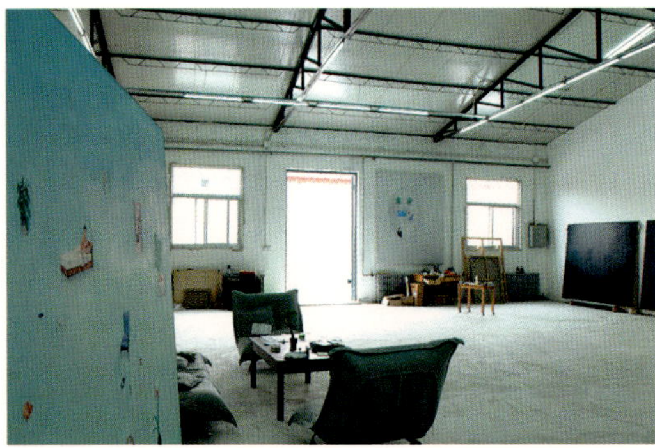

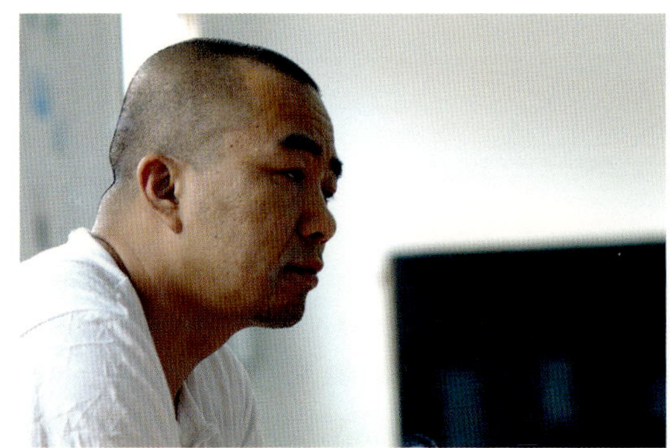

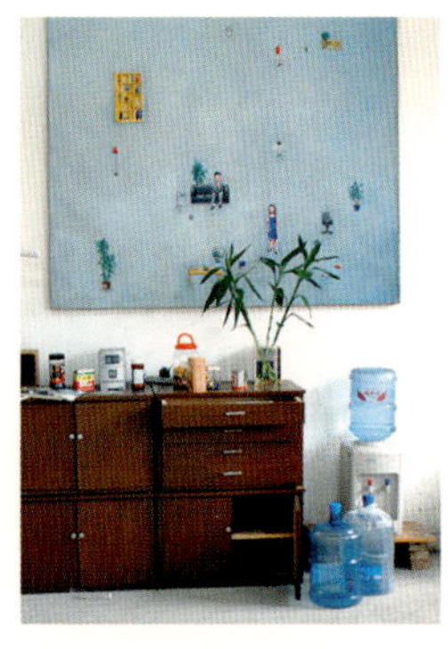

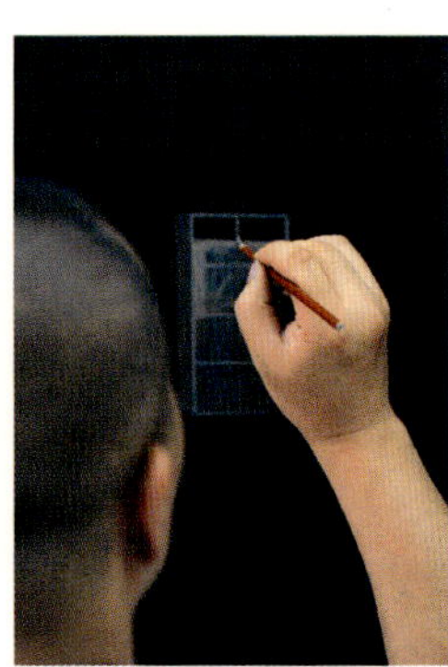

has her arms raised to tidy her hair. The lower part is a swathe of brown. Against this backdrop Zeng Hao has painted a table on which a perfume bottle, a mirror, and a lipstick lie haphazardly. As the following canvases showed, each painting is dated, sometimes to the precise minute—*February 14, 2000, 10:30 A.M.*; *The Afternoon of March 4, 2001*; *Xiao Li and the Others Have Gone Out*; or simply *Five O'clock in the Afternoon*, a painting dating from 1996, more dream-like than the others, with a cloudy brown background that seems to swallow up the objects that float on its surface as if by magic. ¶ The most striking aspect of these paintings is the overwhelming sense of solitude, not only of the people, but also of the objects. The key word is isolation. None of the objects seem to be linked to any of the others. The figures placed in large empty spaces filled with largely neutral colors—pale blue that is almost white, midnight blue that is almost black, gray, blood red, very dark gray—are lonely. They are depicted with their arms hanging down, or with their hands crossed or in their pockets. They are mostly shown facing us. Only one painting, *May 26, 1996*, shows two people—perhaps a couple—sitting side by side on a blue sofa. But they are not looking at each other. ¶ The very furniture looks lonely—armchairs, wardrobes, houseplants, hat stands, electric fans, books, lamps, cupboards, chairs, beds, bottles, chests of drawers, sofas, floating in shadowless, dimensionless space, not entirely flat nor yet quite structured, with no sense of perspective opening onto the world. ¶ In the past—and until very recently—the Chinese were not permitted to buy apartments or houses. Today, things have changed. The urban fabric is being radically altered by programs of demolition and construction, and people are buying homes for themselves. The consumer society has arrived, and there is no going back. Zeng Hao's paintings are a comment on all the consumer desirables—new furniture not traditionally found in Chinese homes, electrical appliances, stereos—that are being bought up so quickly that they do not have time to settle into their new homes, as they would have if they were acquired slowly over a lifetime. They have not had time to put down roots, and so they seem isolated and out of place. They have not yet shed their strange autonomy. They look as if they are on display in a show home. ¶ While we are chatting and looking at Zeng Hao's most recent paintings, someone keeps calling from a taxi on his way to visit. It turns out to be Zhou Chunya, who arrives shortly afterward. We all go out for a meal together, in a dreadful Holiday Inn far from Zeng Hao's home. I think he thought it was a special treat. ¶ Zeng Hao's most recent paintings are a new departure. They all have a dull black background. They now depict cities, skyscrapers, airplanes, and airports rather than household interiors. What made him change tack, I ask? He looks at me, apparently astonished by my question. "Because this is today's world. Look at Beijing and Shanghai. Everywhere, buildings are being knocked down and rebuilt. There are high-rises and skyscrapers everywhere. What I find most interesting is the impact these aspects of daily life have on people." ¶ In his paintings of domestic interiors, the objects were in general sharply defined against the background. In the more recent works, the high-rises, the cityscape, and the airplanes seem to be stuck in the grasp of the background and meld into it to form one undifferentiated whole. ¶ "It used to be said that people could change the world. Now, it is said that consuming changes people. I prefer to look at the way people behave. Not all that long ago, if someone moved a chair, he'd put it back again afterward. Not anymore. Small details like that are important. We've created an environment, but we are progressively coming under the control of objects." ¶ A strange blackness. All this solitude. ¶ And such a gentle smile.

ABOVE AND FACING PAGE: INTERIOR VIEWS OF THE STUDIO. A HOUSEPLANT IN FRONT OF A CANVAS, TUBES OF PAINT ON A TABLE, AN UMBRELLA, AND A PACKAGE WITH SYMBOLS ON THE WRAPPING WARNING THE TRANSPORTERS NOT TO LET THE CONTENTS GET WET.

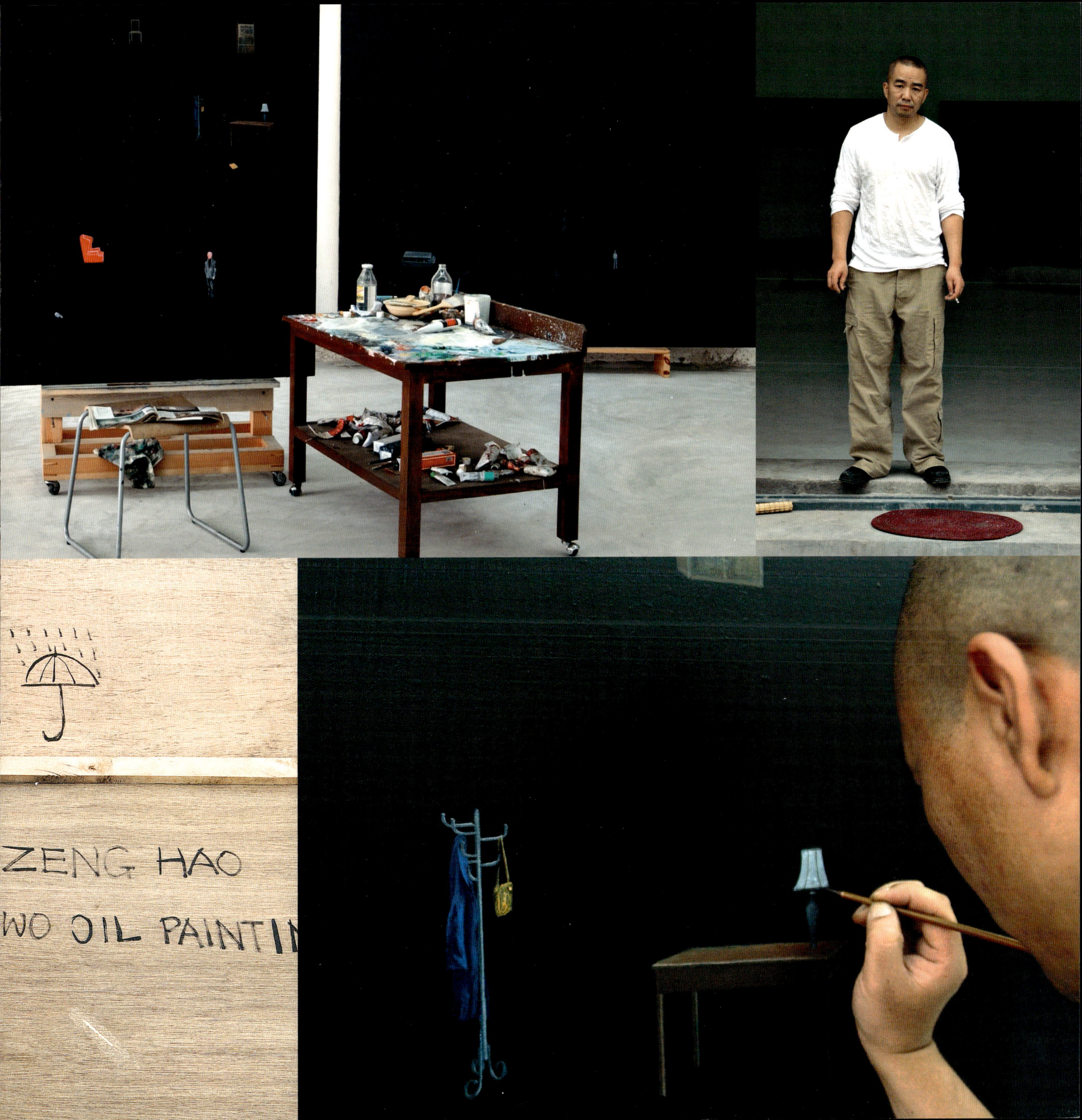
ZENG HAO
WO OIL PAINTI

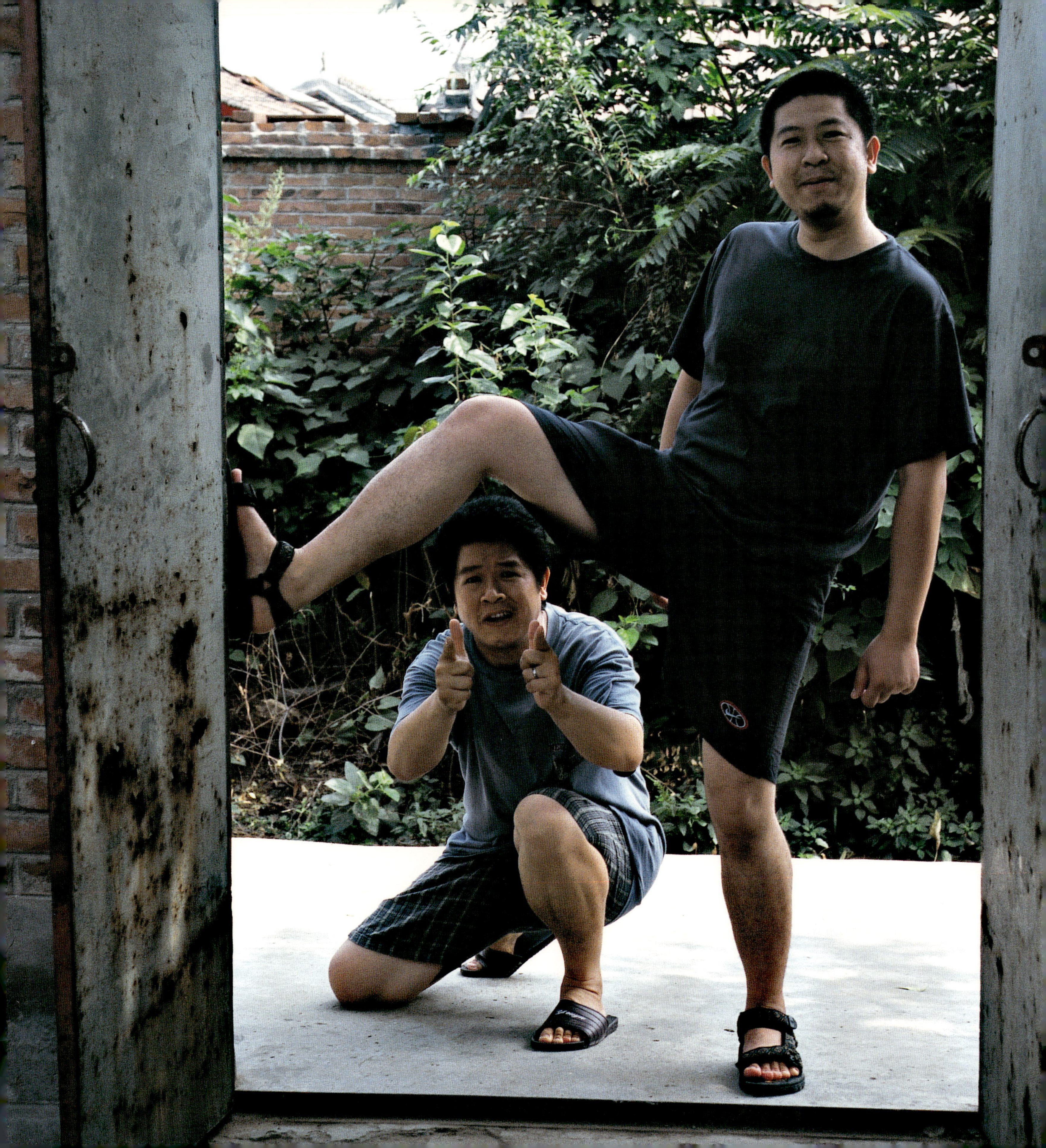

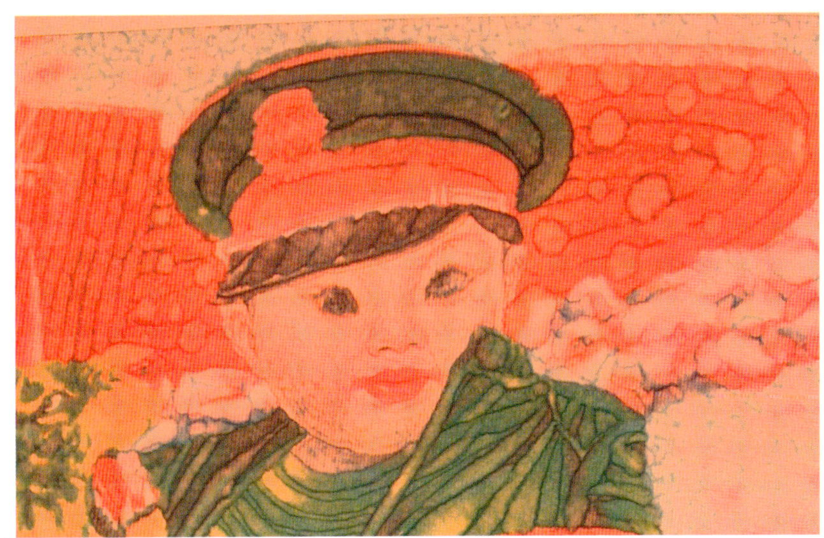

THE LUO BROTHERS

"Guardian of the People's Army" cheats. "Guardian of the People's Army," or Weibing, is the youngest of the Luo Brothers. I challenged him to a game of ping-pong on the table in the courtyard. First, he let me win easily, before beating me in our second game. He plays extremely well, the cheat. He knows all sorts of little tricks, and made me look like a rank amateur. ¶ There are three Luo Brothers. They come from the Guangxi region in southern China, and have been working together as a team since 1986. ¶ They are sometimes known as the Three Ws, because of their names, Weidong, Weibing, and Weiguo. These names denote the revolutionary fervor of their parents—Weidong means "guardian of the nation," Weiguo "guardian of Chairman Mao," and Weibing "guardian of the People's Army". ¶ They enjoy playing up the clownish yet hip personas they have created. They live together in a sort of farm about thirty miles (fifty kilometers) from the center of Beijing, almost in the countryside, in a village called Song, which consists of lots of well-kept little houses, all painted white with a strip of intense blue around the base of the walls. They remind me of buildings in Tétouan, Morocco. ¶ When I first visited the brothers a little over two years ago, my interpreter told me, with just a hint of scorn in his voice, "They are peasants. They only speak the dialect of the southern region where they were born." Apparently, the Luo Brothers belong to the Zhuang minority whose dialect is related to Thai. In 1955, Guangxi province became the Guangxi Autonomous Region for the Zhuang minority. ¶ The Luo Brothers don't seem to care too much. They prefer to see themselves as rock stars. ¶ Their works are stored in a sort of hangar or converted barn. There are small and medium-sized works, in all styles, at a range of prices. Some would suit small apartments, amateur art lovers or serious collectors, while others would only look right in a gallery, a museum, or the marble lobby of a multinational conglomerate. ¶ These works have been labeled Gaudy Art, which is not a movement, as is often claimed, but rather a vision of contemporary Chinese art that could be called kitsch, if the term were not now so widely used as to have become meaningless. The promoters of Gaudy Art see it as an extension of American kitsch in general, and Jeff Koons in particular. Unfortunately, this is to miss the point of kitsch, where American kitsch comes from, and what Jeff Koons is about. ¶ The critic Li Xianting theorized about Gaudy Art. It emerged in China in the mid-1990s. Among its finest proponents are Liu Zheng, whose beautiful young women weep diamond tears, like in Jean Cocteau's film version of *Beauty and the Beast*, and whose 1930s calendar pinups, with their gracious poses, figure on lengths of ornately embroidered brocade, revealing a consummate eye for surprising collages. Liu Zheng spends hours sewing cheap plastic beads onto backing cloth in the shape of American or Chinese bills. The result is fabulously tacky. The hundred dollar bill has a deliciously ironic "Made in China" embroidered to the left of the portrait of Benjamin Franklin, while the hundred yuan bill bears Lui Zheng's signature to the left of the portrait of Chairman Mao. Prior to this, Xu Yihui produced works in padded cloth embroidered with roses, beads, frills, and lace, and now works on ceramic baskets coated in a thick layer of gold, filled with flowers, and with a bundle of hundred yuan notes tied with a ribbon nestling in the center. This is doubtless an allusion to the rush to individual wealth in the post-Maoist period. ¶ The Luo Brothers share a colorful artistic vision inspired by popular art, in particular the garish colors of New Year calendars that abound in symbols of happiness and prosperity, such as laughing, chubby-cheeked infants, gold ingots and coins, and animals associated with good fortune in Chinese mythology—deer, dragons, and bats. They associate these traditional emblems with other, more modern symbols of happiness and wealth that have gained currency in the consumer society that has engulfed China: Coca-Cola, McDonald's, Motorola, and even the fabled Forbidden City, which has become a banal tourist attraction, a product to be

THE LUO BROTHERS ARE CALLED WEIDONG, WEIBING, AND WEIDU. FACING PAGE: TWO OF THE THREE BROTHERS FOOLING AROUND. THEY ARE AMONG THE FOREMOST PROPONENTS OF GAUDY ART. ABOVE: A DETAIL FROM A RECENT WORK.

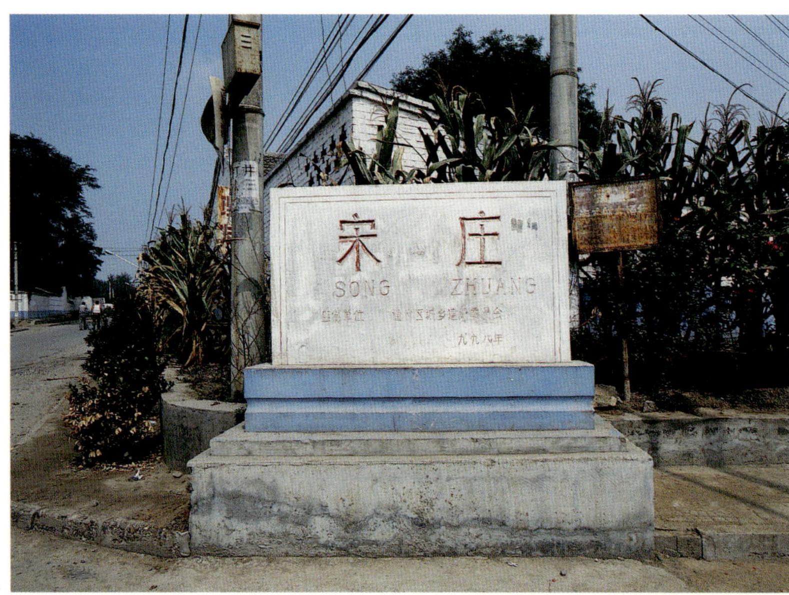

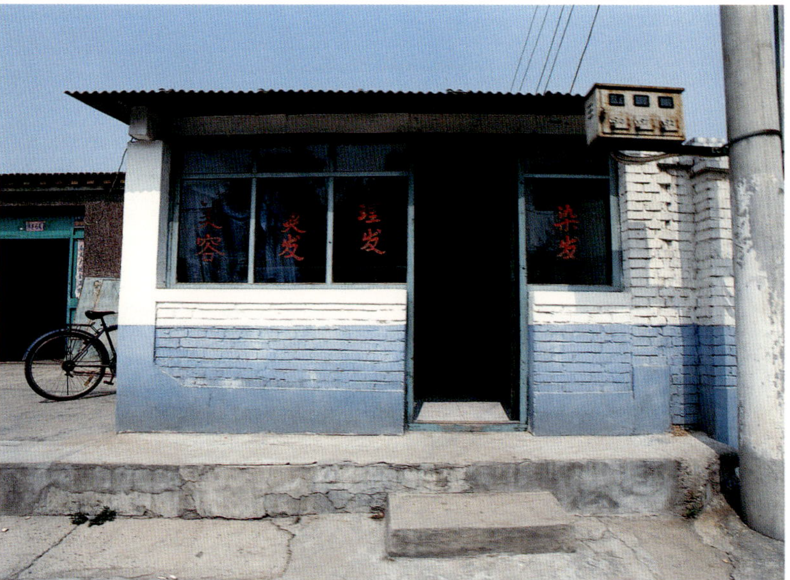

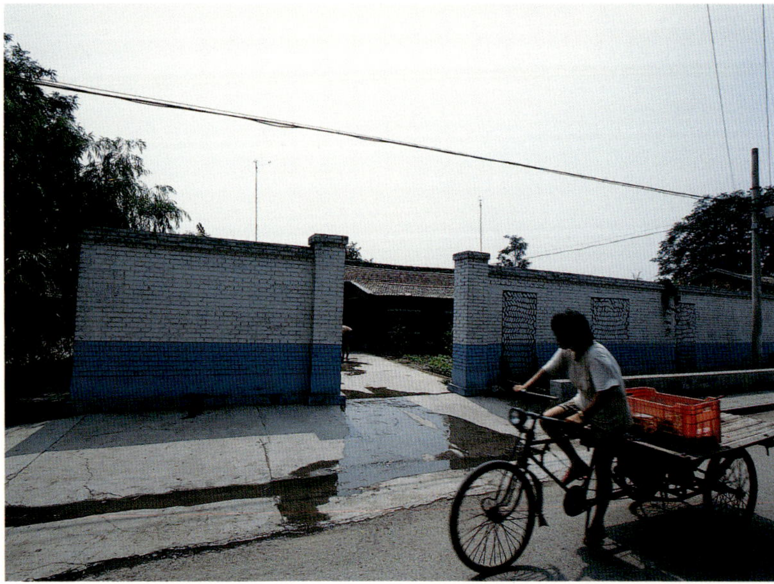

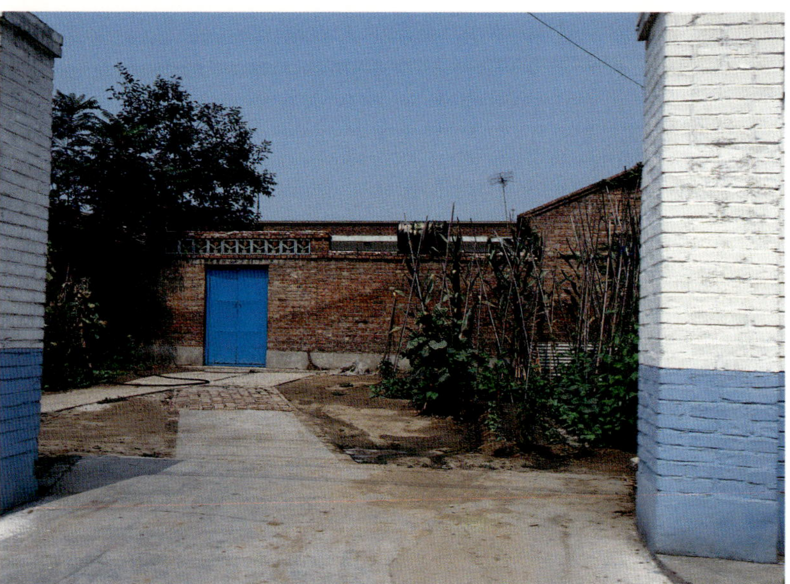

THIRTY MILES (FIFTY KILOMETERS) FROM THE CENTER OF BEIJING WE ARE OFFICIALLY STILL IN THE CITY, BUT THE FIELDS AND NEAT LITTLE HOUSES MAKE IT FEEL MORE LIKE THE COUNTRYSIDE. THE WHITE WALLS WITH BLUE BASES REMIND ME OF HOUSES IN TÉTOUAN, MOROCCO.

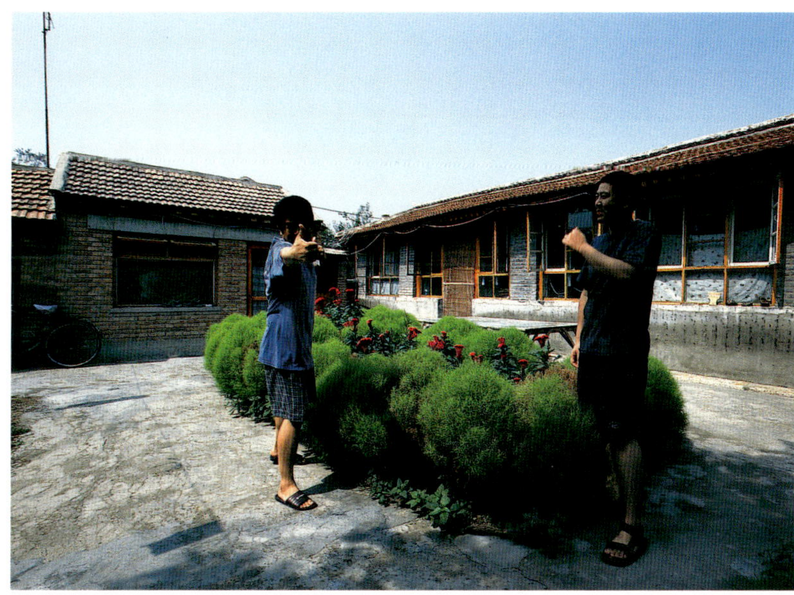

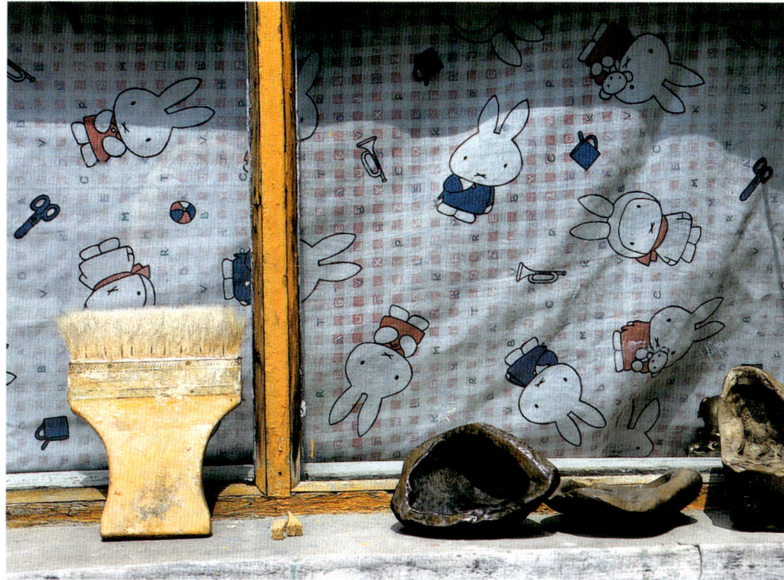

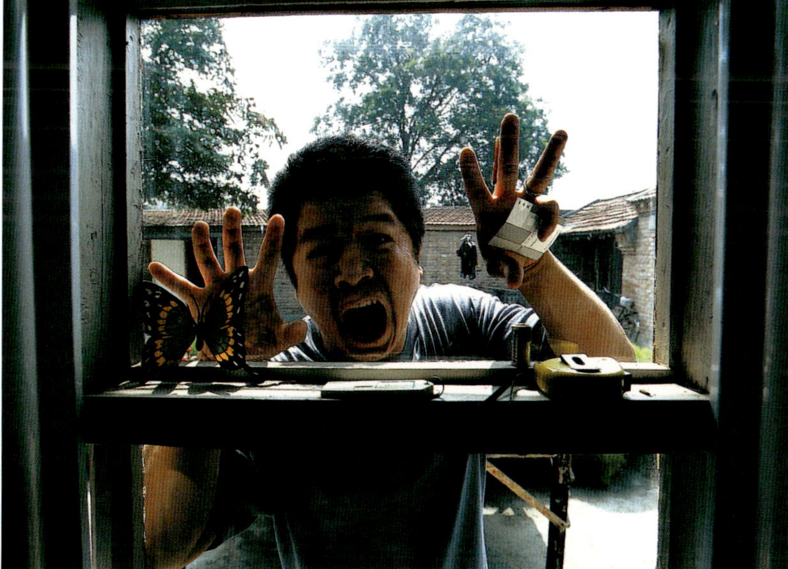

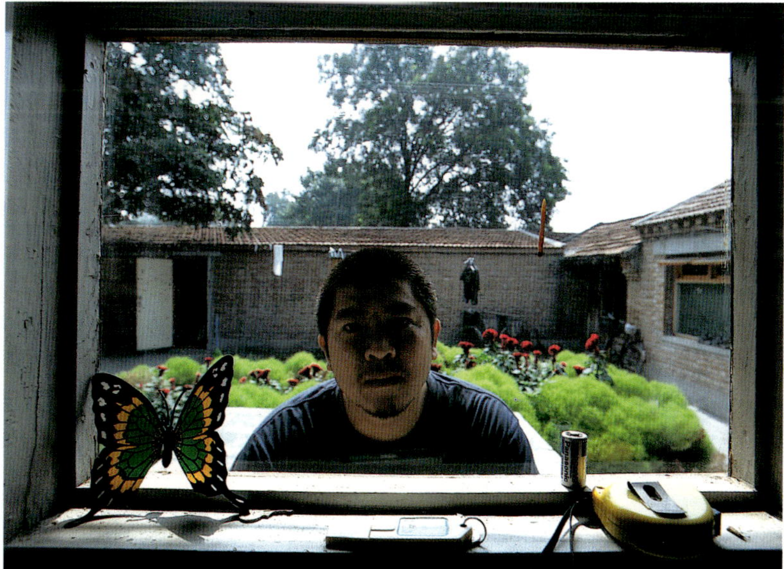

THE LUO BROTHERS LIVE IN A FARMHOUSE THAT THEY RENOVATED THEMSELVES. THEY ARE PICTURED IN THE FARMYARD. THEY BEGIN FOOLING AROUND AS SOON AS THEY SEE THE CAMERA.

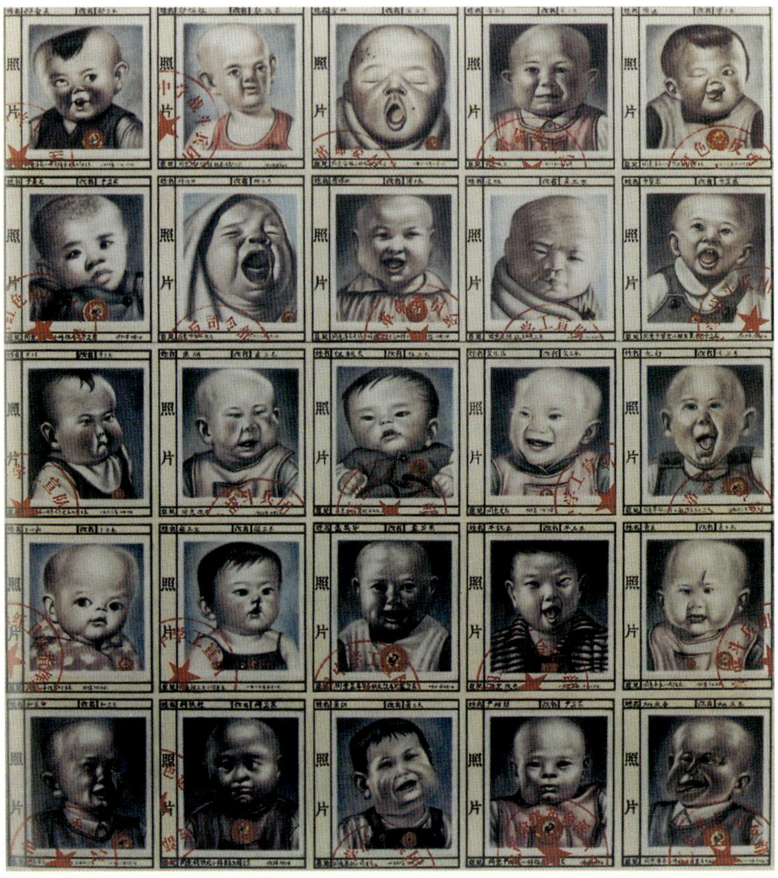

100 FAMILY NAME PRIMER, 1994. LACQUER ON WOOD, FROM THE SERIES *CHANGING NAMES*. FACING PAGE: TWO WORKS FROM THE SERIES *WELCOME THE WORLD FAMOUS BRANDT*, 2000.

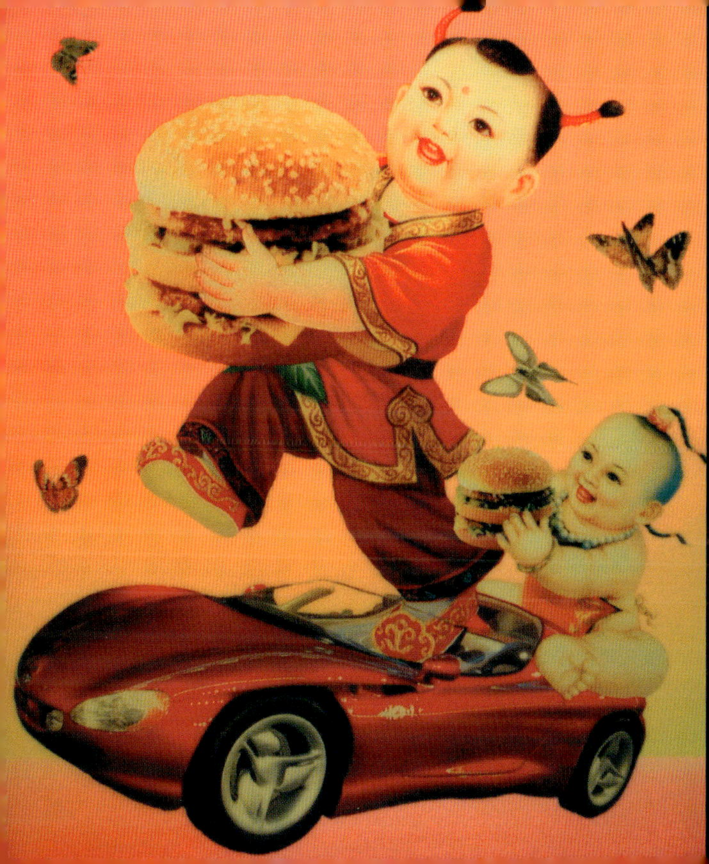

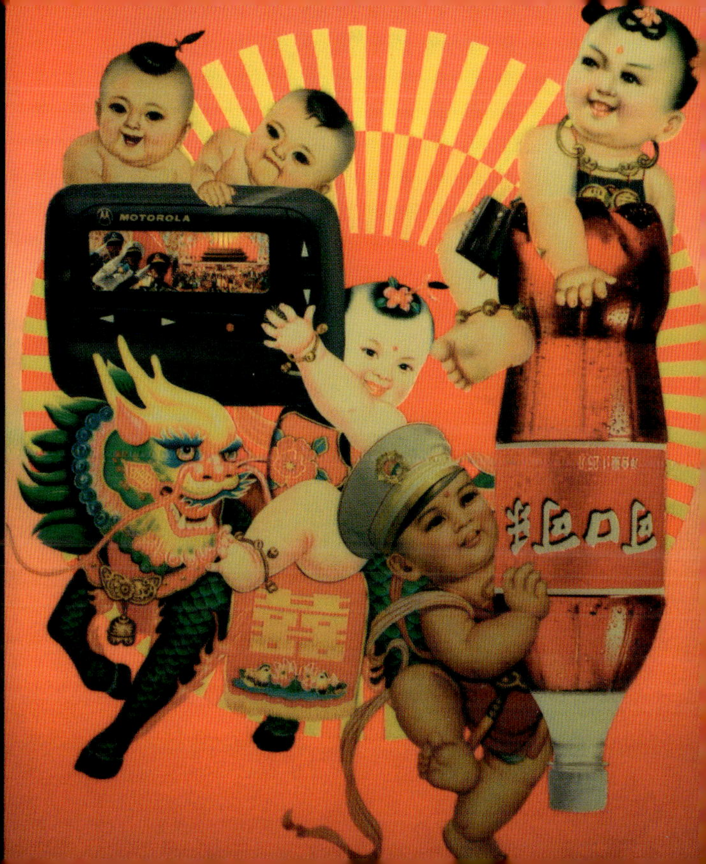

MOTOROLA

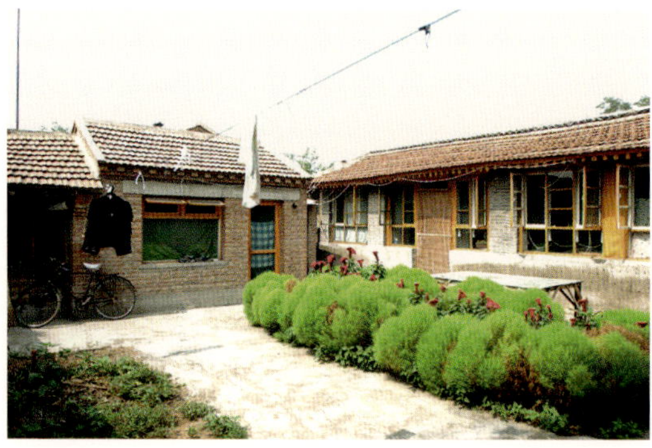

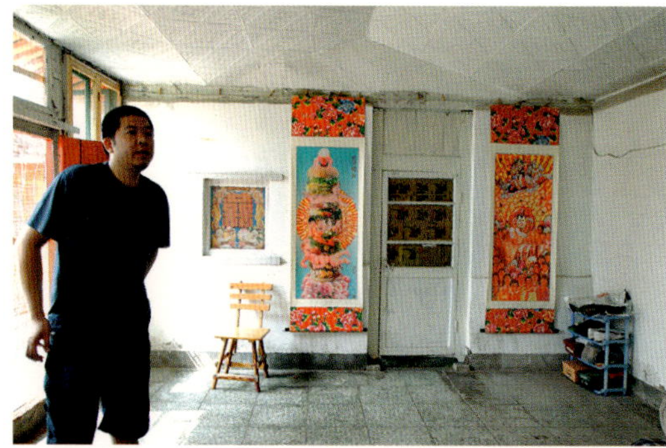

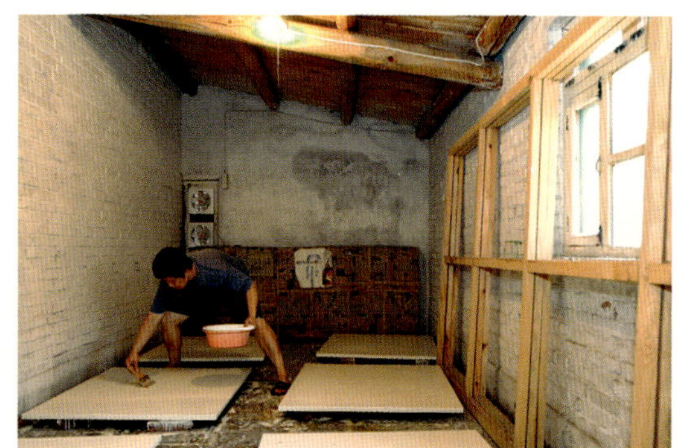

sold like any other. ¶ This very cheery imagery is combined with iconic historical and political scenes that were designed to be just as salutary—Mao Tse-tung greeting the people or swimming (one of his favorite pastimes, along with dancing and parties in the company of charming young ladies), young guards brandishing the Little Red Book, and so on. ¶ In the 1990s, Gaudy Art was a way for the artists to register their wary attitude to the wave of consumerism and the emergence of a capitalist class in China in the early 1980s. Where Political Pop Art could be interpreted as critical of consumerism, Gaudy Art was an unbridled exaltation of its virtues, to the point of caricature. In this, it is indeed close to American Pop Art, which plays with the favorite icons of the consumer society, sometimes magnifying them to the point where a moment of epiphany is attained (although Andy Warhol's art is closer to a poisoned kiss). Kitsch is not in the picture, at least as far as the Luo Brothers are concerned. ¶ Chubby little boys and girls like Renaissance cherubs sit astride a Big Mac, carrying a second with three hands, arms outstretched, while the little boy holds in his right hand a wrapper bearing the Golden Arches logo. Above them are two other infants astride a pair of fish in a field of flowers. Higher up is a scene from the Forbidden City and a view of crowds in Tiananmen Square. Right at the bottom, the Golden Arches logo appears again. ¶ The same view of Tiananmen Square and the Forbidden City features on the Panasonic screen perched at the top of another painting showing a child wearing a crown of pink peonies, with a karaoke microphone in his right hand and a soccer ball in his left, and another between his legs. The boy is flanked by three bottles of Coca-Cola (the labels in Chinese script) on either side, like a decorative motif. Above his head is a frieze of soccer balls. This picture dates back a few years, when neighboring Korea and Japan were preparing to host the soccer World Cup and China was lobbying hard to be awarded the 2008 Olympic Games. ¶ There are chubby infants riding garlands, goldfish, tigers, and deer everywhere you look. The boys and girls fly, skip, dance, hop, smile, hold out Big Macs, and brandish their mobile phones triumphantly. The animals featured, which change from year to year according to the Chinese calendar, each represent a particular quality. The tiger stands for power, the bat good luck, and the deer longevity. But the Luo Brothers turn these symbols on their heads, always with good humor. So while dragons traditionally pursue balls of flame, the Luo Brothers replace them with soccer balls. ¶ Is this the clash of two different worlds? Is Chinese culture being superseded by foreign imports? I would rather say that the Luo Brothers enjoy the give and take between the two worlds—a metaphorical game of ping-pong, if you prefer. ¶ They draw everything by hand using color pencils, cut the shapes out, and put them in place. They then coat them in lacquer to create a perfectly flat, shiny surface. ¶ It's as simple as that. ¶ The Luo Brothers have found their niche. Their art, straightforward, garish, exuberant, paradoxical, and flashy as it is, has met with wry praise, in China, the United States, and Europe. In 1998, the Luo Brothers took part in the twenty-fourth São Paulo Biennial, and in 2000 they were invited to the Sydney Biennial. They have also exhibited in a gallery in New York, then at the museums of modern art in San Francisco and Chicago. In Europe, they were shown almost simultaneously at the Next Generation exhibition at the Passage de Retz Gallery and the Popular Art exhibition at the Fondation Cartier in Paris. ¶ The Luo Brothers do not claim to be great artists, but their work is witty, perceptive, and brilliant. And success obviously agrees with them.

LEFT TO RIGHT: THE FARMYARD WITH FLOWERBEDS AND WASHING HUNG OUT TO DRY. INSIDE THE FARMHOUSE, A FEW OF THE BROTHERS' WORKS ON DISPLAY. THE OUTBUILDING WHERE THE BROTHERS WORK.

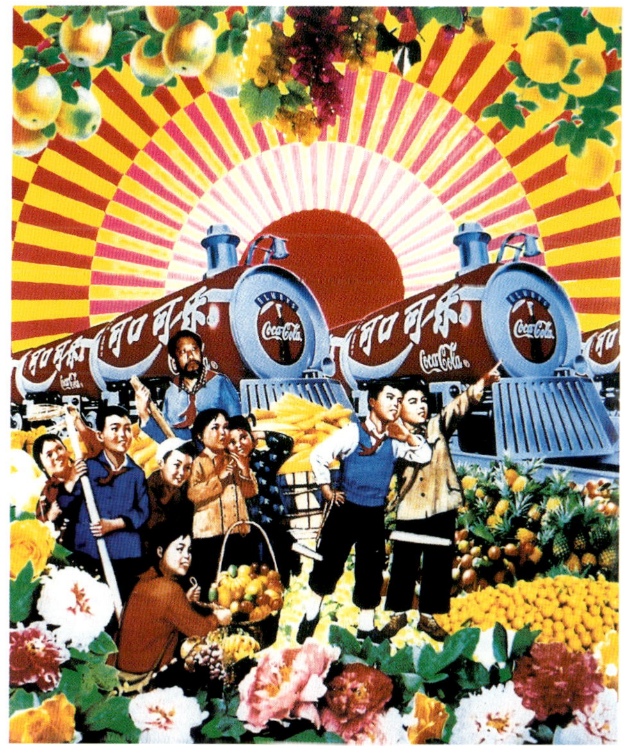

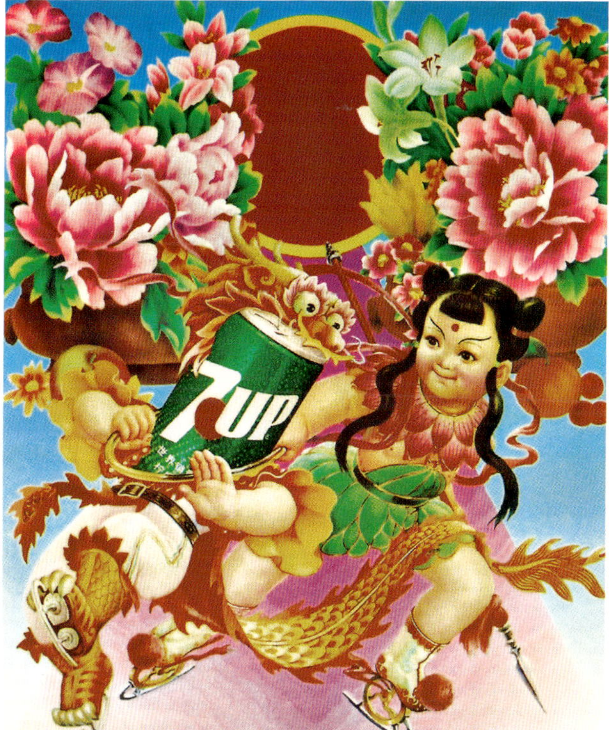

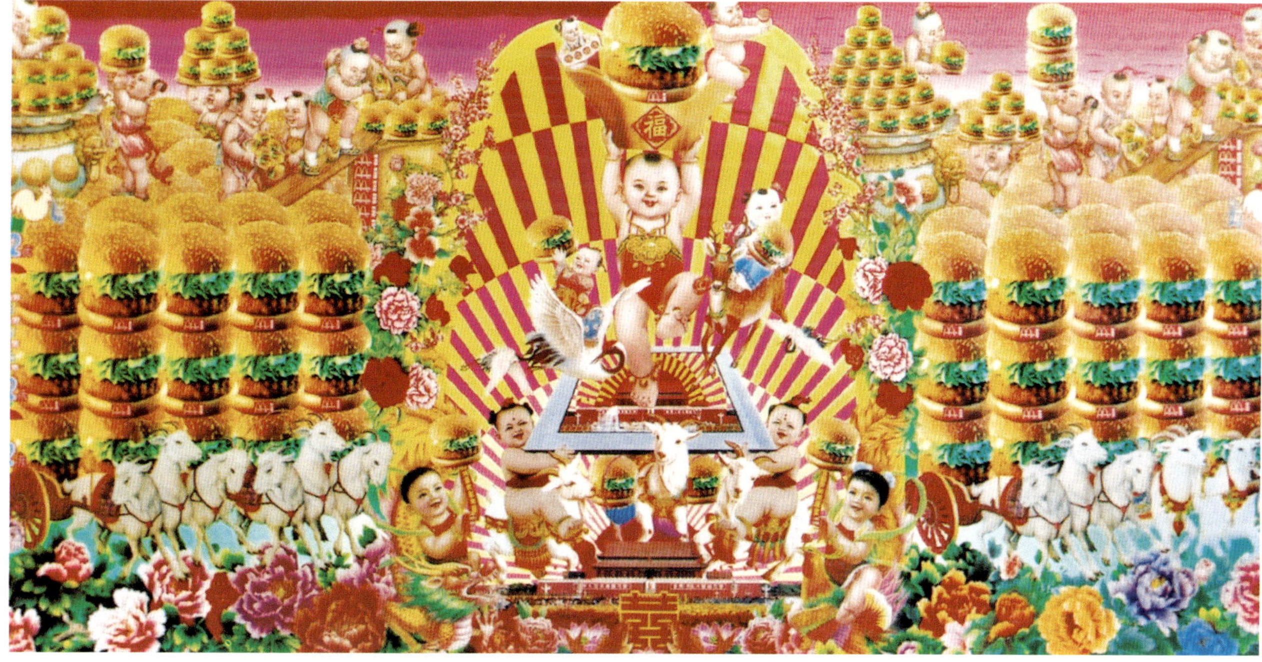

BOTTOM AND TOP RIGHT: TWO WORKS IN LACQUER ON WOOD, ALL WITH THE SAME TITLE AND DATE: *WELCOME THE WORLD FAMOUS BRANDT*, 2000. TOP LEFT: THIS WORK DATES FROM 1995.

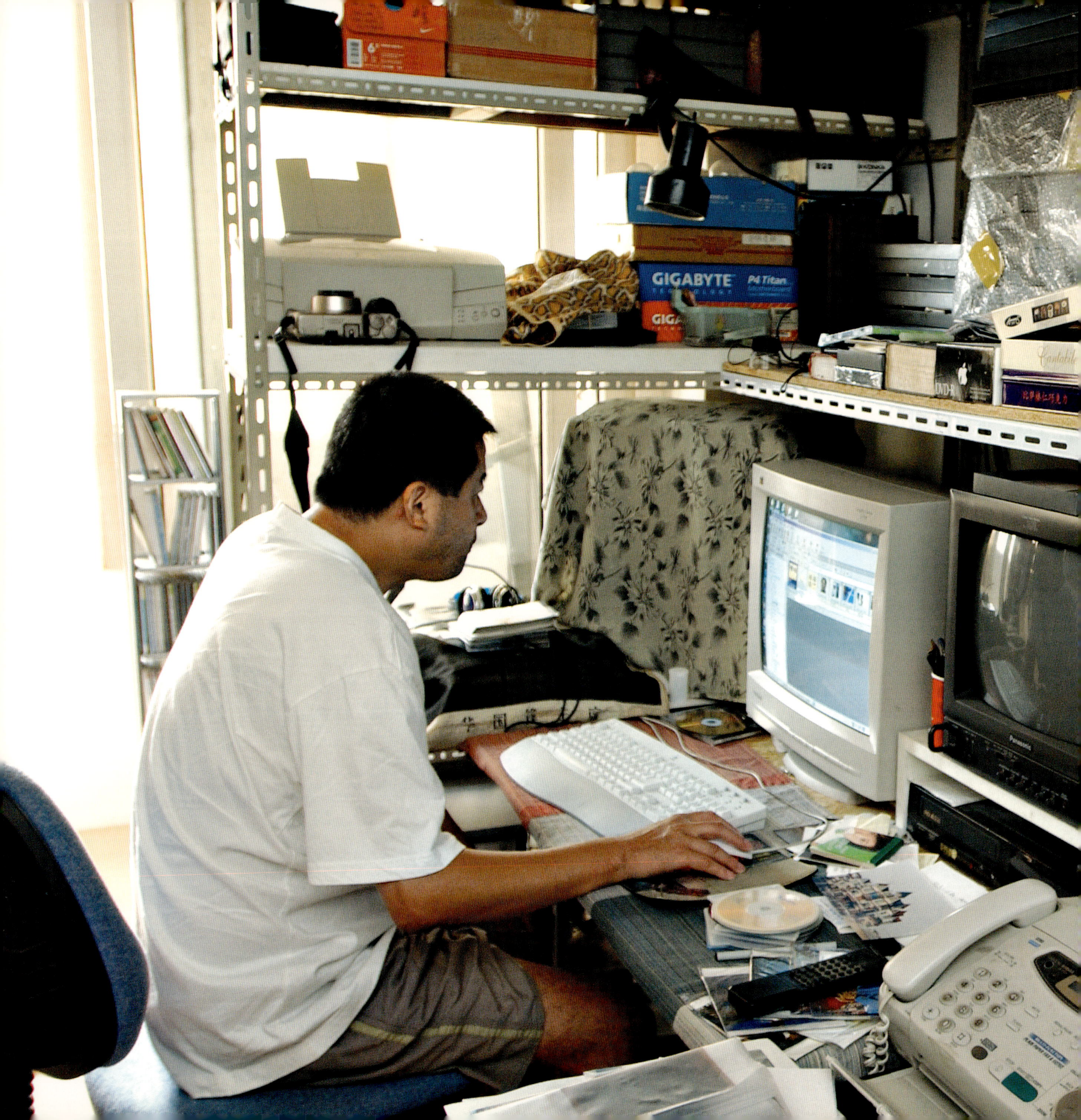
GIGABYTE
P4 Titan

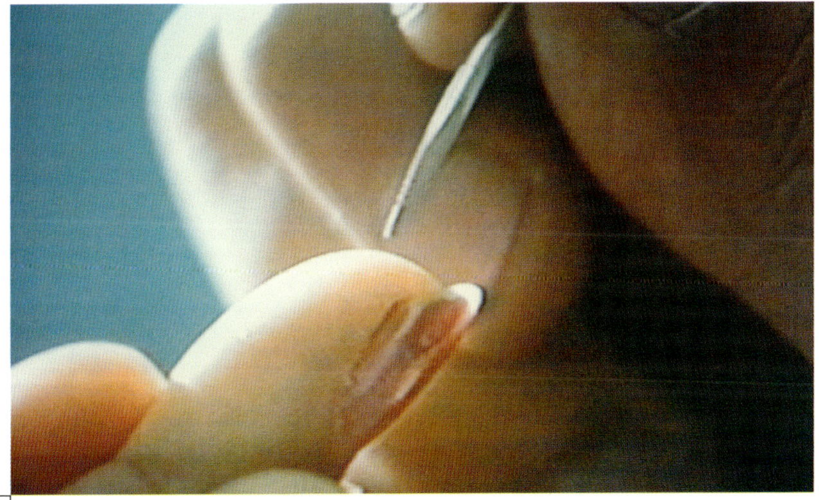

ZHANG PEILI

We are on the train, bound for Hangzhou, ninety-five miles (150 kilometers) southwest of Shanghai. When the train sets off at 7:21 A.M., many of our fellow travelers have already settled down for breakfast. We arrive in Hangzhou two hours later, although it feels as if we have hardly reached the outer limits of the immense urban sprawl of Shanghai. We have seen fields, few and far between, and enormous, impressive mansions with almond-green and candy-pink turrets and bell towers, straight out of Disneyland. These are the homes of the local farmers. I am assured that all the farmers near Hangzhou are extremely well-off. I find this astonishing, and ask for more details. It turns out that the farmers in the mountains and distant plains are poor, but the ones fortunate enough to farm land in the immediate vicinity of Hangzhou are very rich and can afford these horrible, ridiculous Xanadu palaces to flash their wealth around. ¶ Zhang Peili's apartment and studio are in the eastern part of the city. "In the tony neighborhood," our interpreter, a friend of the artist, jokes. We are struck by a powerful odor as soon as we pass the front door. It is a Chinese ginseng-based medicine. There are portraits of Chairman Mao in various styles on the walls. The sitting room is small, and leads onto a sort of studio in a short, narrow corridor where two computers and a television are left on permanently. He takes us to his bedroom where we discover a full-length portrait of Mao. There is also a thermometer showing the temperature of the room 77°F (25°C). This is where he shows his works, on a large screen. A montage. We settle down on the bed to watch. ¶ Surprise—the first video dates back to 1988. I knew Zhang Peili was ahead of his time, but this is astonishing. The video lasts three hours, the duration of a long VHS videocassette. Actually, it is an infinite, looped film, entitled *30 x 30*. This is the size of the mirror that Zhang Peili drops to break it, before sticking the fragments back together like a giant, clumsy jigsaw. ¶ Is it a symbolic work? Is it meant to be read as the image of a shattered human soul trying to put itself back together, or a metaphor for the breakdown of Chinese society and the attempts to patch it up? Again, I ask, is it a symbolic work? "Maybe," he says politely, or hedging his bets, perfectly used to avoiding giving a direct answer to this kind of question. "It's up to the viewer to decide, but that's not what I was thinking of. If there is a symbolic dimension to the work, it's vaguer than that. There's a general parallel with human existence." ¶ Given the inclination of European and American critics to look at their work through a political filter, Chinese artists who, a few years back, greeted such questions with a polite smile, are now more and more likely to respond with a certain hostility. ¶ For Zhang Peili, the most important aspect of the work was simply showing an action repeated over a period of three hours. He tells me that the notions of time and repetition are important components of many of his works. The idea of the cycle is an integral part of his performances. ¶ *Document on Hygiene* (1991), shown in 1993 at the Théâtre du Rond-Point in Paris, features rubber-gloved hands soaping and rinsing chickens in a basin. It is ironic. Zhang Peili says, "Men are often anthropocentric. They apply their own ideas to other cultures and other orders of creation. Some people think that the chickens must enjoy being washed and massaged. Others think that on the contrary, it must be torture for them. But there's no way of knowing. It's like two people looking at fish in water. One says the fish are lucky to be in water, and it must be wonderful for them. The second asks how the first can know whether the fish like being in water or not." The first retorts that the second is not inside his head, so how can he know if he knows whether the fish are happy or not? The title of the work is a reference to an official circular. ¶ *Children Greyhound*

FACING PAGE: ZHANG PEILI ON A VERY HOT DAY IN HANGZHOU, TWO HOURS' DRIVE FROM SHANGHAI, IN THE CORRIDOR HE USES AS A STUDIO, SURROUNDED BY TV SCREENS AND COMPUTERS. ABOVE: ASSIGNMENT NO.1, 1992.

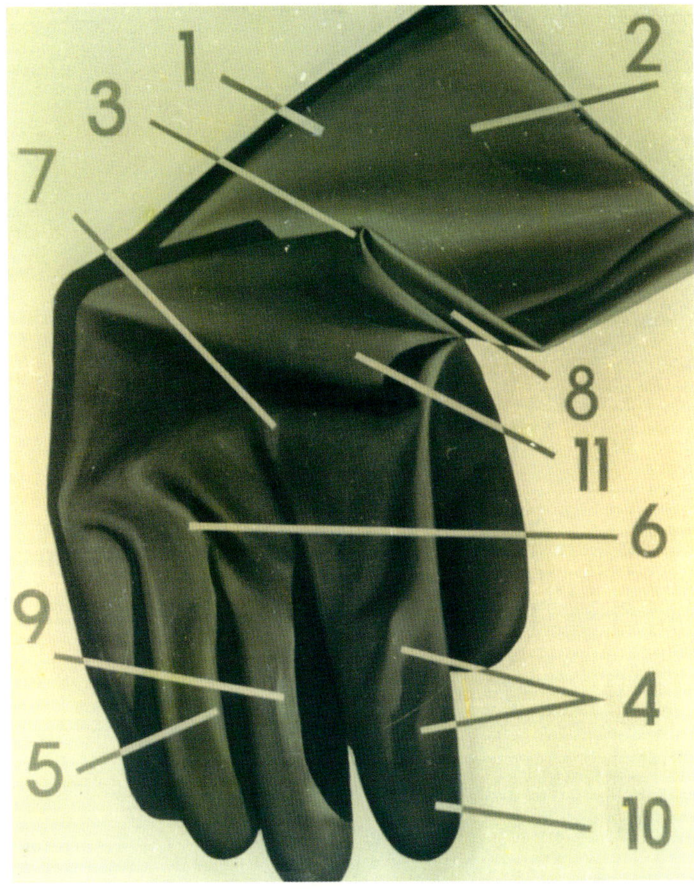

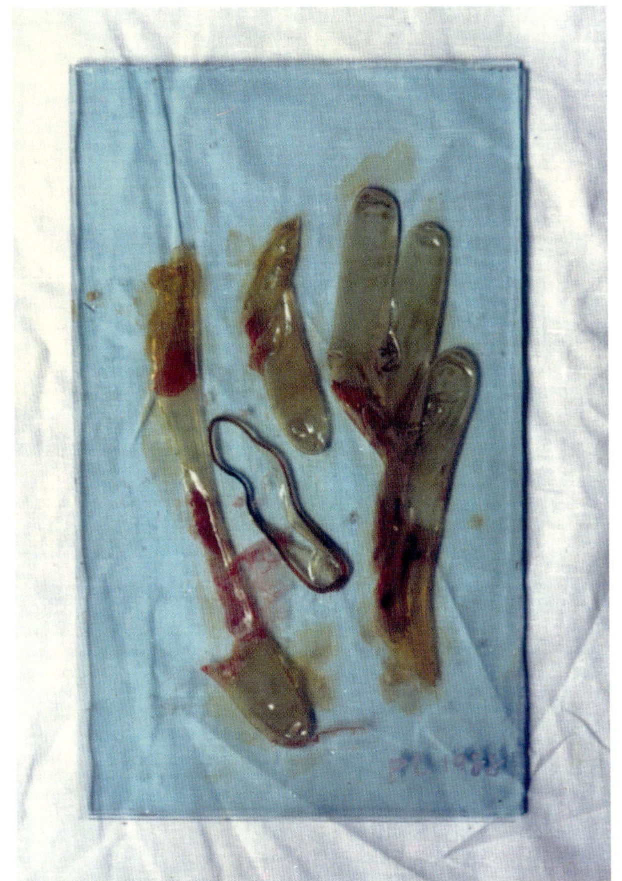

ABOVE LEFT: A PAINTING ENTITLED *X?*, 1986–87. ABOVE RIGHT: A WORK IN MIXED MEDIA *REPORT ON HEPATITIS*, 1988. FACING PAGE: LEFT: *DOCUMENT ON HYGIENE*, 1991. RIGHT: ZHANG PEILI'S FIRST VIDEO, *30 X 30*, 1988.

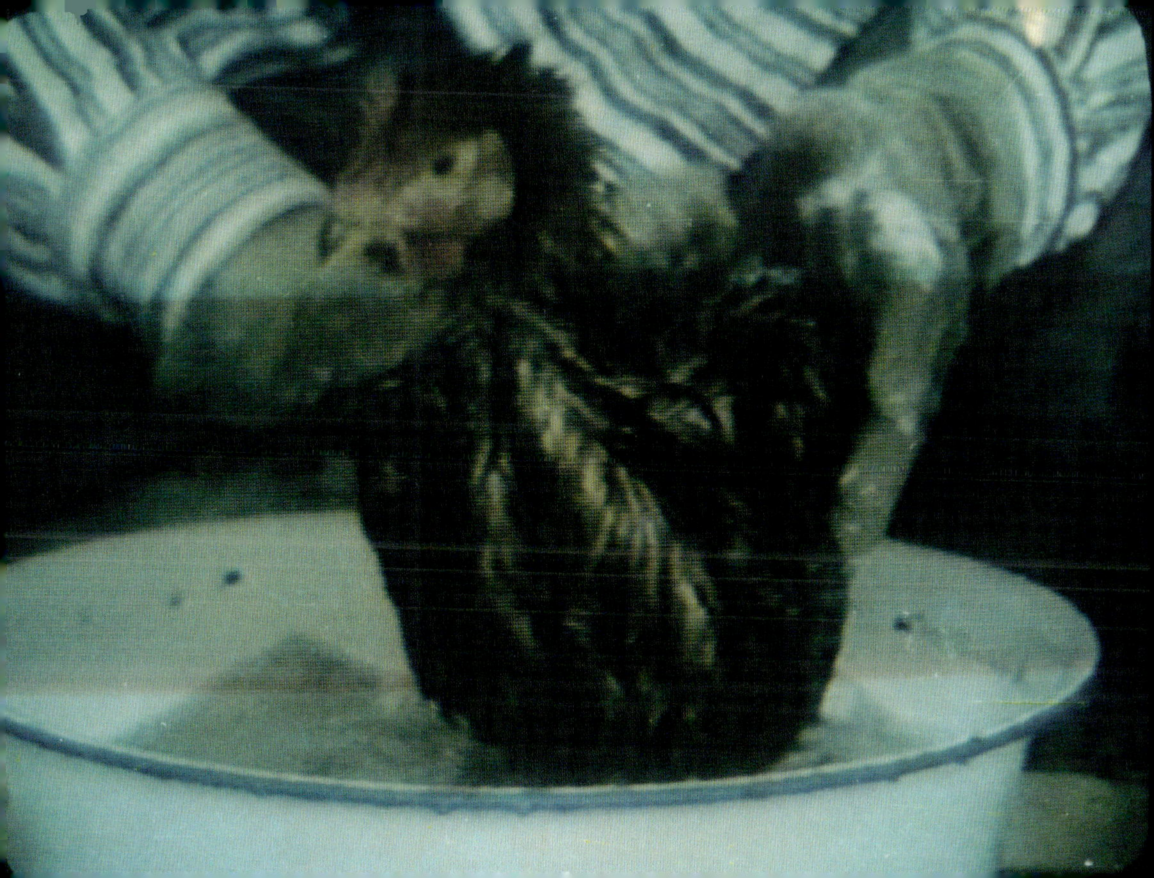

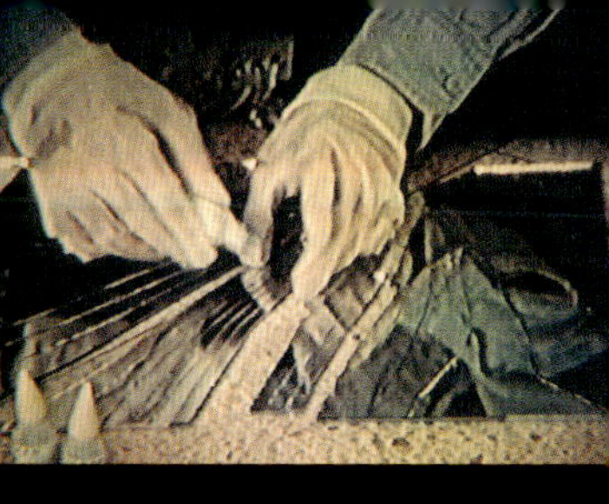
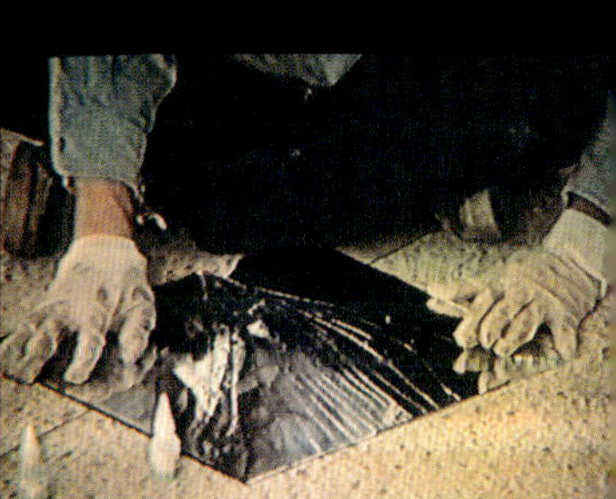
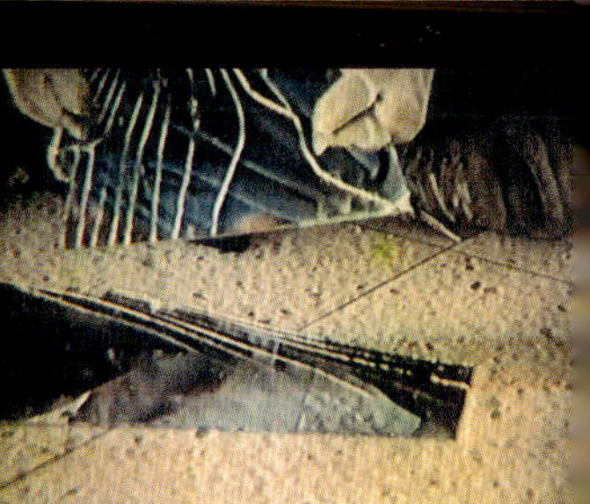

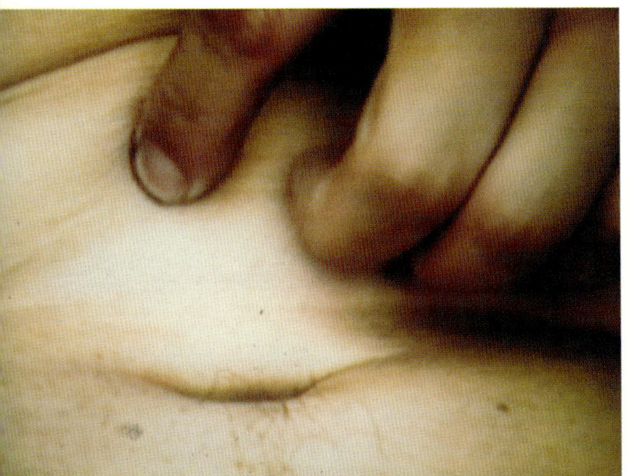

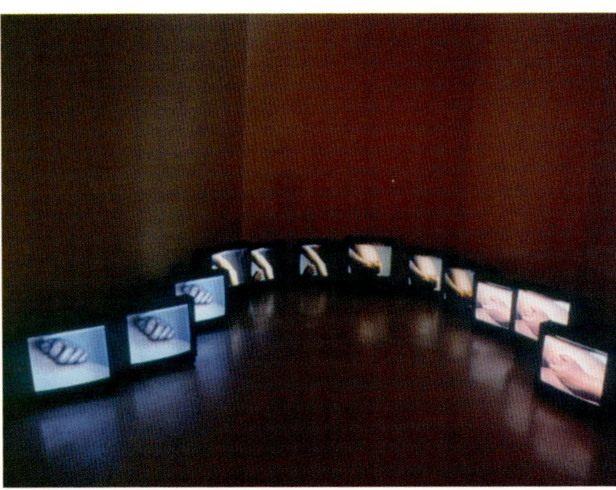

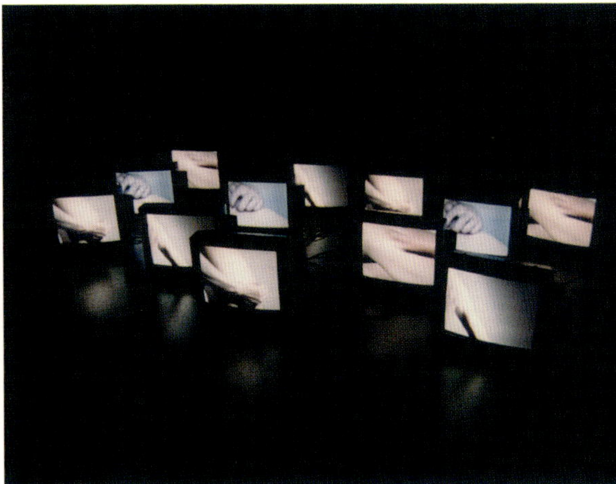

shows a plastic circuit with toy penguins climbing steps and gliding down slides. It is very flashy in bright red and yellow. Zhang Peili showed this looped video, along with an installation in the cellar, at the Chantal Crousel gallery in 1993, shortly after his exhibition at the Théâtre du Rond-Point. He is still with this gallery, which has always paid him regularly. I wonder if this is a veiled dig at other galleries. No comment, he says. ¶ Zhang Peili talks a bit about the difficulties of working with a gallery so far from where he lives, particularly since he is not really familiar with the international art market. He then tells me that his real gallery is in fact Art et Public, which has been representing him since 1996, although, he quickly adds, "Since 2001, I have been wondering whether I am still with this gallery, as I haven't had an exhibition with them since then, and although I still receive invitations to the openings, I hardly get any emails from them these days." His gallery in New York is Jack Tilten in SoHo. He likes Jack Tilten very much, because he was one of the first gallery owners to show an interest in Chinese art. He also works with Max Protech. ¶ *Water* (1992) shows a famous television presenter reading out from a dictionary all the words that include the Chinese sign for water. (There is no reason behind the choice of word: it was completely random). More than a straightforward criticism of television and its influence over people's attitudes, it is an ironic work. "She is a very famous presenter, and what is she doing? She is reading out text, no more involved than a machine would be. She is told to read out the dictionary, and she does, like a machine. If the government suddenly changed and she was given a text to read that was in complete contradiction with what she just read out, she'd carry on reading just the same. And look, see how stereotypical she is, with her hairstyle and her way of smiling." ¶ *Assignment Number 1* (1992) is a close-up of a finger and a bead of blood that wells up as a sort of needle is stuck under the fingernail. Many of Zhang Peili's works from this period deal with issues of the body and hygiene. ¶ *The Related Rhythm* (1996) is shown simultaneously on two screens. This was his first step towards his video installations. He has been the undisputed king of this genre in China for almost a decade. I wonder whether he is influenced by Gary Hill. "No," he answers very quickly. He has probably been asked the same question a thousand times. "I discovered Gary Hill at the Centre Pompidou when I went to Paris in 1996. My work was already completed before then." That may be the case for this particular piece, but not for others that have been presented in installations since then, which have an internal logic very close to the American artist's oeuvre. ¶ His next few works were not quite so interesting. The first showed two landscapes, one with the sun in front of the camera, the other behind. The video camera pans up from the ground and then down again, and we hear the sound of a swing. *Focal Distance* (1996) features a similar scene refilmed, gradually fading until the image vanishes altogether. ¶ 1996. Was it before or after his encounter with Gary Hill's work that Zhang Peili planned his installation *Uncertain Pleasure*? A hand scratching various parts of a body. A perfectly common, simple, repetitive action. A woman, a man, a Chinese man, a French man. Zhang Peili has shown this work all over the world, each time changing the presentation noticeably. "I can show this work as an installation in an almost limitless number of ways. Light or sophisticated," he says. ¶ 1996 was an important year. Zhang Peili threw down a gauntlet, accusing the Chinese avant-garde of creating works with a Chinese "flavor" in accordance with what Western critics and buyers wanted from them. He has always kept them at arm's length. "Chinese artists tend to ask 'Who am I?' too much," he says. "The best thing would be for all artists to

A RECENT VIDEO THAT ZHANG PEILI HAS INCLUDED IN A NUMBER OF INSTALLATIONS, *UNCERTAIN PLEASURES*, 1996–99. LEFT: A CLOSE-UP OF THE VIDEO SHOWING A HAND SCRATCHING SKIN.

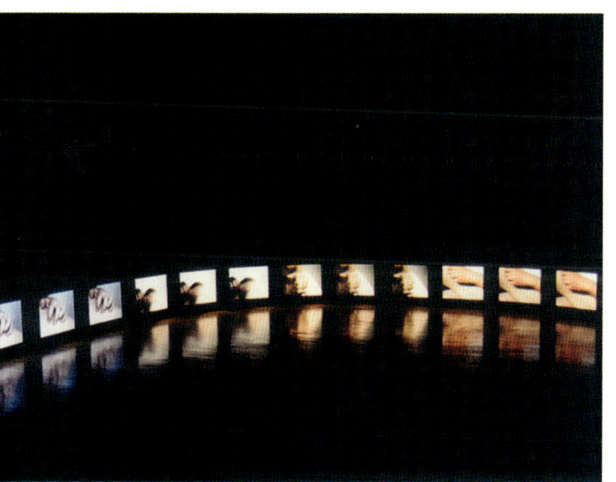
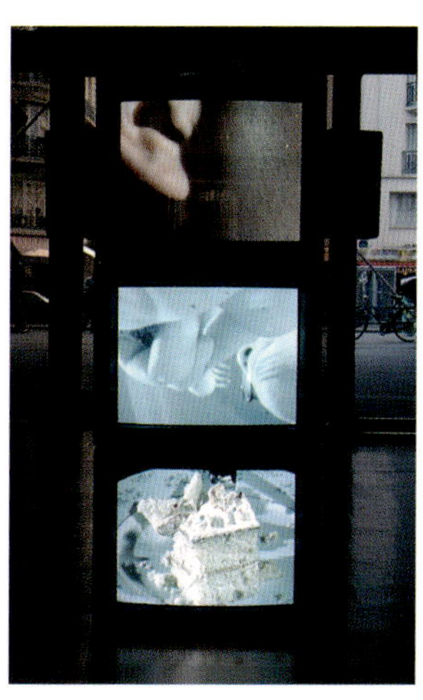
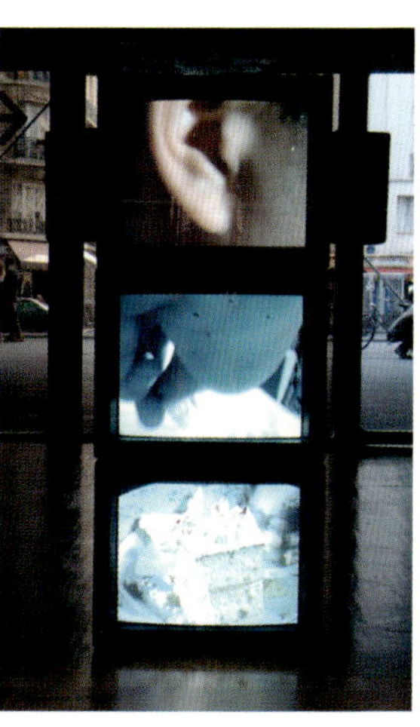
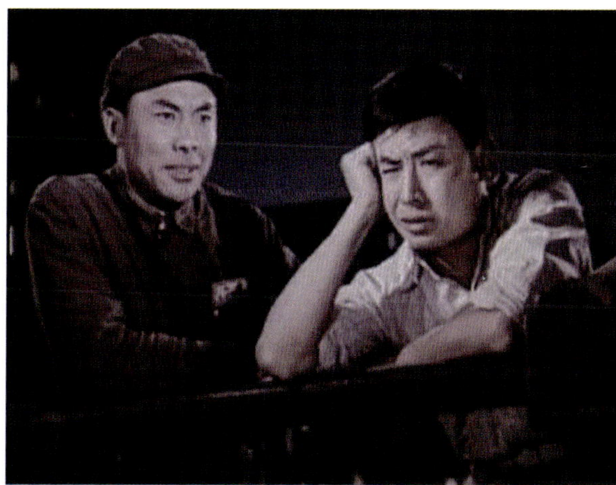

stay natural, just as they are." ¶ What could be more natural than *Eating* (1997), a video shown at the Centre Pompidou's China exhibition in 2003. Zhang Peili filmed someone eating and the plate they were eating from, from a number of different angles and from a very close range. The images are broadcast on three TV screens piled on top of each other. ¶ *Just for You* (1999, shown in Venice) moves from screen to screen in a circle, like children taking turns to sing the lines of a nursery rhyme. A little girl, a man, an old woman, a young woman, and so on, take turns to sing "Happy Birthday" in Chinese. "I filmed people I knew," Zhang Peili says. "Some had good singing voices and had even taken singing lessons, while others did not. But in front of the video camera, they all made the effort to sing nicely. The video has a direct impact on behavior." The title *Just for You* is an obvious reference to the notion of gift giving. ¶ *Endless Dancing* (1999): some professional dancers filmed for a karaoke presenter, and some amateurs Zhang Peili filmed himself at dances or in public squares. OK. Yes, but the song (a waltz, to be precise) is a revolutionary song from the 1970s, sung by nostalgic soldiers. Everything is mixed, squandered, confused, in reference to the state of China (and the rest of the world) today. ¶ Zhang Peili's most recent video work is *Actors Lines* (2003). He took an old sepia propaganda film from the 1960s, a perfect example of the emphatic tone, naïveté, and sheer cunning of the genre. A kindly, attentive soldier asks a young student, "What are you thinking about?" The student confides that he is feeling uneasy. "Why don't you confide in me? We are very close, heart to heart," the soldier replies, keen to get the student to share his burden. Zhang Peili has made just one small change. The end of each sentence is repeated three or four times. It is a neat way of hoisting the open propaganda with its own petard, by repeating the message to the point of absurdity. ¶ Zhang Peili presented his first installation in New York in 1994. A wall of newsprint in the center of a huge hall blocked the view of what was happening on the other side. By climbing up a stepladder, visitors were able to see the artist slowly, methodically, tearing up newspapers. In Barcelona, video cameras placed in two different rooms let visitors see each other in the different spaces. In Beijing in 1995, he showed photographs of landscapes taken with a range of exposures, from the fastest shutter speed to the slowest. Over the photos was a transparent sheet of paper covering the image. A nearby fan would occasionally waft up the piece of paper, giving a clear glimpse of the photo underneath. This was a metaphor of secretiveness, and maybe of the truth which must remain hidden or be denatured, as Nietzsche said about the Greeks. ¶ Zhang Peili, the best-known Chinese video artist, the first Chinese artist to have his work bought by MoMA, only ever produced three copies of his videos on Betacam, although others are available on VHS or DVD, on sale for one-tenth the price (but not in his principal gallery). It sounds a bit complicated, I say to him, not really clear-cut, maybe even a little dangerous. He fires back, "Maybe, but I don't have a contract with any gallery." ¶ Every year, he sells one or two, maybe three, works. The average price is ten thousand dollars. The most expensive was an installation sold for fifty thousand dollars. The first of his three Betacam cassettes is sold for less than the third—an old market tradition. Apart from this income, which averages thirty thousand dollars a year, he earns a salary as a teacher, and now also as the head of the multimedia department at the Hangzhou School of Fine Art. ¶ He was born in Hangzhou, in Zhejiang province, in 1957. His love of the region shines through as he explains, "It's one of the nicest cities to live in all China. It is a happy medium. It's the smallest prefecture in all of China, but it's far from

TWO DIFFERENT TYPES OF INSTALLATION. LEFT TO RIGHT: *UNCERTAIN PLEASURES*, 1999, AT THE FUKUODA MUSEUM IN JAPAN. *EATING*, 1997. ZHANG PEILI'S MOST RECENT WORK, *ACTORS' WORDS*, 2003.

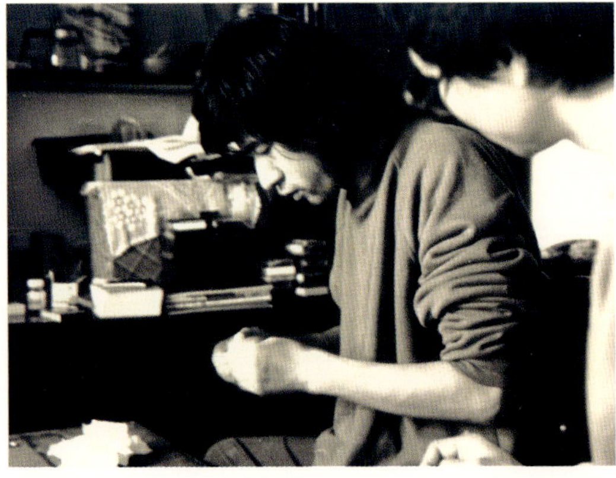

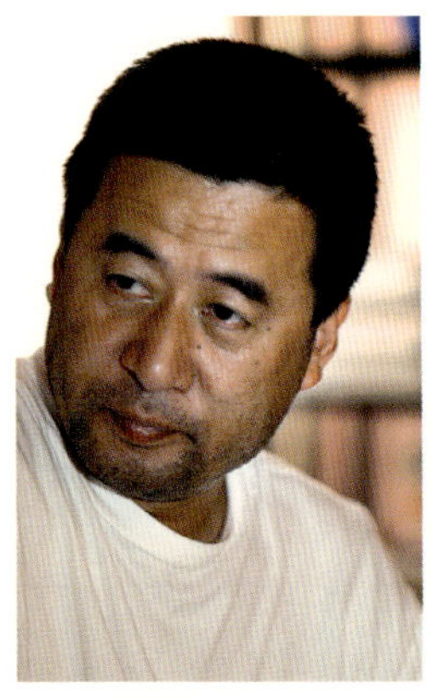

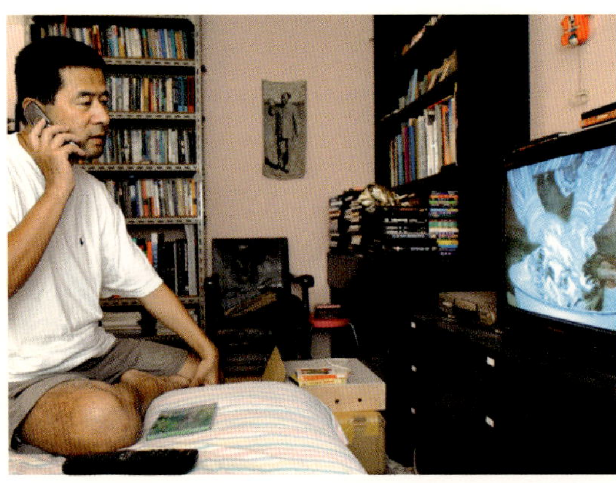

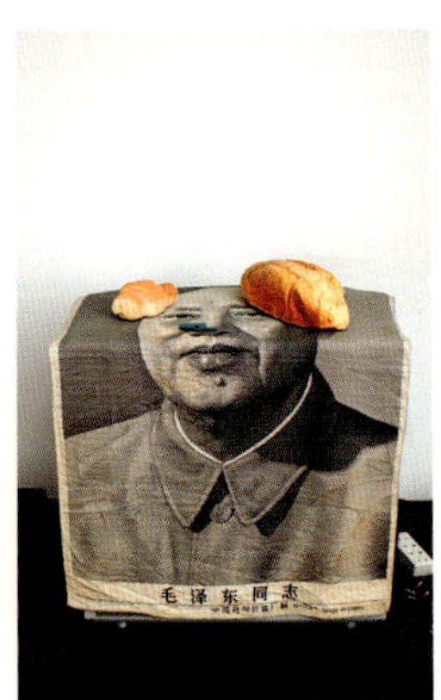

being small-minded and conservative. There are plenty of canals and rivers. The streets are not too wide. There aren't any skyscrapers. But at the same time, it has undergone a terrible program of demolitions. All that is left of its past beauty is a lake and the hills. Anything that could be destroyed already has been. But I love Hangzhou. I grew up here, and I have deep roots and close friendships here." ¶ His artistic vocation became apparent when he was ten, thanks to a neighbor, then aged twenty, whose father was friends with his own father (and who was beaten to death during the Cultural Revolution). The young man introduced him to his drawing teacher. Zhang Peili says, "Very quickly, I knew I wanted to be an artist. That's how it began—simple." ¶ His first job on leaving school, however, was as a laborer. Because of the Cultural Revolution? Let's talk about it. "It's a very complex subject," he says, before pausing for thought. "In some ways it was quite fun yet in others it was absolutely appalling. When I was little, I saw people fighting. We children were allowed to take the train anywhere in China for free, we could criticize our teachers, we could skip classes, and no one would say anything. Our parents were always in meetings and had no time for us. It was absolute, total freedom. It was pretty good fun. Until the day when I saw what happened to the parents of my neighbors when they were criticized. I was scared it could happen to my parents, too." At that time, relations with the USSR were also strained. It was muttered that war was in the cards. There was rationing and coupons were introduced. Food was hard to come by. ¶ Zhang Peili continues, "I began to think about the situation in high school." It was 1975. The Cultural Revolution was nearing its end. Zhang Peili was nineteen. At this point, I dared ask a question about the portraits of Mao that cover the walls of his apartment. The interpreter intervenes: "Mao was the only Communist. Communism can never happen." I get the impression he has some admiration for the utopian vision of the Communist ideal. ¶ Zhang Peili gathers his thoughts before he continues. "From 1949, there was a dream of modernizing the country that figured in the paintings of the day, which bristle with smokestacks. Mao came up against obstacles in Chinese culture and the political system. That's why he didn't succeed straight away with his plan of westernizing China. The plan became reality with Deng Xiaoping. That is when the cities began to change. Since then, they have been totally renewed. Look at paintings from the 1970s, and you will see what I mean." It is obvious that Zhang Peili dislikes this change. "It's like eating in a fast food restaurant. Everything is standardized. There's no room for identity or individual thought in that world." ¶ Today, Zhang Peili is a respected artist and teacher. He has made a name for himself. He is in charge of the brand new multimedia department at the Hangzhou School of Fine Arts, one of the most reputed in all China. I visited the department as it was being built. The building has four floors, and all the facilities are brand new: studios, darkrooms, art rooms, computer labs, and exhibition halls. The staff in the painting department were annoyed, probably because they were jealous. The new department will cost a lot, both in terms of equipment and upkeep. No one is quite sure where the money is going to keep coming from. ¶ All of this must take a lot of time and energy. Isn't his personal creative work suffering as a consequence? "I feel very unsettled," he says solemnly. ¶ We leave the department. I am full of admiration and have dozens of questions. We spend the rest of the afternoon at the local Starbucks, behind a bamboo curtain that opens onto a pond. This is where all the bright young things of Hangzhou hang out. Next door is a Häagen Dazs. The city of Hangzhou, "paradise on earth," has certainly changed.

FROM LEFT TO RIGHT: A YOUNG, SHAGGY-HEADED ZHANG PEILI, A SHOT OF THE ARTIST IN HIS BEDROOM SPEAKING ON THE TELEPHONE WHILE WATCHING A DOCUMENTARY ON HYGIENE, AND WITH A PORTRAIT OF MAO. FACING PAGE: HE HAS BEEN APPOINTED HEAD OF DEPARTMENT AT THE NEW HANGZHOU ACADEMY OF ARTS, WHICH OPENED IN OCTOBER 2003.

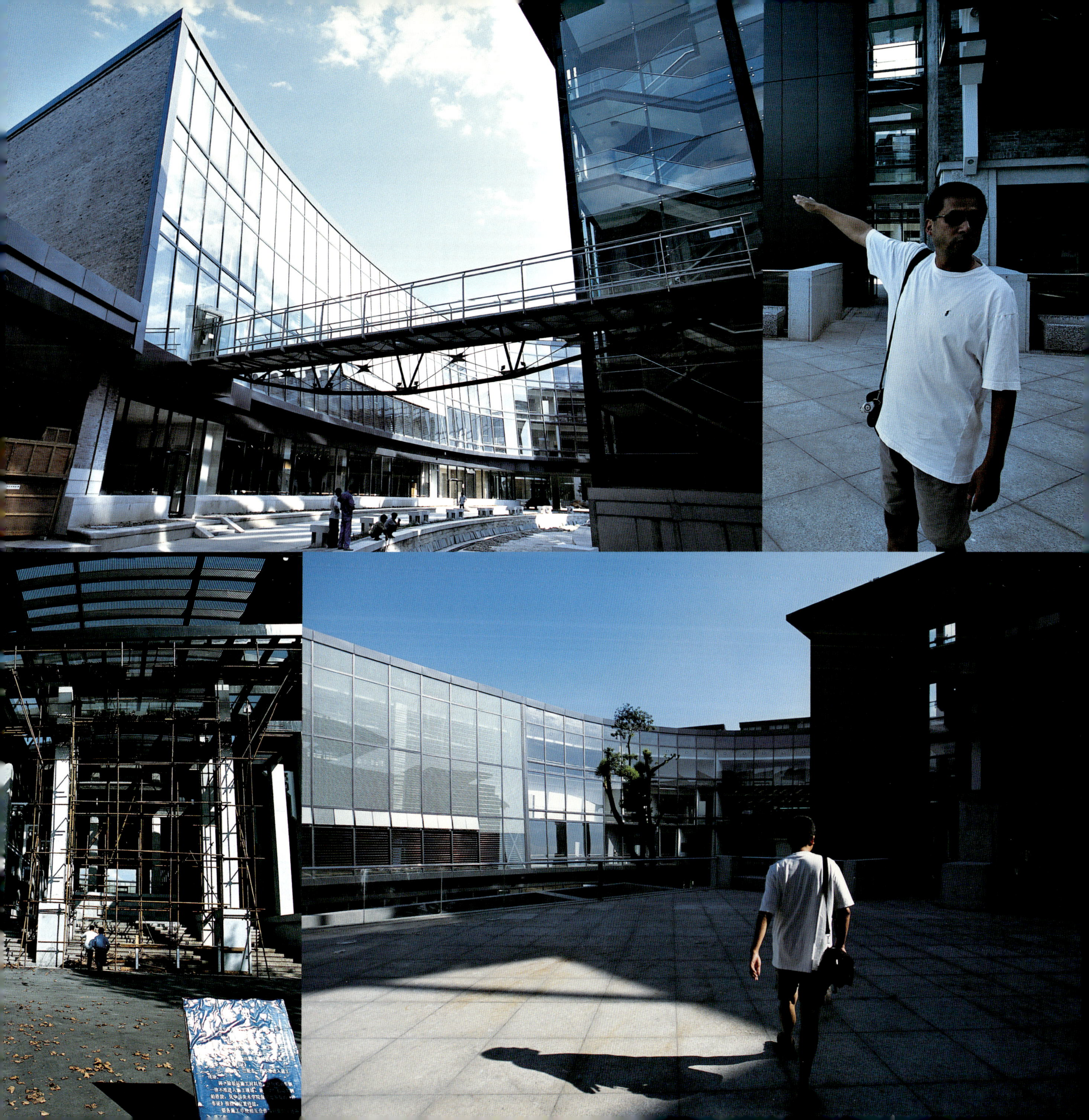
现场。
一律不准进入施工现场，
的停放，凭中国美术学院

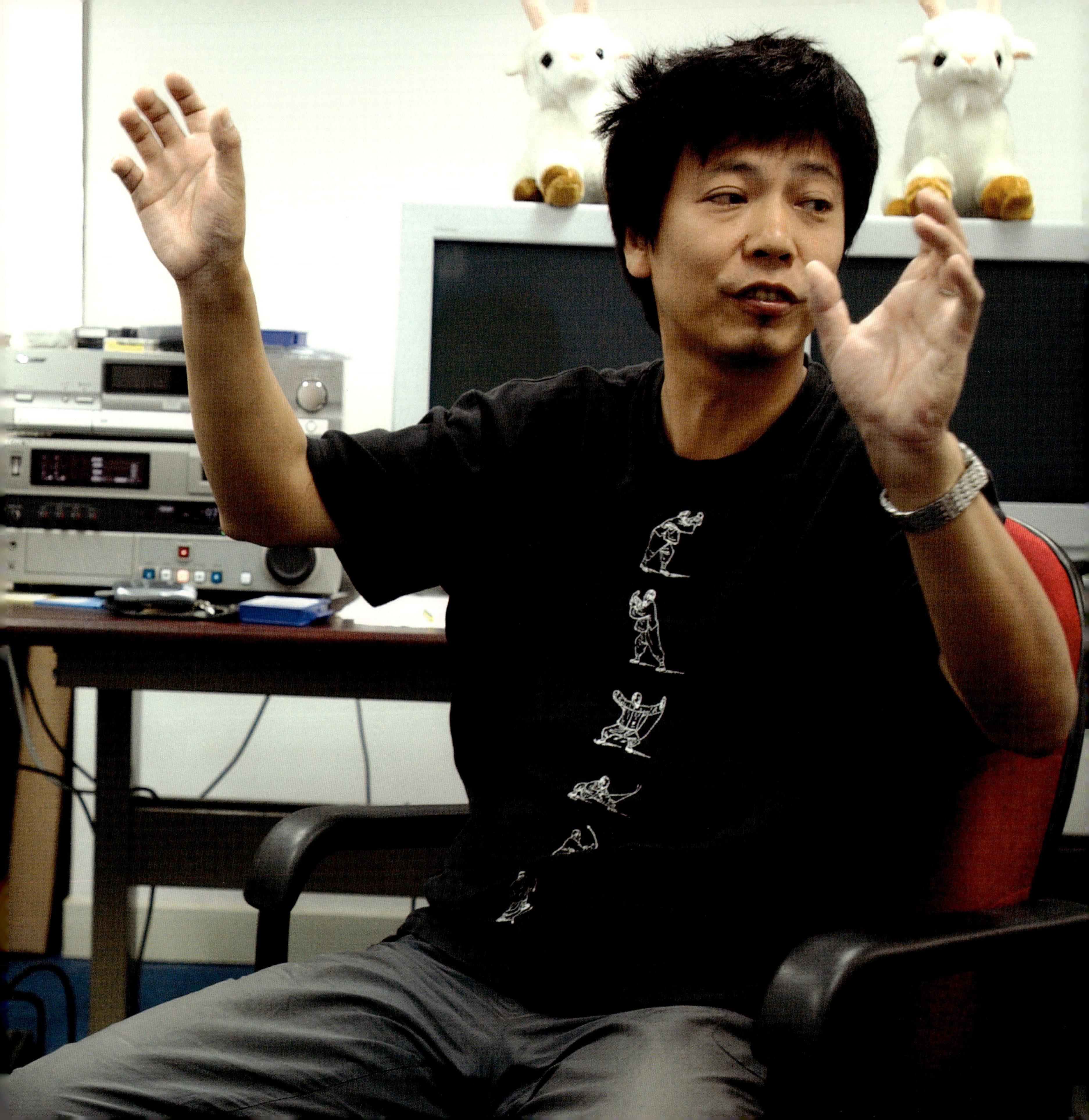

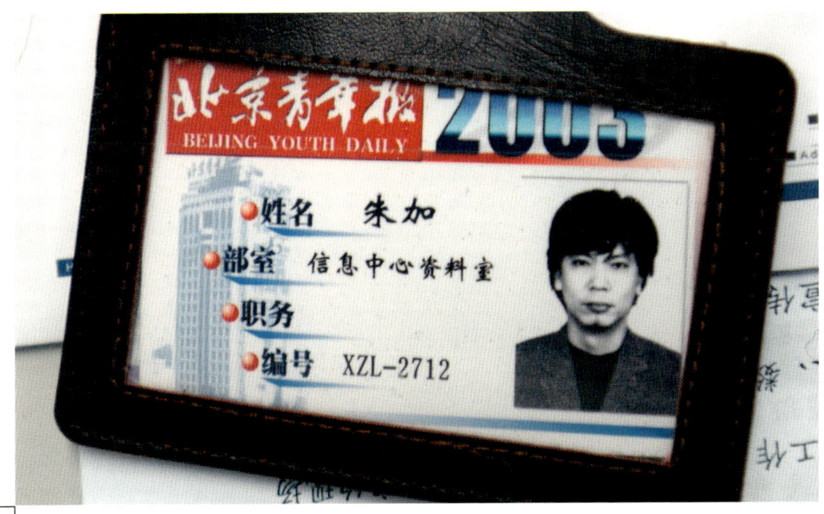

ZHU JIA

He had told us what to expect, but still we—Marc, our interpreter, and me—were not sure we had the right address when the taxi dropped us off in front of a skyscraper in the center of Beijing. Could Zhu Jia's studio really be in this tower block, tall as any New York skyscraper, with an imposing glass and chrome entrance leading into a vast marble and gold lobby with a plush red carpet? "It's not really a studio, more a converted office lent to me by the newspaper where I work," he told us. OK then. ¶ Twenty-three floors: I counted every one. *Beijing Youth Daily*, the name of the newspaper in question, is announced on a large banner just inside the entrance to the offices. To the left is the reception desk with a group of charming desk clerks who give us a message from Zhu Jia. He is caught in traffic and will be late. He wants us to wait for him down on the fourth floor in a little café where you can order ten different types of fried eggs and drink Kona coffee. This is a rarity in Beijing, where coffee is expensive. ¶ Our waiter does not seem overly familiar with the espresso machine, but he tries his best. Zhu Jia turns up quarter of an hour later and orders a glass and the bottle of whisky he keeps behind the bar. It is almost empty. I am surprised by his choice of drink—it is still early, after all—but he replies that it is almost eleven. He drinks as he talks. He smiles, twisting his mouth in a manner that looks almost painful. He scratches his head. He looks rumpled, as if he had spent the night sleeping in the gutter. ¶ We get down to the business at hand straight away—I don't know why. Maybe he is running late because of his late arrival. Maybe he is in a hurry. So here is the gist of our conversation. He was born in 1963, and so was three when the Cultural Revolution began. Before he tells us about his experiences, he turns around to see if our talk is being overheard. An old reflex. He tells us in a low voice, "I don't believe the Cultural Revolution was a Chinese phenomenon. There are many historical reasons why. Back then, in China, we had a certain type of problem." He has either said too much or too little. What? When? What he is telling us is completely different to everything the other artists have said, that for them, the Cultural Revolution was actually rather a fun time, with no lessons. One even said it was a pretty beneficial time. I am intrigued, and await further explanations with bated breath. He continues, "I was very young. Now, I can only talk from where I stand today, from my current point of view. But you know, there wasn't a single family that wasn't affected in some way." ¶ I don't get it. He presses forward, only to slam on the brakes right away. What does he mean? If he doesn't want to talk about it, fine, we'll move on to something else. He slaps me on the thigh wearing a broad smile. Yes, let's move on. We leave the café and go up to the seventeenth floor. That's where his tiny studio is. He is in the middle of moving out of his real studio somewhere

FACING PAGE: ZHU JIA ON THE EIGHTH FLOOR OF THE *BEIJING YOUTH DAILY*, WHICH HAS LOANED HIM TWO SMALL ROOMS WHILE HE MOVES INTO A NEW STUDIO.

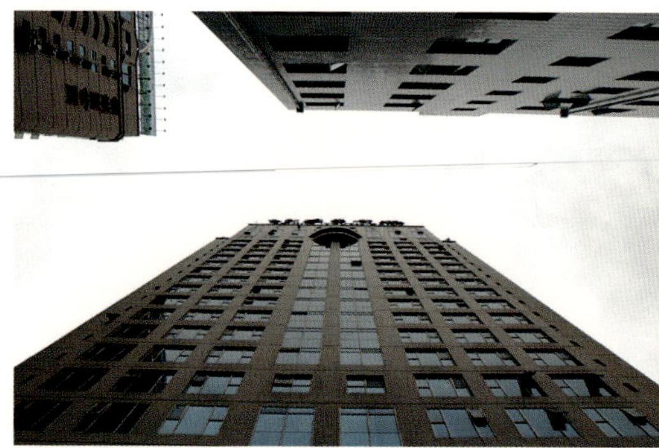

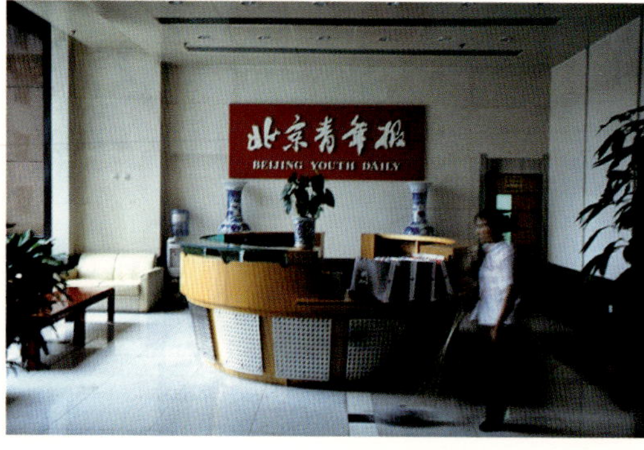

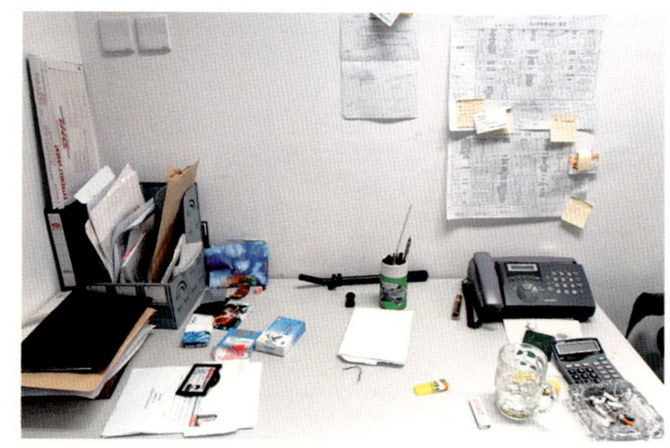

in town. ¶ As we amble through the corridors, then in the elevator, he explains his situation. He works "in video" for the newspaper. What does he do precisely? He laughs, then admits, "They created the job specially for me." So he's paid to do nothing? Yes, basically. ¶ It was Song Dong who first introduced me to Zhu Jia's video work a few years ago. He talked about him in such flattering terms that I was keen to meet him. He lived in a small apartment full of books in an inexpensive part of Beijing. In his apartment, the only signs of his art were two photographs on the wall. He showed me his old videos and some new ones, on an old TV set built into his bookshelves. He didn't speak a word of English, and I spoke no Chinese. We didn't have an interpreter, but we got on fine. ¶ The story of his life? He liked drawing, like all children, but was better at it than his playmates. The one person who really pushed him was his half-brother, a designer. "He really influenced me, and pushed me to study at the School of Fine Art." ¶ He finished his studies in 1988, and for four years, until 1992, he carried on painting just as he had been taught. In 1992, he shot his first video. In those days, he was one of just a handful of Chinese artists experimenting with this medium, starting just after Zhang Peili, whom at that point he had never met. ¶ How did video enter his art and his life? By filming weddings. Because he was a painter, his friends, and then friends of friends, then friends of friends of friends asked him to film their wedding, presuming that because he was an artist, he'd be a natural behind the camera. "And as soon as I had a video camera in my hands," he says, "I knew that was it. Straight away, I knew I'd found the way to express everything I had to say. I loved it!" ¶ In 1994, he shot *Forever*, his best-known work, shown all over the world. The premise couldn't be simpler: he attached the video camera to a wheel on a tricycle pedaled through the streets of Beijing. This simple idea gave a completely new angle on street life in the city—in fact, a completely new angle on life altogether. *Forever* has been shown so often that recently, when I asked Zhu Jia to show it in an exhibition I was curating, for the first time, he refused. His answer was a courteous yet firm "no." ¶ That same year, 1994, he also shot *Repeat on Purpose*, based on an equally simple idea: this time, he placed his video camera inside a refrigerator. When the door is shut, the camera records the blackness. When someone opens the door, the light comes on and shows an arm reaching in for a bottle of milk or a yogurt. Then the door shuts. Cut to black again. The door opens again. Then shuts again. ¶ This work can be interpreted from a political point of view; the metaphor of darkness and light is easily translated. It can also be read with a sociological meaning, as a reflection on interiority and exteriority. Most critics have preferred this reading. Personally, I prefer to read it as a meditation on the import of the medium itself (the "hidden camera") and the creative powers of light, what John Berger calls seeing seeing. ¶ 1995. A photographic interlude with a little-known work entitled *Did They Have Sex?* The principle was for the artist to approach men and women in the street, walking along, chatting, or just happening to be standing near each other, and then take a photograph, holding out a paper bearing the phrase "Did they have sex?" at arm's length so it featured in the shot. Sometimes, the answer is obviously yes, sometimes it is less clear, and sometimes the very idea seems out of the question. Or is it? Why? Because one of the pair is extremely tall and the other very short, or one old and one young, one black and one yellow, one rich and one poor. But we all know people who have ignored similar "impossibilities" to have sex with someone. He is questioning our assumptions.

FROM LEFT TO RIGHT: THE SKYSCRAPER THAT HOUSES THE OFFICES OF THE *BEIJING YOUTH DAILY*. THE RECEPTION ON THE GROUND FLOOR. A CORNER OF ZHU JIA'S STUDIO.

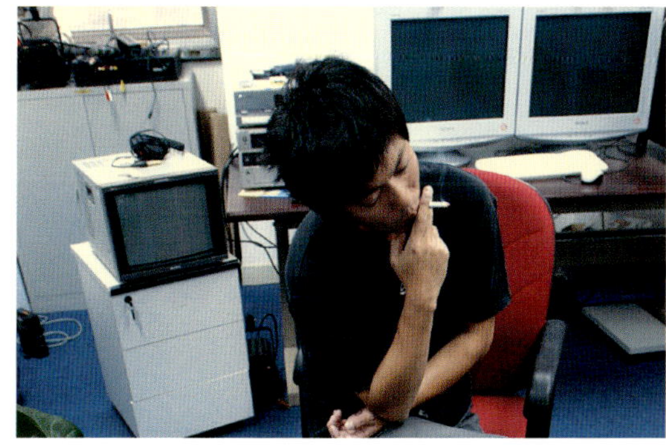

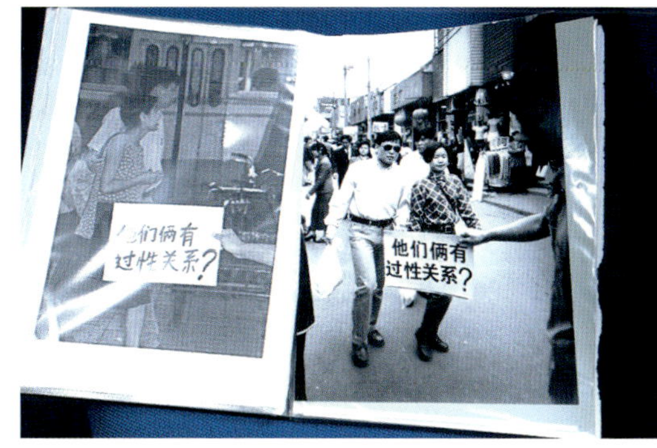

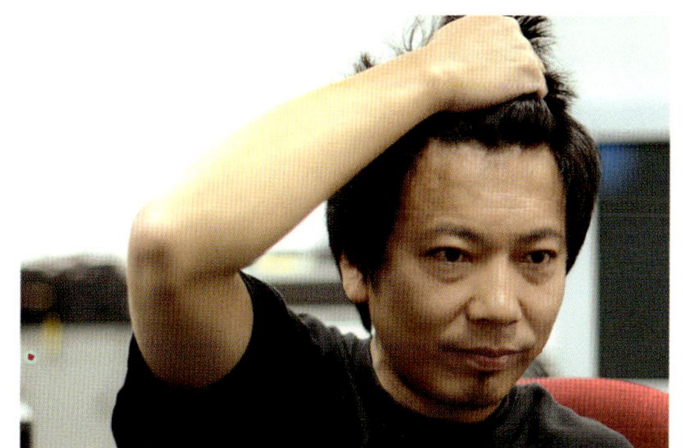

He is questioning the typically Chinese reluctance to talk about such issues. In China, the issue of censorship tends to arise with overly frank depictions of sex just as much as with sensitive political questions. ¶ In 1997, Zhu Jia shot *Related to Environment*, shown at the Fresnoy, the national studio for the contemporary arts in Tourcoing, near Lille in France. It shows a white plate filmed from vertically underneath, with a light above it that is the precise size of the plate. In the middle is a typical Chinese goldfish. Alive. It opens and closes its mouth convulsively, gasping for air. At least, that is what the image suggests at first, but the unwavering eye of the camera films the scene for one, then two, then five minutes. The viewer wonders what the point is: is the artist just showing us a fish dying out of water? But it is taking an awfully long time. Over ten minutes. Now twenty. The point is not to wonder how he managed to create the special effect—because it is a special effect, of course. The important thing is to feel the sense of suffocation engendered by this almost unbearable scene and the endurance of the goldfish. Again, this work can be interpreted from a political point of view. However, it is also the artist's personal meditation about his own life and the conditions of his existence. Maybe the real meaning of the film is the personal and the political intertwined. ¶ *Shine* (1997) is an extraordinary work. The idea is as simple as ever. It is set in a sports center where young people are practicing basketball. The soundtrack resonates with slam-dunks, echoes, and shouts. Zhu Jia fastened the camera beneath his armpit and then threw himself into the melee. He steals the ball from his adversary, whose face is never filmed—we only see his shoulders, torso, hips, and legs, constantly on the move. There are sudden bursts of sound, jagged flashes of light, and a constantly jogged image that almost glitters—hence the title. ¶ From 1997 to 2001, Zhu Jia does not seem to have produced much in the way of art. What was he doing? "Lots of videos and photos, but I hardly showed any of it," he says. He twists a lock of hair and smiles. "I'm not easily pleased with what I do." ¶ After 2001, Zhu Jia began to travel outside China, spending time in Vancouver, but feels he did not make the best use of his time: not speaking English was a big handicap. But he did make one important discovery: the art of Gary Hill. It was a key encounter, leading to his first video installations. ¶ His work *Passages* (2001), recently shown at the *September Spring* exhibition in Toulouse, France, was planned as an installation. It features tall, narrow screens showing a cyclist, a woman crossing the road, a man running, and another looking around him at the city. It reflects the wide-eyed innocence of Zhu Jia's own perception of the city. Why the unusual format for the screens? The answer is simple, as always: "Before, our view was broad and panoramic. Today, the organization of the city has changed. Our eyes frame the view differently." ¶ I watch on his TV screen in Beijing a work shown in Toulouse. The images flow smoothly and simply. Images of life, images of things we see around us every day, but that Zhu shows us with renewed freshness of vision. ¶ He says that, today, he has his doubts about art, or at least about its place in modern society. Maybe that is why he chose to show at the flagship China exhibition at the Centre Pompidou a film showing an airplane about to depart from Beijing airport, gathering speed on the runway, but never actually taking off. This frustrating four-minute video, where the expected event never quite happens, is his most recent work.

LEFT AND RIGHT: TWO CHARACTERISTIC SHOTS OF ZHU JIA. CENTER: A RELATIVELY UNKNOWN WORK ENTITLED *HAVE THEY HAD SEX?* 1995, WHICH ASKS THE QUESTION OF RANDOM PAIRINGS OF PASSERSBY IN THE STREET.

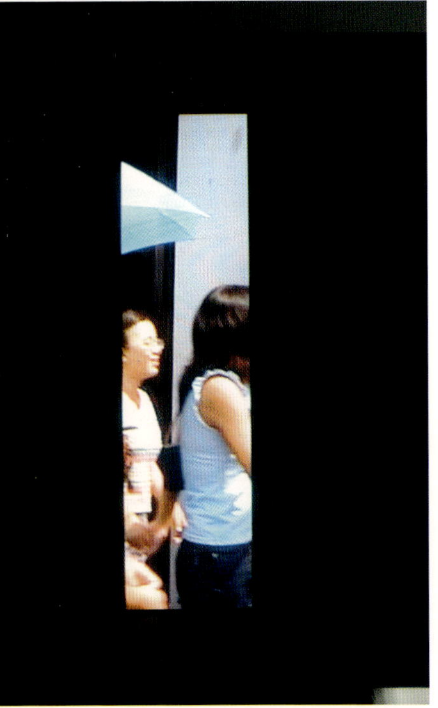

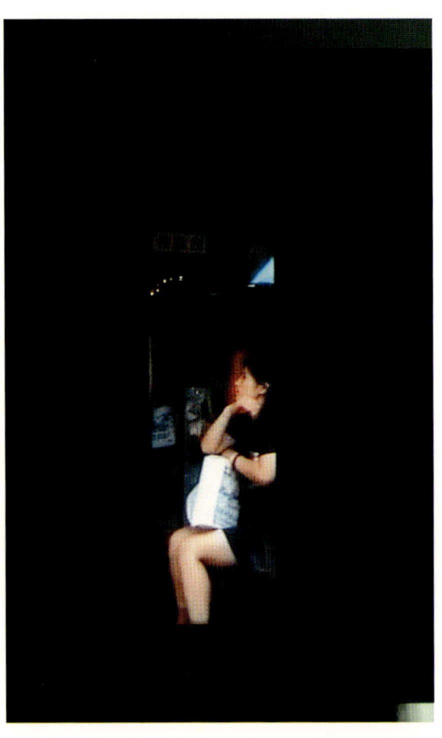

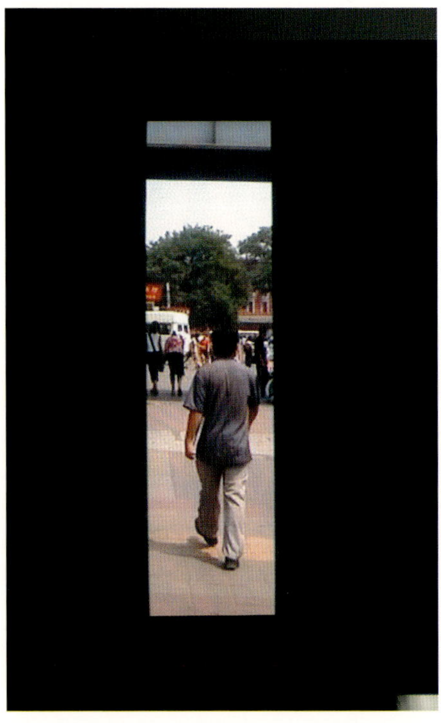

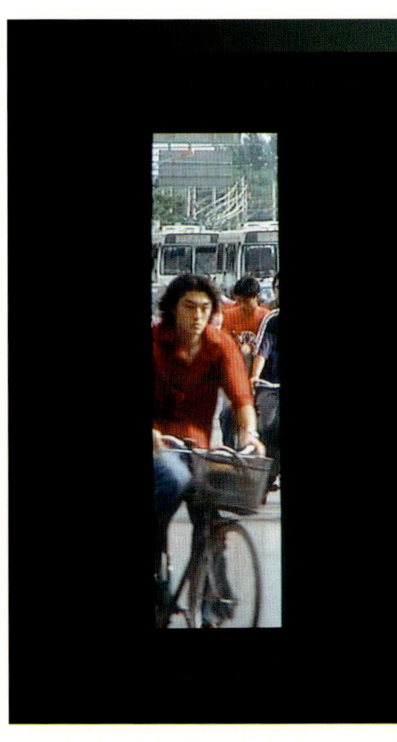

PASSAGE, 2001, IS A VIDEO SHOWN AS PART OF AN INSTALLATION ON EXTREMELY NARROW SCREENS THAT, FOR THE ARTIST, ARE A REFLECTION OF THE NARROW VISION WE ALL HAVE TODAY.

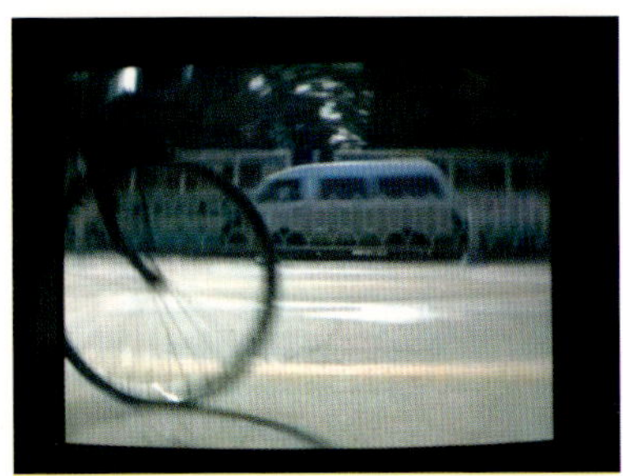

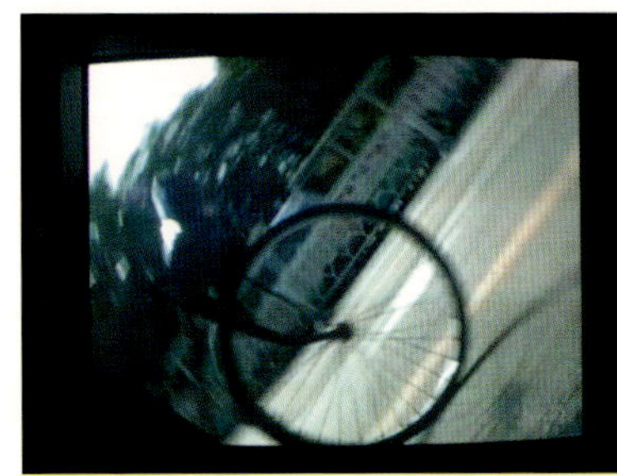

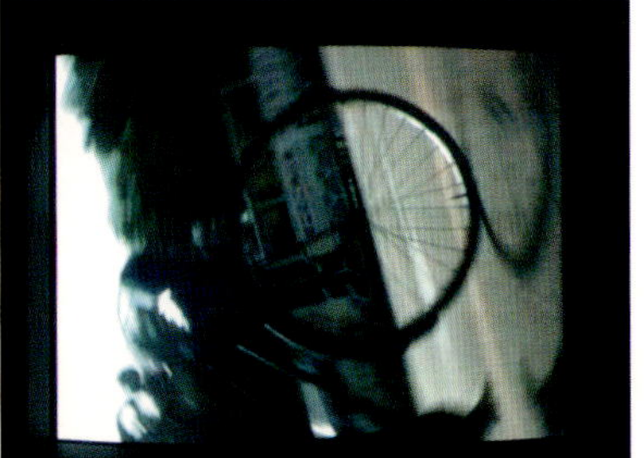

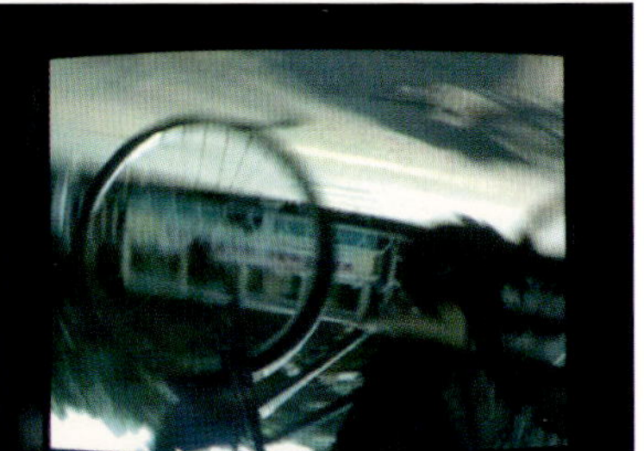

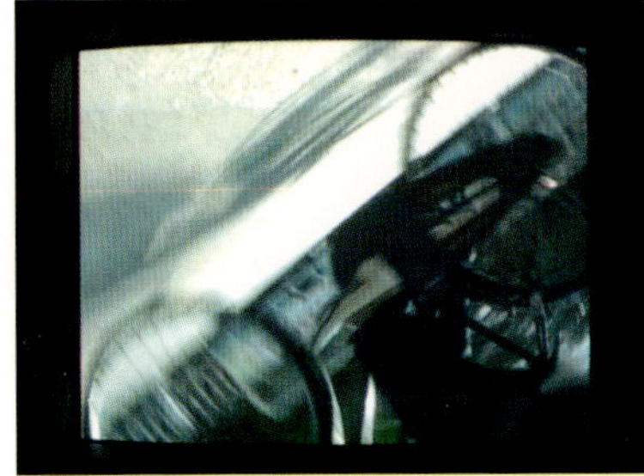

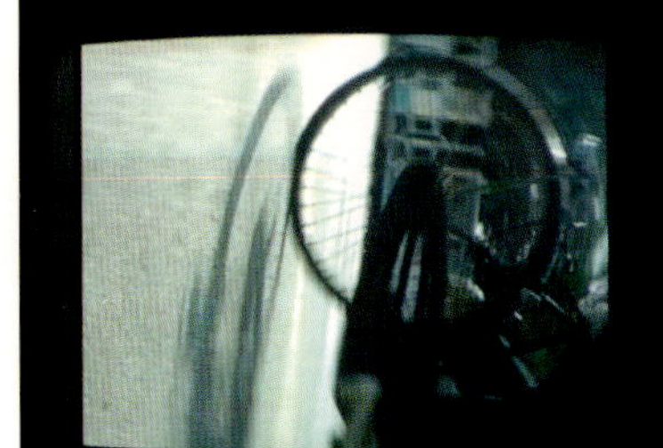

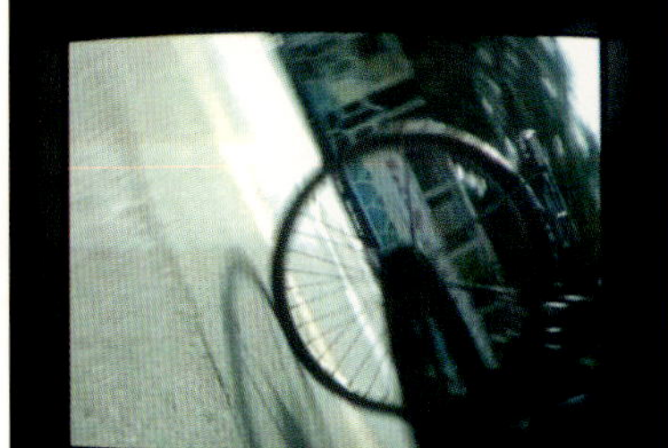

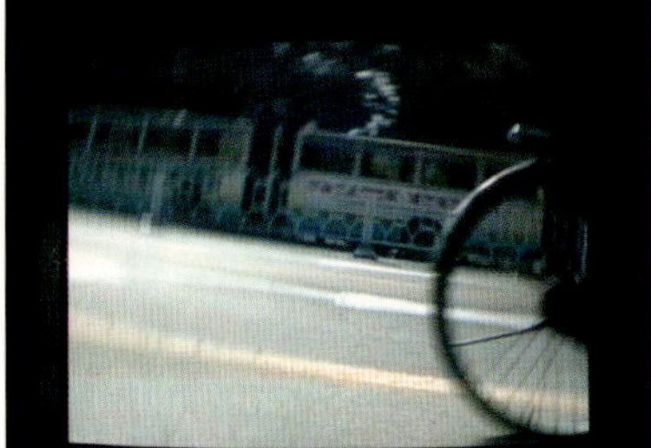

ZHU JIA'S MOST FAMOUS WORK, *FOREVER*, 1994. HE ATTACHED HIS VIDEO CAMERA TO THE WHEEL OF A TRICYCLE TRAVELING THROUGH THE STREETS OF BEIJING.

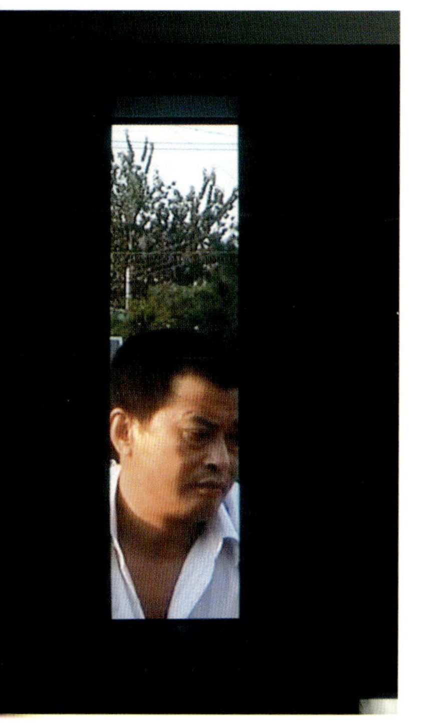
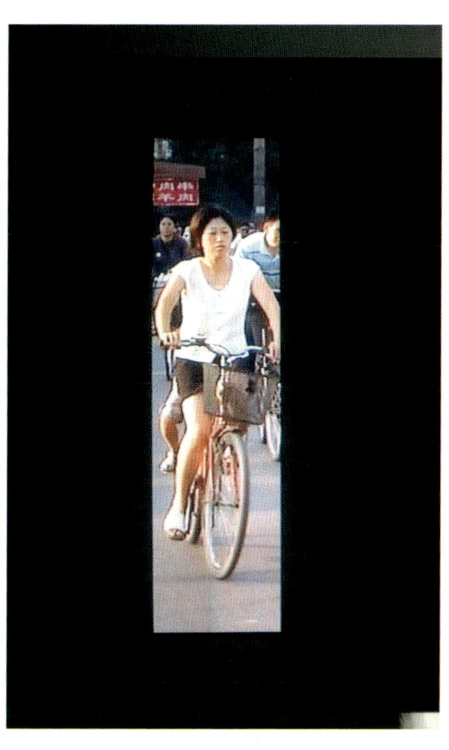
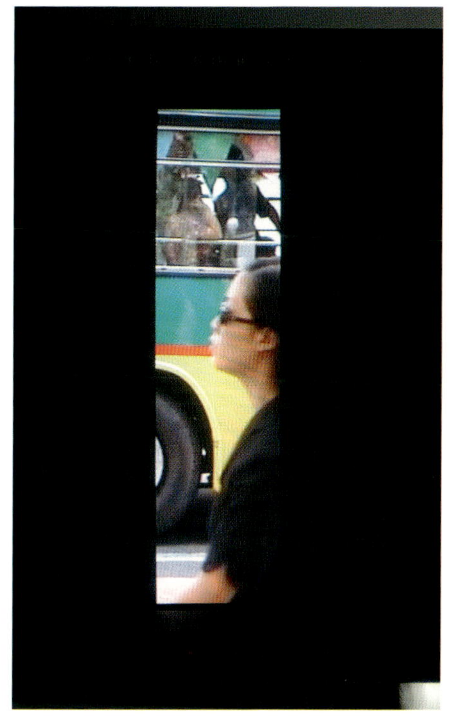
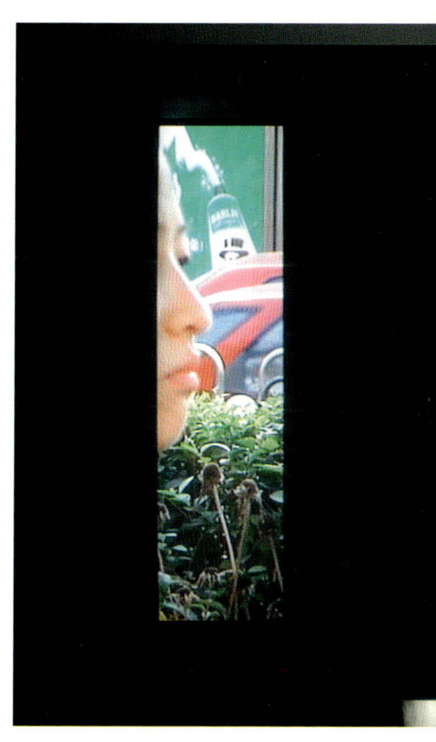
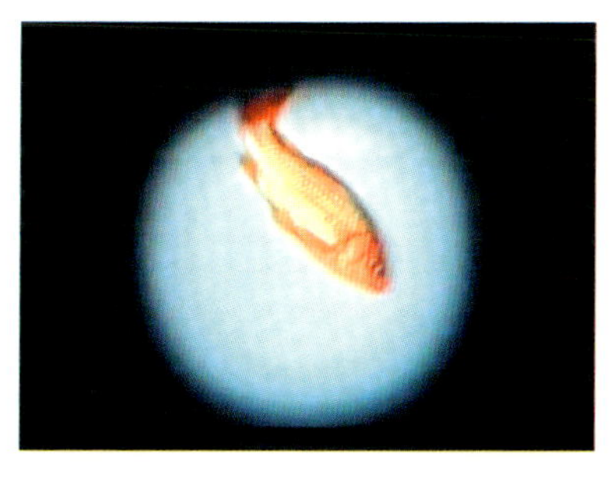
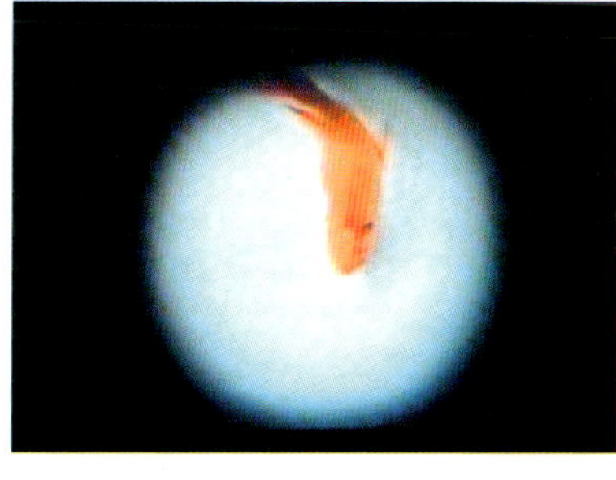
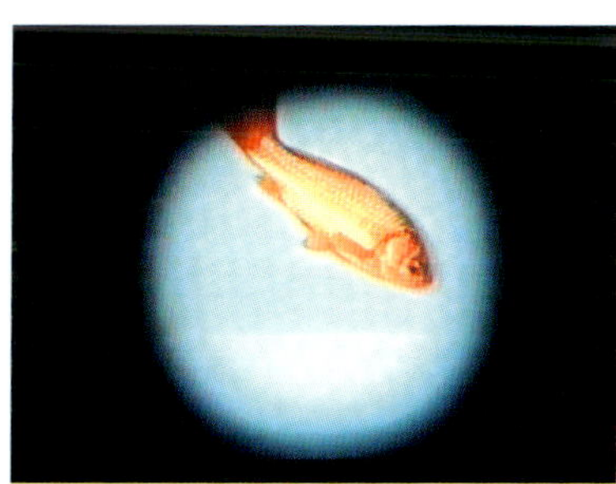
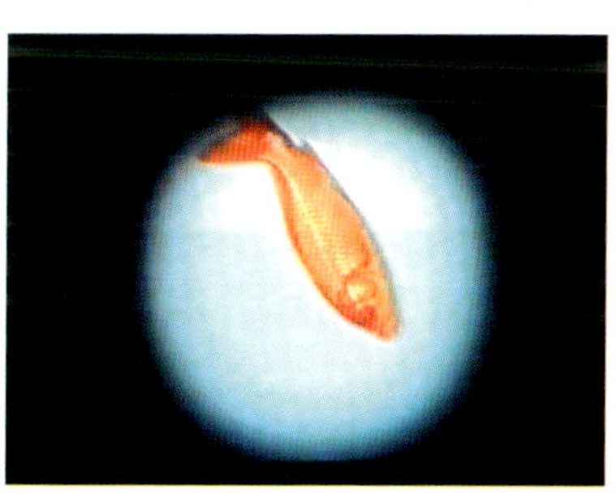
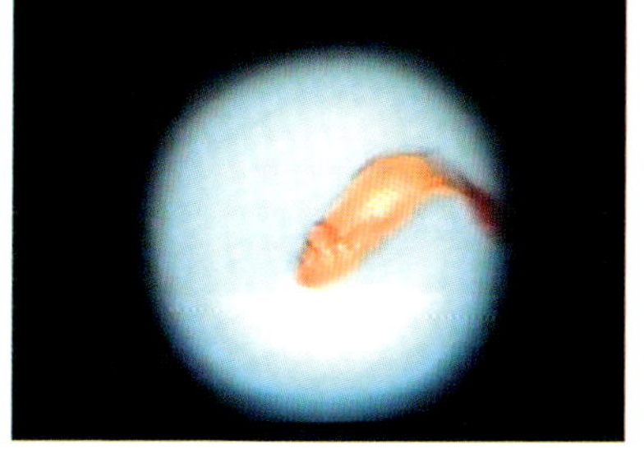
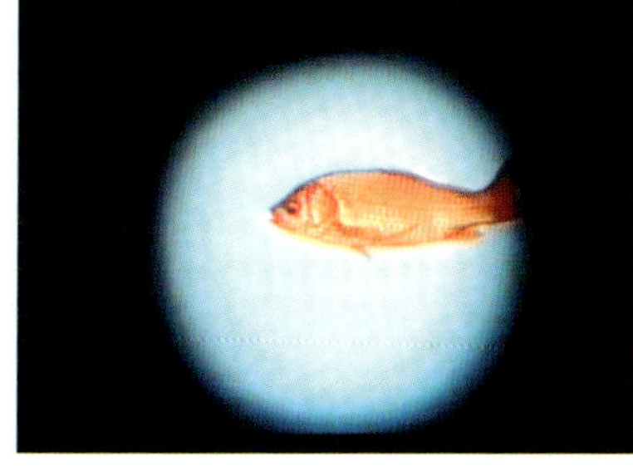
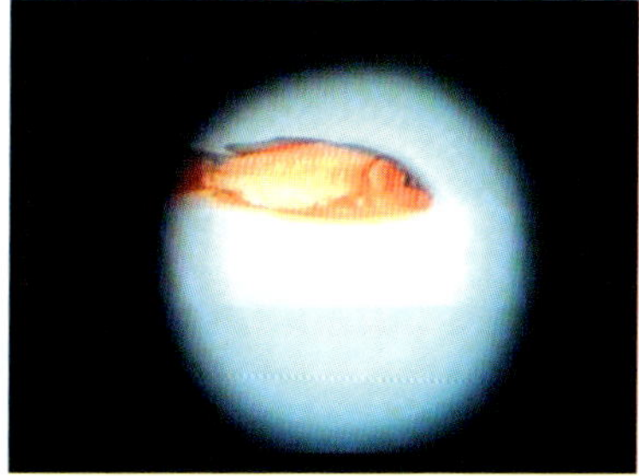
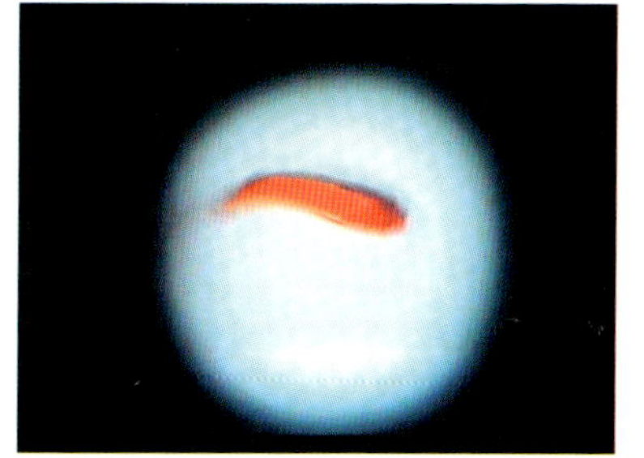

RELATED TO ENVIRONMENT, 1997, FEATURING A GOLDFISH FLOPPING ABOUT IN A DISH FOR TWENTY MINUTES.

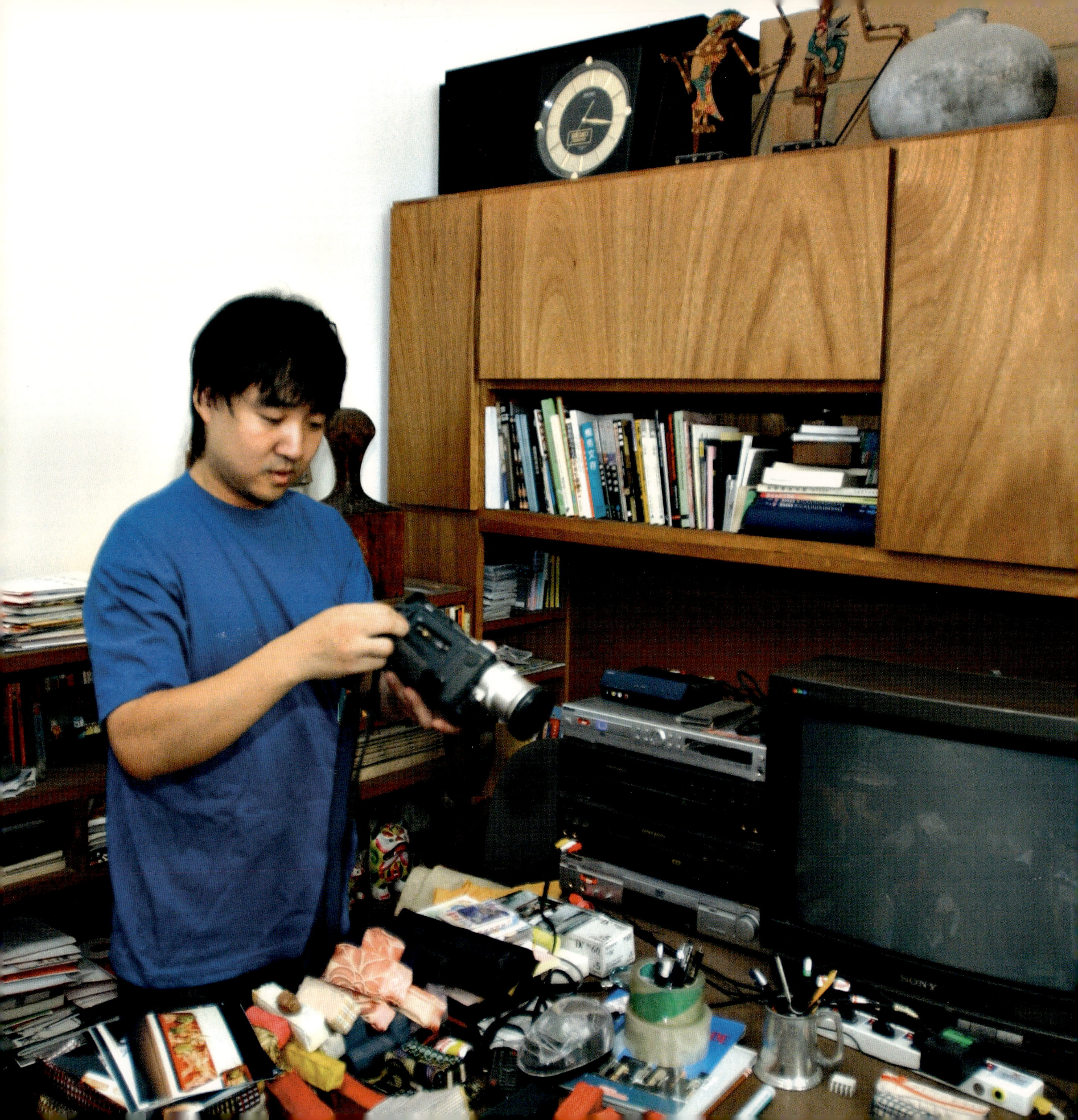
SONY

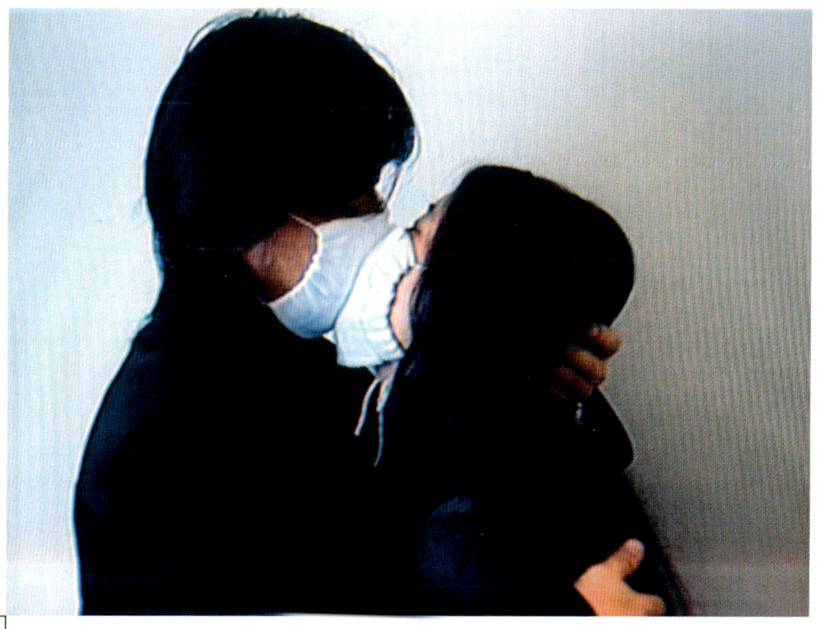

SONG DONG

Song Dong is obsessed with issues of identity, notably his own relationship with his father. One of his most striking works was a video that superimposed his own face on that of his father, the two merging into one. ¶ Song Dong graduated from the National University of Beijing in 1989, the year when the winds of change started to blow across China in earnest—in contemporary art as in every area of life. Song Dong has not tired of experimenting since. He is not just a video artist—ask him, and he will show you his photographs. And then when you have him down as a photographer, he will describe some of his performances. So should we be calling him a performer? But then what about his installations? Like Zheng Guogu, Song Dong has an extraordinarily multifaceted talent. He is remarkably inventive, and does not see the attraction in restricting his artistic activity to one particular art form, which he feels would quickly run dry. ¶ He wanders about, ceaselessly moving, looking for something new to try. In 1999, as the character Mr. Banana, he worked as a guide showing visitors around the exhibition *Art for Sale*, which was a highly influential event. ¶ But while Zheng Guogu has remained a free spirit, insanely talented, buzzing with energy, perpetually on the way to becoming something or someone else, Song Dong, who shares the same qualities, cuts straight to the chase. ¶ His activity—one might almost say his militancy—echoed the anxiety of the time, which was strangely yet inextricably bound with the hope people were daring to express. These contradictory urges were a profound source of energy for him. Because if there were cracks in the façade in the 1990s—a decade characterized by contrast—how to tell if they were real and lasting? And who knows what they might not be hiding? In the past, so many thaws had been greeted with enthusiasm, only to be followed by ever harsher crackdowns. And artists and intellectuals were always the first to pay the price. The limits needed probing carefully, before they could be attacked from all sides. ¶ And what to do with all this information that was suddenly flooding in undiluted from abroad? Did learning to paint in oils mean giving up part of one's Chinese identity? Wasn't oil painting taught in classes in Western art? Should Chinese artists be accepting grants to study in Europe? (Song Dong participated in exhibitions in Berlin, London, and Venice in 1999 and 2000, and in Paris at the Centre Pompidou in 2003.) And once in Europe, should they succumb to the temptation of Western artistic influences, or, on the contrary,

FACING PAGE: SONG DONG IN HIS HOUSE IN BEIJING, WHICH DOUBLES AS A STUDIO. ABOVE: HIS MOST RECENT VIDEO, *SARS TIME*, 2003, FILMED JUST AFTER THE VIRUS STRUCK BEIJING. THE VIDEO FEATURES HIM AND HIS WIFE KISSING, BOTH WEARING SURGICAL MASKS.

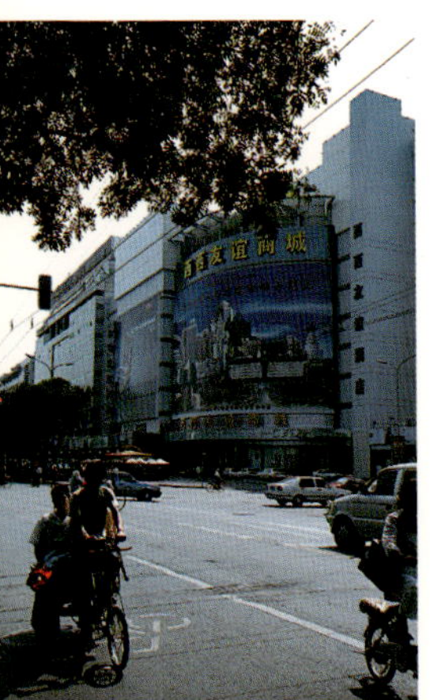
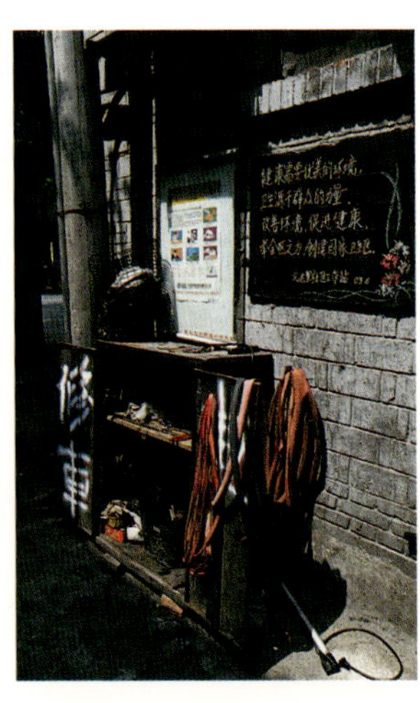
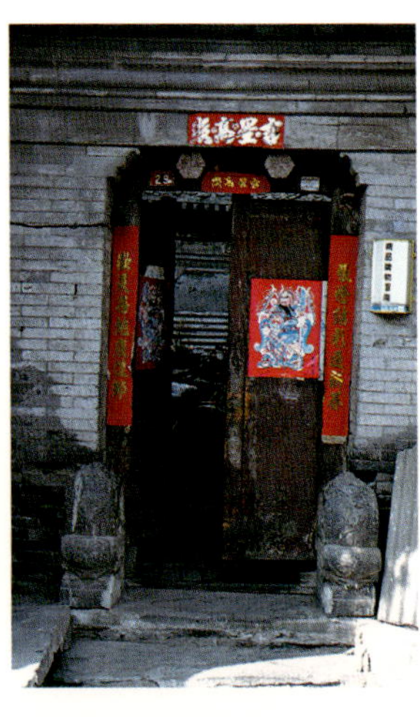
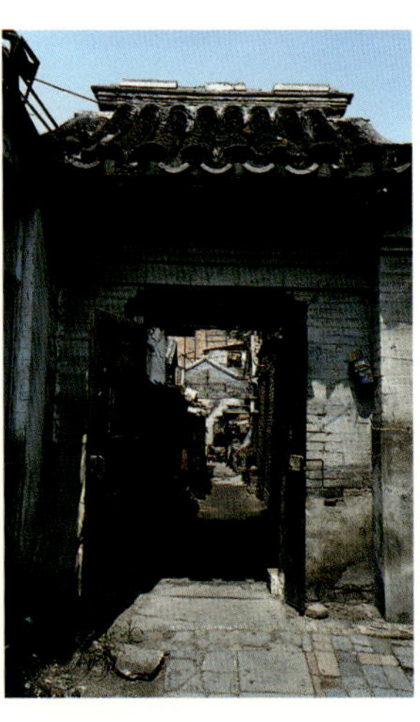
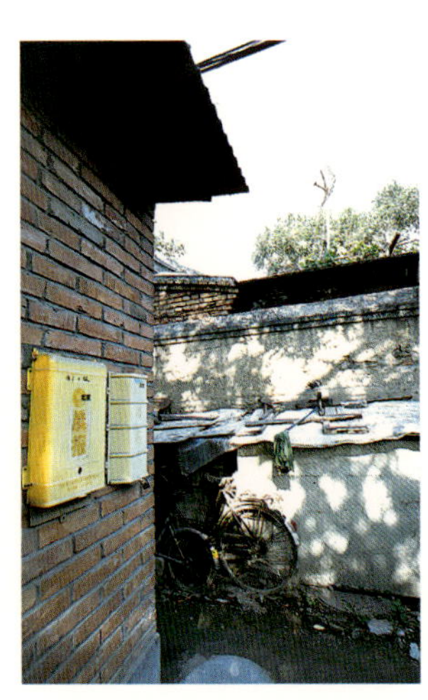
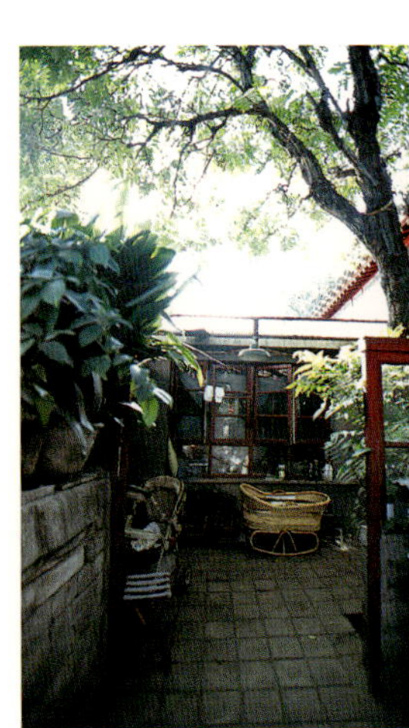

seal themselves off hermetically and preserve their Chinese cultural specificity at all costs? Just one example: All the Chinese artists who took part in the Venice Biennale in the 1980s and early 1990s noted the influence of large formats, unlike their own works which were still floating in the cultural wake of Impressionism. Should they be turning to bigger formats? But then the question was how, when all they had was a tiny studio—there was no way of coming by a large studio space in those days, or even until as recently as two or three years ago. Would it be reasonable to switch from oil painting to video? In a word, in the 1990s, was it possible to be both Chinese—and an artist? To be more precise, was it possible to be oneself? ¶ Song Dong asked himself all of these questions. To find the answers, he set out to pin down his own identity: This is my family, this is me, me and my family, me and my culture. ¶ After dabbling in oil painting at the very beginning of the 1990s and showing a few works at the Cultural Palace, he changed direction and settled on installation art, performances, and their corollary, video. ¶ What does it mean that in 1995 he wrote his diary in water, using a calligraphy brush in the classical manner, held perfectly upright? Of course, we must avoid falling into the trap of clumsily imposing our own Western dictionary of symbols. In Asia, water symbolizes not only wisdom, but also tenacity and continuity. But what continuity? What tenacity? How can we avoid noting that whatever the symbolic tradition, the water dries almost as soon as the brush delicately traces the lines on the stone exposed to the sun and the wind, and that the symbols, simply, well, disappear? The exact opposite of permanence and continuity. Having said that, what is the nature of the water? Is it a river flowing to the sea? Or magical lustral water? The water of life? The water in classical Chinese landscape paintings? ¶ So many simple questions. It was a time when key questions had to be asked and answered. ¶ After the Beijing Spring in 1989, the demonstrations in Tiananmen Square were crushed by Deng Xiaoping, who had previously been—and later became again—one of the most eloquent voices arguing for more freedom. The Communist Party finally embraced the "socialist market economy" in 1992; and in 1999, it adopted amendments designed to encourage company growth. ¶ And then foreign capital came flooding in, lifting China out of poverty but at the same time influencing its development and throwing the country into chaos. Unemployment rose and peasants abandoned their lands to try their luck in the cities, causing social unrest. ¶ Song Dong's art could be compared to a seismograph tracking infinitesimal shifts in the uncertainty and chaos that characterized that generation. ¶ He set out to expose the relativity of experience, the diversity of perceptions, the permanence or impermanence of both human and natural activity, and the part of art that deals with the fleeting moment and, at the same time, the desire for eternity. ¶ From the mid-1990s to the end of the decade, many of his performances dealt with these questions and should therefore be read through this prism rather than from a purely critical stance, as is all too often the case in European readings of art from Communist or formerly Communist countries such as China, Russia, or the countries of the former Soviet bloc. ¶ His 1996 performance in Tibet, for example, during which he spent an hour splashing a lake with a huge wooden seal bearing the ideogram for water, was highly influential. Song Dong told me about it, and showed me photographs and a video. ¶ Another performance took place on New Year's Eve 1996 in a completely empty Tiananmen Square. It was similar in spirit to the lake performance,

AN ABANDONED COURTYARD, A DOOR THAT STILL SHOWS SIGNS OF ITS FORMER MAGNIFICENCE, A TREE, A LITTLE STORE—SONG DONG LOVES THE NEIGHBORHOOD OF XISI, IN THE HEART OF BEIJING, ALTHOUGH IT COULD BE A WORLD AWAY FROM THE MODERN CITY OF SIX-LANE FREEWAYS.

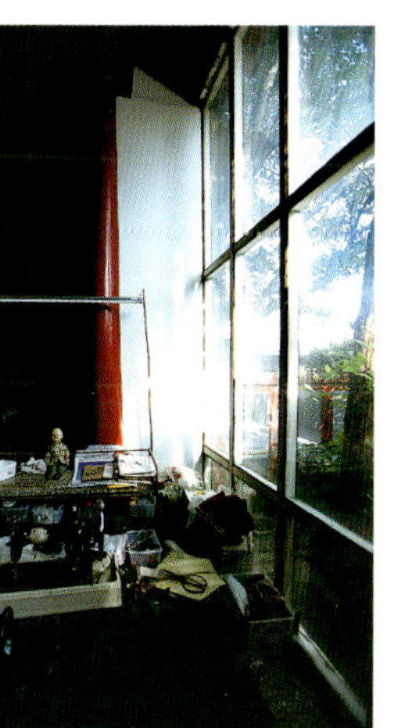

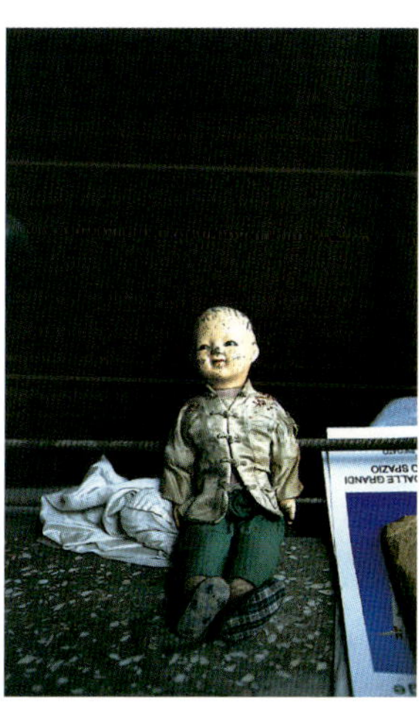

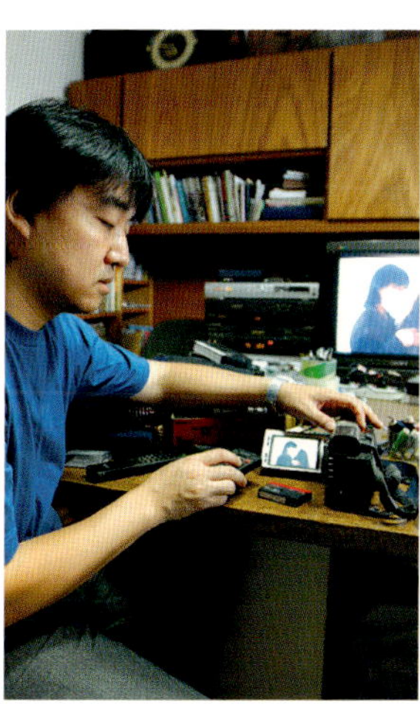

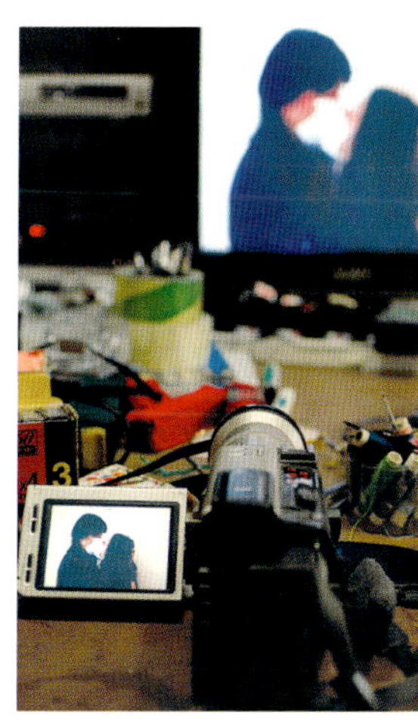

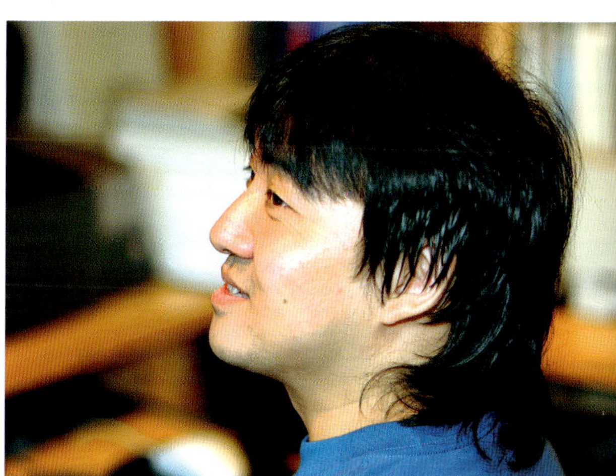

although the fact that he chose as a setting a square that had witnessed such bloody events does tend to give the work a political gloss. Song Dong lay face down on the icy ground (it was 16°F [−9°C]), and simply stayed there for forty minutes. A thin layer of ice formed where he breathed on the ground, only to melt once he got up. No trace of his presence remained the next day. I interpreted this work as an allegory of artistic activity—solitary, difficult, and slightly suspect, fed both by its own ephemeral nature and by dreams of eternity. The political allusion also, of course, colored my reading. ¶ A year earlier, in 1995, Song Dong characteristically turned his artistic practice on its head, tracing ideograms in a bowl full of ink. Writing *on* and not *in* ink is unusual. But what does it mean if in the space of the same twelve months, we also stamp a seal on water? The critical dimension is always there, lying beneath the surface. But by insisting on the essential, meditative face of the work, there is a danger of under-valuing the critical aspect. ¶ In 1995, Song Dong also wrote on ice using a brush and ink. ¶ On the same theme of blurring traces, for the *New Century* exhibition, Song Dong spent the first night of the new millennium outside, writing one ideogram per second in water on stone slabs. ¶ I get the impression that while his performances highlight the ephemeral nature of modern culture, his videos explore the notion of identity—an exploration linked to the notion of challenging reality. ¶ To begin with, Song Dong broke a mirror. *Broken Mirror* is one of his simplest and most striking videos—and also one of the most inspired. He shot it in 1999, when countless old buildings in Beijing were being demolished. It shows an ordinary street full of people going about their business. We settle down to watch, and suddenly a pointed hammer appears violently on screen. We hear the sound of breaking glass, and the image disappears, revealing a second image behind the first. We were watching a decoy. The artist shows us what is on the other side of the mirror. ¶ *Burning Mirror* is a more sophisticated work. It depicts a sheet of reflective paper held at arm's length, showing an ordinary street scene. When Song Dong sets the paper alight, the image distorts as the paper blackens and curls, revealing the reality behind the paper mirror once it is entirely burnt. ¶ Song Dong showed me these magnificent videos and many other works by Zhu Jia, Weng Fen, and other artists a few years ago in his apartment, piled high with books, cassettes, CDs, and DVDs, in the Xisi neighborhood. He is happy to exhibit works by other artists alongside his own creations and those of his wife, also an artist (she exhibited an installation at the Gwangju Biennial in Korea). ¶ Song Dong is a generous man. But that does not mean he shies away from shining a pitiless spotlight on a family history, which is not so much his own as universal. His 1998 work *Father and Son*, for instance, featured his father's face superimposed on his own. His father is talking about his experiences as a Communist Party official. The two faces seem to meld to form a third, which is talking about disobedience. Is this expressing a judgment? ¶ It is more complex and more fluid than that. More human, too. ¶ Song Dong has not managed to avoid the temptation of disobedience. ¶ Some people might see in this video an echo of a work by a young Albanian artist, Anri Sala, discovering his mother's Communist past in a silent black-and-white movie, where she heaps praise on Enver Hoxha, the Albanian Communist leader. Yet Song Dong's work does not reflect the same implacably harsh need to know everything, or the violent insistence. On the contrary, when Song Dong melds his father's face with his own, he is trying to shoulder his

SONG DONG SHOWING HIS MOST RECENT WORK, *SARS TIME*, IN HIS APARTMENT. SONG DONG IS THE SOUL OF GENEROSITY: HE IS LAVISH WITH PRAISE FOR HIS FRIENDS.

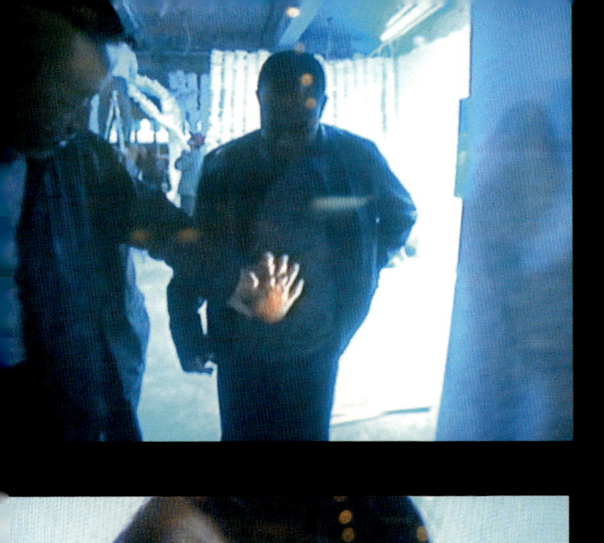
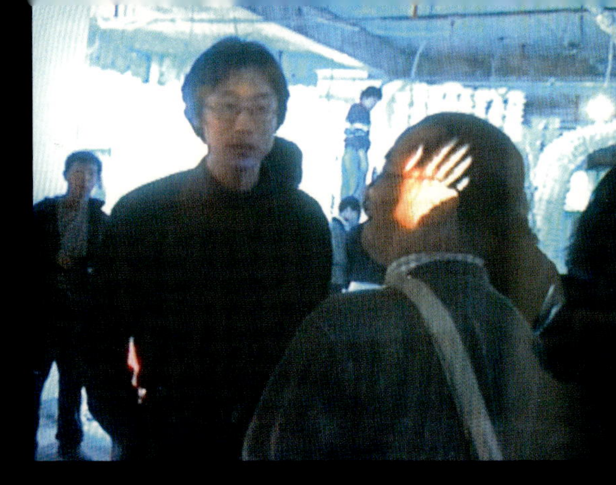
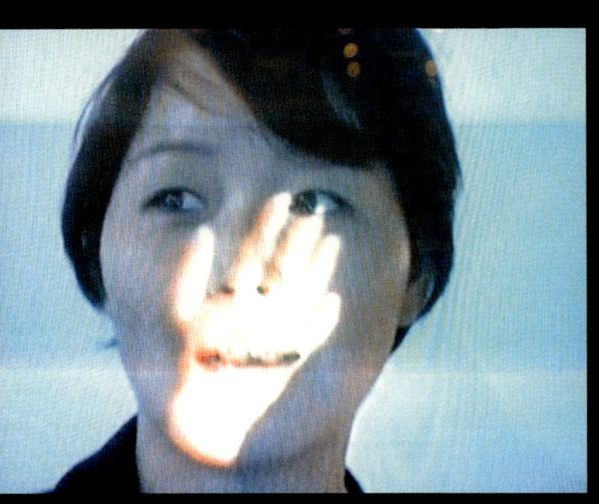
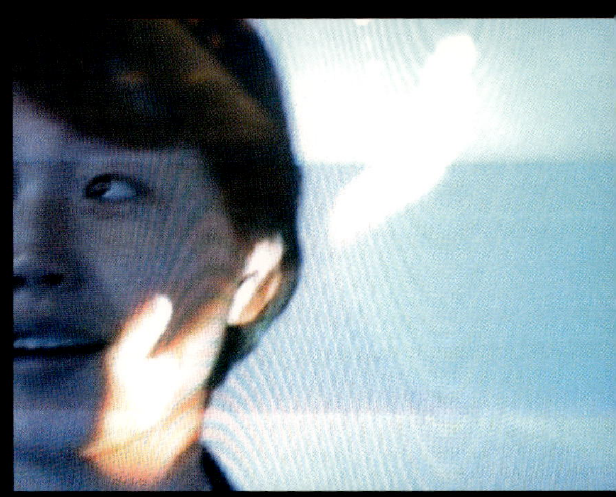
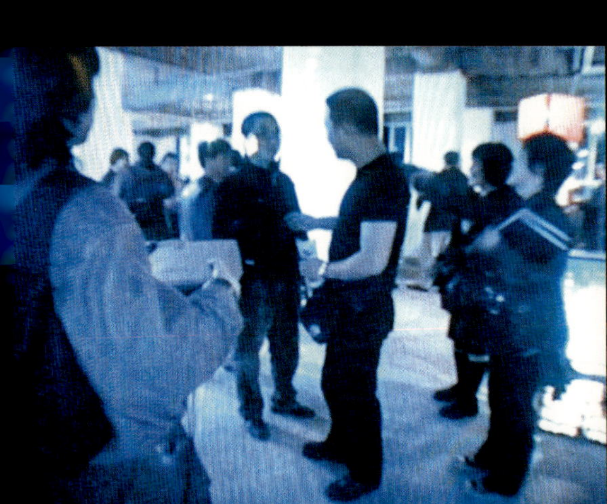
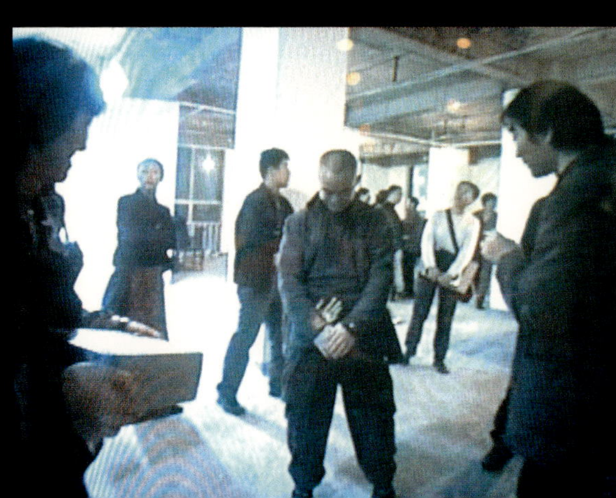

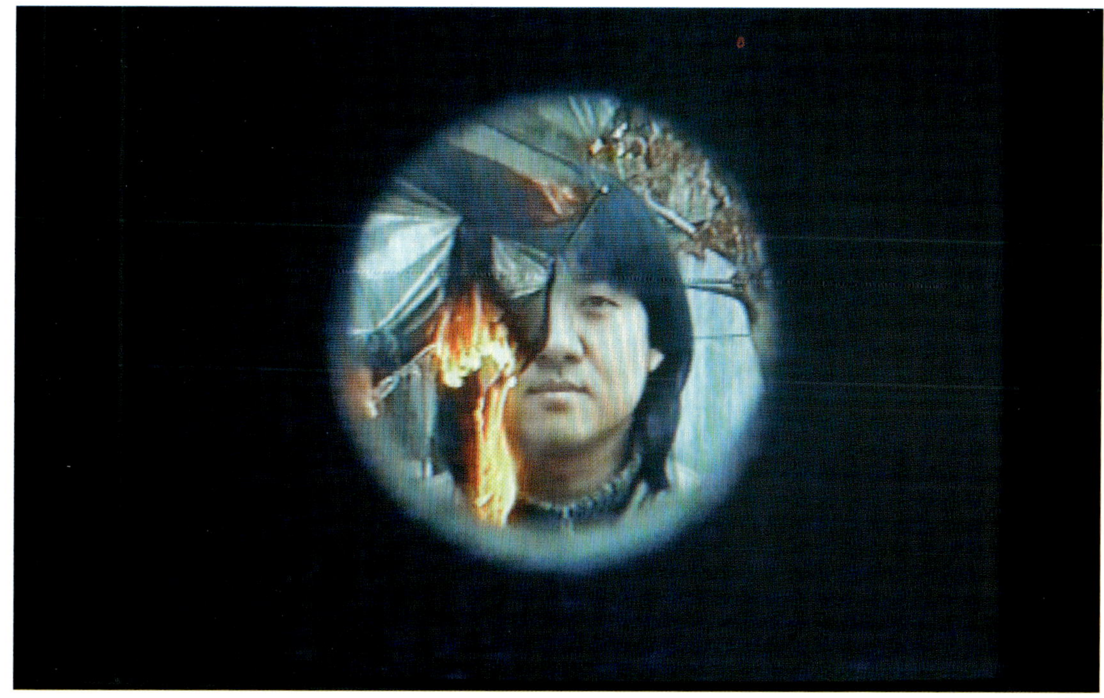

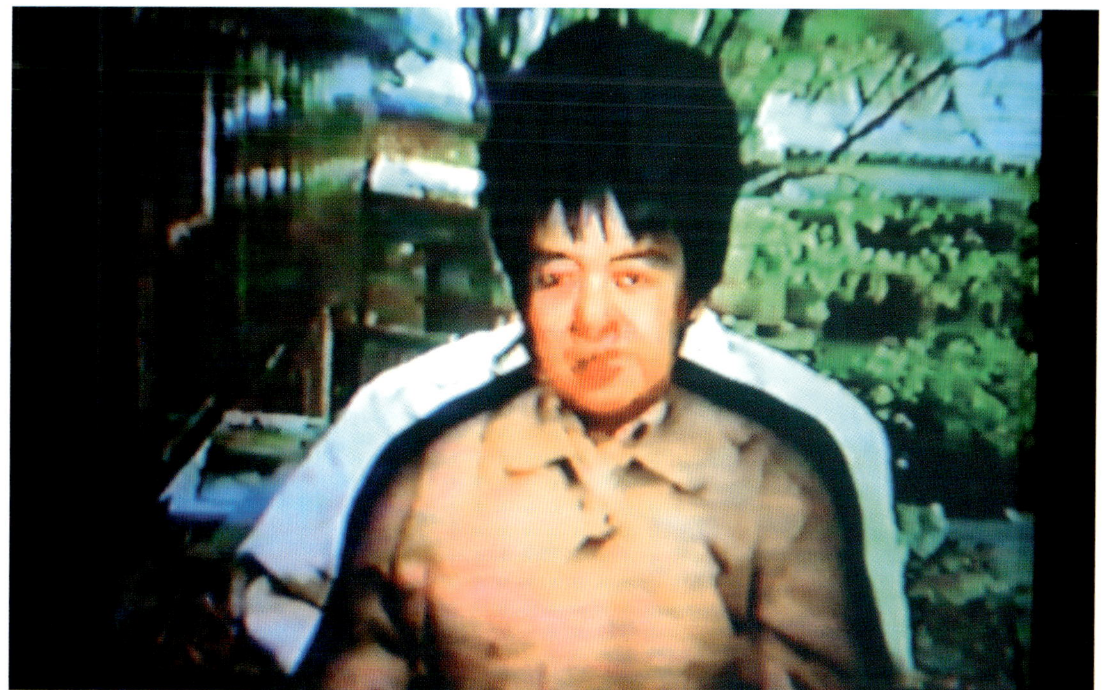

THE VIDEO PERFORMANCE *TOUCH*, 2000, WAS SHOWN IN SHANGHAI, GUANGZHOU, BRISBANE, AND MINNEAPOLIS, AMONG OTHER CITIES. FACING PAGE: BOTTOM RIGHT: CHEN WENBO. ABOVE: A VIDEO OF THE ARTIST'S FACE WITH HIS FATHER'S SUPERIMPOSED IN THE WORK *FATHER AND SON*, 1998, AND HIMSELF REFLECTED IN A BURNING MIRROR.

own responsibility in his father's mistakes or faults, to make them part of himself, and to try and understand them from the inside. To share the burden. ¶ *Family Members*, which dates from the same year, is more firmly anchored in the reality of Chinese society, making it less universal, but nonetheless still enlightening. ¶ He filmed seven members of his family posing for three minutes at a time in twelve different settings in Beijing—in a pretty house, for example, or in a busy street. He then showed the video in a gallery and asked members of the audience to take the place of his family one by one, selecting the person they wished to replace, irrespective of gender or age. He thus created his own extended family. ¶ It was a fascinating experience. Song Dong's family was grouped according to a strict hierarchy, with the father in the middle. On his left was his wife, and on the right his son (Song Dong's brother) with his wife and daughter. Song Dong and his wife were on their left. The group was a study in patriarchal domination. Song Dong noticed that even the young men in the audience chose the place of the father, while even older women chose the role of the artist's wife. ¶ For *Clone*, he filmed himself eating noodles alone in front of the television. Then he played the film backwards, projecting the image onto his own body, and tried to copy his own filmed movements. Sometimes, he managed a perfect imitation, but most of the time it was impossible. Even the most recent past is gone forever. As Heraclitus said, you cannot step into the same river twice. ¶ Here again, there is almost certainly a political dimension to the work. But what is the past in question? Song Dong never makes this explicit, so we are free to interpret as we wish. ¶ In 2000, at the Institute of International Visual Arts in London, Song Dong began another examination of the theme of identity. The video, entitled *Face to Face*, shows his face largely obliterated by the repetition of bright, colored ideograms. ¶ Are writing and image working together or against each other? Are they overlayered or unveiled? More questions. ¶ Have I managed to convey how humorous Song Dong's work is? In the fall of 2003, he showed at the Centre Pompidou in Paris a series of "landscapes" consisting of hunks of ham, bacon, parsley, *surimi*, and other foodstuffs—a feast for the eyes, and for certain visitors, too, it seems. The *surimi* soon started to go bad in the baking heat, but it all got eaten anyway. All that was left to bear witness of the work were a few photographs and a bit of bacon rind. ¶ Song Dong's most recent work is a video shot a few weeks into the SARS epidemic that swept through China, and Beijing in particular, in early 2003. It shows the artist and his wife, facing each other, both wearing surgical masks. They kiss, slowly, seductively, lovingly. But hygienically—because of the virus.

FACING PAGE: FOUR OF SONG DONG'S FINEST VIDEOS: *BROKEN MIRROR*, 1999, *FACE TO FACE*, 2000, *BURNING MIRROR*, 1996, AND HIS MOST FAMOUS VIDEO PERFORMANCE, FILMED IN LHASA, *IMPRINT ON WATER*, 1996. BOTTOM LEFT: THE SEAL HE USED FOR *IMPRINT ON WATER*, PHOTOGRAPHED IN HIS STUDIO.

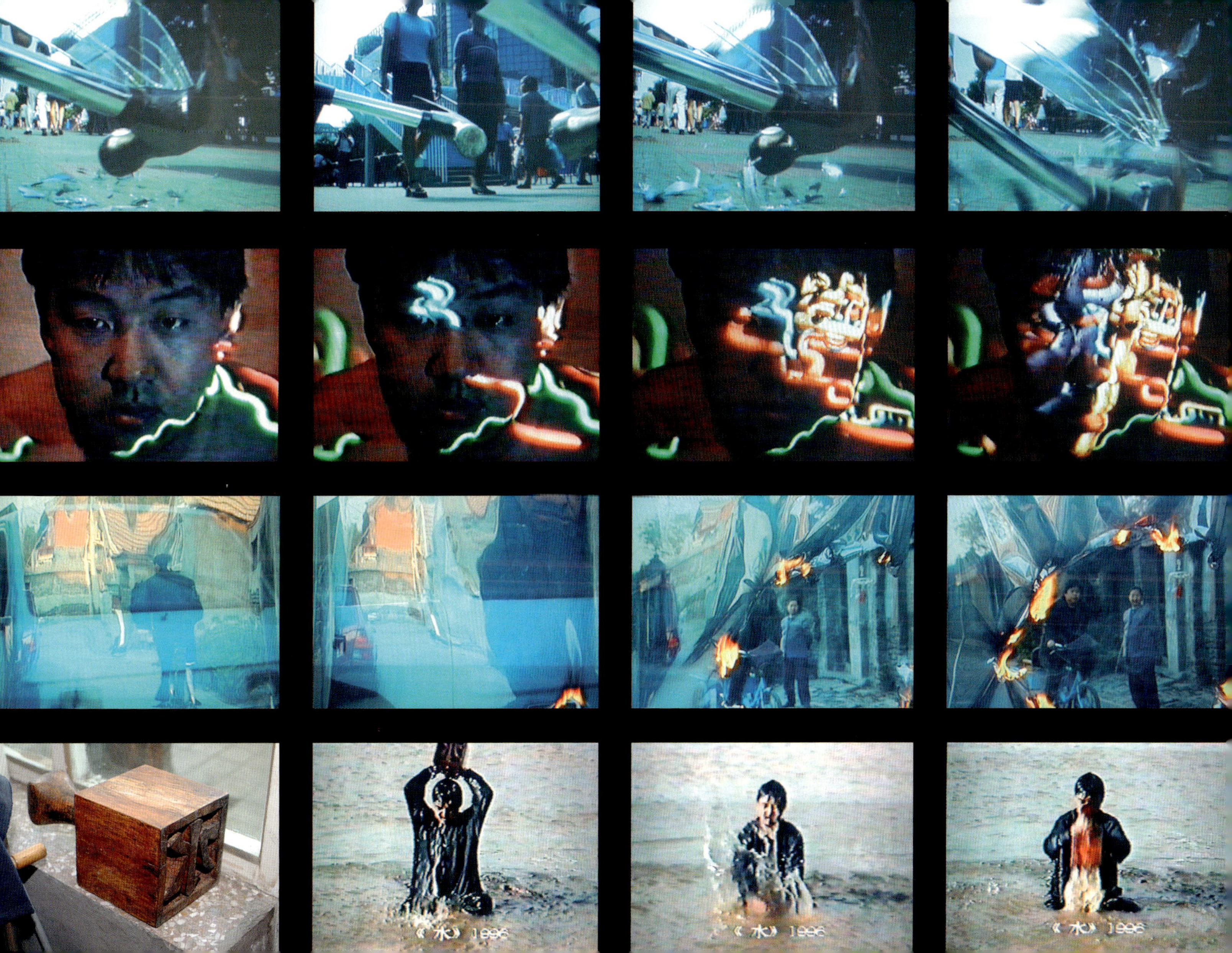
《水》1996
《水》1996
《水》1996

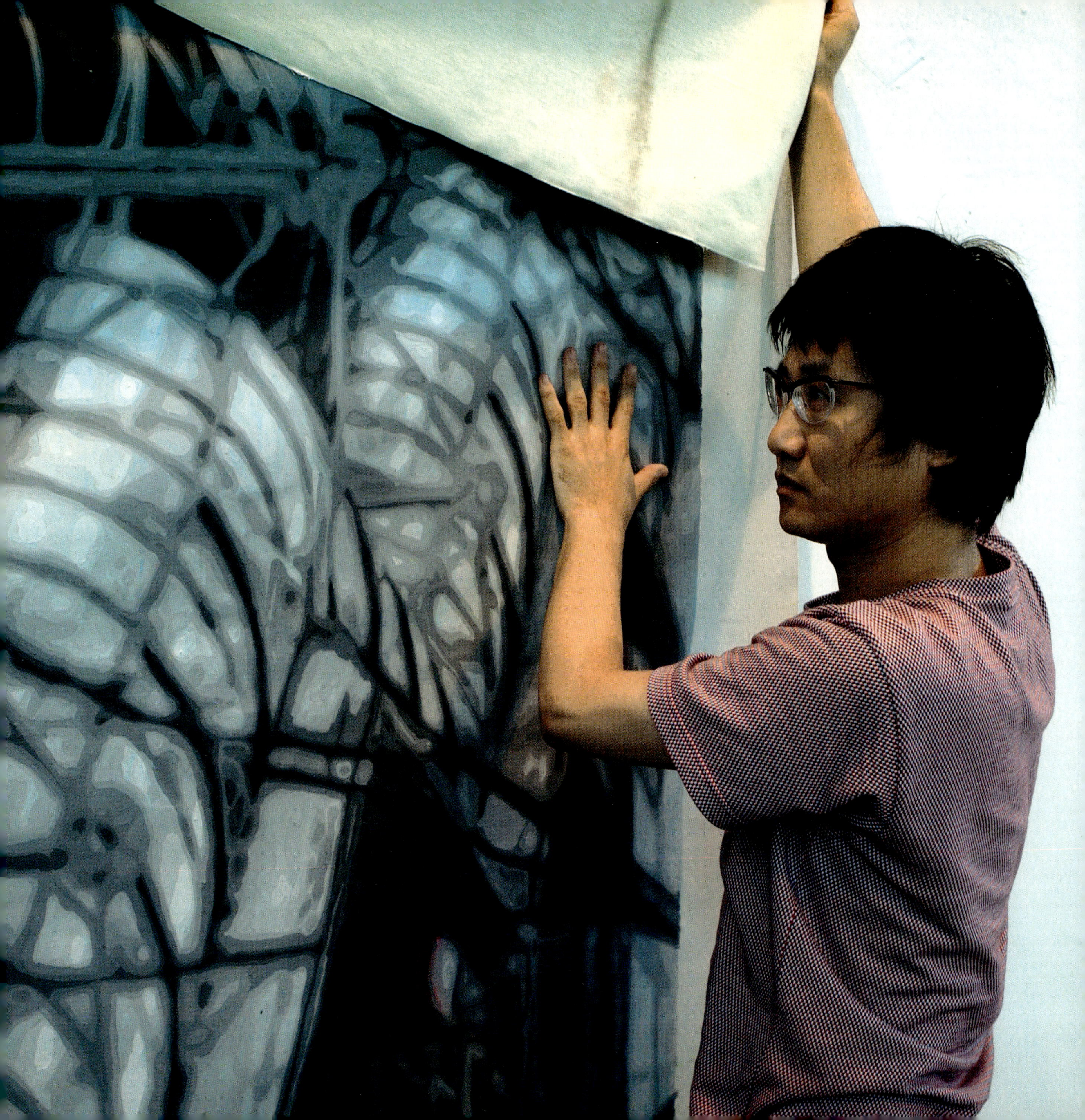

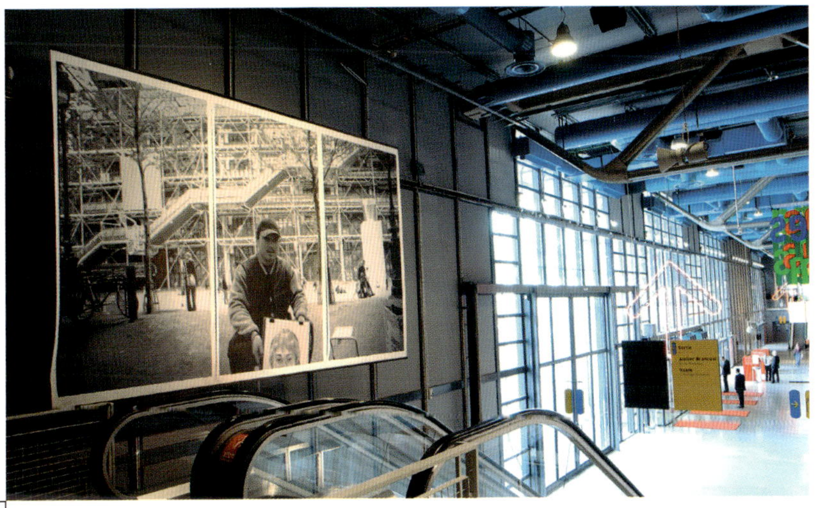

YAN LEI

One evening, late in 2002. Alain Sayag, co-curator of the flagship China exhibition at the Centre Pompidou with Laurent Le Bon, has invited Yan Lei and me to his home for dinner. Yan Lei is arguing passionately, using all his powers of persuasion to convince Alain to let him install a vast work on the façade of the Centre Pompidou, a work based on a photograph of one of the Chinese portrait artists who vie for customers on the piazza opposite the center. The idea is rather amusing, even if Braço Dimitrievic got there first, setting up a giant portrait of some anonymous person on the façade of one of the most prominent buildings in Paris. ¶ The decision was not just up to Alain Sayag. In the end, the work was displayed inside the building, at the top of the escalators, just as Yan Lei had described it, based on a photograph of a Chinese portraitist sketching tourists outside the Centre Pompidou. But did this mean the same thing? The element of ironic confrontation of sitter and portrait was missing—basically, the entire significance of the work was lost. Yan Lei decided to recreate a meaning for his work by producing a portrait of the group of curators in charge of organizing the exhibition and hanging it on the wall on the other side of the escalator, so that his anonymous artist ended up facing the administrators of the center. ¶ Although some of the impact of the work was lost, its spirit remained the same. You can't teach someone who has spent all their life in a Communist country to find their way around obstacles and the use of more or less transparent allusions and more or less covert criticism—they are already experts. The work is open to interpretation, but the clues are there to guide anyone who wants to understand the artist's true intentions. ¶ Strictly speaking, Yan Lei is not a critical artist—in fact, he denies the charge vehemently—but his work is based on his reactions against the world and society. It is true that these reactions contain a dose of criticism, but they also contain—as much, if not more so—a daring desire to take his vision to the logical extreme. This characteristic has provoked reactions of enthusiastic acceptance and violent rejection—extreme emotions

FACING PAGE: YAN LEI IN HIS STUDIO IN BEIJING. ABOVE: ONE OF HIS MOST RECENT WORKS, SHOWN AT THE CENTRE POMPIDOU IN PARIS IN 2003—A PORTRAIT OF A CHINESE PORTRAIT ARTIST LOOKING FOR CUSTOMERS OUTSIDE THE CENTER.

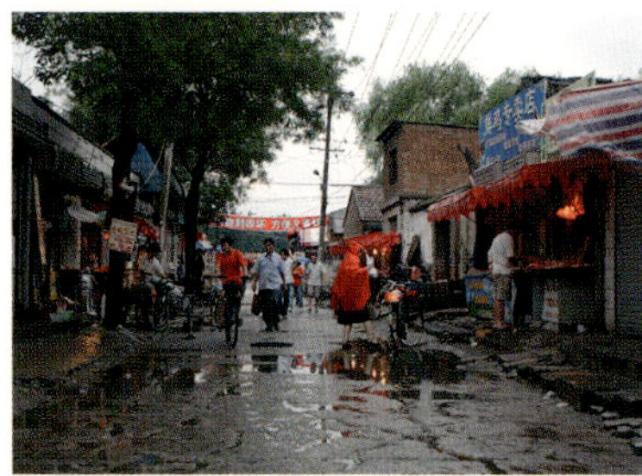
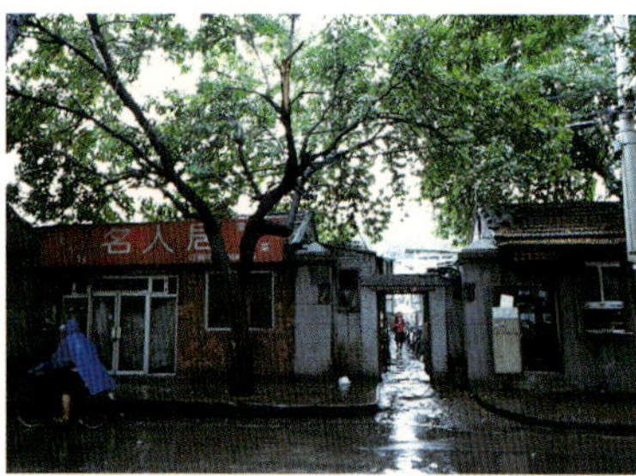
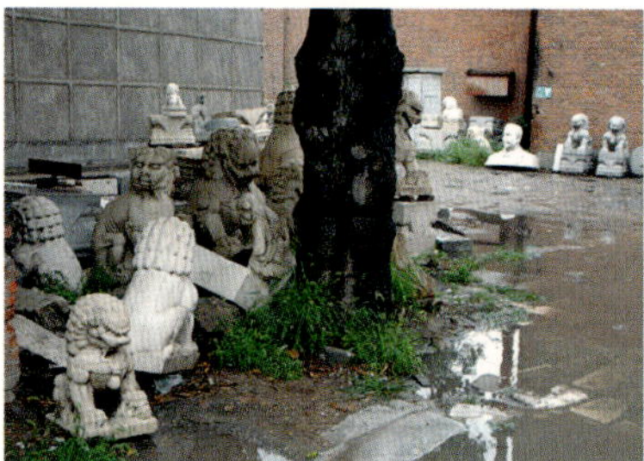
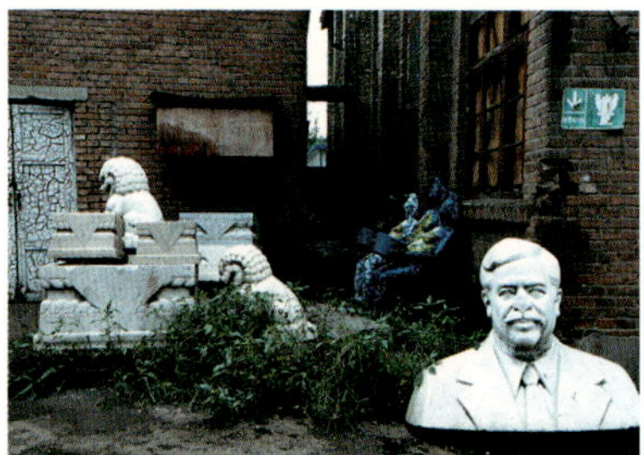
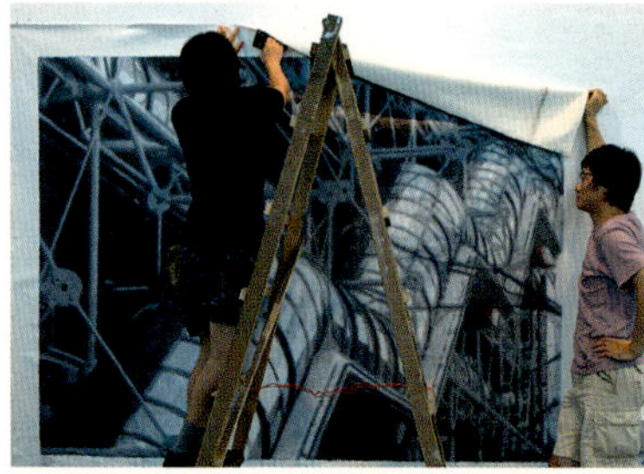
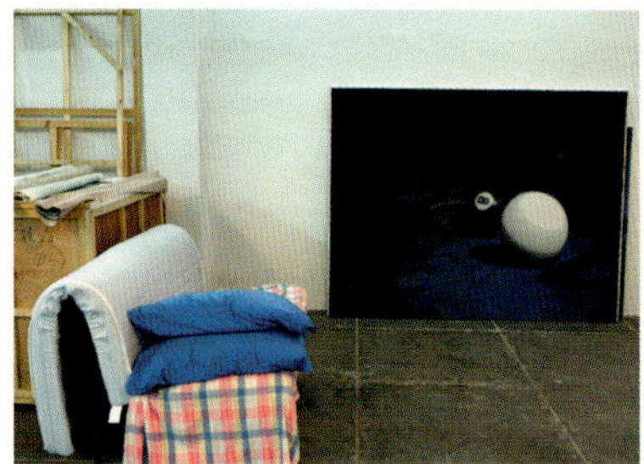
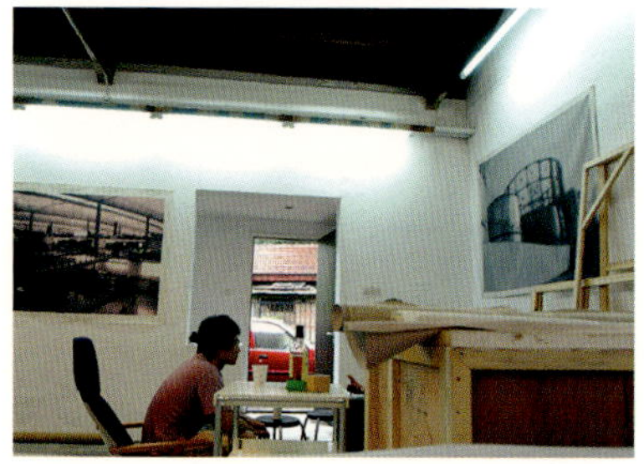
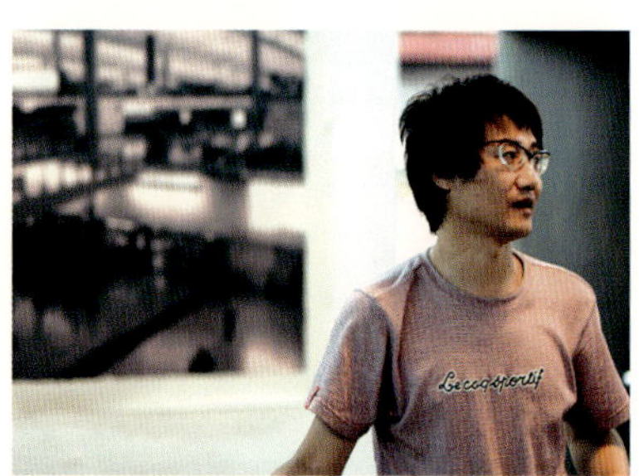

that straightforwardly critical works do not as a rule call forth. Yan Lei does not criticize: he attacks head-on. ¶ I first discovered Yan Lei a few years ago, through works similar to the Centre Pompidou pieces, at the China Art Archives and Warehouse (CAAW) in Beijing. Three of his major works were on display: *Invitation Number 0023283*, *May I See Your Work?* and, on a pedestal, a looped video of *1500 cm*. ¶ *May I See Your Work?* (1997) was on display opposite the entrance in the large downstairs hall. It is both a photograph and a painting consisting of six panels based on the photograph. Both the photographic image and the painted panels are reminiscent of the work of some forbidding seventeenth-century Dutch artist painting the portraits of a guild of austere, self-satisfied shopkeepers. But the title and the interest of the work take it to another level. "May I see your work?" were, almost without exception, the first words uttered by critics and buyers on the international art scene on meeting Chinese artists for the first time—words that betrayed their harsh avidity and their sense of their own importance. At least, that was the impression they made on Chinese artists in the 1990s: they came across not just as interested observers of a newly accessible art scene, but as predators and all-powerful judges. The artists found themselves in such a position of reliance on recognition by foreign critics that they could not but bow to this peremptory request (or order?) "May I see your work?" that might herald the start of a superb international career—or an inglorious end to their hopes. The title of this work thus contains more than a hint of exasperation. The tension apparent in the title and the work meant it had a huge impact both in China and in Europe. ¶ There is a similar hint of exasperation in *Invitation*, an astonishing artistic performance dating from 1997 in collaboration with Hong Hao that takes the form of a series of letters and envelopes displayed on the first floor of the gallery. The target of Yan Lei's barbs this time was the Documenta exhibition in Kassel, which was seen by Chinese artists as their big opportunity to make their mark abroad. Yan Lei sent the same letter to about one hundred artists, exhibition organizers, and critics, on headed notepaper bearing the Documenta logo. The letter, written in German, purported to be from the newly appointed director of Documenta, announcing his forthcoming visit to China to prospect for interesting new artistic developments. The letter gave a telephone and fax number which were in fact the number of a public phone booth. When the artists rang the number, of course there was nobody to answer their call. Yan Lei saw this as corresponding to the failure of the curators of the Kassel exhibition to respond to the needs of the Chinese artists who were, Yan Lei says, "more motivated by taking part in Documenta than they were by producing good art." He went so far as to send all the letters from Kassel. The performance was so convincing that most of the artists who fell for the fake letters were extremely angry, and ironically, those left off the list even more so. There was an enormous scandal. Yan Lei and his colleague Hong Hao were obliged to publish a letter presenting their sincere apologies to the recipients of the letters in the magazine *Jian Su Pictorial*, while relations with the German Embassy were distinctly cool for a while. Could there be a greater measure of success for a work designed to reveal all the intrigues and backstabbing that go on in the art world? ¶ On the second floor, one of Yan Lei's large-format photographs was exhibited. It is a self-portrait of the artist, bruised and battered, as if the work were a police record or a newspaper illustration of a violent mugging. He told me how he signed a contract with some local heavies to come and rough him up, and how, in the heat of the moment, they actually broke one of his teeth. But a contract is a contract. *Number 0023283* (the title of this work) is presented in the form of

TOP LEFT: THE NEIGHBORHOOD OF XI CHENG IN THE RAIN. TOP RIGHT: WORKS BY MEMBERS OF THE ASSOCIATION OF CHINESE ARTISTS IN THE COURTYARD OUTSIDE YAN LEI'S STUDIO. BOTTOM: YAN LEI'S WORKS ON DISPLAY IN THE STUDIO.

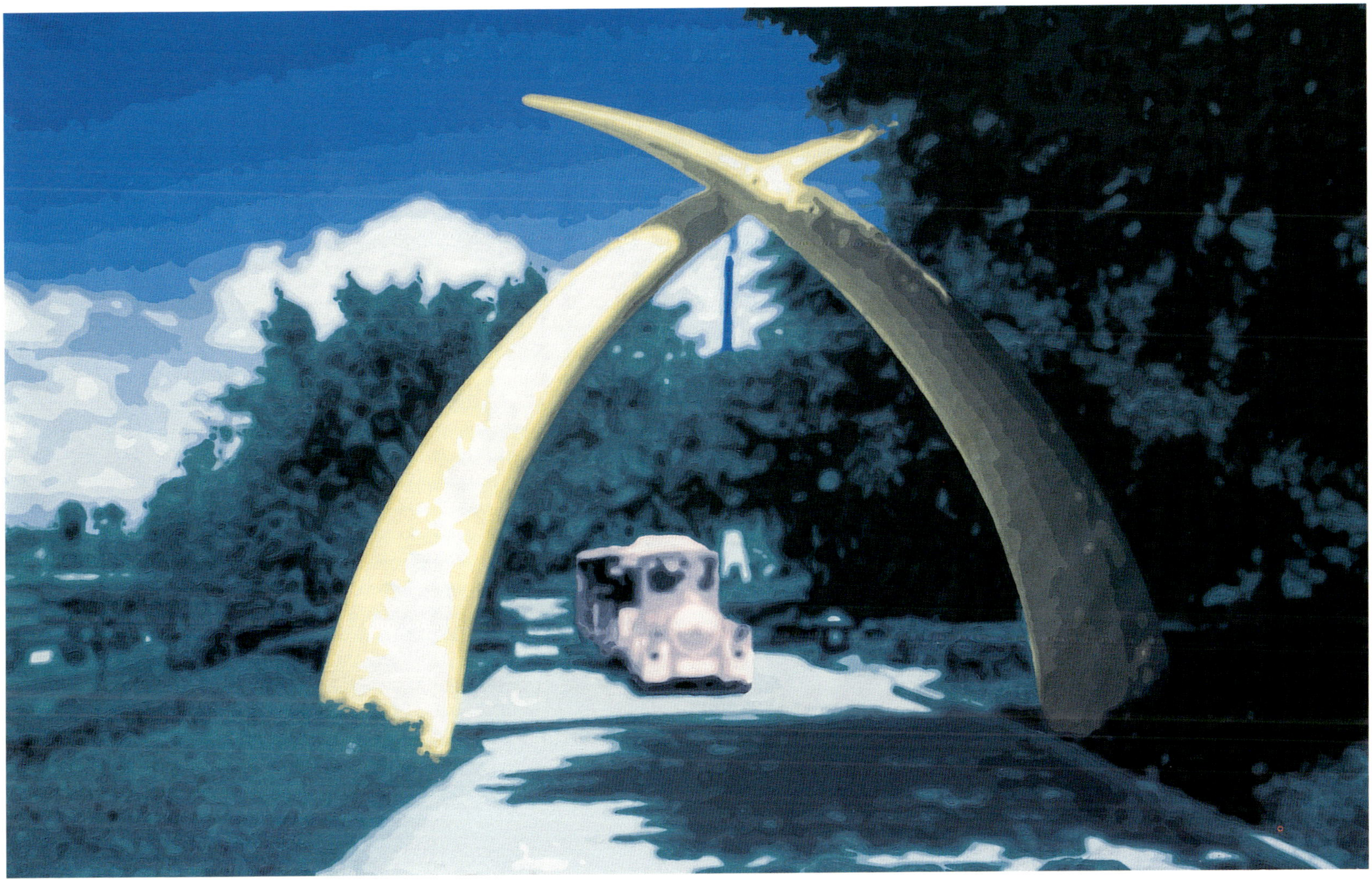

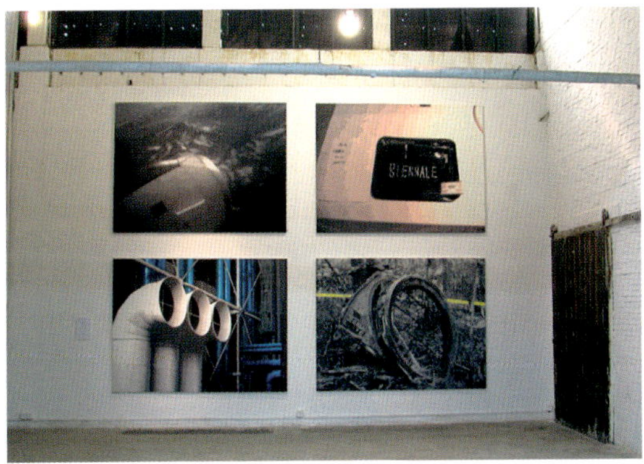

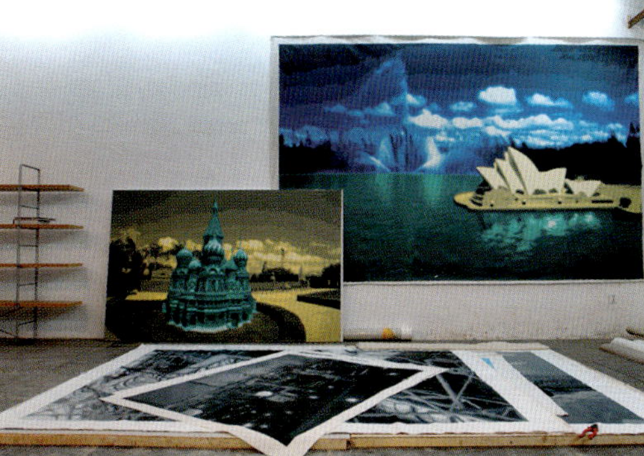

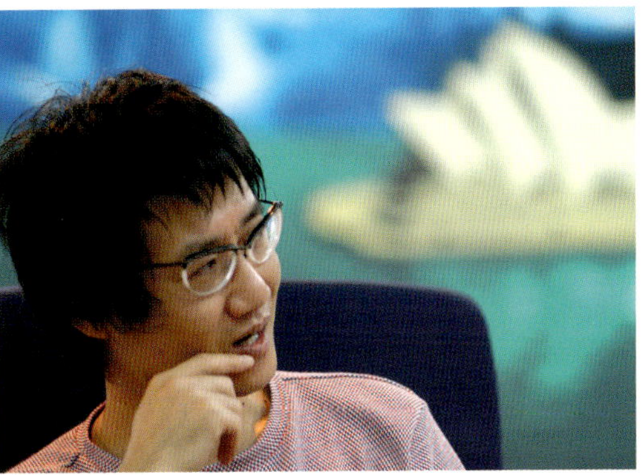

TOP: *INTERNATIONAL LANDSCAPE—ELEPHANT TEETH*, 2003. BOTTOM LEFT: FOUR WORKS COMPLETED IN 2003—*SKY, PIPES, REMAINS*, AND *DISHES*—ON DISPLAY IN THE LONG MARCH FOUNDATION GALLERY. BOTTOM CENTER: WORKS WAITING TO BE MOUNTED IN THE STUDIO.

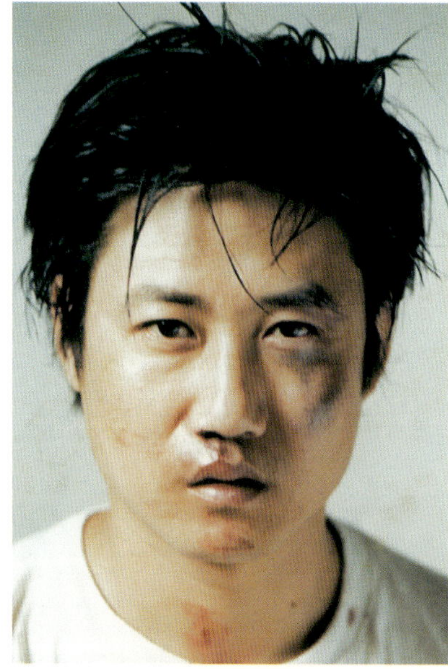
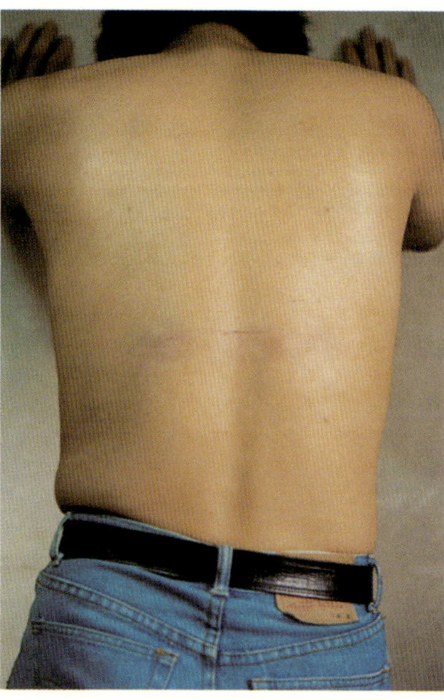
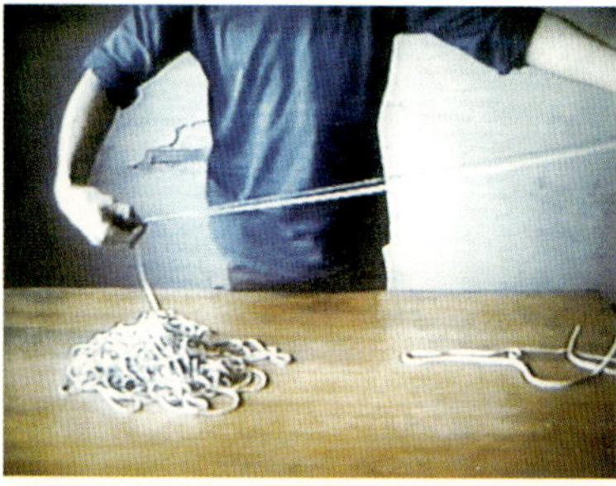
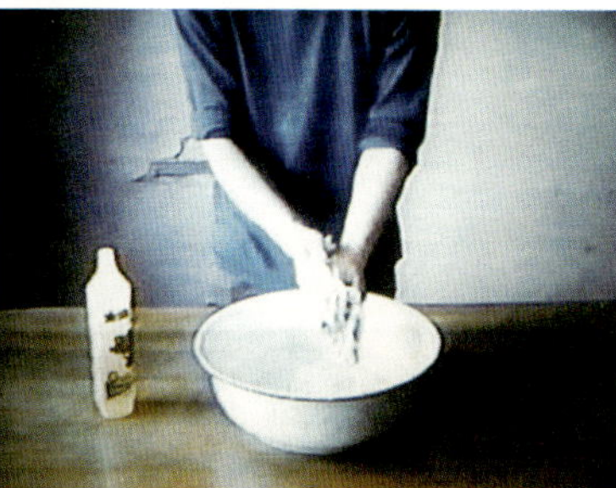
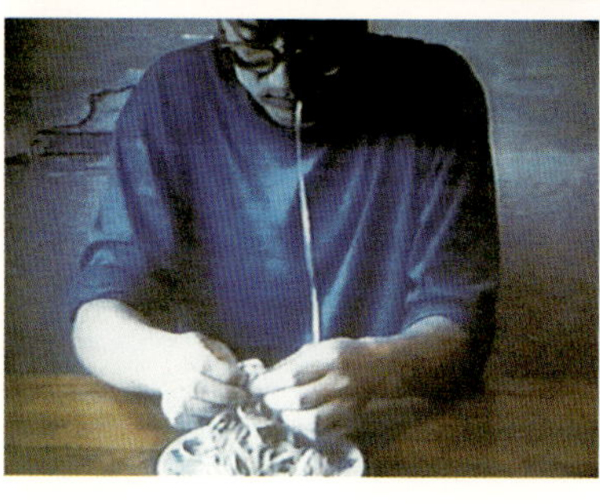
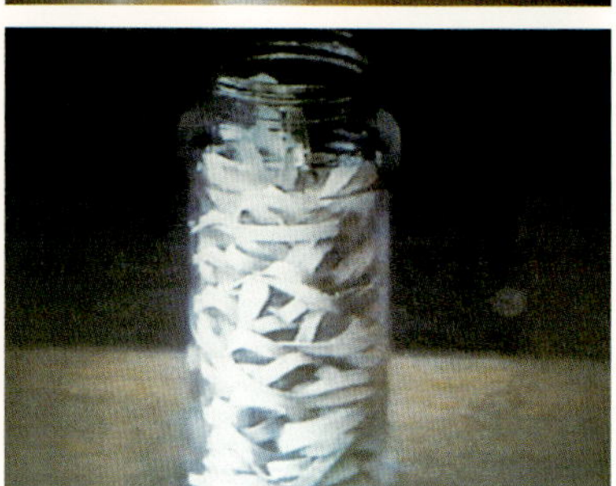

a series of illustrative pieces of evidence, displayed like courtroom exhibits—a medical certificate, X-rays, blood-soaked cotton bandages, and in the middle, a large photograph of Yan Lei looking haggard, with one bruised and swollen cheek, blood streaming from his nose, a broken tooth, and a split lip. The realism of this work was so immediate that it caused extreme reactions among the Chinese audience, including bouts of vomiting. ¶ Critics have seen this unusual performance as a commentary on urban violence. Others have sought comparisons with the Viennese Actionists. But the sheer daring and steely determination shown by Yan Lei clearly transcend these notions and precedents. Yan Lei is neither a sociologist nor a masochist. He just rushes headlong at whatever target he has set his sights on. His attitude itself becomes the form of the work, as the slogan went, back in 1969. ¶ It was the era of Political Pop Art, as Yan Lei takes malign pleasure in pointing out. "Artists were in a difficult position back then. The solution they found was to get together in groups and to work together. But I was never that sort of person. I didn't want to go and live in villages with other people." So he carried on down his own route, alone, exploring the human body's, and society's, capacity for resistance, producing provocative visions of both, throwing caution to the wind. ¶ At the CAAW exhibition, a TV screen next to the photo played a looped video by Yan Lei. The title of the video was *1500 cm*. Shot in 1993, it shows the artist armed with a wooden ruler measuring out fifty feet (1,500 centimeters) of thin ribbon, with infinite patience. He washes it in a bowl with detergent, then rinses it. Having done that, he sits down and proceeds to swallow the ribbon like a long strand of spaghetti. He swallows the whole 1,500 centimeters of ribbon, then slowly regurgitates it into a jar. Inside the jar, the ribbon looks like a stretch of intestine. When I asked Yan Lei about the meaning of this, he tells me that regurgitating is harder than swallowing. He explains that he was just interested in exploring the limits of video technique, which he was unfamiliar with at the time, and to use it in conjunction with a performance. What particularly interested him was the body "as the subject and object of meaning" and testing its limits of endurance. Of course, it is also possible to read the film as an allegory of the artist absorbing information and data, only to regurgitate them transformed by the process of absorption and digestion. ¶ Another time, the artist, dressed in a T-shirt bearing the slogan "No art today," is shown sitting on a hospital chair, alongside a number of other chairs on which a quote by Kam Ping Hiller was written, "I don't care much about art," while an ambulance brought in British beef (this was at the height of the mad cow disease crisis) later shown served up at a poolside barbecue. ¶ It would be wrong to interpret all of these virulent, violent performances as purely stemming from a taste for provocation. It would be wrong to say, as Dai Jinhua did about Yan Lei, that in the 1990s, he had to be in the spotlight. Yan Lei's provocative works deal with issues of identity and the role of the artist in society. When, as Yan Lei says, "everything is art," violence then becomes necessary to engender a reaction. ¶ Incorrigible as ever, Yan Lei hung a banner at the entrance to the exhibition, proclaiming "Shanghai welcomes Yan Lei," which inevitably rubbed a lot of people the wrong way. His most virulent critics demanded that the banner be taken down. Others, while less hostile, were hardly appreciative of such a gesture that diminished the impact of their own work. What had he done more than them to deserve more admiration, more recognition, and pride of place at the exhibition? It must be said that Yan Lei often acts as a catalyst, revealing the truth behind the mask. As he says, "You have to realize that art is a competition." This work was the perfect demonstration. I take my hat off to him. ¶ I went to see Yan Lei on a rainy day in late summer in his brand new studio that he set up in July 2003 in the central

TWO OF YAN LEI'S BEST-KNOWN PERFORMANCES. LEFT: *NO.0310007/NO.00223283*, 1995. RIGHT: *1,500 CM*, 1994. THE FIRST OF THESE WORKS NOW EXISTS AS A PHOTOGRAPH, THE SECOND AS A VIDEO. FACING PAGE: TWO OF YAN LEI'S MOST FAMOUS AND CONTROVERSIAL WORKS. LEFT: *INVITATION*, 1997. A FAKE INVITATION TO THE DOCUMENTA EXHIBITION IN GERMANY. RIGHT: *SHANGHAI WELCOMES YAN LEI*, 1997.

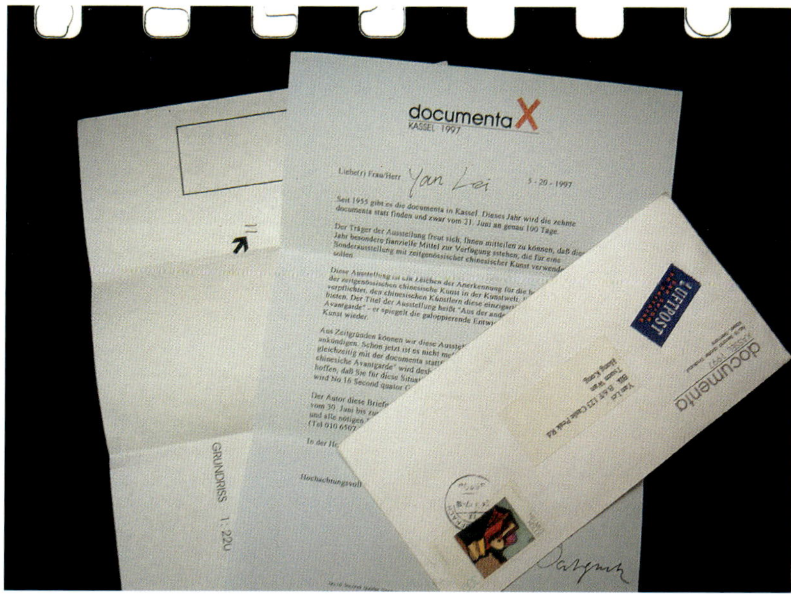

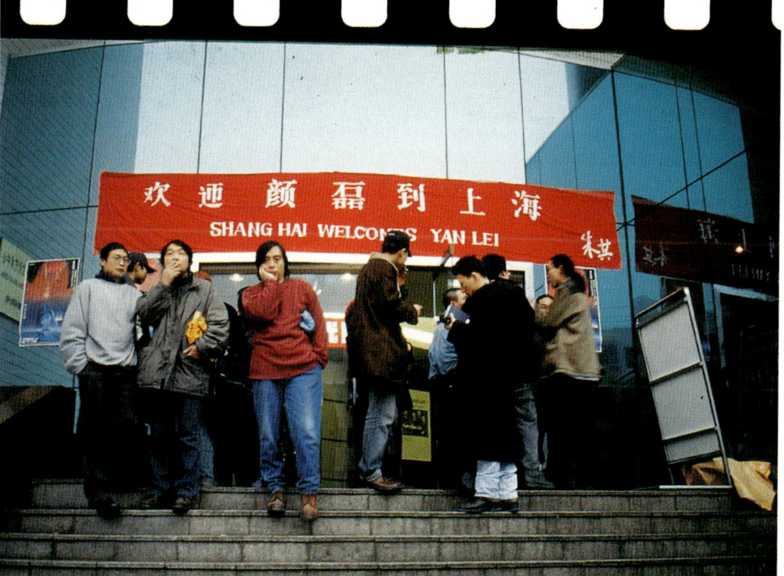

Xi Cheng district of Beijing. In the courtyard, the unfortunately dynamic Association of Chinese Sculptors put on a display of the heights of stilted classicism reached by modern Chinese academic art. ¶ His brother was there, helping him to transport his works and hang some of them on the walls. Yan Lei was wearing a T-shirt he had brought back from Paris with the logo Le Coq Sportif. When he talks, he pouts slightly, as if his mouth is twisted in disgust or nausea. ¶ He was born in 1965, one year before the start of the Cultural Revolution. His mother's uncle was a well-known artist in traditional Chinese painting. His son had also chosen to be an artist. Yan Lei says, "My family was not hostile to art." He had no need to struggle against his family's wishes to exist as an artist. He was lucky, and was very quickly awarded a place at a school specializing in art. ¶ He lives quite a distance from the center of Beijing. His card has given two addresses since 1997, one in Beijing and the other in Hong Kong, but only because his wife is from Hong Kong and the couple lived there for a while. But, he says, "I didn't feel at ease there." ¶ In Hong Kong, he had the impression of being cut off from the art scene in Beijing. He led a very different life, far from other Beijing artists. Now the couple has returned to live in the Beijing region, in Lang Fang, some distance from the city. Yan Lei does not like to live in close proximity to the art world. He often tells people "I am not an artist; I'm a man," as if it were an important declaration of his own principles. ¶ At the Gwangju Biennial, he built a narrow passage in wood, hidden in camouflage. Was it accurate to interpret this in the same spirit as his other works, as a tunnel that blocked out all the other artists' creations? For once, the answer is no. *International Passage*, produced in collaboration with his wife Fu Jie, was built to the exact dimensions of a corridor in his apartment. It was a private space made public. ¶ In 2002, he did not take part in six biennials, as has been said by over-enthusiastic admirers, but two, as he confirmed. But even two biennials in one year—São Paulo and Gwangju—plus one triennial (Guangzhou) is not bad. He turned down an offer to show at the Hong Kong biennial because of problems of organization. ¶ Yan Lei took up painting in 2000, but in his own way, using the canvas to pin down images that he seems to have picked up as a tourist—cities, monuments, an airport, a table, his immediate surroundings, people. These are the images of his life and his experiences. They are part of his past, like pictures in a photo album where people store their key memories. "I don't care if something is important or not, I only paint what is important for me in my life," he says. His technique is to begin with a photo taken with a digital camera and then to play around with it on a computer until he obtains the required effect, when he prints it on canvas. As Marion Bertagna has noted, the result resembles a weather map with lines of isobars. The image consists only of lines separating blocks of color classified by number. All he then has to do is fill in the gaps by numbers with acrylic paint. ¶ This is the technique he has used for most of the works produced in the last few years, including the famous curators in a garden, the hare in a field, the street scene in Sanlintun, and the neighborhood where all the embassies are, and the large painting in three panels featuring a Chinese portrait artist Yan Lei met on the piazza outside the Centre Pompidou, hung over the escalator inside. ¶ This is how he chooses to represent the ever-changing world he inhabits, transforming amateur photographs into paintings. ¶ Faced with this world of latent possibilities and potential, faced with entirely new ways of doing things, Yan Lei, rather like Fabrice Hybert, has turned himself into an art producer, creating a sort of co-operative in Lang Fang where he lives and works, not in a group as such but alongside several other artists. ¶ "I have so many ideas that I need to associate with other people," he says.

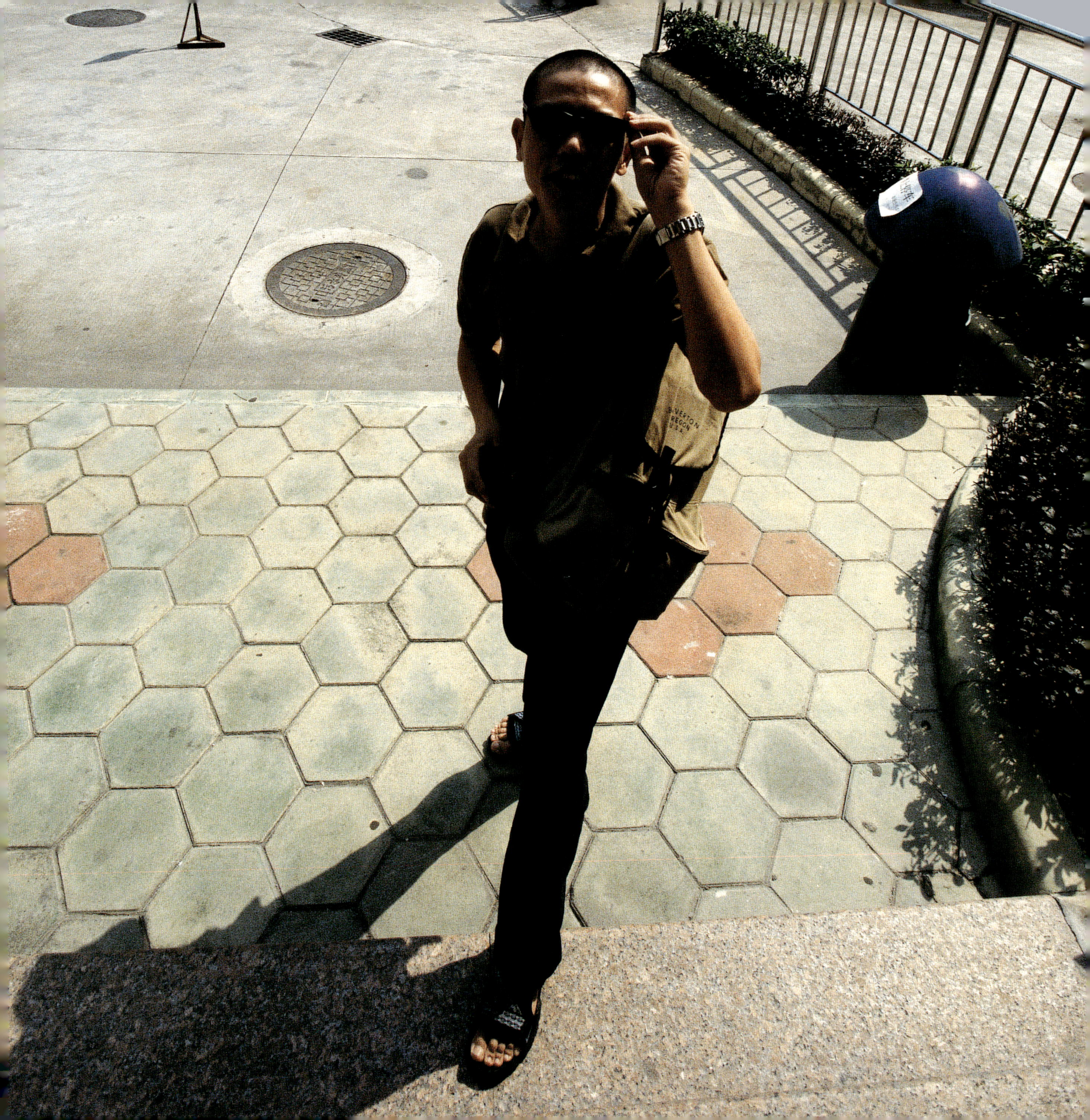

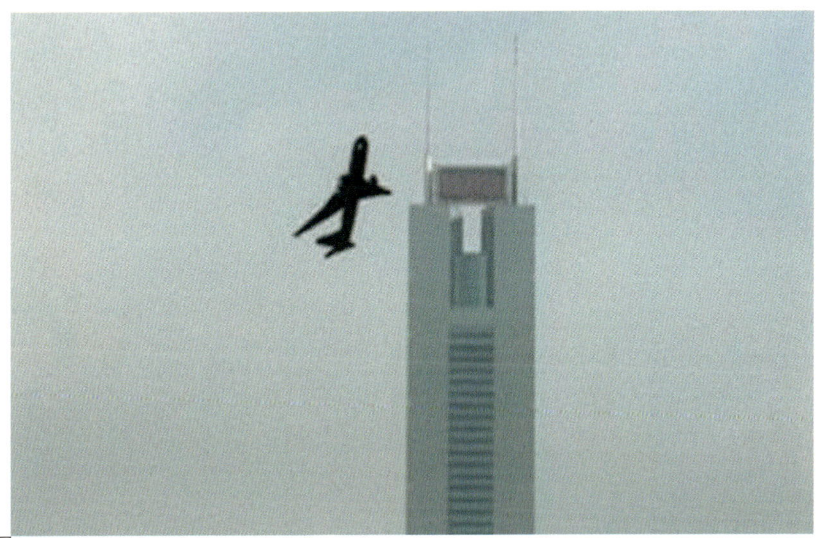

CHEN SHAOXIONG

Chen Shaoxiong is such a multifaceted artist that I get the impression that either he leads several parallel lives or there are several artists using the same name. ¶ I met him in a somewhat unusual way. It was in 2000, on my first trip to Guangzhou. I had expressed a desire to be introduced to a number of young artists and to visit some galleries and schools. The people organizing the trip took this as their cue to get together ten or so artists in the excellent Guangdong Museum for me to have a look at their portfolios. ¶ They all patiently filed past me with their portfolios. I had the unpleasant and horribly embarrassing feeling that they were being paraded for me to choose from, so I called a halt to the proceedings and went to visit them in their studios instead—which led me to make the acquaintance of a number of other artists. One of the original group of ten or so confided that the idea for the "audition" had been imposed by—I think—the Guggenheim, which some time before had made the express request to meet as many artists as possible in a single day. The organizers thus believed that all Westerners wanted the same thing. ¶ Chen Shaoxiong's studio is to the north of Guangzhou, a stone's throw from the Agricultural University of Southern China. ¶ He lives in a pleasant, rather sparse apartment in a sought-after housing development with an outrageously blue swimming pool and luxuriant, Hollywood-style vegetation. On entering his apartment, I was surprised to see a canvas on an easel and boxes of tubes of paint piled high. I didn't realize he painted. I knew of him as a photographer. In Venice, he made a name for himself as a virtuoso video artist. ¶ He makes some tea, Guangzhou style, while he explains to me that he is tired of all the new technologies, or at least the way they are used in China today. He saw that I was astonished by his paintings. He has a most disarming smile that belies the ocean of sadness and seriousness one senses in him, and an off-the-wall sense of humor that I just love. ¶ He was born in 1962 in Guangdong province, in Shantou, some two hundred and fifty miles (four hundred kilometers) east of Guangzhou, not far from the sea. How was his childhood? Quiet, he says. No worries. Really? And what about the Cultural Revolution that began when he was four? "I was very little," he explains. "I didn't know what was happening out in the world. When the Revolution started, I was just old enough to go to elementary school. My mother told me not to go. Instead, I went and played out in the countryside. I enjoyed great freedom. When I said no worries, I meant in comparison with today's children who spend lots and lots of time in school. Lots of people think the Cultural Revolution only brought bad things. But for the children, the revolution had plenty of advantages. That's why I won't say anything, good or bad, about the Cultural Revolution." What? Another artist who refuses to speak out against it? Is he perhaps inhibited by the presence of the interpreter, who more or less works for the government, or does he really believe what he is saying? ¶ Chen Shaoxiong's family was poor and found it hard to make ends meet. But he knew he wanted to be an artist. "Maybe if my family had been rich, things would have been different," he says, with a wry smile. Then, returning to his thoughts on the Cultural Revolution, he continues, "Not everything was cut off by the Revolution. My brother had some friends who were interested in art. One day, after school, they took me as their model. That's how I began to get interested in painting." He was fifteen. Too young to go to university. Instead, he studied in secret with his brother and his friends. "I felt left out of society," he now admits. ¶ "Since my parents were already angry with my brother who annoyed them because his room was always untidy, they were also against the idea of me studying art. So I went to university against my parents' wishes. They didn't understand what I was doing." He studied engraving at the School of Fine Art. "Wait," he says, and goes off to look for an old file that he opens on the floor to show me what he was doing back then. "These are the landscapes of my childhood. Today, I find them incredibly precious. I am constantly seeking this lost world." ¶ He was awarded his degree in 1984 and took part in his first exhibition two years later. He tells me

FACING PAGE: CHEN SHAOXIONG OUTSIDE HIS APARTMENT BUILDING IN GUANGZHOU. ABOVE: A STILL FROM THE VIDEO *ANTI-TERRORIST VARIETY*, 2002.

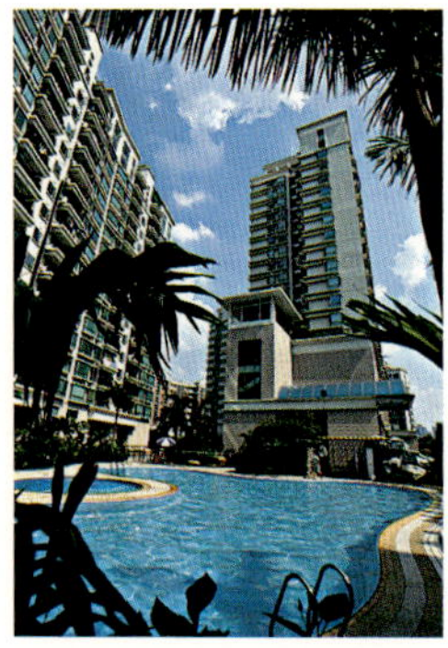

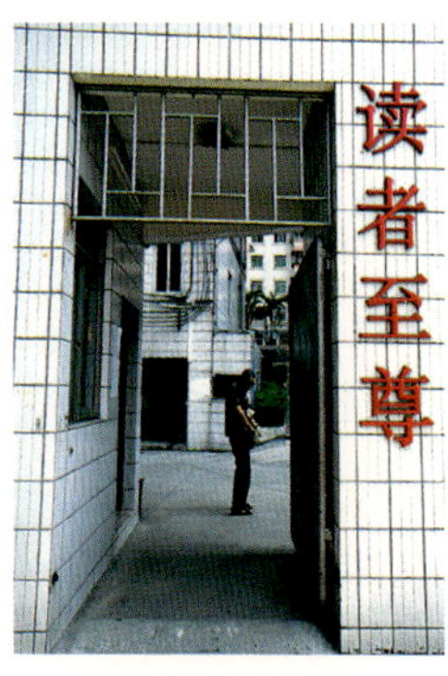

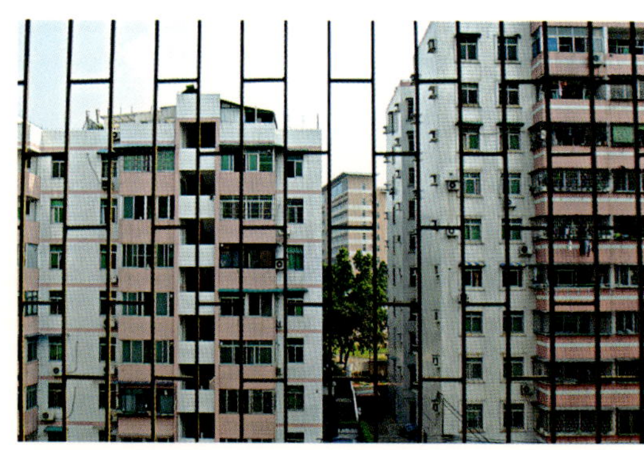

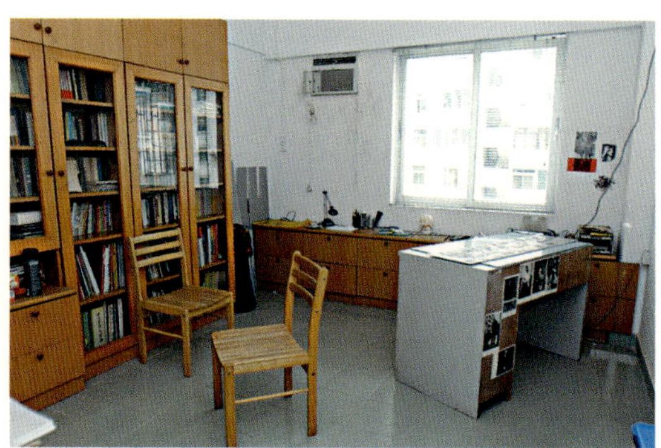

that back then, in southern China, art needed shaking up. Which he did. He organized a Salon of Southern Artists that lasted a whole year. This taught him that he needed to make a clean break with stilted academic art. At around the same time, he discovered Marcel Duchamp and Fluxus, and was prompted to try and make contact with other artists. In 1990, he founded the group Big Tail Elephant. Why, I ask? "Through sheer necessity," he says. "In Guangzhou, the School of Fine Art and the Association of Artists were incredibly powerful. They didn't want to leave even the tiniest amount of elbowroom for artists like us. We created a group so that we could have our own exhibition space and room to maneuver, so we could try out new things. We created this group to create a name for ourselves and to be able to develop." ¶ The Big Tail Elephant group announced the development of a critical strategy to bring about a rapid change in Chinese cultural and economic policy. The group made it clear that one of its defining characteristics would be the absence of any form of personal power. The group of four artists—Chen Shaoxiong, Lin Yilin, Liang Juhui, and Xu Ta—is still more or less active, although one member is now in New York, one in Shanghai, and the other two still in Guangzhou. At least for the moment. They are always on the move. The whole group made it to Venice in 2003 for the Guangzhou Express exhibition at the Biennale, but they were not showing together, and there were few clues to the fact that they work together. ¶ In the 1990s, almost nobody thought of making the trip to Guangzhou to see what was going on in the art world there. Western art critics didn't even bother with Shanghai, restricting their inquiries to Beijing. Chen Shaoxiong says, "The problem was that they thought if they looked at Beijing and understood what was going on there, they automatically assumed they understood all about Chinese art." ¶ So what was the big difference between Guangzhou and Beijing? ¶ "In the early 1990s in Beijing, the artists had a fair amount of access to what was going on overseas, which influenced them a lot. They created political art with political signs. The artists in Beijing were very interested in the theory of the sign. In Guangzhou, we didn't have nearly as much contact with the outside world. We mostly engaged in local dialogue. Today, the situation has changed, because a lot of international exhibitions have come to Guangzhou, and a lot of international exhibitions have included Guangzhou artists. Sometimes it can be difficult to tell art from Beijing and Guangzhou apart today. Artists from Guangzhou are maybe livelier, more active, more animated, bolder. I am thinking in particular of the way they have pushed the limits of photography with 'new photography.'" ¶ Photography, yes. Before he became known as the artist who folded down skyscrapers in Shanghai to stop them from being hit by airplanes in a notorious video, Chen Shaoxiong was known first and foremost—new photography or no new photography— for his work with a camera. I do not wish to devote a discussion to the merits of this "new photography," which claims to be new because before, the key moment was when the photographer pressed the button, while now, the key moments are just before and just after. This is old hat compared to what artists in Europe were doing as far back as the 1970s. What really is interesting, though, in Chen Shaoxiong's photography is not so much the "concept," but rather the much subtler, less clear-cut, slightly unsettling superimpositions that are not quite perfectly in place, creating fissures in a reality which is becoming less and less certain and at the same time more and more unstable, undermined by the possibilities of virtuality. When he superimposes a Bangkok street scene over an almost identical scene in Guangzhou, or vice versa, for example, the camera captures a bizarre collage that is only furtively visible. ¶ Some of his works are in a long, thin layout and show passersby, cars, red traffic lights, benches, motorbikes,

FAR RIGHT: THE STUDIO IN CHEN SHAOXIONG'S APARTMENT IN GUANGZHOU. LEFT: THE VIEW ON THE POOL FROM THE WINDOW. FACING PAGE: CHEN SHAOXIONG SERVES TEA AS HE SHOWS US SOME OF HIS EARLY WORKS.

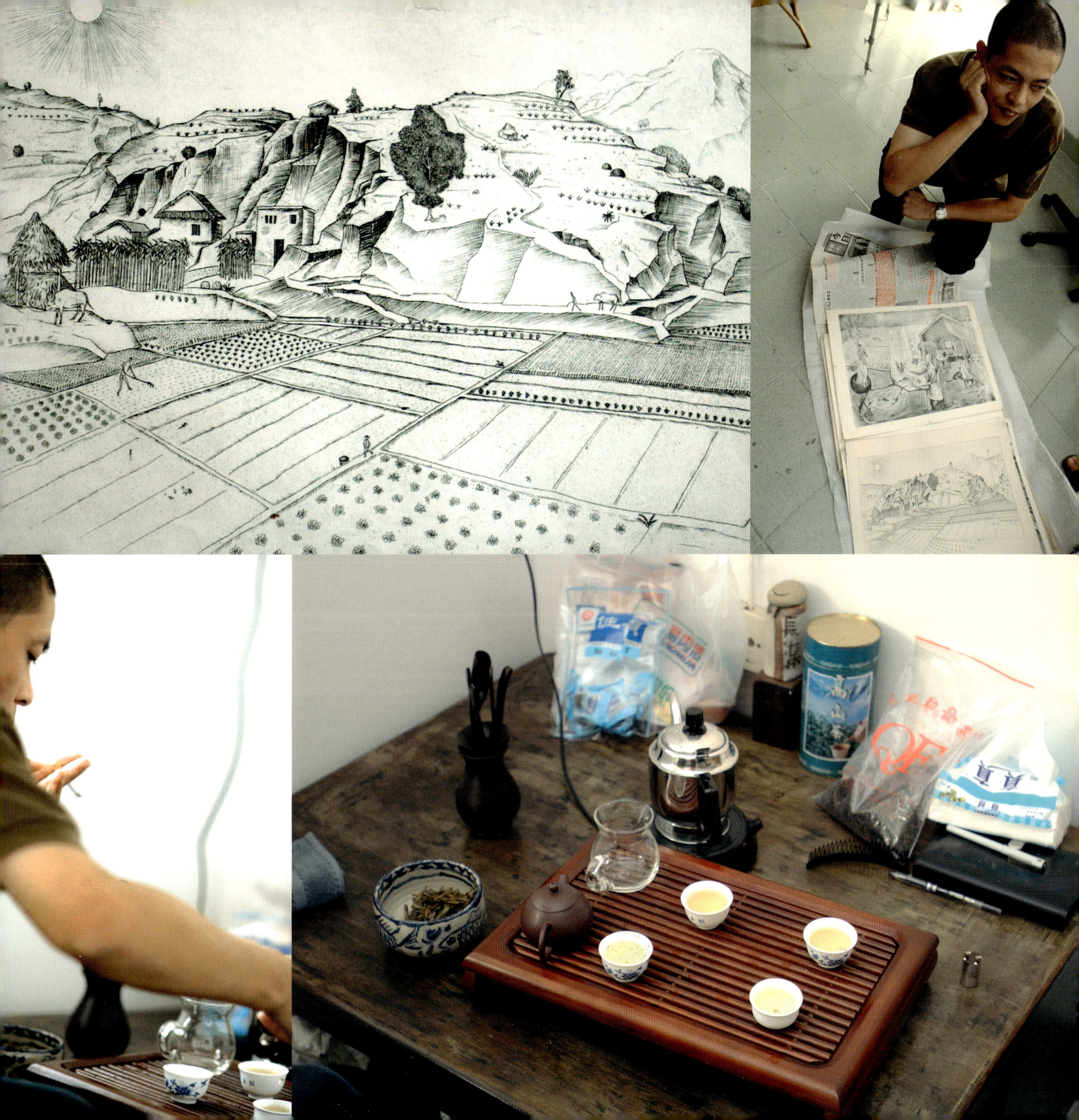
高山茶

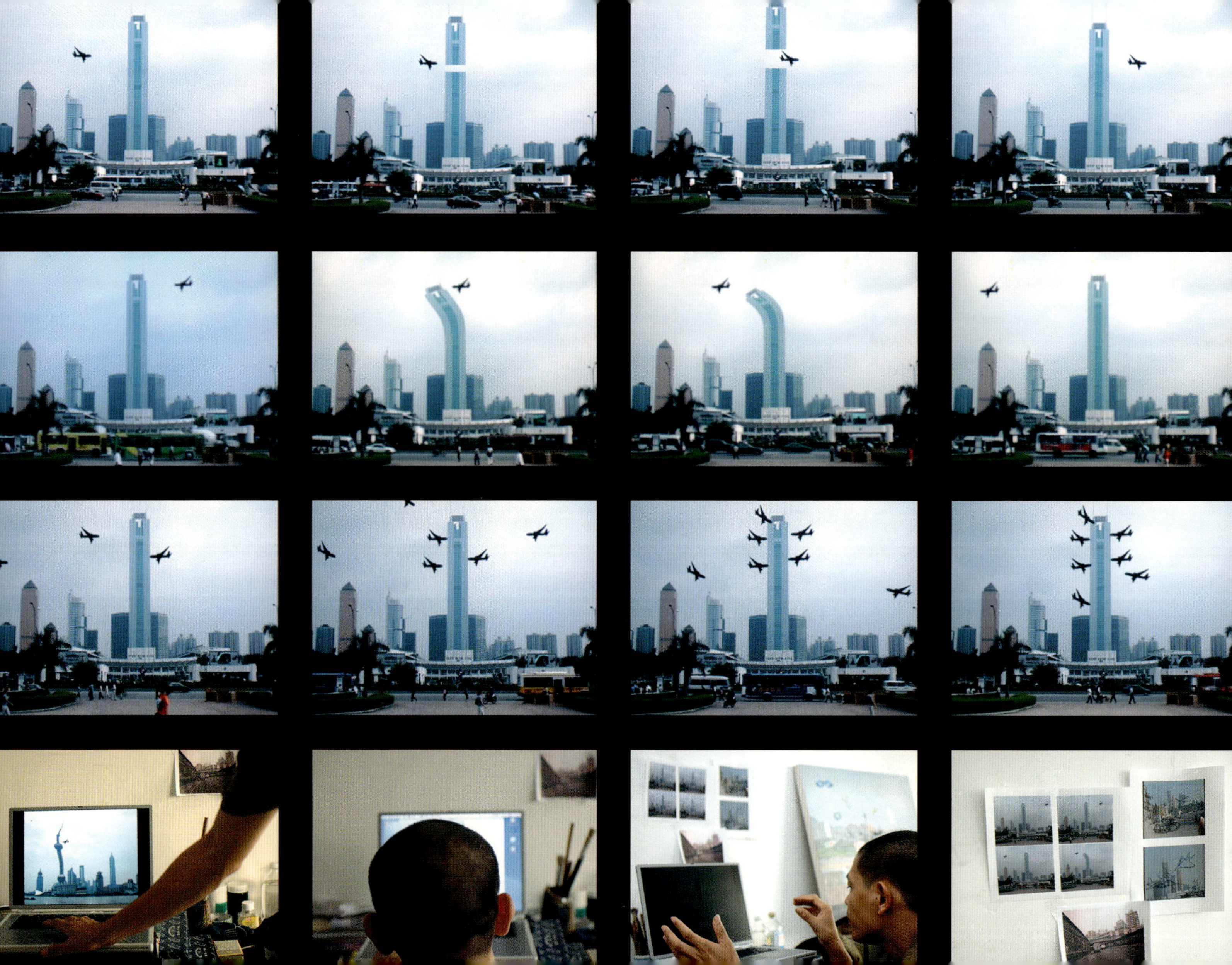

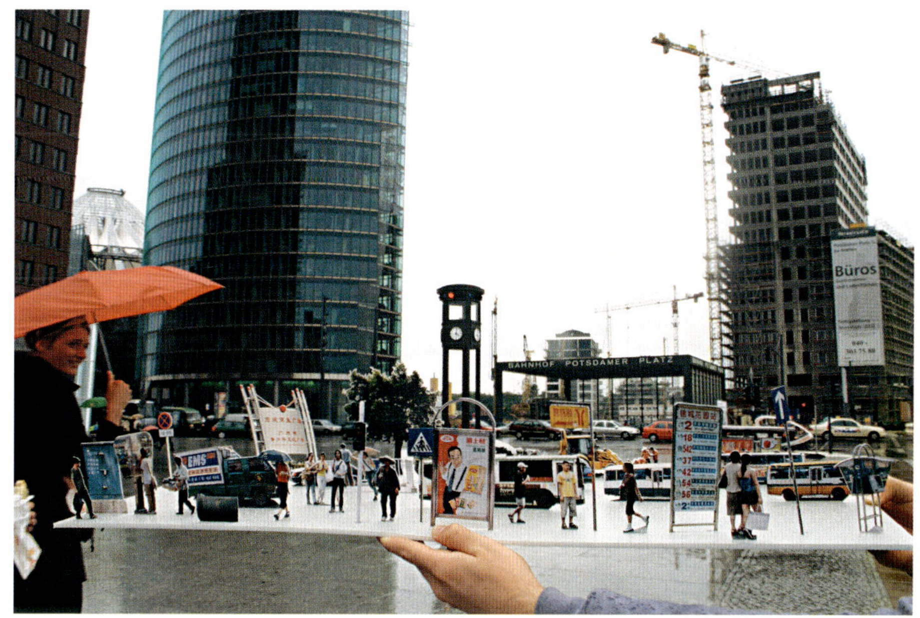

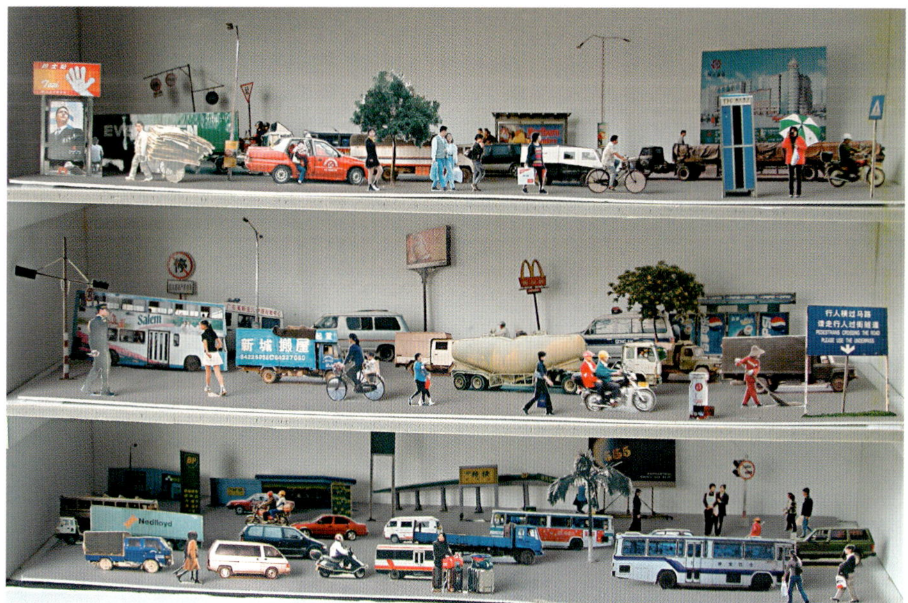

FACING PAGE: CHEN SHAOXIONG'S MOST FAMOUS WORK, *ANTI-TERRORIST VARIETY*, 2002, WHICH WAS SHOWN AT THE VENICE BIENNALE. IT IS AN IRREVERENT TAKE ON THE TRAGEDY OF 9/11. ABOVE TOP: *STREETS*, 1999. ABOVE BOTTOM: *STREETS*, 1998.

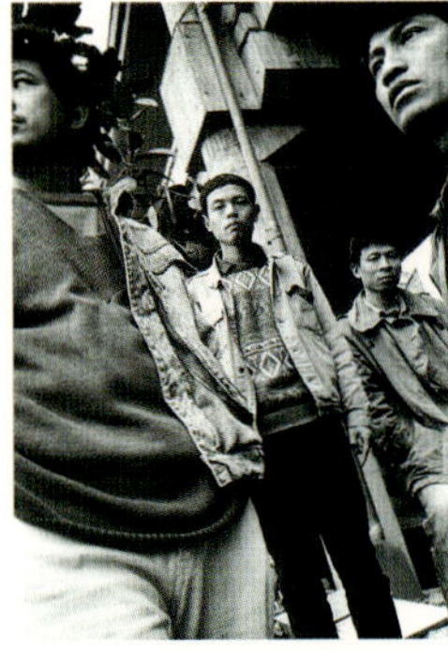
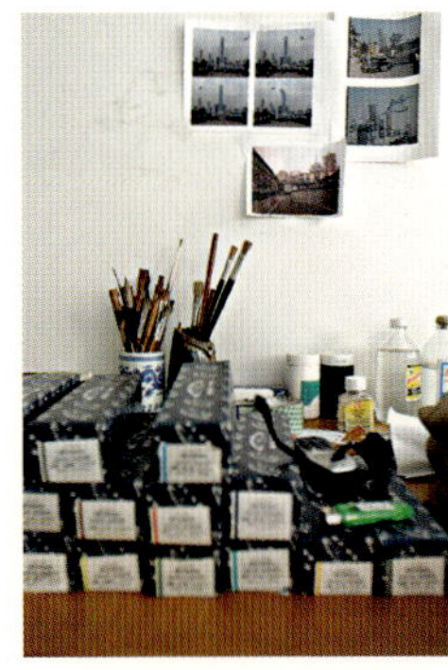
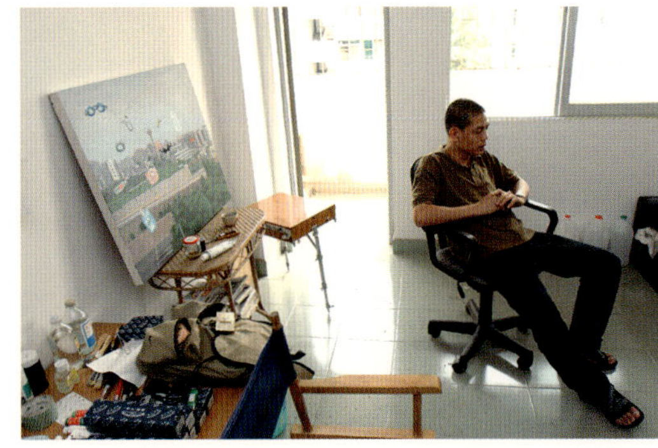
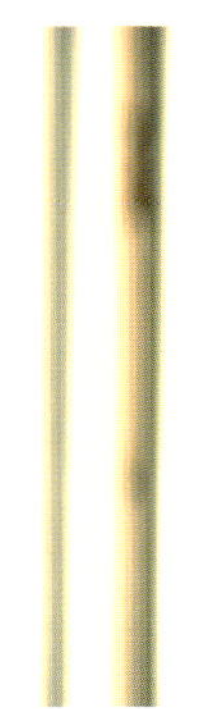
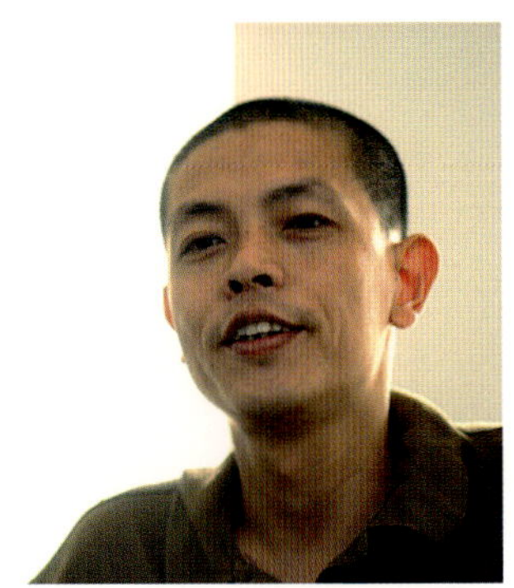

and bicycles, all interfering with our clear view of the road or park, like in the work *Second Avenue* (1997–98), which was shown at the Guangzhou triennial. Every work features a kind of collage that mimics the collages created daily by new technologies, which allow us to be—mentally, at least—in several places at once and to see different things at the same time. ¶ Chen Shaoxiong began experimenting with video art in 2000. *Landscape* makes use of a structure similar to his earlier photographs, and which made them so innovative and widely appreciated. The idea was simple: to place a sheet of glass with a picture drawn on it in marker pen in front of the lens, so that the camera films both the landscape of the work's title and the drawing roughed in on the glass. He asked friends to write a text about an ideal landscape, read by a voice offscreen. The text explores the absence of contact between man and nature, while the blunt outlines of the drawing, as jarring as a swear word, give a vision of a harsh, untamed nature—a vampire clutching a fish in its clawed hands (is there such as thing as a fish-eating vampire?). *Landscape II* depicts our quiet, safe urban surroundings, superimposed with aerial dogfights seen on television—or that we might be seeing tomorrow in reality. But what reality? ¶ The digital videos I saw at the Venice Biennale and then in his apartment were more direct, funnier, and had more impact. They played with notions of special effects, memory, and disappointment and frustration: what you are expecting to happen never quite does. Take the video *Anti-Terrorist Variety*. On the screen, an urban landscape of skyscrapers. An airplane appears, getting dangerously close to the towers. You're thinking of 9/11, right? Everyone does, waiting—I dare not say hoping—for the catastrophe. But just when the planes are about to hit the skyscrapers, the towers gracefully fold and the plane flies overhead as if this were the most normal thing in the world. In China, towers bend, they do not break. ¶ Chen Shaoxiong has produced a number of variations on the same theme. In another work, just as another plane is about to smash into the tower, it peels open so that the plane can fly through the gap that the tower has kindly opened up for it. ¶ The success of these videos, even though they were badly presented in Venice in a setting that could fairly be described as grotesque, has meant that this excellent artist's reputation has spread far beyond the closed circuit of critics and admirers of today's art scene in China. ¶ The last time I visited Chen Shaoxiong at home, he showed me the *Anti-Terrorist Variety* series again on his computer. My attention, however, was captured by a canvas on an easel. "It's unfinished," he said when he noticed I was looking at it. OK, but what does this sudden interest—we can't call it a renewed interest, since hitherto he has hardly shown an inclination to paint—tell us about his career, which has so far been dominated by photography and video? He declines to explain. There is nothing to explain. It's always the same thing: the mix that exists everywhere, in the street, in the landscape, and for Chen Shaoxiong, in his photographs. Look—there is no sign of planned composition. The everyday objects that float against the landscape in the background—a telephone, a bra, a slice of watermelon, a pair of glasses—are not engaged in any form of dialogue. There is no resonance between them. They are simply juxtaposed on a featureless background. No notion of hierarchy. Everything is on the same footing, side by side. Like in the modern world. ¶ On the other painting, the phrase "no war" is clearly outlined. It depicts a group of girls he saw on the Internet demonstrating in favor of the war in Iraq, human shields going to Baghdad, a wounded Iraqi baby, and a helicopter. While he was working on this painting, Chen Shaoxiong watched the TV and scoured the Internet every day. His painting is shaped by news and downloaded files. His latest works; his latest experiments. ¶ A new phase is about to begin.

FAR LEFT: CHEN XIAOGANG WITH THE THREE OTHER MEMBERS OF BIG TAIL ELEPHANT: LIN YILIN, LIANG JUHUI, AND XU TAN. HIS PAINTING MATERIALS AND, BEHIND HIM, A WORK IN PROGRESS.

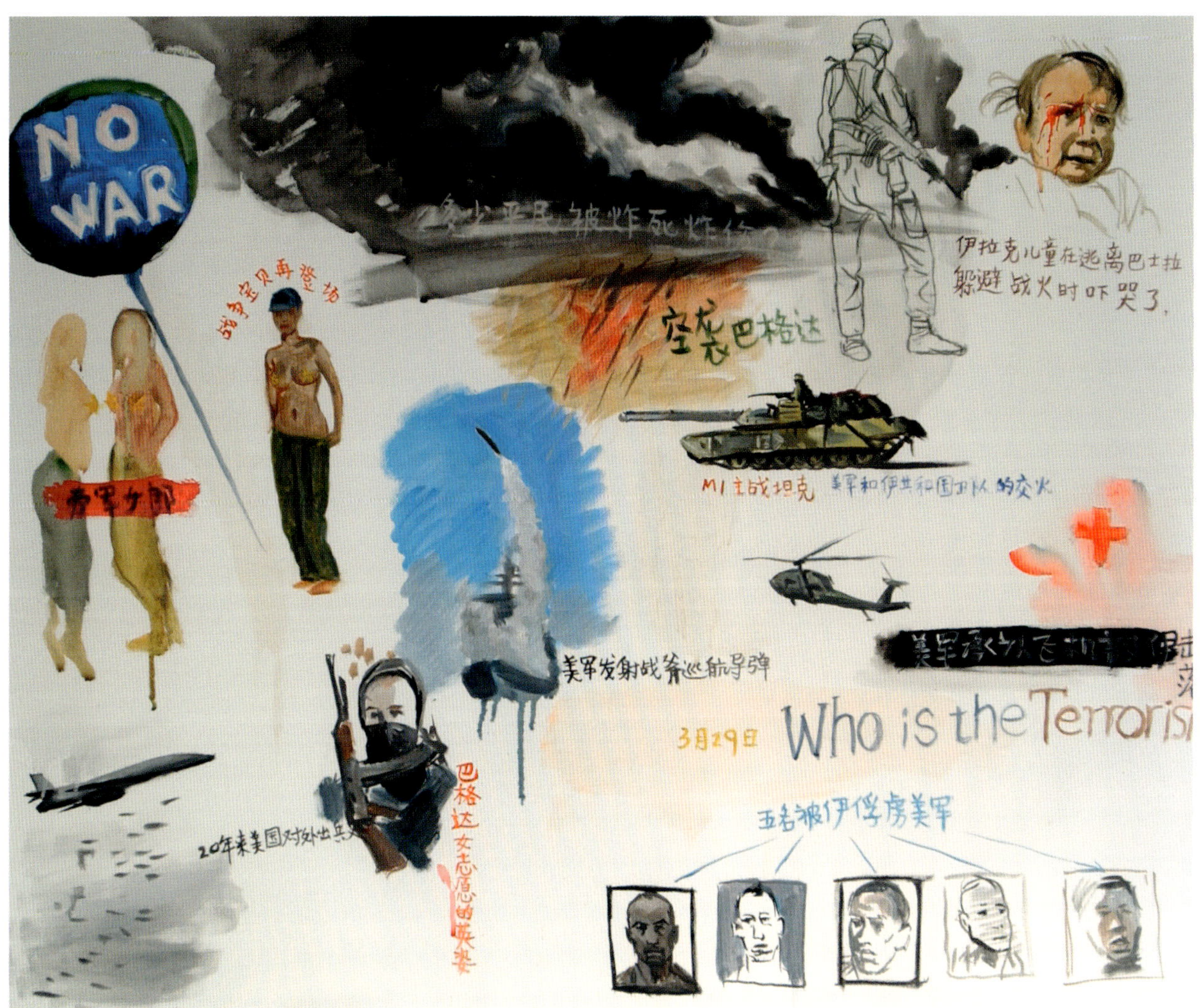

THIS WORK, BEGUN IN 2003 AND INSPIRED BY THE WAR IN IRAQ, IS AS YET UNTITLED. ALONG WITH TWO OR THREE OTHER WORKS ON SHOW IN HIS APARTMENT, IT MARKS THE RETURN TO PAINTING OF AN ARTIST BETTER KNOWN FOR PHOTOGRAPHY AND VIDEOS.

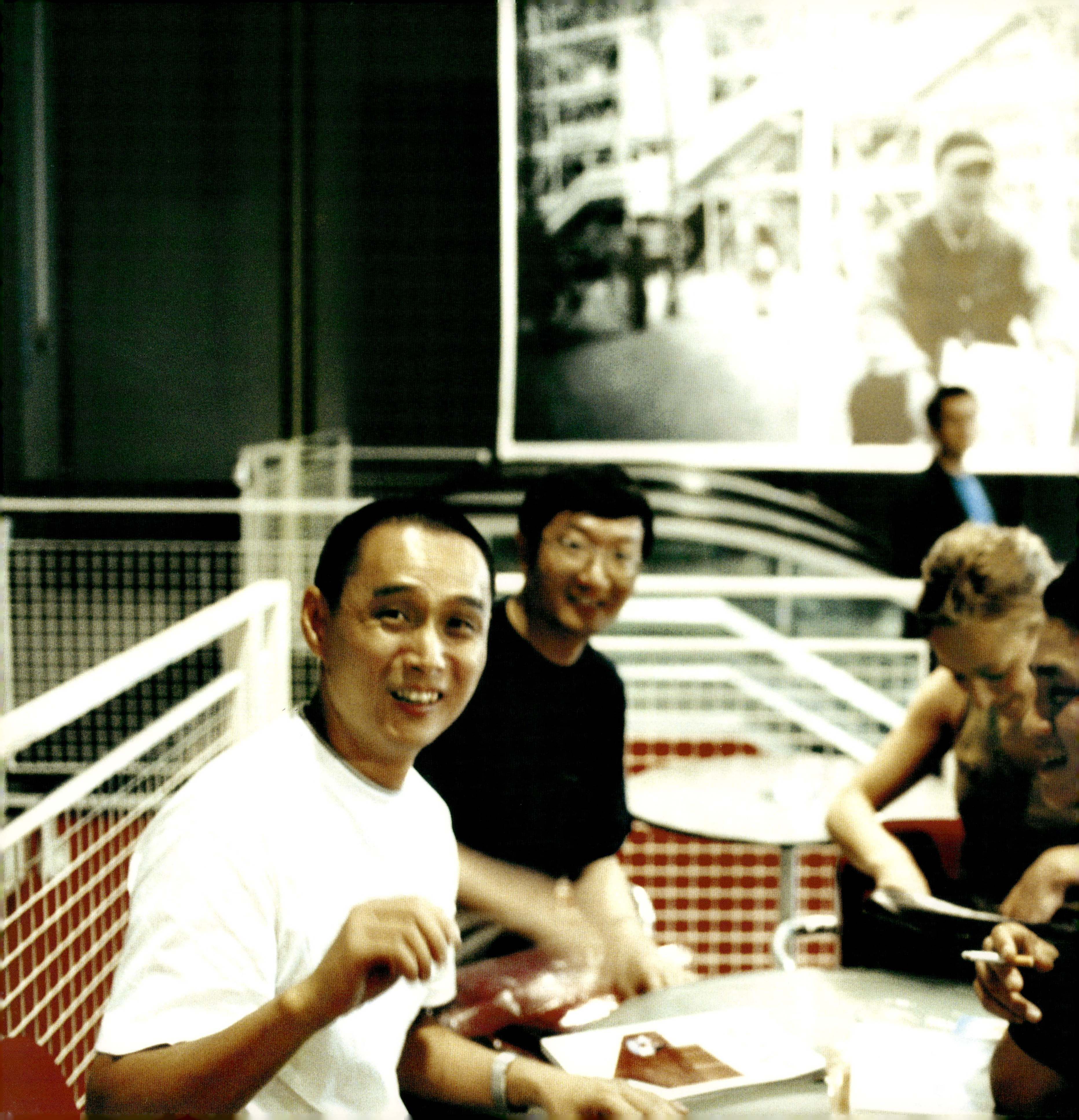

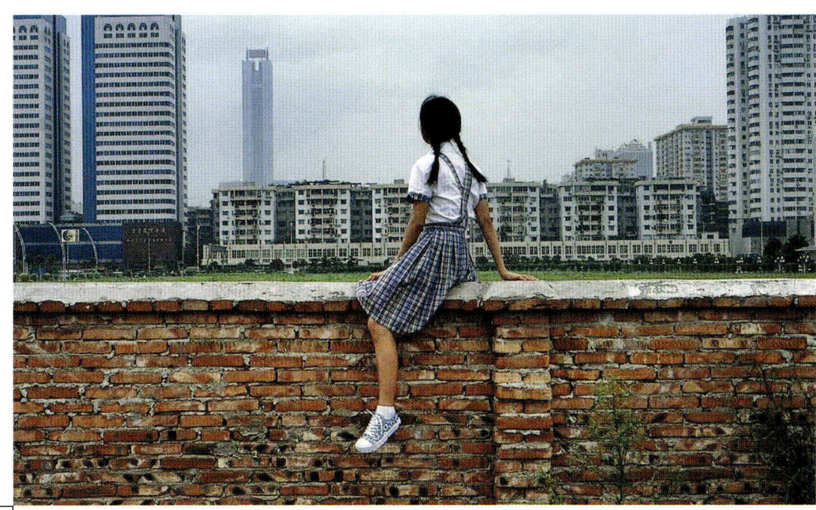

WENG PEIJUN

"The girl on the wall, that's me!" says a shaven-headed, smiling Weng Peijun (Fen). He explains, "I live in a lonely place, Hainan Island. I'm alone, like her, facing the world." ¶ Weng Fen (now known as Weng Peijun) was born in 1961 on Hainan Island in the extreme southeast of China, not far from Macau. Hainan Island is almost a Chinese version of Sicily. The port brings in money, but the locals whisper that the reason the island has the greatest number of Ferraris per square mile of any place in China is actually thanks to the thriving black market. Some people compare Hainan to a Chinese Hawaii. The locals do enjoy the dolce vita; they lead happily indolent lives on the slopes of the magnificent mountains that dominate the superb landscape. ¶ In these tropical climes, Weng Fen is a typical southerner—laid-back, relaxed, slow-paced, and not wanting to rush things. He can name each tree, and tells me how each evokes a particular feeling in him. Each tree gives rise to a new and distinct emotion. He also tells me how he goes to the beach in ten minutes on his motorbike. For the moment, he has decided to spend half the year on Hainan. He feels that "It is absolutely necessary for my mental and physical well-being." The rest of his time is taken up with traveling for exhibitions all over the world—and he is being invited to participate more and more often. ¶ His series of photographs show a little girl seen from behind, sitting astride a wall, against the backdrop of a cityscape that is both glorious and yet faintly menacing. They brought him overnight success, making him one of China's best-known artists, alongside Wang Guangyi. One of the photographs was even chosen to be projected onto the side of the Centre Pompidou in Paris to celebrate the official inauguration of the exhibition held to mark the years of China in France and France in China (2003–05). ¶ Weng Fen was born in a mountain village. Six months later, his parents moved to a nearby town. He stayed there until he was sixteen, when he moved to Guangzhou to study at the Academy of Fine Arts. He first began to show an interest in drawing aged six or seven. Every day, he would sit and draw for two hours, from midday to two in the afternoon, when all the other children went out to play. ¶ What did he draw? Mainly war scenes copied from books, propaganda posters, comic strips, and films, illustrating the combats between the armies of Chairman Mao and the partisans of Chiang Kai-shek, the war against Japan, and any others he could find. ¶ When he was fourteen, his father, who was responsible for cultural affairs in the region, saw that Weng Fen's love of drawing was much more than just a passing whim. He looked for a teacher for his son and bought him books on Rembrandt, the Impressionists, and Ilya Repin (a portraitist and Realist painter who worked in Russia in the late nineteenth century, and was known as the Samson of Russian art). After school, Weng Fen would go straight to the library where he copied pictures he liked. He studied first at the University of Hainan in Haiku, the island's capital, then at the Academy of Fine Arts in Guangzhou. ¶ What then? ¶ His first artistic experiments only date back to 1997. It seems strange that when asked, he dates his artistic awakening to 1998. This is probably for reasons of the heart, since in 1998 he was just married, and began work on an art project alongside his wife. In 1997, he shot a video about his search for identity, as many people did at that time. So in 1998 his search was over, and a new phase in his life began. ¶ So let me see. He was born in 1961, so in 1998, he was in his late thirties. What had he been doing all that time? ¶ He spent years searching for himself. ¶ He frittered away his time. ¶ He became an artist. ¶ On his return from Guangzhou to Hainan, he painted and painted. One day, he was an Abstract Expressionist; the next, he concentrated on geometric abstraction. For example, he would divide the canvas into squares, each painted a different color. "I saw it as an allegory for who I felt I was," he explains. ¶ He met an intrepid German collector who purchased one of his works. This mark of confidence did not, however, stop him from changing direction yet again, this time Surrealism. He confesses, "I found it impossible to settle on one particular style." ¶ He found it difficult to settle down in

FACING PAGE: WENG PEIJUN, IN THE CAFETERIA IN THE CENTRE POMPIDOU, PARIS, WITH FRIENDS INCLUDING GU ZHENQING, ONE OF CHINA'S FOREMOST INDEPENDENT CURATORS, WHO ORGANIZED THE MAJOR INDEPENDENT EXHIBITION *USUAL AND UNUSUAL* AND THE FIRST CHENGOU BIENNIAL. IN THE BACKGROUND IS A WORK BY YAN LEI. PHOTOGRAPH BY JEAN-CLAUDE PLANCHET ABOVE: A WORK FROM THE FAMOUS SERIES *ON THE WALL*, 2001.

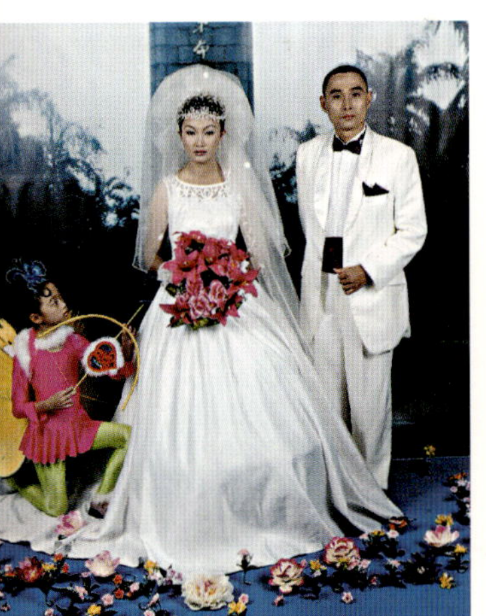
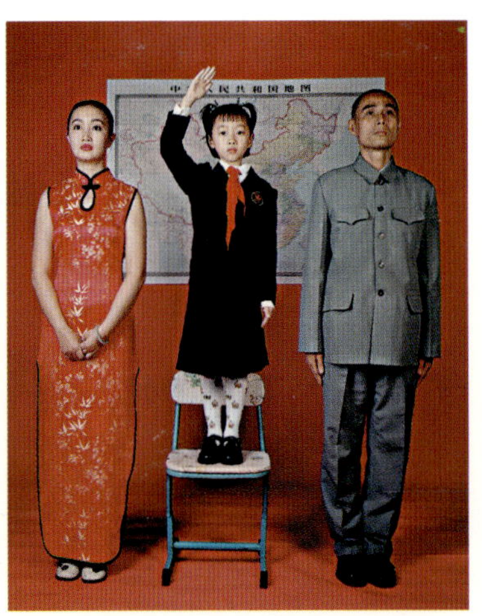
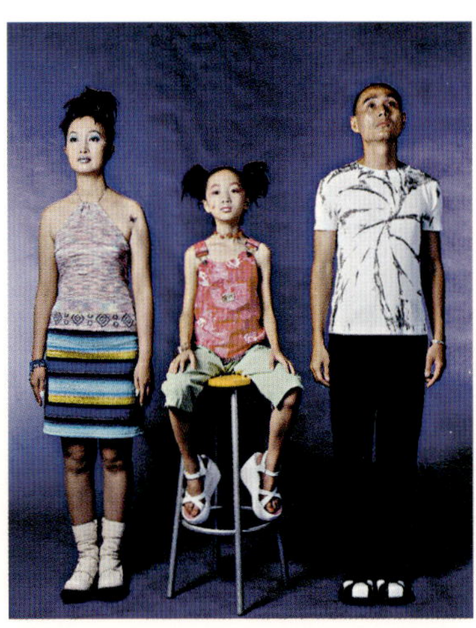
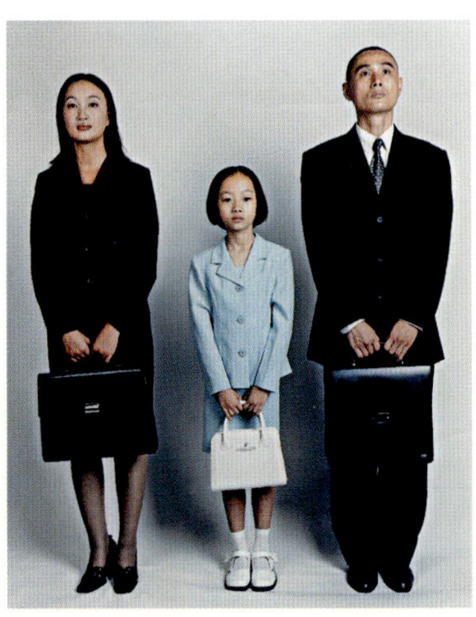
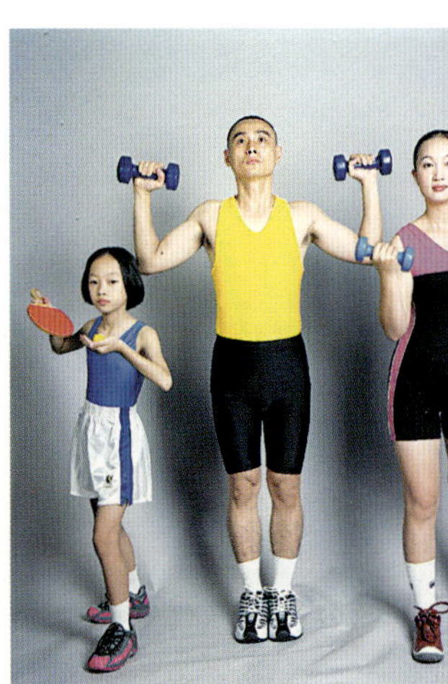

real life, too. When he was twenty-seven, he decided that enough was enough. He had never been in love and was still a virgin. So, coolly and rationally, he decided to focus on one objective at a time: he gave up painting and began looking for a wife. It took him two years. ¶ 1990. The newlyweds had to find a source of income. Weng Fen became a designer. "To begin with," he says, "I thought it was possible to have a career to earn an income, and to devote myself to my art at the same time. I did manage to have a look at contemporary art revues and keep up with what was going on, but I wasn't producing anything worthwhile." So in 1995, he gave up his job as a designer. "I felt as if I was wasting my life. I was earning money, but that was all." He then made a living more or less legally by selling health-care products on a sort of commission system, a long tradition in China that is complicated to explain to Westerners. ¶ In 2000, inspiration struck with his *Great Family Aspirations* series, based on propaganda posters from the Cultural Revolution and even earlier, depicting thought-provoking scenes of families after 1976 and the single-child policy: a father, a mother, and one child. All three are standing at attention, facing the lens, dressed in the mortarboard and gown of Oxford or Cambridge graduates. They thus represent the Chinese intellectuals reviled by the Red Guard but rehabilitated by Deng Xiaoping. In another photograph, they are dressed patriotically, the father wearing a gray Mao suit, the mother in a long red dress, and the little girl reading aloud a propaganda text with the utter seriousness that only the brainwashed can show. ¶ These two photographs are among the best known in the whole series. In both, the little girl is shown standing on a stool, so that the top of her head or her mortarboard is exactly aligned with those of her parents. "There is enormous pressure on children to grow up quickly—too quickly," says Weng Fen. "Chinese parents tend to unload their worries onto the shoulders of their children." ¶ Should this series be interpreted solely in terms of its political, critical dimension, as is often the case when Western critics study contemporary Chinese art? "Yes!" answers Weng Fen, without a second's hesitation. ¶ It was the following series that brought Weng Fen fame. He got a little girl dressed in short socks and a neat skirt to sit astride a wall. She is facing away from the viewer and seems to be gazing out into the far distance, over Haiku, Guangzhou, Shenzhen, or one of the other cities in southern China that have mushroomed in the last few decades, prickly with skyscrapers and high-rises—wounded cities where many building projects have been abandoned halfway through, cities prey to a consumer frenzy. ¶ Is he familiar with Caspar David Friedrich's paintings, which often depict characters seen from behind, who could be the forefathers of this little girl sitting on a wall, her legs dangling on either side? Of course not. Nor does he know Jean-Antoine Watteau's indolent beauties with softly curving napes leading us into enchanting gardens that they fill with their marvelous, golden grace. ¶ No, but it is the same procedure that enables the viewer to identify with the character portrayed looking in the same direction, opening up the cityscape, which, if the little girl were facing us, would remain simply a backdrop, but which here becomes the principal theme of the work: we see it through the child's eyes, through her supposedly innocent gaze. ¶ Was Weng Fen right to take two girls as his subject next, their arms around each other's shoulders, like the best of friends, looking out over the same city scenes? The treatment of the subject undoubtedly gained in refinement, but just as evidently lost in power. The image became more psychological and more anecdotal. "Girls often behave like that together," says the artist. Yes. ¶ And what about the wall? ¶ There is a Chinese proverb about grass growing on a wall, blowing in the wind—a metaphor

ABOVE AND FACING PAGE: WORKS FROM THE SERIES *GREAT FAMILY ASPIRATION*, 2000, A VARIATION ON THE CHINESE NUCLEAR FAMILY OF FATHER, MOTHER, AND ONE CHILD, WHO IS NOW OFTEN REFERRED TO CRITICALLY AS THE "CORRUPT LITTLE EMPEROR." FROM LEFT TO RIGHT: *GOOD MARRIAGE*, *PATRIOTISM*, *IN FASHION*, *WITH COLLAR*, *GOOD HEALTH*, AND, ON THE FACING PAGE, *ACADEMIC DEGREE*.

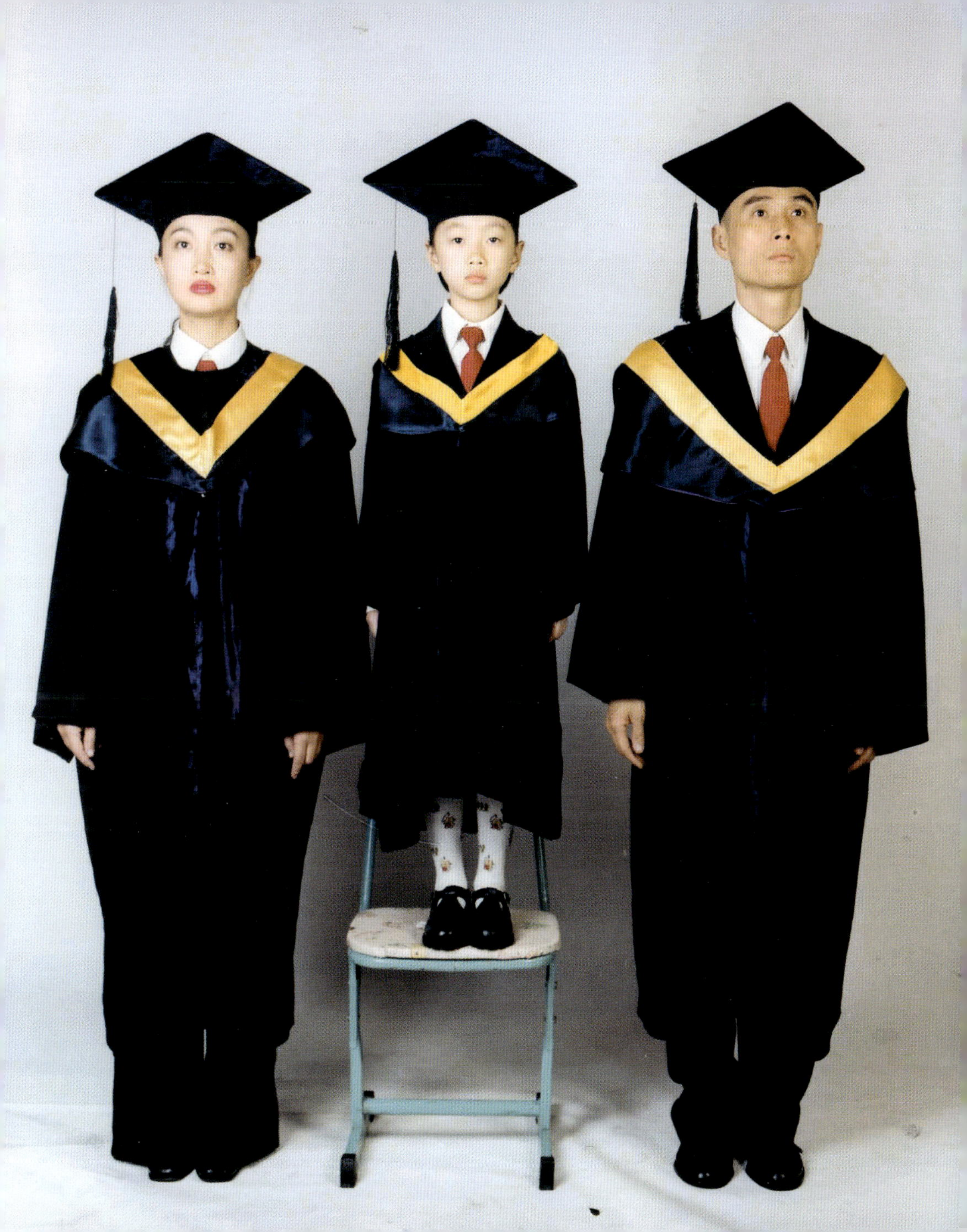

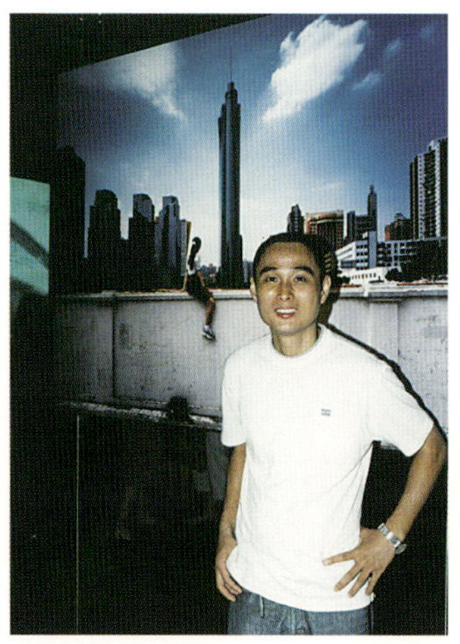

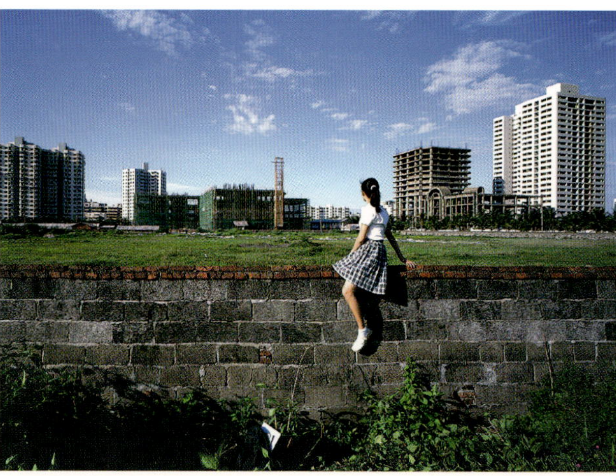

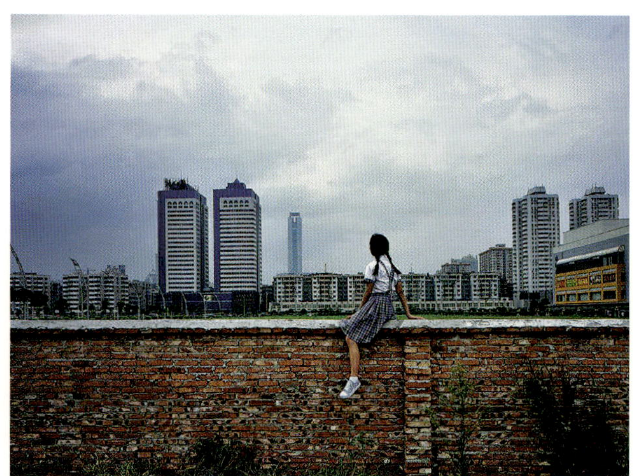

for people who are wavering and easily led. ¶ Walls are there to separate. They stop us from seeing. The other side of the wall is another place, a future about to happen that we can observe and judge from a distance. ¶ Weng Fen adds, "When I was young, I loved going for long walks in the mountains and looking down on things from above. Like in my photos. ¶ Weng Fen started dabbling in video art at the same time as photography, but this aspect of his work has drawn less attention. It has scarcely been shown in Europe. I think I am right in saying that the first time was in June 2003 at the Spazio Consolo in Milan, at Weng Fen's first solo exhibition in Italy. ¶ It was another Chinese artist, Song Dong, who first introduced me to it in Beijing in 2001. He showed me his personal copy of the video *Award Ceremony*. ¶ It was extremely funny. ¶ A sportsman, naked as the day he was born, walks forward towards a podium and climbs onto the top step. A man who appears to be an official steps forward and hangs a medal around his neck. They shake hands, and the official congratulates the naked man. A national anthem is played. Then the scene is repeated with a second sportsman, also completely naked, and then a third. The bizarreness of the video comes from the utter seriousness of the scene, despite the nudity of the three winners. ¶ But part of the pleasure comes from recognizing that the three sportsmen are in fact young artists, while the official is also an older, more established, perhaps more academic artist. ¶ In 1997, as I have already noted, Weng Fen made a film entitled *Identity, Present, Past, Six*. It is his first film, and it shows, although most of the themes he later developed are already there. ¶ The video features six people, shown going about their daily business. The artist has used special effects to add a pinprick of blood on the end of a finger at eye level for each person, as a mark of their identity. Weng Fen wanted to form a link between their bodily and mental selves and the personal history of each of them, with their past and their identity. The video tries to work somewhere between the two extremes and to create passages between the two domains. ¶ *Butterfly*, dated 1998, is more like a butterfly dance inspired by Loie Fuller than anything else. Maybe it simply reflects the pleasure of contemplating and filming a beautiful woman, the artist's beloved. ¶ She is nude, enveloped in gauzy veils. She stretches out her arms and flaps them as if trying to fly. It was filmed in a circular space that some critics have seen as representing the butterfly's eye. In the background, we see what the insect sees. ¶ *My Future Is Not a Dream* dates from 2000, and was shown at the 2002 Triennial in Guangzhou. It is a video installation that now belongs to the museum—one of the few in China to acquire such works. It is shown on two walls. On the left wall are clips from Chinese films, spliced together, where people talk about the future ("I'm going to go to the United States to have my eyes treated," for example). On the right are the artist's friends and family, and some teachers he knows, all of whom live in Haiku. Weng Fen filmed them discussing their vision of a collective or personal future. ¶ It is a remarkable body of work. For Weng Fen, success came when he stripped down his themes and used them as exemplary, allegorical figures. ¶ In the space of two years, he has become so famous that he has chosen to change names. Now he prefers to be known as Weng Peijun. Does he think it sounds more chic? No, he explains. His other name was just a surname and a name that reminded him of a stump [1]. Now Weng has everything he could ever need—including a real first name.

[1] *Although the practice is becoming less common in people under the age of thirty, the Chinese have three names: the family name, followed by a generational name and a given name chosen by the parents.*

LEFT: THE ARTIST IN FRONT OF ONE OF HIS PHOTOGRAPHS AT THE VERNISSAGE FOR THE EXHIBITION *ALORS, LA CHINE?* AT THE CENTRE POMPIDOU IN 2003, AND THE PHOTOGRAPHIC SERIES *ON THE WALL*, 2001–02.

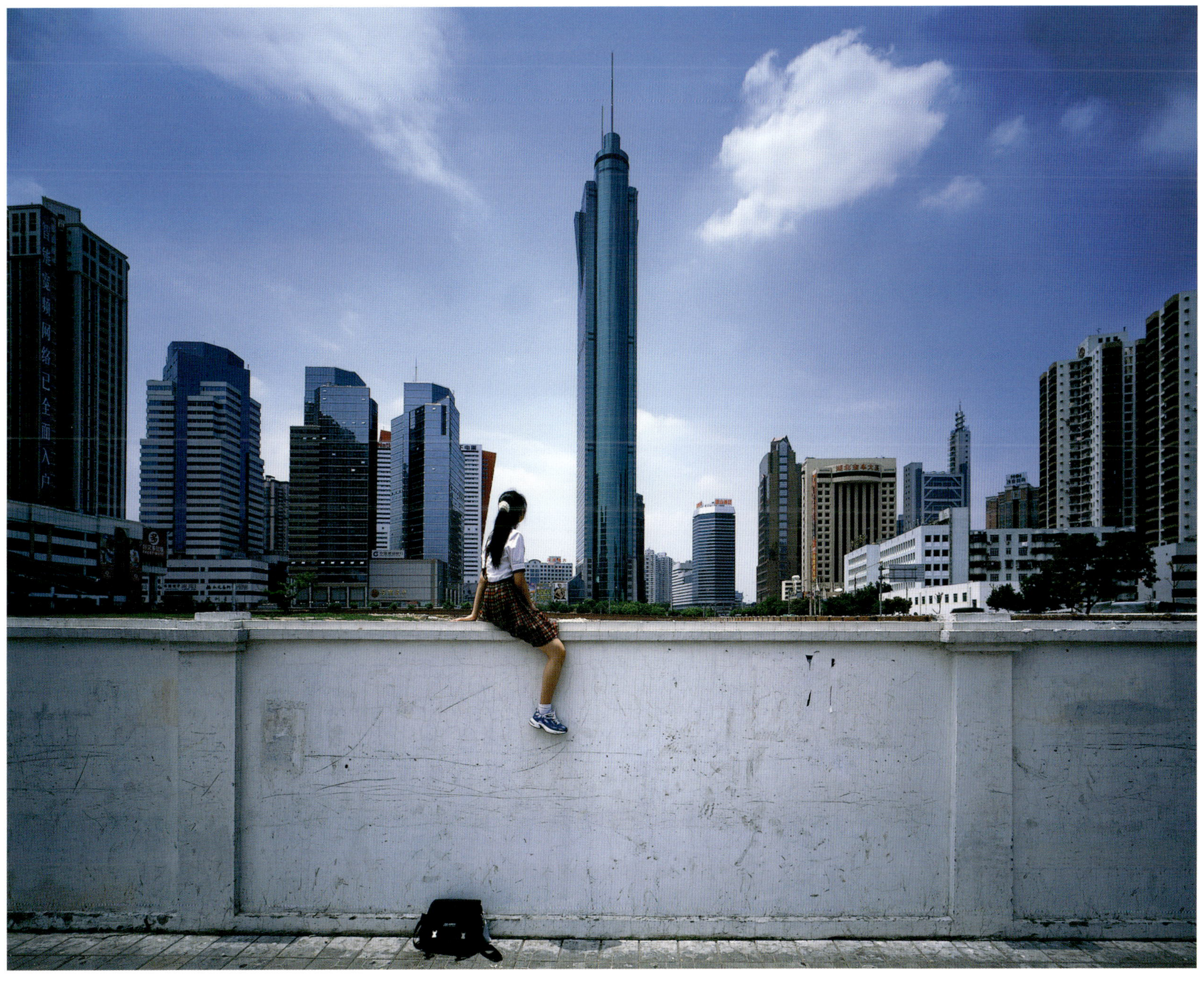

THE LITTLE GIRL SITS ON THE WALL WATCHING THE MODERN CITY SPRAWLED BELOW. THIS IS ONE OF THE BEST PHOTOGRAPHS FROM THE *ON THE WALL* SERIES, WHICH MADE WENG PEIJUN A STAR.

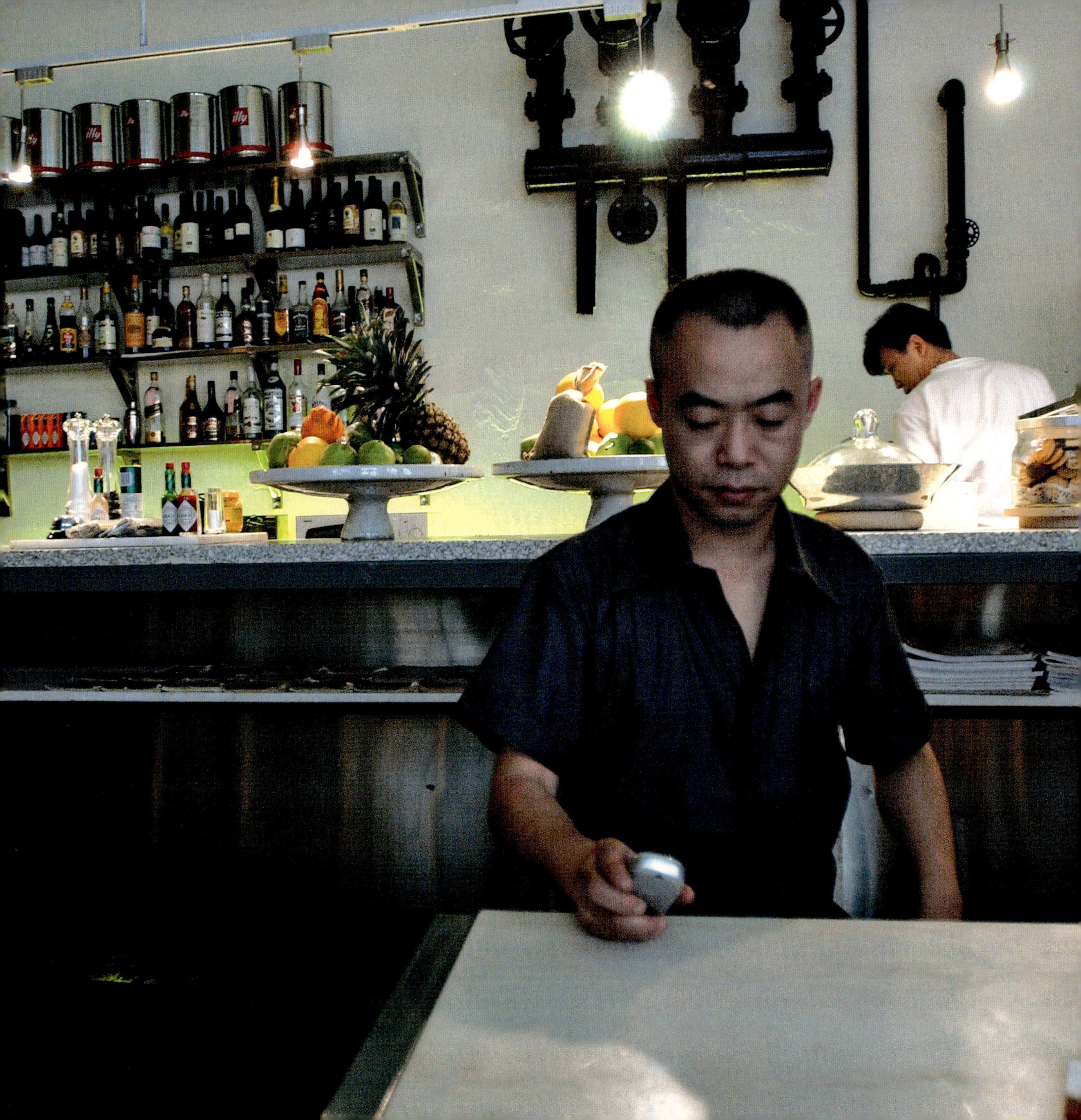
illy

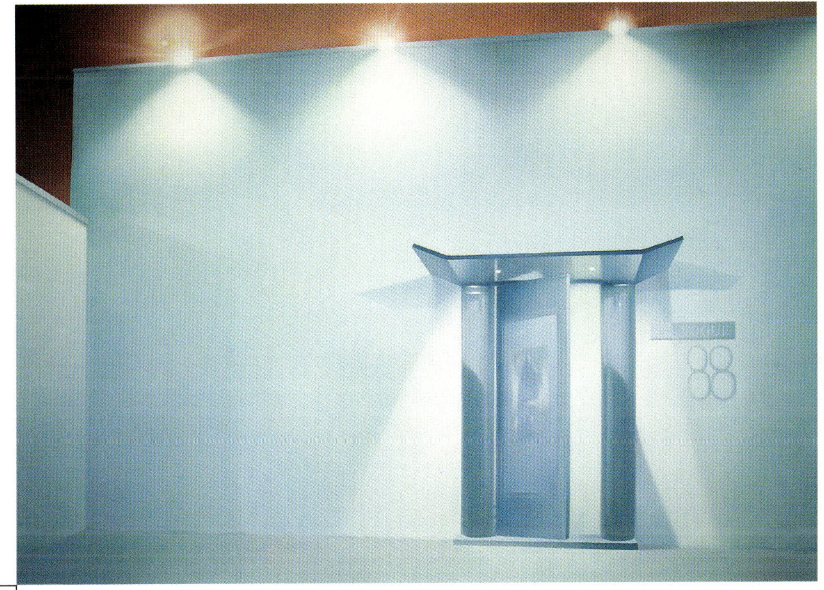

CHEN WENBO

Chen Wenbo's plastic beauties will forever be youthful. Their bald pates gleam. Their pale eyes gaze blindly at you. Their pupils are huge. Their latex skin shines. They are green, blue, orange, or pink. They are magnificent. Their lips are soft—how could it be otherwise? They have an insolent charm. How can I put it? You just want to give in to their temptation. ¶ Then you see that the cyber-beauties have three hands, three arms, and that the fingers reach out to the four corners of the canvas, folding into strikingly unnatural poses. But who cares?! They're sexy as hell, caught in the beam of fluorescent spotlights, which pour monochrome light all around them. ¶ Over all that, Chen Wenbo adds a virtual floating layer of erratic, brightly colored little shapes, such as pills, candies, and mysterious bubbles. Artificial substances in a cotton-candy paradise. ¶ The models are girls that Chen Wenbo met in the Beijing discos where he likes to spend his nights. Pretty but insipid. Interchangeable, all identically sexy. But sexy nonetheless. ¶ This was back in 1996. Chen Wenbo had settled on his chosen subject—pretty pink girls. Adolescence as a foreign, maybe even alien, place. He felt that this was a rich seam, which he mined—but not to exhaustion. He painted about thirty of these works. No more. Chen Wenbo produced a few lithographs, and then decided enough was enough. He moved on to something else. He had no intention of being labeled the man who painted pretty, shaven-headed girls. He did not want to be known as a twenty-first century, Chinese Domergue. ¶ It was a bold move. Many of his more successful fellow artists, such as Yue Minjun with his faces grimacing with frozen smiles or Zheng Fanzhi with his white masks on small bodies with a large head and hands, did not have the same reflex, mining the vein perhaps longer than they should have. ¶ Chen Wenbo chose artistic freedom, while retaining the core aspect of his vision—to paint the surface of things. He replaced the smooth,

FACING PAGE: CHEN WENBO AT THE AT CAFÉ IN SPACE 798 IN BEIJING. ABOVE: ONE OF HIS RECENT PAINTINGS OF THE FAÇADE OF A TRENDY CLUB AT THE START OF THE NEW MILLENNIUM.

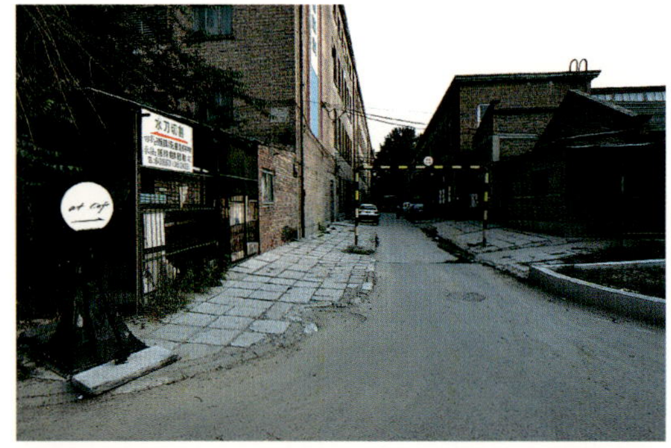
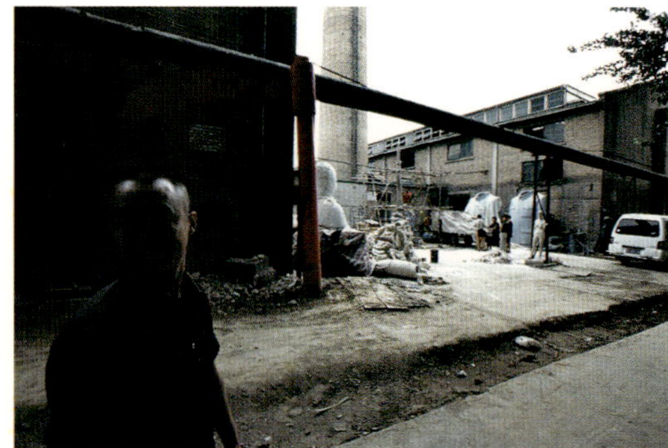
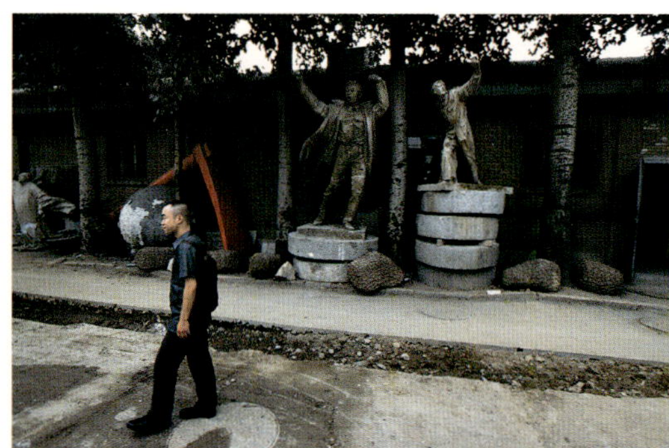
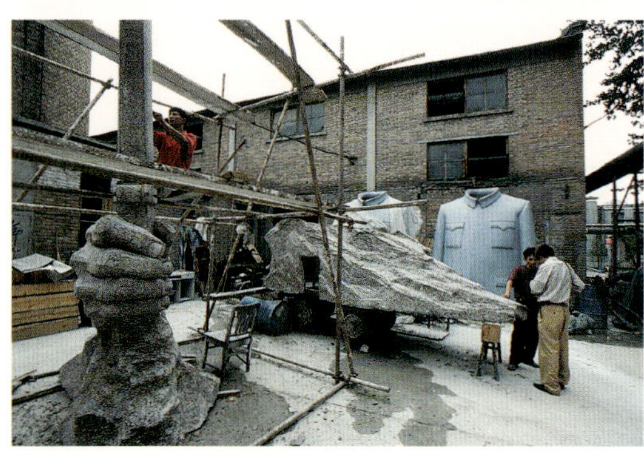
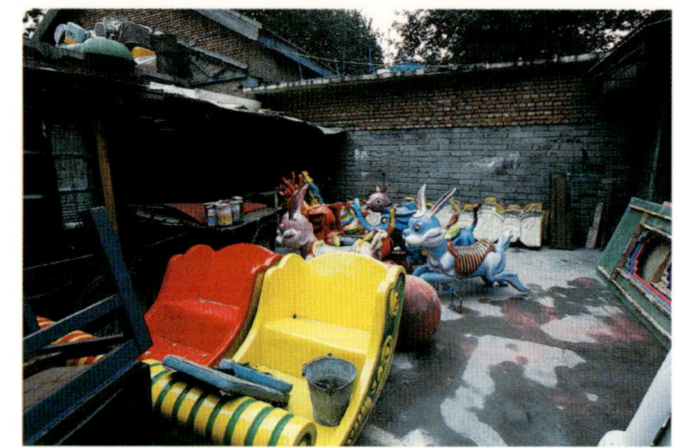
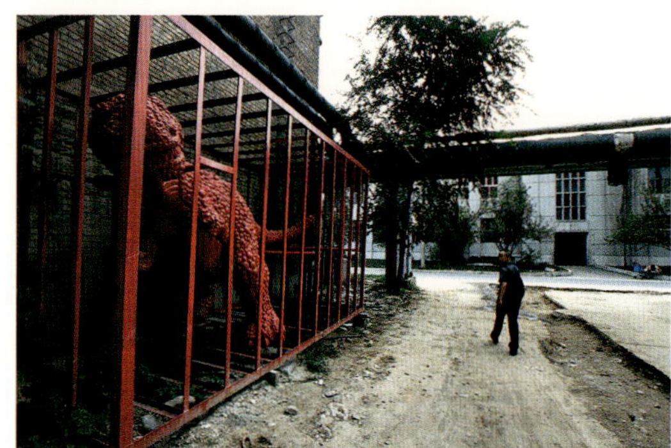
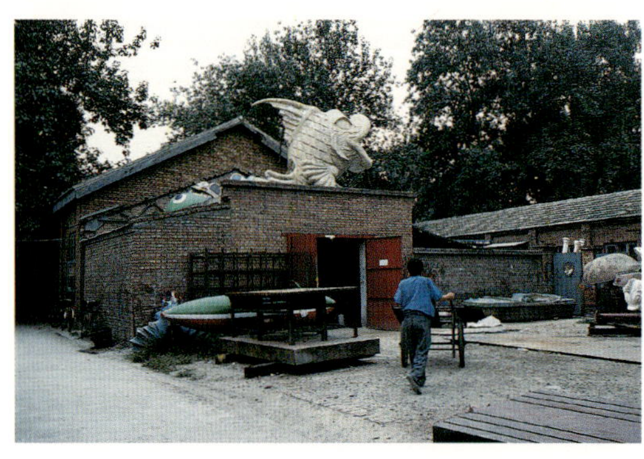
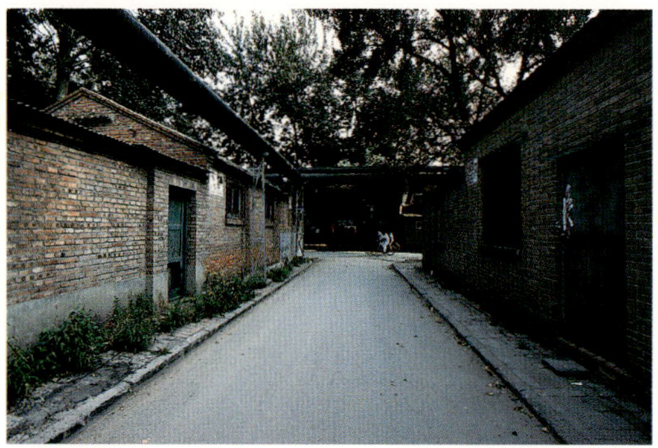
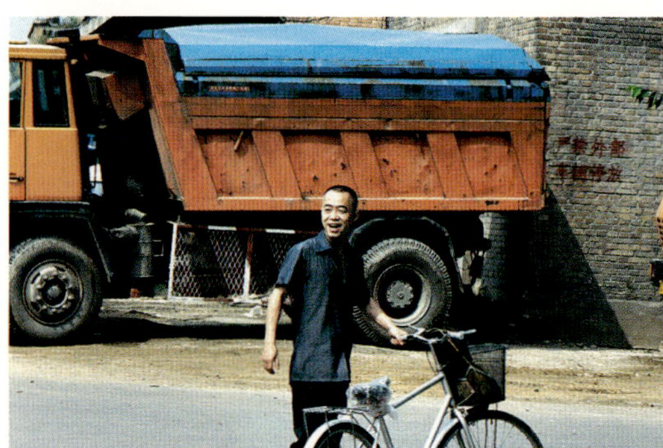

CHEN WENBO'S STUDIO IN SPACE 798, JUST OPPOSITE THE AT CAFÉ.

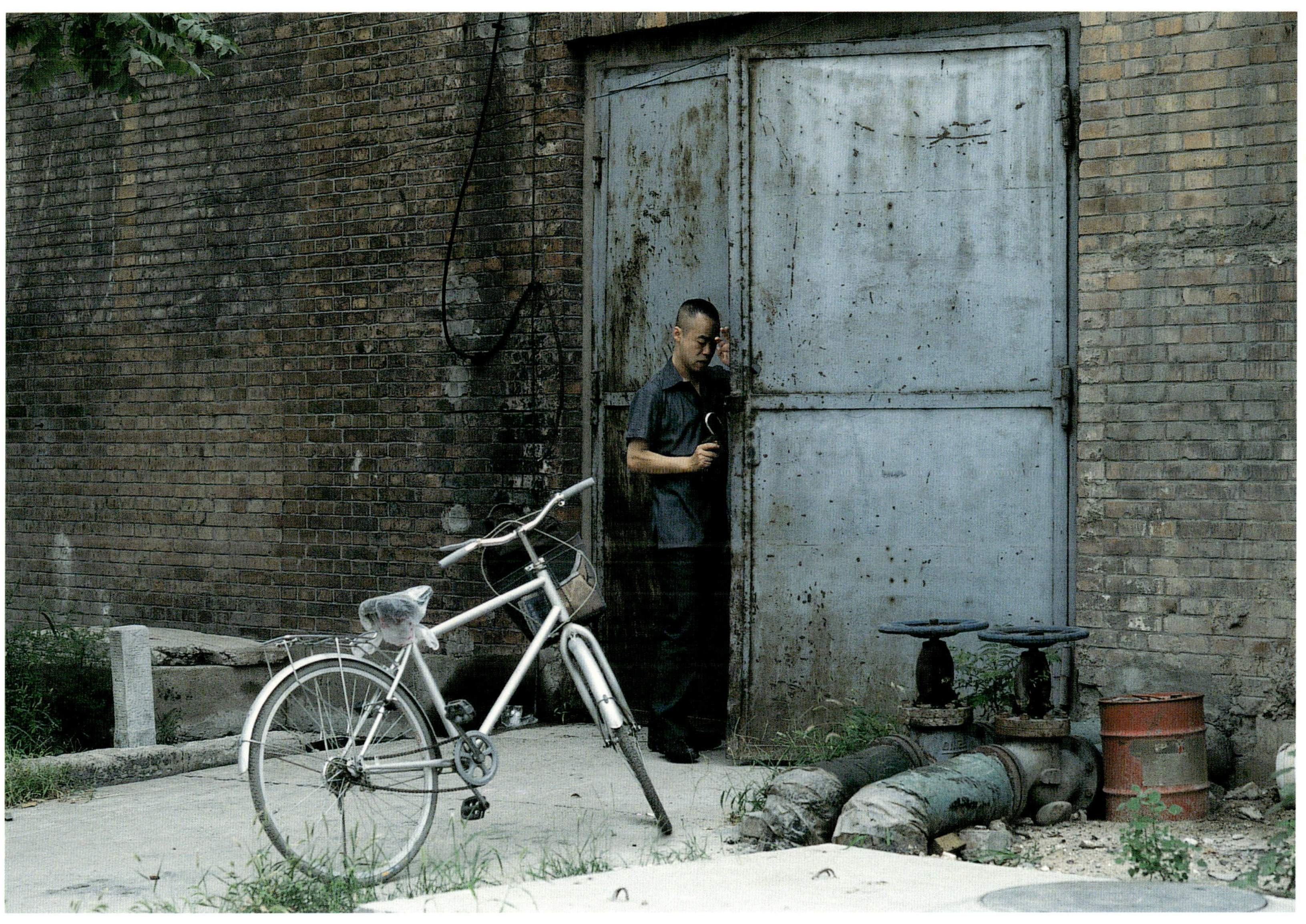

THE ENTRANCE TO CHEN WENBO'S STUDIO. HE HAS A SECOND STUDIO IN HIS APARTMENT, NOT FAR FROM THIS ONE.

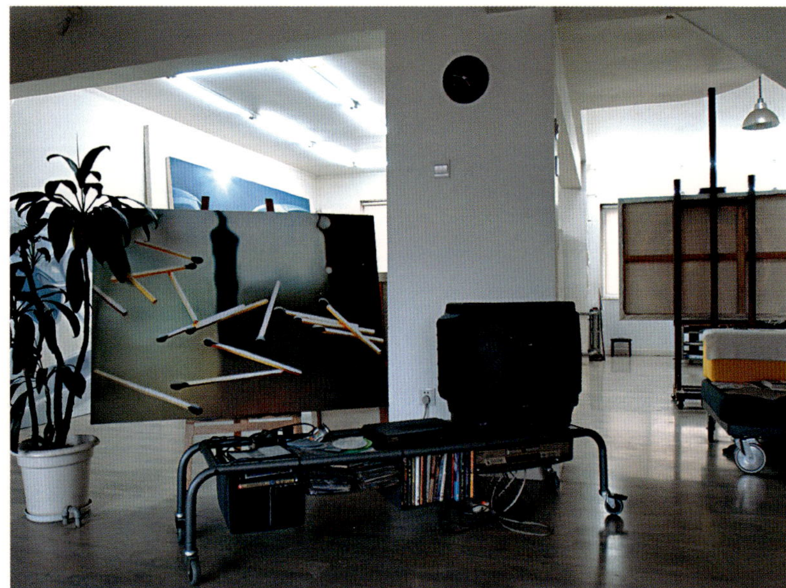

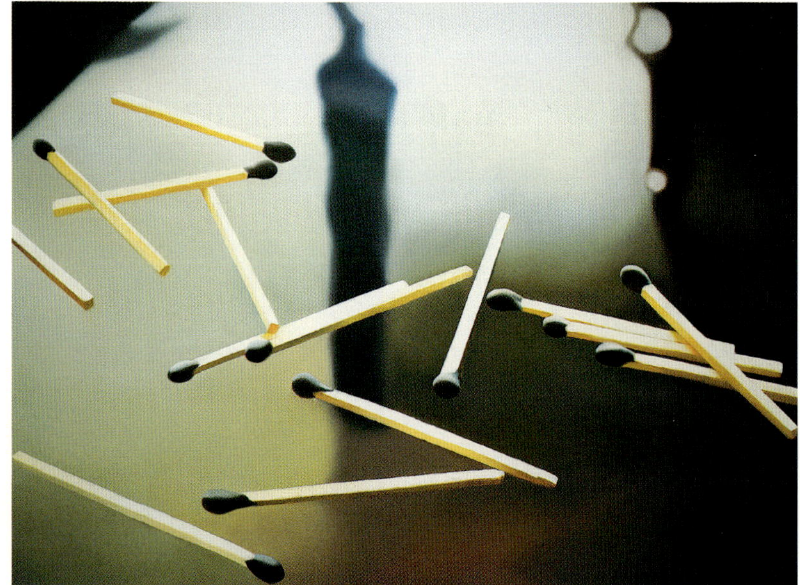

shiny bodies and faces of his celluloid dolls—faces seen as objects—with windows, vehicles, billiard balls—reflective surfaces just as chilly and just as shiny. ¶ This is what Chen Wenbo is working on now, painting the seats in an auditorium; cold, plastic dice; a chandelier; a key ring; matches on a thick glass table. ¶ He manages one painting a month. ¶ He was born in 1969. His parents were shopkeepers in Chongqing, in Sichuan province, east of Tibet. The city is unusual in China in that the streets are not full of bicycles, because the city is built on the flanks of steep hills at the confluence of two rivers. I read somewhere that Chen Wenbo was born into a "Muslim minority close to the Uigur people." He never talked to me about that, although Heaven only knows how many times we met—in Beijing, Shanghai, and Paris. ¶ When he was little, like all children, he loved candy. He suffered from cavities and often had bad toothaches. When the pain became too much, his mother gave him paper to paint on, and he forgot his pain. It's a good story for his future biographer. ¶ Chen Wenbo was not a brilliant student. In fact, he was rather unruly. From age eleven on, painting was the only thing that would keep him calm. Since his teachers were always complaining, his father encouraged him to make the best of his strengths and enroll in art class. Is Chen Wenbo right to say, as he does today, that "painting prevented me from studying normally"? ¶ He began studying at the School of Fine Art in Chongqing in Sichuan province. He claims that it was a very good school and that the student body was dynamic. He had an exhibition in Shenzhen, then a real boom city, not far from Hong Kong, which was then undergoing a period of serious decline. He moved to Beijing in 1999, when he was twenty-eight. "If I hadn't left then," he says, "I would never have got out." He pauses, then adds, "There were new directions in Beijing. I wanted to be part of the movement." ¶ Chen Wenbo began to make a name for himself in around 1995 with his video art and installations. The work *Moisture Content* (1996) was shown at the Guangzhou Triennial. It is a very simple work, showing a cupped hand transferring a blue liquid from a vase to a bottle, then from the bottle to a smaller one, then to a jug, then to a coffeepot, then to a thermos flask, then to a large glass, then to a plastic jerrican, and so on. The liquid gets darker and darker as it is moved from one container to another. The soundtrack is someone making noises that supposedly accompany the pictures, but are far from realistic. It is a metaphor of language that flows, escaping our mouths and our control. "I couldn't show that in painting. That's why I decided to do it in video," Chen Wenbo explains. ¶ His first installation was inspired by the controversial works of Damien Hirst, using meat as the central feature. Lumps of bloody meat set in resin, photographs of slabs of beef or pork. He presents several stages in the cycle of a substance that was once a living being, now set in death as an object to be handled, sculpted, and thrown around. It takes over the space and changes it somehow. The most personal aspect of this installation is its way of looking at the object under the skin of the living being—or rather looking at the skin itself as an object. It may be obvious in this work, but it is less so—in fact, not at all—in the other works that grew out of this one. ¶ Chen Wenbo now lives and works in Beijing. His studio is opposite that of Chen Lingyang, at the entrance to a narrow street where a few small factories struggle to survive in the immensity of sector 798, once full of factories, now practically all shut. The whole neighborhood is one vast building program: all the old structures are to be knocked down. Over the last few years, the neighborhood has become home to the bright young things of Beijing, with the gallery Beijing Tokyo Arts Project and the At Café leading the way. They were followed by a flock of galleries, taking over warehouses

CHEN WENBO LIVES IN A DELIGHTFUL BACHELOR PAD IN NEW TOWN CHAOYANG TO THE NORTHEAST OF BEIJING. THE CANVAS ON ITS EASEL SHOWS THAT HE ALSO WORKS IN HIS APARTMENT. RIGHT: ONE OF THE ARTIST'S MOST RECENT WORKS, EXPLORING THE THEME OF REFLECTION.

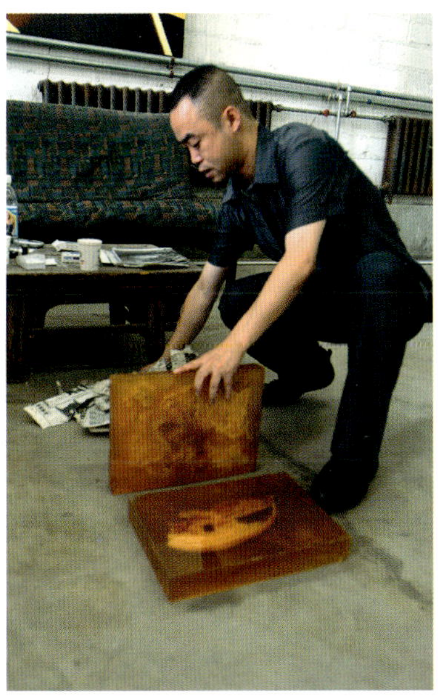

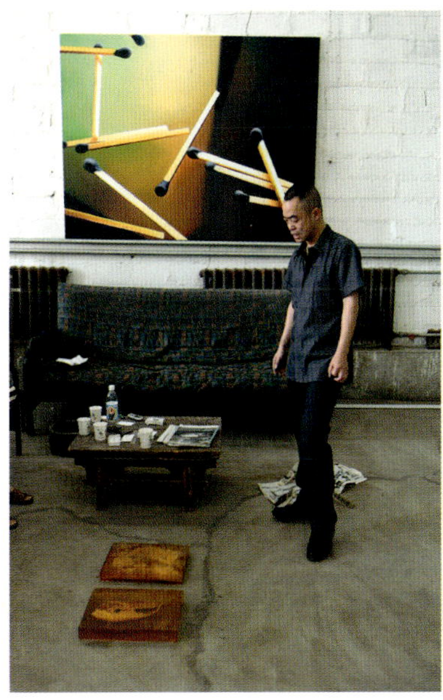

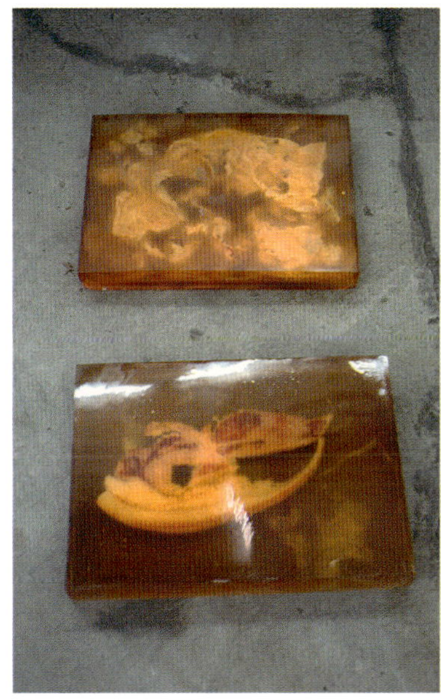

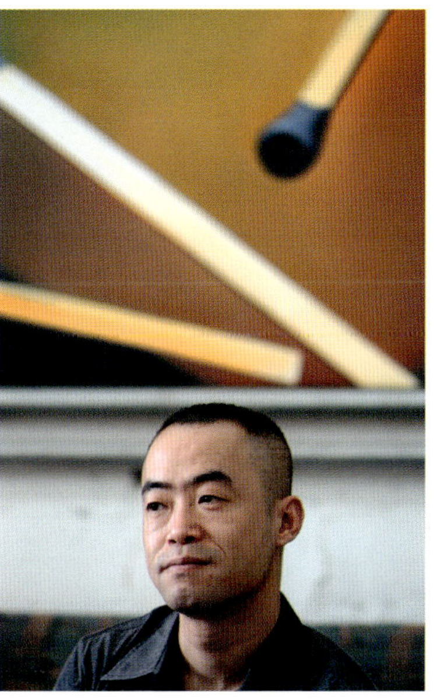

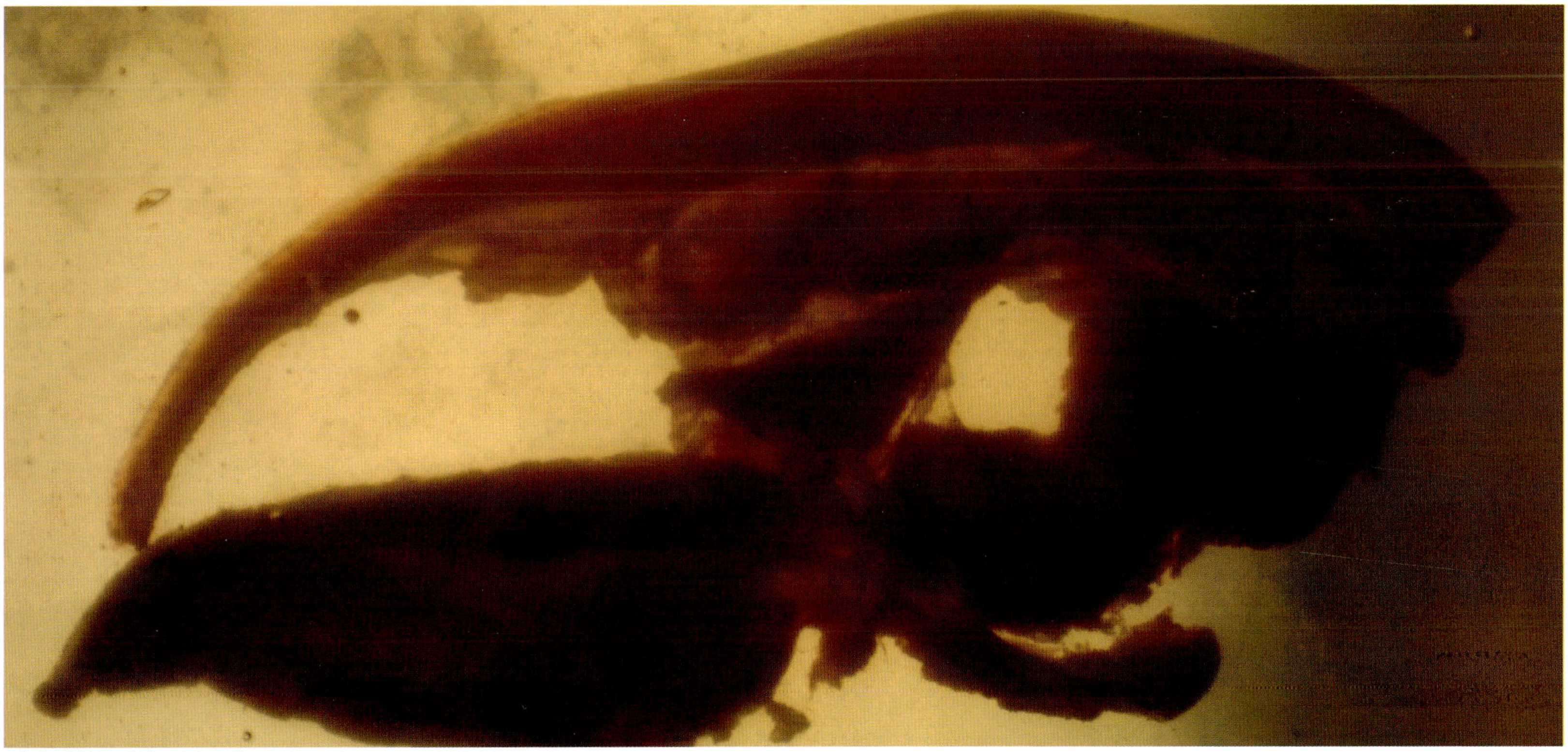

IN HIS STUDIO IN SPACE 798, I DISCOVERED A SECOND VERSION OF THE CANVAS WITH MATCHES AND PART OF AN OLD INSTALLATION, CONSISTING OF HUNKS OF MEAT SET IN RESIN.

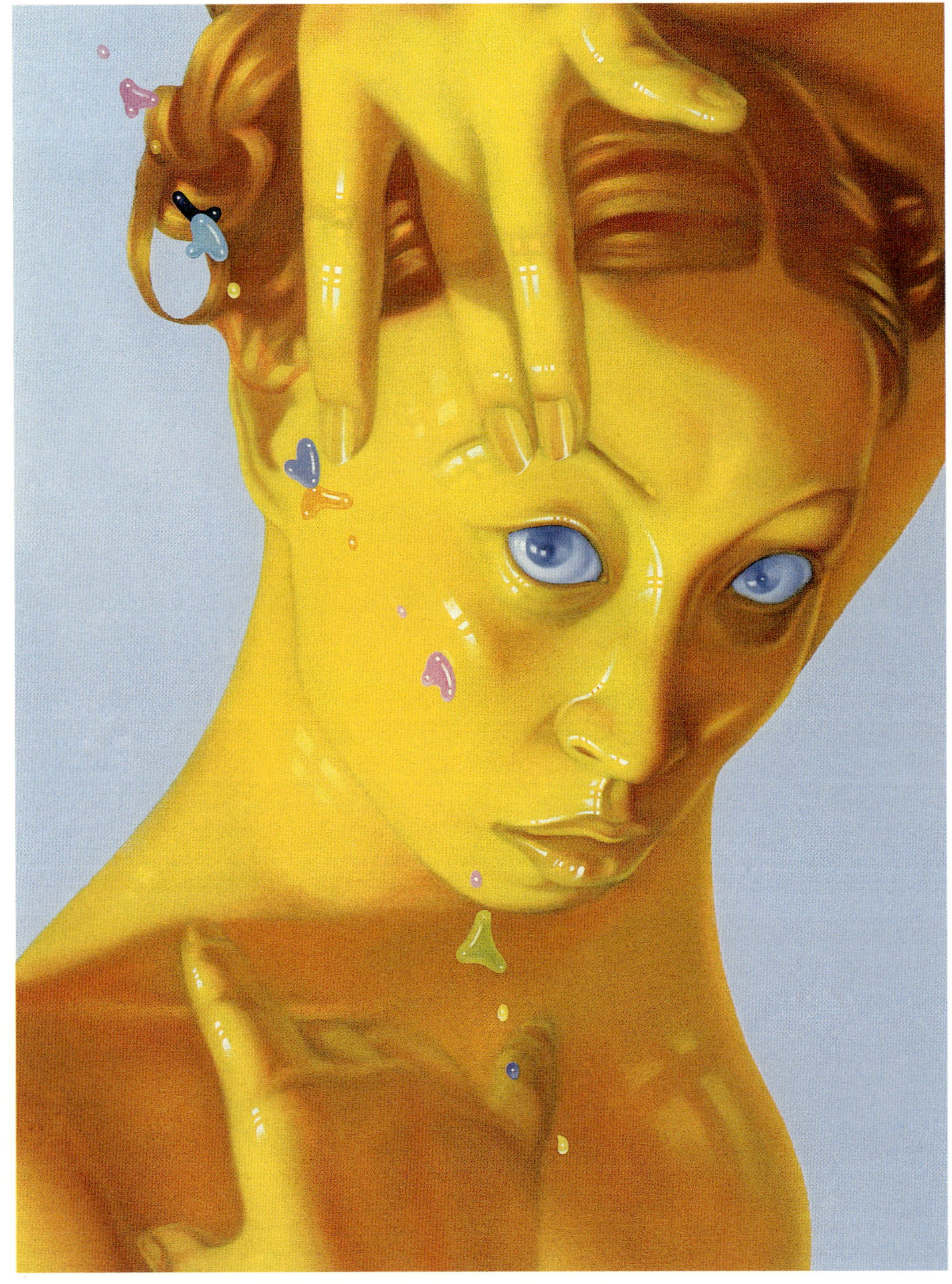

TWO OF THE CYBER-BEAUTIES FROM THE *VITAMIN* SERIES, 1998–2000.

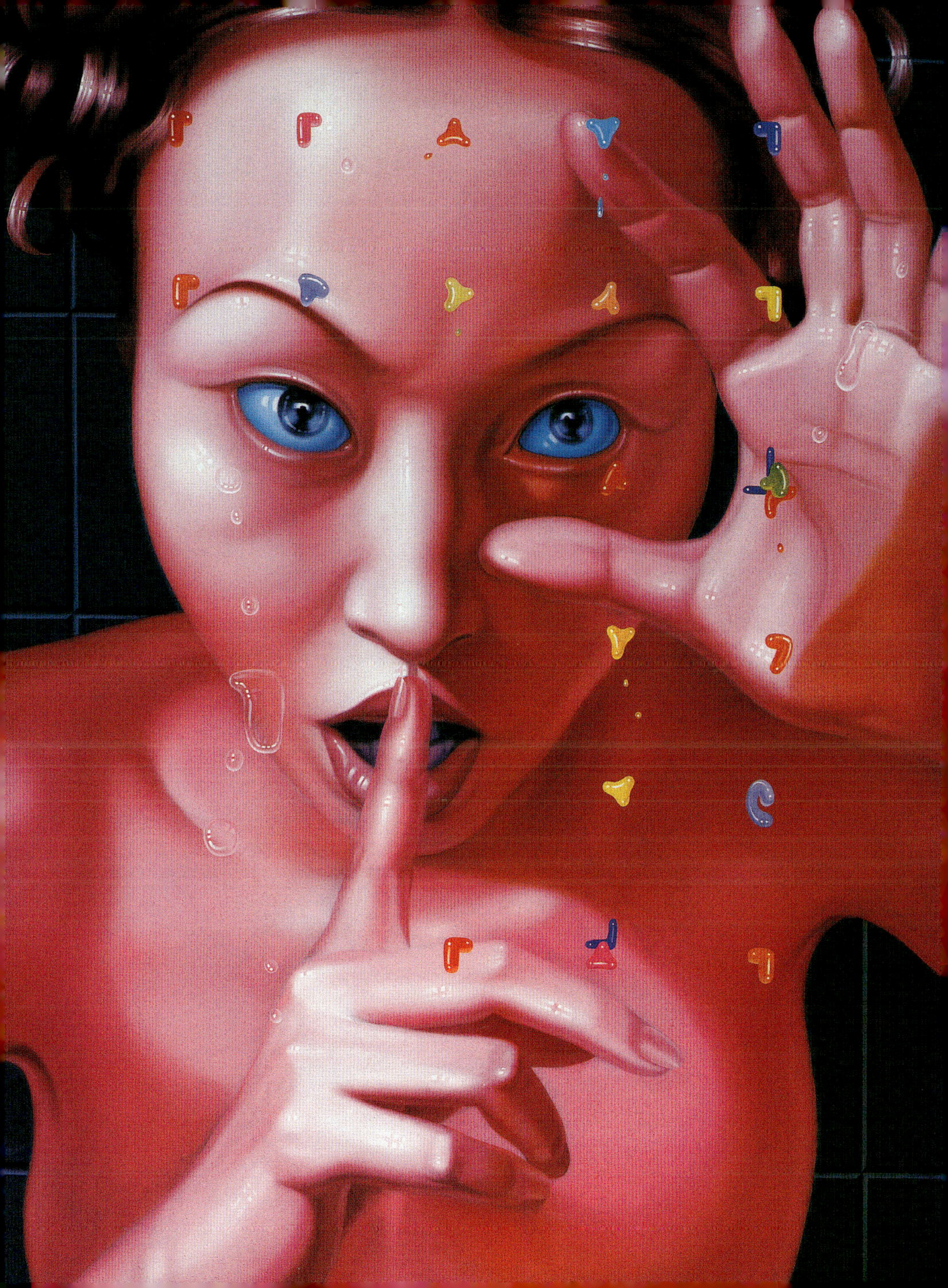

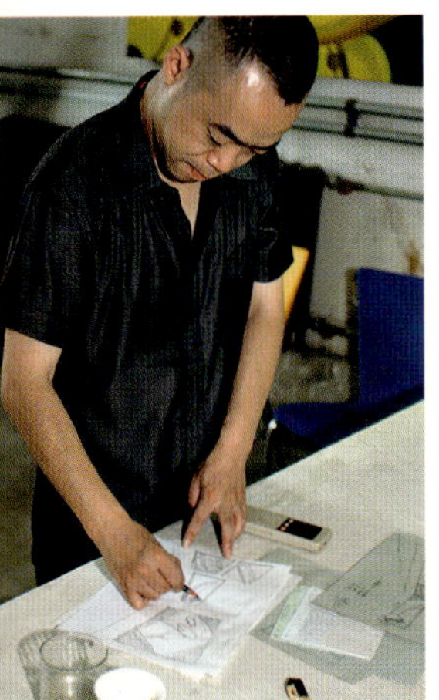

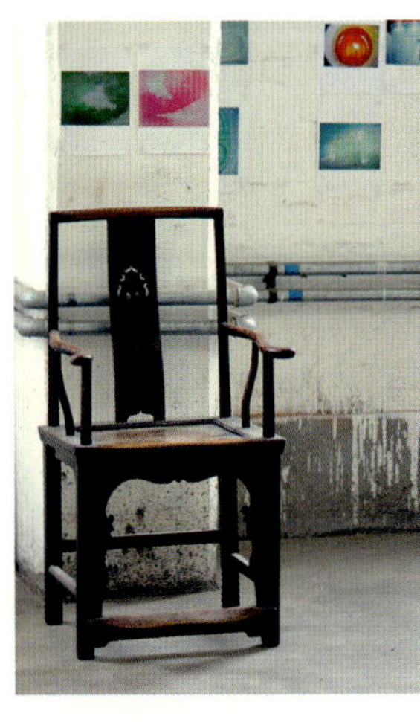

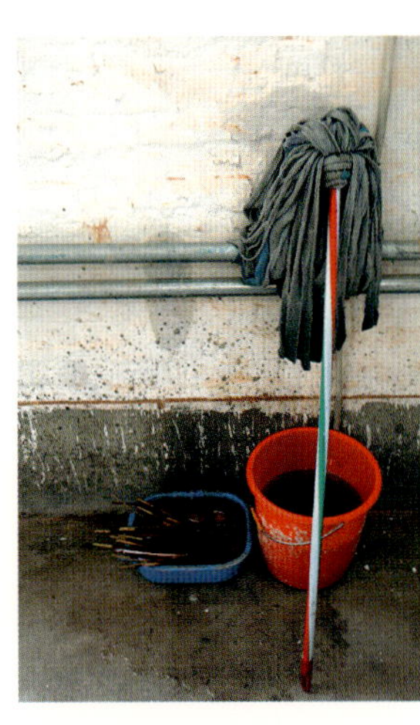

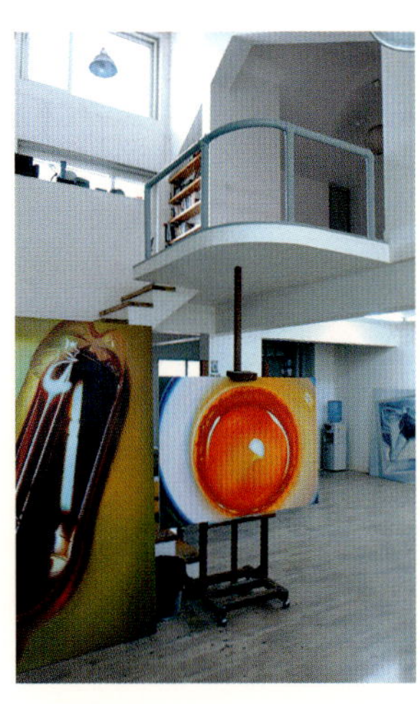

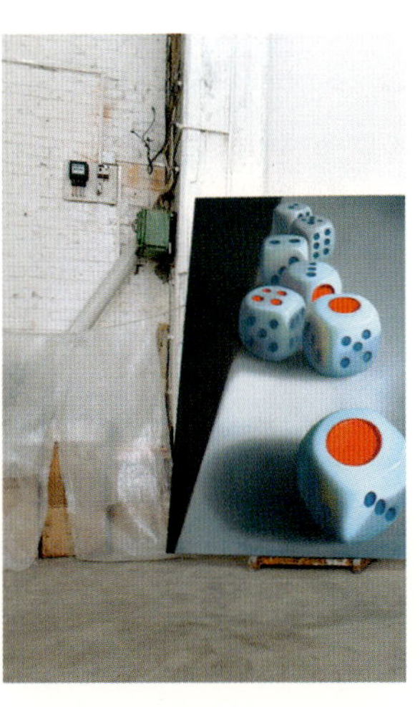

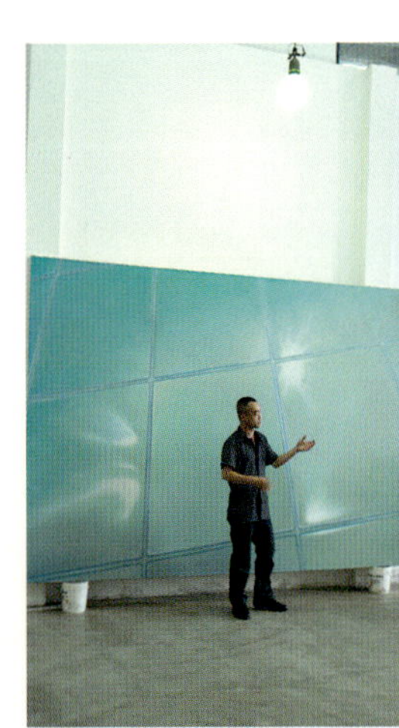

from one thousand square feet (one hundred square meters) to ten thousand square feet (one thousand square meters) at least, and artists who moved into the vast loft spaces. Chen Wenbo was one of the first to settle here. It seems such a long time ago—but it was only in fall 2002. ¶ "The rents here are very cheap, only thirty thousand yuan (about three thousand dollars). Even though prices are going up, like in Manhattan," he says, visibly delighted to be able to compare the situation here to New York, even if it is just to say rent in both places is rising. He adds, "Of course, in two years' time, maybe less, all of this might be knocked down. The government wants to set up an electronic research center. So we're trying to promote the neighborhood as a happening artistic place, to build up a kind of critical mass. It's working pretty well. More and more people are coming here. Even tourists now. It's become the place to be, with all the pros and cons that being trendy brings with it. But it's our only chance to survive." ¶ There are three canvases in progress on the floor. There is little in the way of furniture—one or two sofas, one or two chairs. Two tables, one on castors to carry his palette. A stepladder. Practically nothing. A remarkably high ceiling. ¶ I recognize some of the paintings, having seen them three months earlier at the October 2002 Shanghai Biennial: the chairs in the auditorium, some keys, a glass-fronted store. ¶ His work betrays the same obsession as the pictures featuring girls treated as objects, to show the surface and nothing but the surface by highlighting the glossy sheen and going over the painting until all trace of the brush has been smoothed over. ¶ How to define the glossy, dehumanized poetry that wells up from these strangely entrancing paintings? Chen Wenbo creates a sort of visual epiphany in the flashy electronic virtual world we now live in. It has been compared to the photographic precision of the hyperrealists, yet it is a paradoxical epiphany, lyrical yet reserved, strident yet well-rounded. ¶ The tensions are resolved in a climatic *jouissance*. ¶ Things are going pretty well for Chen Wenbo. At the moment he has two exhibitions in Beijing, one group exhibition at the Courtyard Gallery, which features his billiard balls mirrored in the gallery's highly polished floor, and one at the Long March Foundation, a stone's throw from his studio. ¶ He says, "At the Long March Foundation, you saw on the wall opposite the one with Yan Lei's works and the one that is at right angles to that, how my works were shown. It's of vital importance for me. When I am working on a painting, it's like a word that has an allotted place in my oeuvre, which becomes a sentence written on the wall." He goes over to the table, takes a sheet of paper, and sketches how the canvases were displayed on the wall. "It's the overall effect that counts," he says. ¶ His works sell well. He now keeps the Parisian gallery that wanted him to paint more pretty girls at armslength and sells his own works, "Six thousand dollars a painting. And the people I sell them to sell them for twice that, particularly to German galleries." He has noted that more and more Chinese collectors are getting in on the market. ¶ He turns the lights off and collects his bicycle from the corridor. We set off for his apartment, which is not far away, in New Town Chaoyang, in the northeast of Beijing. ¶ It is a charming little bachelor pad, where he is never quite alone. Right in the middle of the sitting room are an easel and a palette. There are canvases stacked everywhere. "Yep," he says, "I go to my studio and paint everyday, from 1 P.M. to 7 P.M. But even when I get home, I carry on painting. I can't live without it. It's physical. Maybe some kind of anxiety." ¶ Maybe. Or maybe it's just his passion for painting.

A SELECTION OF VIEWS OF CHEN WENBO'S APARTMENT, BALCONY, AND STUDIO. FAR LEFT: CHEN WENBO PRODUCES A SKETCH TO EXPLAIN HOW HE PLACES HIS WORKS ON THE WALL LIKE WORDS IN A SENTENCE.

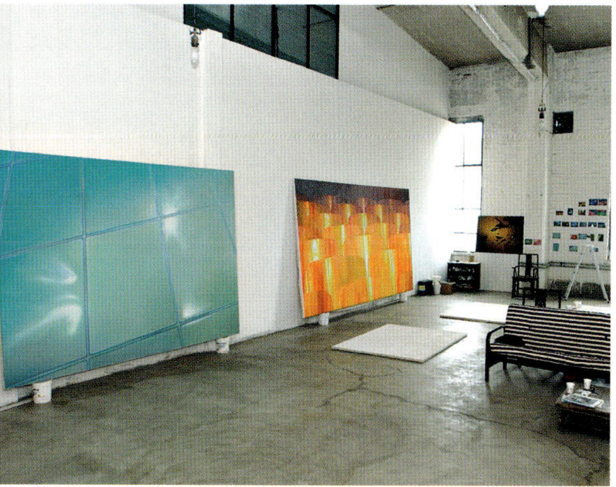

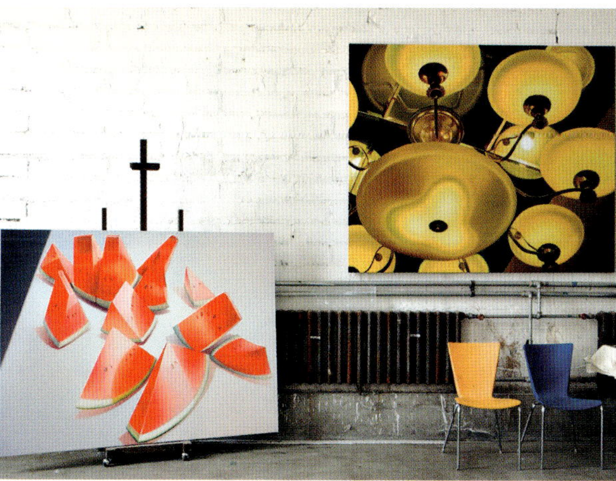

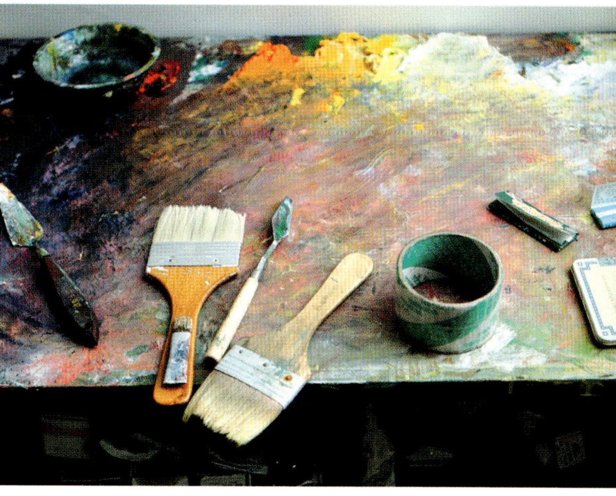

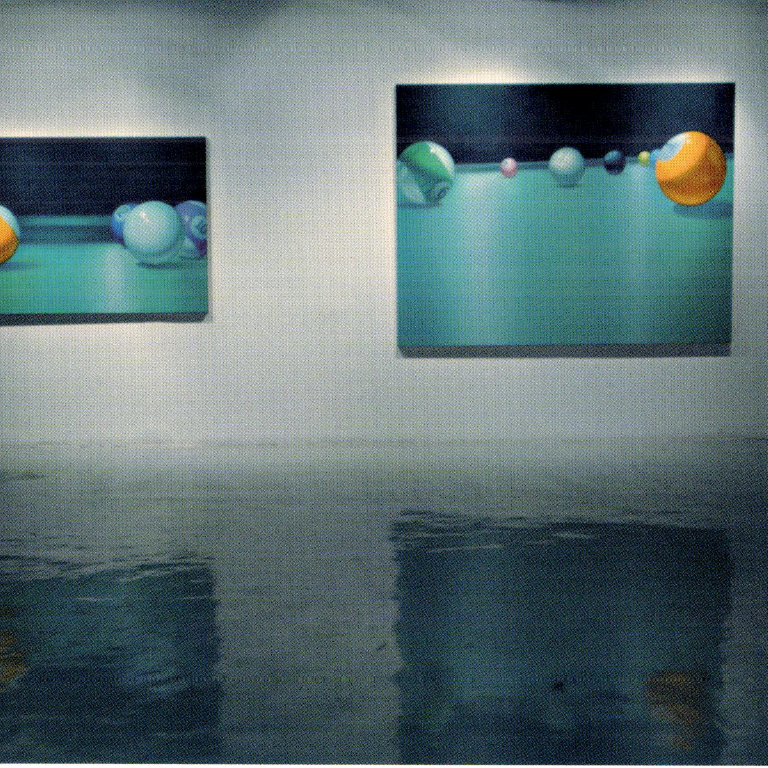

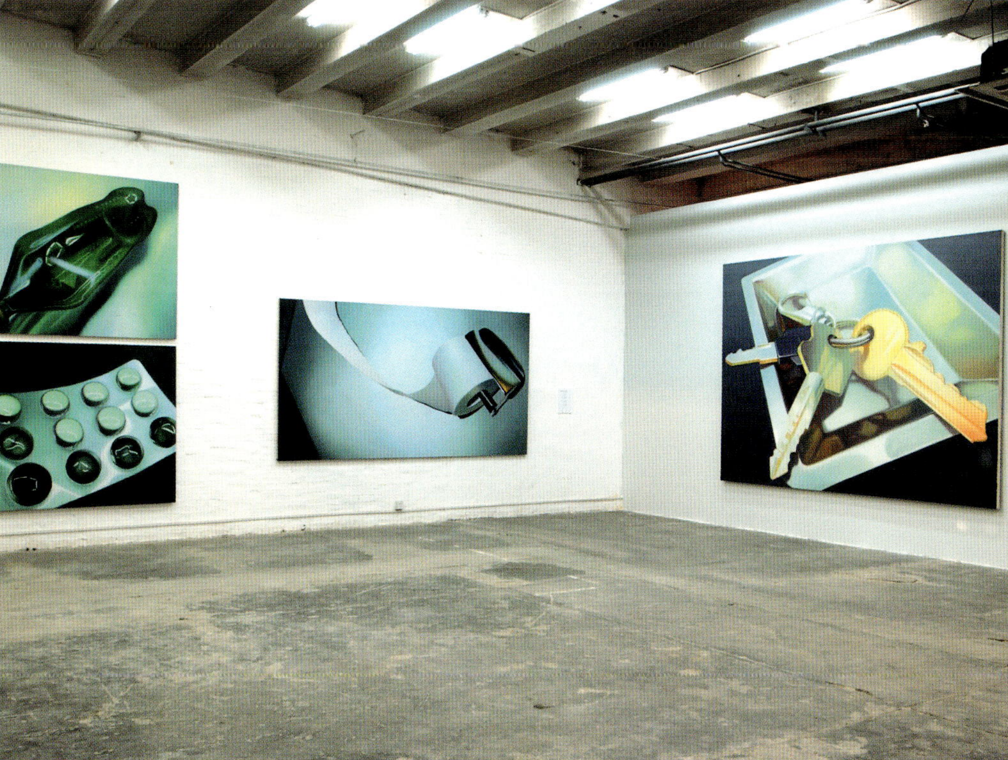

TOP: THE MOST RECENT WORKS ON DISPLAY IN THE STUDIO. TOP RIGHT: CHEN WENBO'S MATERIALS. BOTTOM: TWO EXHIBITIONS. LEFT: THE COURTYARD GALLERY, WHERE THE GLINTS IN THE PAINTING REFLECT GLINTS ON THE FLOOR. BOTTOM RIGHT: AN EXHIBITION AT THE LONG MARCH FOUNDATION GALLERY.

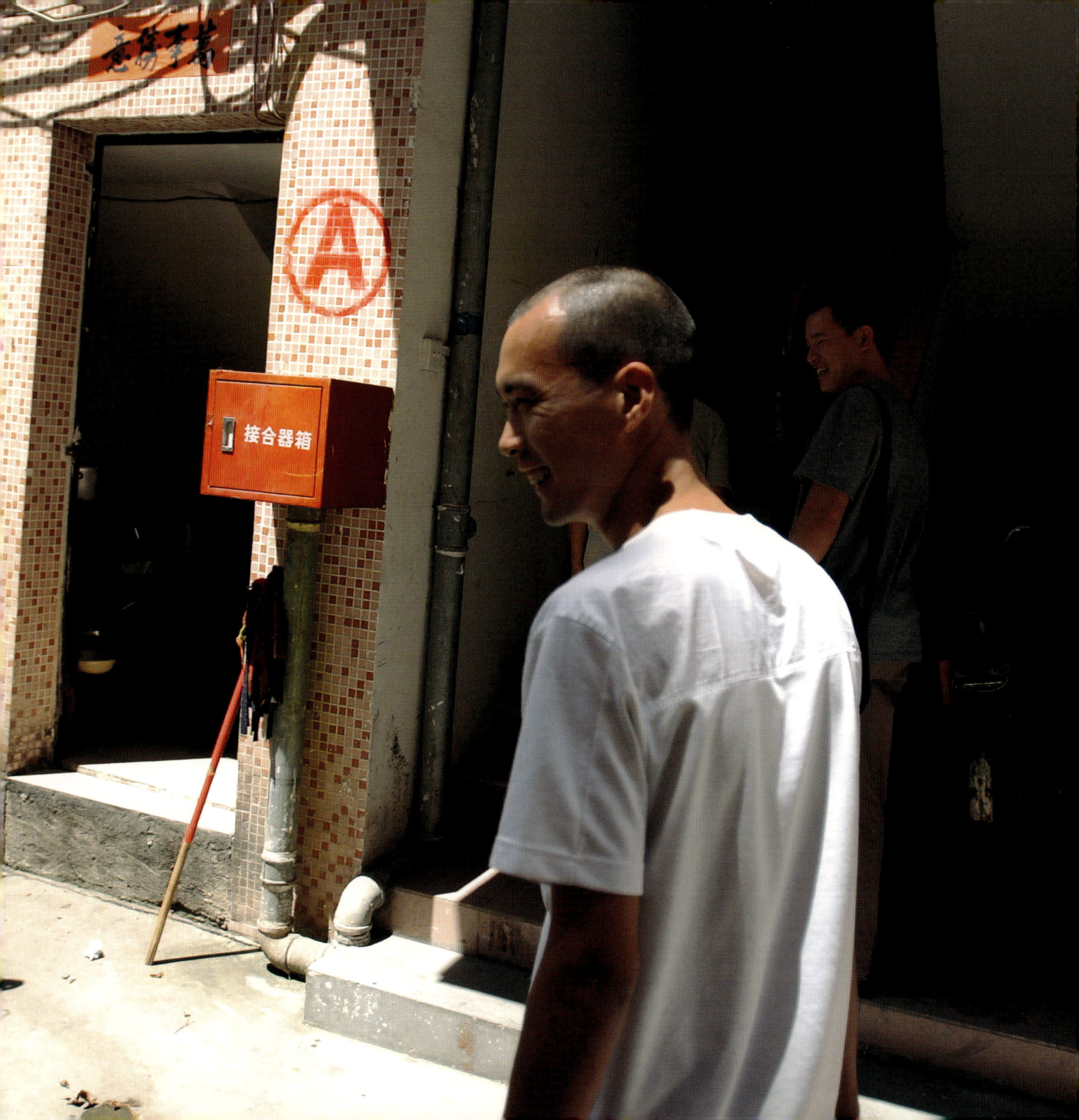
A
接合器箱

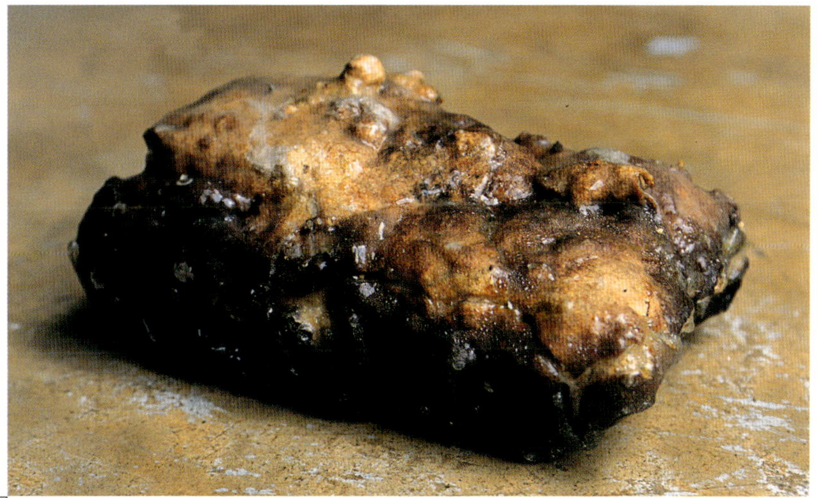

ZHEN GUOGU

He came with a friend to pick us up at the bus station, where we arrived at 11:57 A.M. precisely—on time to the minute. He was driving an air-conditioned Buick, and played with his up-to-the-minute cell phone in the hope of impressing us. He took us to a restaurant that he decorated. Another friend turned up, then two more, and finally a fifth along with his girlfriend, the delightfully named Bang Bang, a writer. Zhen Guogu lives, thinks, works, and parties with his clan. "Everyone has their own ideas, and when you put your ideas together, you get better ones," he says. ¶ Portrait of the artist as leader of the pack. ¶ We are in Yangjiang—a population of two hundred thousand inhabitants, a mere village by Chinese standards—precisely 160 miles (257 kilometers) southeast of Guangzhou, not far from the sea. The bus drove us through a landscape of mountains and rice paddies. In a week, it will be September 11, an important date here, marking the Moon Festival. All over town, tables have been set up to sell little round cakes made especially for the occasion. ¶ Zhen Guogu points out the number of motorcycles, and informs us, for reasons best known to himself, that this is the town with the highest proportion of motorcycle ownership in all China. He has a winning smile and twinkling eyes, close-cropped hair, and a general air of raffish elegance. When he defines himself as a "parasite," he is describing what he is, what he thinks he is, or how he would like to appear. Or maybe he is just ironically espousing the Communist Party's view of undisciplined gangs like him and his friends. ¶ From the outside, his apartment building is exactly the same as all the others. He has transformed his apartment (a triplex with terrace) into an incredibly modish designer pad. ¶ He is handsome, and he knows it. He plays with it, but not in an irritating way, because deep down he doesn't really care, because life is beautiful when you are talented and everything comes easily. He earns more than enough money. The future awaits with open arms. ¶ We visit Yangjiang. Everywhere we go, he points out his studio, then his office, the headquarters of his company, and the place where he works. I begin to get confused. Did he say his company was his studio? Our interpreter for this visit is hopeless, poor girl. Though she tries her best, I am never quite sure what she is trying to tell me. I think, possibly, probably, he did say that. I discovered Zhen Guogu in Venice. The works shown there did not really do him justice: they indicated a half-hearted, dated avant-garde approach. Here, I find an artist who buzzes with talent and a delightful lightness of soul. ¶ A few hours ago, he introduced us to his mother. We took a photograph of the two of them in front of his apartment block. He tells us, "My mother was against my ideas. She didn't understand what I wanted to do, or what I was actually doing. I get the impression that she thought I was a sort of terrorist." He bursts out laughing. Zhen Guogu was born in 1970, so he is thirty-four. He looks easily ten years younger. He is not a terrorist. At least not yet. ¶ He specialized in engraving at the School of Fine Art. He explains, "All the students who study engraving have to change specialty as quickly as they can, because there aren't enough machines for a career in engraving." ¶ His father was a truck driver. When he was little, Zhen Guogu used to dream about driving trucks, but the dreams gradually became nightmares. In order to escape what destiny had in store for him, he decided to go to art school instead. "It was the easiest option for me," he says. His father, inspired by the obvious talent of his son and his determination to make a go of his artistic career, gave up truck driving and pursued his dream of becoming a singer at the Guangzhou Opera, with a certain degree of success. I say to Zhen Guogu that he certainly has an unusual family, but he protests. "No, no, in my family, lots of people sing or play musical instruments." That is probably why he began

FACING PAGE: ZHEN GUOGU, IN THE STREET OPPOSITE HIS HOME IN YANGJIANG. HE SAYS THAT AT HOME, HE FEELS "LIKE A PARASITE." ABOVE: WITH A FRIED TANK, THE REMAINS OF A PERFORMANCE AT THE CAAW GALLERY.

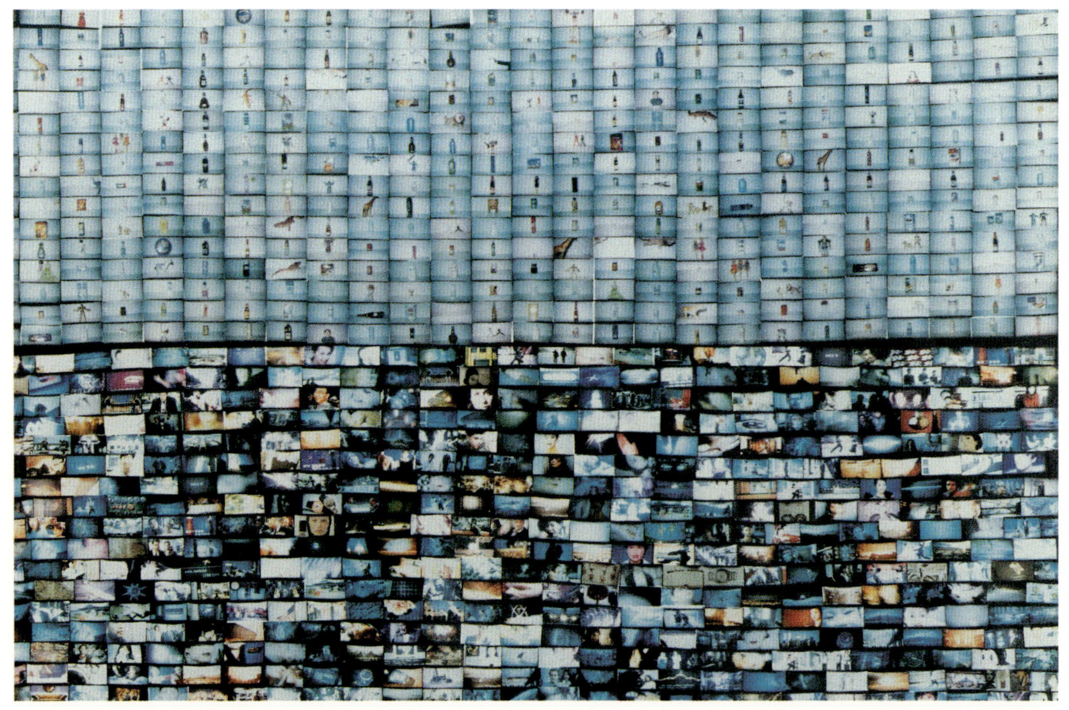

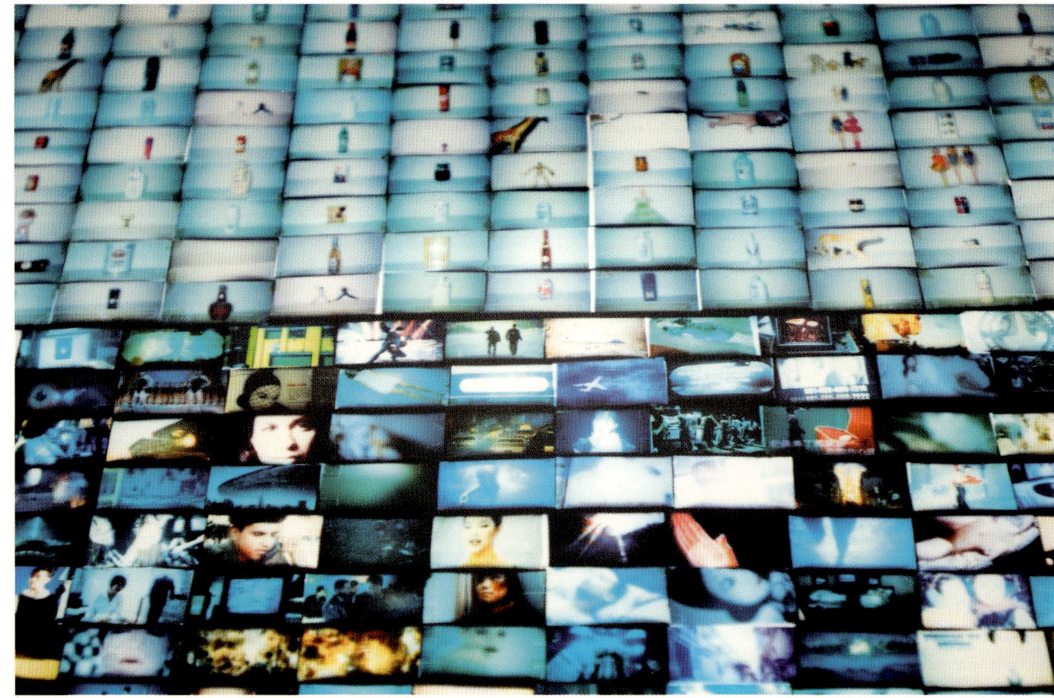

ABOVE: PHOTOGRAPHS BY ZHEN GUOGU IN DRAWERS AT THE VITAMIN GALLERY IN GUANGZHOU. FACING PAGE, TOP: *TEN THOUSAND CONSUMERS 16*, 1997–2000 BOTTOM: *TEN THOUSAND CONSUMERS 8*, 1997–2000.

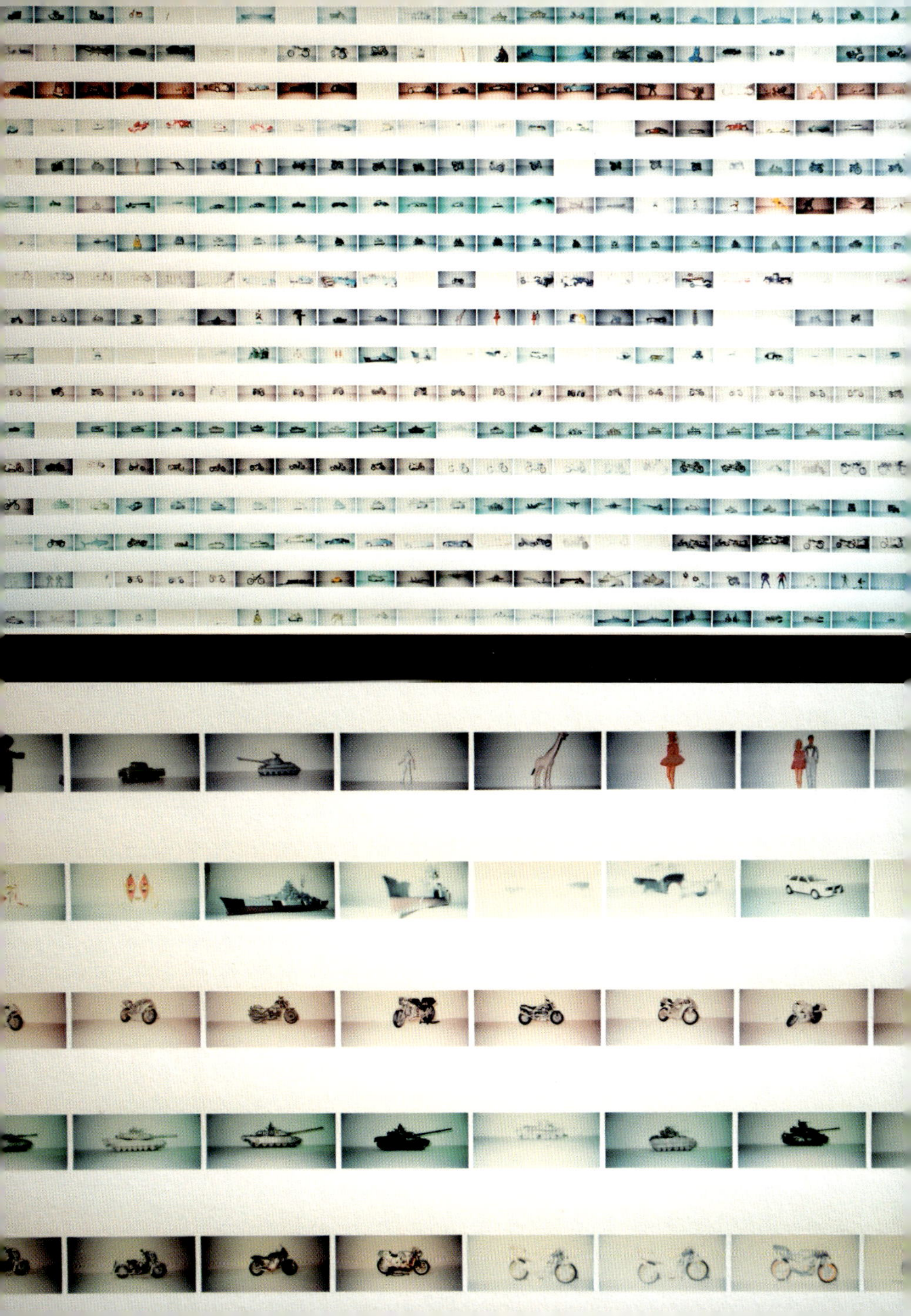

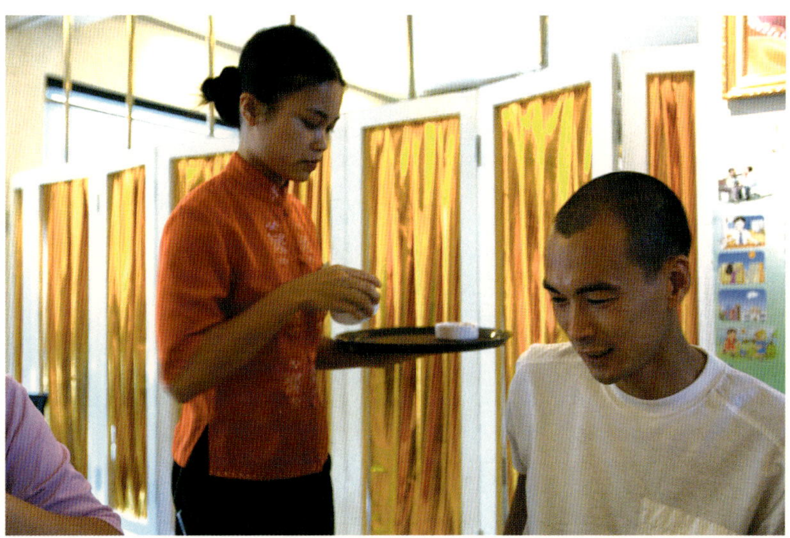

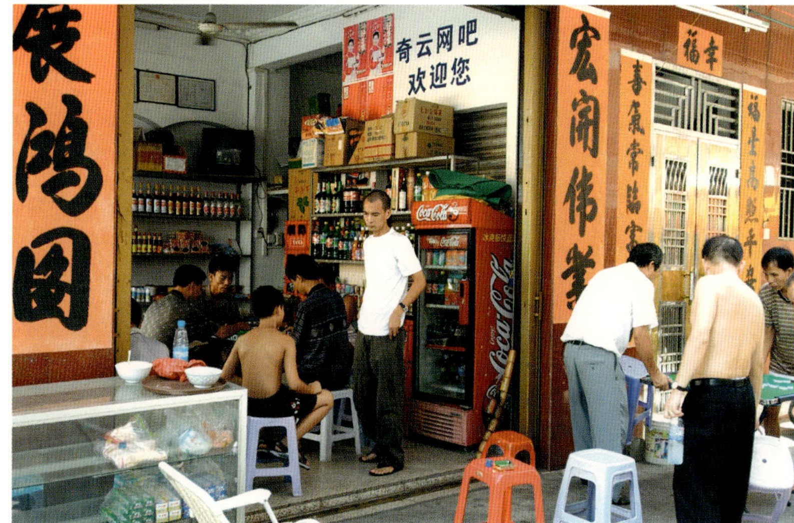

designing bizarre instruments made of recycled materials and junk, planks of wood and old electronic circuitry. All the instruments, shown at the Vitamin Gallery in Guangzhou, actually work. We took a lot of pictures at the gallery, and a good thing too, because he hardly has any works in Yangjiang to show us. "You have to throw out the old stuff to keep moving forward. I consider myself to be a clean slate. My work is elsewhere." ¶ He built one of his homemade instruments from a microwave oven; his father built one using a cheap old electric guitar almost beyond repair. At home, in his studio, the only art in evidence is, on one wall, a magnificent photographic work put together from dozens of shots taken from contact sheets aligned in rows where there is no distinction or hierarchy between good and bad, blurred and overexposed shots. All the photos have been developed in large format and are framed behind glass, all on the same principle, whatever their artistic merit. ¶ "A photo can mean a lot of things," he says. "I want people to read—and I mean really read—my photos, each of them individually and then as part of the whole. Since the pictures are very small, it isn't very easy to read them. I made them small on purpose, so that people had to get up close and look at them carefully. When you just glance at them from a few feet away, they look like abstract works. You just scan them for thirty seconds and then move on to the next work. I hope that people will stay longer, because I have condensed a lot of things into each of my works." Why, I ask. "Because life is powerful stuff," he says, as if this is perfectly obvious. "And in my works, I make every effort to express life as I experience it, precise yet blurred." ¶ In 1997, Hans van Dijk, director of the China Art Archives and Warehouse, organized an exhibition entitled *New Chinese Conceptual Photography*, which was shown in various towns and cities around Europe. One might wonder what was so "conceptual" about this work. Actually, it didn't really matter, the point being to draw the attention of the Chinese to photography in general, and art photography, as opposed to photojournalism, in particular. This is where Zhen Guogu's originality truly stood out. ¶ Copies of the catalog for the mythic exhibition *Fuck Off* are in short supply. Beneath their name and photograph, each participating artist was invited to contribute one sentence that summed up his vision and artistic practice. Zhen Guogu wrote: "TV gives us Chinese the possibility of accessing pop culture from Europe, America, Hong Kong, and Taiwan that has a widespread influence on the younger generation." Is this to say that this lighthearted, fun art has a political dimension? ¶ Who are his contacts? Who are the artists he discusses his vision with? The friends we met this morning. He also has friends in Guangzhou, particularly Chen Shaoxiong. Zhen Guogu took part in the Big Tail Elephant adventure (*No Space: Big Tail Elephant Show* and *Possibility: Big Tail Elephant Show*, both in 1994), although he was not closely involved. In 2003, he participated in the *Guangzhou Express* exhibition—not a resounding success—where he was responsible for the design in a sort of enclave at the far end of the arsenals, at what was easily the worst Biennale so far. He says, "Today it is getting easier and easier to work together with other people at a distance. With email and the Internet, you no longer need to meet people." ¶ He also uses his computer to look for work for his father, who is currently without a job. A worry line furrows his brow: "There is a lot of unemployment. The government is not giving out the true figures. In my family, there are three people without a job." The region is a poor one, with little in the way of natural resources, and the city is a relatively small, provincial backwater. But Zhen Guogu clearly adores it. ¶ "I feel so at home here," he tells us, "that I find it hard to stay anywhere else for any length of time—even in Guangzhou, which is only 150 miles

ABOVE: LEFT: ZHEN GUOGU IN A RESTAURANT. RIGHT: ZHEN GUOGU IN A STORE. FACING PAGE: ZHEN GUOGU IN THE STREET. THE SUNSHADE ON THIS MOPED IS A NECESSITY IN THIS SOUTHERN CORNER OF CHINA. ZHEN GUOGU WITH FRIENDS, INCLUDING THE NOTORIOUS BANG BANG.

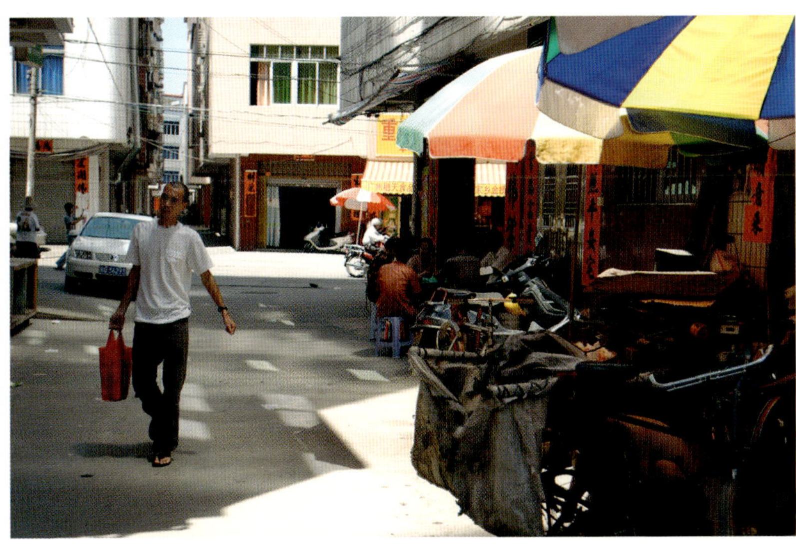

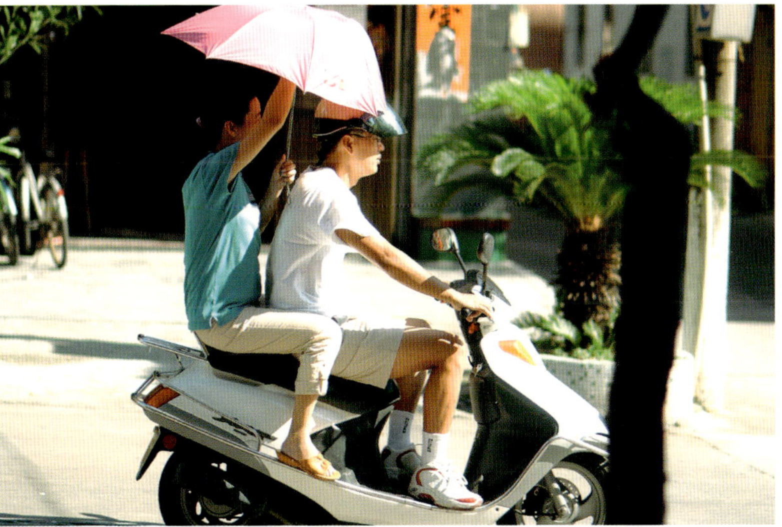

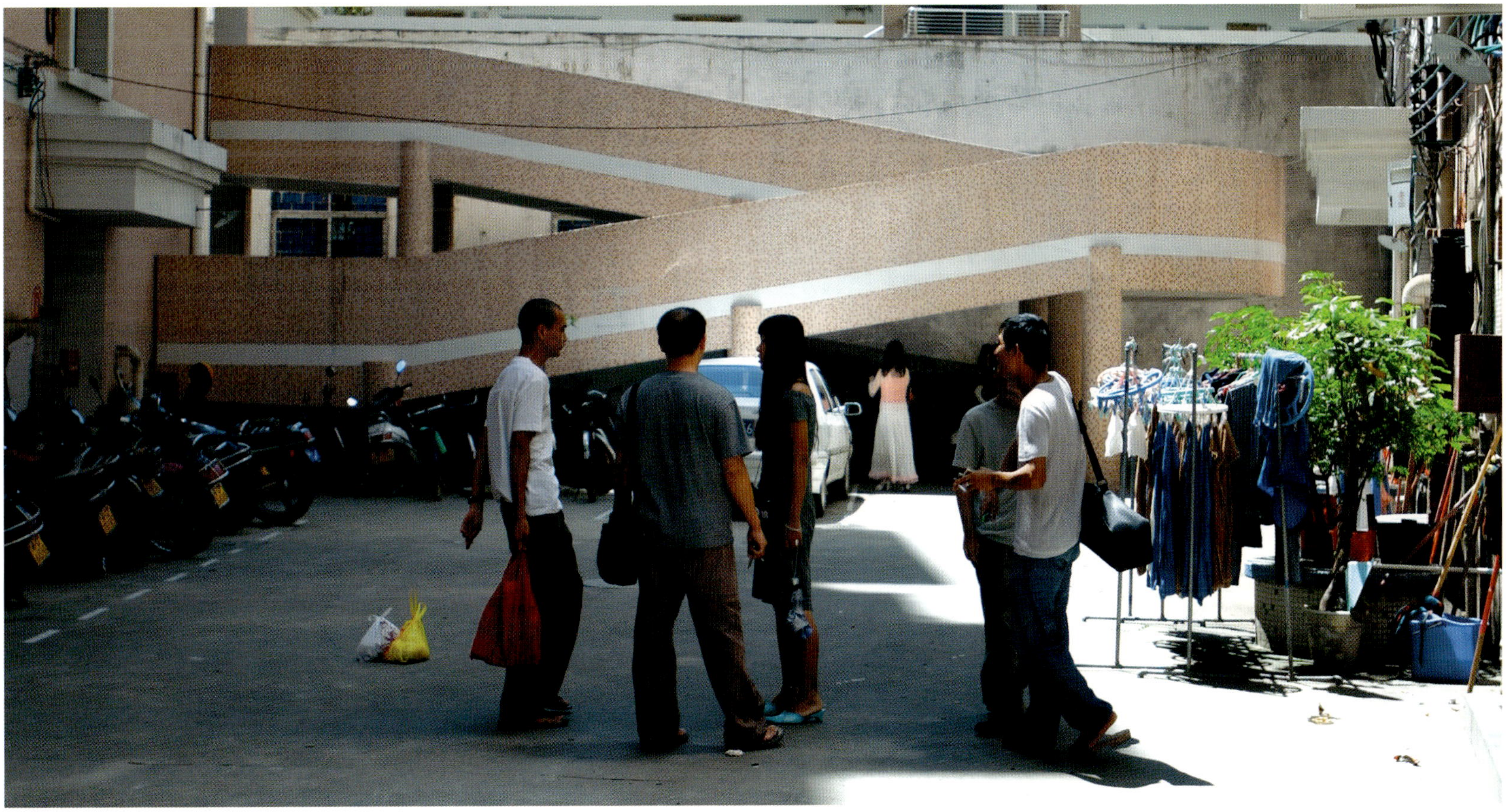

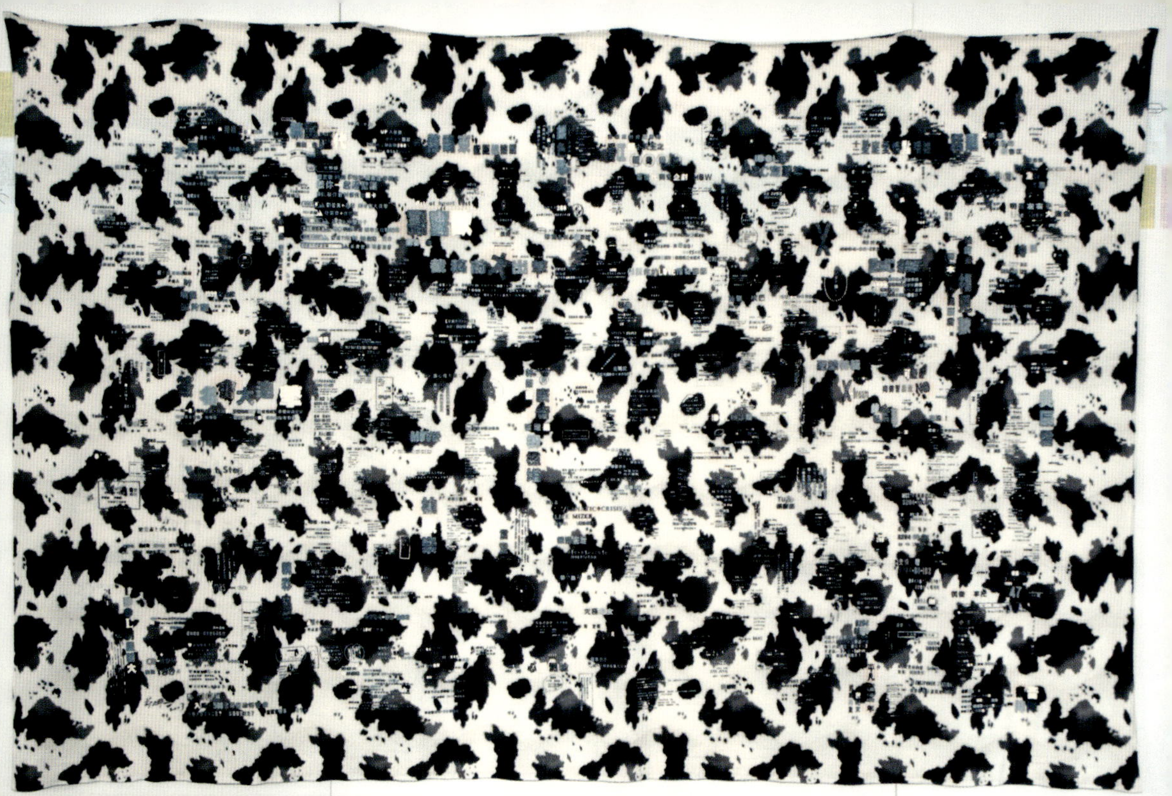

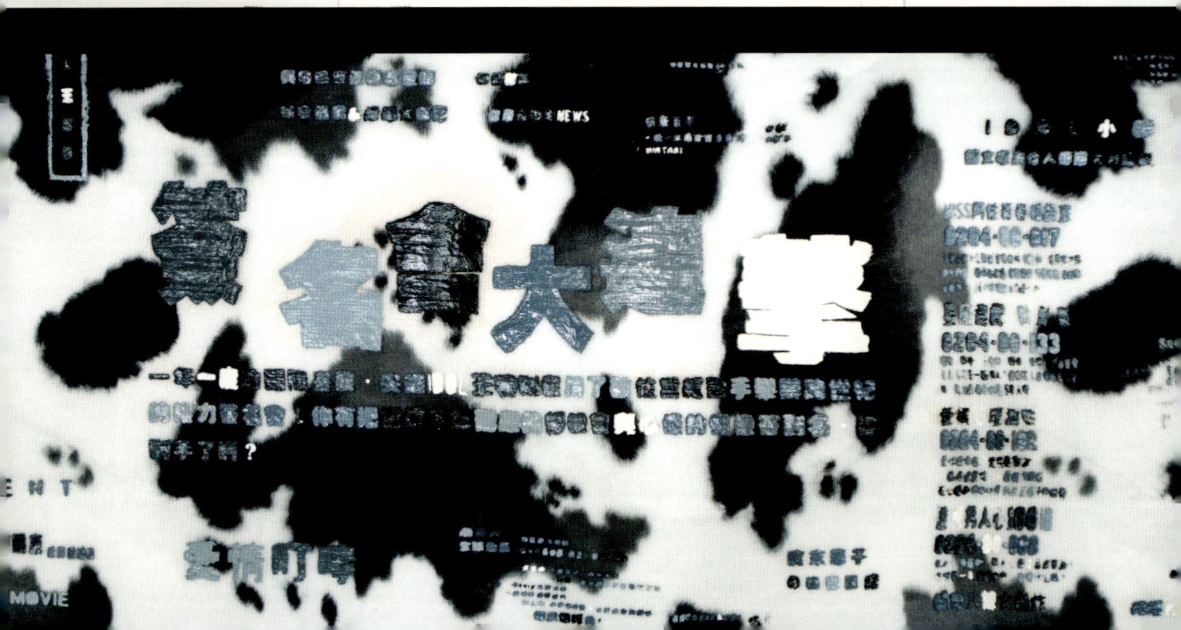

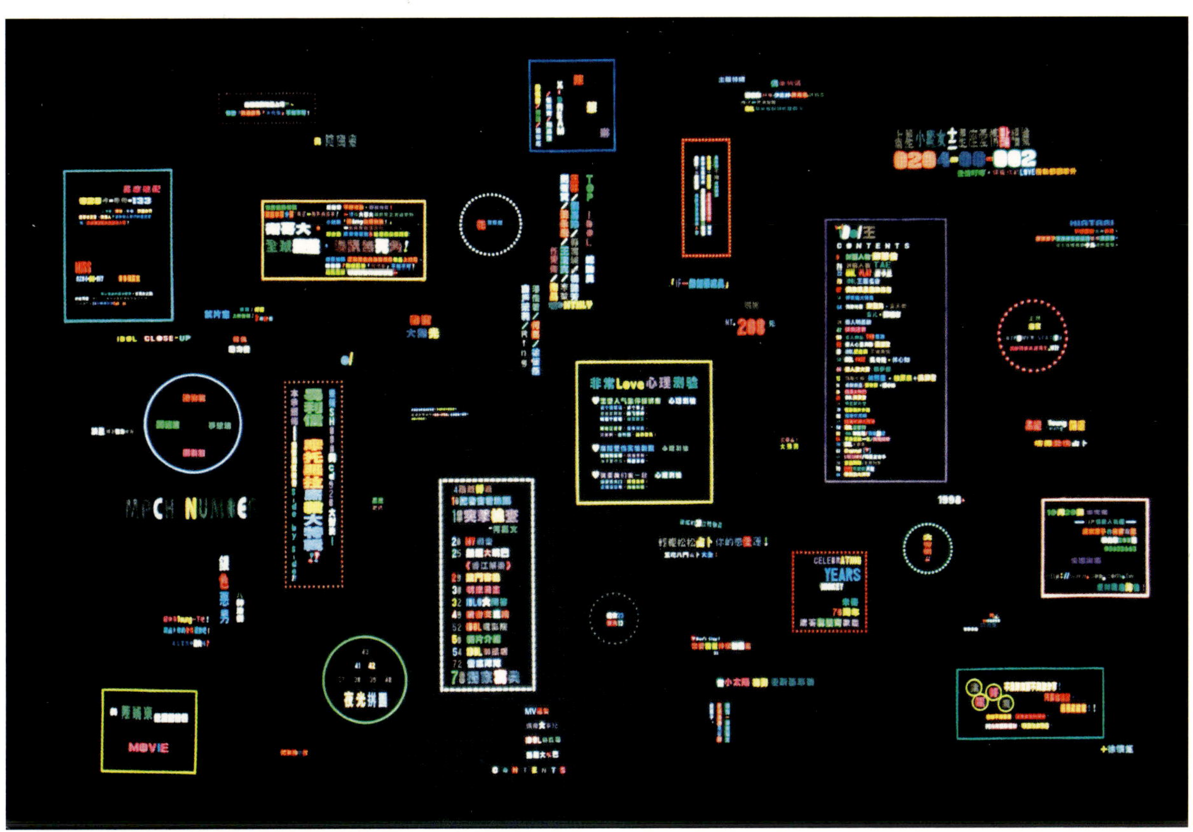

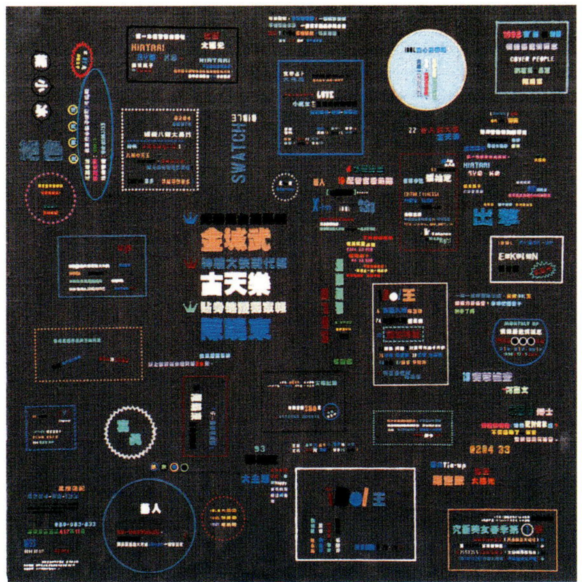

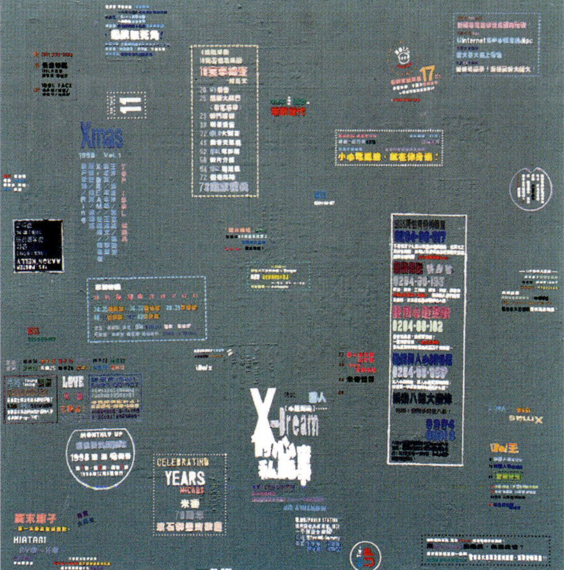

COMPUTER CONTROLLED BY PIG BRAIN, 1999. FACING PAGE: *COMPUTER CONTROLLED BY PIG BRAIN-20*, 1999

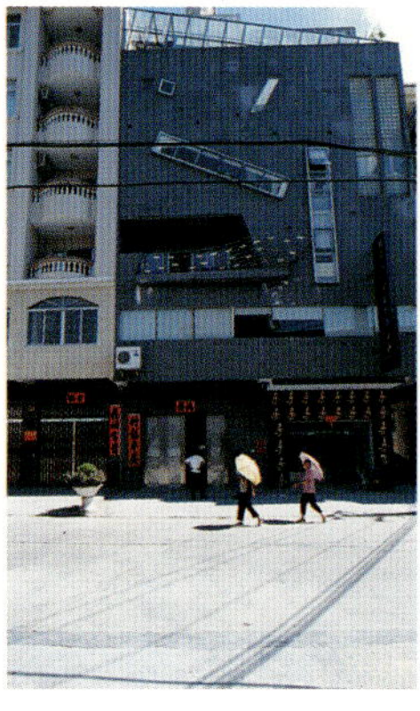
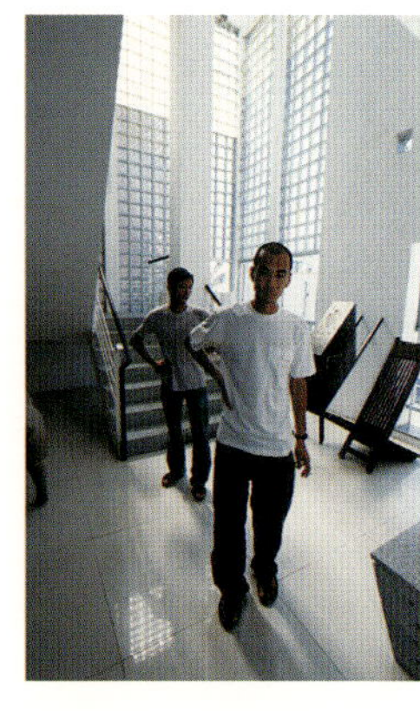
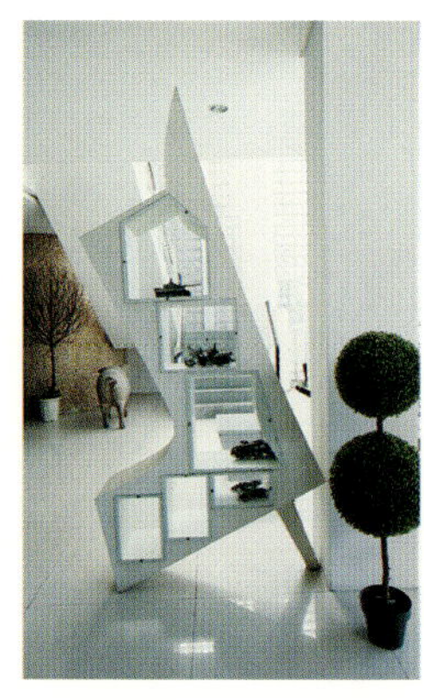
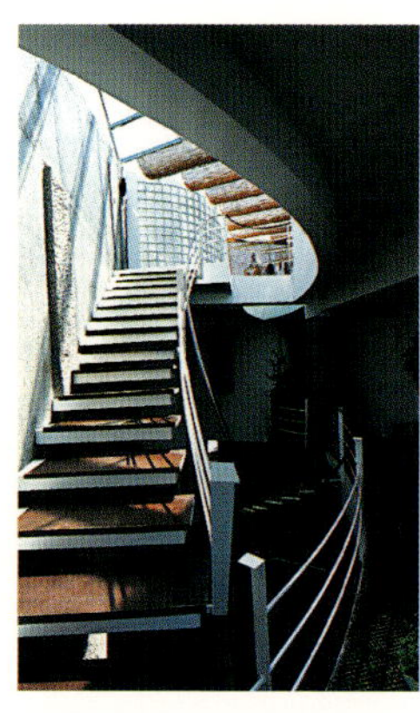
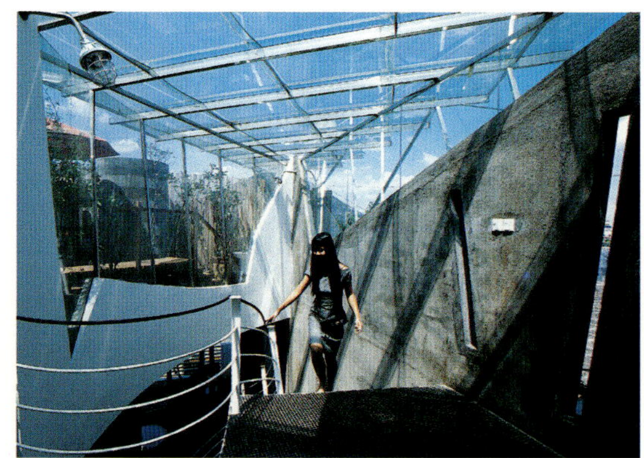

(250 kilometers) away. I get sick whenever I stay there too long. I can't get used to the rhythm of living in a large city. I have to come back to Yangjiang to find the sort of life that suits me. I love being near the beach. And as for traveling abroad, in Europe or wherever, once a year is plenty. And I always come back quickly. My ideal life would be not having to work too hard at anything." And he adds, trying to be provocative, "Luckily, in the contemporary art world, you don't have to live in the cities where your works are shown." ¶ In China, the entire art establishment is at Zhen Guogu's feet. Great things are expected of him. He is an almost perfect fit for the archetype of the young, avant-garde artist. But when you get to know him, he seems less of a pioneer, and more of a virtuoso who can turn his hand to anything, who shows plenty of promise—one has to hope that he can fulfill it. So far he has not turned his brilliant early works into a solid, coherent oeuvre. But does he really want to? At the moment, he is enjoying trying out a range of possibilities too much to tie himself down to one particular style. He does a bit of design work, a few photos, a few experiments with calligraphy, a painting now and then, and the occasional performance. ¶ For example, his golden, crispy "fried tanks" (1999) have become famous, but it is less generally known that they were originally part—or more accurately, perhaps, the leftovers—of a performance. He modeled a series of tanks out of dough, and got a bevy of pretty female cooks to fry them, occasionally lending a hand himself, wearing plastic gloves. ¶ His love of experimenting with new media has not meant that he has stopped painting. A good proportion of his work consists of superb entanglements of geometrical shapes in fluorescent colors on black or gray backgrounds. They are generally referred to as "computer paintings." This, however, reflects a misunderstanding of the works, as they are rather a comment on the process of writing—but writing with a computer. These works are in fact closer to calligraphy than anything else. ¶ He also does (I nearly said "real" here) calligraphy. In a group with his friends. They call it "new calligraphy," just like they called their camera work "new photography." It is calligraphy freed from its constraints, perhaps precisely because none of them specialized in calligraphy, which is a major art form in China. ¶ At the other end of town, the studio where he keeps all his calligraphic works, a sort of hangar also used for storing motorcycles, seems much smaller than the others. However, it is shared by four or five artists, who paint in ink on the floor. ¶ These works could not be further removed from Xu Bing's sophisticated and highly intellectual calligraphy. They paint sloppy ideograms, utterly removed from the classical reference, with ink that runs, smears, and dribbles. They slap the ink down, creating works that are closer to graffiti than any more structured form. If you can read Chinese, you will find a range of international news issues under discussion, like a speech by Margaret Thatcher or how the US attacked Iraq for its oil. One of them, towards the back, is a comment on Damien Hirst's art. Zhen Guogu recently showed his calligraphy at the Vitamin Gallery in Guangzhou, which accepts him as he is, with his eclectic tastes and his search for scattered fragments of truth. ¶ Why has he been so keen to talk about design all day? Because he didn't have anything else to show us? Because the weather was nice? Because he was in the middle of preparing *Guangzhou Express* for Venice? ¶ Back in Yangjiang, when he took such obvious pleasure in showing us the open-plan spaces arranged as he wished, a design full of wit and brio, particularly the strange façade with the diagonal window cutting across it, and the toilets right at the top on the terrace like an observatory, when he was playing at being a designer, it was all a game. He is a dandy, a dilettante. ¶ "Design is my camouflage," he says.

ABOVE AND FACING PAGE: ZHEN GUOGU AT HOME WITH FRIENDS ON THE ROOF OF HIS APARTMENT BUILDING. IT IS ALL VERY CUTTING-EDGE AND MODERN, VAST, AND INCREDIBLE. ZHEN GUOGU IS HAVING FUN. HE LIKES TO THINK THAT FROM DOWN BELOW NO ONE KNOWS WHAT IS HAPPENING JUST ABOVE THEIR HEADS.

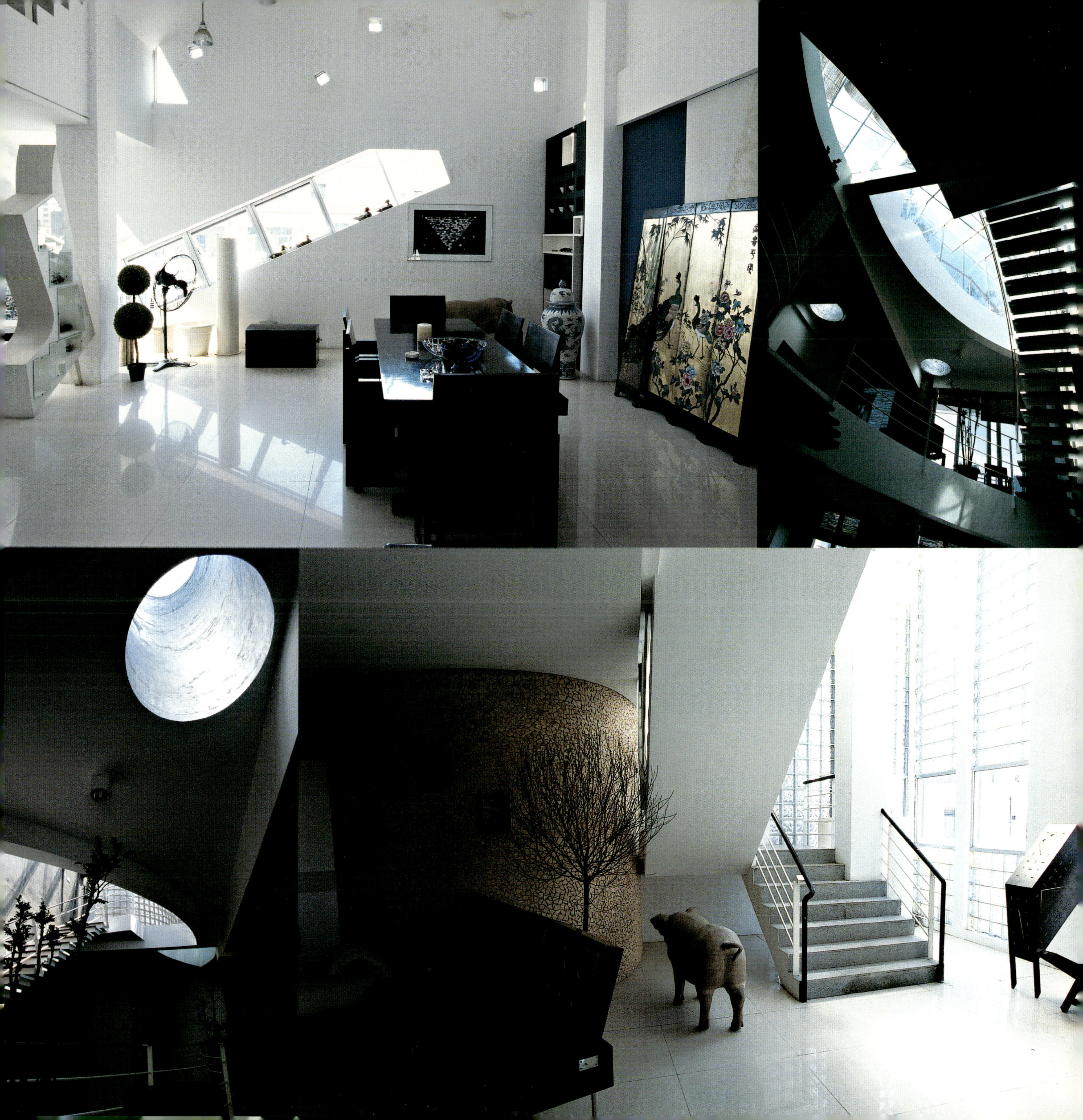

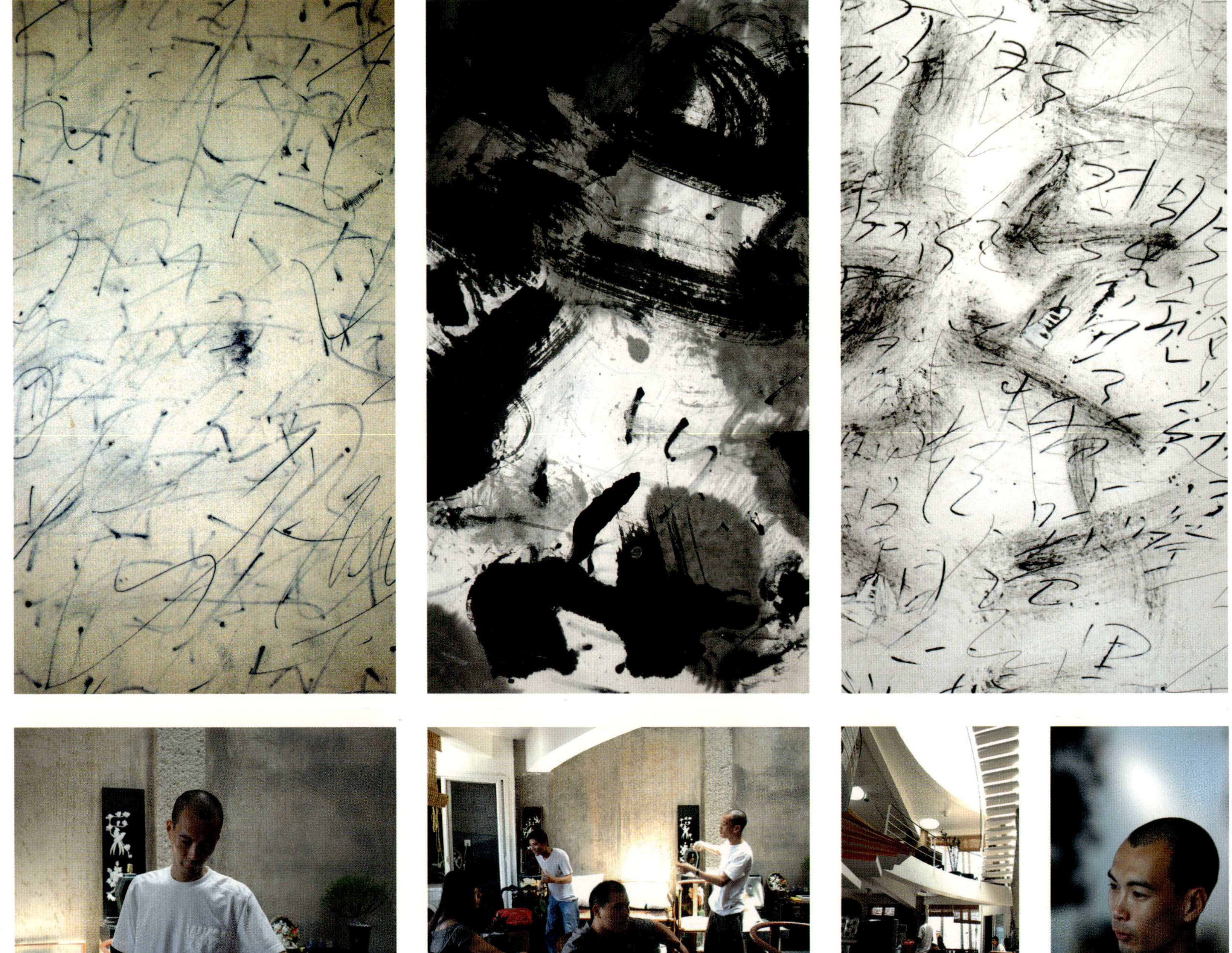

CAN THIS REALLY BE CALLED CALLIGRAPHY? THERE'S NO REASON WHY NOT, ALTHOUGH PERHAPS IT IS CLOSER TO GRAFFITI. IN ANY CASE, ZHEN GUOGU'S WORK IS SUBTLER THAN THAT OF THE OTHER MEMBERS OF THE GROUP.

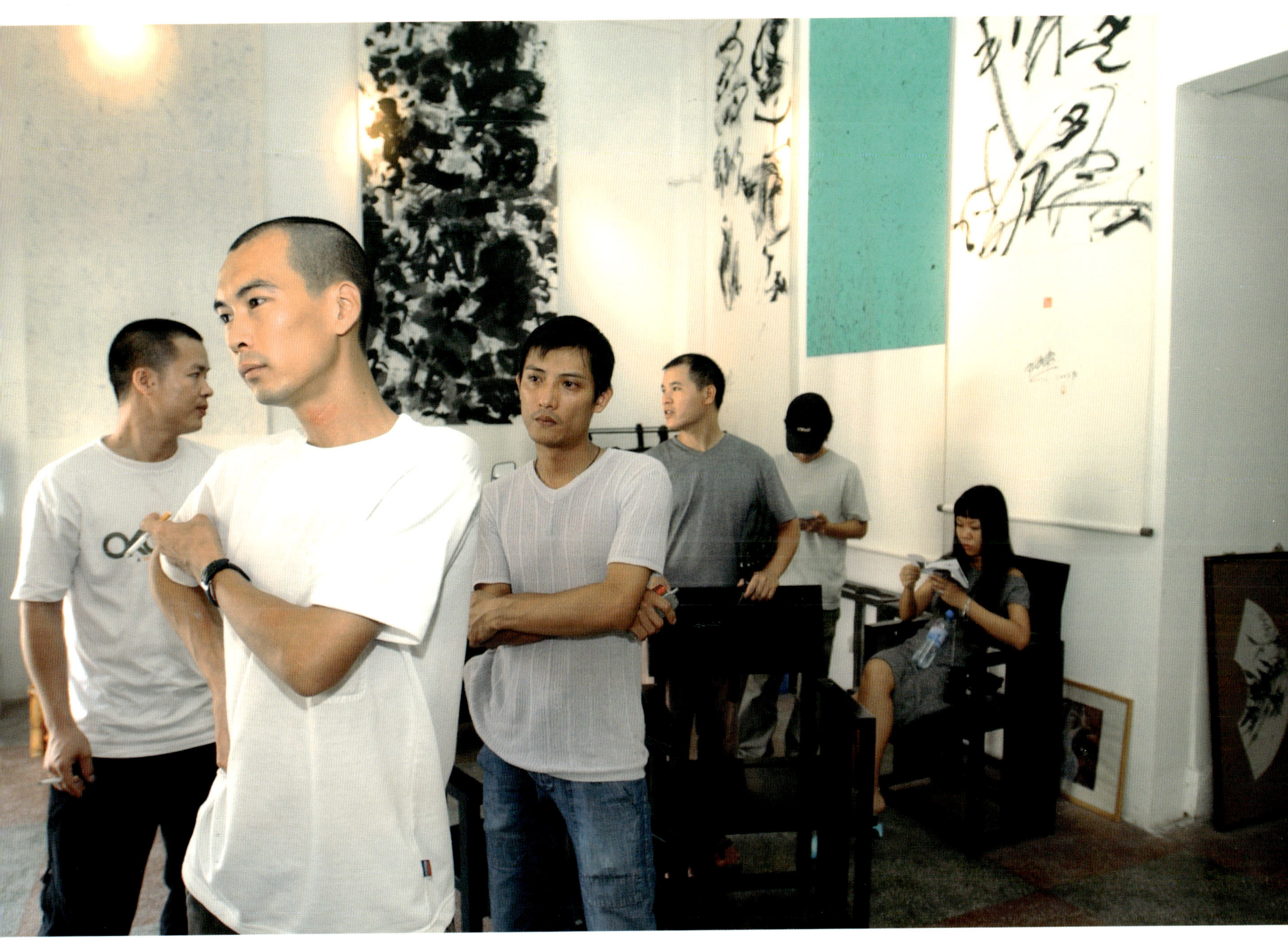

ZHEN GUOGU WITH NEARLY ALL OF HIS GANG, IN THE SMALLEST OF THEIR STUDIOS IN YANGJIANG, WHERE THEY PAINT THEIR CALLIGRAPHY ON THE FLOOR. BANG BANG IS SEATED.

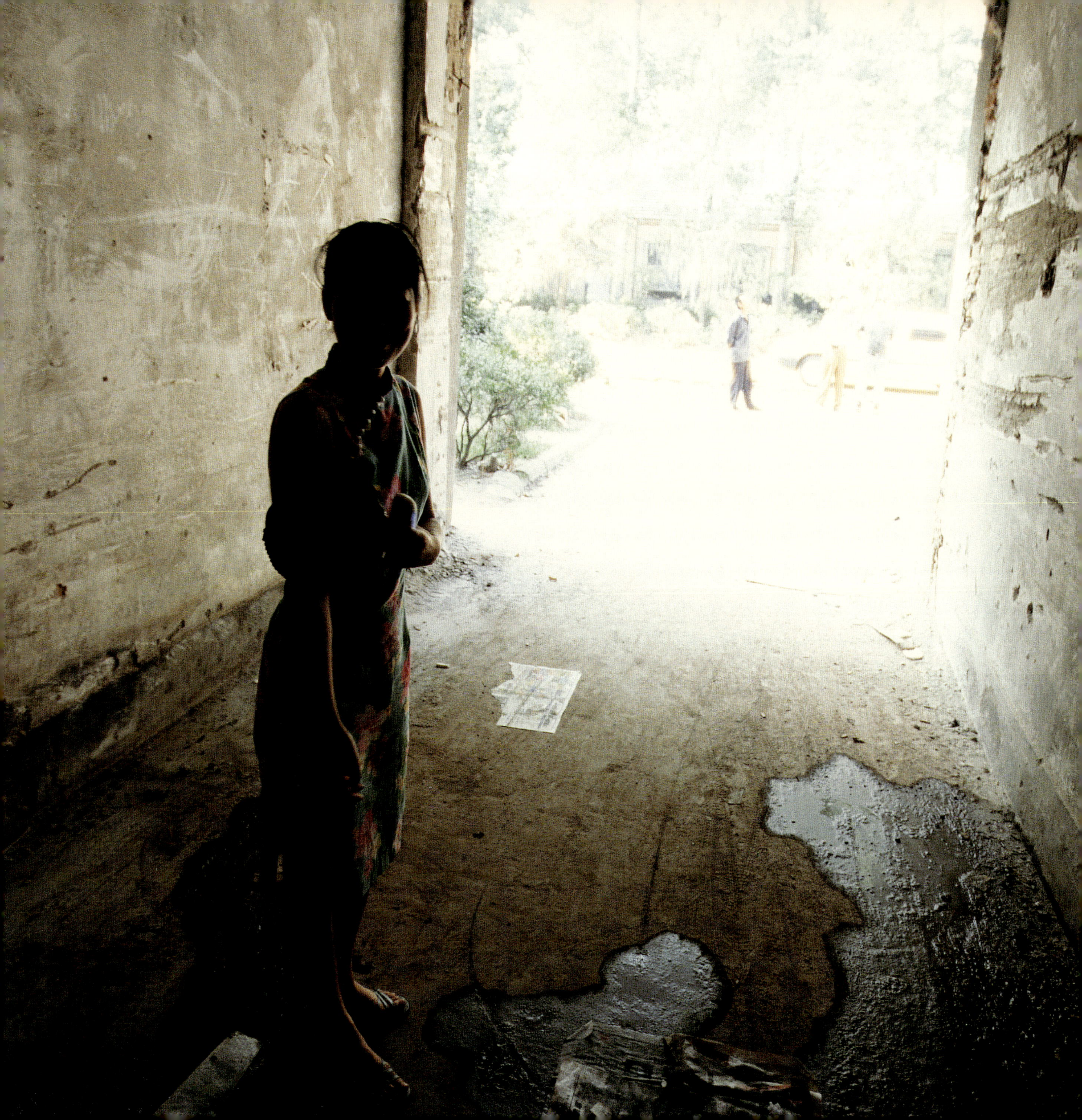

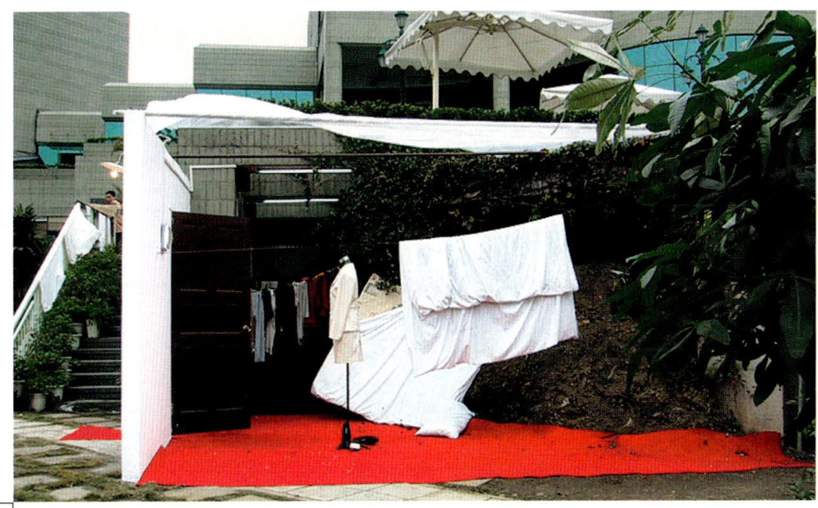

CHEN LINGYANG

She laughs: "When I first invented my alter ego, Chen Lingyang number two, the first thing people asked was 'If your boyfriend is going out with Chen Lingyang number one, does that mean we can sleep with Chen Lingyang number two?'" ¶ She looks down demurely, stifling her laughter in her long hair. She looks back up and glances at us from under her bangs. Chen Lingyang is at once shy and cheeky—or provocative, rather. Maybe pretty. And funny—terribly funny. She is an unpredictable rising star, out of killer, off-the-wall. She does not put herself forward, but the spotlight falls on her nonetheless. ¶ Who are these two Chen Lingyangs? ¶ Listen: This is what she tells us. ¶ She burst onto the Chinese art scene four years ago with a huge scandal. Others might have been crushed by the strict censorship laws in China at the time, but Chen Lingyang—almost against her will—managed to turn the scandal into a launch pad for a brilliant career. The subject of the scandal? One of China's biggest taboos: sex. ¶ Although her shyness is not just play-acting—she actually is introverted—Chen Lingyang is certainly not afraid to stand up to tradition and defy an age-old taboo. Her work of art was a roll of toilet paper, rolled out into a strip eighteen feet (six meters) long by nine inches (twenty-two centimeters) wide. The day she got her period in October 1999, she wiped her vagina with it, drawing trails of blood, forming strange marks that might almost be landscapes. ¶ Was she inspired to paint with her own menstrual blood by Nietzsche's vision of an ideal author writing with his heart's blood? Maybe. Or, more likely, she was exploring her own artistic persona. ¶ Chen Lingyang's work is a contemporary take on the ancient and subtle genre of landscape painting in ink on silk, where the works are displayed rolled out on a purpose-built long narrow table. Traditional Chinese landscape paintings are designed to be contemplated for hours on end, with parts that are more restful, others that are surprising, others still that require great concentration. ¶ Chen Lingyang's spin on this tradition could be taken as an expression of extreme insolence. Not only did it leave far behind all limits of taste as far as sex was concerned, but it also seemed to pour scorn on an ancient and noble artistic tradition. ¶ "Not at all," she explains, "Not only did I not mean to criticize traditional painting, but looking at these silk rolls that show the natural passage of time and the unfolding of experience, I just did the same thing, since this piece of art was all about my own experience and the passage of my own time. The ancient rolls were designed to show the tao, the way the path is constructed by the passing of the seasons, of time—in short, things moving on. My artistic reflection and the process I used are exactly the same thing." ¶ I say jokingly, "So, the traditionalists should have been keen on it." ¶ She answers: "What counts are my intentions, which are far more important than any reaction." ¶ OK. ¶ It would be an understatement to call the reception of her work in China chilly. Even in decadent France four years later, it was given a mixed reception at the exhibition entitled *Twelve Flower Months* at a gallery in Paris's exclusive rue de Seine. Even the French National Commission for Contemporary Art was unsure how to react. The works of art were disturbing. They were *unpleasant.* ¶ The problem is that not only does Chen Lingyang's art undermine traditional artistic representations of Chinese women, who are meant to be beautiful, modest, sweet, and docile—in fact, Chinese critics such as Liao Wen have noted that women are first and foremost shown as *objects*—but it also reflects a vision of the female body that, far from being idealized, is depicted in all its carnal, raw truth. ¶ In the feminist 1970s, the American artists Judy Chicago and Carolee Schneemann worked on the theme of menstruation. In 1971, Chicago produced a close-up photolithograph of herself removing a soiled tampon, and the

FACING PAGE: CHEN LINGYANG IN THE BLINDING SUNLIGHT OUTSIDE HER STUDIO JUST NEXT TO THE AT CAFÉ IN SPACE 798 IN BEIJING. ABOVE: THE INSTALLATION SHE CREATED FOR THE GUANGZHOU TRIENNIAL IN 2002.

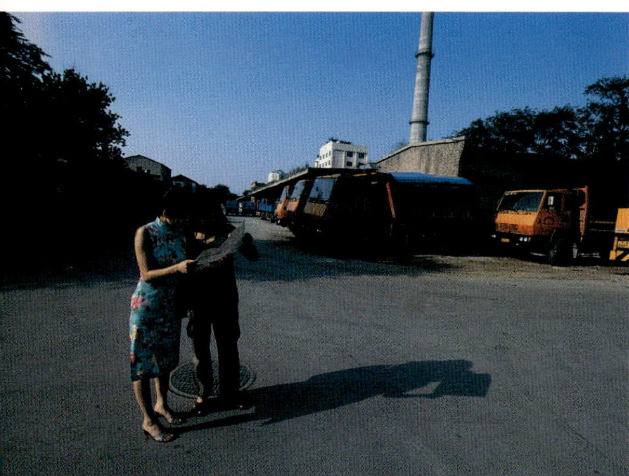

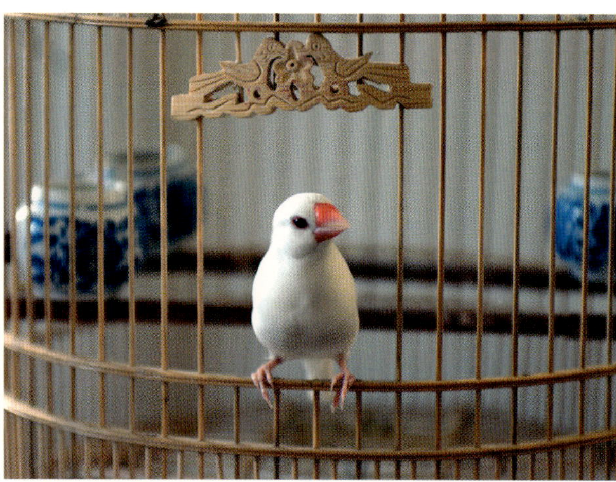

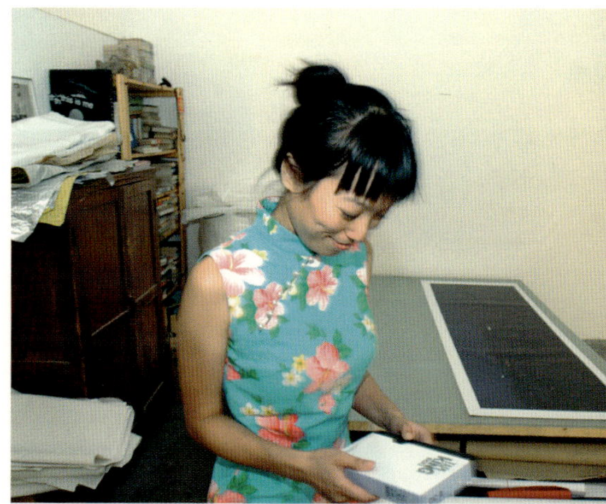

following year, her *Menstruation Bathroom* featured bloody sanitary towels. The performance artist Carolee Schneemann pulled a declaration of female independence from her vagina in *Interior Scroll* (1975). Liao Wen says, "In feminist works of art, it is usual to portray the female body in terms of an artistic concept that undermines the canon of beauty. It is no less usual for artists to use their own body as a medium to represent the truth of the female body." ¶ *Scroll* (October 1999) has gained a cult following in China. Like many other similar works it has hardly been shown at all—just like the legendary canvas hung by Daniel Buren at the Guggenheim in New York in 1971, taken down after twenty minutes after causing a storm of protest, but not before the artist managed to photograph it. As is always the case—and as has happened with *Scroll*—the scandal meant it was brought to the attention of a far wider audience than would otherwise have been the case. In fact, *Scroll* has only been exhibited once, at the *Fuck Off* exhibition at the Eastlink gallery in Shanghai in 2000. It was bought straight away. So, as Chen Lingyang says, "It was taken out of the circuit straight away." But not before the scandal got going. However, the story has a nice twist—the piece was bought by a courageous and visionary art lover, who just happened to be the Swiss ambassador to China. With friends in high places, Chen Lingyang was safe from censorship, and so her career began. ¶ She told me on several occasions that beyond the scandal and the success, *Scroll* is an important, even fundamental, work for her. For the first time, she was doing something that mattered to her. She had found a way to assert her freedom, her will to act. She insisted that whether other people reacted positively or negatively was unimportant. ¶ Even so, other people's reactions did have an impact on her. That is probably how Chen Lingyang number 2 came into being. We will come back to her later. ¶ Suffice it to say for the moment that until then, Chen Lingyang had always worked alone. Now, as she traveled further along her own path, she became progressively more aware of other people's points of view. She met art critics, visited exhibitions, and talked to people. Chen Lingyang number two was born of this apprenticeship, this process of discovering the outside world. ¶ The outside world had given her a cool reception. ¶ That did not stop her from carrying on as before. ¶ With her *Flowers*. ¶ Carrying on with the same theme. ¶ She comes up with a dialogue between Chen Lingyang number one and Chen Lingyang number two to tell us how it began. ¶ "After my diploma, in 1999, I found myself taking the back seat for a while. I didn't have a job, and wasn't often in touch with my friends. I would stay at home for days on end, for weeks and months. I withdrew completely from public life. In such circumstances, you become much more aware of your physiology and everything to do with your body—hunger, cold, and in particular, your period and the anxiety it causes. I observed the daily cycle from dawn to dusk, I watched the plants slowly growing and the seasons changing. But it wasn't just this experience that led me to create this piece. Something just triggered me to become obsessed with my period. I couldn't stop thinking about it. That's when I realized that it was a powerful subject that could say what I wanted to say." ¶ Maybe now is the time to mention that Chen Lingyang was born in a small village in southern China, and that there were no other artists in the family. Her mother was an English teacher. When asked what her father did, Chen is extremely cutting: "He worked in an office doing something completely uninteresting." ¶ Pushed a little further, she reluctantly reveals that he was the pastor of a Protestant church. Her sister played the organ and sang in the choir. Chen says, "I guess they had to teach me something as well; so they decided I should study drawing and painting." She continues, "I had a

ABOVE LEFT: CHEN LINGYANG IN SPACE 798 HELPING A LOST TOURIST. CENTER: THE BIRD IN ITS CAGE. CHEN LINGYANG LEAVES THE DOOR OF THE CAGE PERMANENTLY OPEN. FACING PAGE: TWO DIGITAL PHOTOGRAPHS IN A LIGHT BOX: *25:00 N°1* AND *25:00 N°2*, 2002.

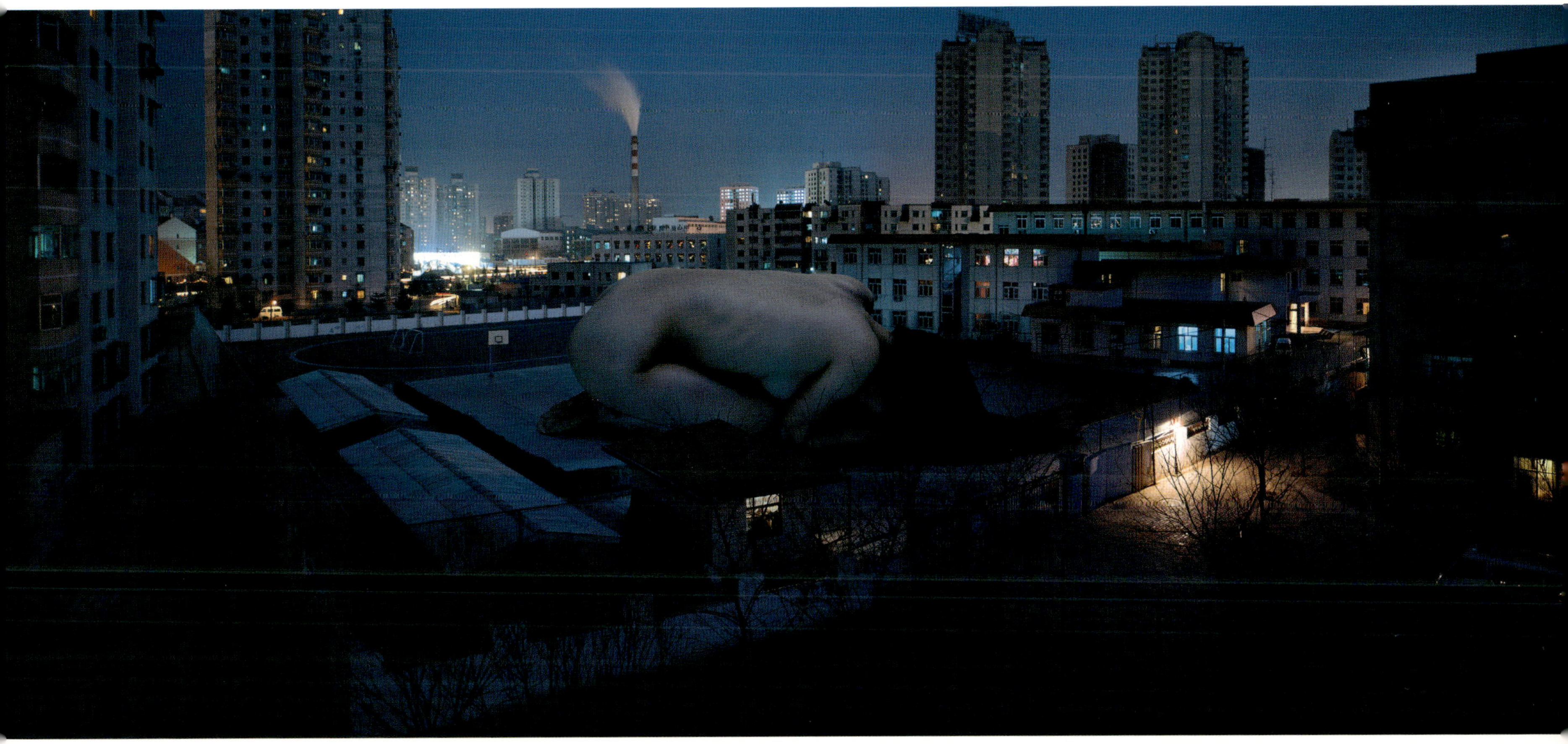

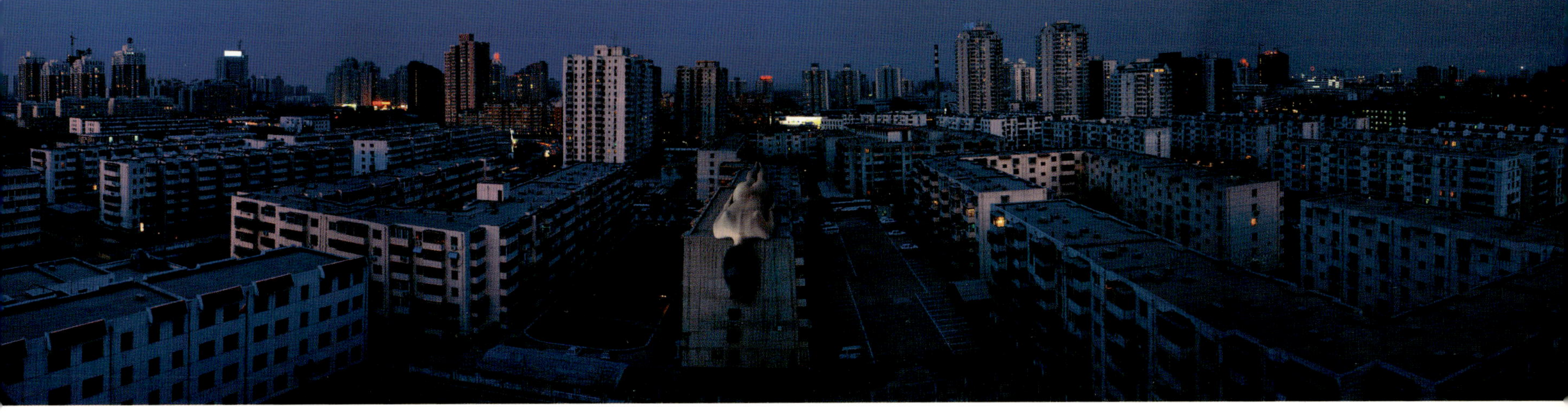

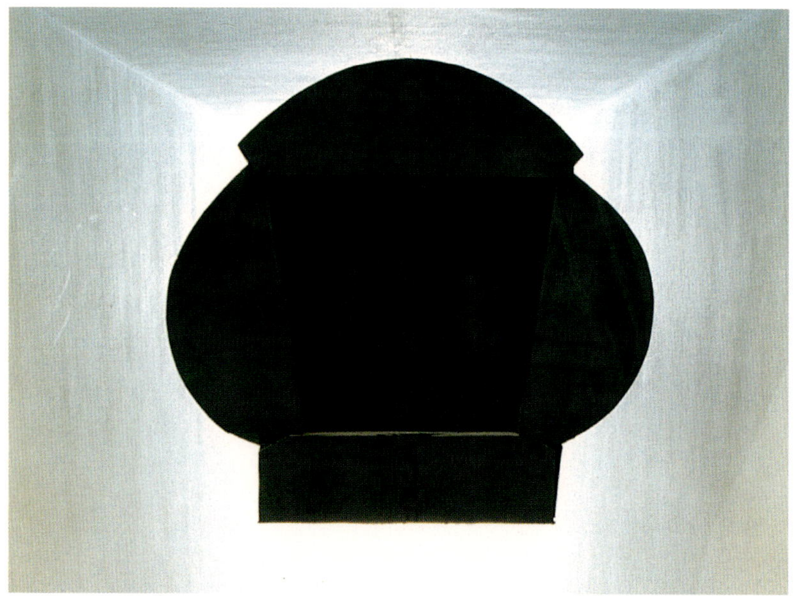

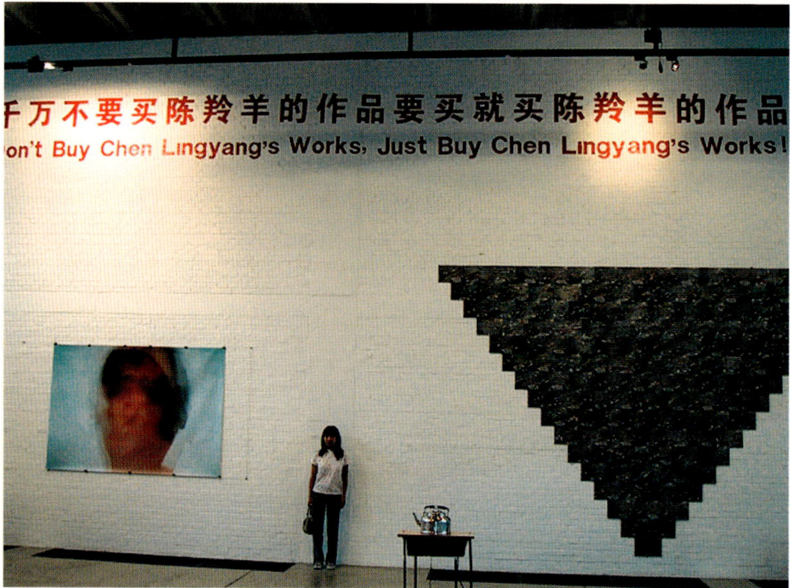

horrible childhood. I didn't have any friends, and I wasn't allowed out. I had to stay at home and draw all day." It might have put her off art forever. It didn't. "But if I chose to study art at college, it wasn't for the love of painting or drawing, but because I thought that was where I would have the most freedom." ¶ Once she had conquered her hard-won freedom, she was not about to let it go. ¶ She certainly needed it to impose her next work, *Twelve Flower Months*, which is another take on an ancient tradition, aestheticizing the female body the better to reveal what she has to say about herself, art, the cycle of the seasons, and nature, with a certain inherent violence. ¶ I first saw the series of photographs entitled *Twelve Flower Months* late in 2000 when I went to visit Chen Lingyang in her little studio—basically just a bedroom—where she handled her photographs with exquisite delicacy. I later came across the same series of photographs in large format (she printed five each of the large formats, and eight of the smaller ones) when I visited her a second time at the tail end of 2002, in her new studio, a huge loft in Xian Qiao Lu in the Chaoyang district of Beijing. ¶ There, surrounded by factories, most of which were closed and all with huge numbers painted on the outer walls, a thriving artists' colony was developing, just like in SoHo at the lower end of Manhattan in the 1960s. Chen Lingyang was joined there by other artists such as Chen Wenbo. ¶ A brand new gallery, Tokyo Beijing Art Prospect, opened in the center of this hive of artistic activity, followed by a trendy bar. Soon the neighborhood was full of artists renting vast studios measuring anywhere from ten thousand to thirty thousand square feet (one thousand to three thousand square meters), organizing exhibitions and happenings, setting up design studios. There was even a French restaurant. ¶ The neighborhood was buzzing. Artists and collectors were drawn there like bees to a flower, and it became the trendiest part of Beijing. The new class of Bobos (bourgeois bohemians) moved there en masse. ¶ *Twelve Flower Months*, as its name suggests, was produced over the space of a year, from November 1999 to December 2000. The photographs are of flowers, of course, budding and blossoming over the year, but also feature mirrors of various shapes and sizes reflecting the artist's vagina during her period. Each shot is framed by a decoupage inspired by the doors and windows of traditional Chinese garden architecture. ¶ The choice of flowers was dictated by the Chinese custom in which each month is symbolized by a particular blossom. The first month is represented by a narcissus. The second, a magnolia. The third, peach blossom. The fourth, a peony. The fifth, pomegranate blossom. The sixth, a lotus. The seventh, an orchid. The eighth, sweet-scented osmanthus. The ninth, a chrysanthemum. The tenth, a poinsettia. The eleventh, a camellia. The twelfth, plum blossom. ¶ Chen says, "This work is linked to the laws and rhythm of nature." She adds, "The reason why I chose not to use digital technology is that I really didn't want people to think that the photographs had been faked." ¶ That is the price of truth. ¶ What the mirrors show us are not the faces of beautiful women, but genitals stained with menstrual blood. Feminine truth, not feminine beauty. ¶ With great charm, not to mention a touch of perversity, Chen Lingyang used the ripe, seductive colors of the flowers, the pleasant shapes of the mirrors, windows, and doors to inscribe the blood-stained genitals in the image, using the very accoutrements of tradition and femininity to question both in a manner that is probing and yet humorous. ¶ First of all her menstrual blood on the roll of toilet paper, then the photographs of her own genitals stained with blood—

LEFT: *BEE HONEY*, AN INSTALLATION FOR THE EXHIBITION *POST-SENSE SENSIBILITY*, 1999. RIGHT: *DON'T BUY CHEN LINGYANG'S WORKS, JUST BUY CHEN LINGYANG'S WORKS!* FOR THE EXHIBITION *VISIBILITY*, HELD IN 2001 AT THE CAAW GALLERY.

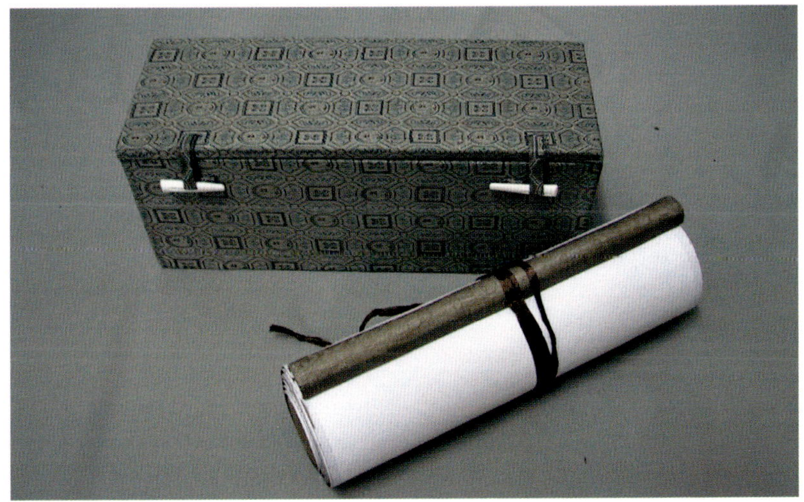

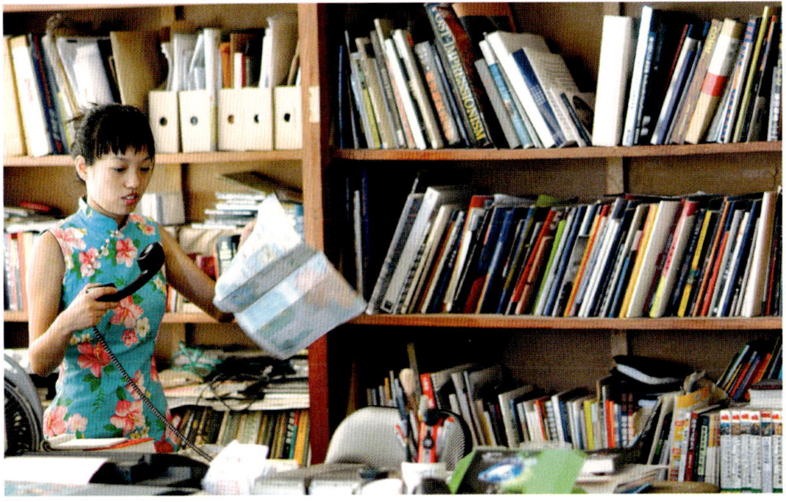

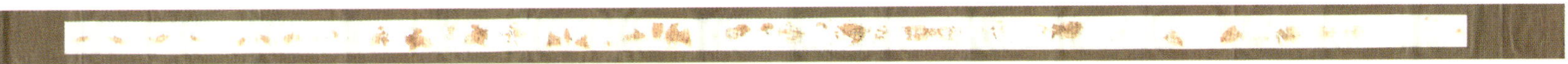

Chen Lingyang was in danger of typecasting herself as "oh, you know, the artist who paints with her own menstrual blood." ¶ So, in order to escape this trap, she created Chen Lingyang number two. ¶ She explained how the idea to split herself into Chen Lingyang number one and Chen Lingyang number two came to her in the aforementioned dialogue between the two Chen Lingyangs. ¶ "It's a long story. For a long time, I felt that there was a sort of fault line, a schism, developing inside me. For example, when I was working, I had the impression that my self was shut in a sort of back room. My relations with the world outside were cut off, and I entered into myself, totally and utterly. When I came out and got back in contact with the world outside, in particular when I talked about my work with other people, I had the feeling of being someone completely different from my other, working self. It was a most unsettling experience. I met Wang Xingwei at New Year in 2001, and he told me how he intended to change his name to Wang Xingwei number two. That way, he could still be the same person, doing the same things, but he would no longer be responsible for what Wang Xingwei did before he became Wang Xingwei number two. To begin with, I found the idea great fun. And after that, we discovered the photographs of Andy Warhol dressed as a woman." ¶ She then tells us how one day, when she was visiting her parents, she saw herself acting the role they expected from her, and how, within the space of a few seconds, she took on an entirely different role when she had to call someone in Beijing. "That's when I decided to begin working on a new series, with one person split into two, working on two oeuvres in two different directions. That's how I had the idea of creating Chen Lingyang number two. Chen Lingyang number two and Wang Xingwei number two look the same as their respective number ones on the surface, but are in fact very different. It's a kind of joke. Greetings to Wang Xingwei." ¶ OK, but in artistic terms, what is the work of the original Chen, and what is the work of the alter ego? She shows me a magnificent, large-format nighttime photograph entitled *25:00 no. 1*, spread on the floor. It shows a large nude huddled on a landscape of roofs. The theme of menstruation is entirely absent. So is this a work by Chen Lingyang number two? "No. Chen Lingyang number one," announces Chen Lingyang. "Because it contains a nude?" "Yeah, that's right" she begins, but then changes tack. "No, only joking. That's not how I decide. Chen Lingyang number one is much more introverted, while Chen Lingyang number two is much more outward looking, open. Chen Lingyang number two is more fun." ¶ She pauses for a second, bursts out laughing, and says, "But in terms of sexuality, Chen Lingyang numbers one, two, three, four, five, and six are all very keen!" ¶ My next question is, "How many of you are there?" ¶ She answers straight away: "Ninety-eight". ¶ My interpreter laughs, and explains, "Why ninety-eight? Because it consists of two beneficial numbers, nine and eight. It also means 'bar,' where you drink alcohol. She chose it for a reason." ¶ That's Chen Lingyang for you. ¶ She doesn't think life in China is much fun. There is just too much economic pressure, and the people have such a utilitarian vision of life. They want to be fit and healthy. They think too much. "I want to give the Chinese a taste of the lighter side of life." ¶ She continues, telling us what she is working on at the moment. It is a sort of installation where all the elements would be constantly being changed and constantly shifted from place to place—an installation where it would be impossible to tell what is part of the work and what isn't, an exhibition that wouldn't be an exhibition in the usual, formal sense of the word. ¶

SCROLL, 1999, IS A TWENTY-FOOT-LONG LANDSCAPE PAINTING USING CHEN LINGYANG'S MENSTRUAL BLOOD. IN HER STUDIO, THE ARTIST UNROLLS A MAP TO GIVE DIRECTIONS TO VISITING FRIENDS.

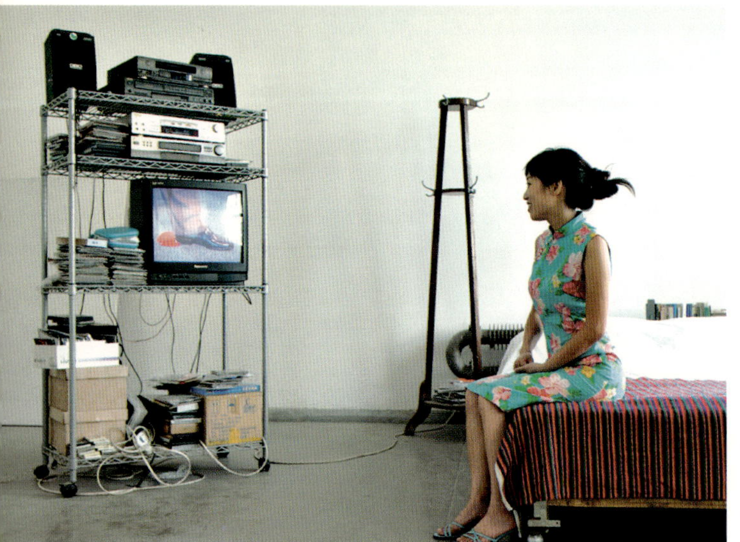

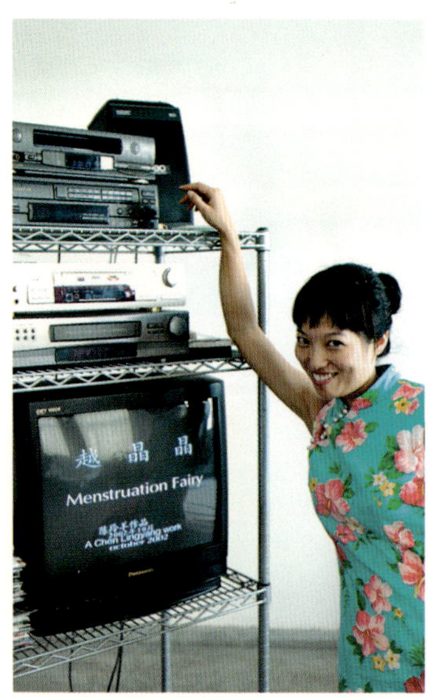

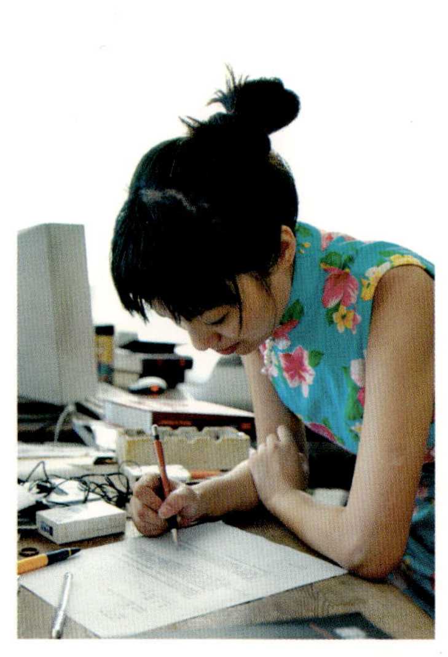

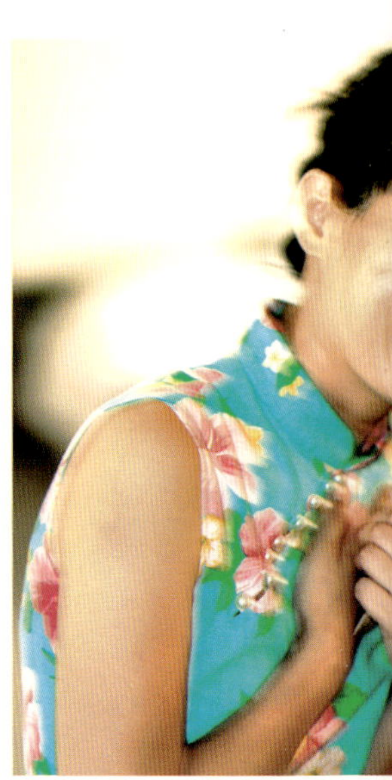

It requires a great deal of organization. I can already tell that with three months to go, she is working out her timetable down to the last minute, organizing the constant changing of the pieces of furniture by delivery men, and tracing out their movements so that they don't bump into each other. "We won't just be changing bits and pieces, bric-a-brac, but large pieces of furniture, really huge and heavy things. I want the place to be transformed totally, to be changing non-stop. Deliverymen will come every ten minutes. It's fiendishly complicated to organize. It's proving a huge amount of work, but it's really exciting! It's like directing a play. The funniest thing is that I won't even be there." ¶ At the unofficial *Twins* exhibition, organized during the 2002 Biennial in Shanghai, the installation was constantly changing. Chen hired assistants to push around columns mounted on sets of castors. ¶ Today in China, information can circulate like nowhere else on the planet. Ideas come and go, are transformed, but whom do they belong to? Nobody knows. ¶ And yet to this day, none of Chen Lingyang's works have been acquired by a Chinese buyer. Only foreign art lovers have purchased a few of her works, bringing her a modest income. ¶ She shows me another photograph, this time of a large nude mysteriously floating over a cityscape. The nude body is beautiful, velvety gray, against a long blue backdrop scattered with pinpoints of light. The titles *25:00 no. 1* and *25:00 no. 2* are explained by a short accompanying text: "Actually, this 'Giantess' is not very brave, which is why she can only become so large at twenty-five hundred hours, as announced in the titles. Often, the domains of reality and of maleness get mixed up in my head. It comes from the outside, and is extremely powerful. Faced with this, I often feel rather lackluster, I don't know what to do, I feel weak. Yet for as long as I live, I won't be able to escape for a single day. So every day I hope there will be a twenty-fifth hour, when I can grow as big as I want and do whatever I want." ¶ I went back to visit Chen Lingyang in August 2003. Nothing had changed much. Oh yes—there was a large bed at the back of the studio, and a bird in a cage whose door she leaves open. I was disappointed not to see many new works. Chen Lingyang burst out laughing when I mentioned this. Don't worry, she told me, she has been working hard, but on installations. ¶ We go for a stroll and stop for coffee at the At Café, just next to her studio. Coffee is a real luxury here—it costs twice as much as any other drink. ¶ The walls are still painted with slogans by Chairman Mao encouraging the workers to step up their rate of production and devote themselves body and soul to the revolution. Scarcely anyone glances at them. ¶ Chen Lingyang explains to me what her next project is: another installation. She plans to drill a hole in the wall between her studio and the café, and set up a video camera and TV monitor to broadcast scenes of herself at work in her studio live in the café. ¶ She laughs again, tickled by the idea. ¶ That's Chen Lingyang for you.

ABOVE: *MENSTRUATION FEAST*, 2002, IS A VIDEO IMBIBED IN BLOOD, SHOWN AS PART OF AN INSTALLATION AT THE GUANGZHOU TRIENNIAL, 2003. FACING PAGE: *TWELVE FLOWER MONTHS*, 1999–2000, PHOTOGRAPHS OF CHEN LINGYANG'S MENSTRUAL FLOW COMBINED WITH THE FLOWERS ASSOCIATED WITH EACH MONTH OF THE CHINESE CALENDAR.

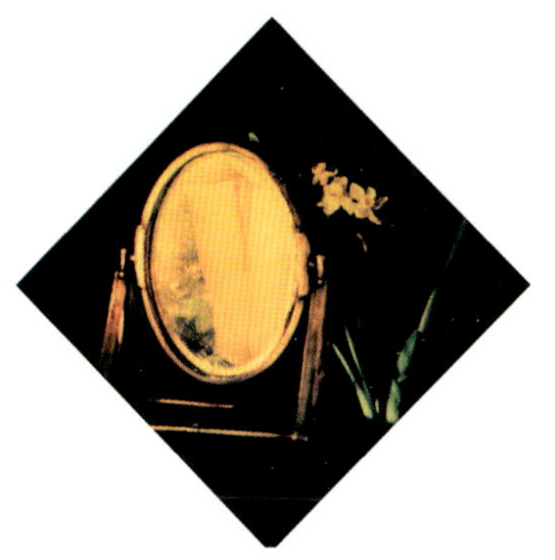
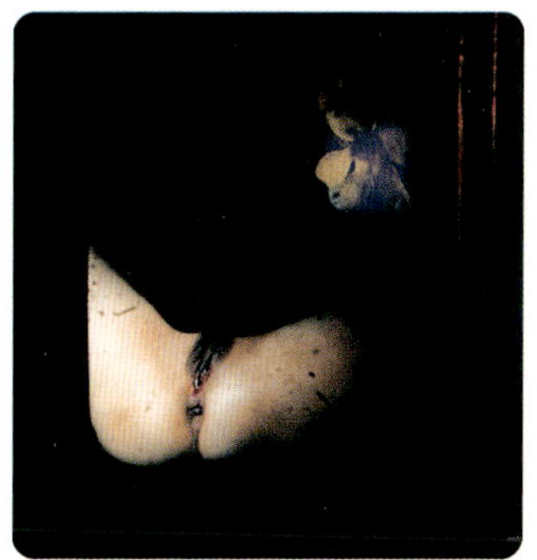
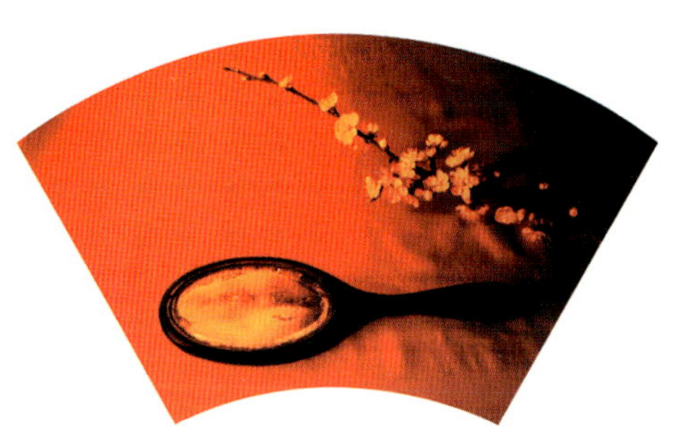
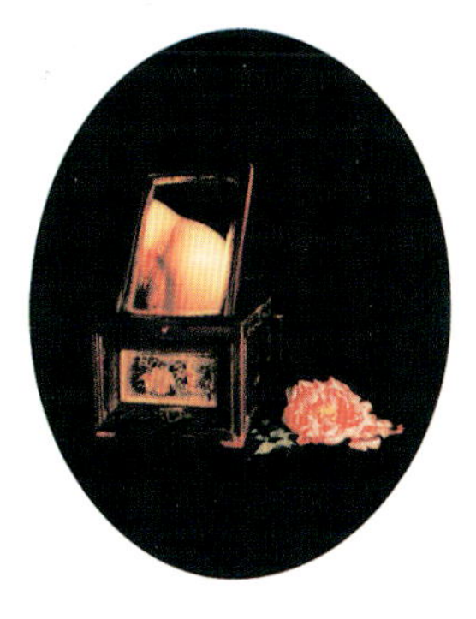
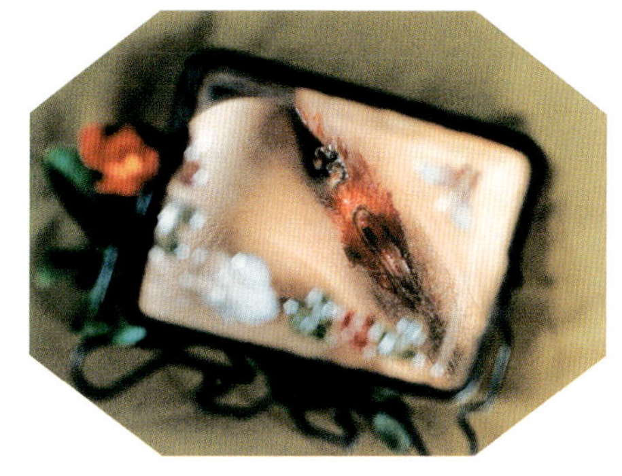
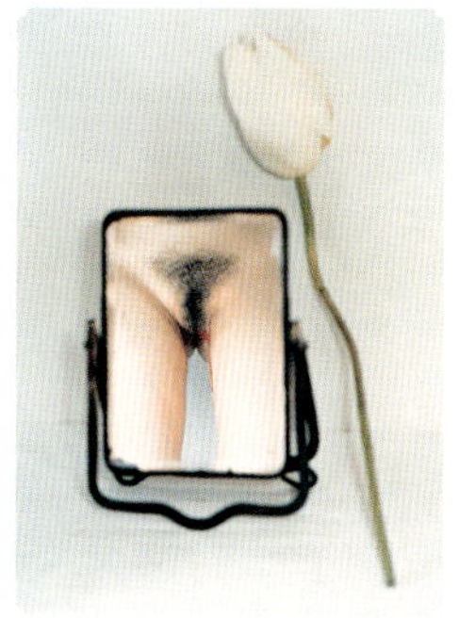
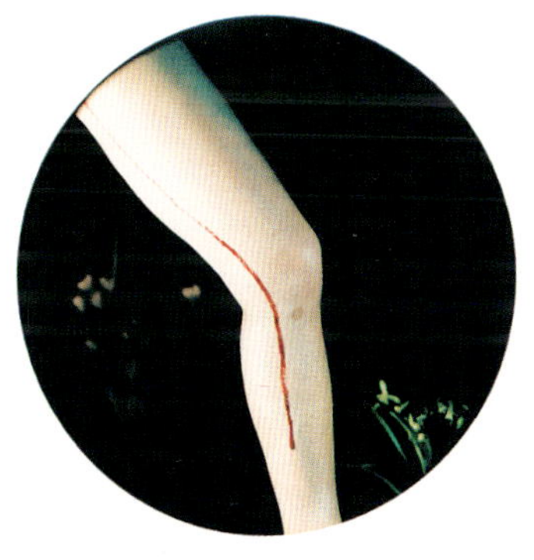
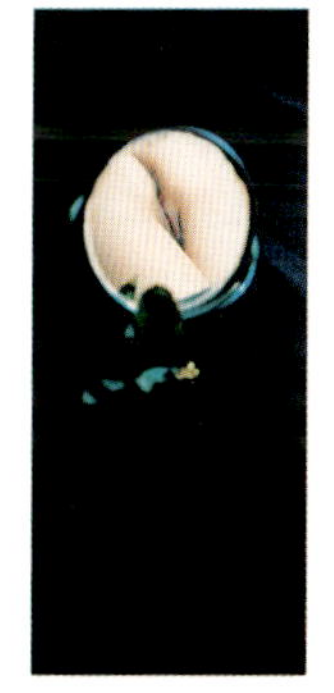
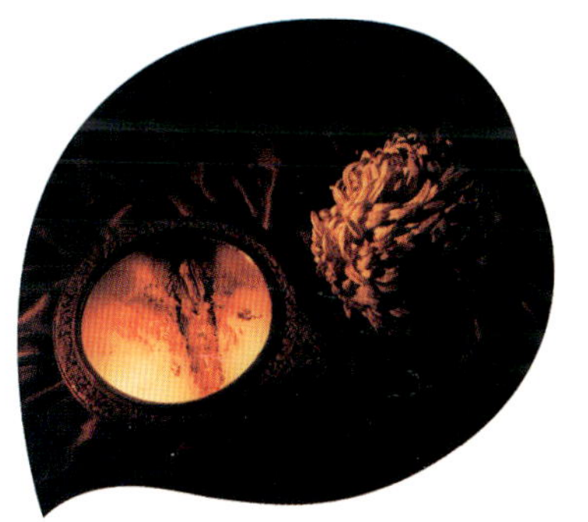
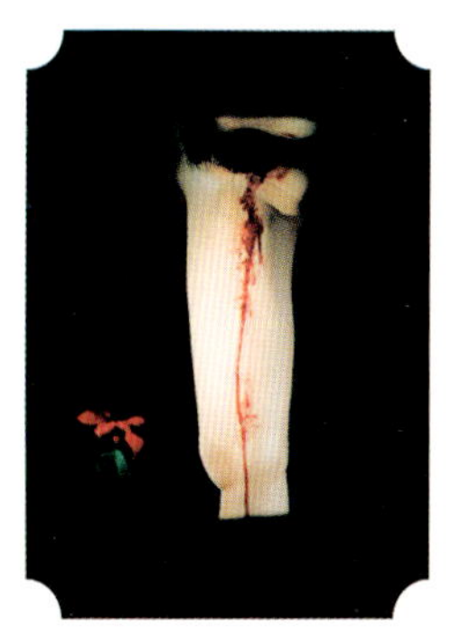
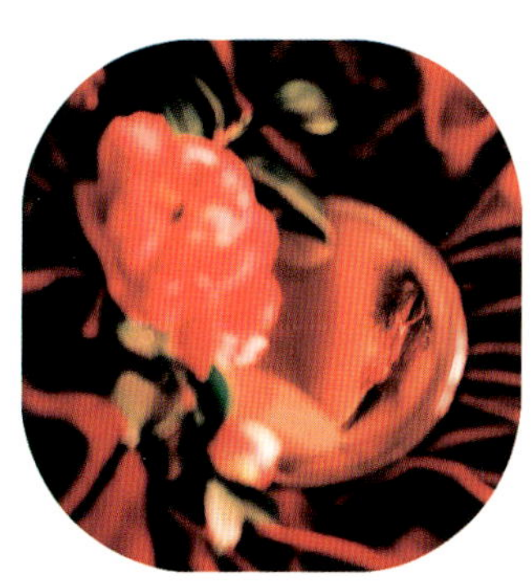
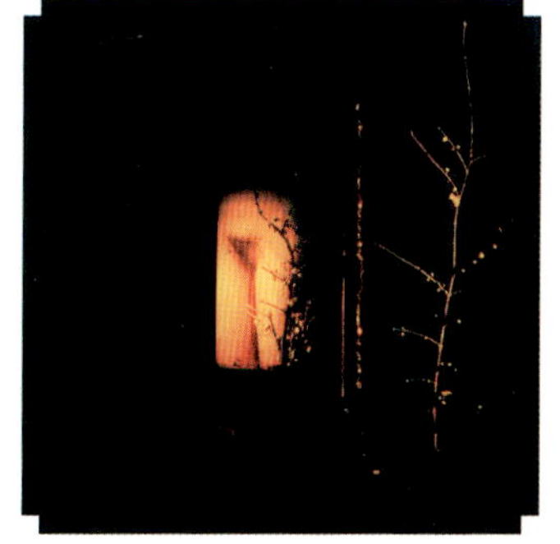

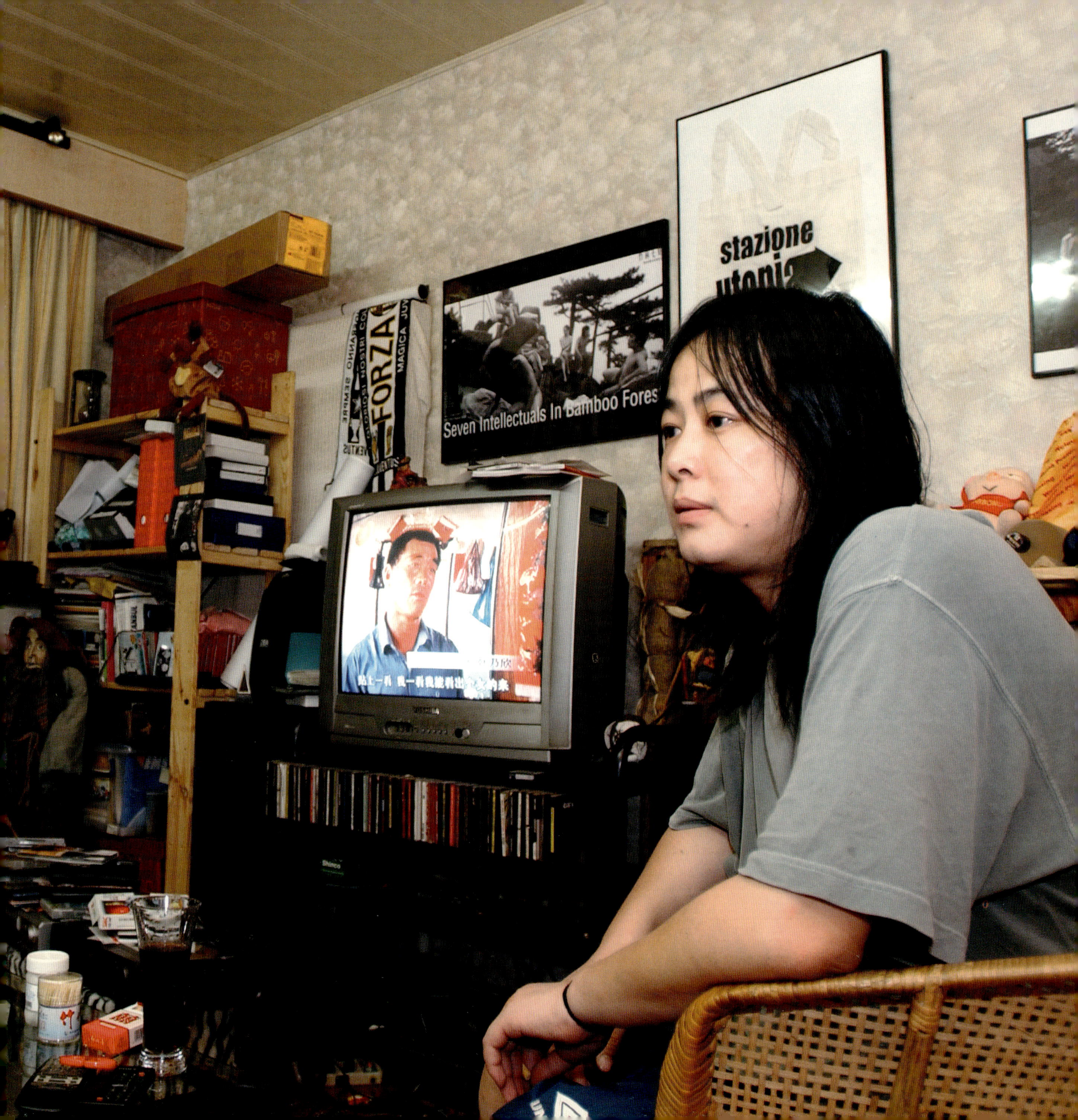
stazione
Seven Intellectuals In Bamboo Fores
FORZA

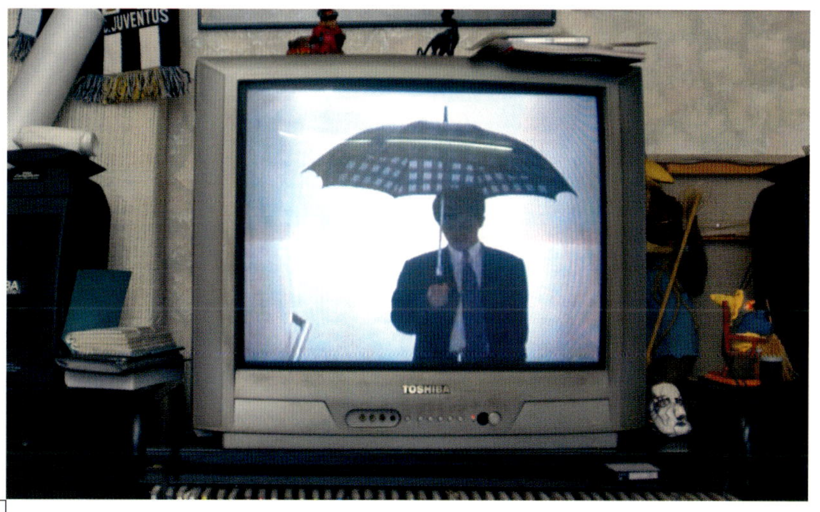

YANG FUDONG

He jumps in surprise when you introduce yourself. He is a sensitive creature, with pale, loose skin and an untidy ponytail that gives him a very modern look. ¶ His works are shot in video or 35-mm film, often in black and white, and show a world that did not suffer under Chairman Mao and the Cultural Revolution, a world focused on typical teenage angst, in China and elsewhere. ¶ Yang Fudong is just as "Chinese" as artists of the older generation, but he is less marked by geographical, political, social, and cultural roots. More at ease on the international scene. ¶ He has been invited all over the world since his superb black-and-white film *An Estranged Paradise* got him noticed at the last Documenta festival in Kassel, Germany. ¶ When I asked him where he comes from, Yang Fudong replied, "Shanghai." Automatically. Without thinking. Maybe he misunderstood, or answered too quickly. Maybe he was thinking of something else. Maybe he just didn't care. ¶ In fact, he comes from Beijing. He says he maintains a strong bond with his family and the city where he was born, grew up, and feels like a stranger in Shanghai, where he now lives. ¶ What did his father do? He was a soldier. "An infantryman," he says. ¶ As a child, all he was interested in was soccer. An injury put an end to his playing. What else could he do to pass the time? He liked reading comics, the sort printed in landscape format, with one large picture per page with text boxes underneath. Like many other children (and artists), he became fascinated by the adventures and battle scenes in the *History of the Three Kingdoms*. ¶ That is how he came to be interested in painting and drawing. ¶ Yang Fudong tells me it was quite by chance that he moved from Beijing to Hangzhou, two hours north of Shanghai by train. It does not sound like chance played much of a part in the decision: at the time, he was studying at a department of the Central Institute for the Fine Arts in Beijing, when for various reasons, four of his friends from the same class decided to transfer to Hangzhou. The Hangzhou Institute for the Fine Arts is generally considered the second best in all of China in terms of its academic reputation, and the best in terms of dynamism and its readiness to embrace new ideas. "All the artists of the new wave and all the most important movements of the 1980s started off there," says Yang Fudong. ¶ He started at the Hangzhou Institute for the Fine Arts in 1991. He remained there for four years, which gave him ample time to become aware that interest in contemporary art and creative freedom were far greater than in Beijing. It was probably the most forward-looking institute in all of China at the time. ¶ And what about Shanghai, where he told me he came from? Only two hours away by train. ¶ Of course, he went to Shanghai regularly to plunge into its dynamic art scene, which I personally first had the opportunity to discover in 1996, when the city hosted the first Contemporary Art Biennial. The city was gutted to make room for the first enormous skyscrapers and overhead freeways stacked in several layers. However, Yang Fudong remained unmoved by the incredible architectural, urban, economic, and financial buzz. ¶ From 1991 to 1995, although the Hangzhou institute was the most open to innovative techniques and media in all China, Yang Fudong chose to study oil painting. Gradually, he became more interested in photography and video, which seemed to offer a range of possibilities. ¶ He left the institute in 1995. He spent his time studying film techniques until he felt he was ready to begin his first work in 2001. ¶ He offers a few banal reasons for his choice of film as a medium: "I felt that film was more powerful than painting," or "When you show a film in a museum, people say it's artistic, but if you show it in a cinema, then suddenly, it's commercial." OK, I see. ¶ His first work—or to be more precise, his first attempt—was a black-and-white work shot in 35-mm film in 1997. It was called *An Estranged Paradise* and was seventy minutes long. He "finished" the images in March 1997, but had no soundtrack—and had run out of money. He was only able to complete the project in 2002, when he was invited to take part in the Documenta festival in Kassel. ¶ The film is a dreamlike account of a young intellectual who moves to Hangzhou, where he meets a girl. Everything looks rosy: the girl loves him, but he begins to wonder whether he is not suffering from some illness. He goes to the hospital time and time again, only to be told that there is nothing wrong. At the end,

FACING PAGE: YANG FUDONG IN THE CHAOS OF HIS SMALL APARTMENT, WHICH HE ALSO USES AS A STUDIO. ABOVE: THE VIDEO *CITY LIGHT*, 2000, ON A TV SCREEN IN YANG FUDONG'S APARTMENT.

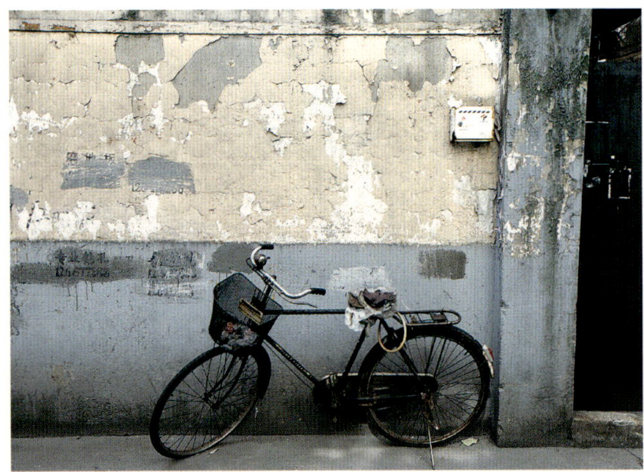

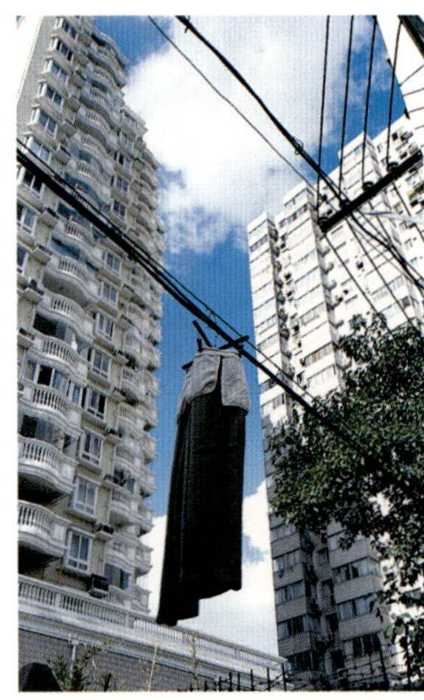

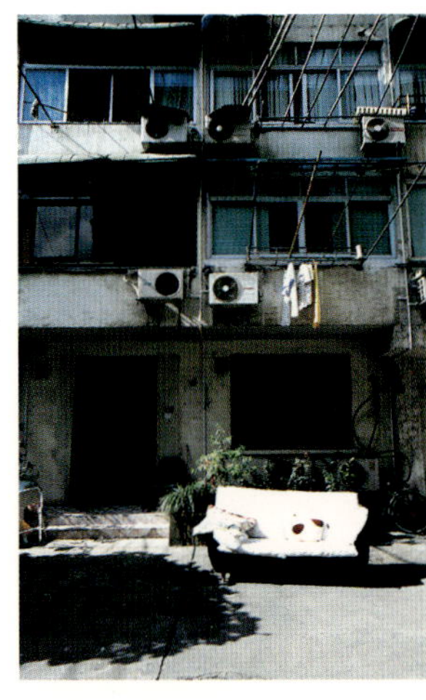

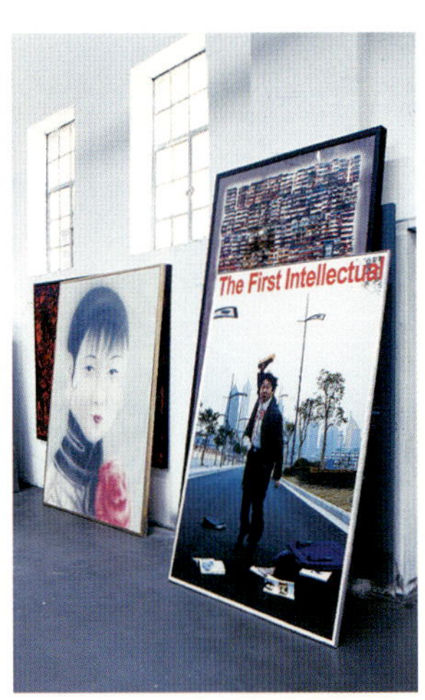

he is going to "try and live." ¶ Yang Fudong explains, "I chose to set the film at the end of winter and early spring, when it rains without stopping for three weeks, because it suited the psychological profile of the character wondering whether he is ill or not." ¶ This *Confession of a Child of the Century* is filmed in short, fragmentary sequences that are not linked by any apparent thread. "Like when you write your diary," the artist explains. Like when you let your pen run away with you. So, no scenario, just a basic framework used as a starting place for improvisations with his fellow students. ¶ The film was a great success in Kassel. Yang Fudong was in the spotlight—although he was far from a complete newcomer to the international art scene. ¶ He had his first success in 1999 at the Hanover Film Festival—another German event. ¶ After that, things moved very quickly. In 2000, he was showing at *Exit* in London and *Our Chinese Friends* in Weimar (again in Germany). In 2001, he was invited to *Asian Party* at the Arco in Madrid and *Living in Time: Contemporary Artists from China* at the prestigious museum Hamburger Bahnhof in Berlin. He also took part in the ultrafashionable Istanbul Biennial, the Yokohama Triennial, and the first Valencia Biennial in the same year, and in 2002, he was at the fourth Video Marathon in New York and Documenta—the crowning glory of his career so far. ¶ When people in Europe discuss the up-and-coming generation of contemporary Chinese artists, chances are they mean Yang Fudong. This is probably due to the subtle qualities of his work, but maybe because the critics who count scarcely glance beyond Istanbul and Kassel. ¶ And so Yang Fudong had success thrust upon him. In February and March 2003, he was invited to the Musée d'Art Moderne in Paris, where he became entangled in the web of an architect playing at being a set designer, or a set designer who took himself for an artist. The upshot was that everybody thought that Yang Fudong and Wang Jian Wei's films and videos were all part of an installation. To say Yang Fudong's work did not come out of it well is putting it mildly. ¶ Two videos were on show, surrounded by an unbelievable setup, supposedly representing a number of cameras. The first film, *Honey*, was a parody of spy films from the 1920s and 1930s. The other, *Liu Lan*, was a dreamlike tale of a beautiful young woman living by a lake and a young student dressed in white, who might be a real figure or a figment of the girl's imagination. ¶ These could not be more different from the films he showed me back in his cluttered little apartment high in an anonymous high-rise next to a shop that boasts "X stores, open 24 hours a day." He showed me *City Lights* (2000), *Backyard: Hey! Sun is Rising* (2000), and the series of photographs *Don't Worry, It Will Be Better* and *The First Intellectual*. ¶ In *Backyard: Hey! Sun is Rising*, four young people wearing a sort of uniform are filmed from a low angle or right up close, as if with a hidden camera. They run around absurdly, lined up in a row, first right, then left, around Shanghai. They hold swords as if they were fighting a war. But what war? Against whom? The enemy is nowhere to be seen. Is it a dream of war? A fantasy? Regret for China's glorious past? Fear of the Cultural Revolution, or another episode from the recent past? ¶ There is no way of telling. Yang Fudong's work is characterized by a certain ambiguity, which here extends to the body, to the gender of the soldiers and to their virile friendship. ¶ The same year, he produced *The First Intellectual*, a triptych of photographs that had a strong impact on people in China. It probes situations, feelings, notions, and facts that are all equally difficult to pin down, all equally ambiguous. We see a young man in a suit, neatly dressed but with his tie back to front, and his face and clothes covered in blood. He is standing facing us in the middle of a broad Shanghai avenue that is completely empty. He looks haggard rather than angry,

ABOVE: LEFT: YANG FUDONG'S NEIGHBORHOOD. RIGHT: THE WORK OF ART SHOWN ON THE FACING PAGE IN THE SHANGHART GALLERY, WAITING TO BE HUNG. FACING PAGE: TWO PARTS OF YANG FUDONG'S BEST-KNOWN PHOTOGRAPHIC TRIPTYCH, *THE FIRST INTELLECTUAL*, 2000.

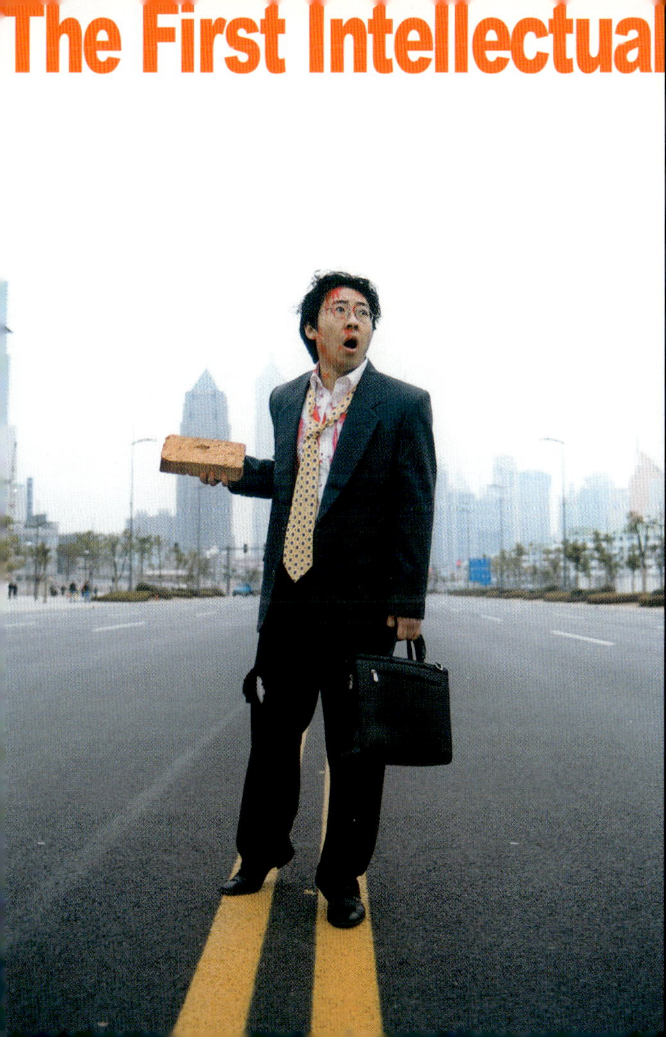

The First Intellectual

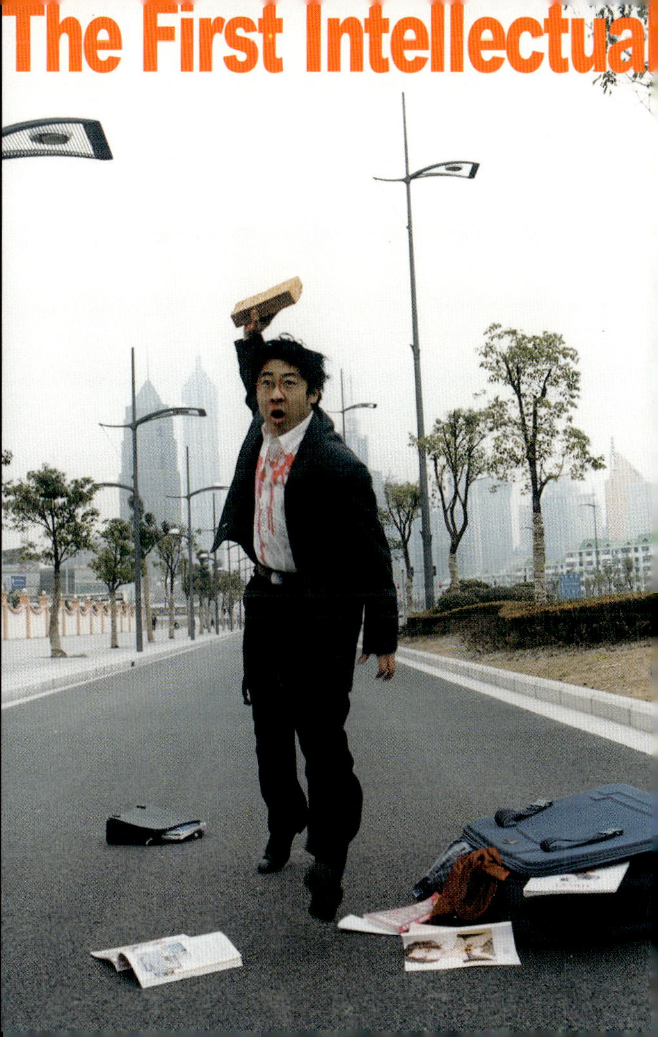

The First Intellectual

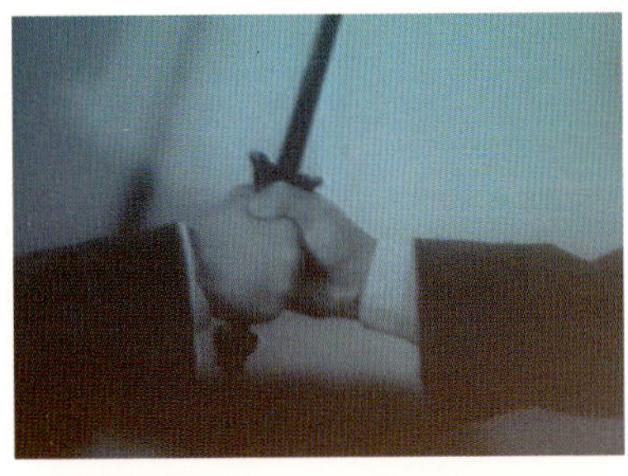
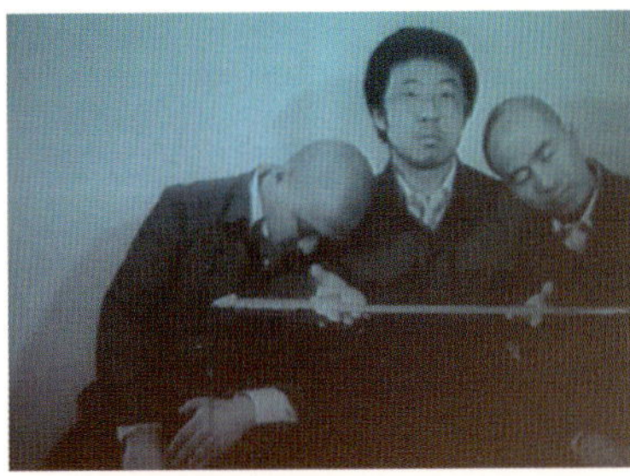
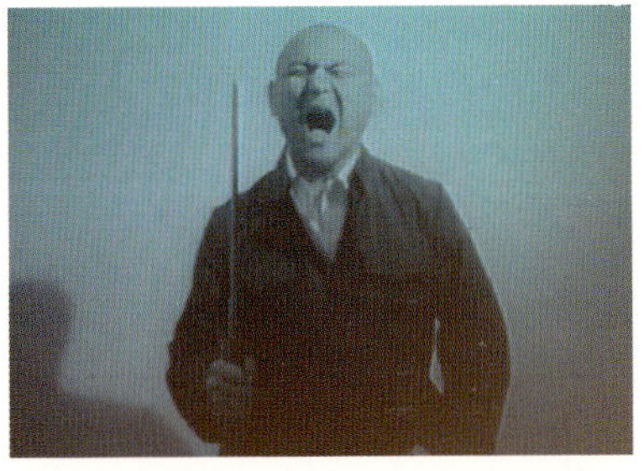
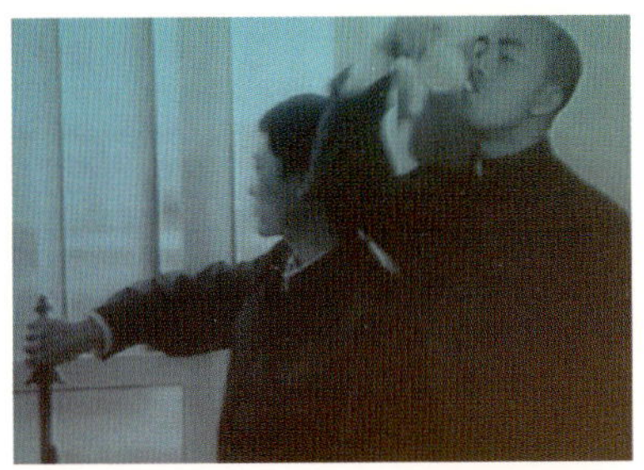
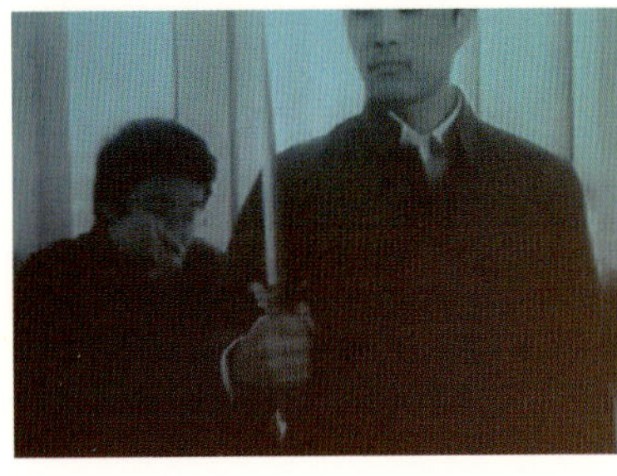
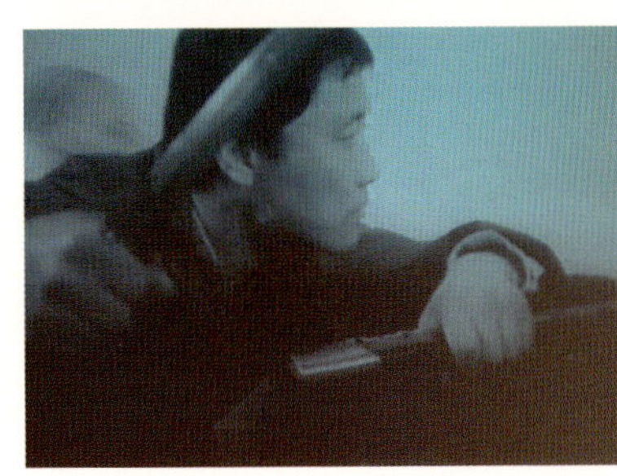
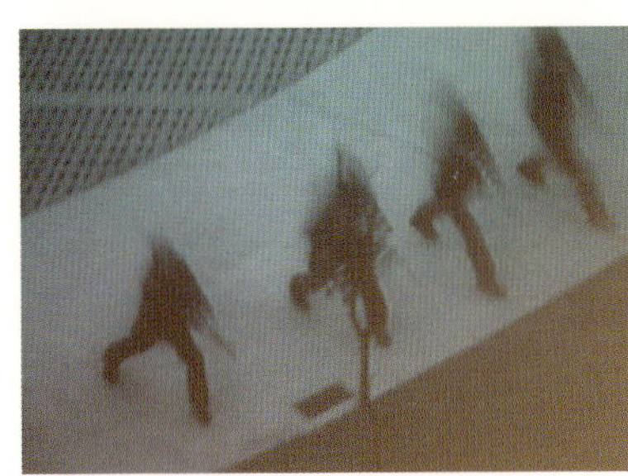
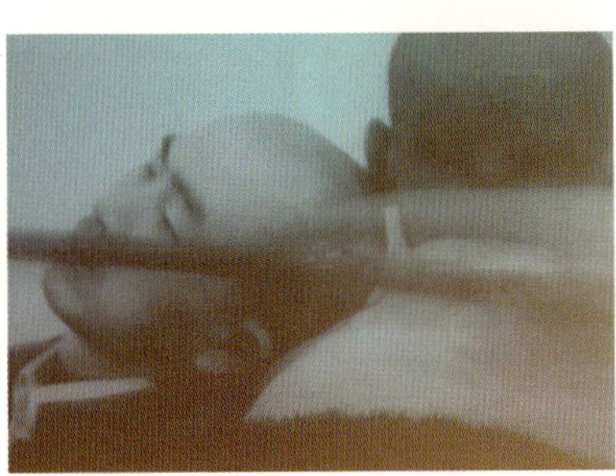

and is clutching a brick in one hand. Is he about to throw it back at his attacker? But the broad avenue is empty. Who is there to attack? Is there an attacker? Was it a real attack, or just a dream? The young man can only trust in the proof his own injuries. But where have they come from? What caused them? He stands there, powerless, faced with a frustrating situation that leaves him unable to react. ¶ When I asked him to explain this ambiguous work, Yang Fudong did not give me a direct answer. He said, "We are all a little bit like him. We want to do great things, but we can't manage to bring them to fruition." He then explains that what he tries to show in general is how young people, when they leave university, want to throw themselves headlong into life and put their grand designs into practice, only to discover that the gap between their ideals and society is vast. "It's not at all what they imagined," he says. ¶ In another series of photographs, *Don't Worry, It Will Be Better*, dating from 2000—a fabulous year for the young artist—he shows a number of well-dressed young bobos (bourgeois bohemians) dancing as they act out the comedy of love and desire. All of these young men and women who look like fashion plates are gazing out to a space beyond the photograph—elsewhere—just as, until recently, people looked with hope to the future. But the future in store for these young people is just as unreal and stereotyped as they are themselves, just as elusive, even if it comes dressed up in the colors of vibrant, international modernity. Their lives, their feelings, and the meaning of both are all a blur. ¶ Yang Fudong has been censured for his propensity for dreaming and fleeing reality. However, this could not be further from the truth—as *City Light* shows. He shot this film in 2000, his annus mirabilis. It features young urban professionals dressed as on TV, all carrying umbrellas and guns, real or pretend, living completely disconnected from reality and other people, locked into the dreams that they turn to for shelter. ¶ Yang Fudong has no time for indulgence or leniency. If these young people are constructing their own artificial paradise, it is because they feel threatened by the realities of social, cultural, and even erotic life. They prefer to invent a life that is a closer match for their needs. ¶ So can we call Yang Fudong a critic of society? Not exactly. His shimmering art, which plays on the theme of frustration, also makes the effort to break free from the stranglehold of easy cynicism and snap judgments. He shows today's society as it is, focusing on the subtle break in continuity to make people stop and think by creating the necessary distance. ¶ *Jasmine* (2002) is the synthesis of his art and his thinking. It is a superb video shown on three screens, and is easily one of his best works. A handsome young man and a beautiful young woman, drunk on love, climb onto the roof of their house to be closer to the sky. What could be more romantic, more lyrical, more abandoned? Yet the two young people talk in Harlequin Romance clichés or as if reading their words from a karaoke screen, gazing straight ahead, toward the viewer, aware that they are on show. ¶ This is the quintessential Yang Fudong—a way of discussing the notion of ideals, a lost or stolen paradise, by introducing an unexpected element into the form or the story—or both. There is always an element of alienation, a hiatus that upsets the balance and creates a fault line in the work. ¶ Finally, one last thought. I cannot recall where or when Yang Fudong said this to me, whether in Paris or Shanghai, in 2002 or 2003, but I noted it on a piece of paper, probably before or after an interview when the microphone was switched off. "Art is absolutely not my profession, but it has become an integral part of my life. Like going to bed every night and dreaming. For me, art is something that is always happening." ¶ He probably gave me a pale, watery smile. Then left, uncertain, as always. ¶ Without once looking back.

BACKYARD, HEY! SUN IS RISING, A WORK DATING FROM 2000, SHOWS FOUR YOUNG MEN RUNNING AROUND AIMLESSLY AS IF THEY ARE ON A BATTLEFIELD. BUT WHO ARE THEY FIGHTING? NOBODY KNOWS.

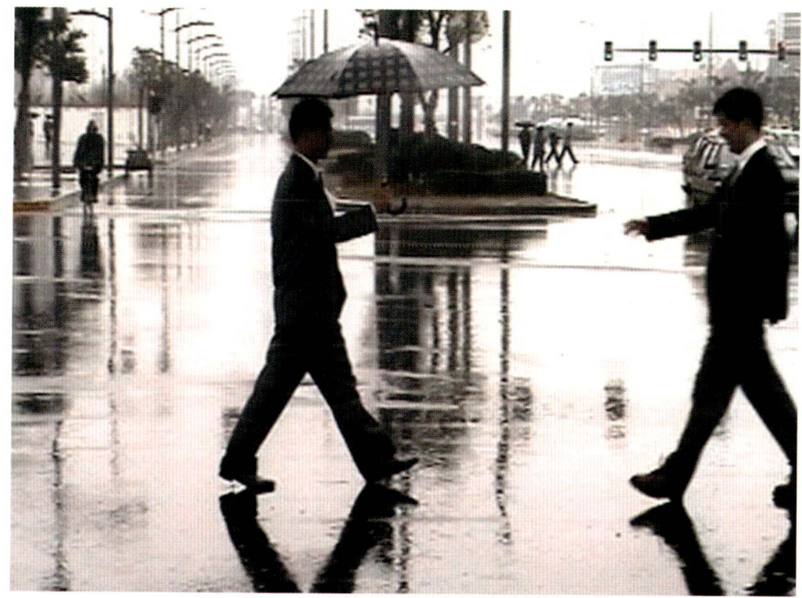

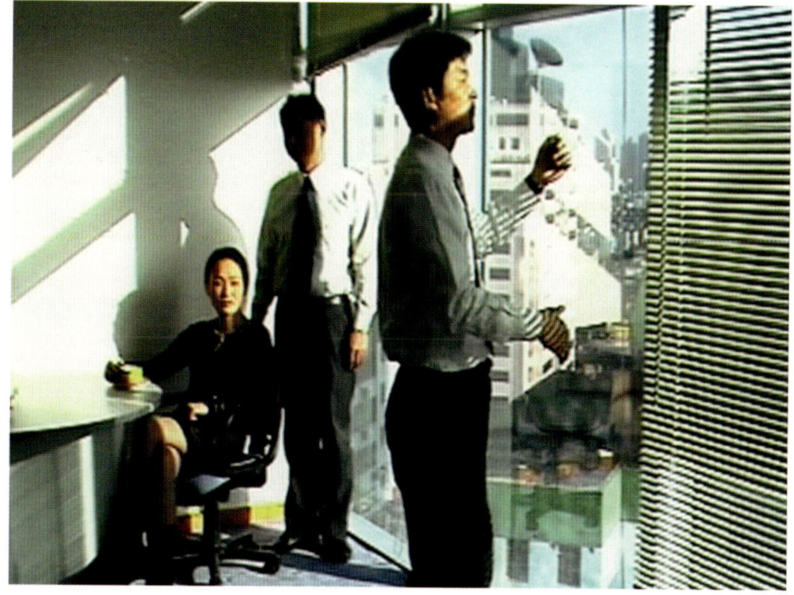

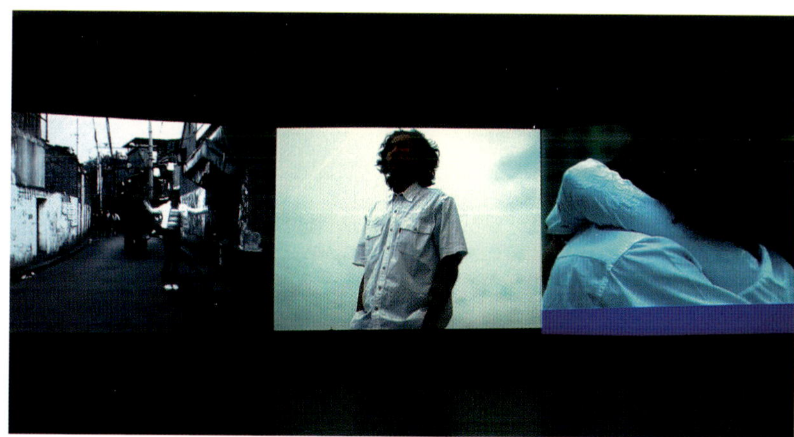

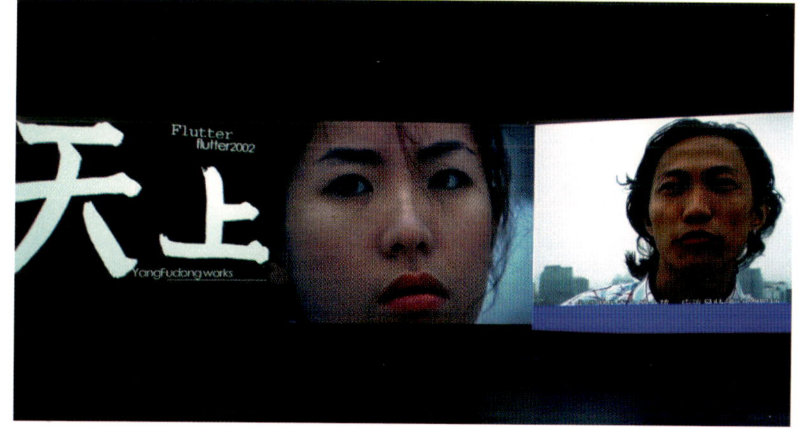

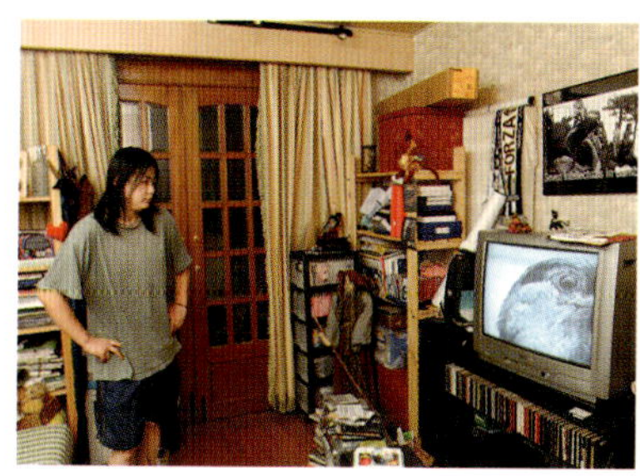

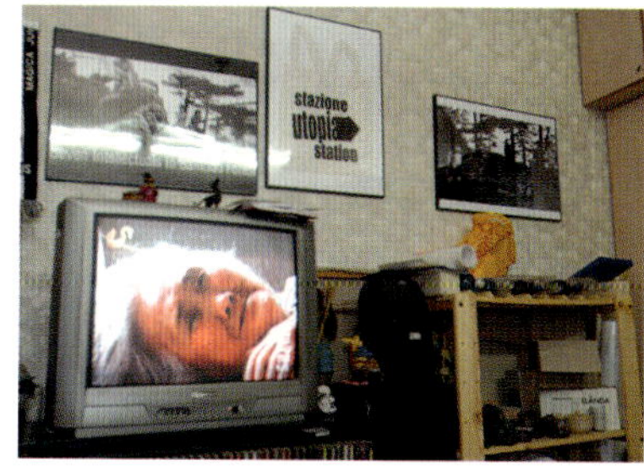

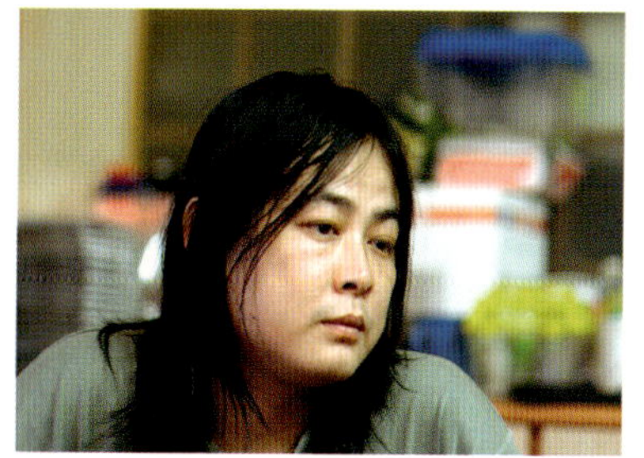

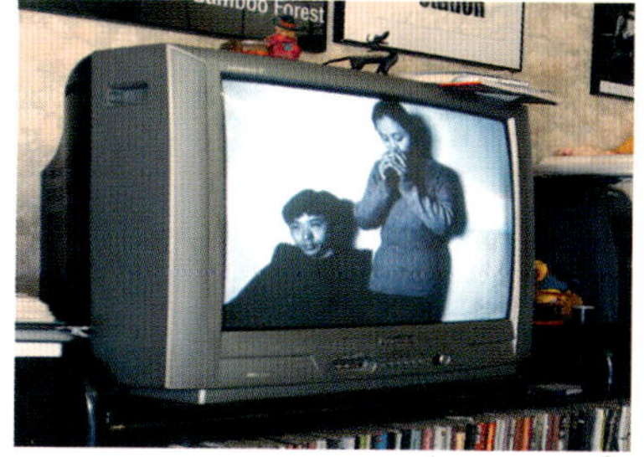

TOP: THE VIDEO *CITY LIGHTS*, 2000. CENTER: *JASMINE*, 2002, SHOWN ACROSS THREE SCREENS AT THE FOURTH SHANGHAI BIENNIAL. BOTTOM: *AN ESTRANGED PARADISE*, 2001, THE BLACK-AND-WHITE FILM THAT MADE YANG FUDONG A STAR AT THE DOCUMENTA FESTIVAL IN KASSEL.

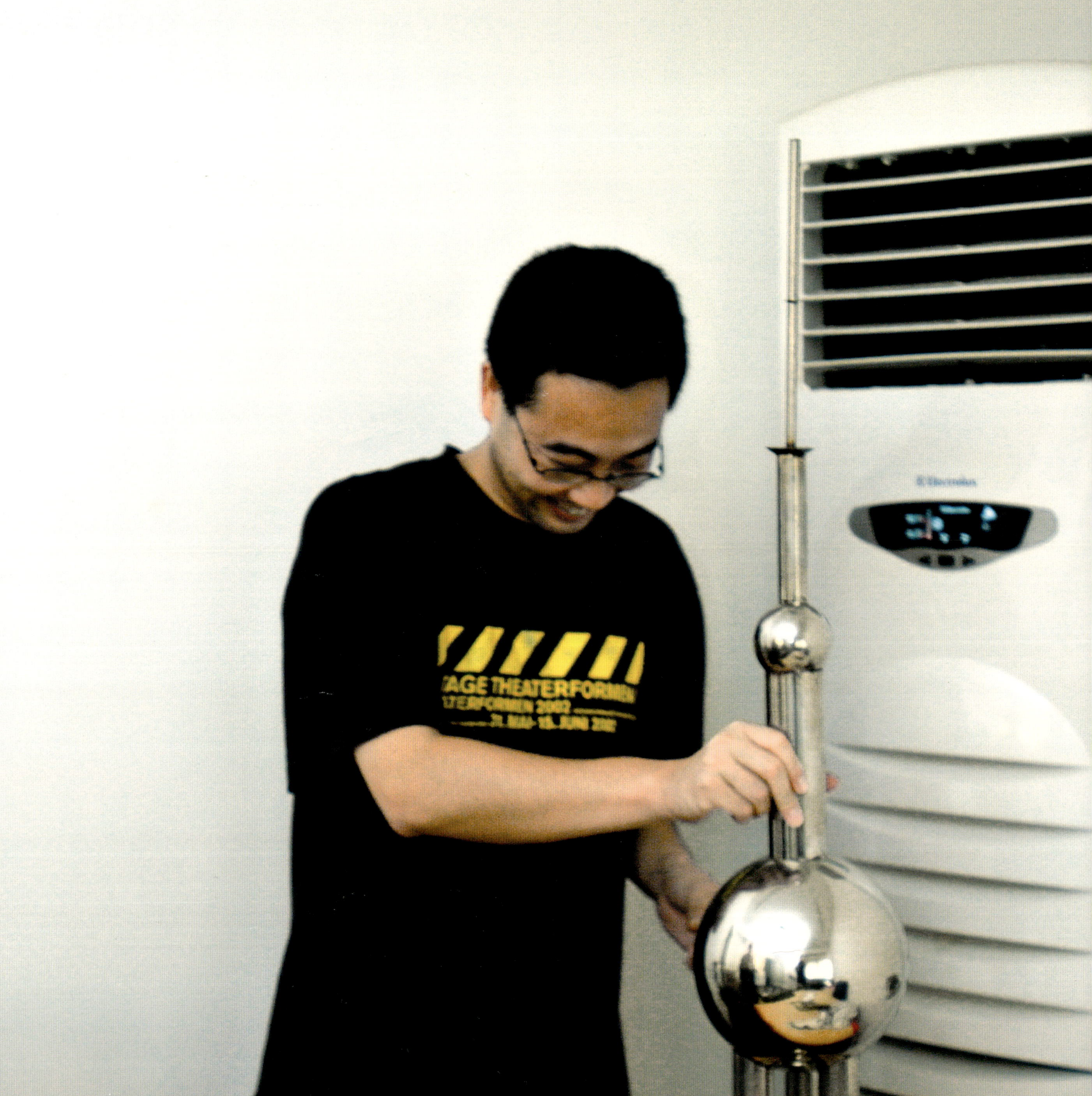
THEATERFORMEN

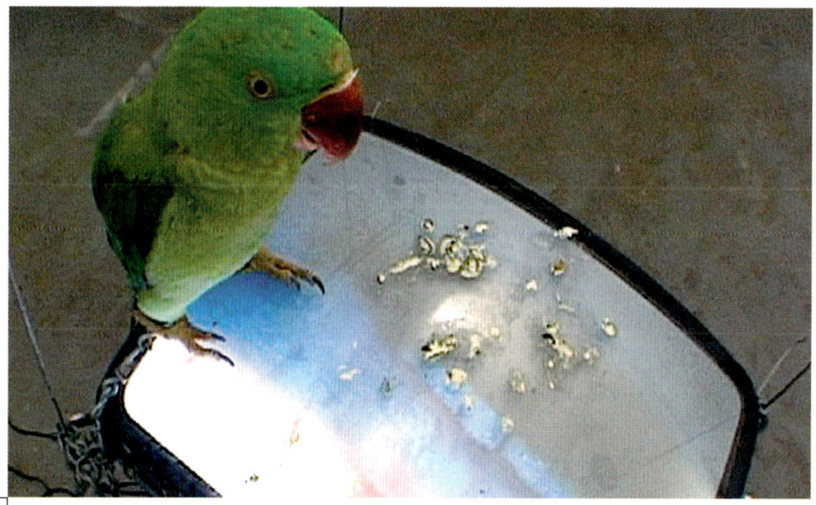

YANG ZHENZHONG

He looks like the kind of young man every mother wishes her daughter would bring home, with his sensible glasses, short hair, and kindly smile. He is one of the most prolific, incisive, and inventive artists of his generation. These are talents he brings not only to his art, but also to his capacity as organizer (or co-organizer, with Xu Zhen) of two of the most influential events on the Chinese art scene in recent years: *Twins* and *Art for Sale*. ¶ Born in 1968 in Xiaoshan, near Hangzhou, this unruffled, gentle, yet brilliant young man now lives in Shanghai. He produces paintings, photographs, films, installations, and performances with equal ease and talent. ¶ The series of photographs *Lucky Family* (1995) has become a cult work, as have the videos *922 Grains of Rice* (2000) and *I Will Die* (2000-03). These works have such a cult following that when people talk about Yang Zhenzhong's art, these are invariably the three works they have in mind. His oeuvre is much larger, however, and most of it is largely unknown. ¶ For example, who remembers the photograph entitled *Happy Birthday*, inscribed with the date November 26, 1994, and featuring a tombstone surrounded by flowers with a birthday cake in front of it? The organizers of the exhibition requested works on the theme of a day chosen at random—November 26, 1994—from ten artists from Guangzhou, Shanghai, and Beijing. "I went to the Nanshan cemetery in Hangzhou and I looked for a gravestone for someone born on November 26," Yang Zhenzhong recalls. "I produced a performance that consisted of wishing the person buried there a happy birthday, with a cake and flowers, and we took a photograph as a record." ¶ *Shower* (1995) is a video of what was also originally a performance. The soundtrack features a brass band. As the title suggests, the work shows a young man taking a shower, but fully dressed. The video is divided into precisely timed sequences: 1 minute 45 seconds to get wet all over, 5 minutes 30 seconds soaping, 6 minutes 20 seconds rubbing himself down with a sponge, 4 minutes to rinse, 4 minutes 10 seconds drying. ¶ This was Yang Zhenzhong's first video. "It's hard washing, because there are always parts that you can't reach, but it's even harder washing while fully dressed," he says in a toneless voice. And it's even harder to wash your brain, he says in the same voice. He doesn't need long sentences or speechifying. It's all simple. Clear. Limpid. ¶ One day, someone will have to write a history of performance art in China to judge its importance. I believe it to be considerable. One day, someone will also have to study the impact of technological developments (or the lack of availability thereof) on contemporary Chinese art—information, books, art reviews, that filter through or are stopped at the border, artists who are granted visas to attend a biennial or whose requests are turned down. ¶ In 1997, the first sophisticated miniature video cameras became available in China. "They could be operated by remote control," Yang Zhenzhong remembers. "So I put one on a remote-control toy car and sent it off to explore the apartment from floor level, an angle that is rarely used." Rarely, but not never—there is a photograph by Jacques-Henri Lartigue as a child taken lying on the floor. There are also pages by Proust describing the world from a worm's eye view in *Remembrance of Things Past*, which inspired Christian Boltanski in the 1970s. The video is entitled *Sleepwalking is a Therapy*. ¶ Like many other Chinese video artists, Yang Zhenzhong is entirely self-taught. When he began experimenting seven or eight years ago, no teachers specialized in video art, whether in Hangzhou or elsewhere. ¶ Like most of the other video artists I met, Yang Zhenzhong studied oil painting. He says, "I loved painting, but I found it impossible to paint two pictures in the same style. I love trying new things. I have no taste for continuity, so I changed style all the time. That's why I began my performances.

FACING PAGE: YANG ZHENZHONG IN HIS APARTMENT THAT DOUBLES AS A STUDIO ON XIANXIA ROAD, SHANGHAI. ABOVE: *IF YOU HAVE A PARROT, WHAT WORDS DO YOU LIKE TO TEACH HIM (HER)?*, VIDEO INSTALLATION, 2001.

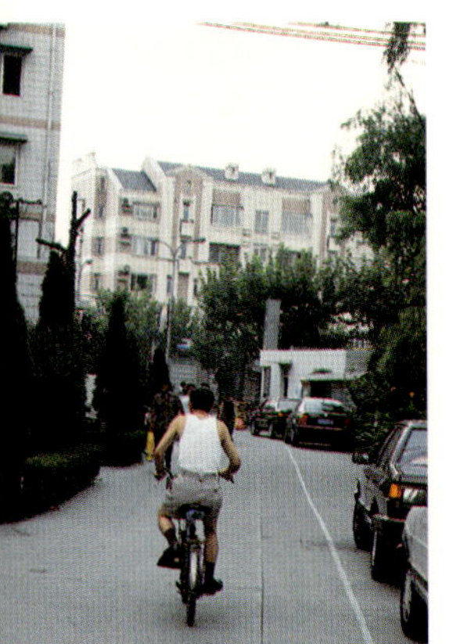

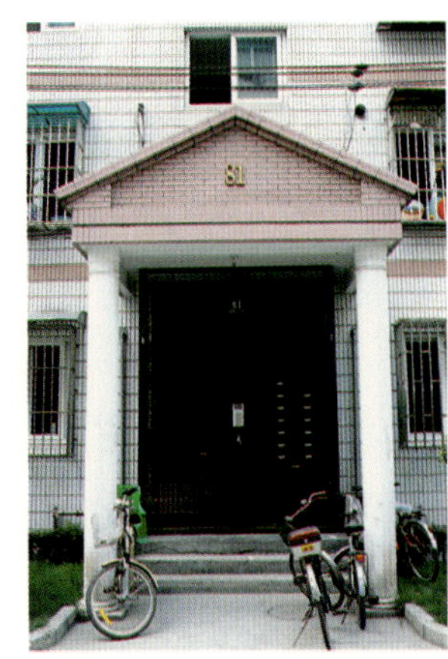

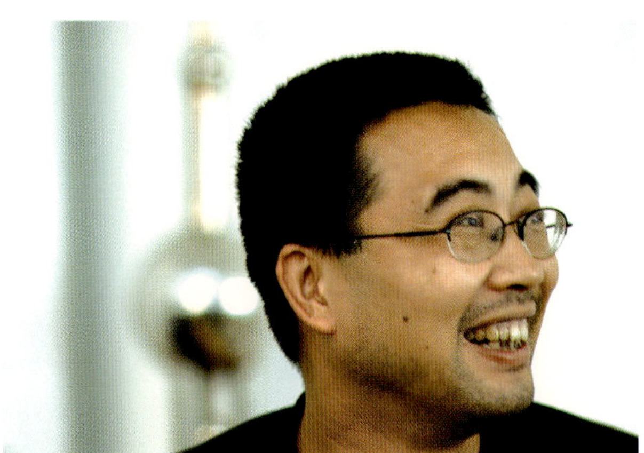

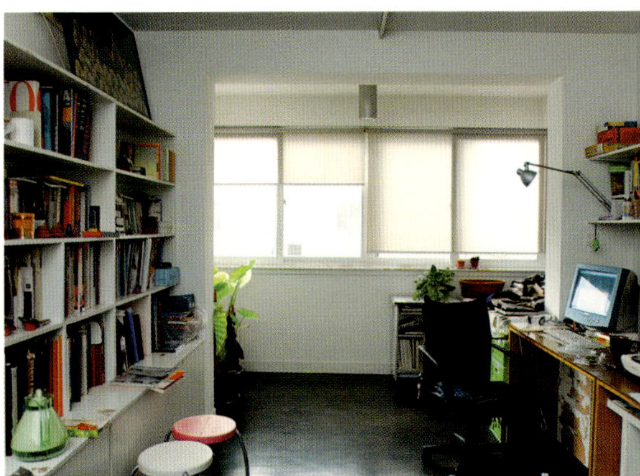

Then in 1995, I borrowed a video camera and shot my first video. It was that simple." He pauses, then adds, "It was pretty good fun, but it was extraordinarily difficult to find opportunities to show my first videos and organize exhibitions." So he decided to create his own opportunities. The video *Shanghai Face* (1999) was first shown at *Art for Sale*, as an installation. Yang Zhenzhong placed a mask with a fixed smile in front of the camera and filmed the crowds in the Shanghai streets from the bridge over the intersection of Nanjing Road (one of the biggest and busiest streets in the whole city) and Xizang Road. Then he showed the video through a tank filled with water, placed between the projector on the ground and the screen on the ceiling. The sound vibrations set up ripples on the surface of the water, which in turn ripple the image. It is a way of tuning into and visually reproducing the nervous tension and anxiety of life in a megalopolis. ¶ A few months later, he used another fairly sophisticated technique for the video installation *Balance* (1998). In a store, the artist placed three TV screens on three columns, each showing his smiling face welcoming the customers. When the customer approaches the screens, the image of the artist on the central screen fades, to be replaced by a slanting shot of the customer himself. To straighten the image on the screen, the customer must lean over. They almost all do. And that is how you induce people to behave in a perfectly bizarre manner, leaning over to straighten their screen selves. ¶ Even simpler: dating from 1998, the work *Trace* is an installation of a video on a plinth behind a table draped in a black veil, on which are placed two photographs framed with a simple black border and a Band-Aid. The video shows a close-up of a hand, probably a man's, slowly peeling a Band-Aid off a piece of hairy skin. The scene is unpleasant enough seen just the one time, but here it is repeated, colored differently each time, using all the colors of the spectrum. The accompanying soundtrack is played extra loud. On the table are two photographs of the skin before and after the Band-Aid was applied, and a piece of the Band-Aid itself. ¶ Even simpler still: *Aquarium* (1996). Three TV screens in a pile, resembling aquariums and apparently filled with water, each showing the artist's mouth in the center of the screen opening and shutting like the mouth of a fish, saying "We are not fish." This was Yang Zhenzhong's first video installation. Does it mean that we should not be treated like goldfish living in goldfish bowls? ¶ *What You Can Tolerate Cannot Be Wiped Off by Your Tolerance*, a video dating from 1999, does not show what you expect, but rather an agitated young man rushing into a subway station, looking anxiously round, heading off left, then right, obviously more and more ill-at-ease, even scared, questioning passersby, until finally he finds what he has been looking for—a public toilet. ¶ This video was shown during the 2000 Shanghai Biennial, at the *Fuck Off* exhibition, one of the most shocking ever seen on the Chinese art scene. There was even a rumor that one artist even showed a fetus being cooked and then eaten. The scandal reached London. The TV station Channel Four broadcast a documentary filmed in Beijing on the performance, dubbing it Chinese cannibal body art. ¶ The year before, in Shanghai, Yang Zhenzhong and Xu Zhen had co-organized an exhibition that, while less openly courting scandal, had in fact struck deeper at the heart of a city renowned for rampant consumerism. The exhibition was called *Art for Sale*, and was held in a department store. It was a huge success, attracting over one thousand visitors in just two days. On the third day, the police evicted the artists who had, naturally, lied on their application form to the Department of Cultural Affairs requesting permission to hold the event. ¶ Song Dong, dressed in bright yellow as the character Mr. Banana, shouting

YANG ZHENZHONG'S APARTMENT IS IN A SORT OF RESIDENTIAL ZONE WHERE ALL THE APARTMENT BUILDINGS HAVE IMPECCABLE LOBBIES. IN HIS APARTMENT, HE HAS SET ASIDE ONE ROOM AS A STUDIO. IT IS FULL OF COMPUTERS LINED UP ON A LONG WORKTABLE.

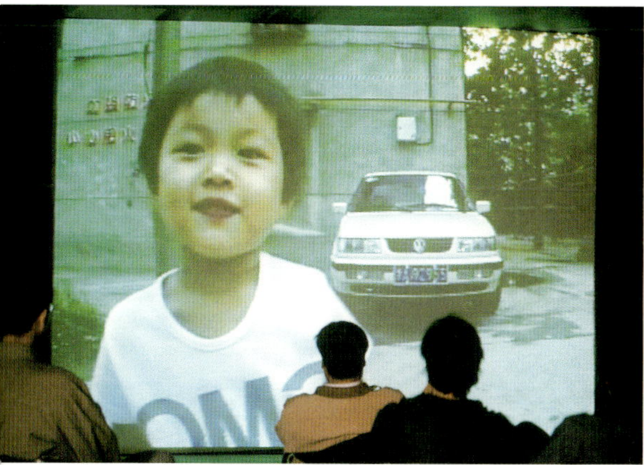

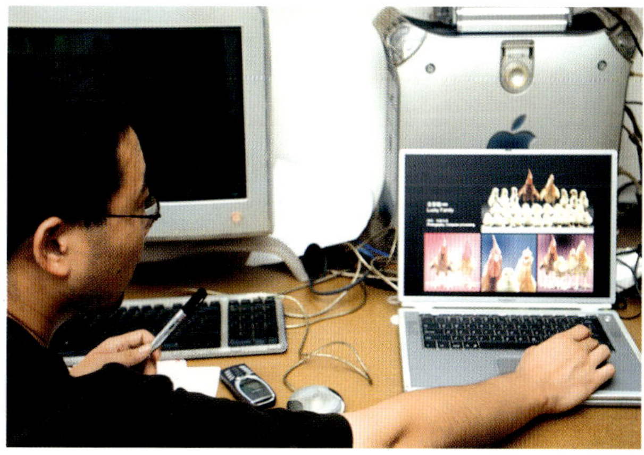

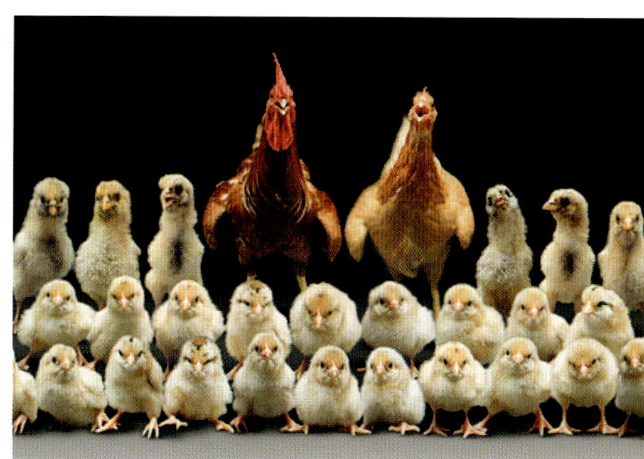

through a megaphone and waving a little flag (a perfectly normal sight in Shanghai, where there is a similar mascot in front of almost every department store), brought the customers in to browse the shelves where the works of art were placed in among the consumer goods. He explained the individual pieces of art and announced the price. ¶ Yang Zhenzhong began his first series of photographs retouched by computer in 1995. The series was based on the type of studio portrait popular with bridal couples. He showed the cockerel as a typical family man, with a hen as the modest wife and three rows of bright yellow chicks, the smallest at the front, the medium-sized ones in the middle row, and the biggest on either side of their parents. They are all perfectly aligned, as if on parade, standing tall in their boots against a black background, lit by the bright, sterile, impersonal light of the photographer's studio. ¶ A variation on the same theme. Two chickens, alone, against a red background. The same two chickens with two large chicks, almost fully grown, against a purple background. The cockerel and hen with a single chick shot close up against a midnight blue background. ¶ The title is *Lucky Family*. Lucky, with twenty-six chicks! In a country where each couple is authorized to have just one child, the title could indeed be considered somewhat provocative. ¶ "Before, there were families with lots of children. That is something our generation is unfamiliar with," comments Yang Zhenzhong with a charming smile. Is there a critical connotation in the work and the comment it has just prompted? I ask. "Not at all. I remain neutral," he replies. Then, as my expression must betray a certain degree of skepticism, he repeats, "I promise it's true. Quite simply because it's so hard to judge. The situation is different in China and in your home country, and from what we knew before. The Chinese population has to be reduced. Otherwise we're storing up huge problems for later on. Yet at the same time, it's not very positive just to have one child. Children get bored if they don't have brothers and sisters. They become depressed." He has one sister. They were born before 1976, after which date couples were no longer allowed to have more than one child. ¶ Another photograph: *Medicine (45° as a Reason)* (1995). It is of a sort of chimpanzee, too human to be a human, in a pretty rosewood frame. Two ceremonial candlesticks holding red candles and sticks of incense stuck in a pot stand in front of the photo as if it were an altar devoted to the memory of some ancestor. "Man descends from the apes; I am descended from my grandmother, who looks like a monkey. So I put in a monkey that looks like my grandmother," laughs Yang Zhenzhong. ¶ He was busy for most of 2002 working on a series of photographs entitled *Light and Easy*, each of which was printed in a limited edition of ten copies. The series depicts the artist in a range of settings, mostly urban, balancing on the tip of his outstretched index finger a number of impossibly heavy, unwieldy objects: a car, a tractor, a rocket, a huge sculpture (probably Ming, or a copy), and even the city of Shanghai. The magic of photography and computer wizardry. He based a video piece on the same idea, with even more striking results. *Light as Fuck* (2003) is a marvel of needle-sharp impertinence and technical virtuosity. The effect is simple yet stunning. ¶ *I Know I Will Die* is a remarkable series of videos begun in 2000 in China, continued in Korea, Japan, Belgium, Germany, and France, and is still a work in progress. It was presented at the China exhibition at the Centre Pompidou. It shows a series of people facing the video camera and uttering the simple, devastating words, "I will die." The impact of the work depends on the attitude of the people filmed—young and carefree, or elderly and therefore likely to be more immediately confronted with the realization of their prediction. It also depends a great deal on the

ABOVE RIGHT: *LUCKY FAMILY*, ONE OF YANG ZHENZHONG'S BEST-KNOWN PHOTOGRAPHS. THE ARTIST HAS THE WORK AND A SERIES OF VARIATIONS ON DISPLAY IN HIS APARTMENT. LEFT: YANG ZHENZHONG'S MOST RECENT VIDEO, *I WILL DIE*, BEGUN IN 2000.

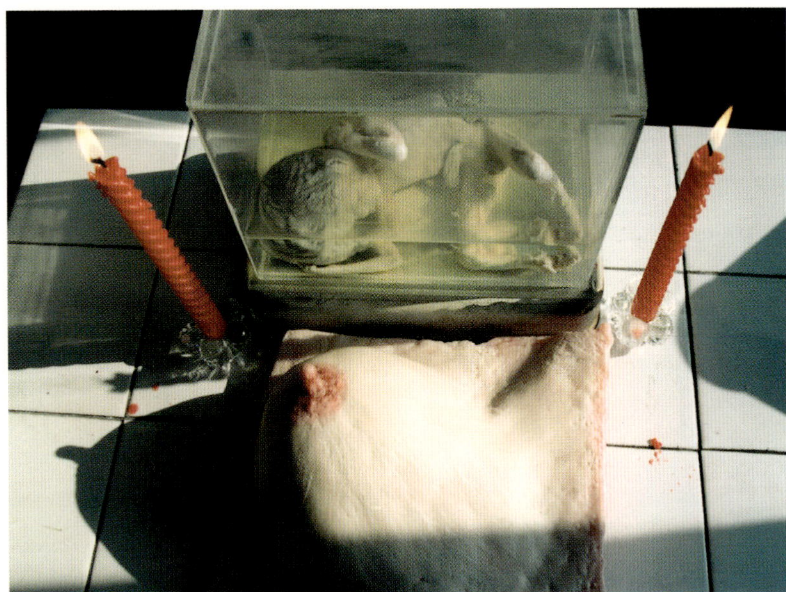

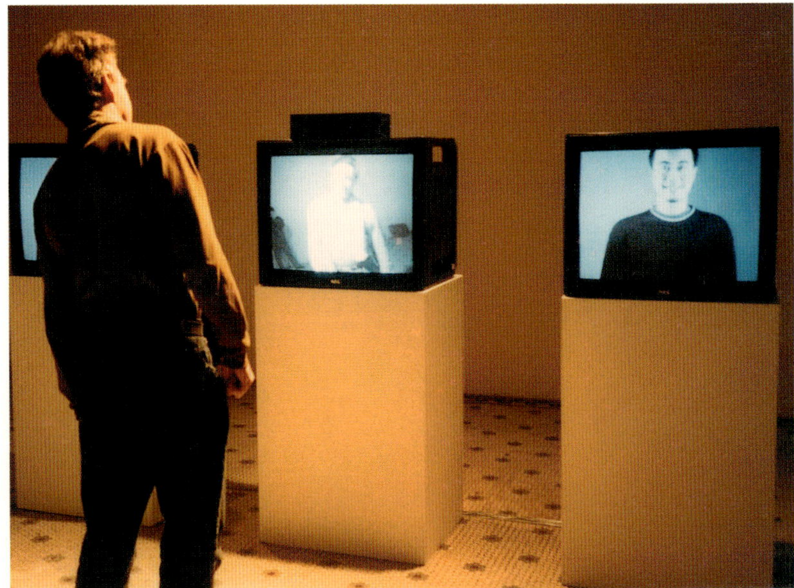

attitude of the people filmed to the act of filming, which represents the essence of neutrality, yet which by its very presence is probing into the private domain addressed by their statement to the camera. ¶ It has been noted that there is often a certain discordance between the speaker, his intonation, and his attitude. Yang Zhenzhong says, "A lot of people gesture and respond automatically. In any case, when you say this sentence to a video camera, it becomes funny, even if the tone of voice is utterly serious. Death, and the certainty that we will all die, is a fundamental aspect of our existence, one of the most absolute of truths. Yet it doesn't sound serious. When I ask people to repeat 'I will die' to camera, they all know they are being recorded. They think about how they look and they lie to the camera, even though what they are saying is true: they are all going to die eventually. I was interested in the expressions on their faces before and after saying 'I will die.' Actually, no one is ready to die. Death terrifies us, but life is fleeting and death is inevitable. Sometimes we think that our image is eternal. Maybe that is why we invented the camera." ¶ The sophisticated video installation, shown in a dark cube at the Shanghai Biennial in November 2002 and again at the Venice Biennale in June 2003, placed two video screens facing each other, with the spectator in the middle. One screen showed one of the most famous streets in Shanghai, and the other a young girl in a sleeveless top blowing as hard as she possibly can. On the facing screen, the street scene seems to move backwards as if shifted by the girl's puffing. When she pauses to catch her breath, the street scene returns to its initial position. The pattern is repeated again and again. Like the rhythm of breathing. Like the effort to break free from a powerful force. What is the video saying? It is recounting the artist's attachment to the city and his efforts to leave. The desire to hold it at arm's length, to leave it entirely—impossible, as it always returns. ¶ Yang Zhenzhong's best-known video depicts a circle of grains of rice in the middle of the screen. A cockerel enters on the left and a hen on the right. At the bottom of the image, three counters detail the number of grains pecked up by the cockerel, the number pecked up by the hen, and in the center, the total of the two. Meanwhile, a couple also tries to count the grains swallowed by each bird, the man counting the cockerel's total and the woman the hen's. They get lost in figures and end up in an argument. After a while the two birds have eaten their fill and wander off. The artist's hand appears and picks up the remaining grains of rice, counting them all: 922 grains of rice. The video is thus entitled *922 Grains of Rice* (2000). It was presented for the first time in Turin, then in Shanghai, and then all over the world. ¶ "With video, it's very easy to count," says Yang Zhenzhong. "I was holding a fistful of rice. I wanted to know how many grains I had in my hand. If I had had to count them one by one, it would have taken too long. So I put it on the ground and got the chickens to help me count. I think it was very clever of me. But the chickens didn't understand anything. I couldn't teach them anything. Sometimes they didn't peck up all the rice, and other times they just fought. I tried recording them several times. It took me more than a week to finish the video on my computer. In the end, I came up with the figure 922. Now, I realize that I am stupid. Chickens never wonder how many grains of rice they have pecked. It's a human problem. Humans are stupid."

ABOVE LEFT: *CHRISTMAS GIFT*, AN INSTALLATION FROM 1994. RIGHT: *BALANCE*, A VIDEO INSTALLATION PLACED IN A STORE IN 1998. FACING PAGE: TOP LEFT: *922 GRAINS OF RICE*, 2000, VIDEO. TOP RIGHT: *SHOWER*, 1995, VIDEO. CENTER LEFT: *BICYCLE GYMNASTICS*, 2000. CENTER RIGHT: *LET'S PUFF*, 2002, VIDEO INSTALLATION. BOTTOM: VIDEO INSTALLATION IN FUXING PARK AT THE FOOT OF THE STATUES OF MARX AND ENGELS.

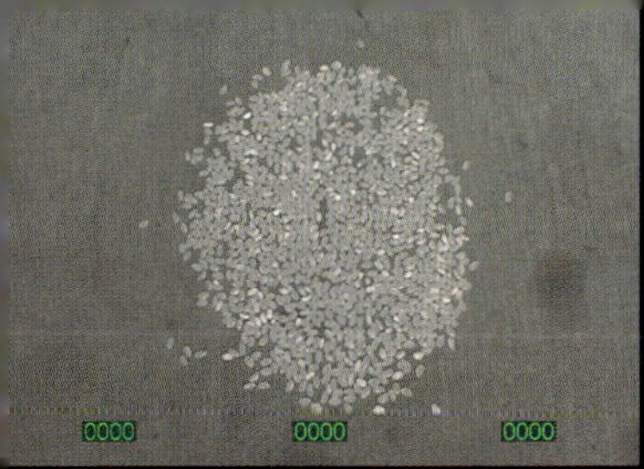
0000
0000
0000
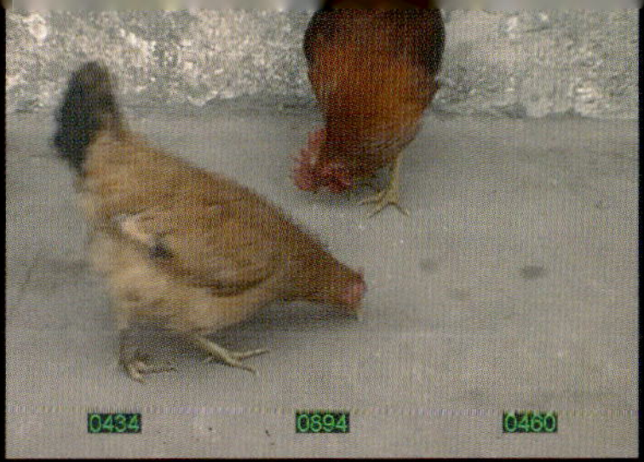
0434
0694
0460
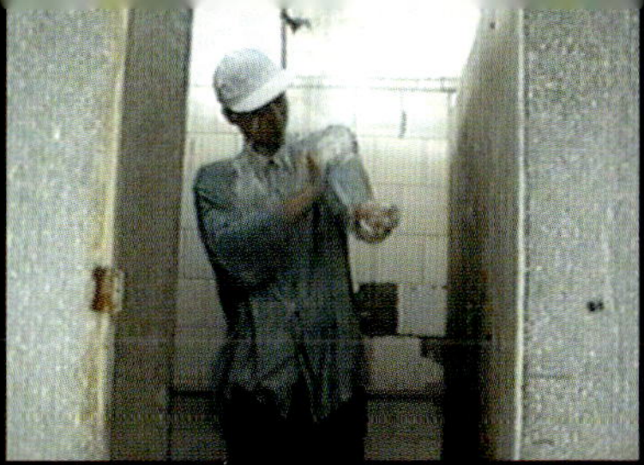
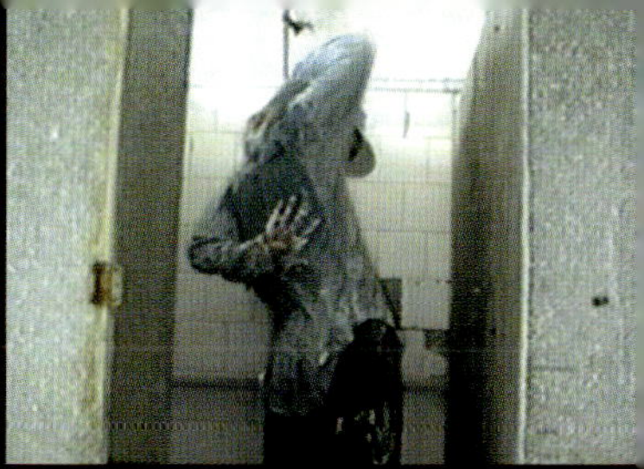
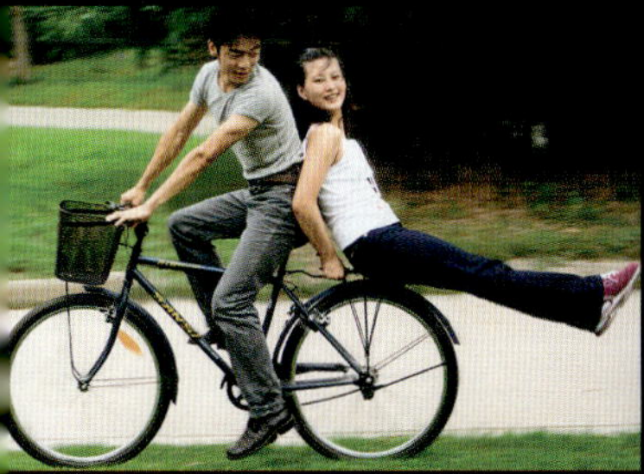
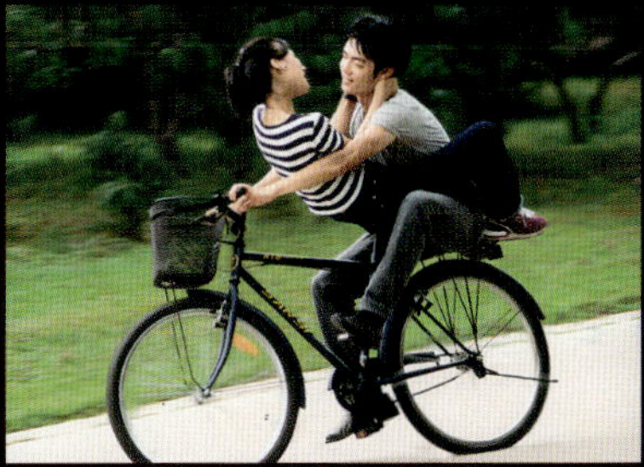
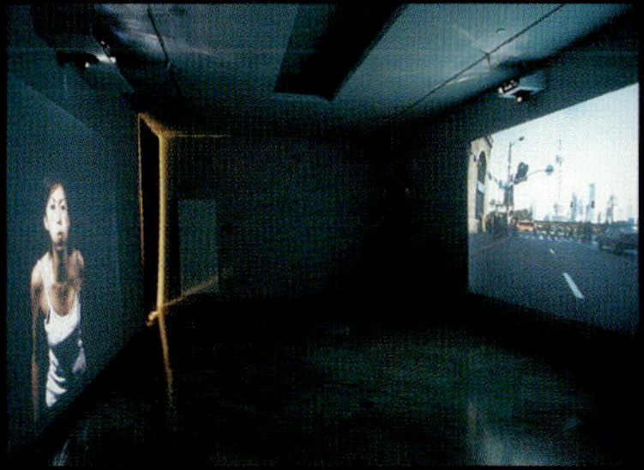
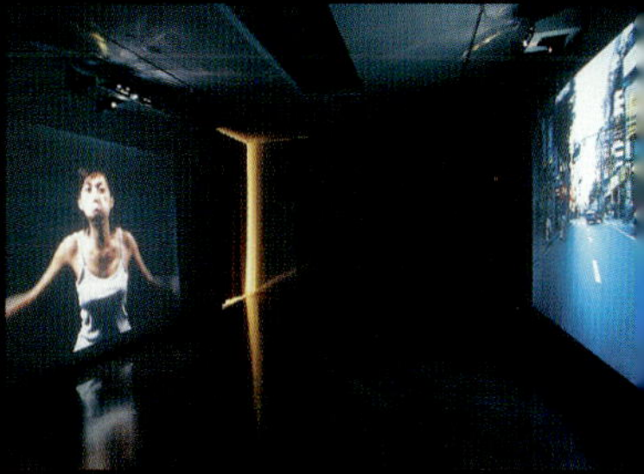
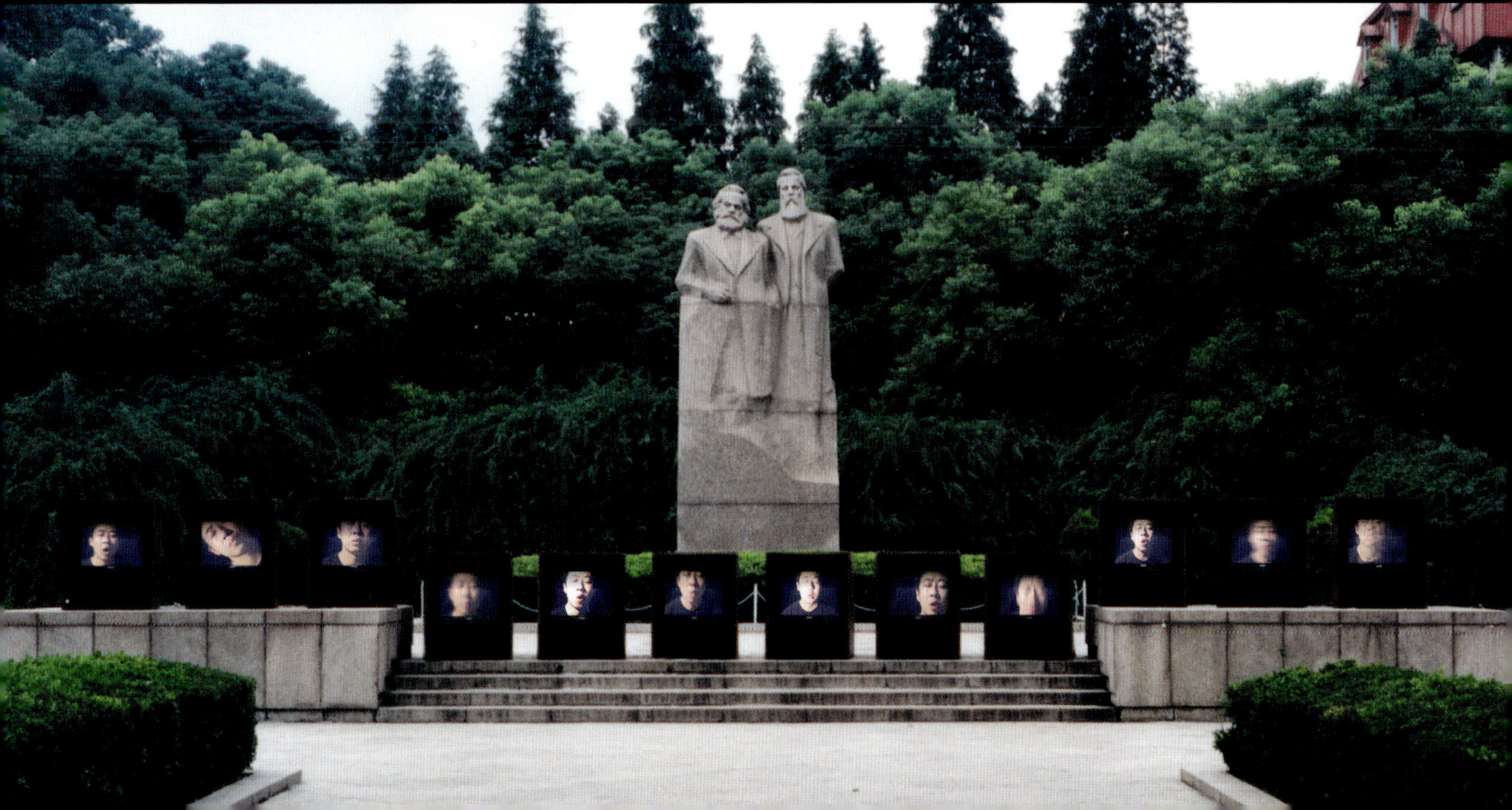

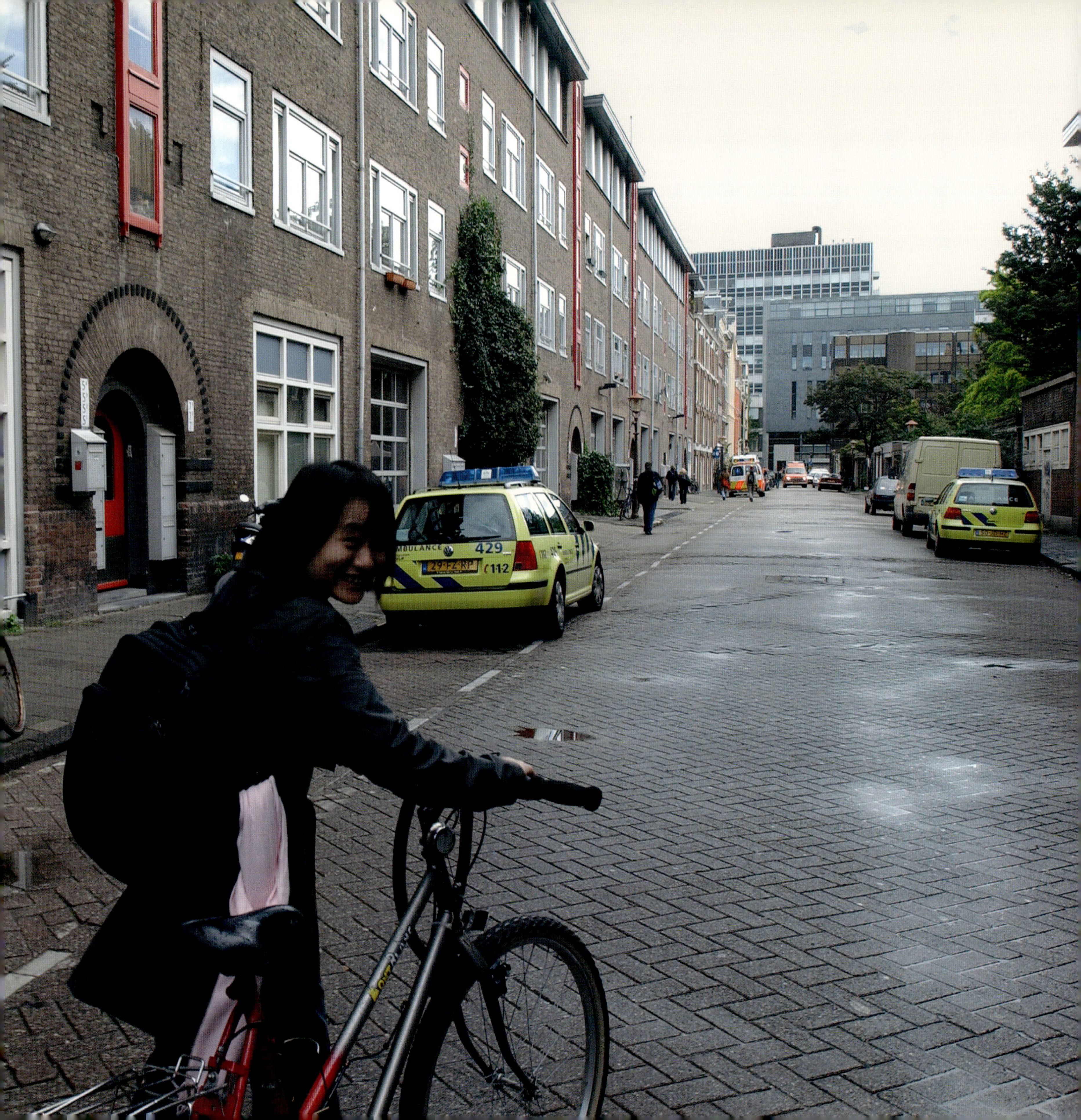
AMBULANCE
429
29-FZ-RP
112

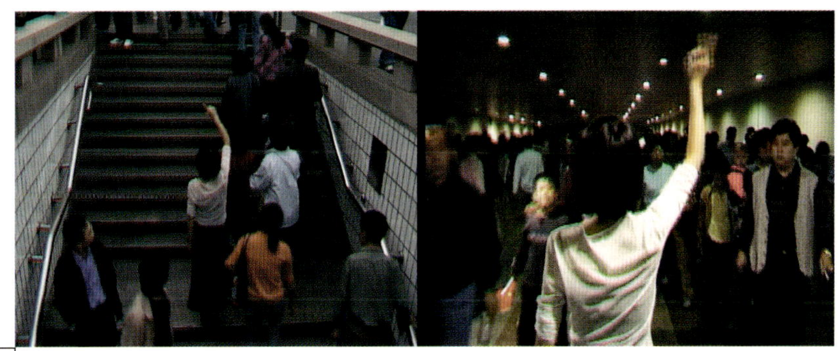

KAN XUAN

We were a little overly optimistic that day. We left the hotel very early, intending to visit several artists' studios. The first lived a fair way from the center of Beijing in one direction, and the second just as far from the center but in exactly the opposite direction. We got stuck in traffic in the city center, and then got lost. I spent a good while wandering through the streets with a cell phone glued to my ear, following the instructions given to me by Wu Ershan, in search of his extremely tasteful studio, all in cutting-edge design. Unfortunately, this meant that by the time we got around to our second visit, to Kan Xuan, in her studio in Zuo Jia Zhang in eastern Beijing, it was 7:30 P.M., and we were nearly two hours late. Our interpreter had been invited to dinner so she just introduced us to the young video artist, made her excuses, and left. ¶ Kan Xuan speaks no—and I mean no—English. She could barely say yes or no. My Chinese is not much better, unfortunately. It was under these rather inauspicious circumstances that I made the acquaintance of one of the most unsettled, imaginative, and fascinating of Chinese artists. ¶ She smiled a lot, talking all the time, constantly on the move, standing up, sitting back down again, turning a machine on only to turn it off again, switching from one screen to another, showing me a number of videos, titled—thank God—in English. ¶ That was how I came to discover *Looking, Looking, Looking For*, an absolutely enchanting video depicting a little spider wandering freely over two bodies—a man and a woman—exploring a patch of body hair here, an underarm there, pausing in a belly-button, then in a nostril. The wanderings of this spider are so funny, simple, and touching that everyone immediately falls under its spell. The audience loves it, the critics' tongues become less sharp, and collectors fall over themselves to buy it—or at least say they do. ¶ Shot in 2000, it is a miracle of grace and humor. The soundtrack is a nursery rhyme sung by two adults (again, a man and a woman) imitating children. The voices, like the words, are at once happy and sad, peaceful and nostalgic. "I am not afraid of the storm. I am not afraid of the rain," the nursery rhyme goes. "Not even if the storm and the rain come together. I want to find it to see it every day. I won't be afraid if the storm and the rain come together. I want, I want, I want to find it and I don't care where it will take me. My sweetheart cannot be found, but please, if you find her, bring her to me." ¶ To be precise, these are the words of the theme songe for a children's cartoon that is very popular in China. It is called *Marco*, and recounts the adventures of a little boy waiting for his mother. Kan Xuan has changed the words. ¶ Was I right to begin discussing this video by using words such as "charm" and "enchanting"? This could give the impression that Kan Xuan is rather a lightweight artist. She can indeed have the very lightest of touches, but this is not the only string to her bow. At times, she has been whimsical, and at others headstrong—and not always when it was appropriate. She is brave, and has proved her devotion to art by working extremely hard to pay for her schooling when she wanted to study painting in Hangzhou. ¶ She has extremely fond memories of her teacher, Gen Jian Yi. He taught her the history of Western art, and she says he was a major influence on her. She even enrolled in his classes as an optional extra course. Back then, Kan Xuan was interested in the same thing as all other young Chinese artists her age: installations. ¶ She learned the tricks of video art and editing on her own. "The only videos I had access to were the ones by Yang Zhenzhong," she says. She formed a group with him and two other friends. They called themselves the 4 x 100 Meters. They exhibited together, worked on projects together, and tested out ideas on each other. The two other members of the group were Wu Chen Feng ("He did some really pretty things. I wonder what's become of him," she says) and Xiang Ligin, who is now a painter and photographer. ¶ She began her studies in 1993 and finished in 1997. She left behind her friends in Shanghai and Hangzhou and moved to Beijing. For a while, she had a job in a multinational advertising and production company, where she became familiar with filming and editing techniques. She spent a large proportion of her salary on videocassettes and other material. After six months, she was

FACING PAGE: KAN XUAN IN A STREET IN AMSTERDAM, WHERE SHE WAS ARTIST-IN-RESIDENCE AT THE PRESTIGIOUS RIJKSAKADEMIE VAN BEELDENDE KUNSTEN. ABOVE: KAN XUAN IN A BEIJING STREET, TRACING NUMBERS FROM 60 TO 1 IN THE AIR, COUNTING SIXTY SECONDS IN DIFFERENT PARTS OF THE CITY, 2001.

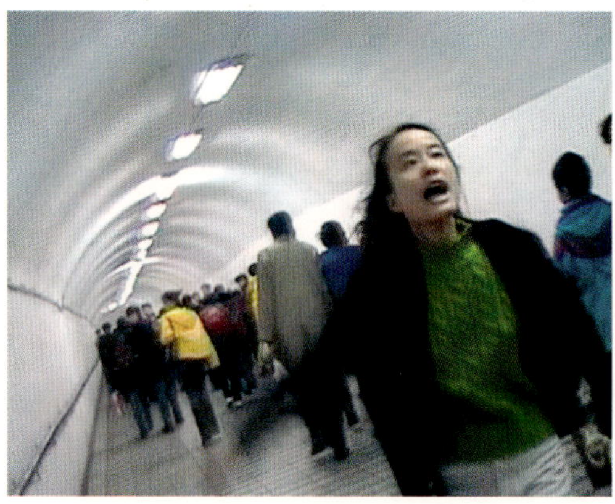

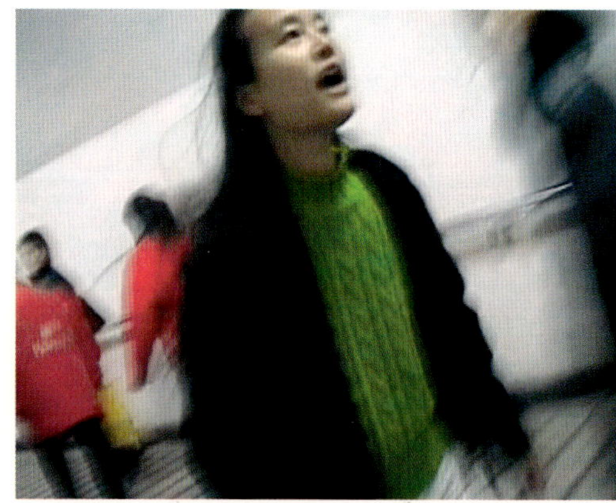

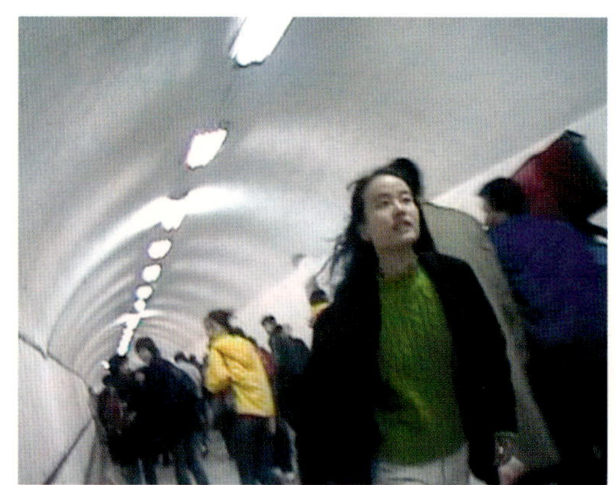

so engrossed in her own video work that her work for the company began to slide. She was fired. The next few months were very difficult. She often found herself without a penny to her name and wondering where her next meal was coming from. This is unfortunately the harsh reality for many contemporary Chinese artists who do not have the good fortune to meet with success at the outset of their careers. ¶ Kan Xuan first began to make a name for herself on the art scene in 1999 with a series of videos, some, but not all, of her performances. ¶ Her 1999 video, *Kan Xuan, Hei!* shows her wandering through subway corridors in a strangely vehement way, apparently in search of someone, and calling out her own name: "Kan Xuan! Kan Xuan!" It should be noted that this video is dated a few years after the *It's Me* exhibition by Leng Lin, which asked a series of questions about Chinese identity and which proved highly influential. Kan Xuan showed this very intense video at the *Art for Sale* exhibition organized by Xu Zhen and Yang Zhenzhong in a Shanghai supermarket. ¶ A later video, where the shots are almost never perfectly horizontal—"more destabilizing," she says—show her swallowing a series of powerful-tasting or nausea-inducing substances (mustard, cinnamon, pepper, monosodium glutamate, and so on) until she vomits. She described this video in the following terms: "Life is boring, so you have to look for a bit of excitement, but at a level that can be controlled." ¶ With the same principle in mind, she filmed herself walking naked up and down the narrow staircases and through the corridors of a monastery, when the temperature was 9°F (-13°C). It was absurd and in fact even dangerous, because the police generally keep an eye on artists. In fact, shortly before starting this work, Kan Xuan's name was given to the police by a journalist. She says the video, EN AVANT, is a reference to her own status as an artist in China. ¶ Chinese critics saw these videos and others that we will examine later as a sort of private diary. Superficially, there is some truth in this. But this would be a better description for Liang Yu's videos. The films by Kan Xuan seem to me to deal with something deeper, more real. How can reality be seen? How can it be felt in a country of "disconcerting lies" like China is (or used to be)—China, where reality is muted beneath a leaden cloak of ideology. Where everything is seen from one particular angle. Where a different ideology—the ideology of capitalism—is preparing to sweep aside the old ways. It is just as much of a lie in its proclaimed defense of fundamental liberties, but in a different way. ¶ All this gets in the way of the heart of the matter. And yet the heart of the matter is what interested Kan Xuan above all in the years of struggle. Years of struggle, but also years of opening to the outside world, and years of lightness. Cracks in the walls. ¶ In 1999, video art was making an appearance in exhibitions all over China. Prior to that, artists had to be extremely persistent, as video cameras were hard to come by and very pricey. Kan Xuan borrowed one for her works. She was only able to afford her own video camera in 2000. It took her a year to pay for it. Such details might seem superficial, but not when you are a penniless artist struggling to make ends meet. ¶ In 1999, she worked on a series of short videos—four or five minutes each—all based on a close-up shot, the camera held motionless. Hands in rubber gloves cracking two eggs together and holding them out in the open palms. The white and the yolk, slippery, organic, dribble between the fingers, reminiscent of unidentified viscera and internal organs. This video was shown at the Centre Pompidou's China exhibition in 2003. ¶ Another video shows the artist's own hands spinning a piece of yellow tropical fruit—a persimmon—which warms and splits under her kneading fingers,

KAN XUAN, KAN XUAN, HEI!, 1999. THIS IS ONE OF THE MOST IMPORTANT WORKS BY THIS YOUNG ARTIST, SHOWING HER WANDERING THROUGH THE CORRIDORS OF THE BEIJING SUBWAY, CALLING OUT HER OWN NAME IN A STRANGELY INSISTENT VOICE. FACING PAGE: KAN XUAN'S MOST FAMOUS WORK, A FAVORITE WITH AUDIENCES AND COLLECTORS, *LOOKING, LOOKING, LOOKING FOR*, 2000.

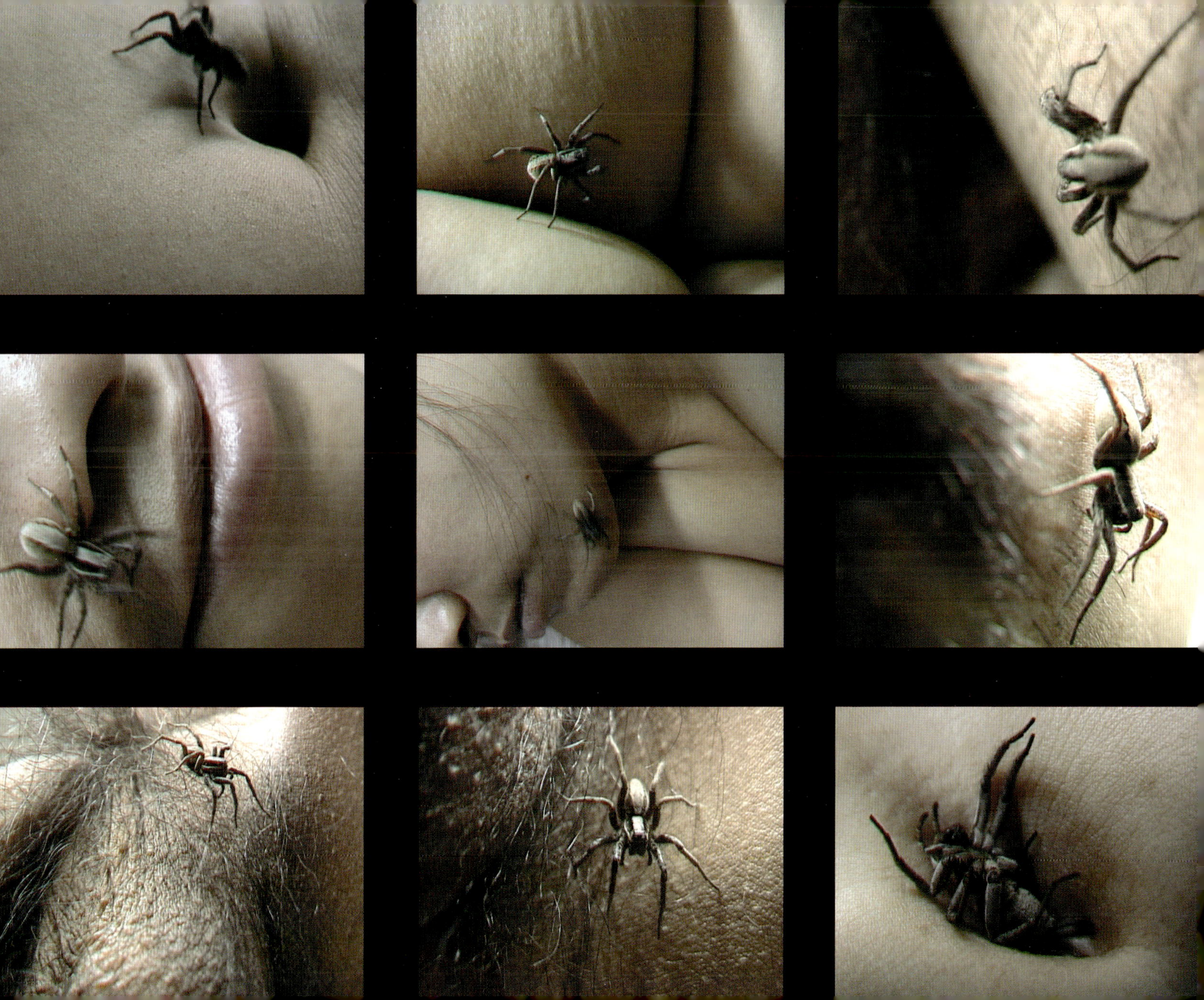

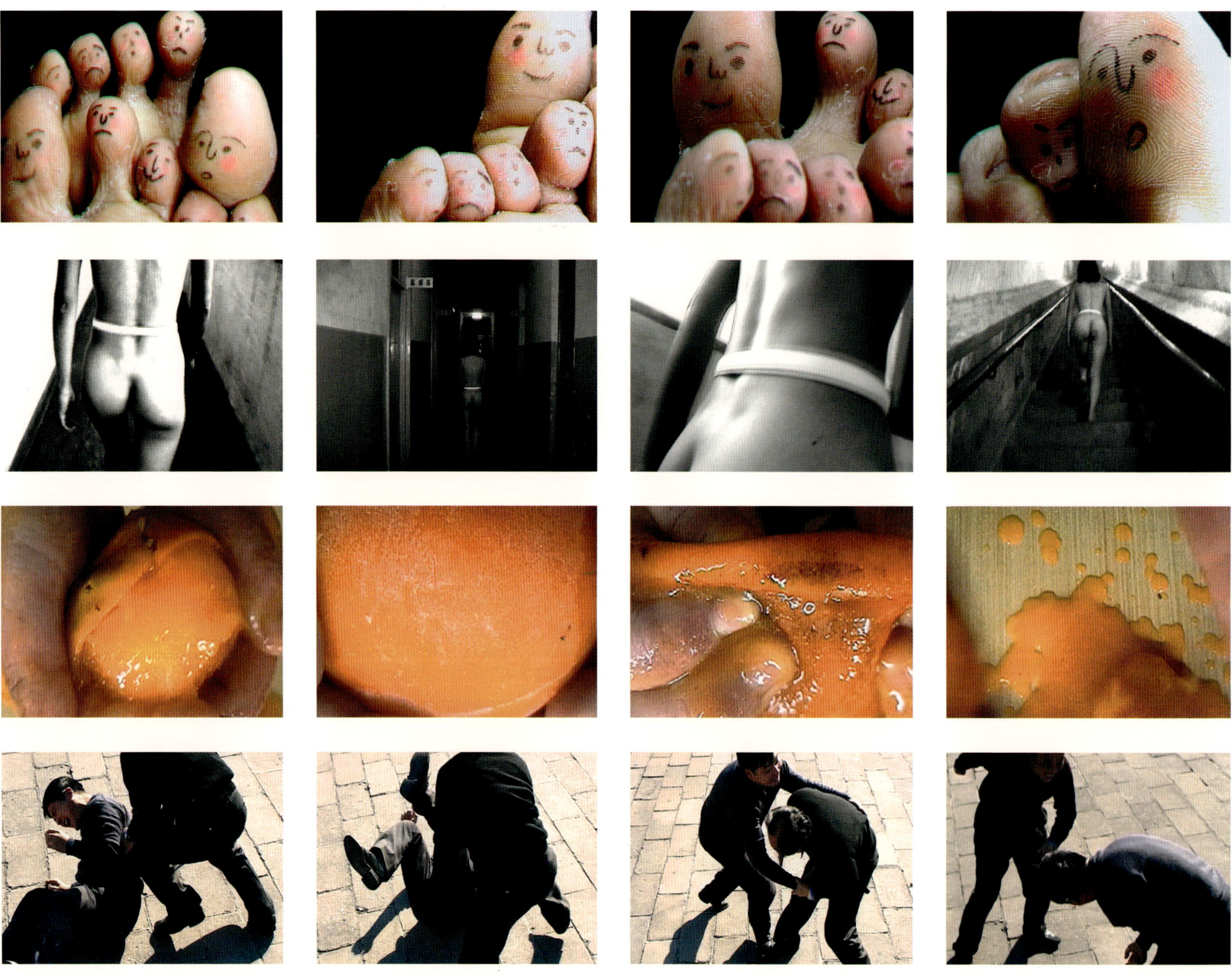

FOUR VIDEOS. ABOVE: FROM THE TOP, *CHORUS*, 1999; *ENDLESS*, 2000; *A PERSIMMON*, 1999; *SUNNY DAY*, 2003.

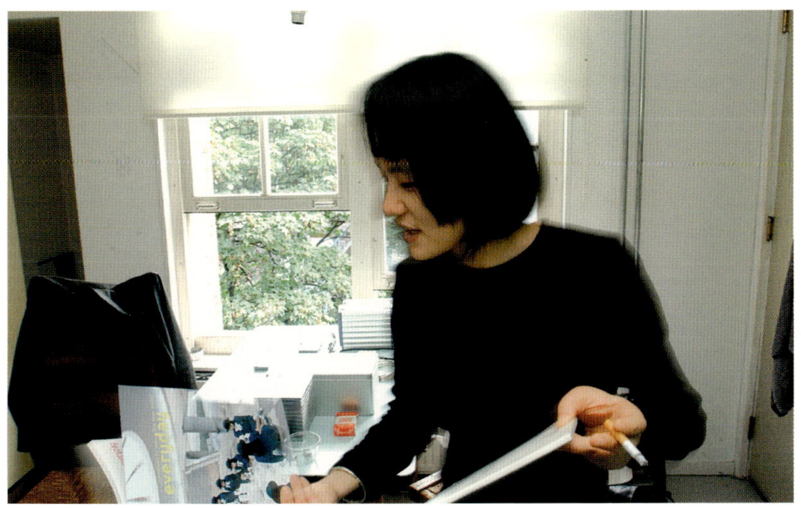

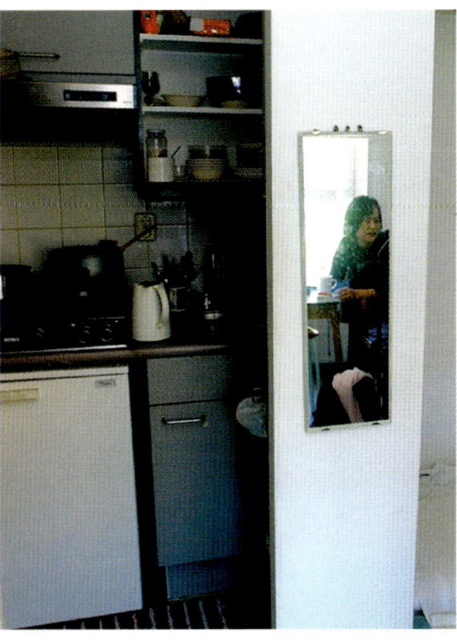

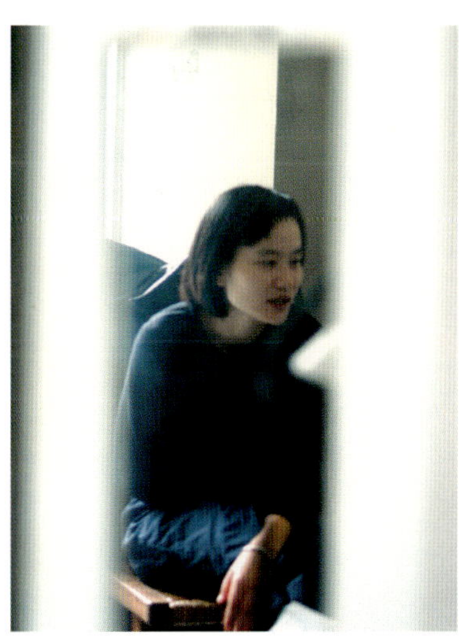

juice spurting out. Another reference to the sticky viscosity of organic matter. This video was exhibited at the Fondation Guerlain, also in 2003. ¶ While Kan Xuan's work undeniably addresses the question of a general attempt to test the boundaries of reality, it must also be read from the point of view of a young woman artist questioning female identity and the female body. When she began working in this field, it was a vast unexplored domain. Kan Xuan, along with artists like Chen Lingyang, Cui Xiu Wen, and Liang Yu, has played a key role in mapping out the female identity in Chinese art. ¶ Kan Xuan has done, so, however, not in the violent, provocative manner of the American feminist artists of the 1970s, or like Chen Lingyang closer to home, but in a vehement tone that still leaves room for ambiguity, for light and shade. Her art is characterized by subtle vehemence, to coin a phrase. ¶ The third video is very different. It shows hands plunging into a trashcan and pulling out various "treasures" that she names as she does so: a packet of Camels, an apple core, a crumpled Kleenex. Pitiful treasures, pitiful revelations. Presentation as opposed to representation. An inventory. ¶ *Choir*, dating from 2001, represents a new direction for Kan Xuan: self-filming. It has been judged over-simplistic. She says, "I began to think about the sound as much as the picture." It is a delightful video of a close-up of the artist's toes. She has drawn a grotesque face on the underside of each toe with some kind of marker pen. She wriggles her toes in time to a bold, invigorating military march. It is a lighthearted way of poking fun at the straitlaced seriousness of the military and political classes. ¶ When I met her, she had just finished this video, whose cheekiness makes a refreshing change from the rather uptight humor of Political Pop Art. I was enthusiastic, and asked her if I could arrange for it to be shown in France. She shook her head frantically, obviously worried about overcurious customs officers and nosy censors. The words of the song, accompanied by a brass band and the thumping of a big bass drum, translate as "If there were no Chinese Communist Party, there would be no new China." ¶ We managed to communicate by gestures, but obviously explaining the finer subtleties of her art was out of the question. That's why I did not understand straight away that most of the videos she showed me, except the last two described, were planned as part of installations. ¶ Why? Because apparently, in Beijing, video installations are considered the *nec plus ultra* of modernity. Relayed by Zhang Peili and Zhu Jia, Gary Hill's influence was spreading throughout Chinese video art. ¶ Kan Xuan changed her mind about video installations when she spent some time in Amsterdam, on a two-year scholarship as artist in residence at the prestigious Rijksakademie van Beeldende Kunsten. She was invited there by a professor she met in Beijing. There, she had time to think, and decided to explore other ways of seeing and feeling. She has developed. Her research became deeper and subtler, while she maintained her penchant for the unforeseen events, accidents, miracles, and tiny tragedies that cross our paths daily, and the occasional chances to kick over the traces, which make the thought of the straight line ahead bearable. ¶ She filmed the video *Rope* towards the beginning of her stay in Amsterdam. In a way, it ties in with her early performances. In it, she is twirling a long red rope, obviously with a great deal of effort. We then see that the other end of the rope is tied to a tree, a good five feet (fifteen meters) away on the other side of a river. The water slows the rope as it skims the surface. At first the film is shot at very close range, but then the camera pans back to finish in a general shot of the whole scene. She looks at me, laughs, and says, "I'd just arrived. I didn't speak a word of English, so I filmed myself. It was easier

KAN XUAN IN HER TINY APARTMENT, SITTING AT THE TOP OF THE STEEP FLIGHT OF STAIRS TYPICAL OF DUTCH HOMES. SHE LIVED IN THE NETHERLANDS FOR TWO YEARS, 2002 AND 2003.

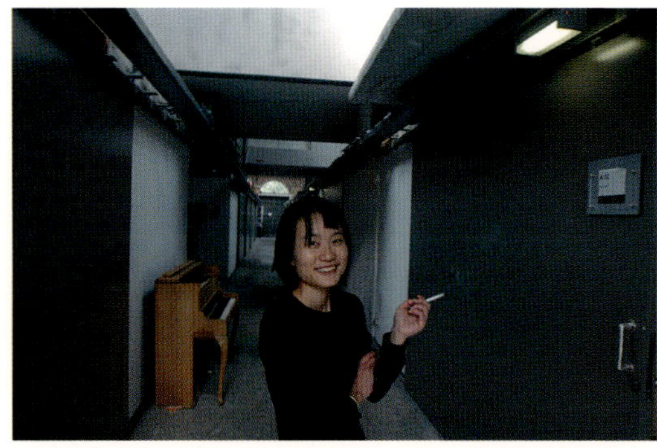

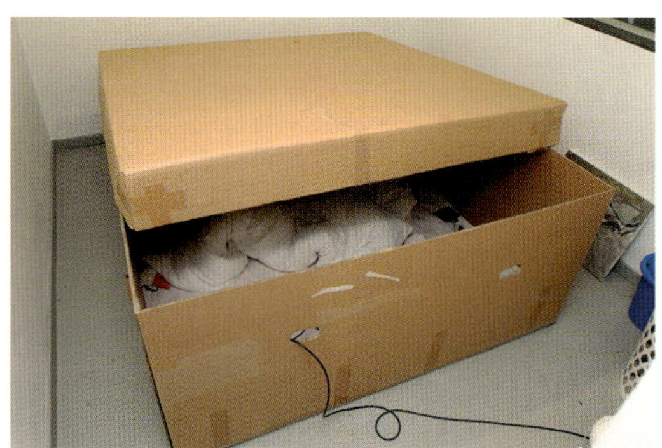

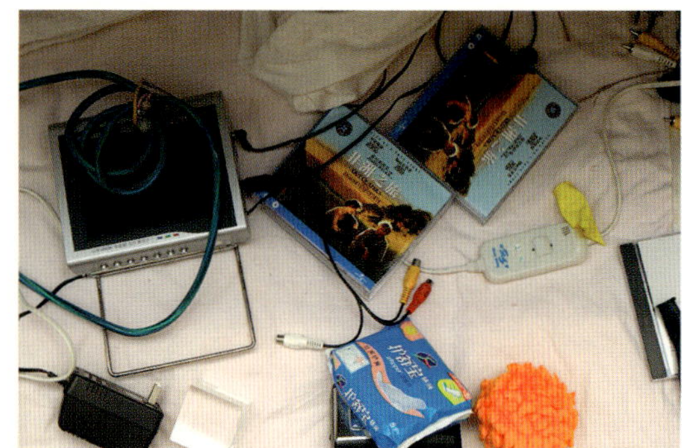

that way." ¶ Kan Xuan worked a lot in Amsterdam, filming a lot, trying out a host of new ideas, many of which didn't work out. Sunny Day, shown in late 2003 at the Fondation Guerlain, represents two men of about forty-five, shot from above, who, while not quite tramps, are obviously down on their luck. They seem to be arguing, but strangely enough, they do not move out of the image. The camera is not totally stable, but the image does not move very much. They are tickling each other and laughing. Again, it is a very simple idea, but the very simplicity is astonishingly effective. Her films are made of interstices, gaps, uncertainties, tiny shifts, laughter that is not really laughter. "I'm interested in laughter," she says. "You get all sorts, like this one, which sometimes becomes piercing. I sometimes catch myself laughing when in my heart, I'm not laughing at all." ¶ Her video *Nothing* (2002) was shown at the Maison Européenne de la Photographie in Paris in early 2004. She described it to me thus: "In our world of information, many people's attention is held by the idea of looking for something. Sometimes it can become an obsession. The video *Nothing* plays with this phenomenon. The sound comes from a normal human voice that has been slightly altered. The sound, somewhere between a human voice and a metallic noise, sounds stupid. The sound and the image together ridicule the insanity of always searching for something, when often we find nothing at all." ¶ Yang Zhenzhong, Xiang Liqin and Kan Xuan, three of the four 4 x 100 Meters artists, met up in Shanghai in 2002 when Kan Xuan made a visit there for the *Twins* exhibition organized by Xu Zhen and Yang Zhenzhong during the biennial. All of these young artists share a way of existing, of being, of reacting, of moving forward. They have identical beliefs. It was superb to see them all together, so united, so sharp, so alive. ¶ Kan Xuan in her tiny apartment in Amsterdam, at the top of a steep flight of stairs typical of Dutch architecture, drawing funny little figures, numbers, and letters on the walls. Kan Xuan in the Amsterdam subway, surrounded by Indonesians. Kan Xuan in the academy cafeteria, eating soup and a slice of bread. In her studio, rather large and almost completely empty, leading onto a long corridor where doors open onto other studios. She put a large cardboard box and a comforter in her studio, along with a selection of the sort of objects people usually take to bed with them to help them to sleep. A performance. She lived there for a week. ¶ In the studio there was also a trashcan that she equipped with an electronic system that opened and closed the lid like the maw of an animal. She laughs. Kan Xuan often laughs. ¶ On the door of the studio, her name and a number. Inside, a table and a computer. That is all. It is not the result of a conscious desire for austerity, but neither is it the opposite. It is just that it is fine as it is. ¶ Her most recent video dates from November 2003. It lasts six minutes, is filmed in black and white, and is called *Object*. It was presented at an open day at the Amsterdam academy, and was one of the works most widely admired by visitors and teachers alike. The video shows small objects such as drips of coffee, milk, or tea, or an apple dropping into water. A woman's voice gives the color of each object. But since the film is in black and white, the voice says, "The apple is gray" or "The coffee is black." ¶ This simple, fluid video—her favorite work—questions not only reality, but also art's claim to represent reality, as well as human vision and language, among other things. Kan Xuan has a special gift for bringing together two or three elements, which by their very juxtaposition undermine the situation and our certainties. ¶ A month later, in January, Kan Xuan flew back to Beijing, where she is now.

FROM LEFT TO RIGHT: KAN XUAN IN THE CORRIDOR WITH STUDIOS LEADING OFF. THE BOX SHE SLEPT IN FOR HER PERFORMANCE. THE ESSENTIALS SHE TOOK FOR HER PERFORMANCE. FACING PAGE: A12 IS THE MILITARY-SOUNDING NAME OF THE STUDIO SHE OCCUPIED IN THE FORMER CAVALRY BARRACKS THAT NOW HOUSES THE RIJKSAKADEMIE. BOTTOM LEFT: KAN XUAN WATCHING THE TRASHCAN SHE PROGRAMMED TO OPEN AUTOMATICALLY.

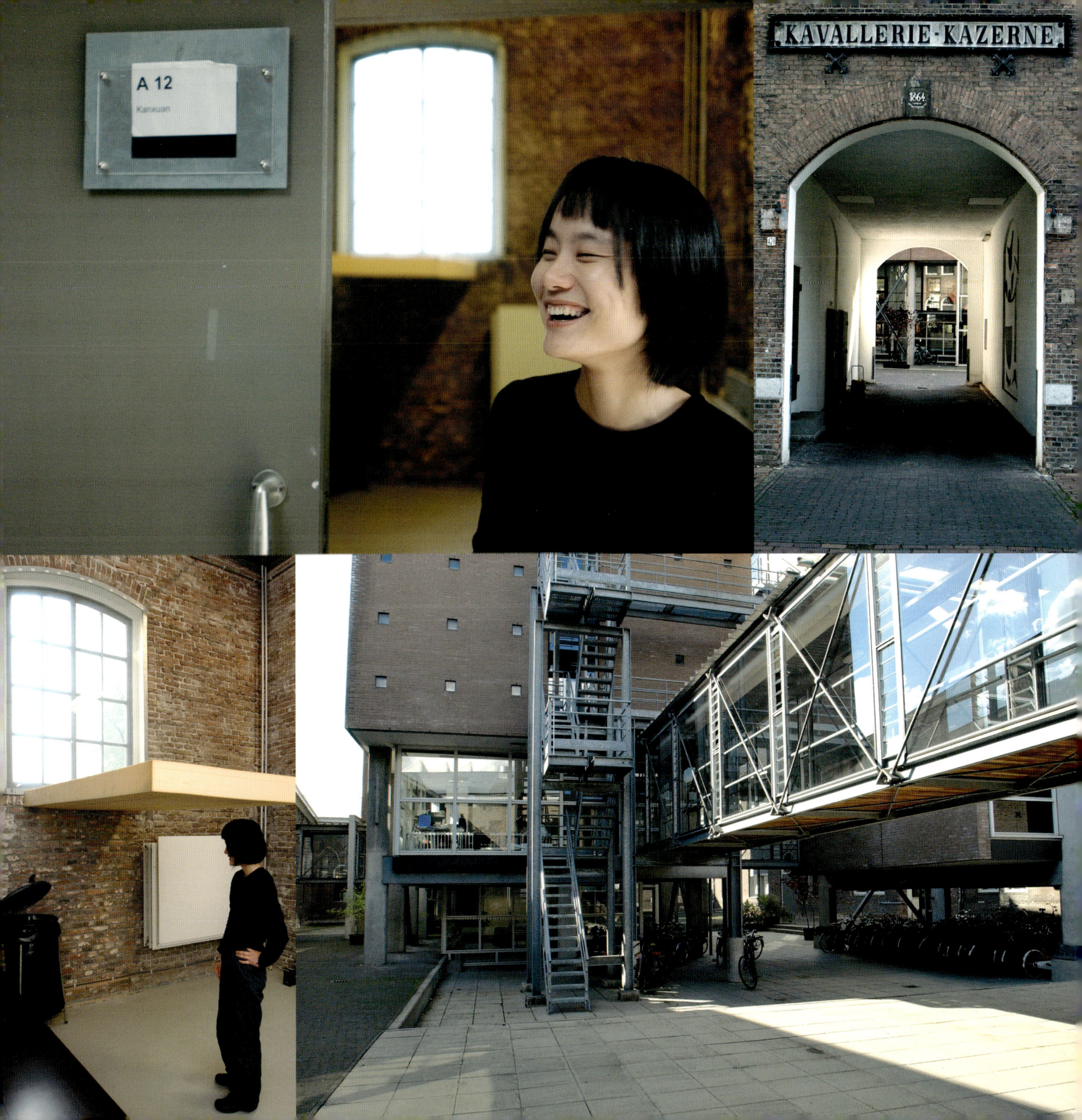
A 12
KAVALLERIE-KAZERNE
1864

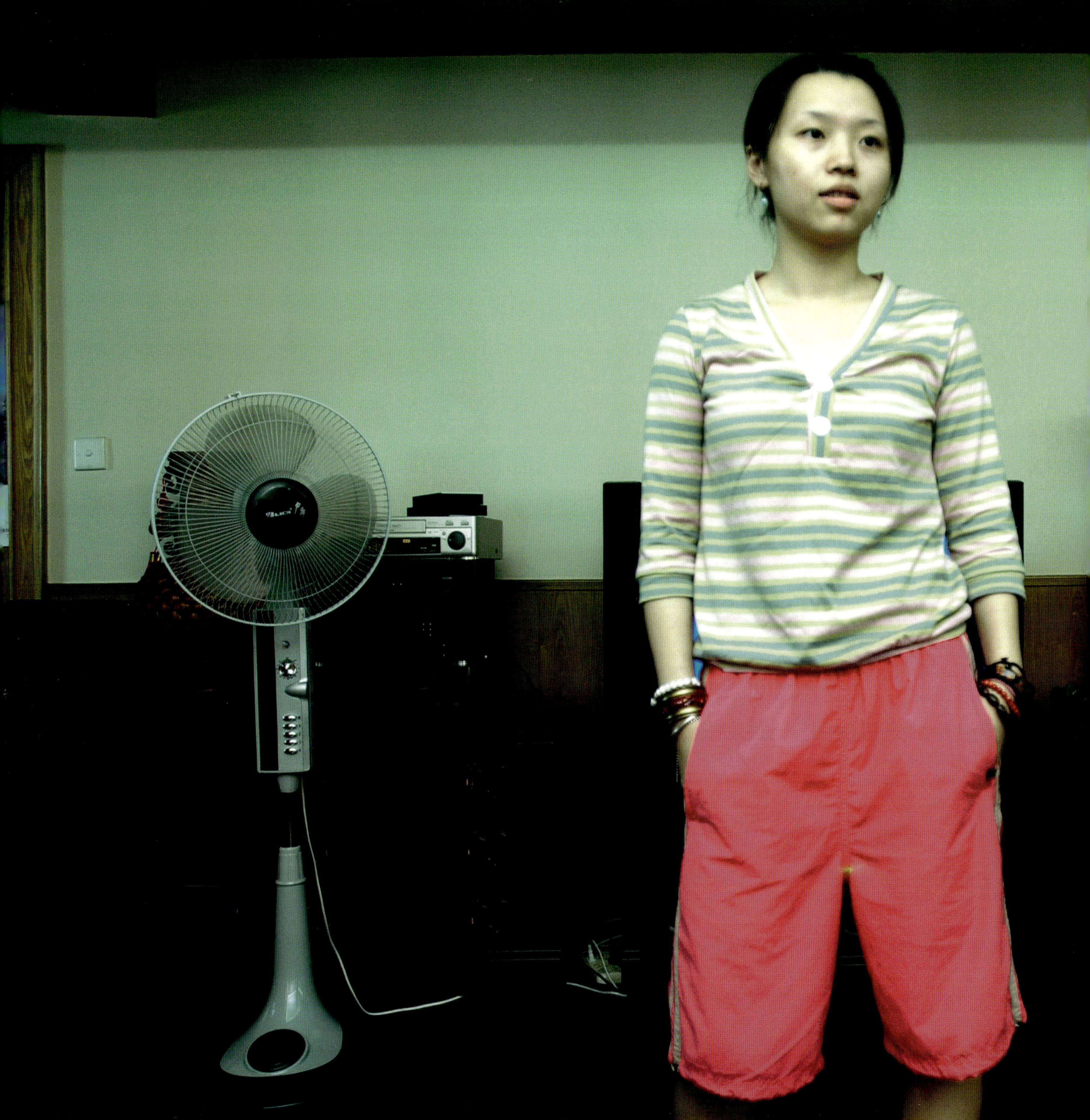

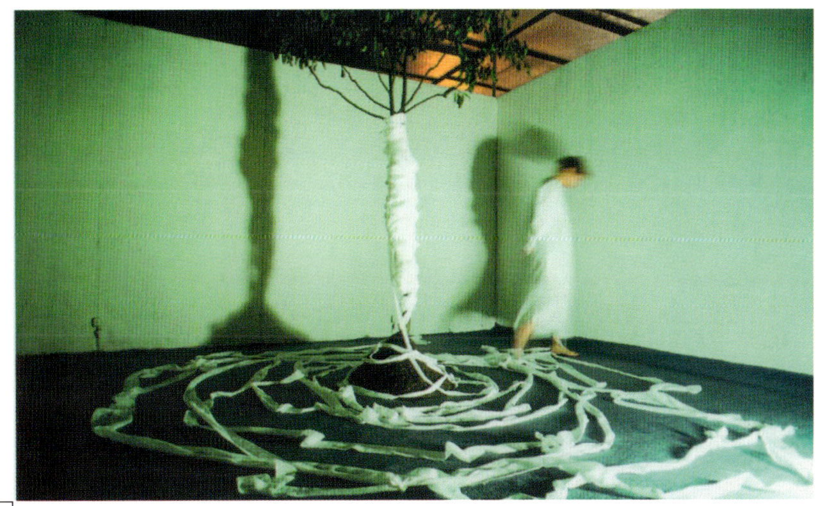

LIANG YUE

A young lady in a hat, swaddled in a padded jacket far too big for her and a shapeless pair of trousers—that was my first impression of Liang Yue when I met her in Shanghai in October 2002 at the Biennale, where she was trumpeted as a brilliant young artist. It was a chilly fall evening. My interpreter told me that she knew of her as a musician rather than an artist. It seems she played the clarinet for an experimental electronic group. ¶ When I met her again in Beijing two months later, she was working on a commercial film, just to earn her keep. ¶ Finally, in Shanghai in September 2003, she was about to leave on the night train for Beijing—cheaper than flying—to shoot her first feature-length film in digital video. Her mother had accompanied her to the station. ¶ She lives with her mother in the southeast of the city, in a fairly well-heeled area, opposite a bizarre hotel and restaurant with an ostentatious façade, almost entirely covered with a gilded eagle. Their apartment is full of heavy, solid furniture. It is large, with several bedrooms, a kitchen, and, near a window in the sitting room, a bar, which looks incongruous in this setting, with its bottle of cognac and the glasses hanging upside-down from a rack. ¶ You take your shoes off before entering Liang Yue's apartment. You sit on the sofa, and you let yourself succumb to the charm of her voice. It is low, modest, and almost too soft. Saturated with nostalgia. ¶ Liang Yue is twenty-four. She is an astonishing mix of quiet and authentic immaturity. ¶ All I knew of her work were two videos I had watched more or less secretly in the back room of the Shanghart gallery in Shanghai, just by Mogashan Lu 50. It was not really enough to judge whether I was dealing with a major talent, but it was plenty to show me that here was a genuine artist. ¶ Over time, it became more and more obvious that Liang Yue is one of the most delightful personalities of what Chinese critics are calling the "new new generation." In my opinion, the other up-and-coming artist on this scene, Song Tao, still has a lot to prove. ¶ Liang Yue joined the art scene through the door marked installations and photography. Her first video, *Lunar Eclipse* (2000), was in fact part of an installation. What is it about? The strange, yet pleasant sensation of being in a familiar place in the dark, where you can put on your makeup without really seeing what you're doing, and where you feel safe. Is that all? Yes. Almost. All of Liang Yue's best work is in this intimate mood, where minute details can prove disconcerting. Like the work of Xu Zhen, who is and has long been a close friend. ¶ *Dandruff*, an eight-minute-long video shot in 2001, plays with the same register, but as a negative. As with most of her work, the video is of the artist herself. Why? "Because I know myself better than anyone, and I know better than anyone what I want to present and represent." In the video, she ruffles her hair and dandruff falls from it. That is all. As normal. She is so young, I can't say as always. ¶ *Poison* is a short video shot as part of an installation, with an obsessive soundtrack that sticks in your mind. "If you listen to this music for too long, you go crazy," Liang Yue tells me, "but I don't lay too much emphasis on it. The music is just to create an ambience." ¶ Another video shows her burning her diary on her birthday—a way of keeping her secrets forever. She whistles as the notebook burns. She says, "I love whistling. I often whistle. Most of the time I use music in my works, but not this time. I wanted something more familiar and ordinary." ¶ And she doesn't just whistle. She plays the clarinet—my interpreter was right—and since 2002 has been an active member of Circus on the Roof, a group of five musicians who were invited to perform at the Museum of Modern Art

FACING PAGE: LIANG YUE IN THE APARTMENT SHE SHARES WITH HER MOTHER. THE FAN IS PROOF THAT IT CAN GET VERY HOT IN SHANGHAI. ABOVE: THE PERFORMANCE *FALLING ASLEEP*, IN 1999.

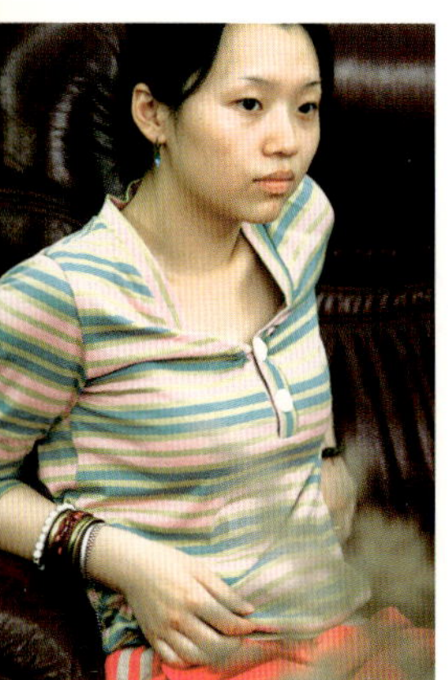

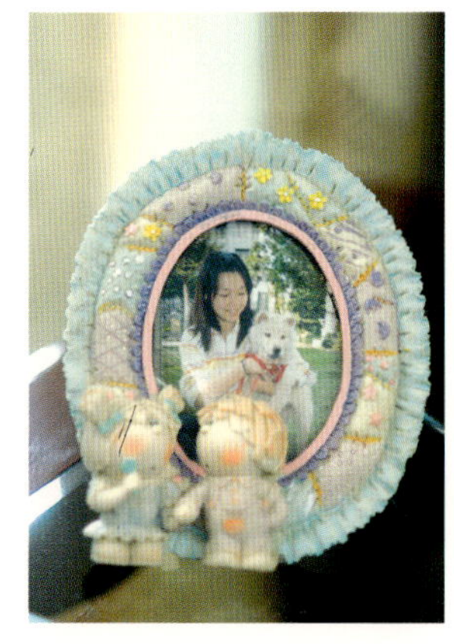

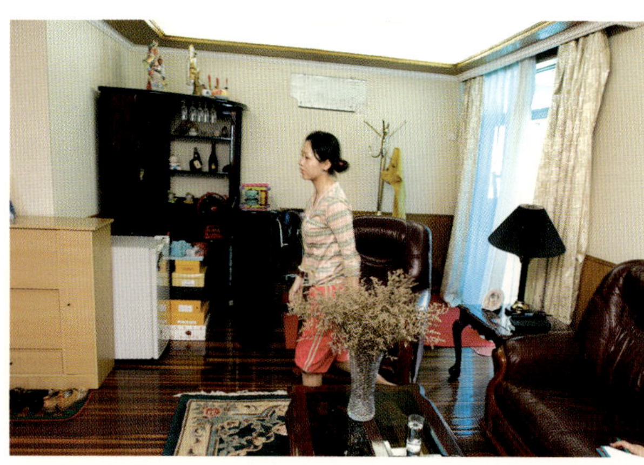

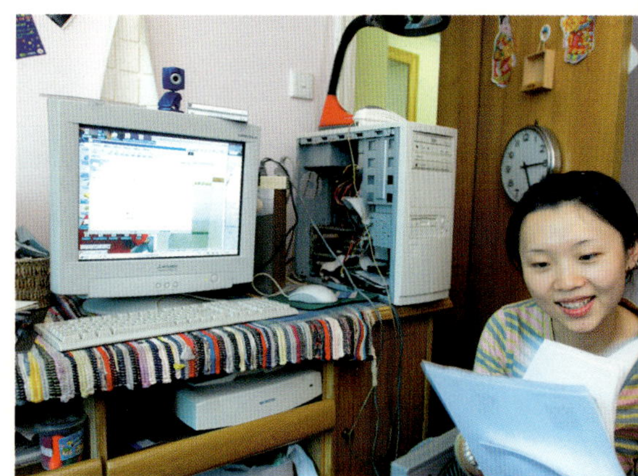

in New York in 2003. In fact, Liang Yue trained as a musician. ¶ What happened, then? How did she become an artist? ¶ By chance, she says—or almost. In high school, she hung out with a group of friends who loved drawing and were enrolled in architecture school. She was fascinated by what her friends were doing and wanted to follow the same path. Instead, she enrolled at the School of Fine Arts, where she studied advertising and design, like many other up-and-coming young Chinese artists. ¶ To begin with, she painted, like everyone else. Oil paintings. Her friends were specializing in photography, video, and performance art, and in 1999 encouraged her to take part in one of the most important exhibitions of the year, *Art for Sale*. She was then in her second year of college. Her art expanded as she explored the immense space of the exhibition hall. She says, "We knew that all that had already been done abroad, but we all talked it over and decided that we wanted to try it ourselves. We had fun." ¶ Liang Yue showed a work entitled *Falling Asleep*. It featured a "tree in a calm space," its trunk wrapped in bandages, which she unrolls and then uses to enchant the rest of the space, wrapping them around the branches to form garlands, all the while falling into a strange sleep-like torpor herself. It was magnificent. Unfortunately, the photographs of the performance do not do justice to the impression of languid sloth that made this unique performance so special. ¶ *Ghost Upstairs* (2003) lasts barely three minutes. It echoes with phrases like "I can't pay my phone bill," and lots of "I hates": "I hate going to work," "I hate laughing in front of my boss," and so on. ¶ *Sky Light* is part of an installation where we watch the light constantly changing around a fixed, unmoving presence. For once, Liang Yue is not the main actress. "It's not easy to act immobile," she says. "To be there without doing anything," as the chosen actress does. ¶ *Nowhere* (2003) has an impressive way of stopping the music in the middle of a shot, and generally fading music in and out more or less abruptly. She tells me in a low, slightly husky voice, "Although life is not difficult, you have the impression of having no future—of not knowing where to go." The music is by Horse and Donkey. The film is dedicated to "young dreamers." ¶ This could almost be a declaration of her intentions. ¶ *The Happiest Winter* is my favorite of Liang Yue's works. It is simple, like all of her works, and intimate, like most of them—but it is enchanted like no other with sleep and enveloping dreams, like the snow that cloaks cottages in German folktales, featuring the artist herself wrapped up snug in padded jackets and woolen hats, crossing the city, sleeping in the bus or the subway, on a bench in some garden or other, against a cement guardrail. The video begins with a shot of Liang Yue in bed. ¶ This film, that could also have been dedicated to "young dreamers," has a fluid rhythm that characterizes her work, which has a curiously somnambulist feel. Although it is early days yet, her work is deeply subtle, licentious, a twirl aside, gradual steps, softness. Liang Yue, the heavenly sleeper, steps forward, eyes closed, transfigured by grace.

LIANG YUE'S APARTMENT, SOUTHEAST OF SHANGHAI, IS IN A RELATIVELY WELL-HEELED NEIGHBORHOOD. VISITORS MUST TAKE OFF THEIR SHOES AT THE FRONT DOOR.

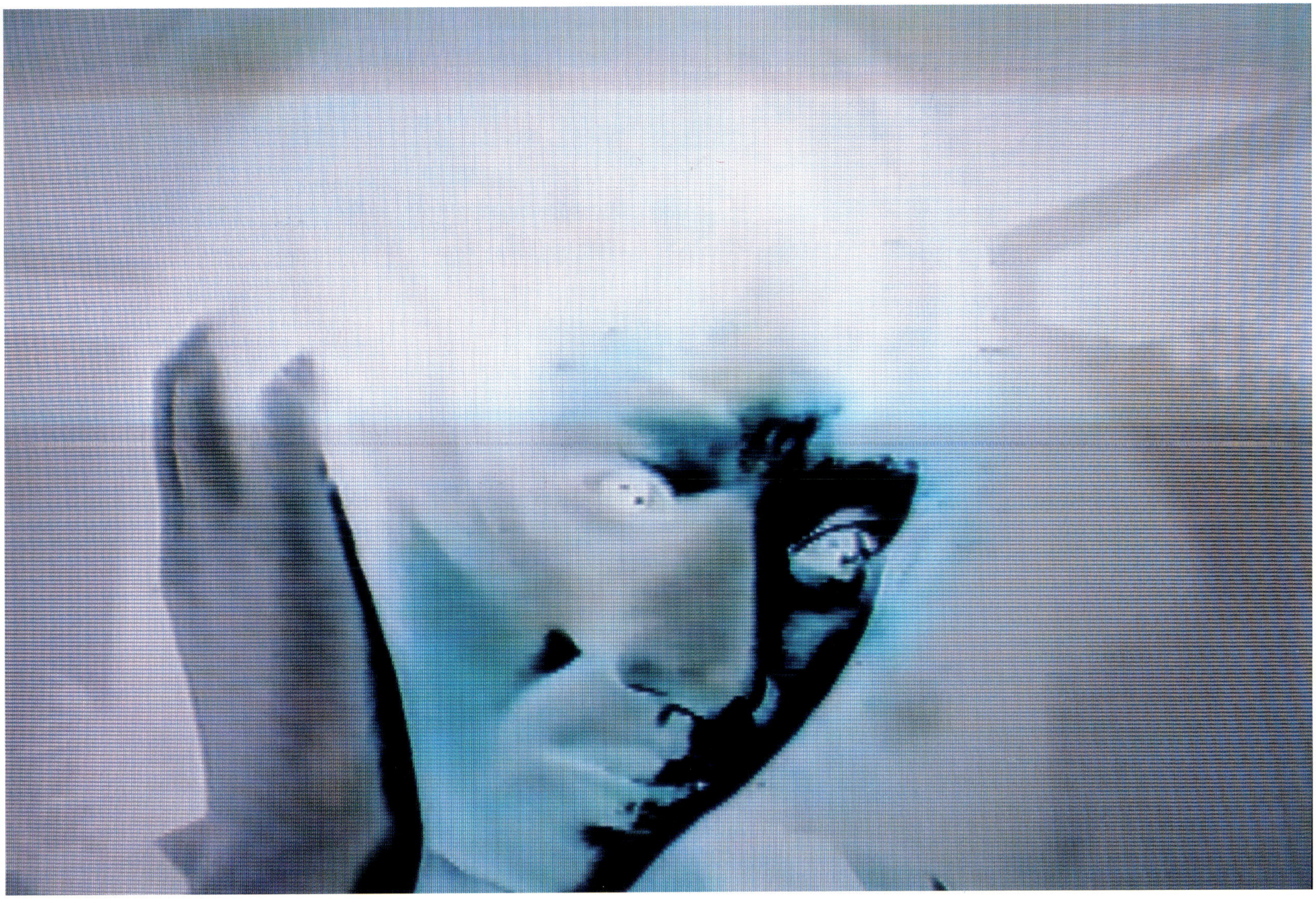

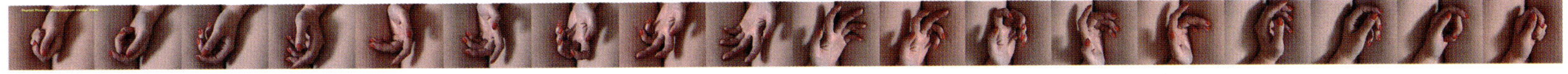

TOP: *DANDRUFF*, 2000, VIDEO. BOTTOM: *PHYSIOLOGICAL CYCLE*, 2000, COMPUTER COPY.

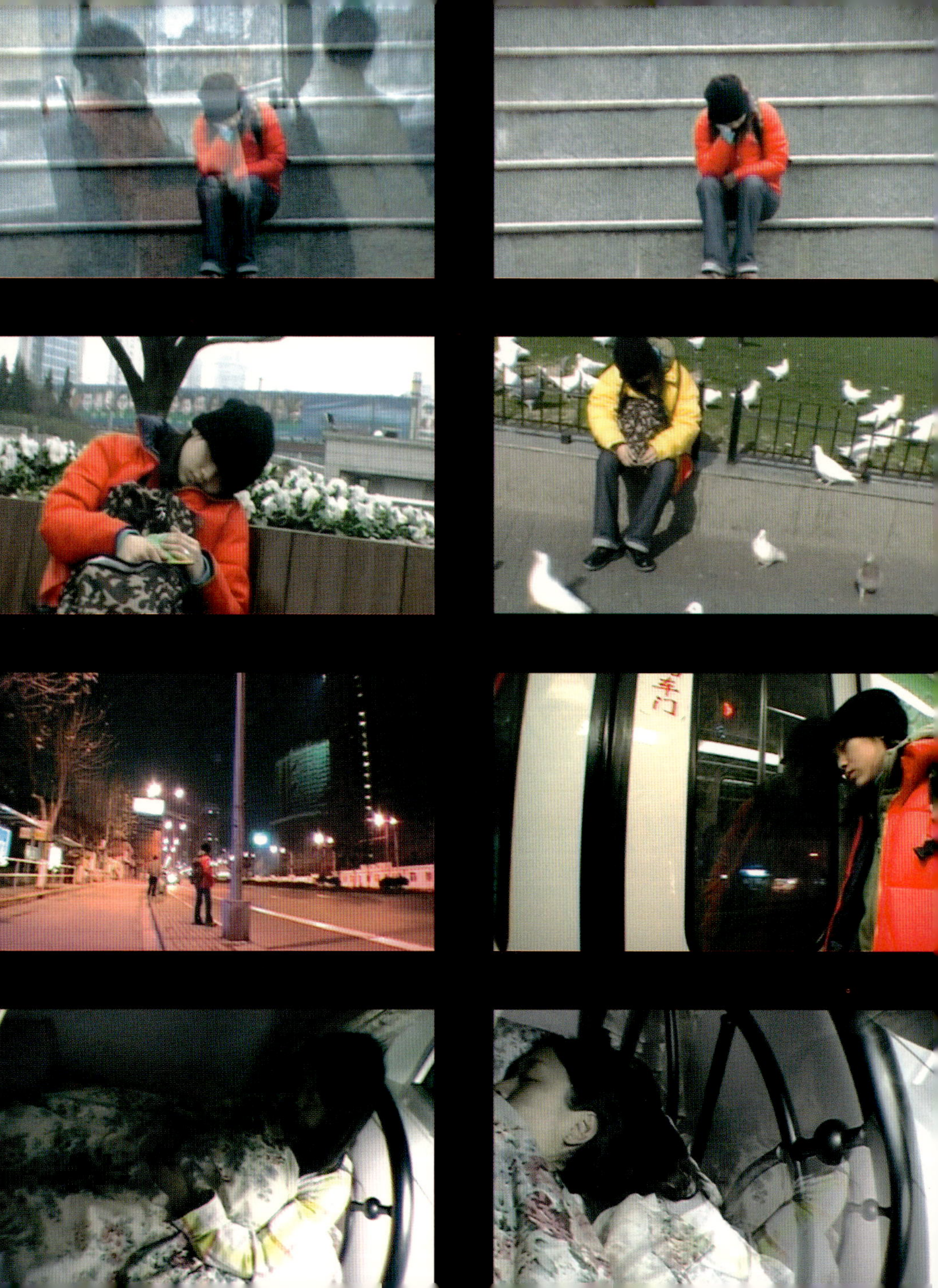
车门

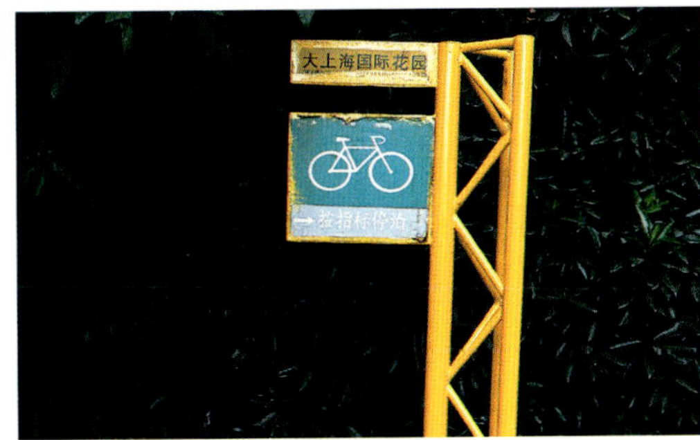

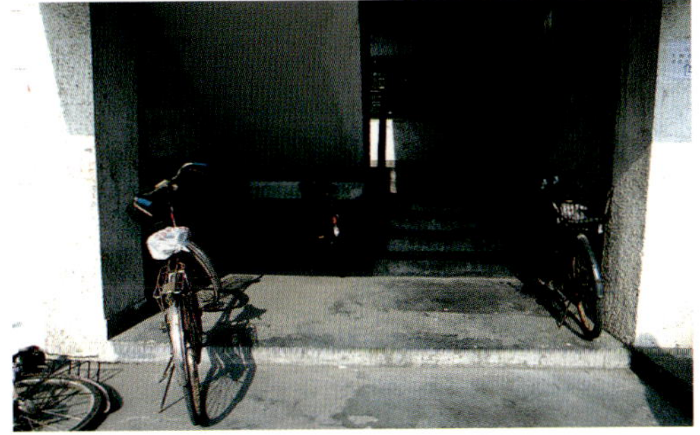

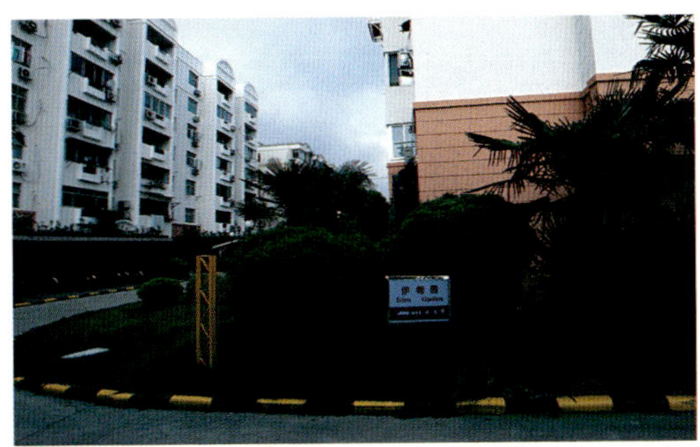

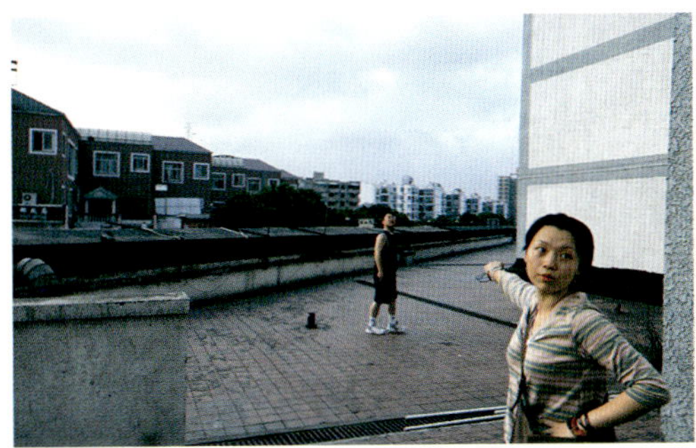

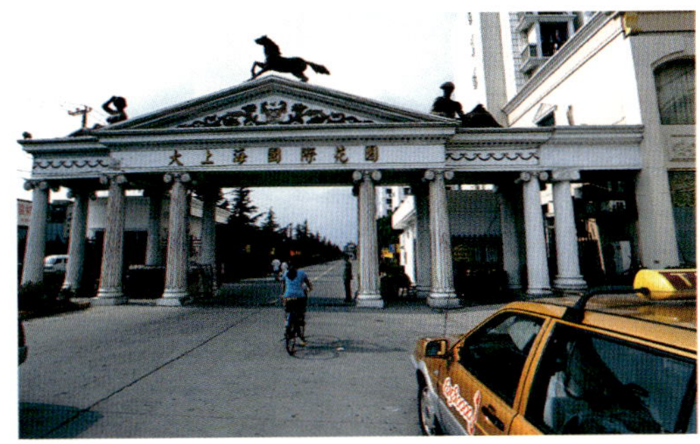

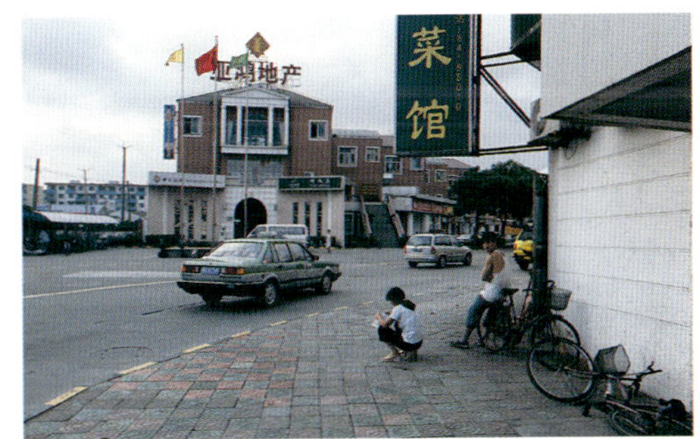

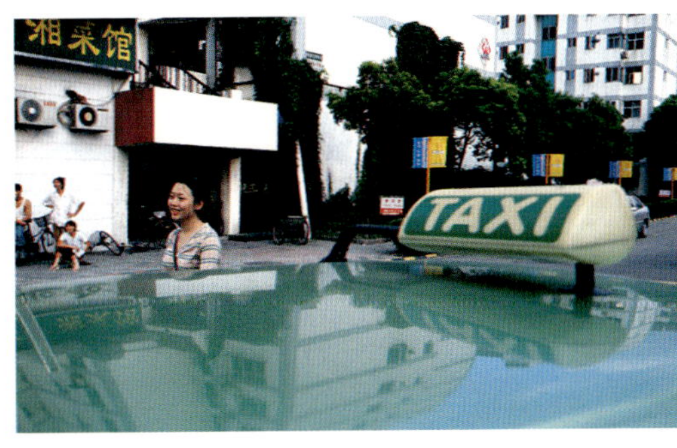

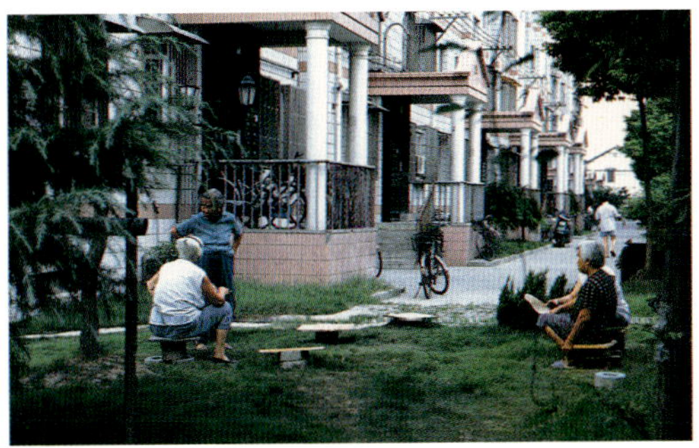

FACING PAGE: *THE HAPPIEST WINTER*, 2003. IN THIS CHARMING VIDEO, LIANG YUE IS ON THE POINT OF FALLING ASLEEP ALL THE TIME, GIVING THE WORK A PLEASANTLY HEAVY FEELING. ABOVE: LIANG YUE TAKING THE TAXI TO THE STATION WHERE SHE MUST CATCH A TRAIN FOR BEIJING.

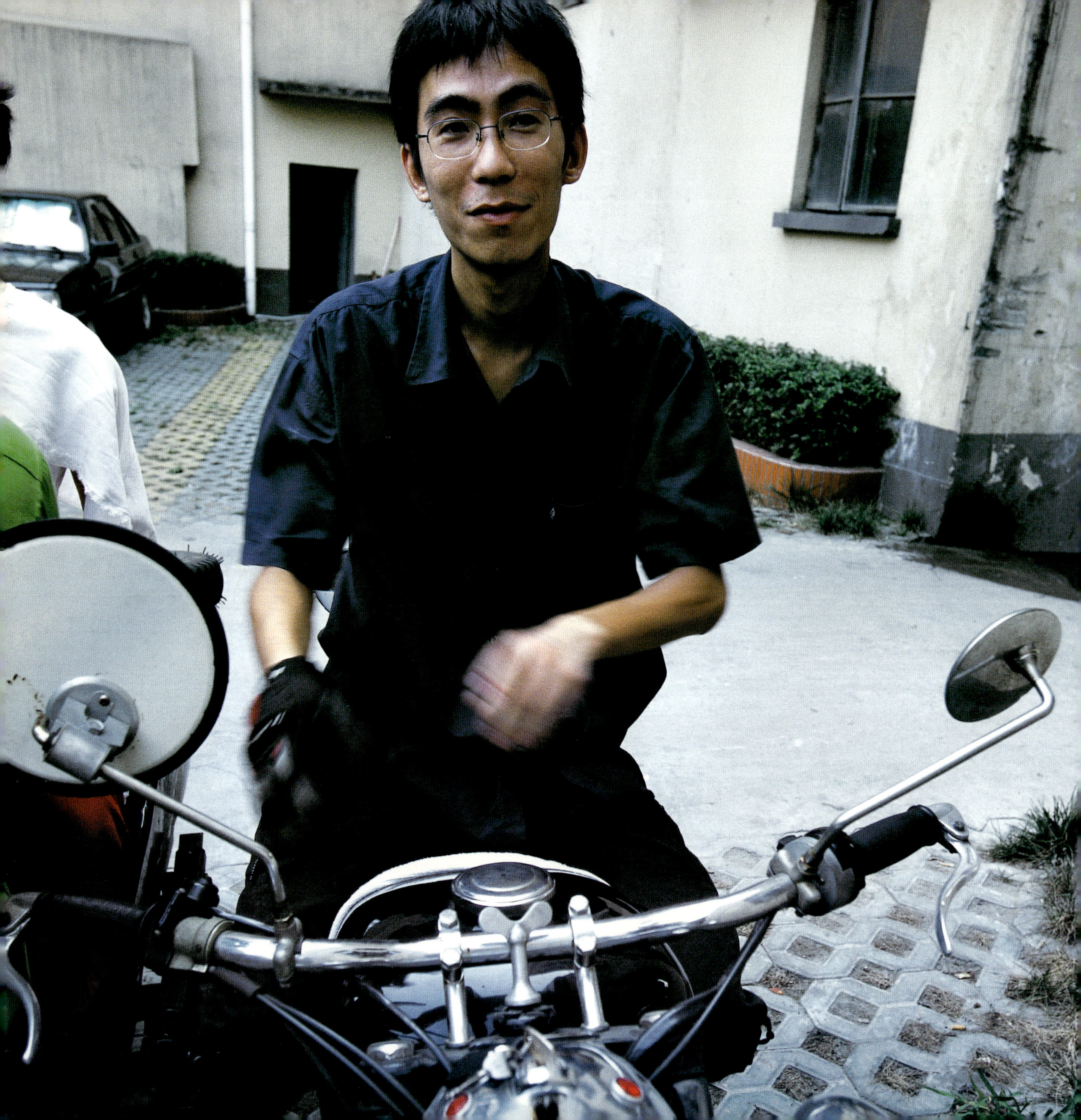

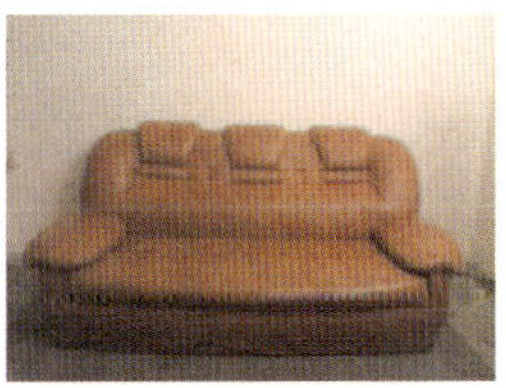
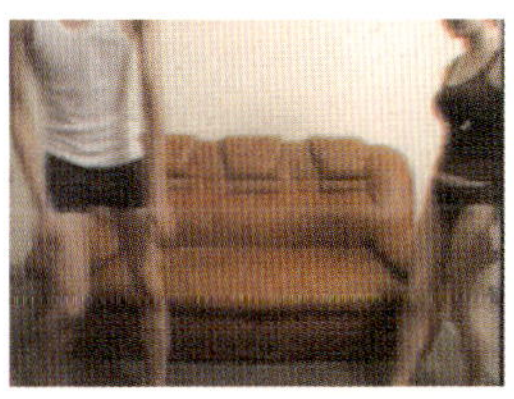
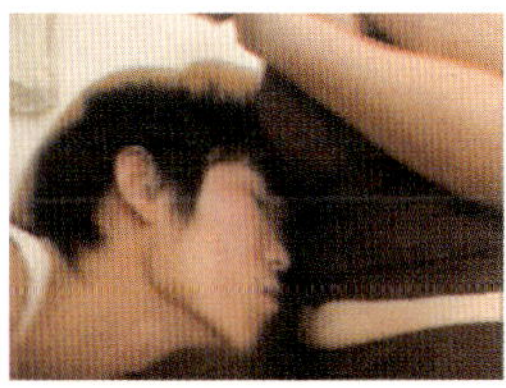
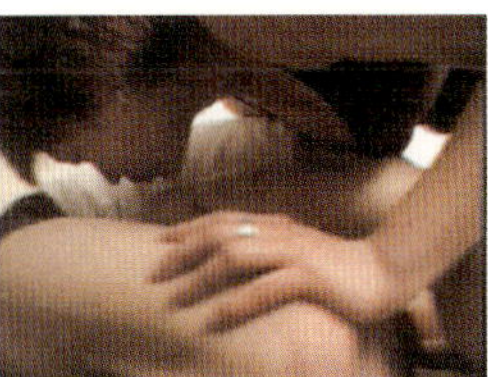
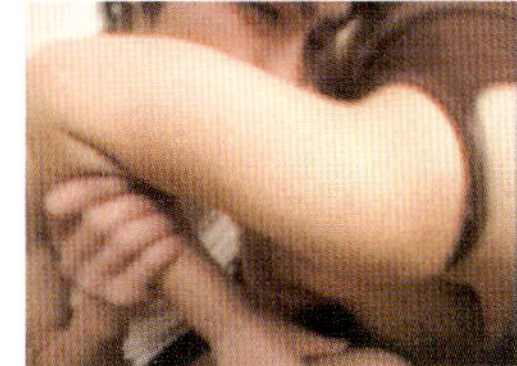
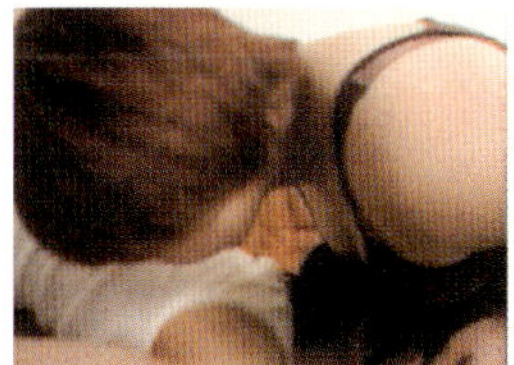

XU ZHEN

He wears glasses. He's a tall, angular young man with long, thin limbs and a graceful, fluid way of moving. We met in the offices of the BizArt Center where he is the brilliant young artistic director. He looks just as languid getting off his motorcycle, involved in a lengthy discussion with an alien with yellow hair, an up-and-coming young artist named Song Tao whose dreamy, hazy creations are beginning to get him noticed in Shanghai art circles. Xu Zhen is extremely mature, and looks older than he really is. That is most unusual in China. ¶ Davide Quadrio, BizArt's director, says he is remarkably intelligent and that he has an extremely precise and clear artistic vision. It's true. He is just twenty-four years old. ¶ Who is this outrageously talented young man? Or rather, who is he first and foremost? Which of his multifarious activities, that would drain the energy of any normal man, defines him best? Is he an artist? The artistic director of BizArt, which is a new sort of art center rather than a traditional gallery? A successful exhibition curator? ¶ He manages to juggle all of these activities, apparently without difficulty. So what does the ironic smile that flits across his face when you ask the question mean? How does he manage to combine all these diverse activities that are less compatible than might appear at first glance? I was to find out, not so much by questioning him directly as I have tried several times in the last few years, but by following his work since 2001, when he struck the Venice Biennale like a thunderbolt. Xu Zhen completed the work shown in Venice in 1998, when he was nineteen. ¶ The work in question, entitled *Rainbow,* was an astonishing four-minute video of a naked man's back from the armpits to the hips. The man's back was repeatedly lashed by a whip—invisible but with sound effects—until the ordinarily rosy pink skin turned a dark purple. Was it an exploration of ways of painting? No, but the strange title of a series of photographs dating from 2000, *Problem of Colorfulness,* shows that this reading should not be rejected out of hand. ¶ What was really happening with this invisible whip, which only existed through sound effects and the marks on the man's back? The viewer is confused, and tries to understand, wanting to see through the film and the trick photography, to discover the special effect. In the end, the viewer hardly reacts to the violence of the image. He is more impressed with the camerawork than indignant at its content. In Venice, the critics generally acknowledged that the unsettling, subtle complexity of the work and the impression of unease that it generates were impressive, as was the talent of the artist—whose name was promptly forgotten. He was neither German nor American. In 2001, China was not yet fashionable. ¶ In his home country, Xu Zhen's talent was quickly recognized. He had certainly done all he could to bring himself to the attention of the people who mattered. He was straight away seen for precisely what he is: an extraordinarily inventive artist, generous with his time, his ideas, and his gifts. From 1998 to 2004, he produced an unbelievable amount of work, directing, exhibiting, organizing, and presenting his creations to the art scene first in Shanghai, then, very quickly, internationally. He was provocative, and he certainly generated some heated reactions. ¶ The photographic series *Problem of Colorfulness* (2000) is as shocking today as when it was first shown. And just as fascinating. It presents what is apparently the lower half of a man's body, from the level of the belly button to the back of the knees, seen from behind. From the genitals (which cannot be seen) there flows a long stream of blood. What is the significance of this blend of genders of a rare intensity? Xu Zhen begins by saying, perhaps prudently, "I love women. But I can only know femininity from the outside. This image is designed to express my love and my regrets. I wanted to show what happens to a woman's body every month, but using a man's body." Like a sort of transfer?

FACING PAGE: XU ZHEN ARRIVING ON HIS MOTORBIKE IN THE PATCH OF WASTELAND THAT NOW HOUSES THE THREE BEST GALLERIES IN SHANGHAI, INCLUDING BIZART, WHERE HE IS ARTISTIC DIRECTOR.
ABOVE: THE VIDEO *FROM INSIDE THE BODY,* 1999.

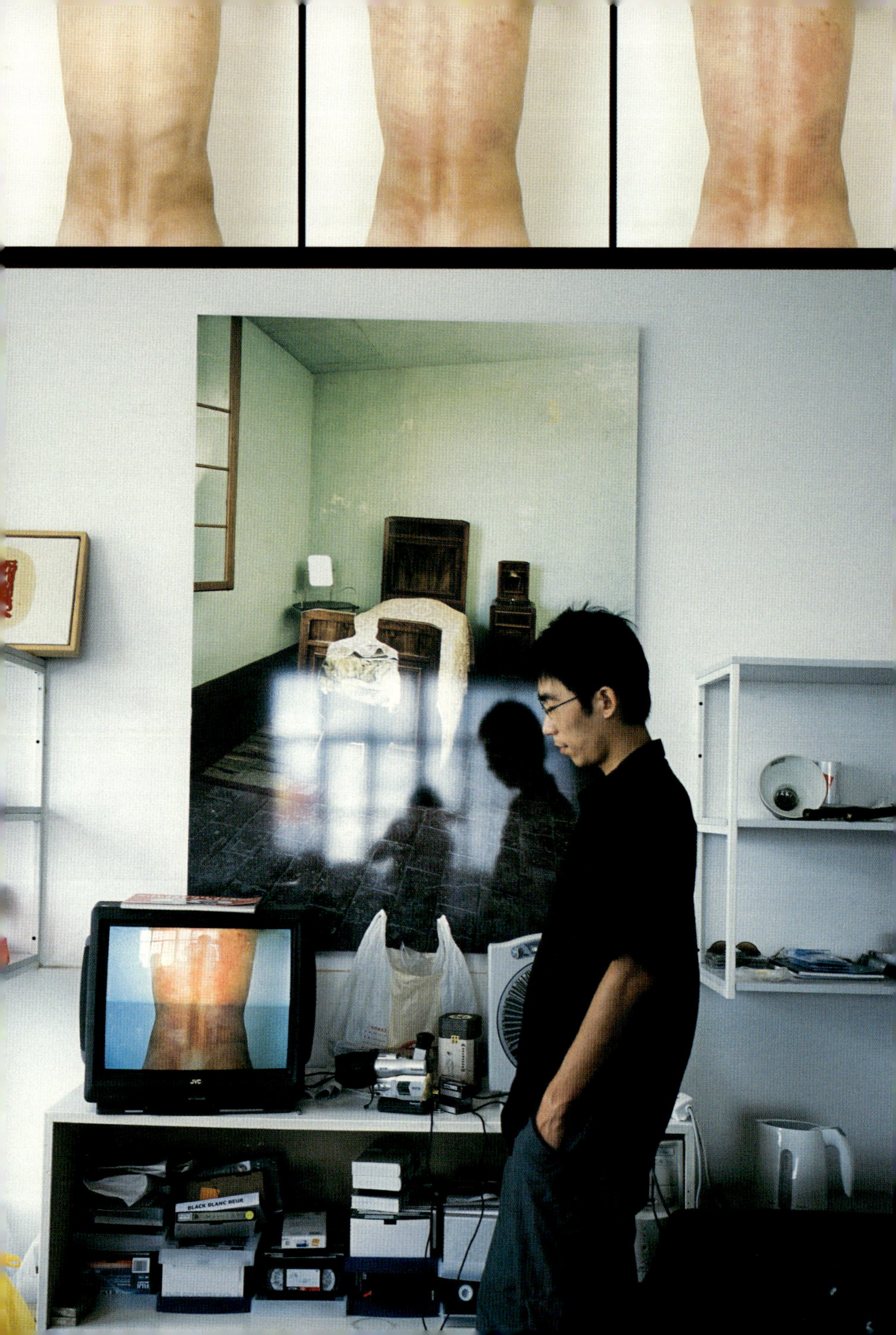
JVC
BLACK BLANC BEUR

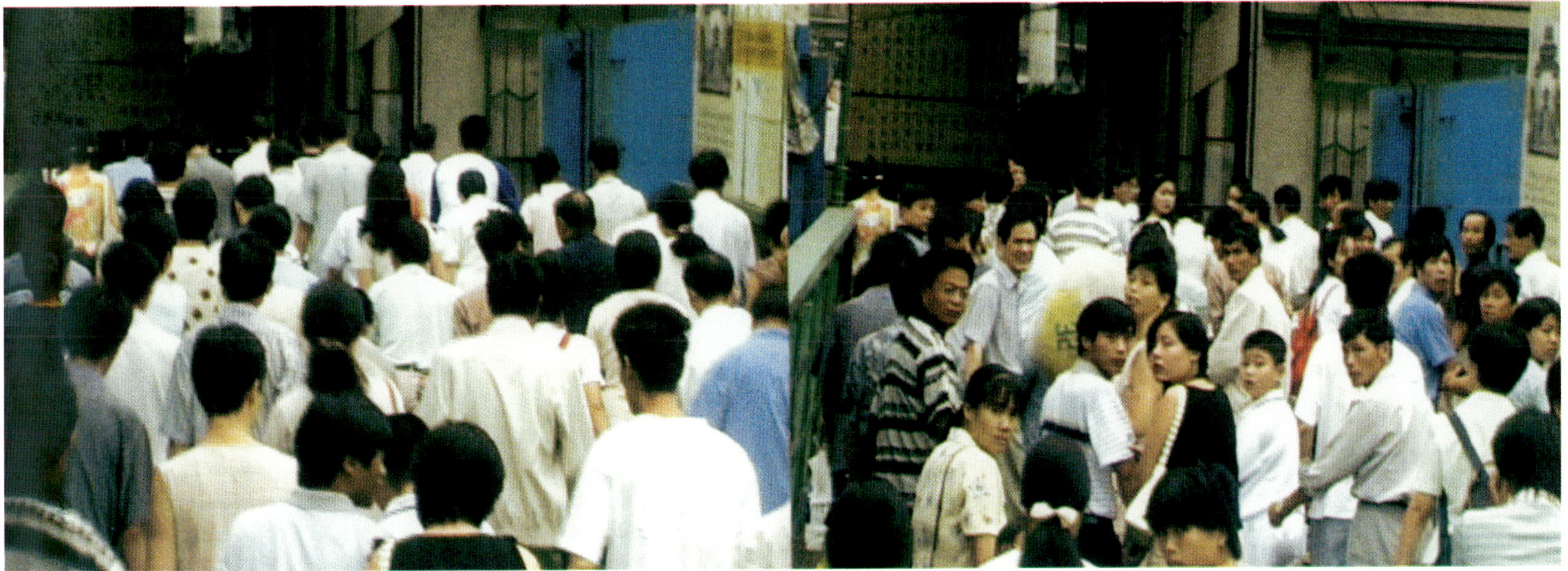

I ask, to see what he makes of the question. But Xu Zhen does not answer. ¶ The animal protection lobby that wrangled with Huang Yong Ping at the Centre Pompidou in Paris, would certainly have had something to say about a 1998 video by Xu Zhen in which he films himself in a small room, grabbing a cat by one paw or its tail and hitting it against the ground for forty-five minutes. The performance was called *Throwing a Cat*, and the video of it *I'm Not Asking For Anything*. Of course, the cat was already dead, but even fully armed with this knowledge, it is impossible to watch the video without feeling queasy. Particularly after reading an interview where the journalist asked, "Why a cat?" to which Xu Zhen replied, "Because cats are sexy." ¶ For the film *Shouting* (1998), Xu Zhen took his video camera to a variety of places, such as the entrances to large department stores, narrow passages, and busy streets, to film the passersby—without any particular motive in mind. We settle down to watch. The passersby walk on, the shoppers ride up and down the escalators in the department stores elbow to elbow, people come in and out of offices. So far, so good. Then, suddenly, a long, howling cry rips through the air, a little like Kan Xuan shouting his name against the tide of the crowd or in the subway, but more gut-wrenching, more from the heart. Xu Zhen records the reactions of the passersby, who hardly seem concerned, maybe turning round to see if they can locate the source of the animal shriek, but more interested by their discovery of the impassive eye of the video camera than the cry and what it could mean. ¶ Xu Zhen does not observe reality. He attacks it. He makes it pay. He is out to get it, like a thug out to get a rival or someone to beat up. ¶ Somewhere else, another time. A street corner, a sidewalk, or a view from a doorway. People walking along, chatting, smoking, running, cycling, stopping. Normal activities in a normal street. Then something out of the ordinary happens. Someone looks towards the camera, at you, the viewer, and comes towards you, intrigued. As he approaches, a few locks are ruffled by the wind, which grows progressively stronger. The person turns his head; the wind is too strong and it is becoming difficult to walk. Other people around are astonished to find that suddenly, the wind is tousling their hair and flapping their coats and dresses. But it is a strange wind, which only affects this little street corner where people smile and laugh as they stare at the lens. Xu Zhen simply set up a wind turbine at the entrance to his exhibition, and put a video camera down next to it to record what happens when a mysterious wind sweeps through the dullness and banality of an ordinary street. ¶ Many other young—or even less young—artists have borrowed from Xu Zhen's innovations, drawing on his manner of intervening in reality, of observing the body and testing its limits, not to the point of outrage, but at least to the point of provocation. ¶ I had never been to Xu Zhen's studio. I wasn't sure he even had one. As his Korean biographer Kou Jeong-A wrote, he "lives and works everywhere." He shows his work wherever it is practical to do so, wherever there is a TV screen and a VCR or DVD player—basically anywhere. He often puts on shows in the offices of the BizArt gallery. ¶ BizArt used to be in Shanghai, at 758 Julu Road, through the vast square courtyard and on the left, up on the fourth floor. There, he would gladly show you, for as long as you wanted or for as long as you could spare, videos and photographs by Yang Zhenzhong, Yang Fudong, and Zhen Guogu. If you said you had come to see his own work, he just as willingly took his videocassettes (often of mediocre picture quality, unfortunately) down from a shelf high up on the wall. ¶ His most recent video, *On the Boat*, shows a man and woman in a boat, filmed from the thighs to the neck, reduced to nothing more than their gestures. They take out of the zipper of their pants a pack of cigarettes, then a lighter.

FACING PAGE: XU ZHEN EXHIBITING HIS VIDEO *RAINBOW* IN THE BIZART GALLERY OFFICES. TOP: THREE STILLS FROM A VIDEO SHOWING A MAN'S BACK GROWING BLOODY FROM THE LASHING OF AN INVISIBLE WHIP. ABOVE: *SHOUTING*, 1998, VIDEO.

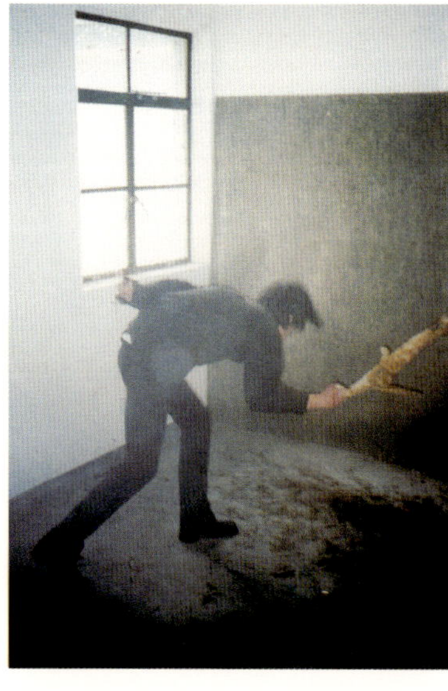
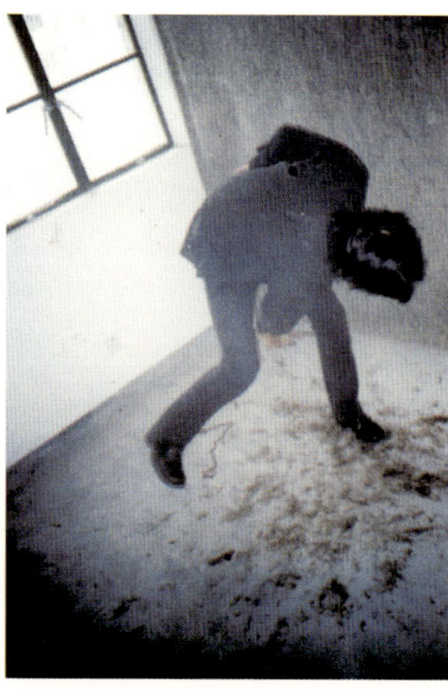
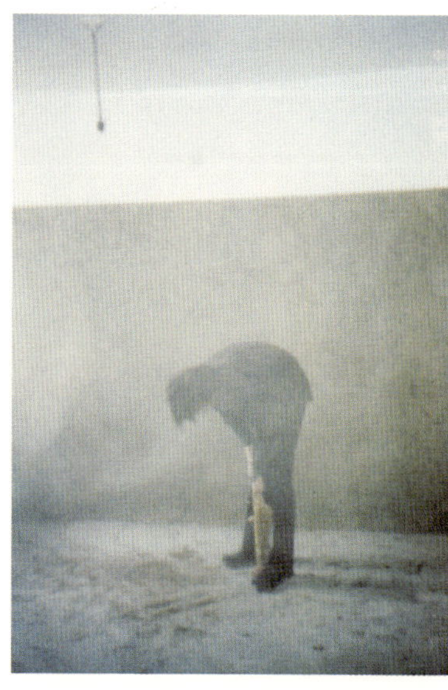
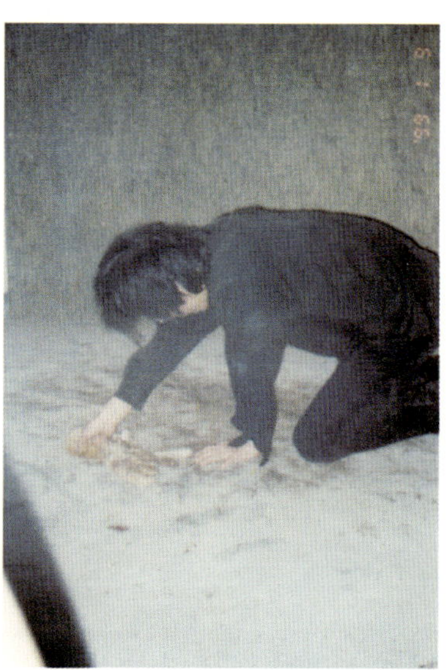

After lighting the cigarettes, the girl takes a lipstick out of the zipper of her pants and touches up her makeup (we do not see this happening as her face is off-camera). Meanwhile, the young man removes yet another item from his zipper. Everything passes through the zippers of their pants. Is this a way of saying that all these consumer desirables are worthless as piss? No: Xu Zhen's work reflects his very powerful affirmation that young men and women of his generation are no longer bothered with politics, and don't want to become involved. At least, he adds with a sly smile, not in Shanghai. Maybe artists in Beijing are a different matter. . . . So what about the video? It shows a new way of living and behaving. It may be abnormal, but it certainly is modern. ¶ An enormous sheet, pinned to a wall. Holes have been cut in the fabric. Arms poke through the holes. If you have seen Jean Cocteau's *Beauty and the Beast*, the image will be familiar. But there is nothing decorative or Surrealist about it. The arms point towards the audience and then fold down back against the sheet. People walk up to them, shake the hands, kiss them, or stroke them. The object is to create a new kind of relationship based on close proximity yet keeping the idea of distance. ¶ *Tour Show* is a performance with the artist on stage holding a microphone, not singing into it as might be expected, but just blowing. The noise of his blowing starts softly, slowly, but then builds up, getting faster and stronger until in the end it becomes a moaning, mewling growl. It sounds as if he is making love. It lasts for quite a while. When the performance is over, he waves to the audience like a pop star. It is a comment on the way nowadays, even the most intimate spheres of life are exposed to the public gaze. ¶ Xu Zhen's work is a combination of humor and irony. He is provocative, something of an exhibitionist, yet at the same time he looks on his immediate reality—his own life, that of his girlfriend—with astonishment as if he were encountering it for the very first time. It is this strange yet seductive blend of humor, cynicism, and refreshing bluntness that makes his work so original. The 1999 work *From Inside the Body* (two minutes) shows the artist and his then girlfriend taking off all their clothes, then sniffing each other's bodies, concentrating particularly on the shadowy, intimate folds and creases of skin. They are discovering themselves as much as they are exploring each other. ¶ An installation of giant tampons hanging from the ceiling, in the middle of an exhibition, like punching bags. When you walk past, it is infinitely tempting to hit them. ¶ One last video: in a gallery somewhere in Germany, in 2002. A small electronic toy car driving around and around the gallery floor. The car is propelling a fine stream of spray, and the visitors step aside quickly as it passes, squealing with disgust. The liquid is saliva "donated" by twenty visitors—sixty-four fluid ounces (two liters) in total. Xu Zhen, or portrait of the artist as a demonically intelligent young rebel. ¶ And that is not all. As I have already mentioned, Xu Zhen is the artistic director for BizArt, an arts center that also has its own production facilities. Many of the best-known artists of the new Shanghai generation have come to work at the center precisely because Xu Zhen was there. ¶ Together with Yang Zhenzhong, his colleague and friend, Xu Zhen has proved a bold and energetic co-curator for some of the most important and spectacular exhibitions of recent times in Shanghai. His intelligence, his off-the-wall sense of opportunity, and his in-depth familiarity with the young art scene are a perfect foil for Yang Zhenzhong's intelligence, knowledge of art, and gently crazy ways. Together, both as artists and key figures on Shanghai's art scene, the two men are at the very heart of the most innovative and inventive artistic trends in one of the most dynamic cities in China. ¶ And they always bring their own riotous brand of humor to everything they touch.

I'M NOT ASKING FOR ANYTHING, A PERFORMANCE LASTING FORTY-FIVE MINUTES, RECORDED ON VIDEO IN 1999. FACING PAGE: THE VIDEO, *ON THE BOAT*, 2003.

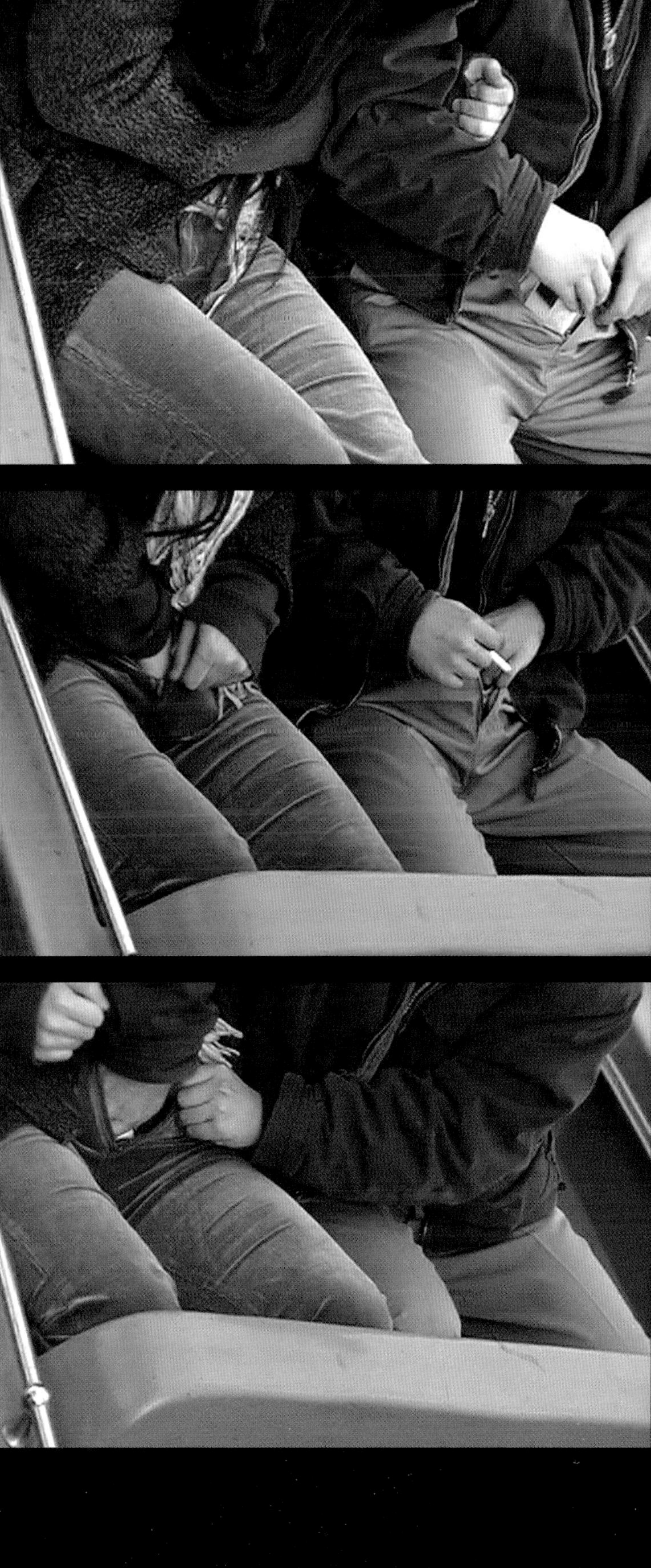

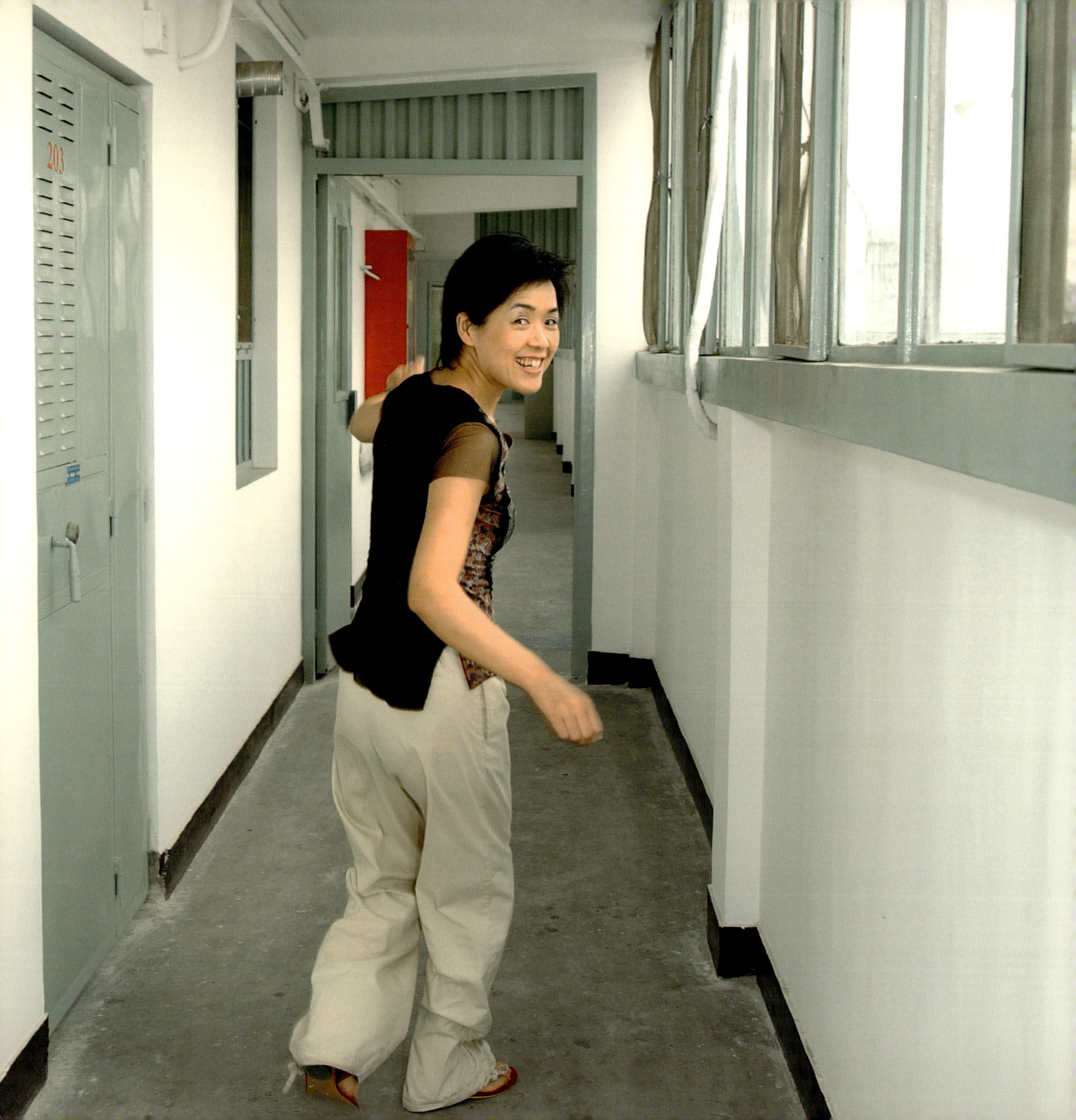
203

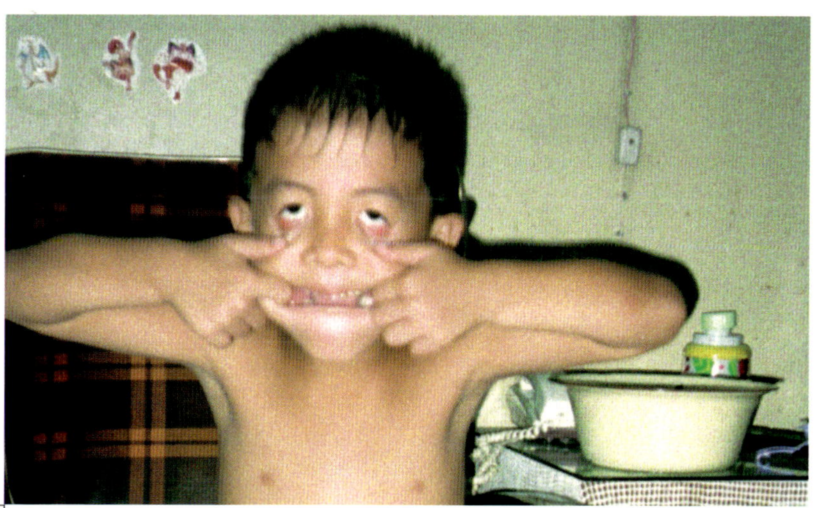

CUI XIU WEN

We are in a tiny restaurant just a stone's throw from Cui Xiu Wen's equally tiny studio. Cui Xiu Wen did not dare order pig's stomach for us, as usually "foreigners aren't very keen on trying it." Instead, we are served a dish of pork in its rind, chestnuts, and large white beans. It is lightly caramelized and surprisingly refreshing. It reminds me of the Corsican dish of tripe with beans I shared with Raymond Hains in a restaurant in rue Mazarine in Paris before the dish was taken off the menu because no one ever ordered it. Except me. Cui Xiu Wen tells me, "This was Mao's favorite meal. It's a traditional dish from my hometown." Her hometown is Harbin, in northwestern China. ¶ Her parents were ordinary workers. It was her brother and sister who got her interested in art. How, I ask? I am at a loss to know whether the curious turn of expression of the answer is hers or the interpreter's: "That was the generation that did not labor in the fields." What does that mean? Simply that her generation was fortunate enough to escape the years of deportation and reeducation of the Cultural Revolution, when students were sent to be toughened up by spending months on end breaking rocks and laboring on farms. Cui Xiu Wen's family, including her brother and sister, were able to stay in their hometown. They had plenty of free time, which they put to good use by studying. Her brother, whom she says is extremely intelligent, was passionate about all forms of art, except, curiously enough, the visual arts. He sang and played several instruments. Her older sister was fascinated by fashion. Today, she manages a clothing factory. ¶ Cui Xiu Wen is obviously deeply attached to the memory of what was clearly a happy, if not wealthy, childhood. Her brother sang all day long, and his friends, who loved to listen, would often sing along. The house was always full of a cheerful atmosphere. Is that where the sparkle in her eyes comes from? And the charming little wrinkle in her nose? And her unwavering smile? ¶ Her brother, who was such a strong influence on her childhood, encouraged her to sing and study music. "I loved it when he told me I had a gift." And what about her drawing? "I copied characters from the TV," she says. ¶ At this point she shares with me a touching anecdote about her brother, as always. One day, in a town on a mountain slope in the province of Harbin, he came across a worker struggling to pull a heavily loaded cart up a steep slope. Her brother rushed to help the man and pushed the cart up to the worker's home. As a mark of gratitude, the man gave him a roll of paper, telling him to unroll it only when he got home. When her brother got home and opened the roll, he found a number of reproductions of great works by famous artists. He gave them to his little sister, who copied them. ¶ That is how Cui Xiu Wen began painting. She had never taken any formal lessons, but just decided one day to take brush in hand. She had struck gold. Even her first effort was sold—not for much, but even so, she was thrilled. She still remembers with excitement how the buyer said, "This girl's got talent." With the money, her brother bought her a book on van Gogh. She began taking private lessons with an art teacher who taught a group of six teenage pupils. With him, she finally learned the basic techniques in a formal setting. Over the year, the other five students dropped out one by one. Cui Xiu Wen was the only one determined enough to stick with it. ¶ She says, "It was hard. I had to get up incredibly early to go and paint from nature, on the banks of the river, but I was absolutely determined to keep on with it. It was just a matter of willpower. I realize that now." ¶ End of school. University. The School of Fine Arts, one of the best in northeastern China. Then on to Beijing, where she followed her then boyfriend, whose family lived in the suburbs. She earned a meager living by giving art lessons.

FACING PAGE: CUI XIUWEN IN THE CORRIDOR TO HER LITTLE APARTMENT AND STUDIO IN BEIJING. ABOVE: DETAIL OF ONE OF HER SERIES OF PHOTOGRAPHS OF CHILDREN.

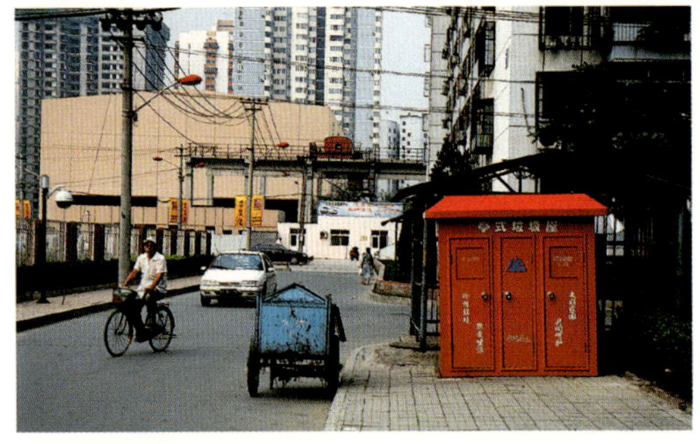
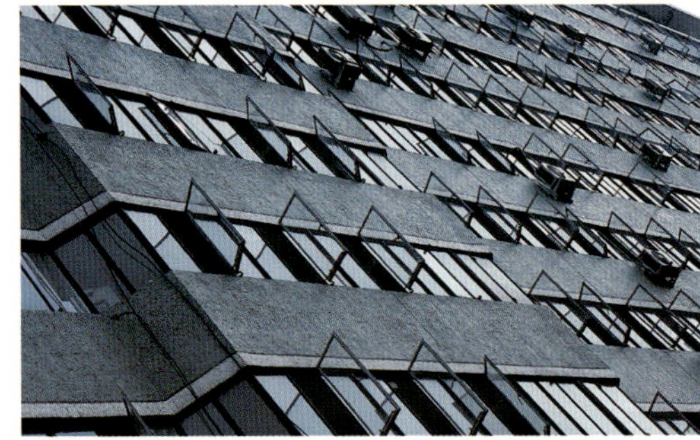
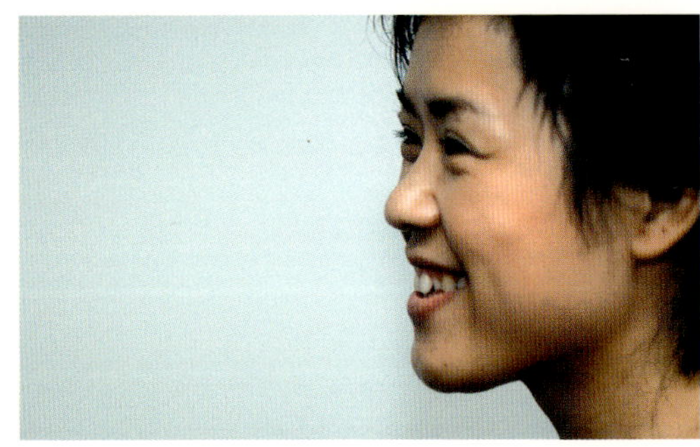
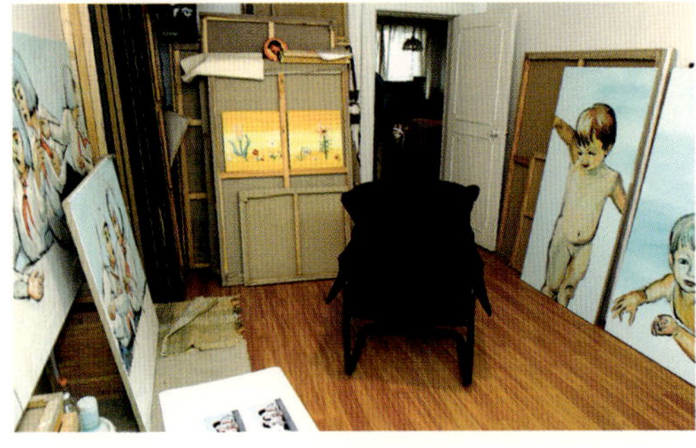
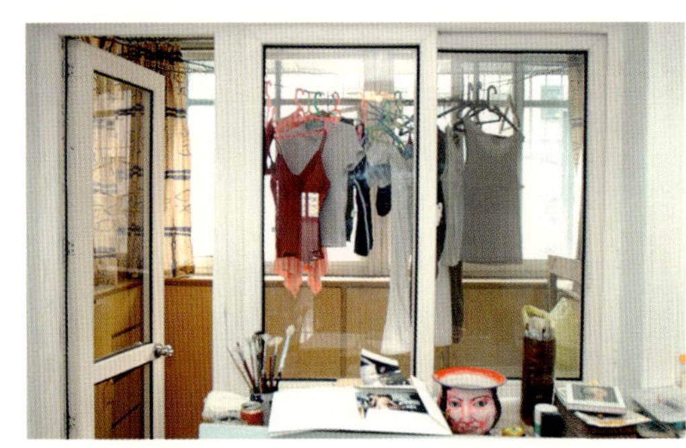
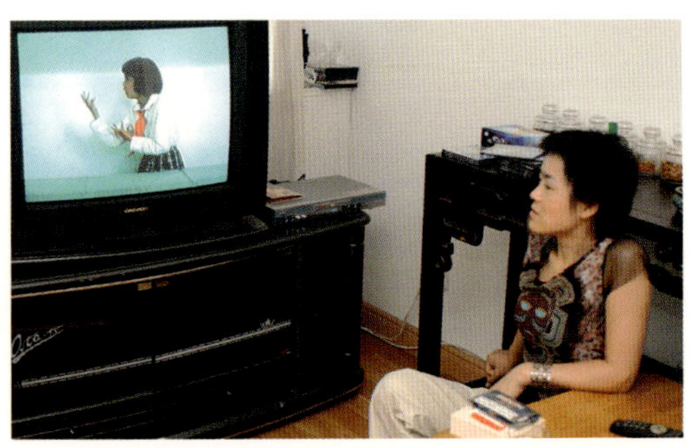

She met other artists also scraping together a living by teaching. "I was painting. I started to think," she says jokingly. ¶ You mean painters don't think? ¶ Of course they do. But she became intrigued by the limits of painting, and very soon, of video. She laughs that she also became interested in the possibilities of sex as an artistic subject. This was in 1996. Since she is a very attractive girl, she was invited to play a role in a made-for-TV film. She watched carefully how the film was shot. In 1998, she presented her paintings in Hong Kong, as part of an exhibition by women artists. There, she met a collector who took her back to Beijing where he took her to a nightclub where she discovered the seedy underbelly of the city's nightlife. She was fascinated by the phenomenon of prostitution (which was just beginning to become a problem in China) and the lives of the girls who spent their lives hanging around in bars waiting for clients. She was inspired to shoot the video *Lady's* with a sophisticated video camera that was small and therefore easily hidden. ¶ I first watched *Lady's* at the Shanghai fair, vastly out of place amidst a host of tacky, horrid views of the Bridge of Sighs in the snow, peasants in traditional costume, and copies of traditional silk paintings on flimsy paper. There were several floors of this junk. I even came across several French galleries, all completely unknown, and with good reason if their displays were anything to go by. ¶ There was one stand, however, that stood out from the crowd. There was a Dalí sculpture that Chen Xindong sold quite quickly, organizing in the evening a huge party at La Maison, a French restaurant in one of the trendiest parts of Shanghai, full of French, Italian, and even German eateries. This stand was showing the only video in the whole fair: *Lady's*. I stood and watched it, moved on, then came back to watch it again. The video revealed a way of visualizing reality that for me was brand new and intriguingly personal. I asked Chen Xindong if he knew the artist, and if it would be possible to meet her. It was possible, but I'd have to go to Beijing. That worked out nicely, since we were actually off to Beijing the next day. ¶ In Beijing, Chen Xindong introduced me to Cui Xiu Wen at his lovely home in the old neighborhood near the Forbidden City. There, Cui Xiu Wen showed me *Lady's* again, explaining that she had first had the idea for the video in 1998, but that she only made the decision to make the film in 2000, that it had been a dangerous undertaking, but that she liked taking risks, and that she had had to film five or six takes in what was, back then, the most exclusive nightclub in Beijing (she never told me its name). ¶ The video was filmed in the nightclub's ladies' room, where the ladies of the title come to touch up their makeup, check that their fake breasts are still giving a generous cleavage, brush their teeth, count their earnings, or call a client, away from the prying eyes of the men in the bar. Women together or, more precisely, women snatching a few moments to be alone, fleeing the reality of their sordid lives for a few instants. The most enthralling, almost miraculous aspect of the work was the impression that these shots capture a moment beyond time, where the women, unaware of the presence of the camera, were able to breathe and be themselves. It is as if they are actors in the wings of a theater, relaxing before stepping back into the spotlight. ¶ At my request, Cui Xiu Wen showed me her other works. She brought me two short videos that she had recently finished. What a disappointment. They were nothing but sketchy, narcissistic performances, filmed with no definite point of view in mind. She was wrapped in bandages like a mummy. Someone rolled them off her, and then I think she was wrapped up again. I don't really remember. It was completely uninteresting. ¶ So was *Lady's* a miracle or just a happy accident?

THE EXTERIOR AND INTERIOR OF CUI XIUWEN'S APARTMENT BUILDING. BOTTOM LEFT: EXAMPLES OF HER PAINTING. BOTTOM, FAR RIGHT: CUI XIUWEN'S MOST RECENT VIDEO, *SANJIE*, 2003. FACING PAGE: HER BEST-KNOWN VIDEO, *LADIES*, 2000.

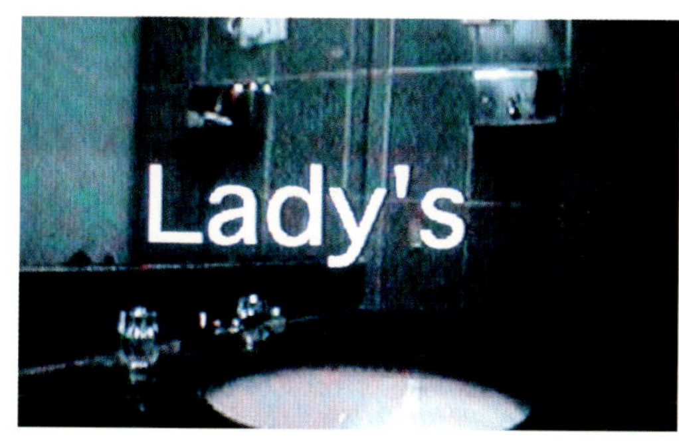
Lady's

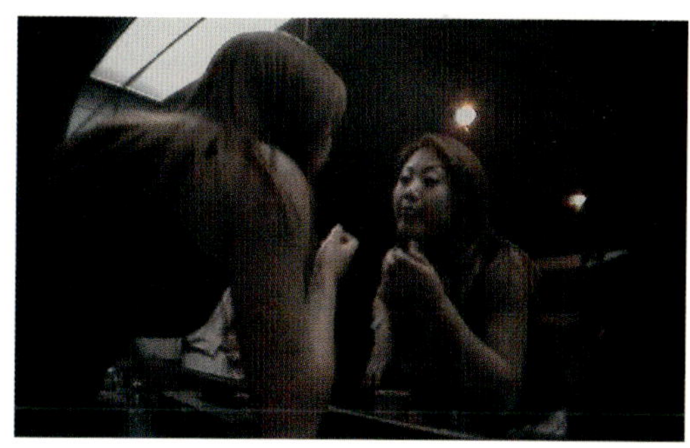

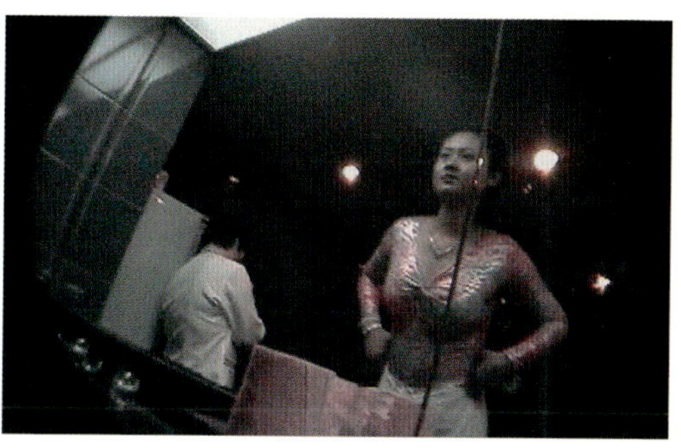

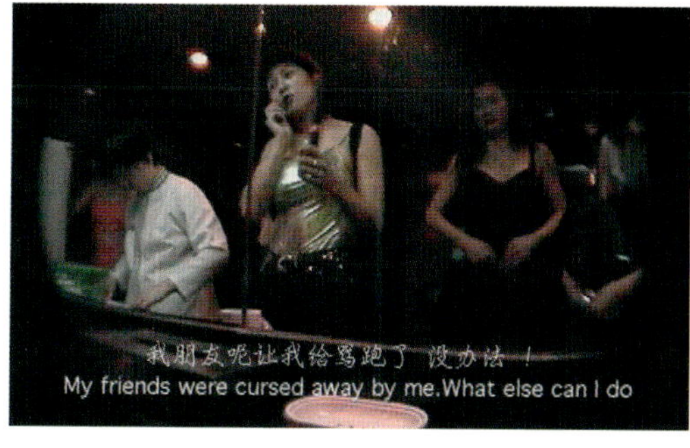
我朋友呢让我给骂跑了 没办法！
My friends were cursed away by me.What else can I do

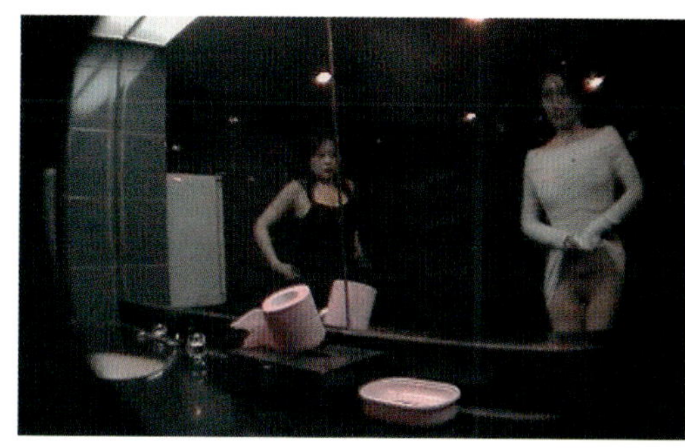

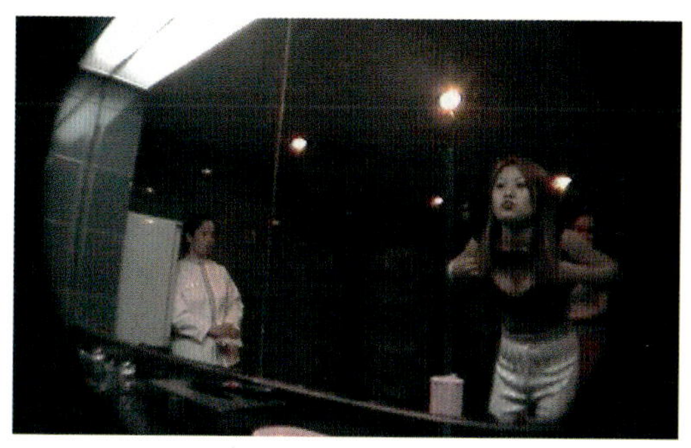

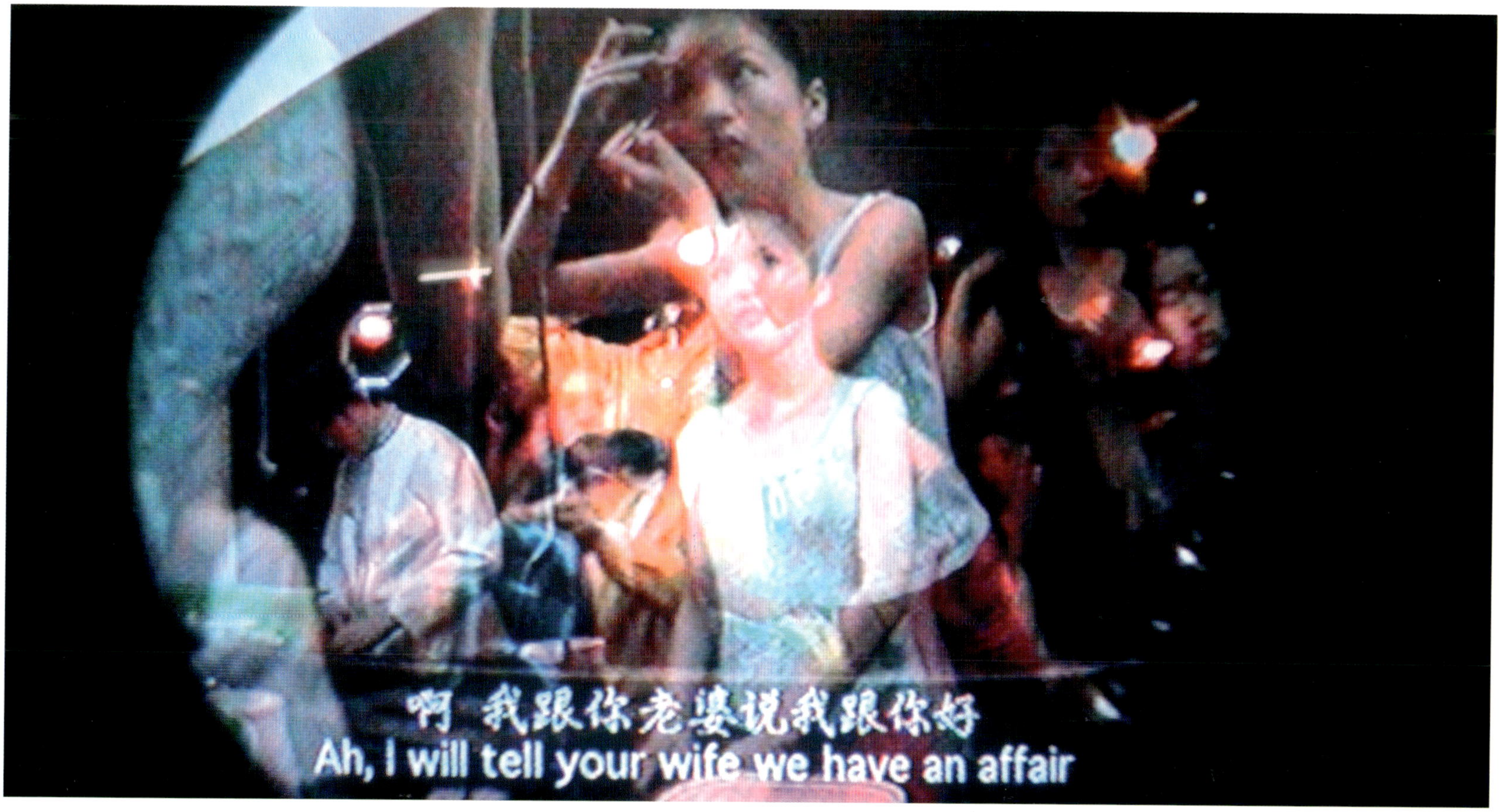

啊 我跟你老婆说我跟你好
Ah, I will tell your wife we have an affair

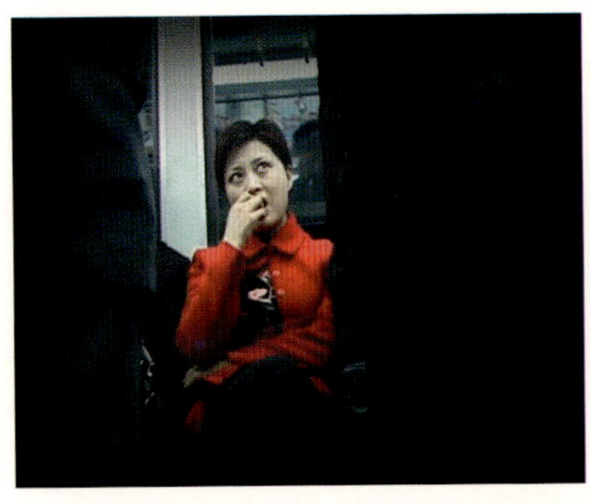
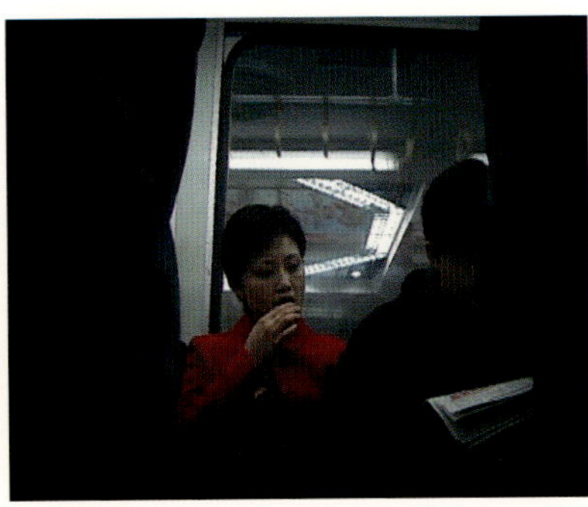
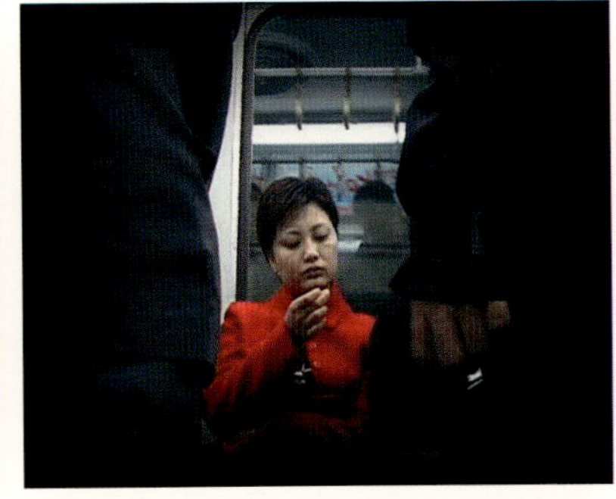
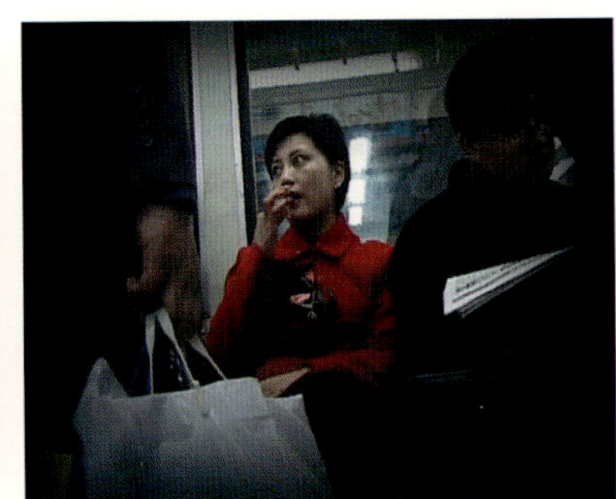

A promising debut or a one-hit wonder? ¶ I came back to Cui Xiu Wen, thanks to Alain Sayag, during the preparations for the China exhibition at the Pompidou Center. Alain told me about a video filmed in the subway that he had seen in Beijing, and which he had found particularly worthy of interest. It was Cui Xiu Wen's latest work. ¶ So I went back to Beijing to see her again, this time in her studio. The walls were covered with photographs of naked children facing the camera, making faces and showing off their genitals. There were also paintings of women together and couples making love. Tubes of paint everywhere. A video artist's studio in China today. ¶ Cui Xiu Wen makes a living by teaching painting, not video. Likewise, most of the works she has sold have been paintings, not videos. She also has a sideline writing articles for fashion magazines. She has surprisingly few books. She says, "I do read a lot, though. Philosophy, in particular." ¶ She shot the video that Alain Sayag liked so much in 2001, in the subway, on line 1, which cuts across Beijing from east to west. The credits date the film to 2002, because of two or three cuts that were all she did in the way of editing. It lasts nearly three hours, based on twenty minutes of film slowed down. It has a deliberately unrealistic soundtrack that is never quite synchronized with the image. ¶ What does the video show? For the three hours of the film, we see a woman in a bright red jacket, filmed from directly in front in a single, unmoving shot, with a video camera held on the knees. The woman is totally indifferent to everything around her. She is framed by two people in overcoats who barely move at all throughout the film. She is utterly focused on her tic, repeatedly sticking her index finger into her mouth to scratch the inside of her cheek and then rubbing the index finger on her thumb. That is all. It could be dull or leave the viewer indifferent. But it is not, and does not. It is fascinating. Because of the insistent repetition of the gesture. We, too, become wholly focused on this woman, her dreams, her madness, her reality. Even if—or precisely because—the camera does not move, her unwavering focus is palpable, on the verge of unbalanced obsession. ¶ Cui Xiu Wen confides, "I am not very prolific," and it is true that she is a rather slow worker, producing little. For this film, she spent days and days in the subway, looking for someone with an obvious tic. "I often observe people. I particularly notice people who repeat the same gestures over a relatively long period of time," she tells me. Women are her favorite theme. "When the women of *Lady's* are in the bathroom, the world outside no longer exists," she says. "I find that fascinating. Just look at the way the woman in the subway's gaze is turned in on herself." She adds, "I find plunging into the psychological depths of other people absolutely fascinating." And she laughs. ¶ 2003 saw an entirely new departure in Cui Xiu Wen's art. I visited her again in the tiny apartment that she uses as a studio. Her most recent work—entitled *Sanjie*—is inspired by Leonardo da Vinci's *Last Supper*. It is shown on thirteen screens—one for each apostle, and one for Christ. Each apostle, and indeed Christ himself, is played by the same little girl, very bright-looking, wearing a little skirt and a white blouse with a red kerchief over it. The little girl takes her place, standing very straight in front of the camera, and then exceedingly slowly, takes up a pose, like an actress, with an astonishing intensity and verity. And when she has taken up the exact position of the model, she suddenly straightens up, bursts out laughing, and is once again a little girl. ¶ This video, shown as part of an installation, is a real gem, on the fringes of Cui Xiu Wen's oeuvre, on the fringes of politics, on the fringes of everything. ¶ Just like Cui Xiu Wen herself—she is not a regular on the art circuit. ¶ She is happy just to offer, from time to time, nuggets of pure gold. Astonishing little masterpieces.

ABOVE: *UNDERGROUND N°2*, 2002, FILMED IN THE SUBWAY. FACING PAGE: *SANJIE*, FILMED IN 2003, SHOWING A YOUNG GIRL MIMICKING THE APOSTLES IN LEONARDO DA VINCI'S *LAST SUPPER*.

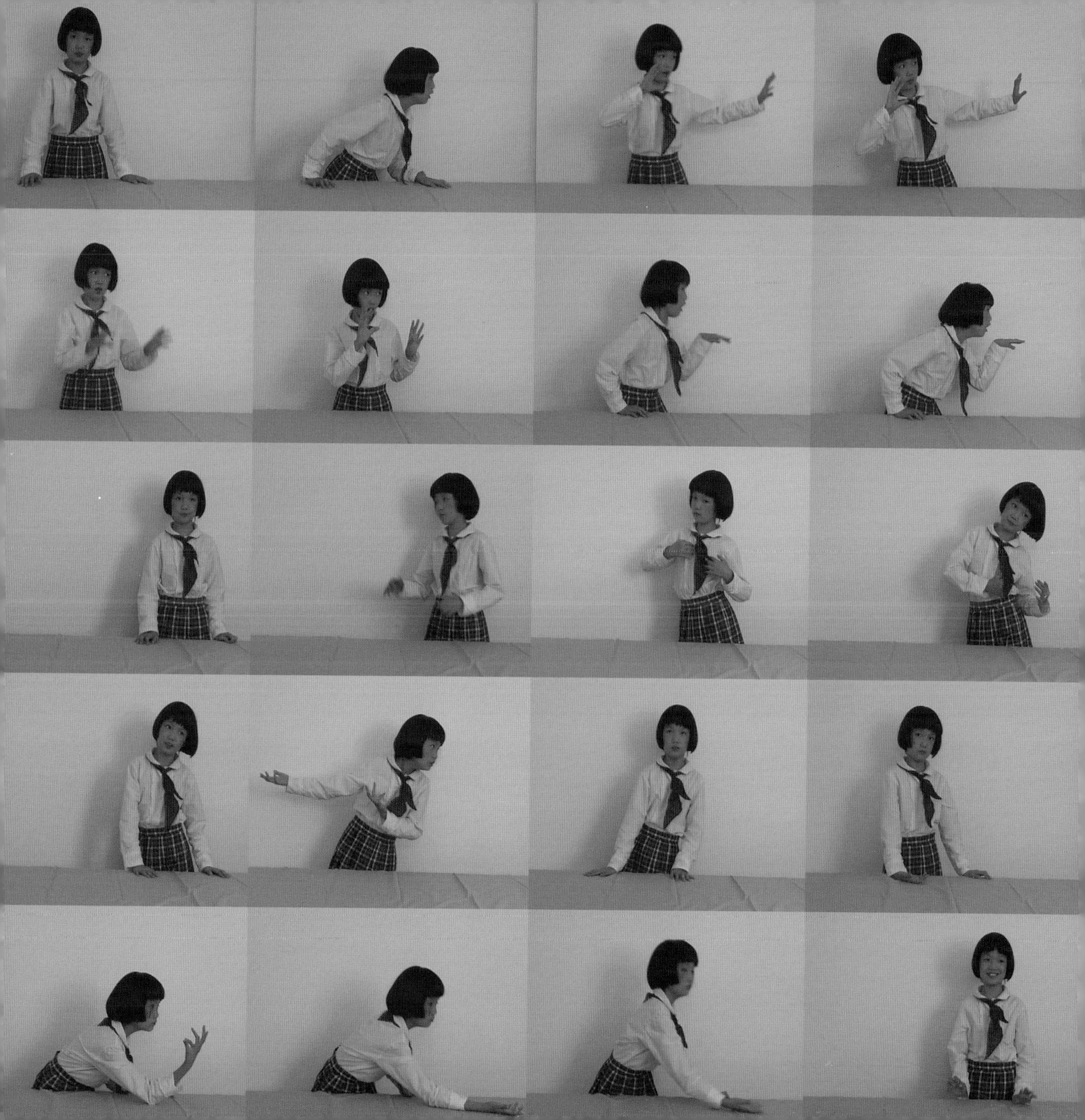

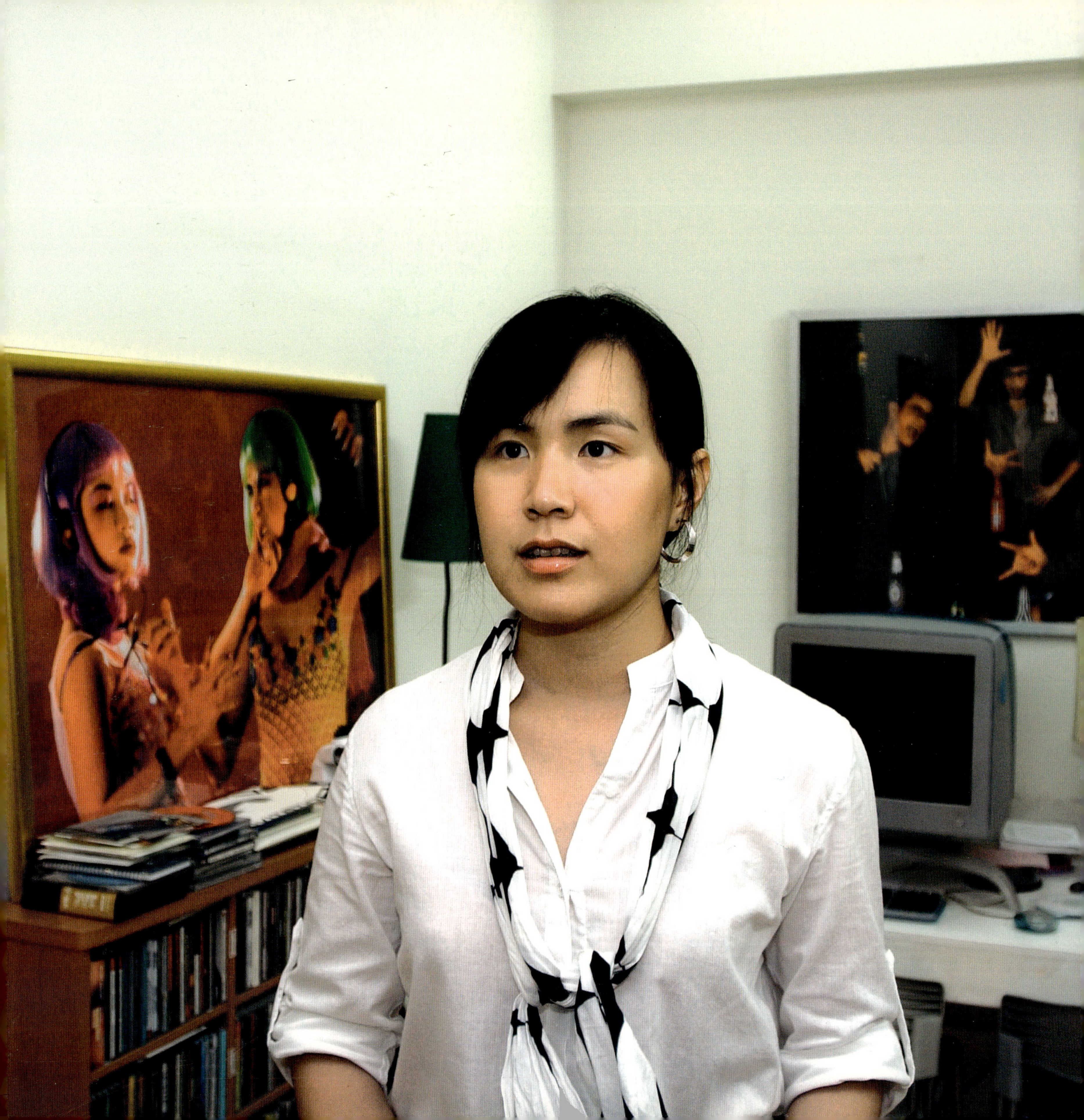

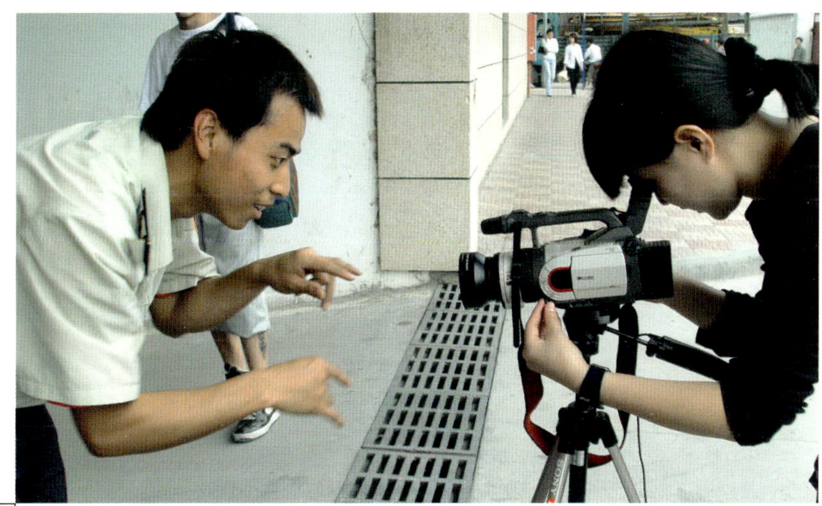

CAO FEI

Funny things, reputations. People told me that she was a kind of muse for the art scene in Guangzhou, hanging out in bars, leading the crowds. I even seem to remember someone rather spitefully calling her "the little local muse." ¶ When I first met Cao Fei in Guangzhou, Block 3, Xinhe Guangchang, Changgang Zhong Road, I discovered a robustly healthy-looking young woman with a blunt cut and bangs. She was shy almost to the point of coldness. Yet her talent shone through. Since then, I have met her five or six times, in Guangzhou, Venice, and Paris, where her sister has been living since 1999. She has always given me the same impression of reserve and self-control. I suppose it's her professionalism. ¶ She switches on her computer to show me her video. She vanishes, then comes back as soon as she hears the music heralding the end of the film. She switches it off. That's all. ¶ Her apartment is light and airy, impersonal, almost trendy. There are vast numbers of CDs scattered everywhere. There are posters on the wall. Her boyfriend, who is a designer, is hanging around in the background. He worked with her on her recent work *San Yuan Li Project*, to be presented at the 50th Venice Biennale. Her studio is just an office at the far end of the apartment. ¶ Let's watch the videos. ¶ The first to appear on the computer screen is called *Chain Reaction* (five minutes long, 2000). It was shot using digital video. It did not have a script as such, but rather a storyboard that Cao Fei describes as instinctive. "Written, directed, and filmed by Cao Fei," says one of the boards, which also lists the names of the actors (Zhang Xiaochuan and Song Jiaqi), the cameraman and his assistant, the studio, the stylist, and the sponsor. The music was by Dickson Dee. The name of Ou Ning, co-artist on the *San Yuan Li Project*, features once in tiny writing in the sixteen-page landscape-format brochure printed to accompany the film. He is credited as being in charge of design and the "editorial concept"—rather a grand term for such a modest brochure. In fact, this was Cao Fei's second video, freely inspired by a local television hospital drama. ¶ "I wasn't in the circuit at that time," says Cao Fei. "I was hugely impressed by Cindy Sherman. Not by any of her works, but by a quote of hers that I read in an article." ¶ Deliberately aggressive, with violently contrasting lighting and unreal, clashing colors, the video shows amputated ears being extracted from a glass basin full of blue liquid using metal tweezers, syringes stuck in flesh, surgical scissors being passed from one white-gloved hand to another, internal organs in cocktail glasses, characters in surgical masks, others with all-white makeup, their eyes extravagantly outlined in black, wearing clothes that could be surgical gowns bristling all over with pointed cones. ¶ She showed demiurges, nurses and doctors looking like devils, handling God only knows what, swept into a shocking chain reaction of events that summed up the philosophy of the *Fuck Off* exhibition at the Eastlink Gallery in Shanghai, in which Cao Fei participated in 2000. ¶ Cao Fei is very young. It was the first time she showed her work. She says, "I found myself promoted into the category of contemporary artists, although I didn't think I belonged in the group. My work was more individual. They wanted to cause scandal for scandal's sake. The violence in my film was more poetic and lyrical. I just wanted to open up the dark side of existence, and observe it." ¶ *Chain Reaction* can be characterized as a schizophrenic film driven by an absurd logic and an independent thinker acting quite alone—like a force of nature. The film begins abruptly and cuts off just as brusquely. There is no real beginning or end. ¶ "*Chain Reaction* is an allegory of evil, but without the dimension of the possibility of redemption that exists in

FACING PAGE: CAO FEI IN HER GUANGZHOU OFFICE, IN FRONT OF HER COMPUTER, SURROUNDED BY PHOTOGRAPHS. ABOVE: FILMING HER MOST RECENT WORK, *HIP HOP*, 2003.

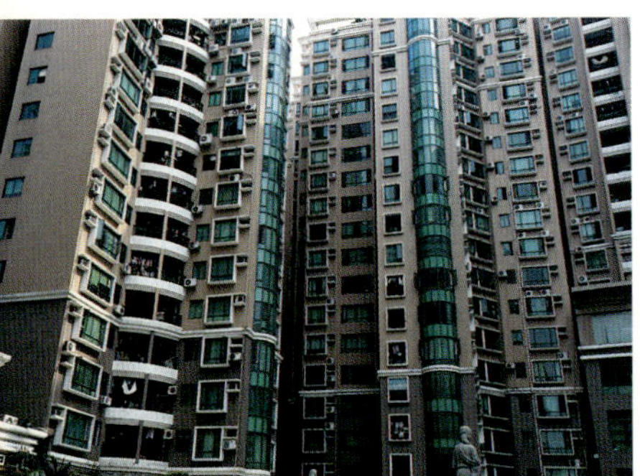

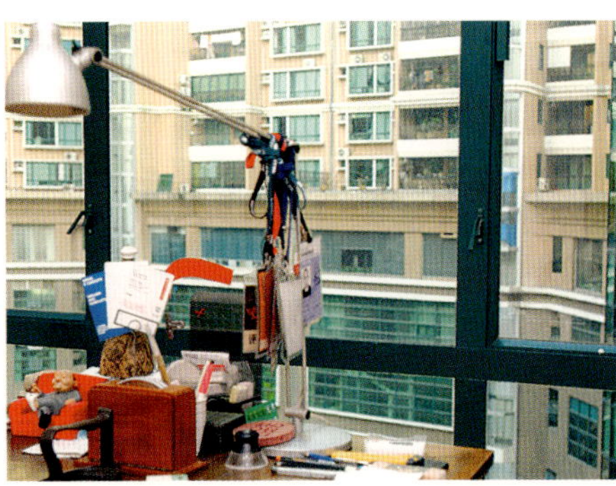

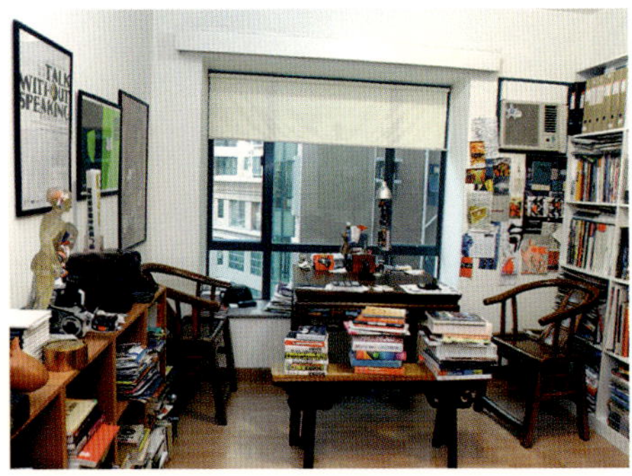

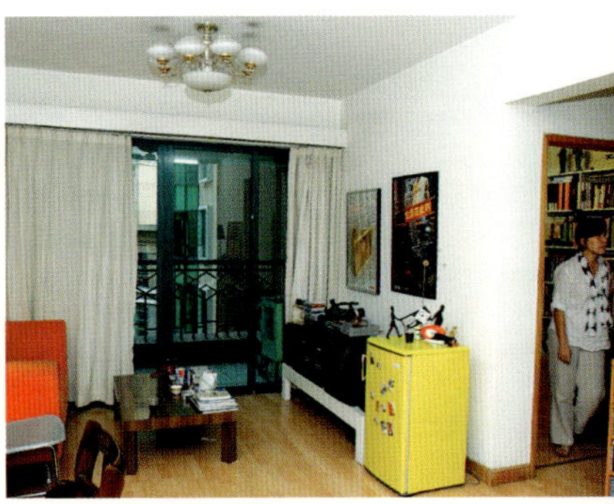

most allegories," Cao Fei explains. ¶ We could call it a film noir, in line with the artist's constant need to test the limits and feel danger. We could also evoke the violence inherent in her work, which becomes more disquieting on closer acquaintance. "Are you a violent person?" I ask her. "Yes," she replies, with a gentle smile. ¶ Perfect self-control, as I said. ¶ In the sixteen-page brochure printed for the film, Cao Fei, exploring the transformation of the images, admits: "I find my real pleasures, anxieties, and fears in my images, which exist independently of the objective world." ¶ I mentioned absurdity. It was already present in Imbalance 257 (twenty-six minutes, 1999), her first video, which took as its subject the lifestyle of the young generation that "tries to dismantle the limits of all the old accepted truths and certainties, and transform rationality into absurdity (and vice versa) and to laugh at objective reality and legality." ¶ This video strips our souls bare. The mere act of watching it encourages us to broaden our perceptions of both happiness and despair, to throw our selves into question, and to embrace change. ¶ Would it be an extrapolation to say that the true subject of *Talk without Speaking* (two minutes, 2001) is an attempt to show a visual thought—that of the artist in particular? ¶ It shows a close-up shot of hands, the fingers forming strange shapes. Talking. They are the hands of deaf-mutes. They are expressing themselves through signs that bear meaning. ¶ The hands sign a number of taboo words that are violent in their breaking of boundaries of Chinese taste: "Do you make love with your daughter? Are you homosexual?" It lasts two minutes, because afterwards there is nothing left to say. ¶ *View on the Move* (five minutes, 2001), as she reminded me recently, is a graduation piece. It was a miniature revolution in itself—the first time a student presented a video for their final diploma in the department of decorative arts where she studied. It is a virtuoso demonstration; the images are doubled, pulled about, deformed, and multiplied to explore the possible transformations of the image, featuring "guest stars" such as Andy Warhol, Picasso, and a few others, their images crackling and clicking like the rest. ¶ *Rabid Dogs* (eight minutes, 2002) features brightly colored characters made up as animals, imitating dogs imitating human behavior. So while they are crawling around on all fours, they use a typewriter, stick their tongues out, mimic sex, and shit on the floor. "We don't dare bark," Cao Fei explains. "We work docilely, faithfully, patiently, like dogs. We want to behave like animals and be locked into the cages of modernization." ¶ This is probably the most obviously allegorical of Cao Fei's videos. It was immediately followed by one of her best films, shot in black and white. It was less glossy, maybe, but it was certainly more poetic, simpler, more tense, and more intense. Called *Give Me a Kiss* (five minutes, 2002), it depicts a middle-aged man, dreaming away, in a world of his own. He is neither a middle-class man down on his luck nor a tramp who has managed to keep up appearances. He is not completely sane, nor is he mad. He is just there, in the street, trying out some dance moves with his arms and hands. He is not practicing tai chi—he is dancing. It is hard to tell whether they are masculine or feminine dance moves. ¶ And to be truthful, it doesn't matter. ¶ What is fascinating is to watch the man in his short-sleeved shirt, ruined, alone in his dream, smiling to himself, oblivious of the passersby who in turn ignore him as they walk on by. He is miming a dance. Blowing kisses into the air. Seeing only with his inner eye. ¶ For the music, Cao Fei chose a lightly jazzy air from 1930s Shanghai. Surprisingly, it fits perfectly. It is almost as if the man in the white shirt is following the music. "Give me a

CAO FEI'S NEIGHBORHOOD, BLOCK 3, XINHE GUONGCHANG. LEFT: AN EXTERIOR VIEW. RIGHT: AN INTERIOR VIEW. MANY OF HER PHOTOGRAPHS ARE DISPLAYED ON THE WALLS.

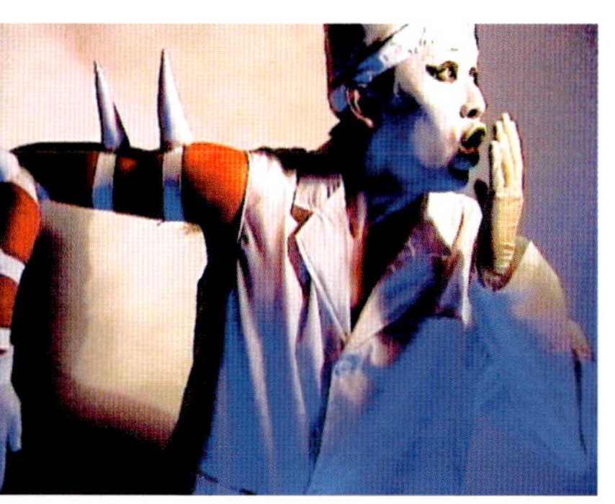

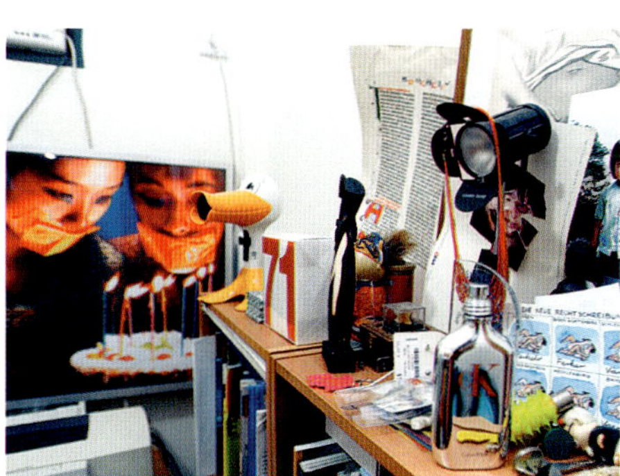

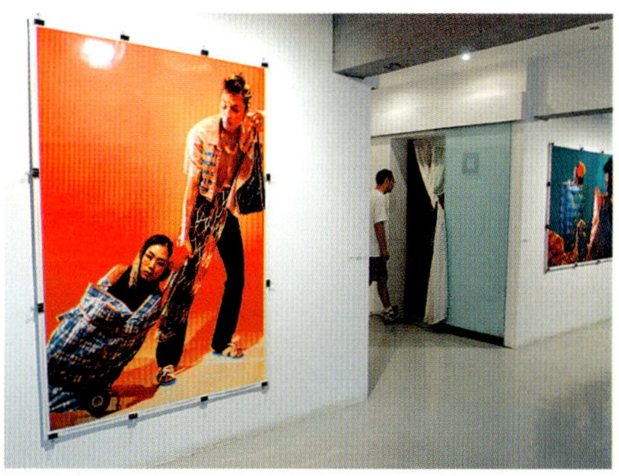

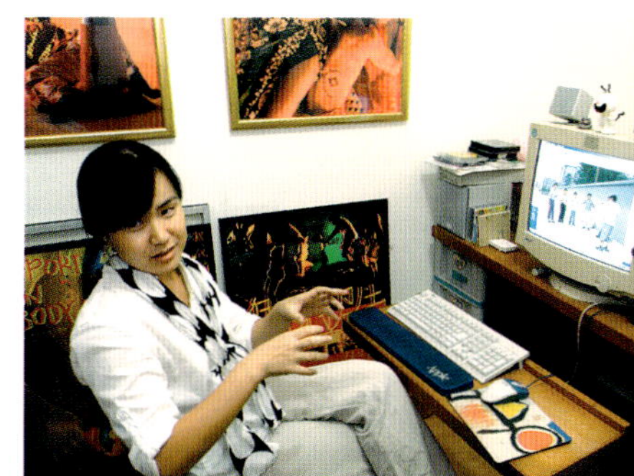

kiss, look at me." But the passersby rush past without a glance. The man opens his arms wide, but no one stops. ¶ In this piece, has the artist abandoned the overly "simply complicated" aspect (as Thomas Bernhard might say) of some of her earlier works, seeking liberty instead? When I asked her, I think I saw the shadow of a smile flit across her face. What I do know for certain is that she then immediately began telling me about her new film: "I'd like to do something on Guangzhou. Show my city." Since then, she has finished her film; it was a great success at the Venice Biennale when it was shown at the press launch on June 12, 2003. This was the *San Yuan Li Project*. It consisted of a video shown in a dark room, and on the other side of the wall, where the projector was, a range of equipment—chairs, a desk with the brochures explaining the project, and a bank of computers connected to the U-theque Web site. ¶ And what is the U-theque? ¶ This is where Ou Ning comes into the picture. The U-theque is his brainchild. The *San Yuan Li Project* likewise. ¶ Ou Ning is a go-getter. He is the art director of several cinema, music, and arts magazines. He hangs out with poets, has been known to write his own poetry, and enjoys meeting film and video directors. It was inevitable that he should one day end up behind the camera. ¶ The U-theque came about on September 11, 1999, thanks to the shared love of films of two poets and Ou Ning himself. They set about organizing art-house screenings in a region of southern China that had never seen anything quite like it. They began with Salvador Dalí and Luis Buñuel's *An Andalusian Dog* and Kenneth Anger's *Fireworks*. They began in Shenzhen, between Hong Kong and Guangzhou, then very quickly moved to Guangzhou itself, in spring 2000. By then they had moved on to films by Chinese directors and a short video by a young Cantonese artist—Cao Fei, who thus became one of the first members of the U-theque. ¶ The cinema club soon became a place to discuss films, encouraging the emergence of free speech. The debates led to the founding of a fanzine like those of the punk generation in the 1970s. ¶ Ou Ning and his friends, like many people of the Beuys generation, believed that anyone could become an artist. They thought that new technologies brought art within their grasp. Video, in particular, was held to be an easy means of artistic expression. ¶ You must understand that it was a particularly euphoric, effervescent period for the art scene in Guangzhou, sharing in the dynamism of the Chinese art world in general in the 1990s and after 2000, when artists did not bother to ask themselves to what extent they were borrowing or inventing ideas—whether they were seventy years behind Dziga Vertov or whether they were pioneering a new way to experience art. ¶ From 1999 to the present, the U-theque has naturally evolved, moving on from simply organizing screenings, often of DVDs, to producing and directing films and videos. ¶ *San Yuan Li*, directed by Cao Fei and Ou Ning, is a black and white documentary lasting thirty-five minutes, divided into sequences, extremely well filmed and brilliantly edited. Rather than simply accompanying the images, the bewitching sound track actually seems to carry the film forward. ¶ San Yuan Li is a village on the outskirts of Guangzhou, and was a major base for attacks against the English during the Opium Wars. The village has been sucked in by Guangzhou's massive growth, but has not entirely lost its character in the urban sprawl. In the video, we discover a village surrounded by an immense city—a shadowy zone in the glittering development of the megalopolis, with its fair share of problems—fly-by-night contractors, drug dealers, rising prostitution, uncontrolled immigration, the noise of airplanes taking off and landing at

FROM LEFT TO RIGHT: *CHAIN REACTION*, 2000, VIDEO. BRIGHTLY COLORED RECENT PHOTOGRAPHS IN HER APARTMENT, IN THE COURTYARD GALLERY IN BEIJING, AND IN HER OFFICE.

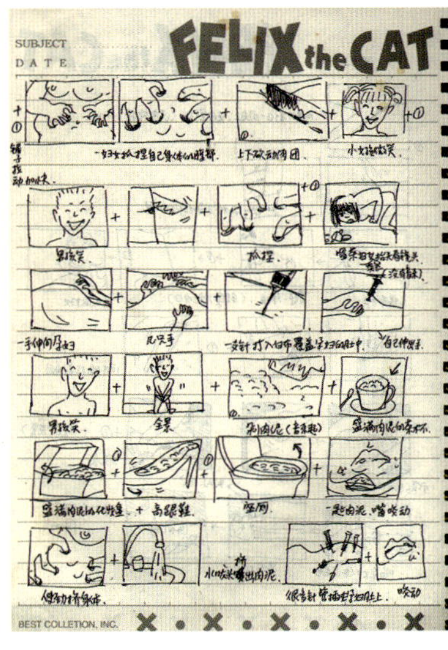

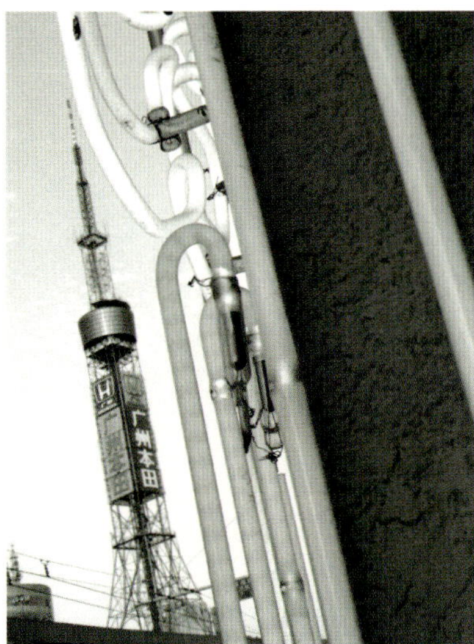

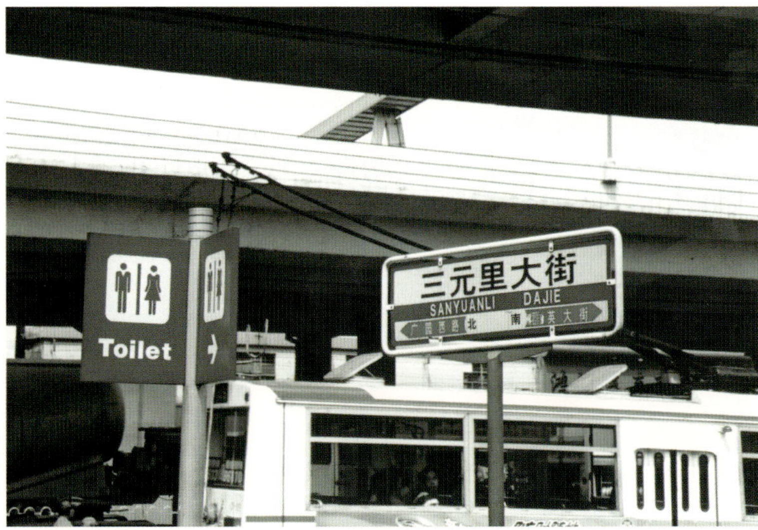

the nearby airport thundering through the narrow streets and rattling the windows in the flat-roofed houses with a few chickens in the garden. Here people like to play music, tend their garden, and mind their own business. ¶ It frequently reminded me of Dziga Vertov's *Enthusiasm*, with the additional theme of sociological inquiry, not just because of the many high- and low-angle shots, but also because of its busy rhythm. Magnificent! When I mentioned this to Ou Ning, he confirmed that the film made deliberate references to Vertov's work. ¶ In the brochure printed to present the film at the Venice Biennale, Cao Fei discusses the difference between a town and a village. Fortunately, the film itself does not attempt a definition, but rather explores the question by taking us straight to the heart of life in the village, leading us through the narrow streets so that we gradually become permeated with the ambience and sense the smells, the charm, the horror, the appalling hygiene, the lack of privacy, and all the difficulties that gnaw away at life there like an infection. ¶ As always, Cao Fei (and Ou Ning) produced a wealth of material documenting their experiences shooting the video. They included some at the end of the brochure. Does this perhaps reveal a certain narcissism? Or should we read it as a sort of Brechtian alienation effect designed to stop the viewer getting too close to the illusion? ¶ "Actually," Cao Fei says, "It's to show that the film was made on a shoestring budget." She adds, "We were filming people strolling, and we wanted to show that we, too, were just that—people strolling." ¶ Cao Fei's photography does not predate her video work—it is an accompaniment and a prolongation of the same themes. She shoots series of theatrical images in brash colors, violently lit and deliberately unreal. The series *Games* dates back to 2000, *Storage Box* to 2001, *Fresh Series* and *Room 807* to 2002. In a short text entitled *My Photographs*, Cao Fei in fact only talks about her generation and her relationship to it. She sees it as a generation that cannot imagine a future and does not recognize the past—a generation characterized by (willful) indifference. She is worried by the way her contemporaries seem to take life as a game. ¶ That is what she writes. ¶ When asked, her response is less black and white. "We are living in a consumer age, where society is advancing at top speed. There is no time to think about the past, which for us is completely abstract. We must constantly adapt to new things and ideas. It isn't easy. It takes up all of our time and drains much of our energy." ¶ Her most recent video, *Hip Hop*, which she showed me in September 2003 in her studio, is one of her best works, alongside *Give Me a Kiss*. It is also based on a simple idea: people in the street (they are in fact actors) breaking into more or less complicated hip hop dance moves. The effect is more or less astonishing depending on what we expect from the characters, chosen to be representative of various social positions—a policeman, a tramp, a construction worker, and so on. Above all, the film is meant to undermine the heroic vision of Chinese society that until recently was the only one permissible, relayed by the government, art, and the media alike. ¶ Cao Fei is not attacking the government or society head-on. She prefers to defend her vision of the daily lives of her contemporaries using weapons they will understand—their words, their logic, their way of talking, which make power and domination completely redundant, unthinkable. Absurd. ¶ Like the times she is living in. Like today's China. ¶ You just need to go there to see, and believe, what I mean.

LEFT: *STORYBOARD*. CENTER AND RIGHT: STILLS FROM THE FILM SHE CO-DIRECTED WITH OU NING, *SAN YUAN LI*, 2003. *PHOTOGRAPHS BY OU NING, CAO FEI AND U-THEQUE ORGANIZATION*. FACING PAGE: *HIP HOP*, 2003, CAO FEI'S LAST VIDEO.

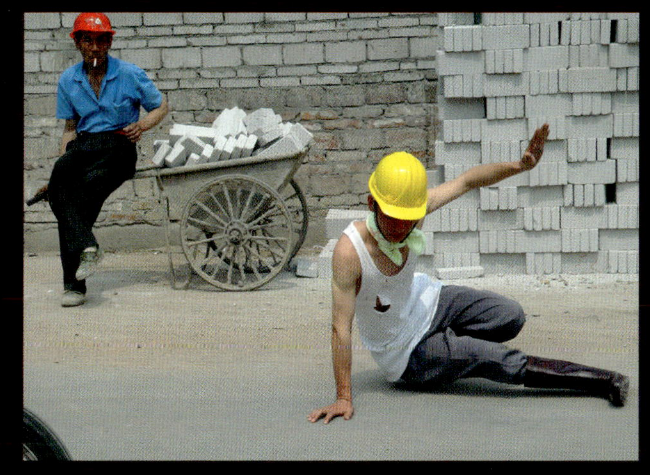

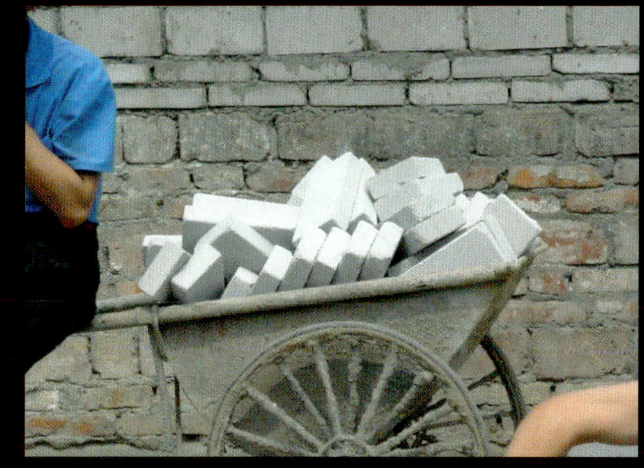

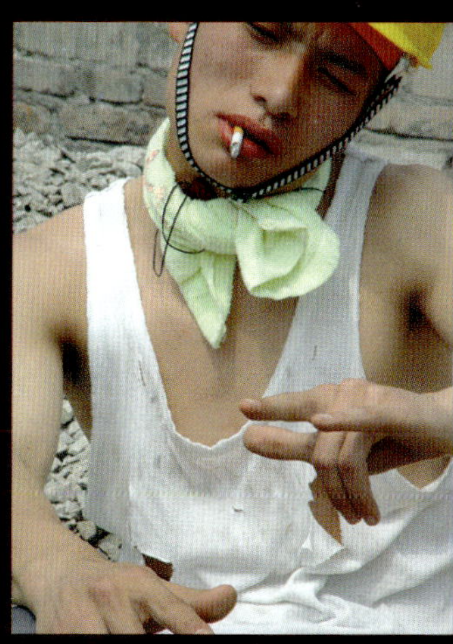

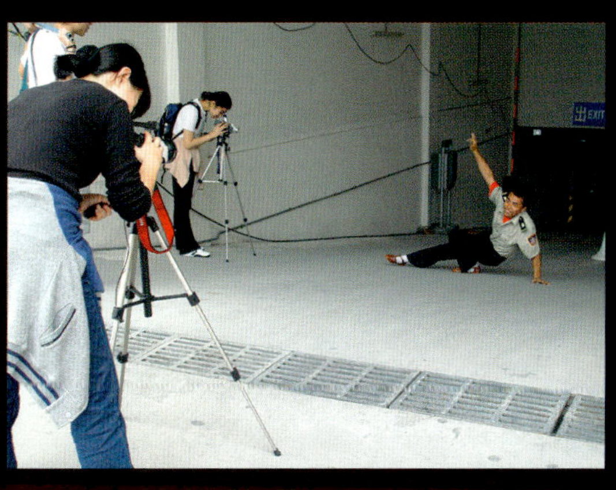

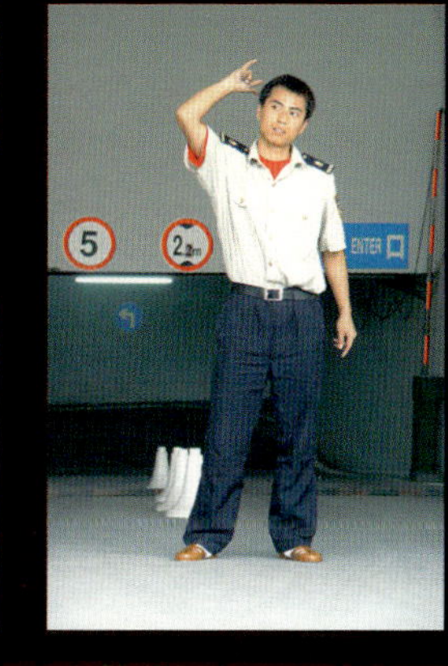

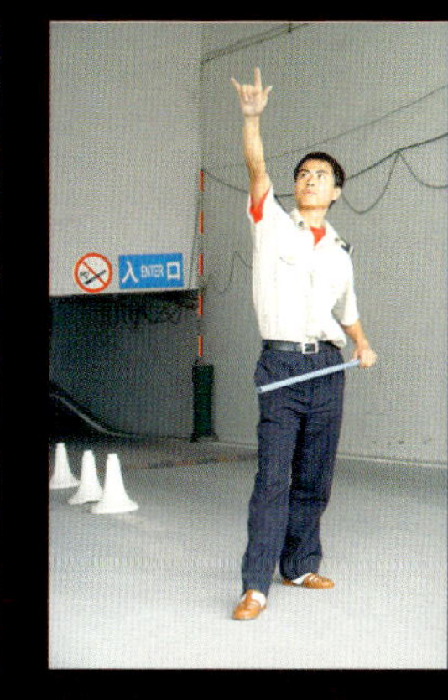

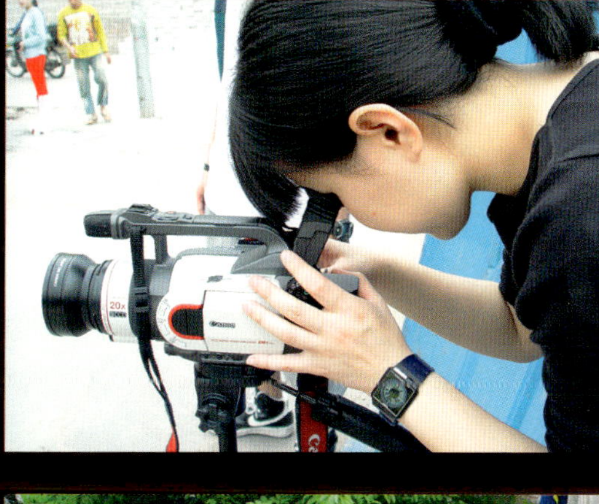

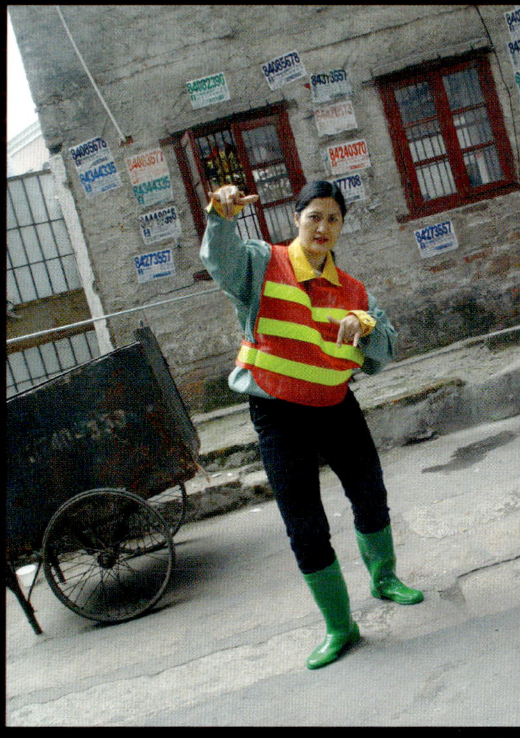

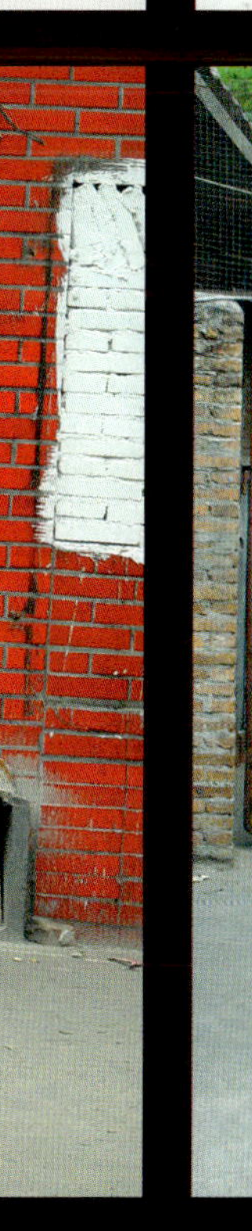

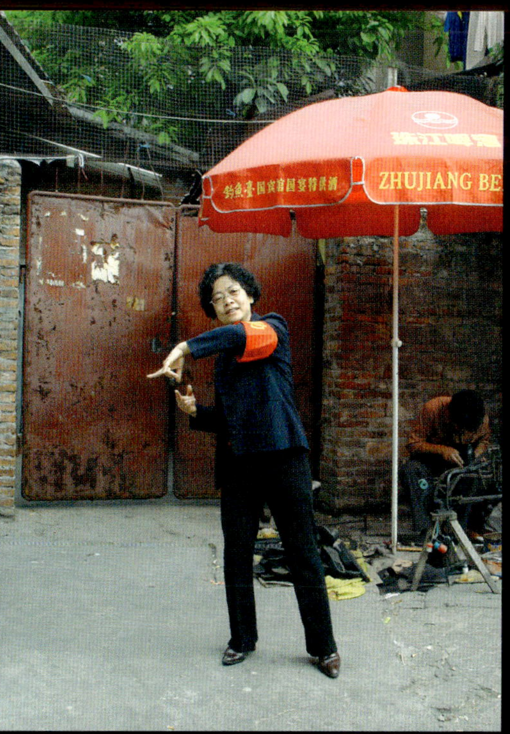

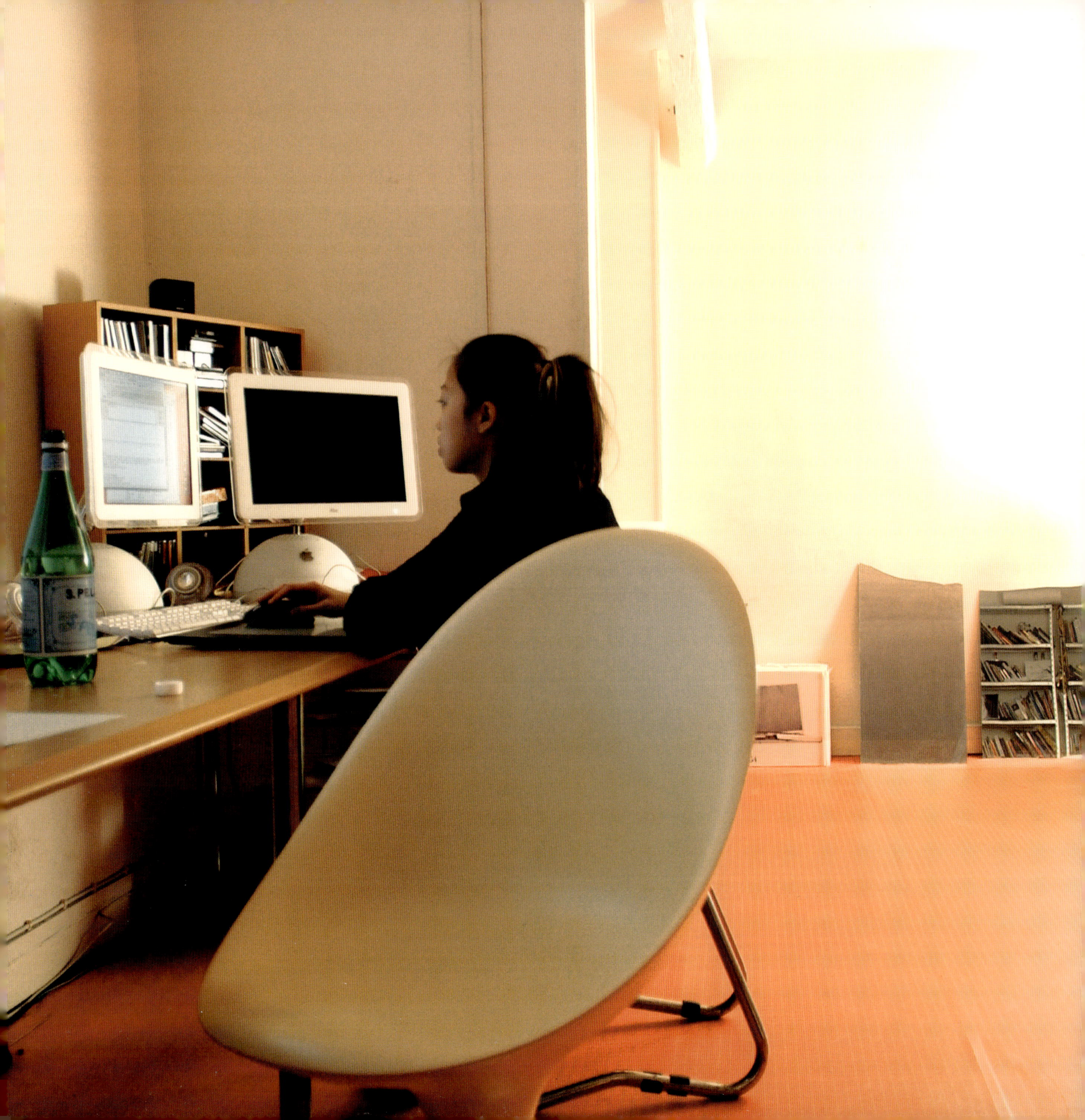

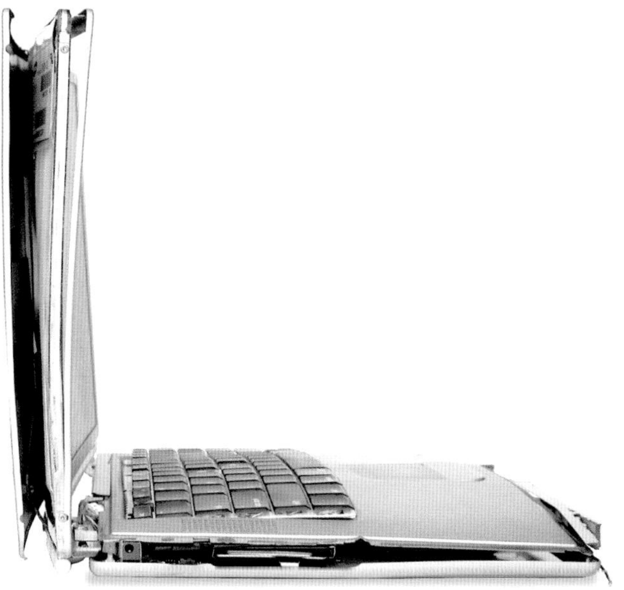

ZHOU YI

With Zhou Yi, everything moves so quickly that I sometimes—often—forget that she only started out a year ago. She has already accomplished so much, come so far, negotiated her way past so many pitfalls, tried so many avenues, and saturated so many paths on the information superhighway with her frenetic messages. ¶ Zhou Yi is gifted. A blessing and a curse. Or is it? She first held a calligraphy brush in her pudgy little hand at the age of two or three. She could already read and write. She was granted special permission to go to primary school early, but did not fit in, since she was two years younger than all the other children. ¶ Fast-forward a few years. When she was nine, her father took the family from Shanghai to Rome for work. There, she learned to enjoy drawing again. On Piazza Navona, she would watch the portrait artists churning out formulaic sketches of gawking, flattered tourists. "I loved it!" she says, still flushed with excitement at the memory of this astounding adventure. "I went there every day!" And she began to imitate the street artists. She sketched everyone she knew, from her family and close friends to neighbors and vague acquaintances. It became an obsession. One day, her mother said, "Why don't you study brush and ink painting with a proper teacher?" So she took lessons for a year. She was granted authorization to attend lessons at the School of Fine Art in Rome in the afternoon, after high school in the morning. And after that? ¶ "After that, I gave up because it was always the same thing. I wasn't getting anywhere." She moved from Italy to London, where she studied at the London School of Economics for two years. And again, she felt she wasn't getting anywhere, so in her last semester she moved once more, this time to Paris. She obtained a degree in political science at the age of twenty-one. ¶ Yi has always been in a rush. Her father wanted her to be a diplomat, at the very least. Meanwhile, she was telling herself, "I have to go for it. I have to get my studies over and done with as quickly as possible, and afterwards, I can do whatever I want." She was heading for a clash with her parents when she made contact with the art scene. She had promised her parents she would go back to London to study for a master's. Instead, she met Paola Pivi, Claude Closky, Xavier Veilhan, and Miltos Manetas, and her studies were forgotten. ¶ Contemporary art is a powerful drug. Zhou Yi set sail on a stormy sea. Fortunately, Paola Pivi proved to be a fine mentor. She began by taking her new protegee to her exhibition at Castello di Rivoli, and taught her that in

FACING PAGE: ZHOU YI AT HER COMPUTER IN HER STUDIO IN PARIS. ABOVE: THE COMPUTER WHERE SHE STORED ALL HER WORK, SMASHED BY A BOYFRIEND. SHE DECIDED TO EXHIBIT THE SMASHED COMPUTER INSTEAD.

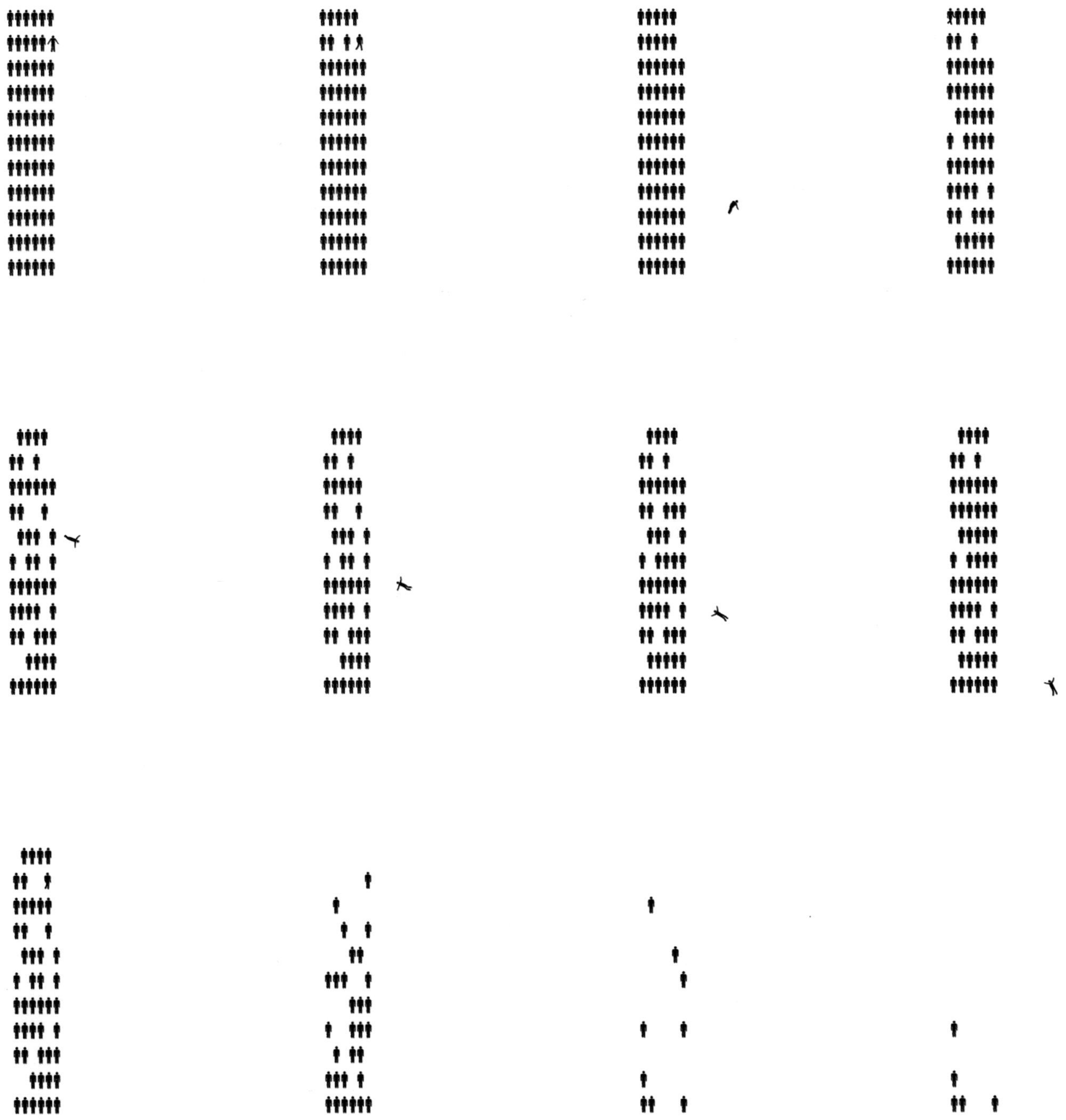

JUMP2MORROW, 2002. THIS FLASH ANIMATION SHOWS A TOWER CONSISTING OF LITTLE PEOPLE WHO SLOWLY FALL UNTIL THE TOWER HAS ENTIRELY DISINTEGRATED. WHEN IT IS OVER, THE WORDS "GAME OVER" APPEAR ON THE SCREEN, AND THE ANIMATION BEGINS ALL OVER AGAIN.

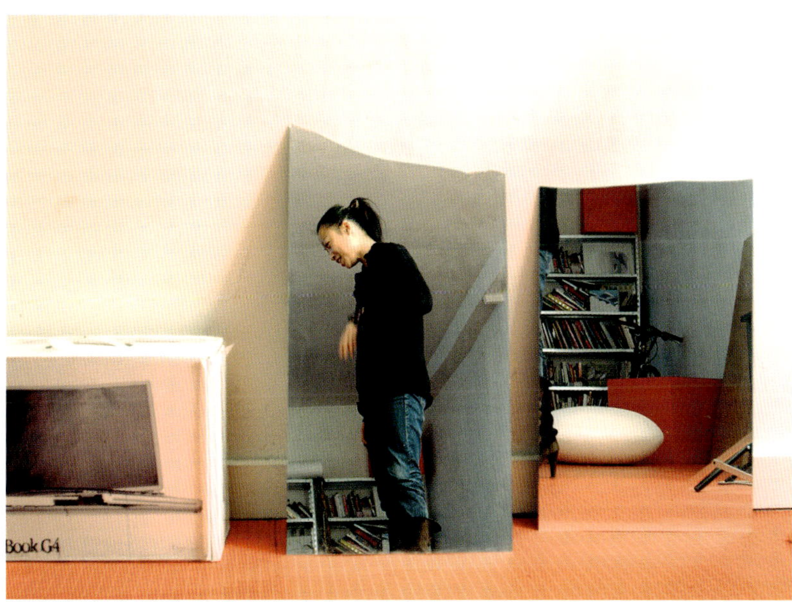

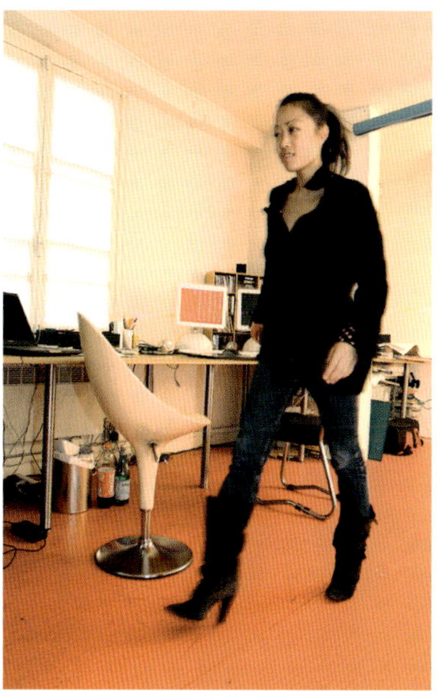

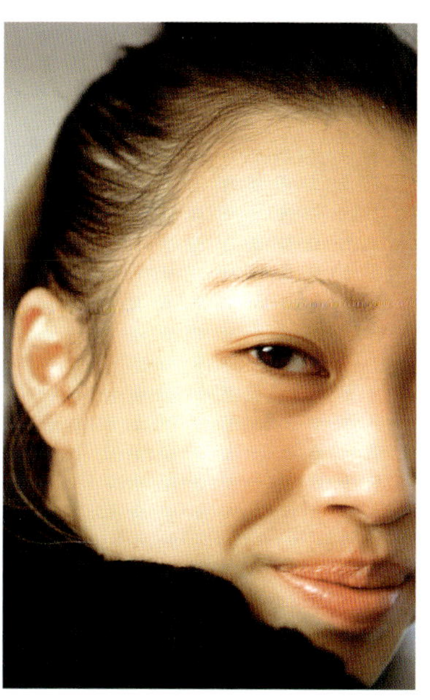

art, truly anything goes. ¶ Yi helped Paola to place an order for beads by telephone, calling China in the middle of the night. She said, "I need three thousand beads of such and such a size." In the end, she says, "I became aware that there really wasn't that much of a difference between the people making the beads and the artists." ¶ It was the same with Claude Closky. She helped him translate a text from English into Chinese for the Taiwan Biennial. Xavier Veilhan asked her to pose for him. But it was Miltos Manetas who really encouraged her to produce her own work. ¶ For the first time in her life, the size of the challenge caused her to hesitate. She began writing a book on the subject of camp. "It was an excuse to meet all sorts of people I wanted to meet." Ah, so she felt she needed an excuse. ¶ It was about this time that I first met Zhou Yi. I certainly didn't need an excuse. She was attending the Venice Biennale with Fabrice Bousteau, editor in chief of *Beaux-Arts* magazine. I met her again a few months later at the São Paulo Biennale, once again with Fabrice Bousteau. ¶ It was bizarre. She seemed to know absolutely everybody, and yet nobody really knew what she did or who she was. She would join a group of people, talk, laugh, and then all of a sudden leave, walking off with long, decisive strides. Alone. She was in a different hotel from the rest of us. From time to time, we would bump into her, and she would walk with us for a bit. That is how I happened to take her to see the superb collections of Luiza Strina and Bruno Musatti—two artists that I have long held in great esteem. It was then that my curiosity overpowered me, and I asked her to show me what she was working on, if anything, when we got back to Paris. ¶ She did. ¶ The first thing I saw were a clutch of small, kitsch cushions scattered on the floor, embroidered with sequins and frills. They were hardly the most original things I had ever seen. My first impression was not good. ¶ Then she showed me what got her started—a computer that a furious ex-boyfriend had smashed by throwing it on the floor. All her work was on the hard disk, so she decided simply to show it as it was. There you are. Take it or leave it. ¶ Straight away, I thought to myself, this girl is an artist. Good or bad, only time will tell—but she is definitely an artist. Showing the computer like that is not just strikingly arrogant, it's also the mark of a true artist. ¶ I told her so. I encouraged her as best I could, and visited her often. I showed her works whenever I could. ¶ To this day, I remain thunderstruck by that astonishing discovery. ¶ She says, "It was immensely personal. I have an almost symbiotic relationship with my computer. I spend most of my time with it. Everything passes through it—love, whatever. We have an almost fetishistic bond." ¶ *Yo-Yo* is a crackling sound. Words, hurled, swallowed, jostled, illegible. They flit so rapidly that all you can see is the crackling, the rhythm, the bombardment. Like in music videos that cut from one beautiful girl to another, toying with the viewer's frustration. ¶ *Yo-Yo* puts everything on the same footing, like the TV news, cutting from horror to seduction, from entertainment to tragedy. It is all equally valid. It is all blended together to form a homogeneous mass. Up and down. *Yo-Yo*. ¶ The following video shows towers of little black figures piled in rows of four or iver, stacked ten or eleven high. It is similar in style to *Yo-Yo*. Of course, there is a reference to the Twin Towers, to September 11, but there is no sense of tragedy. When we all watched those terrible TV pictures, first live then looped over and over again, it felt unreal, as if we were watching a disaster movie rather than a human tragedy. It took minutes, hours, even days for the reality of the images to sink in. Here, the little figures

ZHOU YI'S STUDIO IS A LONG, NARROW ROOM CONTAINING A TABLE WITH FIVE COMPUTERS. LEFT: THE BOX ZHOU YI HAD MADE FOR HER BROKEN COMPUTER.

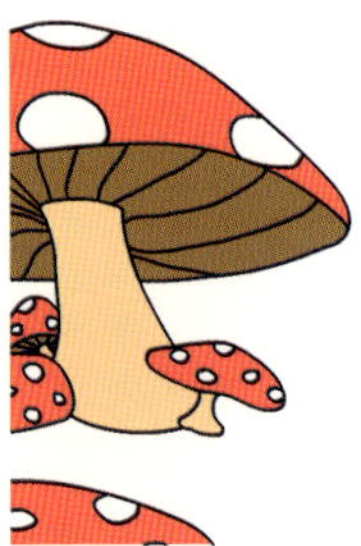
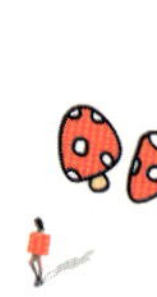
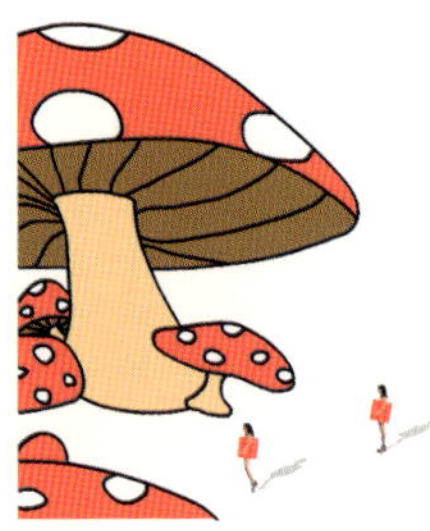
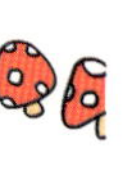
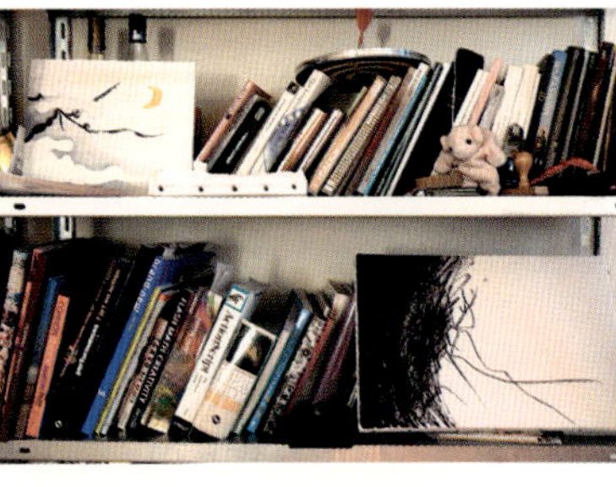
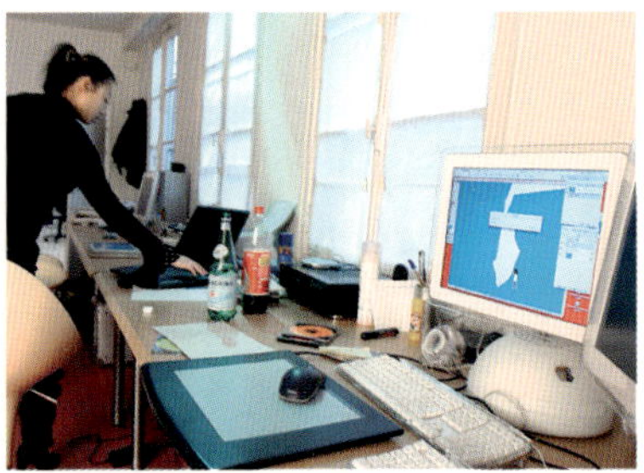

fall, like the people leaping from the burning buildings in New York, but here they fall softly, dreamily, almost playfully. And since these bodies were the tower itself, it crumbles rather than exploding or collapsing. ¶ I watched these two videos a few days apart in her studio in rue Charlot in Paris, behind a workshop filled with dresses on wheeled racks. I pushed open the door at the back of the workshop, and there it was. ¶ The floor was covered with linoleum, and there were a few sparse bookshelves on the wall. In the middle of the room was a long wooden trestle table, with an impressive array of computers. ¶ Computers here are gregarious creatures. ¶ There is also an assistant, who changes from time to time. ¶ They communicate in numbers, in English, in computer-speak. ¶ With Zhou Yi, the collapse of communism takes fifteen seconds. Here is a red flag with stars. The stars peel off and fall lazily, one by one. Nothing dramatic. It could be a game, like a pinball machine. "Like in a cartoon," she says. ¶ Her videos are starting to look more and more like cartoons. Here is a swathe of blue. Drops of rain fall gently. That is all. The sound lags a little behind the image. In the past, Zhou Yi's work was fun and above all quick. Is she moving towards more poetry? So it would seem. "It's a very Asian style of painting, in perpetual movement," she says. "In Asian culture, raindrops symbolize tenacity, wisdom, and continuity. If enough raindrops fall in the same spot, over time, they will wear a hole in a stone. The way the sound is not in step with the picture and is more haphazard is the Western side." ¶ Her Puck is also highly poetic. It shows three identical donkeys at the bottom of the screen forming a kind of barrier, and a broad swathe of space above them. She explains, "It is very minimal. Just a little barrier with a large breathing space above. Life reduced to the minimum, with the refreshing rapidity of acceleration." ¶ Poetry, again, in the large mushrooms, their caps dotted with red spots, underneath which Yi has depicted herself in electronic form as a little elf, spinning, jumping, raising an arm or a leg, like a miniature Alice in Wonderland. ¶ These mushrooms and the dozens of tiny jumping Yi figures were featured on the picture rails in Jérôme de Noirmont's gallery in Paris, alongside the video of *Pucks* and opposite another showing a butterfly flitting from flower to flower, fluttering across to the other walls and all over the gallery. The whole room vibrated to the butterfly's wings. ¶ One of her most recent videos was shown at the Fondation Guerlain at an exhibition organized to celebrate the Year of Chinese Culture in France. ¶ In an idealized, dreamlike Oriental landscape, where long lianas led from a mauve tree like tresses of hair, swirling lazily in the liquid air, a yellow crescent moon—the sort a child might draw—rose gently in the blue-gray sky. The moon rose, transcribing a hypnotic, dreamy circle. The tinkling of a music box created an ambience of soft, warm, gentle wonder. ¶ So Zhou Yi is a video artist, then? ¶ For the moment. ¶ Recently, she told me that she was going to begin painting. "What do you think?" she asked me, but didn't really listen to my answer. ¶ Then she recorded a track for Sony, which was not bad at all, and produced a video to go with it. ¶ Is she an artist, then? ¶ Yes, but "a surprising one." Never where you expect her to be. ¶ Yi is around. Just like when I met her in São Paulo. I bump into her occasionally. She sits down for a moment, then gets up again and wanders off, head held high, taking great strides with her long legs. ¶ Call her, and you'll see what I mean. Her answering machine message simply says, "Leave a message, and I will get back to you. Maybe."

FROM LEFT TO RIGHT: *Y-GAME*, 2002, FLASH ANIMATION. ZHOU YI'S SMALL COLLECTION OF BOOKS WITH A FEW ATTEMPTS AT PAINTINGS. THE TABLE THAT IS COVERED IN COMPUTERS AND PRACTICALLY NOTHING ELSE.

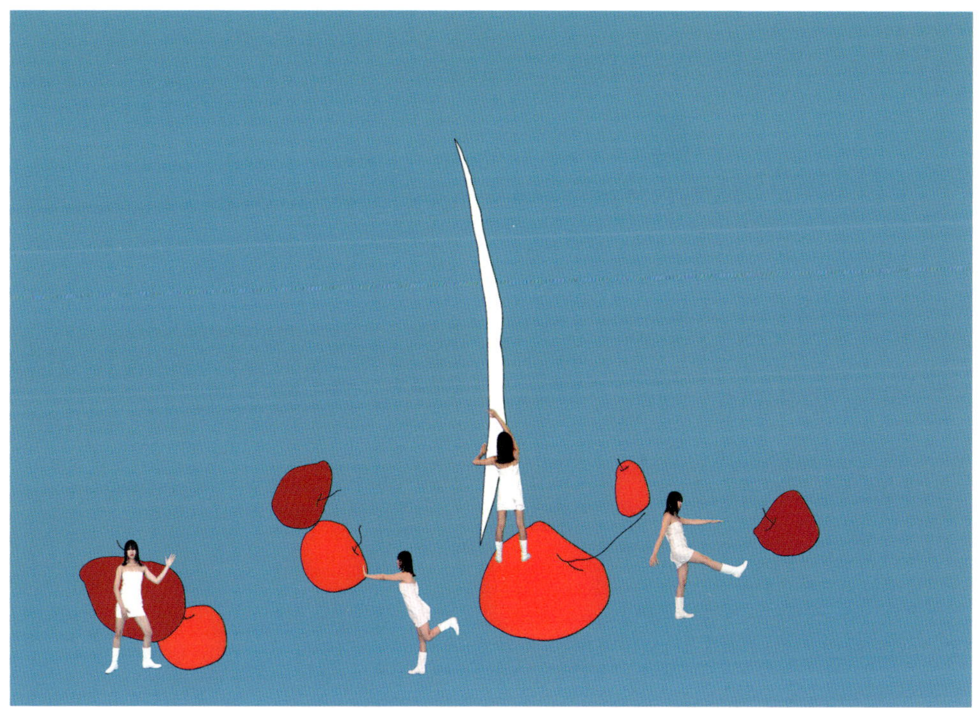

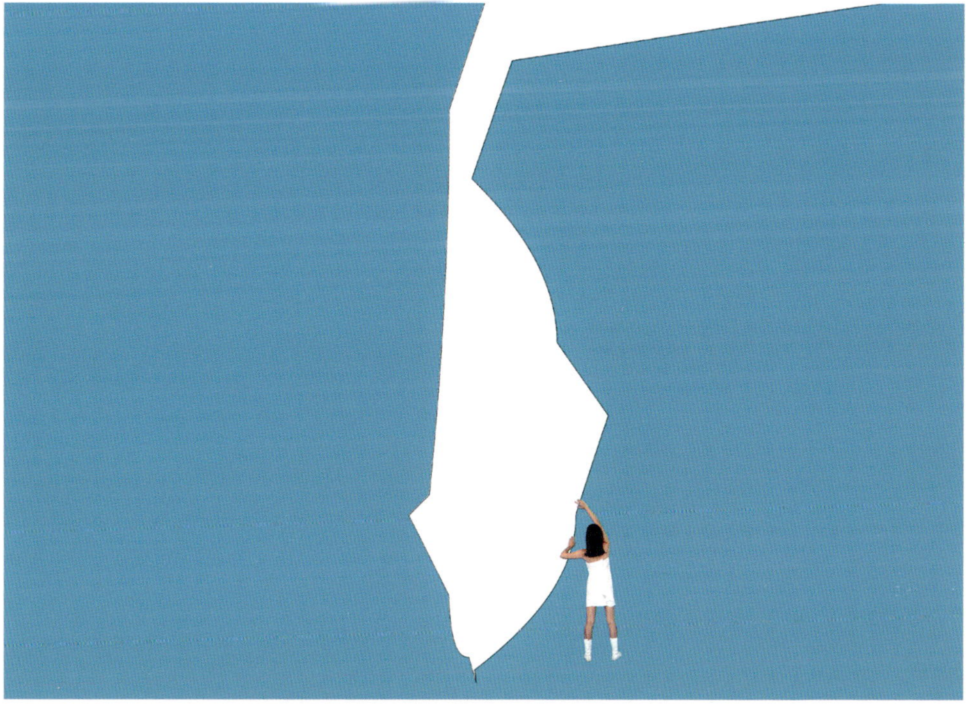

YIOUTOFTHEBLUE, 2003, FLASH ANIMATION. THE WORK ALSO EXISTS IN THE FORM OF A PHOTOGRAPH.

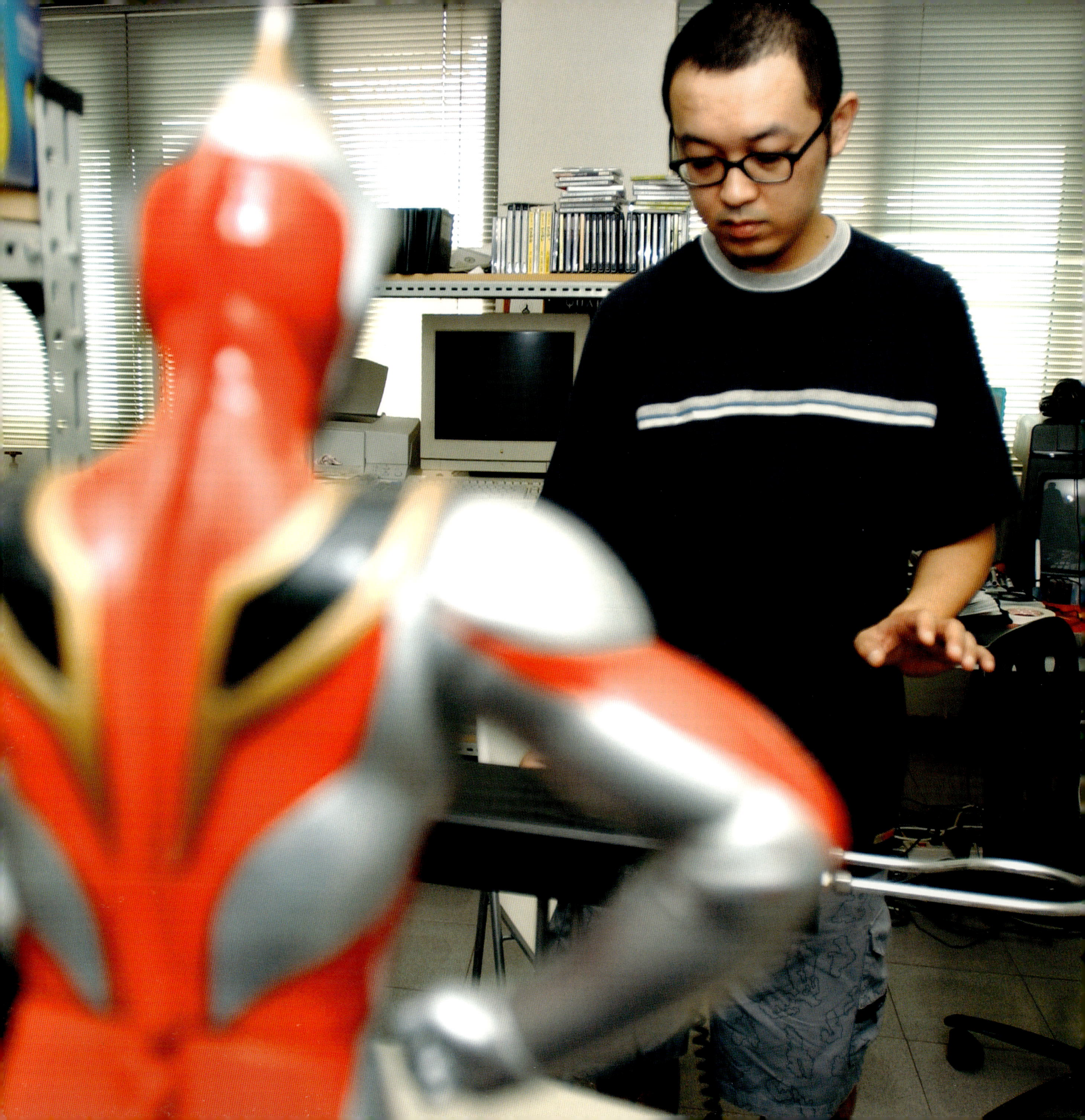

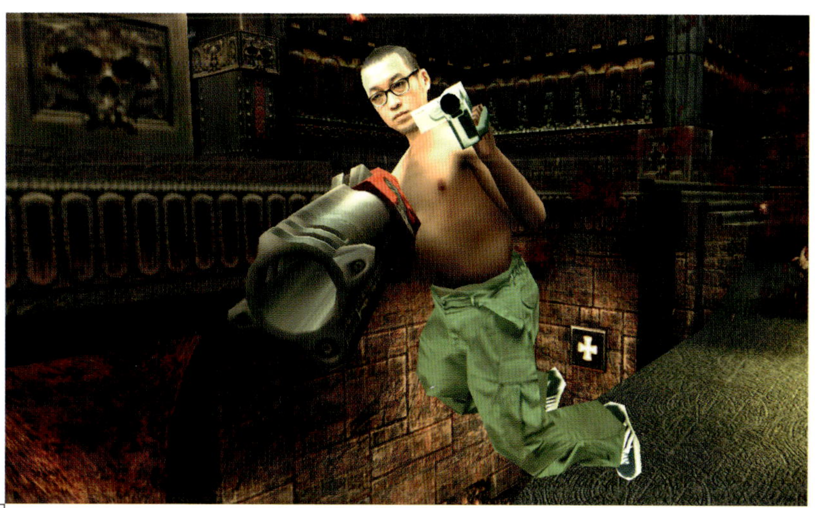

FENG MENGBO

Craaaassshhhh! Shhhriieeekkk! Zooooommmm! Whhhizzz! Feng Mengbo's soundtracks are really something else. The pictures are just as loud, hacking, slashing, spurting, splattering, exploding. An arm is sliced off and glides almost gracefully through the air before it hits the floor and spins round. Kerrannnngg! There is Feng Mengbo himself, right there on the screen, in combat gear and a helmet and his trademark tortoiseshell glasses. In his hand is a machine gun—or is it a video camera? He can fly, just like in a kung-fu film or a video game. The film cuts quickly from one scene to another. The action is just as rapid. The camera whips around, spins, shooting accelerated flashes of action. The image roars, screeches, and snaps from place to place. The aim of the game: kill or be killed. You have to find out how—easier said than done. ¶ I challenged Feng Mengbo to a game at the last Documenta in Kassel, Germany, where pride of place was given to his *Q4U* with three consoles, three screens, and the artist himself in the prime central position. It took him less than thirty seconds to flatten me. Feng Mengbo is a real pro. He is in permanent contact with players from all over the world. It's hardly surprising, then, to discover that he is currently putting the finishing touches to a documentary on Rocket Boy, the greatest Quake gamer in all of China. This is his world. "I'm a child of the Cultural Revolution and of electronic games," he says, just like in 1968, Jean-Luc Godard was a child of Marx and of Coca-Cola. He adds, "Ever since I was small, I have thought that the real heroes were ordinary people." ¶ He pauses, then continues, "When the screen is switched off, the world disappears." With all the fervor of an addict. ¶ In principle, it was easy to get to his home. In fact, I'd already been several times, always with the same driver, and although I knew that on arrival it was not always easy to tell his house from the dozens of other almost identical ones around it, I wasn't too worried. What a mistake. This time, the freeway came to a sudden stop. Roadwork. We tried to cut around them and got stuck in the rutted track. We did a U-turn, but where next? My chauffeur gazed into the distance, looking for telltale landmarks, trying to work out the best route. I rang Feng Mengbo. No answer. We set off, traveling under road bridges, even at one point cutting across another freeway under construction. We went around in circles for half an hour only to end up back where we began. We asked everyone we could find. We even called Song Dong, whose number I had on a scrap of paper. Feng Mengbo was still not answering the phone. We drove on at random. At nearly eleven A.M. (we were supposed to be at his place at ten A.M.) he finally answered the phone. He had switched off his mobile. It took another three or four calls for him to give us directions. I didn't recognize the house. The only clue was when I peeked in the window and saw some science-fiction

FACING PAGE: FENG MENGBO, ON THE SECOND FLOOR OF HIS HOUSE IN BEIJING, DISPLAYING A PASSION FOR MUSIC. HE COMPOSES HIS OWN PIECES USING THE LATEST ELECTRONIC EQUIPMENT. ABOVE: *Q4U*, 2003.

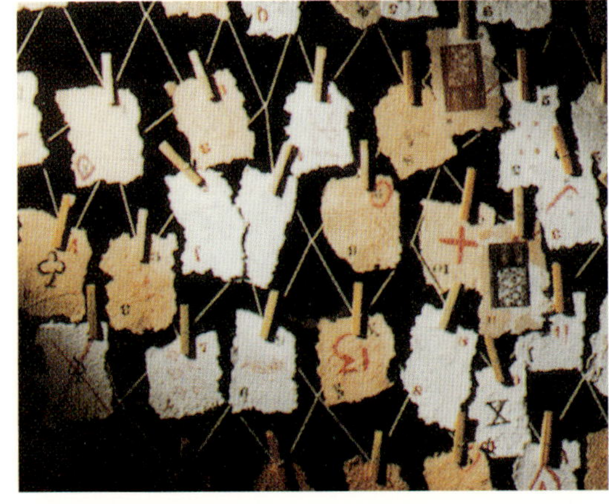

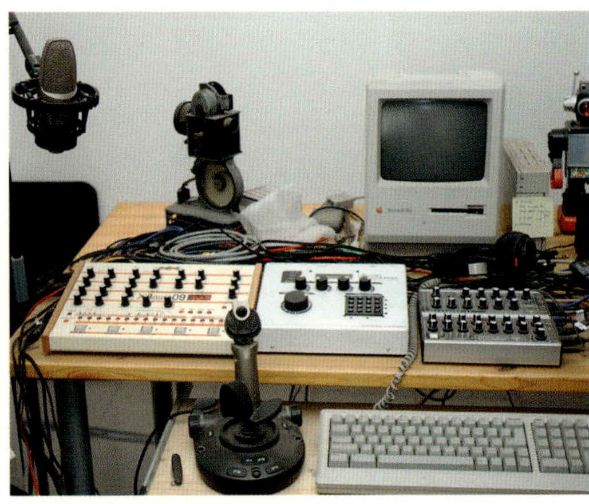

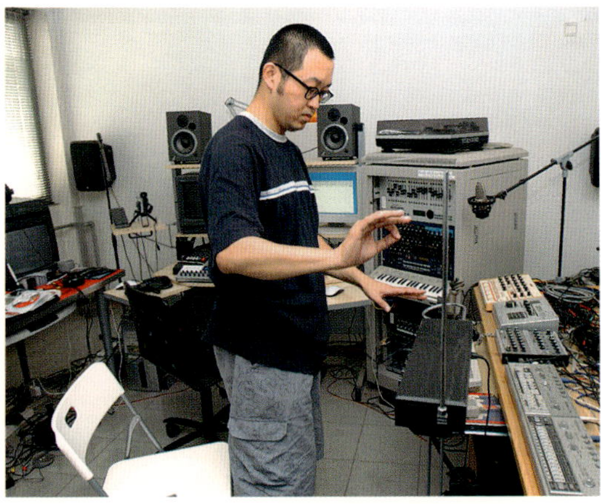

magazines lying on a table. ¶ This is it. We've arrived. We have come a long way east of Beijing, to a rather exclusive residential zone with plenty of green spaces. The house has hardly changed. The first-floor living room is vast, with the television right in the middle. The floor is scattered with toys. Two years ago, on my last visit, there were already plenty of them, but now the amount has to be seen to be believed. Feng Mengbo's son is now four years old. The world—this house—is his oyster. ¶ Is this ostentatious display of toys a way for Feng Mengbo to finally lay to rest the ghosts of his own childhood, which was poor although his father was an engineer and his mother a clerk. He once told me how his father made him a bed using whatever wood he could find. Feng Mengbo is the soul of discretion. You have to read between the lines when he says simply, "My parents suffered during the Cultural Revolution." ¶ He was born in Beijing in 1966, the year when the Cultural Revolution began as one of the biggest social experiments in human history. When I tell him that another artist had tried to persuade me that if it were not for the Cultural Revolution, modern China would not exist, he shoots back, quick as a flash, "That's as stupid as saying that the modern world would not be what it is but for the Second World War." ¶ He doesn't have any exhibitions on at the moment. "I'm on holiday," he says, before explaining that in China, exhibitions only began very recently, with the Guangzhou Triennial in 2002. Before that there was the Shanghai Biennial in 2000—the first exhibition worthy of the name—and two earlier, local shows that barely even deserved to be called mediocre. Why? "In China, the appropriate conditions have not really been met yet." ¶ When he began to specialize in the visual arts as a teenager, he chose to study design, like many Chinese and American artists. He was awarded his diploma in 1985, and a second in engraving in 1991. "I love working with instruments that are a bit complicated and technical," he exclaims. But in 1991, for one of his earliest works, he did not turn to complicated technology. Instead, he simply took a blender, filled it with different colors of paper, and blended it to a pulp, which he then used to make models inspired by pop culture, such as TV stars, as well as pairs of jeans and even ID cards. As early as 1992, he began to explore the possibilities of video games in the series *Video Endgames*, which depicted the heroic figures of revolutionary opera popularized by the Cultural Revolution, painted as simplified characters from video games. Such clear-cut oppositions have led some critics to read Feng Mengbo's works as Political Pop Art, and he does not deny this aspect of his oeuvre. In fact, many of his friends have made their mark in this genre. But the essence of his work lay elsewhere. He had just bought his first Nintendo console. "It was just a game, but I found it absolutely fascinating," he says. In 1993, he was chosen for the Venice Biennale. He has always been quick off the mark. He demurs. "I got lucky. For the first time, one of the Biennale's directors came to China. It was Achile Bonito Oliva." ¶ 1993 also saw the launch of Doom, the first superstar game—the first to have a named author, John Romero. It was also the first game where the gamer was an integral part of the action. Since then, like many children born in the 1960s (the video game culture first appeared in China in the 1980s), Feng Mengbo would spend hours every day playing on his console. In the end, he became bored, and decided to find out "what was going on behind the screen." His moment had come. He was to make his mark in the world of video games. ¶ In 1994, he acquired his first Macintosh Model Mac LC II (known in China as a Chuany), "4MPB, MAM, 40 MD HD System 7.0," he says proudly, as if announcing the weight of his newborn son. In 1994 and 1995, he used this new equipment to produce five works based on the idea of an on-screen slide show with a variety of

FROM LEFT TO RIGHT: *AIRDRY SERIES, DISH POKER*, INSTALLATION, 1990-1991. THE ARTIST IN HIS STUDIO WITH THE LATEST TECHNOLOGY.

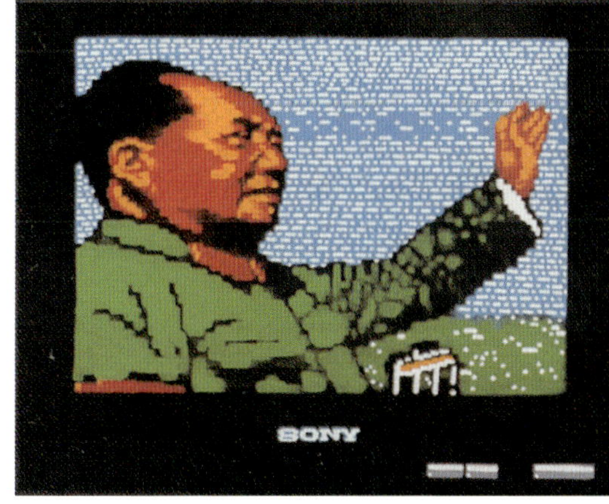

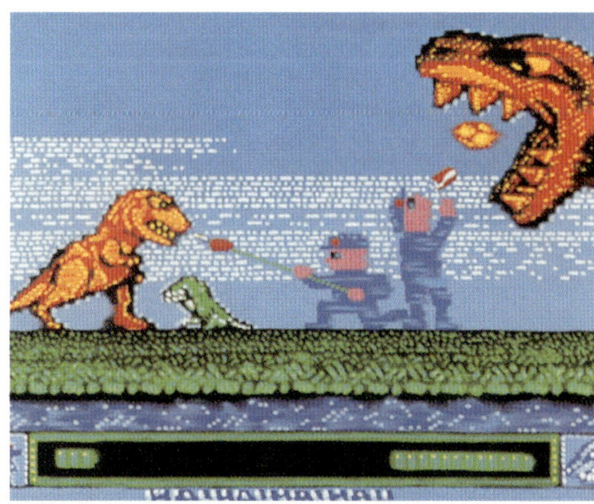

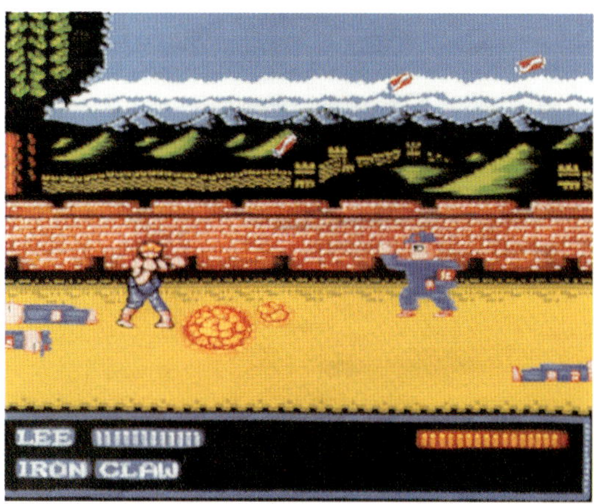

effects as the images melded into one another. He also painted a lot. The series entitled *Streetfighter* (1995) shows a revolutionary soldier wearing a Red Guard uniform, fighting assassins and monsters on the computer screen. The screen and the denizens of the electronic world were the subjects of his painting. ¶ Over the years, Feng Mengbo gradually bought more and more of the latest equipment, occasionally inventing add-ons as and when needed. He also built up an extensive collection of miniature figurines. In 1996, he produced *My Private Album*, initially planned as a collection of slides documenting his family history. He fed a heap of old photograph albums, pages torn from books, postcards, drawings, paintings, scenes from old films, and LPs into his computer to produce a record of his family over three generations, noting births, old age, deaths, and periods of hardship, with a warmth and affection that anyone who knows Feng Mengbo instantly recognizes as his defining characteristic. The work describes the struggles his family—along with countless others—underwent in days of historic change. Alongside the private family pictures he included some images taken from official sources. "My art deals with the ordinary lives of everyday people," he tells me. ¶ This was Feng Mengbo's first interactive display. It was shown in the Fruitmarket Gallery in Edinburgh; the Nouvelle Galerie in Graz, Austria; the Aaltonen Art Museum in Turku, Finland; and at Art Focus in Jerusalem. More recently, it was on show at the Guangzhou Triennial in 2002-03. "With *My Private Album*, I wanted to produce something on a grander scale, and in better conditions. I especially wanted to give a gift to my parents." ¶ The heartfelt accompanying text explains how and why the work came to be: "Not so long ago, photographs were a luxury in China. Now, twenty years later, my parents are sitting in front of my computer. They are moving the mouse with hands that a lifetime's labor has made clumsy and callused. They are transfixed by the photographs that appear on the screen before them. Sometimes their eyes fill with tears. When I tell them that this CD-ROM will be shown in exhibitions in Europe and the United States, they ask in wonder whether something like this can be considered art. What can I say to that? That it's just an example of an ordinary family." ¶ But Feng Mengbo also draws my attention to other facets of the question. "This interactive CD-ROM was not produced solely for the impressive walls of an art gallery. It has been produced in a format that is accessible to everyone. Which means that everyone can come up with his or her own version. Aside from the technical reasons that made me choose the CD-ROM format, I wanted to give the audience more freedom to handle my works, because my family history is shared by countless other Chinese families. In addition, I thought that an interactive CD-ROM would free me from the constraints of the linear narrative format and would make the work closer to the palimpsests of memory itself." ¶ Shortly after, Feng Mengbo produced a series of interactive multimedia works using the structure of commercial software packages cloaked in Chinese themes, such as *Game Over: The Long March* and *The War of Resistance against Japan*. He combined cultural themes from ancient China, traditional opera, and more recent tales from the Cultural Revolution or Hong Kong action movies and film stars, dressing them up in a romantic, heroic style, with a moral or political flourish to finish off. ¶ "People see me as a game artist," he says, "Rather than a political Pop artist. But that doesn't mean that I'm not interested in history. It's just that I'm not responsible for the past." He adds, "My art is full of imagination and memories. I draw on cultural icons. They can be political, but I don't think of my art as having a political message." 1997: *Taking Mount Doom by Strategy* is shown on three computers and three screens at the Haggerty Museum in Milwaukee, the *ISEA 98 Revolution*

GAME OVER: LONG MARCH, 1994.

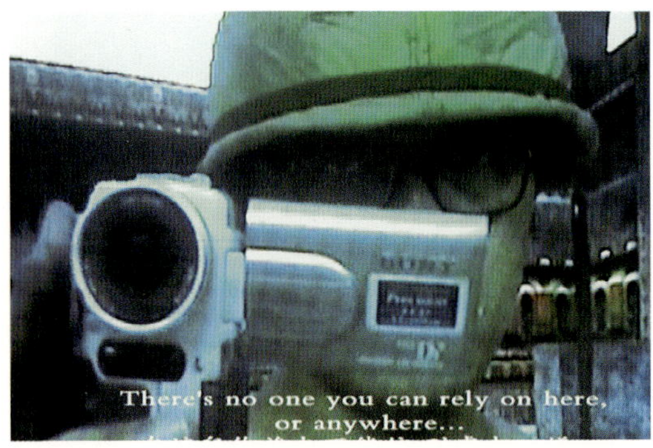

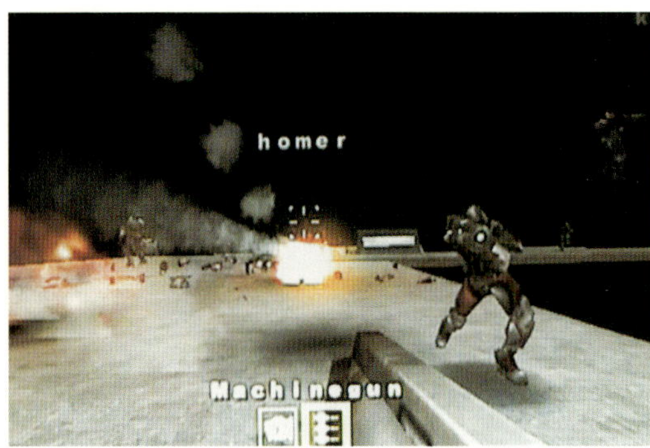

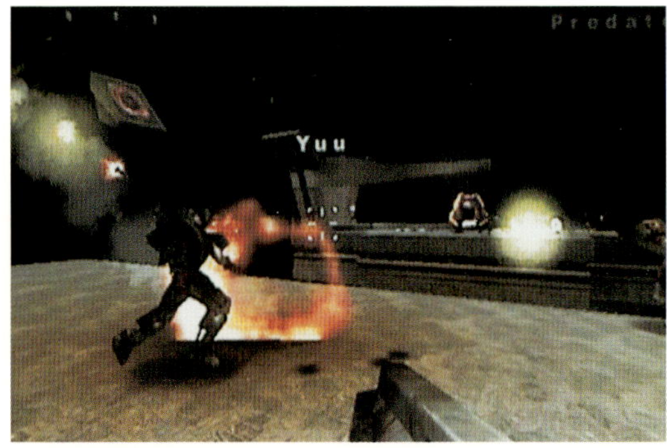

exhibition in Liverpool, and the first Fukuoka triennial in Japan. The work caused a certain amount of controversy because of the way it melded two extremely different cultural references—Doom, the aforementioned hi-tech video game launched four years earlier, and one of the six model operas authorized by the Gang of Four led by Mao's wife, Jiang Qing, for the education of the masses during the Cultural Revolution. The opera was called *Taking Tiger Mountain by Strategy*, and Feng Mengbo's work also included forty-two scenes from *Taking Tiger Mountain*, a popular 1970s film. Feng Mengbo combined all of these elements with wit and a fine sense of irony, underscoring the way the film and the opera both drew on the struggle for power, the thirst for blood, and the need for heroes, and contrasting this with scenes from his own life with flair and imagination. ¶ This was Feng Mengbo's second interactive CD-ROM installation. It was more mobile, freer, funnier, and faster than the first. "I have always believed that playing is a vital component of art. Games are full of imagination and fun. Moreover, they are always interactive. But the most important thing is maybe that a good game comes out of nowhere, just like a work of art," he explained in a text written to accompany *Taking Mount Doom by Strategy*. ¶ This work heralded Feng Mengbo's success in America with a solo exhibition at Holly Salomon's gallery in 1997. "Oh," I ask, "You work with Holly Salomon, do you?" He answers evasively, saying he is not sure: "I had one exhibition with her and I haven't heard anything since." These days, with a few honorable exceptions, relations between Chinese artists and their European and American galleries are often unusual, to say the least. They all dream of being invited to Documenta (Feng Mengbo has shown there twice, in 1997 and 2002), to MoMA in New York, the Centre Pompidou in Paris (Feng Mengbo's art featured in the China exhibition in 2003), and maybe one or two major biennials (Feng Mengbo has been to Venice, Johannesburg, and Gwangju). However, they don't really know which are the most important biennials, and in terms of sales, they rely on a few enthousiastic collectors who are ahead of the trend. They are perfectly up-to-date for some things, and are hopelessly lost for others. ¶ Feng Mengbo tells me, "When I was little, I had two ideals. I wanted to be either a soldier in the People's Liberation Army or an artist. I thought it was pretty much the same thing—the best way to have an extraordinary life and to be a hero. In the end, I chose the second route. I wanted to create things. But I changed my mind after I discovered the fun I could have with video games. We can't create anything from scratch. All we can do is destroy things. But can we build them up again? Look at our marvelous cities. Do you think we'll manage to find a way to protect them from pollution? Maybe it would be better to keep them as street scenes like the ones in games like Quake or Street Fighter—all black and dirty in the icy rain. That's too pessimistic. Of course, you could say that all the successful games software is completely commercial and that that's not what real life is about. But why, then, are there millions of young people who love them so much? Why do they love pretending to be characters such as serial killers in bloodthirsty games? What are they thinking about when they mow people down on screen with a machine gun? What do they feel when the people on screen explode and die?" ¶ Question: Is it up to the artist to provide the answers? ¶ Feng Mengbo is not the only person to be both attracted and repelled by the violence of video games. They reveal the dark side of human existence. ¶ When, in 1998, Feng Mengbo downloaded a basic version of Quake, he quickly realized that he was onto something. "The game was so straightforward, and yet so powerful. The possibilities were endless!" he recalls. His interpretation was rapidly forthcoming—a digital video entitled *Q3*

Q3, 1999. INTERACTIVE VIDEO GAME.

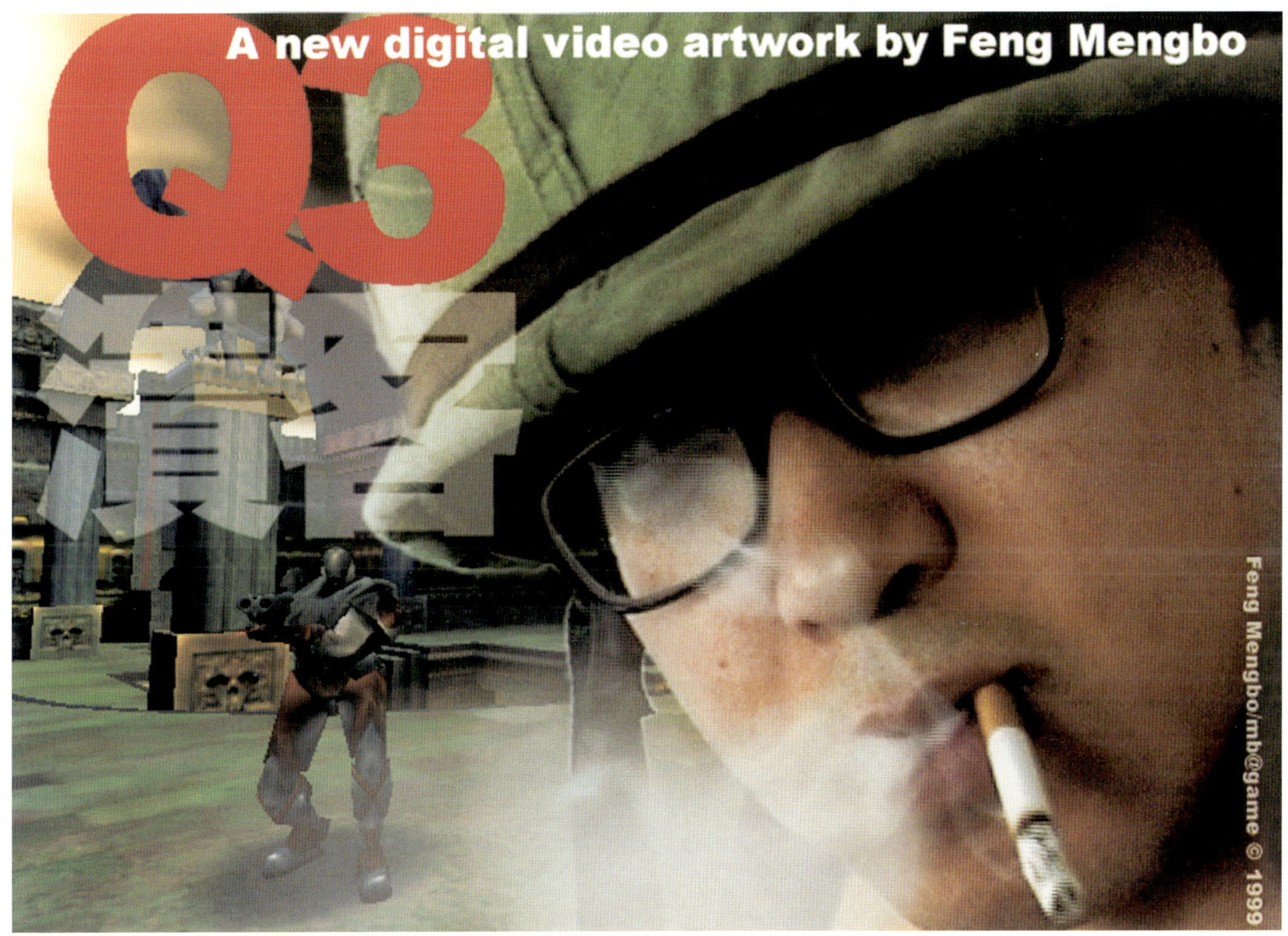

Q3. 1999. INTERACTIVE VIDEO GAME.

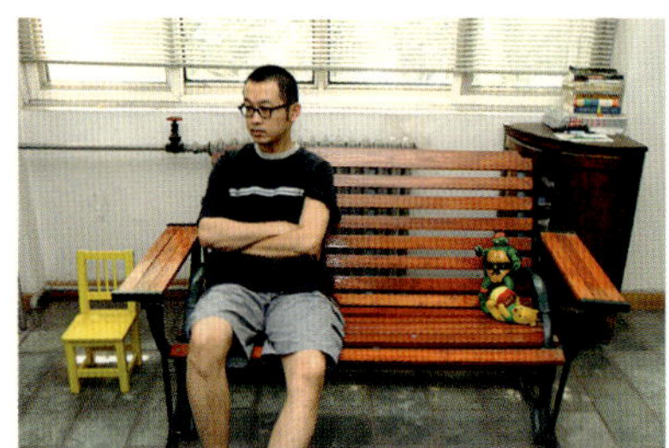

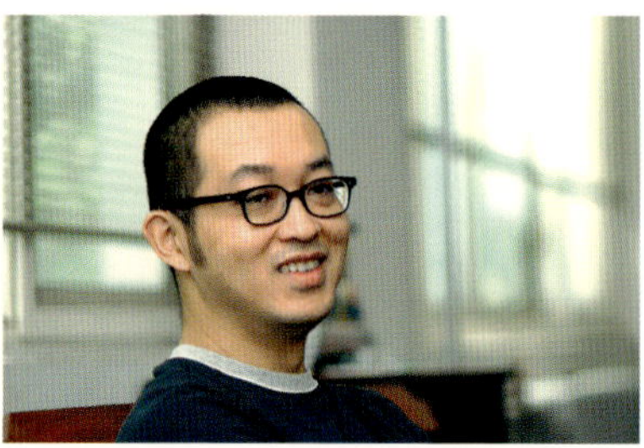

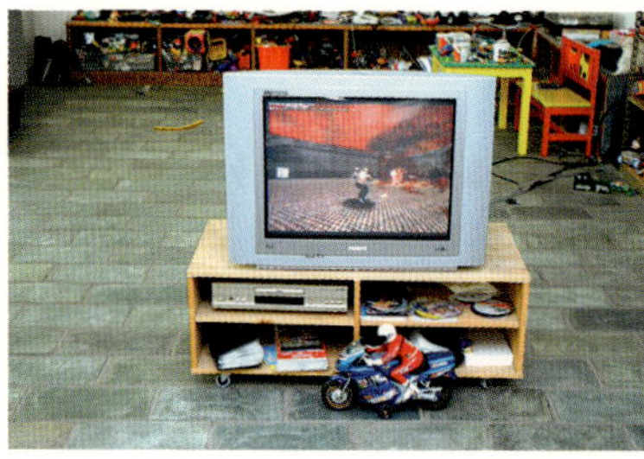

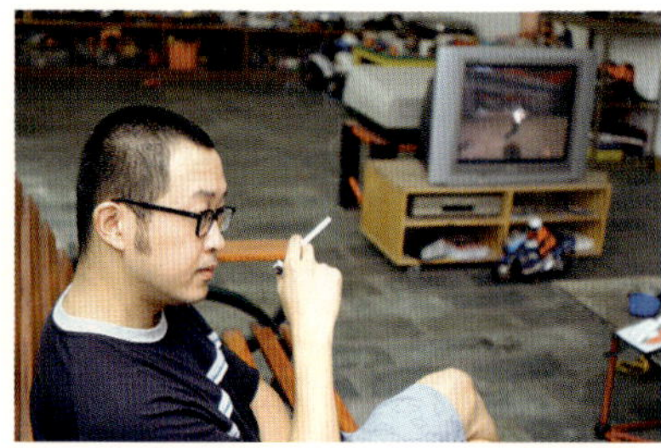

(mini DV wide screen, 32 minutes) adapted from the ultraviolent game Quake III Arena. *Q3* featured Feng Mengbo himself as a war correspondent, a cigarette permanently drooping from his lip, interviewing a clone warrior in the midst of a virtual war, shells exploding around them and bullets whistling past. It is a remarkable combination of violence and humor. A curious blend. ¶ *Q4U*, first shown at the most recent Documenta, is the follow-up. It uses three Pentium 4 computers, each loaded with Quake III Arena, on three ten by twelve foot screens. The game requires three players who have downloaded the Feng Mengbo character, and who can also play over the Internet. There can be as many as sixty-four Feng Mengbos on the screens simultaneously, and the content of the game changes constantly depending on who is playing. *Q4U* is a real nightmare. "I meet people through *Q4U*. I'm part of the game, but I'm also a real person. I play every day, which means something brand new as far as I'm concerned." ¶ The work was presented at the University of Chicago Renaissance Society, and caused a heated debate as to whether it could be considered art. This question is never far away when new technologies are involved. Feng Mengbo can barely be bothered to answer. In fact, he adroitly avoids the question. "I am tired of art that tries at all costs to be new and different. I scorn people who seek aesthetic effect." ¶ *Ah Q* is the rather poetic title of his most recent creation, which tickled the somewhat bemused crowds at the entrance to the China exhibition at the Centre Pompidou in 2003. It is an interactive game developed with his friend Lu Yue, a 3-D graphic designer, where the controls are in a carpet that the gamer must dance around on to operate the Feng Mengbos that appear and disappear on the screen, blowing them up, missing them, killing them or letting them live. The letter Q in the title is the only reminder of the game Quake that this game is based on. ¶ The Quaker artist does not go out much, and steers clear of the Chinese contemporary art world. He prefers to stay home and communicate with the whole world over the Internet. "The whole world is one big game," he says. ¶ Upstairs in his house, I find paradise. A large room full of screens, keypads, joysticks, levers, mice, LEDs, electric cables, and nameless bits of computers in all shapes and sizes, from clunky old models to recent sleek, streamlined beauties. Here, Feng Mengbo can record anything he likes and then work on the images and sounds to his heart's content. Bring things to life. Resuscitate them, even. He is like a little boy in a candy store. ¶ He sits down, stands up again, shows me what he has done and what he is planning to do, grabs hold of a machine that looks nothing special and caresses it as if it were his firstborn. The machine bleeps. He twiddles the buttons, evidently enjoying himself, astonished by the result. He tells me he loves composing like this, and that he is planning to record an album. He turns to his keyboards, but gets up again almost immediately. "I've had enough of keyboards. I'd love to be able to work everything just from a joystick with two buttons that you could use for whatever you want and that you could twiddle in all directions. Actually, what I would love would be to develop whatever I need right here. I'd love to be a sort of video DJ. My dream is to input directly into the screen with my joystick and direct the action live, as it were." ¶ Feng Mengbo smiles, picturing himself in action. ¶ Who said that technology and dreams were incompatible?

ABOVE: IN THE BIG LIVING ROOM ON THE GROUND FLOOR. FACING PAGE: *Q4U*, 2003.

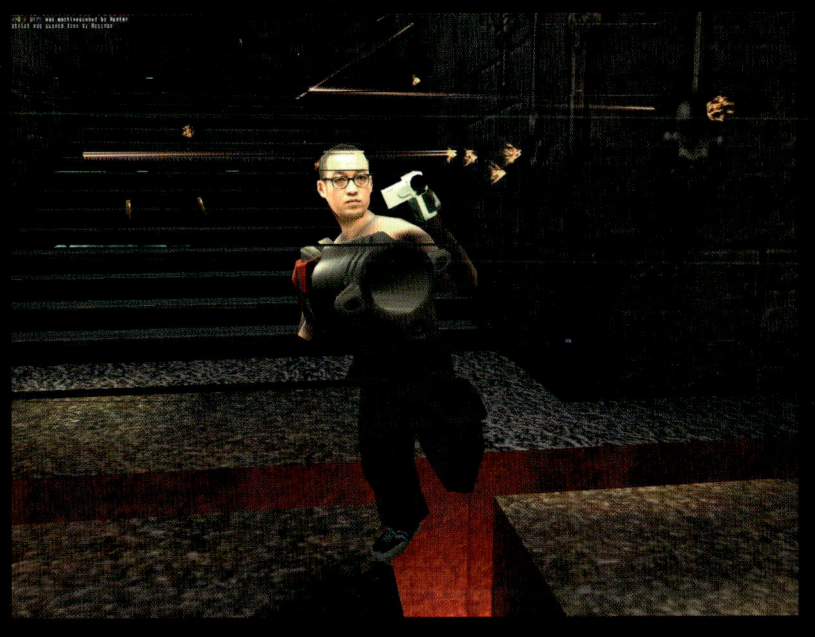
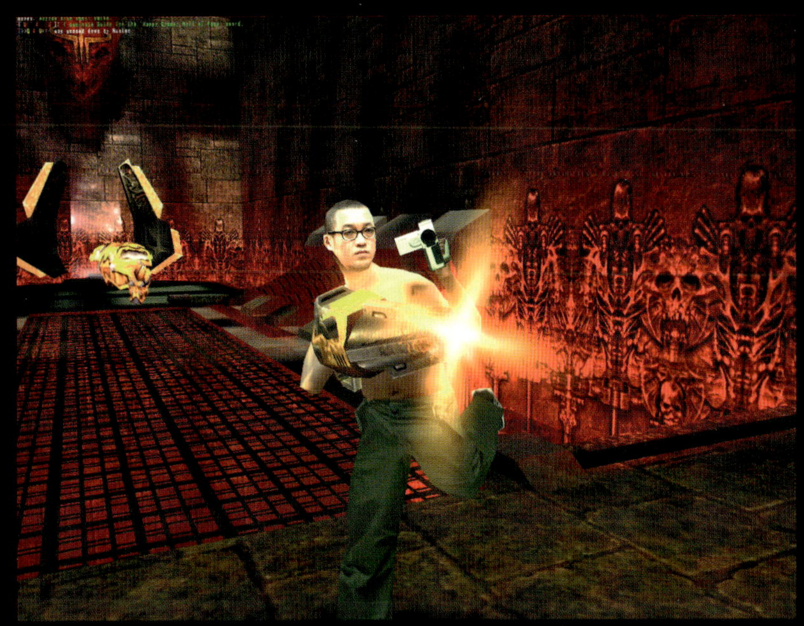
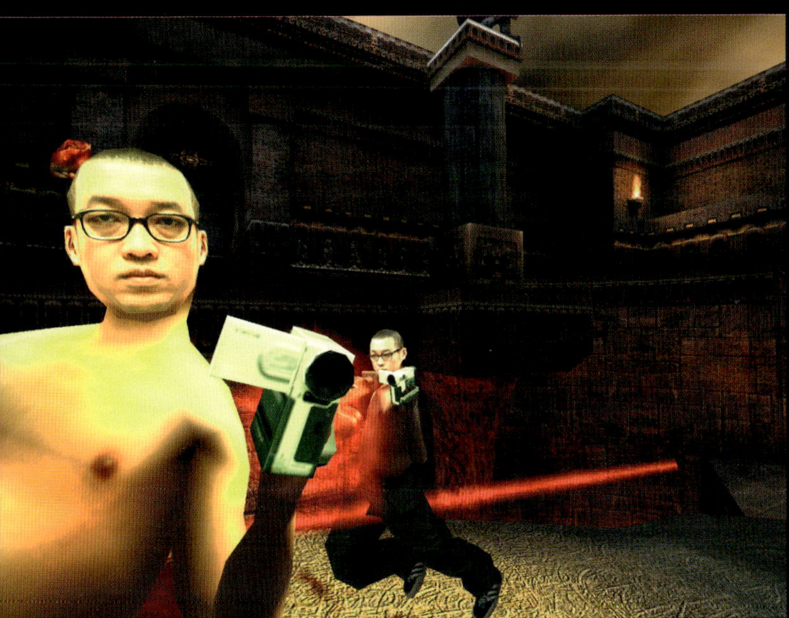
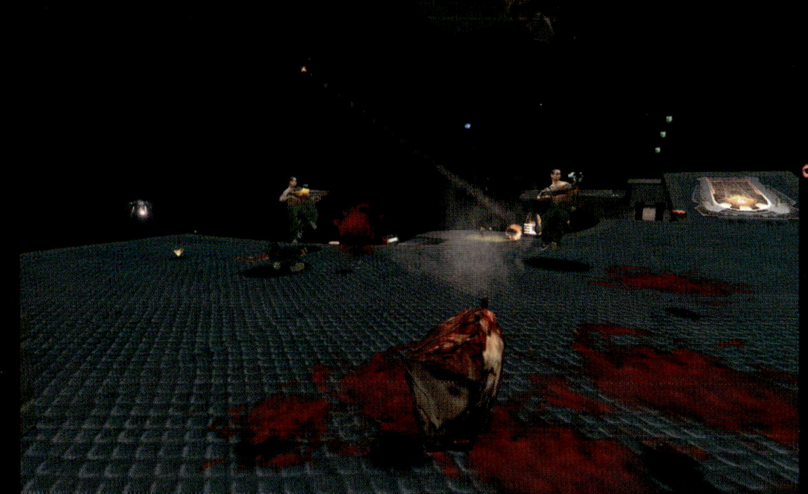

CHRONOLOGY

1949: October 1. Foundation of the People's Republic of China, with Mao Tse-tung as leader. Zhou En-lai is prime minister and foreign minister.
The nationalists flee to Taiwan.
1949–52: The Communist Party promulgates first reforms: laws on marriage, schooling, and agricultural reform. Private companies are nationalized.
1951: Campaign to root out counterrevolutionaries.
1953–57: First Five-Year Plan.
1958–60: Mao Tse-tung's Great Leap Forward. Priority is given to the development of heavy industry and creation of people's communes.
1959: Repression of an uprising in Lhasa. The Dalai Lama flees to India.
1960–62: Industrial output falls 43 percent. The emphasis on steel production instead of agriculture results in famine. An estimated forty million people starve to death. Rumor has it cannibalism is common all over China.
1961: A policy of "economic readjustment" is introduced. The start of de-collectivization.
1962: Armed conflict with India.
1965: Mao Tse-tung launches the Cultural Revolution.
1966: The insurrectionary phase of the Great Proletarian Cultural Revolution. Distribution of the Little Red Book. Organization of squadrons of Red Guards.
1967: China is on the verge of civil war. Persecution of Communist Party cadres and intellectuals.
1968: Disbanding of the Red Guards.
1969: The Chinese Communist Party is divided into two camps: radicals and moderate intellectuals represented by the Prime Minister Chou En-lai and Deng Xiaoping.
Border skirmishes between China and the USSR.
1971: The People's Republic of China is granted international recognition as it joins the United Nations, replacing Taiwan, which represents Nationalist China.
Death of Lin Biao.
1972: Visit from President Nixon. Relations start to improve between China and the United States.
1975: Chou En-lai launches a program of economic modernization.
Chiang Kai-shek dies in Taiwan.
1976: Chou En-lai dies in January. Violent skirmishes in Tiananmen Square.
Mao Tse-tung dismisses Deng Xiaoping and names Hua Guofeng Prime Minister.
July **28:** The Tangshan earthquake kills some 270,000 people.
September **9:** Death of Mao Tse-tung. The Gang of Four is arrested.
1977: End of the Cultural Revolution. Deng Xiaoping is rehabilitated and returns to power. Economic reforms. China begins to open up to the outside world.
1978: A new, more liberal constitution is drawn up, providing for collective leadership. A "Wall for Democracy" is built in Beijing. The first news posters begin to appear.
The first independent exhibition is held at the Shanghai Children's Palace. For the first time, works that explicitly reject Socialist Realism are allowed to be shown.
One month later, a second exhibition is held in Beijing, breaking with the heroic themes imposed on artists by the Communist regime and showing still-life paintings and landscapes.
A Shanghai daily newspaper publishes a short story by Lu Xinhua entitled *The Scar*, denouncing the excesses of the Cultural Revolution and describing the hardship faced by the young intellectuals sent to the country to be reeducated.
1979: Deng Xiaoping announces a new economic policy. He visits the United States and diplomatic relations are restored. Armed conflict with Vietnam.
September: The first exhibition of the now legendary Star Group in Beijing. The artists hang their canvases on the railings of the park next to the National Museum of Art. Two days later, the police intervene to stop the exhibition. The group organizes a second exhibition in Behai Park two months later.
The magazine *Fine Arts World* is launched with an article on developments in Western art.
1980: Creation of the Special Economic Zones designed to bring in foreign capital and technology. The goods produced in these zones are for export only.
The Star Group has an exhibition at the National Museum of Art. It is a great success.
1981: Introduction of new policies leading to the liberalization of the Chinese economy.
The city of Xi'an organizes its first contemporary art exhibition.
1982: Campaign against what is termed "spiritual pollution," or Western artistic influences.
An abstract sculpture on the Gezhou Dam is a source of heated debate.
A play entitled *Alarm Bells* describes the problems faced by young people, particularly unemployment.
1983: Beijing: The Picasso exhibition at the National Museum of Art is followed by a Munch exhibition five months later.
Shanghai: An exhibition featuring experimental paintings is shut down by police four days after it opens.
Xiamen: Huang Yong Ping takes part in an exhibition of five modern artists.
Suzhou: The National Art Association meets to discuss ways of eliminating "spiritual pollution in the art world."
1984: Abolition of the people's communes.
The National Art Association inaugurates its sixth national art exhibition in nine cities as part of the campaign against "spiritual pollution." Opponents organize the *New Wave 1985* movement.
1985: Censorship of cultural products is relaxed. The number of exhibitions increases dramatically.
Foundation of the Northern Art Group with Wang Guangyi as a leading figure.
Beijing: Exhibition of progressive young artists at the National Museum of Art. Works from the New Wave 85 movement figure prominently.
Shanghai: The first exhibition featuring the new figurative art including works by Zhang Xiaogang. The exhibition is later shown in Nanjing.
Wuhan: Exhibition of recent paintings in the traditional Chinese style, including works by Gu Wenda.
The Rauschenberg exhibition in Beijing, then Lhasa, Tibet, makes headlines.
Hangzhou: The *New Space 1985* exhibition featuring works by Zhang Peili.
Changsa, Hunan province: Foundation of the Zero group.
Taiyuan, Shanxi province: The Three Steps Studio organizes an exhibition, which is shut down by the police a few hours after it opens.
1986: Student demonstrations in Beijing. Deng Xiaoping declares, "Reform must include reform of the political system."
Shenzhen: The Zero group organizes a street exhibition.
Hangzhou: An exhibition of installations is held.
Guangzhou: Wang Du organizes the first Salon for artists from southern China.
Nankin: Exhibition of new Fauvist works and formation of a Surrealist group.
Xiamen: Huang Yong Ping and his group organize the *Xiamen Dada: Postmodernism* exhibition.
Beijing: Exhibition of works by young artists from Hunan at the National Museum of Art.
1987: Zhao Zyang becomes leader of the Communist Party. Student demonstrations on Tiananmen Square. *The People's Daily* condemns the students. Riots quelled in Tibet.
The first Chinese rock album recorded.

Changchun, Jilin province: Wang Guangyi organizes the first biennial of artists' groups in northern China.
Beijing: The exhibition *Let Us Turn to the Future*, featuring works by young Beijing artists, is held at the National Museum of Art.
1988: The hardliner Li Peng becomes prime minister. The Chinese Communist Party accepts the principle that the state controls the market, and the market guides companies. Yang Shangkun is elected President of the People's Republic.
Beijing: Xu Bing and Lu Shengzhong show installations at the Museum of Art.
Nankin: A magazine devoted to Chinese fine art organizes an international symposium on developments in Chinese contemporary art.
Performances are held on the Great Wall of China.
1989: Gorbachev visits Beijing. Relations between China and the USSR return to normal.
Riots in Tibet and the proclamation of martial law. The Beijing Spring. Students announce an unlimited strike in support of their demands for press freedom and dialogue with the government. June 4: Deng Xiaoping sends tanks to crush a demonstration in Tiananmen Square.
Zhao Ziyang is sacked and replaced by Jiang Zemin.
Beijing: The *China/Avant-Garde* exhibition at the National Museum of Art is the biggest of its kind so far, showing works by 185 of the most representative Chinese contemporary artists. Two months later, a Tàpies exhibition is held.
Hong Kong and Taipei: The Star Group celebrates its tenth anniversary with an exhibition of works by twelve members at the Hanart TZ gallery.
Paris: The *Magicians of the Earth* exhibition includes works by three Chinese artists: Huang Yong Ping, Yiang Jiechang, and Gu Dexin.
1990. End of martial law in Beijing. China's international isolation ends as a result of the Gulf War. The magazine *Chinese Fine Arts* is closed down by the authorities.
Xu Bing produces rubbings of the Great Wall.
Chen Shaoxiong and three friends found the Big Tail Elephant group in Guangzhou.
1991: China's relations with Vietnam are restored to normality.
Beijing: Twenty or so young artists take over the artists' village in the old Summer Palace.
Pasadena, California: The first major exhibition of contemporary art from China abroad, entitled *I Don't Want to Play Cards with Cézanne*.
Guangzhou: Big Tail Elephant's first exhibition at the Workers' Palace.
Beijing: Feng Mengbo and Zhang Bo's installations are to be shown at the gallery of the Central Academy of Arts high school, but it is closed down before it has a chance to open.
1992: The Chinese Communist Party adopts a socialist market economy.
Relations with South Korea are restored.
Beijing: The emergence of Cynical Realism with Fang Lijun and Liu Wei's exhibition at the Central Fine Art Gallery. The artists in the artists' village at the Summer Palace hang their works from the trees.
Guangzhou: The first biennial where Political Pop Art makes its mark. Big Tail Elephant show their works at the Guangdong Radio and Television University.
Hong Kong: The Hong Kong Art Center and the Hanart TZ Gallery organize an exhibition of Xu Bing and Gu Wenda's installations, *Desire for Words*.
1993: Jiang Zemin becomes the Chinese president.
Berlin: *China/Avant-Garde* featuring works by seventeen artists is shown in Berlin, then later in Rotterdam, Oxford, and Odense, Denmark.
Hong Kong: The Hong Kong Art Center shows works by fifty-four artists at the *China New Art, Post 89* exhibition.
Beijing. A Jorg Immendorf exhibition is held at the International Art Palace, and Gilbert and George show at the National Museum of Art. In October, a performance here by Zhang Huan leads to the closure of the exhibition on the 1990s.
Guangzhou: Big Tail Elephant have an exhibition in the Red Ants bar.
Venice: Achile Bonito Oliva throws open the biennial to China. Among the artists shown in the *Road to East* section are Feng Mengbo, Wang Guangyi, Zhang Peili, and Xu Bing.
1994: The yuan falls 40 percent on the currency markets. The Three Gorges Dam project is launched.
Beijing: At the National Museum of Art, the exhibition featuring Song Dong's performance *One More Lesson: Do You Want to Play with Me* is closed down after less than an hour. Nine months later, the exhibition *12-12* at the Zhaoyao gallery shows experimental works by five female artists.
Shanghai: *94 Art Paragraph*, an exhibition of installations at Huashan Technical School.
São Paulo, Brazil: Six Chinese artists are invited: Li Shan, Yu Youhan, Wang Guangyi, Zhang Xiaogang, Fan Lijun, and Liu Wei.
Ma Luming and Zhu Ming organize a series of performances. They are sentenced to two months in prison for pornography.
1995: Beijing refuses to acknowledge the successor of the Panchen Lama named by the Dalai Lama.
Beijing: Yan Lei's works are shown at the Beijing Number One Theater.
Chengdu: A series of performances on the theme of water conservation, *Defender of the Water*.
Gwangju, South Korea: The first biennial includes works by Wang Jianwei, Feng Mengbo, Song Dong, Fang Lijun, and Lu Shengzhong.
Venice: The forty-sixth biennial shows works by three Chinese artists: Zhang Xiaogang, Liu Wei, and Yu Youhan. Fei Dawei organizes the *Asiana* exhibition.
1996: Missiles fired over the Taiwan Straits.
Shanghai: The first biennial is held, showing mostly oil paintings.
Beijing: The Wan Fung Gallery hosts *Gaudy Life*, including works by Wang Qingsong and Liu Zheng.
Hangzhou: The video art exhibition *Image and Phenomena* at the Academy of Fine Arts gallery.
Edinburgh: The Fruitmarket Gallery shows *Reckoning with the Past*, the first experimental exhibition grouping works by artists from mainland China, Taiwan, and Hong Kong.
Guangzhou: Big Tail Elephant have their fifth exhibition.
Bonn: *China! Zeitgenossische Malerei* (an exhibition of contemporary painting).
Creation of the Annie Wong Foundation, which gives financial support to Chinese artists exhibiting abroad.
1997: The British hand Hong Kong back to China. Demonstrations by Chinese democrats demanding political reform.
Deng Xiaoping dies.
Beijing: Song Dong has an exhibition of video installations in the gallery of the Central Academy of Fine Arts high school.
Shanghai: *New Asia, New City, New Arts*, an exhibition of Chinese and Korean art at the Contemporary Art Museum.
Vienna: *Cities on the Move* begins with works by Wang Du, Chen Shaoxiong, Zhang Peili, and Zheng Guogu, among others.
Kassel, Germany: Feng Mengbo and Weng Jianwei take part in the tenth edition of Documenta.
Venice: Cao Guoqiang's work is selected for the forty-seventh biennial.

Lyon, France: Harald Szeeman presents works by Yan Pei Ming, Chen Zhen, Pu Jie, Xu Yihui, Zhang Peili, Feng Mengbo, and Wang Xinwei.
Seoul: Ten artists are selected by Fei Dawei for the *In Between Limits* exhibition at the Sonje Museum.
Gwangju: The artists chosen for the second biennial are Xu Bing, Huang Yong Ping, Chen Zhen, and Feng Mengbo.
1998: Zhu Rongji becomes prime minister and launches an ambitious modernization program, reforming Chinese housing, finance policy, and the rural economy.
Beijing: The exhibition *It's Me*, organized by Leng Lin, is canceled the day before it was due to open.
Changchun, Jilin province: An exhibition of video and computer art is held at the Industrial Design School.
Shanghai: The first major exhibition of contemporary Japanese art in China, *Beyond the Everyday*.
Bonn: *Half of the Sky: Contemporary Chinese Women Artists* at the Women's Museum.
New York: *Inside Out: New Chinese Art* at PSI, featuring sixty artists from mainland China, Taiwan, and Hong Kong. The exhibition was later shown all over the world until 2000.
Luxembourg: *Gare de l'Est* brings together three Chinese artists based in Paris: Wang Du, Huang Yong Ping, and Chen Zhen. The curator was Hou Hanru.
1999: Celebrations to mark the fiftieth anniversary of the founding of the People's Republic. The government passes an amendment in favor of free enterprise. A major commercial deal is struck between China and the United States. The Portuguese hand Macao back to China. NATO mistakenly bombs the Chinese Embassy in Belgrade.
Shanghai: Xu Zhen and Yang Zhenzhong organize *Art for Sale* in a supermarket.
Beijing: The inauguration of the China Art Archive and Warehouse (CAAW), a new exhibition hall in a former factory.
Chengdu: *Gate of the Century* brings together works by two hundred artists from 1979 to 1999.
Chicago: Twenty-two artists present their work in *Transience: Chinese Experimental Art (at the End of the Twentieth Century)* at the Smart Museum of Art.
Venice: The forty-eighth biennial sets a new record, with nineteen Chinese artists participating in *Apertutto*.
2000: One month before the presidential elections in Taiwan, Beijing threatens military intervention if there is no progress in the process of reunification. The People's National Assembly promulgates laws to restrict Internet access.
Shanghai: The third biennial proves to be decisive. The scandal caused by *Fuck Off* at the Eastlink Gallery casts doubt on the future of the biennial.
Xieyang, Guangxi province: *Ways of Life in the Future*, a festival of performances. Xu Zhen, Yang Zhenzhong, and Yang Fudong organize *Useful Life* and, on the fringes of the biennial, *Heads, Figures, Couples, and Group Portraits* at the BizArt Gallery.
Changchun: *2000 Internet Art in China*, an exhibition on the use of new media at the Academy of Fine Arts.
Beijing: *Food as Art* at the Vogue Club. *Screen* by Wang Jianwei, using video, theater, and multimedia, is shown at the Ju'er Theater.
Lyon: Jean-Hubert Martin invites a number of Chinese artists to the biennial, including Gu Wenda and Yan Pei Ming.
2001: The first official transport link between China and Taiwan. China joins the WTO. Eighty-nine people are executed in a single day as part of a new drive to root out crime.
Beijing: Qiu Zhijie organizes an artistic event entitled *Post Sensation: Spree*.
Paris: The exhibition *Next Generation/Contemporary Asian Art* brings together artists from Taiwan, Korea, Japan, and China, including Feng Mengbo, Chen Lingyang, Zhen Guogu, Zheng Hao, Wang Guangyi, Ding Yi, Song Dong, and Chen Wenbo.
2002: Beijing is awarded the 2008 Olympic Games. The People's Republic acknowledges the existence of a huge public health scandal involving tainted blood products in Henan province.
Shanghai: The fourth biennial builds on the success of the third. On the fringe, Yang Zhenzhong and Xu Zhen curate *Twins*. A video exhibition is organized in Fuxing Park with works by Yang Zhenzhong, Song Tao, and Liang Yue.
Chengdu: The first biennial is held at the Museum of Modern Art.
Tirana, Albania: The first biennial. Feng Mengbo is invited.
Berlin: *Living in Time* at the Hamburger Bahnhof is the first exhibition of Chinese contemporary art abroad sponsored by the Chinese government.
Nice, France: As part of a month celebrating the art of photography, Claude Hudelot organizes an exhibition of photographs from China and of China.
Tourcoing, France: The exhibition *C'est pas du Cinéma* brings together sixty video artists, including ten from China: Cui Xiu Wen, Du Haibin, Song Dong, Wu Ershan, Wu Wenguang, Kan Xuan, Liang Zhao, Yang Zhenzhong, Zhou Yi, and Zhu Jia.
2003: Shanghai is to host the Universal Exhibition in 2010.
Hu Jintao replaces Jiang Zemin as head of state. The respiratory disease SARS appears in Guangdong province and quickly spreads all over China and beyond. The health minister and mayor of Beijing resign.
China sends its first astronaut into space.
Beijing: *Chinese Maximalism* by Gao Minglu at the Millennium. Reconstruction 798 builds a reputation as the most dynamic exhibition space in Beijing, with its lofts and vast halls.
France celebrates the Year of China. A flagship exhibition is devoted to Chinese art at the Centre Pompidou in Paris.
2004: Paris: *China: Video Generation* at the Maison Européenne de la Photographie in Paris.
Shanghai hosts its fifth biennial.
President Hu Jintao visits France.

BIOGRAPHIES

HUANG YONG PING

Born in Xiamen, Fujian province. Lives and works in Paris.

1986 Xiamen Dada group exhibition, Fujian Art Museum. **1989** *The Magicians of the Earth*, Centre Pompidou, Paris. **1994** *Chinese Hand Laundry*, New Museum of Contemporary Art, New York. **1996** Fondation Cartier, solo exhibition. **1997** Johannesburg Biennial. Gwangju Biennial, Korea. *Cities on the Move*, first shown in Vienna. **1998** *Inside Out: New Chinese Art*, P.S. 1, New York. **1999** Forty-eighth Venice Biennial, French pavilion. **2002** Barbara Gladstone Gallery, solo exhibition. Gwangju Triennial. **2003** Venice Biennial.

YAN PEI MING (MING)

Born in 1960 in Shanghai. Lives and works in Dijon, France.

1988 ARC, Musée d'Art Moderne, Paris. **1991** *Mouvements 2*, Musée National d'Art Moderne, Paris. Exhibition, Galerie Anne de Villepoix, Paris. **1994** Nouveau Musée Nouveau, Villeurbanne, France. **1996** Venice Biennial. *Portrait d'un inconnu* (*Portrait of an Unknown Man*), Galerie Durand-Dessert, Paris. **1997** *In Between Limits*, Sonje Museum, Gwangju, Korea. **1999** *Kunstwelten* (*Art Worlds*), Dialog Museum Ludwig, Cologne, Germany. **2000** Lyon Biennial. Fourth Shanghai Biennial. **2003** Fiftieth Venice Biennial.

WANG GUANGYI

Born in 1958 in Haerbin, Heilongjiang province. Lives and works in Beijing. **1987** Biennial of the Northern Art Group. **1989** *China Avant-Garde*, National Art Museum, Beijing. **1990** *I Don't Want to Play Cards with Cézanne*, Pacific Asia Museum, Pasadena, California. Salon for Young Artists, Paris. **1992** First Guangzhou Biennial. **1993** *Mao Goes Pop, China Post-1989*, Museum of Contemporary Art, Sydney, Australia. Forty-fifth Venice Biennial. **1994** São Paulo Biennial, Brazil. **1996** Second triennial of contemporary art from Asia and the Pacific Rim, Queensland Art Museum, Australia. **2001** *Towards a New Image: 20 Years of Contemporary Chinese Art*, Beijing, Shanghai, Guangzhou, Chengdu. **2002** First Guangzhou Triennial. **2003** *Alors, la Chine? (So, China?)*, Centre Pompidou, Paris.

WANG DU

Born in 1956 in Wuhan, Hubei province. Lives and works in Paris. **1986** First experimental exhibition in Guangzhou. **1989** *China Avant-Garde*, Beijing. **1997** *Cities on the Move*, Vienna, first stage of the touring exhibition. **1998** *Inside Out: New Chinese Art*, New York. *Gare de l'Est*, Casino Luxembourg, Luxembourg. **1999** Venice Biennial. *Marché aux puces* (*Flea Market*), Art et Public Gallery, Geneva (solo exhibition). **2000** *Réalité jetable* (*Disposable Reality*), Le Consortium, Dijon, France. Taipei Biennial. **2002** *No Comment*, Palais de Tokyo, Paris.

WANG JIAN WEI

Born in 1958 in Sichuan. Lives and works in Beijing.

1991 Cultural Palace of Nationalities, Beijing. **1993** *China New Art Post '89*, Hong Kong. *Mao Goes Pop, China Post-1989*, Sydney. **1995** First Gwangju Biennial. **1997** *Another Long March: Conceptual Chinese Art of the 90s*, Breda, Netherlands. Documenta X, Kassel, Germany. **1999** Melbourne Biennial, Australia. **2000** International Video Festival, Amsterdam. Shanghai Biennial. **2001** *Living in Time*, Hamburger Bahnhof, Berlin. **2002** São Paulo Biennial. **2003** *Alors, la Chine?* Paris.

GU WENDA Born in 1955 in Shanghai. Lives and works in Brooklyn. **1989** *China Avant-Garde*, Beijing. **1993** First stage of the *United Nations-Poland* project at Lodz Museum. **1994** *United Nations-Italy*, Milan. **1995** *Mao Goes Pop, China Post-1989*, Sydney. *United Nations-USA* Untitled Gallery, New York. **1996** *United Nations-Sweden*, Stockholm. **1997** *United Nations-Africa*, Johannesburg Biennial. **1998** *Inside Out: New Chinese Art*, New York. Performance of *Confucius Diary*, Vancouver. **1999** *United Nations-The Babel of the Millennium*, San Francisco Museum of Modern Art. **2000** Performance of *Tang Poem*, Utsunomiya Art Museum, Japan. Gwangju Biennial. **2001** Forty-ninth Venice Biennial. **2003** *From Middle Kingdom to Biological Millennium*, University of North Texas, Dallas.

DING YI

Born in 1962 in Shanghai. Lives and works in Shanghai.

1985 Modern art exhibition featuring six artists, Fudan University, Shanghai. **1989** *China Avant-Garde*, Beijing. **1993** Forty-fifth Venice Biennial. First triennial of contemporary art from Asia and the Pacific Rim, Queensland Art Museum, Australia. **1996** *China!* Bonn Art Museum. **1997** *In Between Limits*, Sonje Museum of Contemporary Art. *New Art from China*, Flanders Contemporary Art Museum, Minnesota. **1998** Eleventh Sydney Biennial. **2000** *Fuck Off*, Eastlink Gallery, Shanghai. **2001** *Next Generation*, Galerie Passage de Retz, Paris. **2002** First Guangzhou Triennial. **2003** *Chinese Maximalism*, Millennium Art Museum, Beijing.

ZHOU CHUNYA

Born in 1955 in Chongqing. Lives and works in Chengdu.

1987 *Five international artists*, Bielefeld, Germany. **1991** First annual exhibition of Chinese oil painting, Historical Museum, Beijing. **1993** *China, New Art Post '89*, a touring exhibition. **1996** First Shanghai Biennial. **1998** *Quotation Marks*, Singapore Museum of Art. **2001** First Chengdu Biennial. *Towards a New Image: 20 Years of Contemporary Chinese Art*, Beijing. **2003** *Alors la Chine?* Paris.

ZHENG XIAOGANG Born in **1958** in Kunming, Yunnan province. Lives and works in Beijing. **1985** *New Space 85*, Zhejiang Academy, Hangzhou. **1989** *China Avant-Garde*, Beijing. **1991** *I Don't Want to Play Cards with Cézanne*, Pasadena. **1993** *Mao Goes Pop, China Post-1989*, Sydney. **1994** Twenty-second São Paulo Biennial. **1995** Venice Biennial. **1996** *China!* Bonn. **1998** *Inside Out: New Chinese Art*, New York. **2000** Third Gwangju Biennial. **2001** First Chengdu Biennial. **2002** Guangzhou Triennial. **2003** *Art from China*, National Gallery, Jakarta, Indonesia.

ZHENG HAO

Born in 1963 in Kunming, Yunnan province. Lives and works in Beijing. **1992** *1990s Oil Painting*, Guangzhou. **1994** Second exhibition of the painting department at the Guangzhou School of Fine Art. **1996** *Recent Works from Five Studios*, Munich. **2000** *Contemporary Chinese Painting*, Padua, Italy. **2001** *Next Generation*, Paris. First Chengdu Biennial. *Hot Pot*, Kunsternes Haus, Oslo. **2002** 25th São Paulo Biennial.

LUO BROTHERS

Luo Wei Dong born in 1963; Luo Wei Guo born in 1964; Luo Wei Bing born in 1972—all in Guangxi. They now live and work together in Beijing.

1997 Wang Fung Gallery, New York. **1998** 28th São Paulo Biennial. **2001** *Next Generation*, Paris. **2003–4** Courtyard Gallery, Beijing.

ZHANG PEILI

Born in 1957 in Hangzhou, Zhejiang province. Lives and works in Hangzhou.

1993 Solo exhibition, Galerie du Rond-Point, Théâtre du Rond-Point, Paris. Solo exhibition, Galerie Chantal Crousel, Paris. Forty-fifth Venice Biennial. **1997** Fourth Lyon Biennial. *Cities on the Move*, Vienna. **1998** Museum of Modern Art, New York. **1999** Forty-eighth Venice Biennial. Solo exhibition, Jack Tilton Gallery, New York. **2001** *Living in Time*, Berlin. **2002** Fourth Gwangju Biennial. **2004** *Génération vidéo* (*Video Generation*), Maison Européenne de la Photographie, Paris.

ZHU JIA

Born in 1963 in Beijing. Lives and works in Beijing.

1997 *Cities on the Move*, Vienna. *Another Long March: Conceptual Chinese Art of the 90s*, Breda. **1998** Sixteenth International Video Festival, Amsterdam. Eleventh Sydney Biennial. *Asia City/Asia Contemporary Art*, The Photographers' Gallery, London. **1999** *Un matin du monde (One Morning in the World)*, Galerie Eric Dupont, Paris. **2000** *Documents on Chinese avant-garde art in the 1990s*, Fukuoda Asian Art Museum, Japan. PhotoEspaña. **2000** International Photography Festival, Madrid. **2001** *Living in Time*, Berlin. **2002** *C'est pas du cinéma* (*For Ree/al*), Studio National, Le Fresnoy, France. **2004** *Génération vidéo*, Paris.

SONG DONG

Born in 1966 in Beijing. Lives and works in Beijing.

1987 First national painting exhibition, Shanghai. **1992** First Guangzhou Biennial. **1994** *Outdoor Art*, Beijing. **1995** First Gwangju Biennial. **1998** *Inside Out: New Chinese Art*, New York. *It's Me*, Tai Temple, Beijing. **1999** Performance on Tiananmen Square, Beijing. **2000** *Expo 2000*, Hanover, Germany. International Video Festival, Amsterdam. *Song Dong in London*, installation and performance, Tablet Gallery, London. **2002** *C'est pas du cinéma*, Le Fresnoy. **2003** *Alors la Chine?* Paris.

YAN LEI

Born in 1965 in Langfang, Hebei province. Lives and works in Beijing and Hong Kong.

1989 *China Avant-Garde*, Beijing. **1993** *Post 89 China New Art*, Hong Kong Art Center. **1995** *Post 89 China New Art*, Vancouver Art Gallery. **1998** *It's Me*, Beijing. **2001** First Chengdu Biennial. *Next Generation*, Paris. **2002** Twenty-fifth São Paulo Biennial. Fourth Gwangju Biennial.

First Guangzhou Triennial. **2003** Fiftieth Venice Biennial. *Alors, la Chine?* Paris.

CHEN SHAOXIONG

Born in 1962 in Shantou, Guangdong province. Lives and works in Guangzhou.

1991 First exhibition by the Big Tail Elephant group, Workers' Palace, Guangzhou. **1997** *Demonstration of Video Art '97, China*, central gallery of the Beijing School of Fine Art. First stage of *Cities on the Move*. **1998** International Video Festival, Amsterdam. *Inside Out: New Chinese Art*, New York. **1999** *Art for Sale*, Shanghai. **2000** *Fuck Off*, Shanghai. **2001** *Living in Time*, Berlin. **2002** Shanghai Biennial. Gwangju Biennial. Guangzhou Triennial. **2003** *Canton Express*, Fiftieth Venice Biennial. **2004** *Génération vidéo*, Paris.

WENG PEIJUN (WENG FEN)

Born in 1961 in Hainan. Lives and works in Hainan.

1998 Contemporary art exhibition, Asia Pacific Museum, Fujian province. **1999** *Departing from China*, Design Museum, Beijing. **2000** *China Avant-Garde*, Artists Documentary Exhibition, Fukuoda Museum, Japan. **2001** First Chengdu Biennial. Sixteenth Exhibition of International Asian Art, Guangzhou. **2002** Fourth Shanghai Biennial. *New China Photography*, Courtyard Gallery, Beijing. **2003** *Alors, la Chine?* Paris. First Prague Biennial. **2004** International Center of Photography, New York.

CHEN WENBO

Born in 1969 in Chongqing, Sichuan province. Lives and works in Beijing.

1992 First Guangzhou Biennial for 1990s oil painting. **1993** Biennial for oil painting, China Art Gallery, Beijing. **1994** *Fragmentation*, Sichuan School of Fine Arts, Chongqing. **1996** *South-West China Exhibition of Conceptual Art*, Chengdu. **1997** Chinese Video Art, Central School of Fine Art, Beijing. **1999** *Post-Sense Sensibility: Alien Bodies and Delusion*, Beijing. **2000** *Future*, Center of Contemporary Art, Macao. **2001** *Next Generation*, Paris. First Chengdu Biennial. **2002** *Chinese Modernity*, Armando Alvares Penteado Foundation, São Paulo. First Guangzhou Triennial. **2003** *Out of Focus: A Dimension for Painting*, Long March Foundation, Beijing.

ZHEN GUOGU

Born in 1970 in Yangjiang in Guangdong province. Lives and works in Yanhjiang.

1994 Third Contemporary Art Exhibition, Library of Eastern China, Shanghai. **1997** *Cities on the Move*, Vienna. **1998** Biennial of the Image, Centre National de la Photographie, Paris. **1999** *Art for Sale*, Shanghai. *Post-Sense Sensibility: Alien Bodies and Delusion*, Beijing. *Love*, Tachikawa Art Festival, Japan. **2000** Arles Photography Forum, France. **2001** *Next Generation*, Paris. *Living in Time*, Berlin. **2002** Fourth Shanghai Biennial. Gwangju Biennial. **2003** *Canton Express*, Fiftieth Venice Biennial.

CHEN LINGYANG

Born in 1975 in Zhejiang province. Lives and works in Beijing.

1998 Solo exhibition, *Paradise or Lost Paradise*, Beijing. **1999** *Post-Sense Sensibility: Alien Bodies and Delusion*, Beijing. *Art For Sale*, Shanghai. **2000** *Documentation of Chinese Avant-Garde Art in the 90s*, Fukuoka Asian Art Museum, Japan. *Fuck Off*, Shanghai. **2001** *Take Part*, Urs Meile Gallery, Lucerne, Switzerland. *Next Generation*, Paris. *Visibility*, Chinese Art Archives & Warehouse, Beijing. **2002** *China New Photo*, International Festival of Photography, Pingyao, China. First Guangzhou Triennial. **2003** *Alors, la Chine?* Paris.

YANG FUDONG

Born in 1971 in Beijing. Lives and works in Shanghai.

1999 *Art for Sale*, Shanghai. Hanover Film Festival, Germany. **2000** *Fuck Off*, Shanghai. **2001** Istanbul Biennial. *Living in Time*, Berlin. Yokohama Triennial, Japan. **2002** Documenta XI, Kassel. Fourth Shanghai Biennial. **2002** First Guangzhou Triennial. **2003** *Camera ARC*, Musée d'Art Moderne, Paris. *Alors la Chine?* Paris. Fiftieth Venice Biennial.

YANG ZHENZHONG

Born in 1968 in Hangzhou. Lives and works in Shanghai.

1992 First Guangzhou Biennial. **1995** *4 x 100 m*, group performance, Hangzhou. **1997** *Chinese Video and Photography*, Max Protech Gallery, New York. **1999** *Art for Sale*, Shanghai. **2000** Arles Photography Forum. **2001** *Living in Time*, Berlin. **2002** Fourth Gwangju Biennial. First Guangzhou Triennial. *C'est pas du cinéma*, Le Fresnoy. **2003** Fiftieth Venice Biennial. *Alors, la Chine?* Paris. **2004** *Génération vidéo*, Paris.

KAN XUAN

Born in 1972 in Xuan Cheng. Lives and works in Beijing.

1999 *Art for Sale*, Shanghai. **2000** *Inertia and Masks*, Shanghai. **2001** *Or Nothing!* Shanghai. *Next Generation*, Paris. **2002** *C'est pas du cinéma*, Le Fresnoy. *Contemporary Chinese Art*, Guangzhou. **2003** *Alors, la Chine?* Paris. Echigo-Tsumari Short Video Festival, Tokyo. *Lost and Found*, Amsterdam. Hedah Film Festival, Maastricht, Netherlands. **2004** *Génération vidéo*, Paris.

LIANG YUE

Born in 1979 in Shanghai. Lives and works in Shanghai.

1999 *Art for Sale*, Shanghai. *The Same but also Changed*, Shanghai. **2000** *Fuck Off*, Shanghai. **2002** *Liang Yue: Don't Think about Anything*, BizArt, Shanghai. **2003** *Chinese Maximalism*, Beijing. *Several Dusks*, ShangArt Gallery, Shanghai. **2004** *Generation vidéo*, Paris.

XU ZHEN

Born in 1977 in Shanghai. Lives and works in Shanghai.

1999 *Art for Sale*, Shanghai. Maya Maya Biennial, Portugal. *Love*, Tachikawa Art Festival, Japan. **2000** *Fuck Off*, Shanghai. **2001** Venice Biennial. *Living in Time*, Berlin. *Inside the Body*, ISE Foundation, New York. **2002** *Careful, Don't Get Dirty*, Waldburger Gallery, Berlin. **2004** *Génération vidéo*, Paris.

CUI XIUWEN

Born in 1970 in Harbin. Lives and works in Beijing.

2000 *About Me: Chinese Conceptual Photography*, New Vision Gallery, Shanghai. **2001** *Dialogue: Others*, Bari Museum, Italy. *Cross Pressure: Contemporary Photography and Film from the Beijing Photography Museum*, Helsinki. **2002** *C'est pas du cinéma*, Le Fresnoy. First Guangzhou Triennial. *Australia New Media*, Australia New Media Department. *Post Material*, Red Gate Gallery, Beijing. Second International Photography Festival, Pingyao. **2003** Prague Biennial. *Alors, la Chine?* Paris. **2004** *Génération vidéo*, Paris.

CAO FEI

Born in 1978 in Guangzhou. Lives and works in Guangzhou.

1999 Eighth Biennial of the Moving Image, Saint-Gervais, France. **2000** *Fuck Off*, Shanghai. PhotoEspaña **2000** International Photography Festival, Madrid. **2001** *Living in Time*, Berlin. *Virtual Future*, Guangdong Art Museum, Guangzhou. **2002** Clermont-Ferrand Short Film Festival, France. Guangzhou Triennial. **2003** *Canton Express*, Fiftieth Venice Biennial. *Alors la Chine?* Paris. **2004** *Génération vidéo*, Paris.

ZHOU YI

Born in 1978 in Shanghai. Lives and works in Paris.

2002 *Première Vue* (*First Sight*), Galerie Passage de Retz, Paris. *C'est pas du cinéma*, Le Fresnoy. *Y Game*, Noirmont Prospect, Paris. www.whitneybiennal.com, on-line exhibition. *Alter Ego*, Museum of Art History, Luxembourg. **2003** Tirana Biennial, Albania. *Loverforevernornever*, Palais de Tokyo, Paris. *Forty Views of an Icon* for Comme des Garçons; Hermitage Museum; Moscow, and Spazio Consolo, Milan. *Something about Love*, Casino Luxembourg. *Made in China*, Fondation Guerlain, Les Mesnuls, France. **2004** *Génération vidéo*, Paris.

FENG MENGBO

Born in 1966 in Beijing. Lives and works in Beijing.

1993 Forty-fifth Venice Biennial. **1995** First Gwangju Biennial. **1996** *Contemporary Chinese Painting*, Fruitmarket Gallery, Edinburgh. **1997** Fourth Lyon Biennial. Second Johannesburg Biennial. Documenta X, Kassel. **1999** Fukuoda Asian Art Triennial. **2001** Solo exhibition, *Fantastic Story*, DIA Center, New York. First Tirana Biennial. *Next Generation*, Paris. **2002** Documenta XI, Kassel.